Bonfire of Creeds

BOOKS BY ASHIS NANDY

THE ROMANCE OF THE STATE
And the Fate of Dissent in the Tropics

THE INTIMATE ENEMY
Loss and Recovery of Self under Colonialism
(Oxford India Paperbacks)

AT THE EDGE OF PSYCHOLOGY
Essays in Politics and Culture
(Oxford India Paperbacks)

ALTERNATIVE SCIENCES
Creativity and Authenticity in Two Indian Scientists
(Oxford India Paperbacks)

THE SAVAGE FREUD
And Other Essays on Possible and Retrievable Selves
(Oxford India Paperbacks)

Omnibus Editions

EXILED AT HOME
Comprising: At the Edge of Psychology / The Intimate Enemy
Creating a Nationality

RETURN FROM EXILE
Comprising: Alternative Sciences / The Illegitimacy of Nationalism
The Savage Freud
(Oxford India Paperbacks)

Bonfire of Creeds
THE ESSENTIAL ASHIS NANDY

Ashis Nandy

OXFORD
UNIVERSITY PRESS

OXFORD
UNIVERSITY PRESS

YMCA Library Building, Jai Singh Road, New Delhi 110 001

Oxford University Press is a department of the University of Oxford.
It furthers the University's objective of excellence in research, scholarship,
and education by publishing worldwide in

Oxford   New York
Auckland Bangkok Buenos Aires Cape Town Chennai
Dar es Salaam Delhi Hong Kong Istanbul Karachi Kolkata
Kuala Lumpur Madrid Melbourne Mexico City Mumbai Nairobi
São Paulo Shanghai Taipei Tokyo Toronto

Oxford is a registered trademark of Oxford University Press
in the UK and in certain other countries

Published in India
by Oxford University Press

ISBN 0 19 566412 4

Typeset in Sabon MT
by Eleven Arts, Keshav Puram, Delhi 110 035
Printed in India by Maha Laxmi Printers, New Delhi 110 020
and published by Manzar Khan, Oxford University Press
YMCA Library Building, Jai Singh Road, New Delhi 110 001

To Dhirubhai Sheth, my most reluctant reader and
uncompromising critic, and to the memory of Giri Deshingkar,
a fierce sceptic who never turned cynical,
in gratitude for decades of intellectual and spiritual sustenance

A Note on the Essays

THE ESSAYS IN this book were written over a period of thirty years, but they are not arranged here in a chronological order. Thus, the collection ends with three essays that were written in the early 1980s. Hence the intrusion, in one or two places, of the presumption of a tripolar world and the pre-postmodern use of the term postmodern. Some of the early essays also use disciplinary technicalities and other formalities that the author has avoided in his later works. For instance, diacritical marks in two of the essays have not been removed. The order imposed on the collection and the division of the book into four parts are designed to give the reader some idea of the way the author sees the relationship between the empirical and the visionary, the outer and the inner, and the political and the ethical.

Contents

1

Introduction
A Dialogue with Ashis Nandy
By Gustavo Esteva and Madhu Suri Prakash

FOR MORE THAN a year, Ashis' articles, essays, and books have been with us, even in our excursions into small villages or big cities in Mexico, India, and other parts of the world. Travelling with such a companion has been a matter of continuous discovery, an invitation to us to revisit his thinking and to participate in the open-ended adventure defining his life and works. These essays continue to challenge us, forcing us to ask ourselves new questions, even as they offer us guidance in the regeneration and re-enchantment of our own selves.

Our previous acquaintance with Nandy as an author came a long time ago. He was one of the pioneers in radical critiques of development. He became, for many of us, a world public intellectual, supporting our resistance to development and, later on, accompanying us in our journey beyond it. He was at his best in dismantling the intellectual underpinnings of the development enterprise and baring its damaging cultural and psychological impact. 'Culture, Voice and Development', included in this volume, is a good illustration. In revealing development as a state of mind and a social process with ethnocidal features, he became a spokesperson for development's victims at a time when they were hardly heard and even their self-appointed representatives were ready to betray them, unable to accept the victims' views, contaminated as they were by the victims' own terms, categories, and theories.

For years we also followed Nandy's radical critique of modern science. Well before the postmodern plague struck, accompanied by the irrationalism and fundamentalism to which some followers of the new fashion succumbed, Nandy positioned himself as an internal critic, a well-known, if controversial scientist, who, no matter how much he distanced himself from the scientific community, did not disown science. He shared the self-criticism of many practitioners of the scientific method and the critical traditionalists who do not see modern science as alien (no matter how alienating they find it) and can use it for critical and limited purposes within their own traditions, as part of a new cognitive order.

As the essay, 'Science, Authoritarianism and Culture', in this book shows, Nandy identified an inbuilt tendency in modern science 'to be an ally of authoritarianism'.[1] He declared two decades ago that the main contemporary civilizational problem lay with the ways of thinking associated with the modern concept of rationality:

Modern science has already built a structure of near-total isolation where human beings themselves—including all their suffering and moral experience—have been objectified as things and processes, to be vivisected, manipulated or corrected. According to this view, the irrationality of rationality—as Herbert Marcuse might have described the pathology—in organized normal science— as Thomas Kuhn might have described the system—is no longer a mere slogan. It is threatening to take over all of human life, including every interstice of culture and every form of individuality.[2]

The critiques of development and modern science were, for Nandy, two pivots of his work on the political psychology of violence and on cultures of knowledge. Development, he wrote, 'has entered the Southern world as an analogue of two processes: modern science, wedded to evolutionism and the theory of progress, and modern colonialism, seeking legitimacy in a new civilizing mission'.[3] His critique of the modern nation-state is rooted in this insight. Aware of the failure of most countries in the Southern world to create viable nation-states along the lines prescribed for them, he speaks of the resilience of their cultures: 'Increasingly, cultures are refusing to sing their swan songs and bow out of the world stage to enter the textbooks of history. Indeed, cultures have now begun to return, like Freud's unconscious, to haunt the modern system of nation-states.'[4]

[1] Ashis Nandy, 'Science, Authoritarianism and Culture', *Traditions, Tyranny and Utopias* (New Delhi: Oxford University Press, 1988), p. 110.
[2] Ibid., p. 106.
[3] Ashis Nandy, In 'Development, Science and Colonialism', *Interculture*, Winter 1996, 29(1), p.8.
[4] Ashis Nandy, 'State', in W. Sachs (ed.), *The Development Dictionary: A Guide to Knowledge as Power* (London: Zed Books, 1992).

Nandy's fear of social engineering, in all its forms, and his radical critique of development, modern science and the nation-state (redefined as the only available model of the state and as the only available tradition of social and political organization in the contemporary world) came at an appropriate time. In the 1960s and 1970s a postcolonial mood had spread all over the world. The struggles for 'national liberation', in Africa, seemed to bring to a conclusion the process of decolonization initiated by the 'revolutions of independence' in Latin America in the nineteenth century. The grip of colonial powers, which did not loosen for almost 500 years over most peoples of the South and the East, at last relaxed, when the colonizing powers were forced to leave the territories they occupied. President Harry S. Truman seemed to speak in the name of all the colonial powers when he announced the end of that era, on 20 January 1949, the day he took office: 'The old imperialism—exploitation for foreign profit— has no place in our plans.'

True, old-style military and political interventions, shorter and more limited in scope, continue even today. Though the colonial powers, for the most part, have given up direct political and military domination of other peoples, the threat of their military intervention is always present. But such intervention is now a last resource and is carried out only to re-establish, whenever and wherever it is challenged, the new 'social order', the Pax Americana, which Truman proclaimed. 'What we envisage is a program of development based on the concepts of democratic fair dealing.'⁵ Development has thus become the emblem chosen by the Americans for a campaign in which they use their hegemonic power to reshape the old-world 'order'.

As a result, the definition of 'colonial powers' has itself got blurred. Today, among the 100 biggest economies of the world, only 49 are nation-states or countries; 51 are corporations. General Motors is bigger than Denmark; Wal-Mart is bigger than Norway; General Electric is bigger than Portugal. Five hundred global corporations have sales amounting to almost half of the GNP of the world. The richest 1 per cent of the world has a larger income than the poorest 57 per cent. Most governments, 'democratically' elected, are now at the service of these corporations, controlling with guns and police the very citizens who 'freely' elected them. But, even though their domination is more pervasive and complete, the corporations do not exercise that domination in the style of the 'classical' colonial powers. In fact, calling the new 'social order' by the

---

⁵Harry S. Truman, Inaugural Address, 20 January 1949, in *Documents on American Foreign Relations* (Connecticut: Princeton University Press, 1967).

old name of 'colonialism' has become contentious, since the term colonialism implies, for many, the old political and military domination of other peoples by one or more nation-states.

The new cosmetics of colonialism did not fool Nandy. Trained in the use of formal categories, he was never comfortable with them and systematically refused to reduce to reified, abstract constructs, a diverse world. Trained to explore the complexity of the selves of real men and women, and convinced that the whole cosmos, not only society and culture, is present and represented in every person, he discovered colonialism in the people around him and focused on their colonized selves that survived the departure of the colonial powers. In an era of flux and confusion, he was among the very few concerned with the resilience of colonialism.

The age of global development was heralded by Truman on the very day the United States, through the same speech of Truman, declared the Cold War. Forty years later, after four failed Development Decades, the fall of the Berlin wall marked the end of that war. A new emblem for American hegemonic power was now constructed, globalization. It was a timely substitute for the now frayed flag of development. The 'end of history' was proclaimed and a new era of unlimited prosperity for everyone was announced.

Globalization is, thus, the emblem of a new phase of an old, universal, economic project. It seeks the transformation of every man and woman on earth into *homo economicus*—the atomized, possessive individual in the West and the main, in fact the sole, actor in the industrial mode of production. That project now has a political face—representative democracy, and an ethical face—human rights.

The 'new social order' promoted under such an emblem requires the obedient, active participation of 'proper' or 'good' subjects. They are subjects who find in their condition as *homo economicus* a true identity and a satisfactory way of being and who now constitute a significant social minority in both the North and the South. However, to uphold such an 'order', a vast global army and police, national and international, is essential for controlling the social majorities, particularly the 'bad subjects' among them—those who oppose the constitutional powers and the oppressiveness of the system, and have recently expressed their discontent in Seattle, Genoa, Ottawa, Bangalore, and Okinawa, for that matter, all over the world many times over.

Nandy argues that both 'good' and 'bad' subjects, the victims and the victimizers, are trapped in the web of the colonial enterprise, in its old and, more inescapably, its new incarnations. The 'non-subjects', who refuse to play the game, are disqualified or ignored, or declared 'bad subjects'. Once in a while someone like M.K. Gandhi demonstrates what it means to have the autonomy, dignity and freedom of the 'non-subject'— to be neither the colonizer nor the colonized; neither the oppressor nor the oppressed; neither the hawk nor the dove; neither the terrorist nor the terrorized; neither the empowerer nor the empowered; neither the conscientizer nor the conscientized. Inevitably, Gandhi was classified as a 'bad subject'—from the very beginning of his struggle until well after his assassination. Being a bad subject had to be an inevitable part of being a successful rebel against the old colonial order, and he succeeded in gently but firmly bringing the first global superpower to its knees. But even those who did not write off Gandhi as an impossible eccentric, even those who celebrated his struggle, chose to see him as merely using non-violent means for the same ends for which other rebels were fighting colonialism. Even though he clearly, passionately, and unequivocally said that he was not interested in natives governing an independent, western-style nation-state; that his revolutionary, non-violent struggle was for *Hind Swaraj* (India's self-rule). The educated élite misunderstood him almost universally.

Venerated as the saintly Father of independent India, a new national state, Gandhi was summarily dismissed as a political thinker. It was assumed that he had no role to play in the development of the new state, busy 'catching up' in the global race defined and initiated by the industrial mode of production. The meaning and depth of Gandhi's revolutionary ideas were either not understood or, worse, distorted and mutilated by India's western-educated elite. For that matter, his ideas were radically rejected even by those who called themselves his heirs and brain-children and were now leading the new India towards its 'tryst with destiny'. Few cared to see how and why Gandhi, looking ahead, sought to bypass the industrial revolution. They re-read Gandhi's non-cooperation as a means of keeping them behind in the race set up by the western industrial project.

In this context, in the recognition and celebration of both heroic and unheroic 'non-subjects', the role played by Nandy's work for many of us can be understood, particularly the role by the two brilliant essays constituting *The Intimate Enemy*.[6] In that book, Nandy uses the tools of

---

[6]Ashis Nandy, *The Intimate Enemy: Loss and Recovery of Self under Colonialism* (New Delhi: 1983). There are plenty of references to Gandhi, in this book, illustrating Nandy's attitude towards him. What we love the most in this respect, however, is a short piece, 'Gandhi After Gandhi: The Fate of Dissent in our Times', *The Little Magazine*, May 2000, pp. 38–41.

his trade, psychology, to conceptualize the modern West as a psychological category and to take seriously the idea of psychological resistance to colonialism, shifting the locus of criticism from the purely psychological to the psycho-political (demystifying in the process, conventional psychological techniques of demystification). It is an indication of the book's strength that we are not too sure if we could have written the above paragraphs before his writings sedimented in our own thinking and action. Nandy has guided the decolonization of our minds.

'The West', Nandy claims in his book, 'has not merely produced modern colonialism, it informs most interpretations of colonialism. It colours even this interpretation of interpretation.'[7] How to escape from this condition without being a player or a counter-player? His examination of the psychological structures and cultural forces that supported or resisted the culture of colonialism also becomes an exploration of post-colonial consciousness. For he borrows and deliberately misuses concepts from modern psychology and sociology, not to fit the experiences he examines into existing theories, but to pursue his conviction that an 'ethically sensitive and culturally rooted alternative social knowledge is already partly available outside the modern social sciences.'[8] Unable to fully shed his professional baggage, he seeks to do consciously what the subjects of western colonialism did unconsciously. An example is his analysis of the torn self of the first non-western psychoanalyst in 'The Savage Freud', included in this book—originally a contribution to a collective research on decolonizing knowledge, led by Frédérique Apffel-Marglin and Stephen Marglin, in which some of us participated.

In his Foreword to Nandy's *Traditions, Tyranny and Utopias*, Roger Garaudy writes:

[T]o talk of developed and underdeveloped countries; in reality there are only the sick and the deceived. The Western countries are sick—with their blind economic growth and underdeveloped culture, wisdom and faith—which in turn breeds violence and pointless lives, incapable of proposing and realizing human ends. The deceived countries are those made to believe that their future lies in imitating the sick countries.[9]

How does one explore those sick and deceived selves? From where does one begin, especially if, as Garaudy claims, the West 'has confiscated

---

[7] Nandy, *The Intimate Enemy*, p. xii.
[8] Ibid., p. xvii.
[9] Roger Garaudy, 'Foreword', in Nandy, *Tradition, Tyranny and Utopias*, p. x.

the universal' and Nandy has exposed this 'imposture', showing how even the modern idea of history has itself become a major means of oppression.[10] Nandy's effort, Garaudy says, is 'not to repudiate or reject the western culture in its entirety but to relativize it' and the effort is 'of major importance for the fate of this planet'.[11] We cannot but wonder what this relativization is? From what vantage is it possible to formulate it? Who is relativizing what?

Nandy himself covers much ground in his radical critique of western universalism and examines it in many different forms, but never falls into the trap of cultural relativism, which so often gets transmogrified into another fundamentalism. However, the question remains: is his suggestion of a competing theory of universalism or his vague alternative universalism—however open, inclusive, and tolerant—the best or even the only option to escape the illegitimate, closed western universalism and cultural relativism?

We can deepen this question by giving it a personal touch. While reading Nandy, we are not comfortable with his frequent use of the word *bicultural*, to describe a whole generation of Indians, including Gandhi, Kipling, and a large cast of characters whose lives and deeds he explores. Can anyone be bicultural? Are we bicultural? One of us was born a Punjabi and has been teaching for the last 20 years in an American university and has an American son. The other is a deprofessionalized intellectual, raised in Mexico City in a fully westernized, indeed Americanized middle-class family, and claims his Zapotec ancestry, which his own family has consistently disowned. Like Nandy, we can fluently participate as insiders in both western or westernized activities and debates, and in deeply-rooted indigenous movements in India and Mexico. Where are we culturally located? Are we bicultural?

Of course, we do not have an answer, which in our view lies at the deepest level of Nandy's life and work and, in a sense, define them as open-ended adventures. Because his works, during the last one year, have continuously challenged us, we do not want to complete this reflection on him without confronting the challenge. We want to accept his invitation to engage in the open inter-cultural dialogue he persistently initiates in his work, personal conversations, and social interactions.

For this purpose, we borrow some of the insights our common friends, Robert Vachon and Kalpana Das of the Intercultural Institute

---

[10]Ibid.
[11]Garaudy, 'Foreword', pp. x–xii.

of Montreal, offer building upon the ideas of Raimon Panikkar, a person
who is conspicuously bicultural, even multicultural, apart from being a
pioneer in the theory and practice of intercultural dialogue.

At this point, let us state a basic agreement. We also long for the
'intercultural communion', which for Nandy is almost an obsession (if
he allows us to use a term contaminated by the language of his trade).
We also accept the two 'intellectual co-ordinates' that he uses in 'Towards
a Third World Utopia' in this volume, on which could be plotted all intercultural communion:

The first of them is the recognition that the 'true' values of different civilizations
are not in need of synthesis . . . . The second co-ordinate is the acknowledgement
that the search for authenticity of a civilization is always a search for the other
face of the civilization, either as a hope or as a warning.[12]

While using these coordinates, however, Nandy adds that the 'true'
values of those different civilizations are, 'in terms of basic biopsychological needs, already in reasonable harmony and capable of transcending
the barriers of particularist consciousness'. That is something we cannot swallow: in our view, only a long and deep intercultural dialogue, of a
kind not yet attempted, will be able to discover or create such harmony.
Nor can we agree with Nandy's observation that 'the principle of cultural
relativism . . . is acceptable only to the extent it accepts the universalism of
some core values of humankind'. We cannot accept, as yet, the existence
of these 'core values' that may or may not, be uncovered by inter-cultural
dialogues. We can identify in non-western cultures some homeomorphic
equivalents, as Panikkar calls them, of the West's 'core values', but they
are not, for those cultures, 'core values', or even 'values'. We suspect that
when people rooted in those cultures and in the West talk about the
'humankind' they talk of different things. Our doubts in this regard, which
prevent us from sharing Nandy's convictions, will become clearer from
the following.

Like Nandy, we approach culture without reducing it to a mental
category, a concept, a reality of the logico-epistemic order, a system
of meaning, signs and representations, or to a logical–reflexive angle, or
essence. Like Panikkar, we believe that 'all human culture is a texture
of myth and *logos*'; each culture is a galaxy hosting the experience and
perception of the world from which the understanding of one's self, others

---

[12]Ashis Nandy, 'Towards a Third World Utopia', in Nandy, *Tradition, Tyranny
and Utopias*, pp. 54–5.

and the reality around us emerges.[13] Like Vachon, we believe that at the heart of every culture 'there is a deeper and more universal and consistent stratum, quite real, although invisible, un-thought, un-said'.[14] This stratum 'is the encompassing myth, the mythic, primordial, ontonomous matrix, the unifying, integral, encompassing reality which is the wellspring of every thought and belief system.'[15] In both anthropological jargon and ordinary language, the word 'myth' alludes to legends, stories, allegories, and fables of a people. The idea of 'myth' used here usually nourishes the legends and stories, but should not be confused with them or reduced to them. It is the horizon of intelligibility of a people, in which all its perceptions of reality make sense; it is the people's territory of meaning. It is what allows and conditions any interpretation of reality. As Panikkar might say, it is what you believe without believing that you believe in it. It is not what you see, or what you believe, but what you believe that you see (Machado). It is what gives transparency to words and perceptions allowing you to see, but it itself, like light, cannot be seen.

Using the analogy of a tree, Kalpana Das compares the *morphological* dimension of culture with foliage. It is entirely visible and includes history, behaviour, customs, language, *techné*/technology, arts, food, and habitation. The *structural* dimension of culture represents the trunk. It is partly visible and partly invisible, and includes family, community, society, the person, nation, social organizations and practices, religious practices, language, and norms. The *mythical* dimension constitutes the root. It is entirely invisible and is the source of meaning—the world-view, the concept of the self and the cosmos, the meanings of the divine (supernatural) and the human, spirituality, the meanings of time and space, psyche, mind, knowledge.

The Zapatista movement, in southern Mexico, and Rigoberta Menchú and other Amerindian movements, have been using in recent years an old saying that apparently comes from the *Popol Vuh*, a Maya homeomorphic equivalent of the *Mahabharata*: 'They wrenched off our fruits .... They ripped off our branches .... They burned our trunk .... But they could not kill our roots.' They are saying what we want to say here: the amazing resilience of cultures, after 500 years of the ravages of colonialism, comes from their roots. No matter how much the foliage

---

[13]Robert Vachon, 'Guswenta or the Intercultural Imperative', in: *Interculture*, 28(2), issue no. 127, p. 53. The quotes from Panikkar and the analogy of the tree given by Das are taken from this essay.
[14]Ibid.
[15]Ibid.

and trunk might have been damaged, if your cultural roots are still alive, you can exert 'cultural control' on what happens to the foliage or the trunk and, in time, regenerate them in your way.

We are living in a world of unprecedented intercultural experiences that integrate the daily life of most people on the earth, with principles and practices coming from different cultures. The integration can be fluid and harmonious; it can be conflictual. Every year, millions of Mexican migrants quickly adjust to American norms, to earn money, and later they bring back to their communities what they have learnt or bought there. Some of their children use the indigenous language at home or in their community. They speak English in their schools in the US. But they are unable to learn Spanish, the official language of Mexico. More and more people, all over the world, learn in the school or from the TV, ways of thinking and living entirely alien to their cultures, which they immediately apply to their daily lives. Are they all bicultural?

A limited concept of culture can be applied to a community or a small group of communities which fully share that culture. They 'breathe' the cultural texture of the community in which they are born and in which they live; they are always aware of their uniqueness. When they visit another such community, they can also see what makes the other community culturally unique. Like the visitors, the other community also belongs to a culture and that culture belongs to them. But the visitors may also intuitively discover that they share with the other community the same ultimate horizon of intelligibility and experience; they may feel at home. Thousands of communities in the south of Mexico and Central America, belonging to different peoples and cultures and speaking different languages, seem to share the same mythical horizon. Any member of those communities can be called bicultural or even multicultural, if he or she has assimilated and adopted the cultural patterns of different communities and peoples that share the same basic horizon of intelligibility. Something similar can be said about most persons in western Europe, who may be born and raised in a specific local culture or country and may settle down in another. They share the same horizon of intelligibility.

Given the idea of culture we are using here, the question of biculturality or multiculturality acquires a different meaning when it refers to cultures whose ultimate horizons of intelligibility and experience are contradictory or radically incompatible. Is biculturality possible in such cases? Can a person experience life from incompatible horizons of intelligibility or fluidly move from one horizon to another?

It is of course possible to adopt ways of life (morphological stratum) or ways of organization (structural stratum) from other cultures: (*a*) as a condition for survival, when culturally alien principles or practices are imposed and you cannot survive without adopting them (as has happened during the last 500 years among the colonized peoples, forced to behave, and to even think, according to alien patterns); or else, (*b*) as freely or autonomously adopted practices or principles observed or experienced in other places, adopted for the sake of convenience or as a preference by a person or a community.

At this level, all cultures are hybrid: all people are culturally *mestizos*, mixed. They have adopted principles, elements and practices coming from other cultures. There have never been individuals, communities or peoples not exposed to hybridization, whether in ancient times or now. However, reality is necessarily experienced from one's own horizon of intelligibility. The alien elements are understood (or not understood or misunderstood) from that horizon. That is the tacit limit or boundary of knowledge, experience, or interest. Without such a limit, thinking becomes vacuous or overly abstract; no experience takes place.

The horizon itself can be 'fecundated' by other cultures and transformed through cultural interactions. All cultures have been exposed and continue to be exposed to such mutual fecundation. A culture loses its distinctive character, the character that defines it and distinguishes it from others, only when its horizon gets dissolved and a new all encompassing myth takes its place. The previous horizon is now perceived from outside, from the new horizon, the new culture.

Mythology, the attempt to reduce myth to *logos*, the rational examination of the myth, destroys and dissolves it and transforms its character. However, as Vachon observes:

[Myths] when visited by *logos*, are 'demythicised', but do not disappear altogether. They have a way of retreating strategically to a perhaps deeper level, in a mythical region that has not been touched by the invading light of critical reason. Just as reality is not given once and for all, but is constantly creating itself, so is the primordial myth of every culture. Hence the depth of cultural resistance. Since a myth is always part of a community of myths (it is never isolated or autonomous), not only does it resurrect in various ways, and under multiple traits within the ontonomic order to which it belongs, but it also enters into osmosis with other myths, so that new myths spontaneously emerge, without one having control over them or being able to predict them or to define a priori what they should or will be.[16]

---

[16]Vachon, 'Guswenta or the Intercultural Imperative', p. 54.

It is not possible to live without a mythical horizon of intelligibility. Since everyone is rooted in his or her culture, no biculturality is possible. A person cannot experience a rain dance calling or convening rain, with all its real and symbolic power and, at the same time or in quick succession, experience the phenomenon called 'rain' (or the lack of it) based on a scientific-technological interpretation of the natural or artificial factors producing it. That is, it is not possible to be convinced that the dance has the capacity to produce 'rain' through the proper ritual invocation of the benevolence of the gods and, at the same time, believe that rain is produced by meteorological factors that can describe and explain it. A person may fully understand the medical factors causing the death of a person, without abandoning his or her religious beliefs. But he or she cannot attribute the death to those factors and at the same time consider the death determined by the will of God or by some 'hidden forces'. As a compromise, the person may 'rationally' conclude that God or the 'hidden forces' seem to have chosen the factors described by the doctor to cause the death. Apparently, this establishes compatibility between the two modes of perception. However, at a deeper level, the contradiction persists. The scientific explanation specifies the pattern or chain of events which may have caused death. It may establish, for example, that a bullet pierced the heart and stopped it. It can also estimate statistically the probability of such a pattern or chain causing death. Within the scientific–technological frame, however, it is impossible to demonstrate a causal connection, say, by interlinking all possible causes. To *affirm* the cause of the death, one must turn to an extra-scientific element such as God, reason, a 'hidden force', or bad luck. In the same way, rain can be attributed to a certain combination of natural phenomena, that is, to the normal operation of natural 'laws' in which a person believes and which are considered knowledge; or, else, rain could be attributed to the appropriate performance of a prescribed ritual. What cannot be done is to simultaneously believe the two explanations. And the preference for or use of one locates a person within one or another horizon of intelligibility, one or another culture.

As Nandy knows well and explicitly says in his work, no culture can remain static without destroying itself and the living tradition in most cultures is the tradition of changing traditions in a traditional way. That gives the cultures historical continuity and allows for the mutual fecundation of cultures. The resilience of cultures seems to have allowed for such fecundation even in the middle of all the suffering imposed by the violence of colonialism. However, we now face a situation that seems to have no historical precedent. One single culture, which for convenience we all call the western culture, is not only trying to impose itself on every man and women on earth, dissolving all other cultures, but also seems to have the ways and means of succeeding in the enterprise. (Others might have tried to do so earlier but never had the capacity.) The idea of 'One World', which can be traced back to ancient history, is no longer a theory, an aspiration or an ideal, but a project being implemented. The fact that the universalism embedded in that project is under siege, theoretically, ethically and politically, does not stop the promoters of the project from continuing with it. There is thus a sense of urgency in all those searching for alternatives to such universalism and to the project itself, as well as to the so-called 'shock of civilizations', which may be but another face of the search.

In 1996, in the Intercontinental Encounter convened by the Zapatistas to look for alternatives to the new name of that project, globalization, the main proposal of the convenors was immediately accepted by the representatives of the myriad social movements attending the encounter. The time had come, they said, *to create a world in which many worlds can be embraced.*

Particularly, after 11 September 2001, in response to an act of unacceptable intolerance, many sensible calls to tolerance have been given. But, these calls are not mere olive branches; they also include thorns of intolerance. They sting, and they wound. Intolerance can never embrace. Tolerance means to suffer with patience. The person who tolerates perceives the other as someone who lacks the right colour of skin, the proper God, and correct behaviour. The tolerant is aware of his or her generosity when tolerating the other, when suffering the other with patience. At times, however, the tolerant one loses patience and is no longer able to tolerate the other. Though gentler and more discreet, tolerance is merely another form of intolerance. 'Toleration' Goethe observed, 'ought in reality to be merely a transitory mood. It must lead to recognition. To tolerate is to insult'.

Tolerance is a cherished word for Nandy. It is one of the elements of the western tradition that he wants to retain, while he continues identifying its homeomorphic equivalents in other cultural traditions. We are pretty sure that he will also embrace the necessary transformation of that early liberal, western ideal. As John Gray has observed, we cannot do without it; but it cannot be our guide in late-modern circumstances:

For the ideal of toleration we have inherited embodies two incompatible philosophies. Viewed from one side, liberal toleration is the ideal of a rational consensus on the best way of life. From the other, it is the belief that human beings can flourish in many ways of life. If liberalism has a future, it is in giving up the search for a rational consensus on the best way of life.[17]

If that is the case, and Nandy has contributed much to heal us of the pathology of western rationality, we are no longer in the realm of tolerance, but in that of hospitality. In contrast to toleration, suffering with patience, hospitality is a recognition, an association, a coming together of an entirely different sort. In being hospitable, you recognize the plurality of reality. You host the others even when you disagree with their arguments and their versions of the multiverse. To be hospitable does not mean to follow others, to adopt their views, to affirm or negate them. Hosting the others simply means opening one's arms and doors for them, to accept their existence in their own places—and to celebrate that existence.

As never before, we are now compelled to take a stance in the presence of the other. The reality of our daily life makes it impossible to avoid mutual intertwining, intermeddling and the conflicts emerging from them. What we now suffer is an impasse that is implicated in every form of violence: the incompatibility of world-views. The question of pluralism has thus become urgent for everyone of us: the current global situation throws us into the arms of one another. Are we going to hospitably open our arms or arm ourselves?

Democratic procedures—appropriate when different opinions, views and attitudes interact—offer minorities consolation prizes and the possibility of improved power positions in future political contests. It is better than fighting and, oftentimes, the best or the only feasible solution for many conflicts. But democratic procedures cannot resolve the confrontation between incompatible world-views. A plural world requires pluralist accords, not democratic, provisional agreements.

What we need is the creation of mutual openness to the concerns of the other. We do not share ideas, concepts, beliefs, even words with one another. But we can find and share something that can offer both of us some guidance, inspiration, insights, ideals—whatever both sides acknowledge and neither side controls. And we can thus re-enact a dialogue, transcending our logos, rising above our conceptual systems.

The time has come to bury not merely the project but very idea of one world, of any colour or shape. It is an idea that has divided us for so

---

[17]John Gray, *Two Faces of Liberalism* (New York: The New Press, 2000), p. 1.

many years, and for centuries has harassed, threatened and damaged even the last, isolated indigenous village. It is an idea that has diminished or eradicated cultures and peoples, often in the name of a unity that would disregard economic, political, or religious creeds.

Some try to compare civilizations, others to 'prove' the superiority of one civilization over another. All fail to recognize that everything, even thought, is rooted in a particular cultural soil. There exist no supra-cultural criteria enabling anyone to make such comparisons. Incomparability of cultures, their incommensurability, is one of the certainties of our times. We can assume cultural diversity and live with that assumption, never trying to compare cultures or to establish a hierarchy among them. But there is nothing intrinsically wrong in believing in the superiority of one's own culture. We may even consider it a reasonable desire if some want to share the blessings of their cultures with others. All of us may even be, in a sense, universalists, if we accept Nandy's position that in every person the whole cosmos is present and represented, every person may have and usually has, while being rooted in his or her culture, a cosmic view, a vision of the universe. What has been and continues to be the problem is the absolutization of that specific view, and the pretension to impose on others a particular idea of good, one's own idea of good, for their benefit. That is what colonialism is all about. The Others—as barbarians, infidels, savages, natives, the underdeveloped or the undemo-cratic—have been seen, at different times, as peoples in need of evan-gelization, civilization, marketization, development, or democracy. Some even seem to believe that they should and can actually choose the others with whom to share their blessings. They have even ended up bombing people into accepting their gifts.

Perhaps we are now witnessing the process of the creation of a new myth, a new horizon of intelligibility: the myth of interculturality. This new myth is the child of a form of pluralist attitude that is, in one sense, the opposite of the now-fashionable idea of multiculturality. It not only assumes the diversity of cultures, but also recognizes the limitations of everyone as a part of the awareness of the existence of other cultures, and accepts that no culture can experience or understand the totality of the human experience. This pluralist attitude has important historical pre-cedents in many indigenous and native cultures and in some self-critical trends of the western culture. With such an attitude, it is possible to attempt an intercultural dialogue to explore possibilities of communion among cultures. If such a dialogue finally takes place and a new intercul-tural myth emerges, the people will not become bicultural or multicultural: everyone will remain rooted in his or her own culture, within his or her own horizon of intelligibility, while sharing with others, at another level, the elements of the new myth.[18]

Given that Nandy's life and work continuously induce him to focus on the selves of the people around him and on the sources of their experiences, he also often reaches the depth of their horizons of intelligibility, their myths. He has resisted the temptation to reduce these myths to the formal categories in which he was educated. He has struggled against every kind of reductionism, be it scientific, ideological or religious. He has been, thus, forced by the current condition of the world, particularly his world, to engage in mythopoetic interventions, a kind of intervention that has become urgent at this point in time, when only a new myth, the myth of interculturality, can help heal not merely the many fragmented selves produced by colonialism among the colonizers and the colonized, but also heal the devastated planet in which we live.

These words, arising from the joyous and challenging experience of accompanying Nandy in his mythopoetic adventures, can also be read as an invitation to the readers of this 'essential Nandy'.

[18]To be precise, we are talking here about an attitude, not a philosophical or theoretical position. As we have already said, in our terms, no one can be culturally plural.

2

Cultural Frames for Social Transformation
A Credo

Culture, Critical Consciousness and Resistance

AMILCAR CABRAL, THE African freedom fighter, spoke of the 'permanent, organized repression of the cultural life of the people' as the very core of colonialism. 'To take up arms to dominate a people is', he said, 'to take arms to destroy, or at least to neutralise . . . its cultural life.' Cabral also seemingly recognized the corollary of such an understanding: that the reaffirmation of cultural traditions could not but be the heart of all authentic anti-colonialism.

In many ways, however, Cabral borrowed heavily from nineteenth century Europe's world image. He could not be fully sensitive to the other reason why a theory of culture has to be the core of any theory of oppression in our times: a stress on culture reinstates the categories used by the victims; a stress on cultural traditions is a defiance of the modern idea of expertise, an idea which demands that even resistance be uncontaminated by the 'inferior cognition' or 'unripe' revolutionary consciousness of the oppressed. A stress on culture is a repudiation of the post-Renaissance European faith that only that dissent is true which is rational, sane, scientific, adult and expert—according to Europe's concepts of rationality, sanity, science, adulthood and expertise.

Viewed thus, the links between culture, critical consciousness and social change in India become, not a unique experience, but a general response of societies which have been the victims of history and are now trying to rediscover their own visions of a desirable society, less burdened by the post-Enlightenment hope of 'one world' and by the postcolonial idea of cultural relativism.

Criticisms of Modernity: Internal and External

Cultural survival is increasingly a potent political slogan in India. When the religious reformers of nineteenth-century India spoke of protecting cultures, it seemed an obscurantist ploy. Today, when the juggernaut of modernity imperils every non-western culture, the slogan no longer seems a revivalist conspiracy. It has become a plea for minimum cultural plurality in an increasingly uniformized world.

The plea has been accompanied by a growing concern with native resources and ideas, even though only to the extent they serve causes such as development, growth, national integration, security and even revolution. As if culture were only an instrument. Perhaps the time has come to pose the issue in a different way. I shall do so here in terms of the binary choice which underlies most responses to modernity in complex non-western societies.

Unmixed modernism is no longer fashionable, not even in the modern world. The ultra-positivists and the Marxists, once so proudly anti-traditional, have begun to produce schools which criticize, if not the modernist vision in its entirety, at least crucial parts of it. Lionel Trilling and Peter Gay have gone so far as to call such criticisms—and the modernist dislike for modernity—a unique feature and a mark of modernity. One can offhand think of several examples: the 'solar plexus' of D. H. Lawrence; the crypto-Luddite critique of industrialism by Charles Chaplin in *Modern Times*; the 'primitivism' of Pablo Picasso; and the defiance of science and rationality in the surrealist manifestos of André Breton, *et al.* And now have appeared in the western and westernized intellectual circles schools that claim to be nothing less than postmodern. They are all indicators of how modernity at its most creative cannot do without its opposite: anti-modernity.

However, to the extent these criticisms try to abide by or use as their reference the values of European Enlightenment, and to the extent modernization is an attempt to realize these values, such criticisms are internal to modernity. Let us call them forms of critical modernism. Other examples of such critical modernism are: those models of scientific growth or technological transfer in the Third World which do not challenge the content or epistemology of modern science; critiques of the existing world order which take for granted the modern nation-state system; and the social criticisms which vend the belief that if you displaced the élites or classes that control the global political economy, you could live happily with the modern urban–industrial vision ever after.

At the other end of the spectrum are the criticisms of modernity from outside. These criticisms reject or bypass the Enlightenment values and thus seem insane or bizarre to the modern man. Blake, Carlyle, Emerson, Thoreau, Ruskin and Tolstoy have been some of the better-known external critics of modernity in the West. In our times, Gandhi has been by far the most consistent and savage critic of modernity and of its best-known cultural product: the modern West. Gandhi called the modern culture satanic; and though he changed his mind about many things, on this point he remained firm. Many Gandhians cannot swallow this part of him. Either they read him as a nation-builder who beneath his spiritual facade, was a hard-headed modernist wedded to the nation-state system. Or they see him as a great man pursuing crazy civilisational goals (the way Isaac Newton, when not working on proper mathematical physics, worked on alchemy and on the science of trinity). They divide Gandhi into the normal and the abnormal, and reject the latter either as an aberration or as an embarrassment. 'Bapu, you are far greater than your little books', Nehru once charmingly said.

An unabashed Gandhi, however, took his 'insanity' to its logical conclusion. He rejected modern innovations such as the nation-state system, modern science and technology, urban–industrialism and evolutionism (without rejecting the traditional ideas of the state, science and technology, civic living and social transformation). Not being a Gandhian, I often watch and applaud from a distance the contortionist acts many modernists put up to fit Gandhi and his strange views into the modern paradigm. They can neither disown the Mahatma nor digest him.

Yet, Gandhi was no Ananda Coomaraswamy. Both hated modernity, but they parted company when it came to traditions. Coomaraswamy theoretically kept open the possibility of assessing or altering traditions from the point of view of traditions. But perhaps because he was single-handedly trying to do for past times what the anthropologists as a community were trying to do for distant cultures, there was no criticism, or at least no significant criticism, of traditions in his works. The attitude was unashamedly defensive (examine, for instance, his comments on the concept and practice of sati).

Gandhi never eulogized the Indian village nor called for a return to the past. He supported the ideas of the village and traditions, and India's traditional villagers, but not the existing Indian villages or traditions. Coomaraswamy, too, at one plane made this distinction, but the tone was different. This would be obvious to anyone who reads Coomaraswamy and Gandhi on caste. Coomaraswamy defended the pre-modern caste system because he found it more human than the modern class system. Gandhi also did so but went further; he sought to reorder the hierarchy of skills—to re-legitimize the manual and the unclean and delegitimize the Brahmanic and the clean. (I remember anthropologist Surajit Sinha once saying that while Rabindranath Tagore wanted to turn all Indians into Brahmans, Gandhi sought to turn them into Shudras. This can be read as an indictment of Gandhi; it can be read as a homage. And every Indian social thinker and activist has to make his or her choice some time or other; for to say glibly that one must in the long run abolish both the categories is to fight in the short run for the Brahminic world-view. Exactly as to work for the future removal of poverty without touching the super rich in the present is to collaborate with the latter.)

Such examples can be multiplied. Compare Coomaraswamy's appraisal of the Indian village—or Nehru's—with Gandhi's description of Indian villages as 'dung-heaps'; compare Dhanagopal Mukherji's passionate defence of India against the attack of Catherine Mayo in her *Mother India* with Gandhi's advice to every Indian to read what he called Mayo's 'drain-inspector's report'. Recently, sociologist Triloki Nath Madan, analysing Raja Rao's *Kanthapura*, has shown how the novelist construes Gandhi's movement against the tradition of untouchability as the other side of his struggle against modern imperialism, to stress the point that neither of the two struggles could be conceived of without the other.

Unlike Coomaraswamy, Gandhi did not want to defend traditions; he lived with them. Nor did he, like Nehru, want to museumize cultures within a modern frame. Gandhi's frame was traditional, but he was willing to criticize some traditions violently. He was even willing to include in his frame elements of modernity as critical vectors. He found no dissonance between his rejection of modern technology and his advocacy of the bicycle, the lathe and the sewing machine. Gandhi defied the modern world by opting for an alternative frame; the specifics in his frame were frequently modern. (The modernists find this hypocritical but they do not object to similar eclecticism when the framework is modern. Witness their attitude to the inclusion of Sarpagandha in modern pharmacology as reserpine, even though the drug has been a part of Ayurveda.)

Today, the battle of minds rarely involves a choice between modernity and traditions in their pure forms. The ravages of modernity are known and, since the past cannot be resurrected but only owned up, pure traditions, too, are a choice not given to us. Even if such a choice were given,

I doubt if going back 2500 years into the past is any better than going 5000 miles to the West for ideas, especially in a post-Einsteinian world in which space and time are inter-translatable variables. Ultimately, the choice *is* between critical modernism and critical traditionalism. It is a choice between two frames of reference and two world-views.

Oppression, Innocence and Voice

Some scholars object to the foregoing formulation. They find the concept of critical traditionality soft on obscurantism and internally inconsistent. One of them, T. G. Vaidyanathan, has suggested that I should use the expression 'critical insider' instead of 'critical traditionalist'.

Frankly, I have little attachment to the words I use. If by changing them some process can be described better, I have no objection. I recognize that my descriptive categories are partly the ashes of my long romance with some versions of the critical theory, especially the early influence on me of scholars such as Theodor Adorno, Herbert Marcuse and Erich Fromm. They are not always adequate for non-western realities. However, my categories are also partly a response to the argument of some scholars—Pratima Bowes being the last in the series—that traditional Indian thought never really developed a true critical component. I argue that (*a*) Indian thought, including many of its *puranic* and folk elements, can be and have been used as a critical base, because critical rationality is the monopoly neither of modern times nor of the Graeco-Roman tradition, and (*b*) that some aspects of some exogenous traditions of criticism can be accommodated in non-western terms within the non-western civilization.

Let me further clarify my position by restating it differently. Critical traditionality refers to the living traditions which include a theory of oppression, overt and/or covert. No tradition is valid or useful for our times unless it has, or can be made to have, an awareness of the nature of evil in contemporary times. If the term 'evil' seems too Judaeo-Christian to Indian ears—it should not though in a civilization that has known and included the Judaeo-Christian traditions longer than Europe has—one can talk of the nature of man-made *dukha* or suffering in our times. This is the obverse of the point that no theory of oppression can make sense unless it is cast in native terms of categories, that is, in terms of categories used by the victims of our times. As a corollary, no native theory can be taken seriously unless it includes a subtheory of oppression.

This is not an odd restatement of the ideology of instrumentalism which dominates most modern, secular theories of oppression. I am not speaking here of a strategy of mass mobilization which includes certain compromises with the language or the so-called false consciousness of the ahistorical societies. I am speaking of the more holistic or comprehensive cognition of those at the receiving end of the present world system. I am speaking of the primacy that should be given to the political consciousness of those who have been forced to develop categories to understand their own suffering and who reject the pseudo-indigenization of modern theories of oppression using—merely using—native idioms to conscientize, brainwash, educate, indoctrinate the oppressed or to museumize their cultures. The resistance to modern oppression has to involve, in our part of the world, some resistance to modernity and to important aspects of the modern theories of oppression. The resistance must deny in particular the connotative meanings of concepts such as development, growth, science and technology, history and revolution. These concepts have become not only new 'reasons of the state' but mystifications for new forms of violence and injustice. The resistance must also simultaneously subsume—and here pure traditionalism fails to meet our needs—a sensitivity to the links between cultural survival and global structures of oppression in our times. The critical traditionality I have in mind is akin to Rollo May's concept of authentic innocence, as opposed to what he calls pseudo-innocence. Authentic innocence is marked by an updated sense of evil; pseudo-innocence is not, for it thrives on what psychoanalysis calls 'secondary gains' for the victim from the oppressive system.

This also means that the living traditions of the non-western civilizations must include a theory of the West. This is not to make the facile point that the West is a demon, but to recognize that the West and its relationship with the non-West has become deeply intertwined with the problem of evil in our times—according both to the West and to the non-West. Contrary to what the modern world believes, this non-western construction of the West is not morally naive, either. It does draw a line between the western mainstream and the cultural underground of the West, between the masculine West and the feminine—exactly as it draws a line between the authenticity and pseudo-innocence of the non-West.

All said, it is the culturally rooted, non-modern understanding of the civilizational encounters of our times for which I am trying to create a space in public discourse. I am not trying to provide a new theory of oppression from within the social sciences.

Language, Survival and the Language of Survival

Is there an Indian tradition with a built-in theory of oppression? The question is irrelevant. The real issue is: can we construe a tradition which will yield a native theory of oppression? The issue is the political will to read traditions as an open-ended text rather than as a closed book.

This civilization has survived not only because of the 'valid', 'true' or 'proper' exegesis of the traditional texts (though a sophisticated hermeneutic tradition has always existed in India), but also because of the 'improper', 'far-fetched' and 'deviant' reinterpretations of the sacred and the canonical. If Chaitanya's dualist concept of *bhakti* (evolved partly as a response to the pure monism of Advaita that had till then dominated the Indian scene) seems to have been posed too far in the past, there is the instance of the *smarta* text, Gita, acquiring the canonical status of a *shruti* text in the nineteenth and early twentieth-century India. And, of course, there is the instance of the first great social and religious reformer of modern India, Rammohun Roy (1772–1833), 'legitimately' interpreting Shankara's monism as monotheism, and the instance of Gandhi 'legitimately' borrowing his concept of *ahimsa* or non-violence from the Sermon on the Mount and saying so, while claiming it to be the core concept of orthodox Hinduism. Howsoever odd such 'distortions' may seem to the westernized Indian or to the scholastic, Brahminic traditionalist, they are the means the Indian civilization has repeatedly used to update its theories of evil and to ensure cultural survival while allowing large-scale social interventions.

To appreciate such reinterpretations, we must learn to acknowledge or decode three languages which often hide the implicit native theories of oppression in many non-western traditions. These are the language of continuity, the language of spiritualism and the language of self. They may look like aspects of a primitive false consciousness to the moderns, but they continue to be the means of indirectly articulating the problems of survival for the non-modern victims of history.

The language of continuity (which accounts for the image of the savage as change-resisting and stagnant) assumes that all changes can be seen, discussed or analysed as aspects of deeper continuities. In other words, the language assumes that every change, howsoever enormous, is only a special case of continuity. The perennial problems of human living and the perennial questions about human self-definition are common to all ages and cultures, and all disjunctions are apart of a continuous effort to grapple with these problems and questions. This position is radically different from the modern western concept of continuity as only a special case of change or as only a transient period in time which is only overtly continuous or which, if it is truly continuous, is for that reason less valuable. In the dominant Indic tradition, each change is just another form of the unchanging and another reprioritization or revaluation of the existent.

At one plane, the difference between the language is exactly that: a difference in language. Yet the fact remains that the language of continuity is mostly spoken by the victims of the present global system; the language of disjunction by the powerful and the rich and by those dominating the discourse on cultures. The fact also remains that the language of disjunction today has been successfully, though not wholly, co-opted by those who are for the status quo. The Shah of Iran spoke of modernization and social change; his opponents spoke of cultural survival and conservation; the military juntas in South America, Africa and in the ASEAN countries speak of changing their societies into powerful nation-states; their opponents speak of American-Indian rights and of the traditions of non-white cultures; Ronald Reagan and Indira Gandhi have spoken of scientific and technical growth, their critics of ecological issues, traditional sciences and rural technologies. For a long time the weights were differently distributed: the language of continuity was mainly used by those who ran the older oppressive systems. Now, development, maturity, scientific temper, revolutionary consciousness—these are keywords in the vocabulary of those who see themselves either as deservedly ruling the world or as its future rulers.

The language of spirit, including both its 'respectable' versions and the versions which the spiritually-minded themselves reject as confidence tricks, serves a number of this-worldly purposes of the oppressed. It often expresses, when decoded, an analysis of oppression which rejects the analytic categories popular with the oppressors and with the modern sectors from which the oppressors come. Such analysis in the language of spirit is seen by us as a camouflaged statement of hard self-interest and *simultaneously*—and here lies a fundamental contradiction in the modern concept of the politics of cultures—as woolly sentimentalism and a subjectivist hoax. Obviously, if it is only woolly sentimentalism it cannot at the same time be a camouflaged statement of self-interest; and if it is an indirect statement of self-interest it is not that subjectivist, after all. Marx recognized this when he spoke of religion as expressing the pain of the oppressed. But he was mired too deeply in Eurocentric nineteenth-century scientism and evolutionism. He did not go so far as to take seriously the cognitive frame which went with the pain. Nor did he notice (*a*) that the frame often used the language of spirit to articulate a set of values which criticized or defied the society as it existed; (*b*) that it rejected the conventional concepts of science and rationality as potentially irrational, inhuman, sectarian and collaborationist; and (*c*) that it included the potentiality, as Gandhi was to later demonstrate, of a renunciation of renunciation which would shun spiritual exercises for the sake of political intervention on the assumption that suffering is never unreal and a moral truth has to be acted out at both the subjective and the objective planes.

A subcategory of the language of spirit in societies like ours is the language of anti-history that rejects the idea of history, especially the idea of historical laws, as a new tool of oppression. The language seeks to reinstate the mythopoetic language which is closer to the victims of history. The understanding of oppression expressed in myths and other forms of shared fantasies—or expressed through alterations in existing myths and shared fantasies—transcends the barriers of regions and sub-cultures in a complex civilization. For most savages, myths communicate life experiences and cultural roots; history hides them. That is why the theory of oppression expressed in mythopoesis does not come as a special module prepared by outsiders (to which the oppressed must learn to adapt); it comes as an analytic statement of the emic kind which may or may not be translatable into the languages used by the dominant theories of man-made suffering. History, as a modern myth, selects for us what should be remembered on grounds of objectivity. Myths, as self-consciously selective memories, not only aid memory but also select for us what should be forgotten on grounds of compassion.

Finally, the language of self in which the oppressed often package their story. It includes, as does the language of spiritualism, the so-called fatalism of the savage and the primitive against which conscientization and other similar processes seem such good medicines. The language of self emphasizes variables such as self-control, self-realization, self-actualization and self-enrichment, and it apparently underplays changes in the not-self or the outer world. The language has been especially emphasized by the humanistic psychologists and others who have tried to base their theories of consciousness, psychological health and human creativity on insights into self processes rather than on insights into psychopathologies of social life. I am, however, drawing attention to the language from another vantage ground. The language of self, I want to stress, also has an implicit theory of the not-self—of oppression and social transformation. To borrow words from modern psychology, autoplasticity does in this case include alloplasticity. In many of the non-western traditions the self is not only included in 'external' laws of nature and society; nature and society, in turn, are subsumed in the self. Self-correction and self-realization include the principle of intervention in the outside world as we have come to understand the world in post-Galilean and post-Cartesian cosmologies. Bhikhu Parekh has drawn my attention to the Gandhian emphasis on purifying the self as a means of serving the world, and serving the world as a means of purifying the self. The emphasis is built into the more sensitive traditional theories of self-in-society.

Critiques of Critiques

Modern theories of oppression may or may not help the oppressed; but they certainly help the theorists a lot. To the extent they speak the language of discontinuity, ultra-materialism or impersonality, they become a part, often a fashionable part, of the modern world and of the valued streams of dissent within that world. To the extent they presume to represent the sanity of the oppressed, these theories sometimes become the livery of a new elite—whether known as the revolutionary vanguard, the expert demystifier, the trained psychotherapist, or the scientist trying to break-down the prescientific temper of the masses. Perhaps we have reached the point where one must learn to take more seriously other categories used by those victimized by the modern oppressive systems. For these systems not only oppress in the way older oppressive systems did—by openly legitimizing violence, greed and dominance. These systems successfully tap the human ingenuity (*a*) to produce systems that are unjust, expropriatory and violent in the name of liberation or freedom; and (*b*) to develop a public consciousness which would include an explicit model of proper dissent. In such a world, dissent, unless it seeks to subvert the rules of the game and the language in which the rules are framed, becomes another form of conformity.

George Orwell realized this. He felt that the oppressed, when faced with problems of survival, had no obligation to follow any model or any rule of the game. Now, it is possible to argue that this 'methodological anarchism', too, can, in turn, produce over time its own special brand of violence. I have no foolproof answer to that argument. But I like to believe that perhaps one way of containing such second-order violence is to work with a perspective which (*a*) retains, and persistently struggles to retain, the sense of immediacy and directness of the experience or perception of man-made suffering, and (*b*) keeps open the scope for criticism of every criticism.

In the short run, however, one may have to be even less demanding. Protest or dissent cannot, and should not, wait for that golden moment when the protestor or the dissenter gets hold of, or is converted to, the correct theory in the correct way, be that theory modern or traditional. In fact, any theory which believes that such correctness or conversion must come before liberation can be talked about is, to that extent, an incorrect theory, following the Orwellian principle mentioned above. Yet, some stipulations can perhaps be made about the minimum scepticism towards contemporary structures of authority and authoritativeness which an activist or a social critic must show in order to qualify as useful for our times. Such stipulations may give meaning, not only to the resistance of the illiterate savage pitting his naked body against the might of the high technology of his oppressors, but also to the passions of the young activist moved by the plight of his fellow humans and trying to understand that plight in terms of the highly technical modern theories of liberation.

First, scepticism has to be directed at the modern nation-state. This, I am aware, is easier said than done in postcolonial societies. The folk-theories of politics popular among the middle classes in these societies would have us believe that all the ills of these societies are due to their inability to produce or to sustain proper nation-states. Once such nation-states are built, the argument goes, the first problem of social engineering and collective survival would be solved. Scepticism towards the nation-state in such an environment looks, at best, simple-minded; at worst, treacherous. Yet, the fact remains that in most Asian and African societies, the state has increasingly become, not only the major instrument of corruption, expropriation and violence towards their own people, but also increasingly ethnocidal. Even if one does not take an anarchist position on the state in such societies, one could at least be wary of the idea of nation-state as an end in itself and be sceptical of state-sponsored anxieties about national security, specially when this concept of security is invoked to demand sacrifices from social sectors least able to make them.

Second, there must be scepticism towards modern science. I am not speaking of the usual scepticism about some forms of technology or about the usual criticisms of the control on science exercised by social forces. I am speaking of modern science as the basic model of domination in our times and as the ultimate justification for all institutionalized violence. I am speaking of the criticism of criticism which is aware that the acceptance of the social determination of science and technology can hide the refusal to be sceptical about the philosophical assumptions and

texts of modern science, about the modern scientific imagination itself.
Unless one builds checks against the basic model of domination in
modern science, I doubt if one can have any check on the newer forms
of institutionalized violence.

Third, there must be scepticism towards history, specially towards
the so-called larger forces of history, unless the awareness of such larger
forces is matched by an awareness of their implications in everyday life.
I am not very clear here. Let me try again. I have mentioned here and
there in this essay the name of Gandhi; and it may be appropriate to
end this statement with a reference to his attitude to history. One reason
why Gandhi aroused deep anxieties in Indian middle-class *literati* was
that he always pushed social analysis to the level of personal lifestyle,
to the level of what can be called the smaller forces of history. Gandhi
did not allow the rhetoric of historical awareness to be a substitute for
the political morality of everyday life. He was willing to suspend his
suspicion of history, but he was unwilling to let anyone forget one's
personal responsibility to live out one's understanding of historical and/
or perennial truths. This terribly, terribly fuddy-duddy demand for
internal consistency—between the public and the private, and between
the collective and the personal—is particularly anxiety-provoking to those
who specialize in speaking the language of making history while only
passively living in history.

Now, it is possible to argue that all accountability is odious, that
ideas are important in themselves and independent of the personal lives
of their proponents. But Gandhi was always sceptical of the modern
claim that perfect institutions would one day eliminate the social need
for individual morality. He therefore believed that accountability should
be demanded at least of those whose theories of social intervention
demand sacrifices and accountability of others. He believed, too, that
accountability should likewise be demanded of those whose theories claim
to bridge the private and the public, and the personal and the historical.

For those who feel uneasy with any talk of personal morality in the
public realm I can word the issue differently. Many political economists,
Immanuel Wallerstein being a recent example, have drawn attention to
the fact—uncomfortable to the Third World élites and intellectuals—
that the Third World societies usually maintain within their borders
exactly the same violent, exploitative, ethnocidal systems which they
confront in the larger world: the same centre and periphery, the same
myth that the sacrifices made by people in the short run will lead to the
beatitude of development and scientific advancement in the long run,
the same story of over-consuming élites fattening themselves to early death

at the centre and starvation, victimhood, and slow death at the periphery. Because of this, the demands of the Third World for more equitable and just terms in North–South exchanges often sound dishonest or hollow. I believe that many traditional as well as some modern systems of psychology allow us to extend the argument to the level of the individual. In other words, they allow us to claim (*a*) that we model our interventions in the world on our interventions in our own selves, and (*b*) that the world does to us what we do to ourselves. This is the reverse of what I have called elsewhere the principle of isomorphic oppression, according to which each level of an integrated social structure neatly reproduces within it the oppressive dynamics of the whole. The principle of isomorphism says: what you do to others you ultimately do to yourself, for 'the wages of sin is the kind of person you are'. When reversed, the principle becomes: what you do to yourself or to your kind cannot but invite others to do the same to you and to your kind.

It should be obvious that this way of looking at social intervention and culpability dissolves the crude dichotomy between the study of the élites and the study of the masses or, as some have begun to call them, subalterns. Following traditional wisdom, I like to believe that the story of the prince can never be told without telling the story of the pauper, and that the cause of the pauper can never be independent of the cause of the prince. My life's ambition is to write an interpretation of poverty by focusing entirely on the lifestyle of the super-rich. As Franz Fanon recognized, the suffering of the victims cannot but be the sickness of their oppressors and the inter-translatability between two sets of life-experiences is complete once the rules of translation are identified.

The three scepticisms are tied together in my case—I have a right to end a credo on a personal note—by a general scepticism towards all ideas which are used as sources of legitimacy by the winners of the world. I should like to believe that the task of a person living a life of the mind is to make greater demands on those who mouth the certitudes of their times and are closer to the powerful and the rich, than on the faiths and ideas of the powerless and the marginalized. That way lie freedom, compassion, and justice.

*Earlier published in *Alternatives* 15.

Politics of Tradition

3

Sati
A Nineteenth-Century Tale of Women, Violence and Protest

Authority and Defiance

THERE ARE SUPERSTITIONS, and superstitions about superstitions. For over 150 years, the legal abolition in 1829 of sati, the Hindu rite of widows committing suicide after the death of their husbands, has been considered the first victory of the modern world over Hindu obscurantism and primitivism. I contend in this essay that the epidemic of sati in the late eighteenth- and early nineteenth-centuries was mainly a product of British colonial intrusion into Indian society; that the popularity of the rite and its abolition in response to a reform movement were two phases in Indian society's attempt to cope with large-scale environmental and cultural changes; and that both these changes involved the invalidation and distortion of traditional attitudes to woman and femininity. I also contend that Rammohun Roy (1772–1833), who led the movement against the rite and partly on that ground is known as the father of modern India, represented society's attempt to work through its ambivalences towards the rite, towards traditional concepts of womanhood and women, and towards the sexual identities the colonial culture was helping to crystallize.

This alternative interpretation of sati assumes that to walk the razor's edge between makeshift adjustments and total surrender to its changing environment, a civilization constantly needs to generate new concepts, symbols and structures of authority and to renegotiate terms with its older gods. It is this social need which defines the importance of the person who evolves new sources of legitimacy and designs alternative controls of transgression, and yet makes his innovations reflect the unique history and genius of his people. If society helps such a person to take care of his private conflicts, gives him the chance to relate his world-view to the needs of his contemporaries, and appreciates his interpretation of traditions as authoritative, a creative anastomosis between man and society is established. Social change then comes to mean not only changes in rites, rituals and practices, but also a changed relationship between cultural symbols and individual motives.

Starting from such an assumption I shall explore in this essay the relationship between the reform of sati and the world of Rammohun Roy to illustrate how a person's private conflicts with the immediate authorities can get intertwined with aggregate responses to public issues, how older controls of transgression can become a threat and a challenge to the person, and how a person's personal ethics and private symbols can become valid tools of social intervention. I shall do so in two stages. First, I shall examine the culture of sati in historical and psychological terms and show how the ritual became a battleground between the old and the new, the indigenous and the imported, and the Brahminic and the folk. I shall try to show that these three intersecting conflicts were given meaning by the central conflict between traditional concepts of womanhood and the emerging man–nature system, political authority and social organization. In the second stage I shall try to show how Rammohun Roy subverted the rite of sati by introducing his society to alternative symbols of authority which constituted not merely the first serious reinterpretation of Hinduism in modern times, but also carried the intimations of a new lifestyle and new principles of masculinity and femininity more compatible with the large-scale industrial, social and economic changes then taking place in Indian society.[1]

To sharpen the analysis, I shall avoid details of the history of the reform

[1]In this context, the recent controversy among historians over who was ultimately responsible for the decision to legally proscribe the rite is both misleading and irrelevant. The fact remains that Roy was an embodiment of the anti-sati movement to both anti-sati and pro-sati groups as well as to the British rulers (who in turn were ambivalent towards the rite because of their non-interventionist social policy). And it was only he who provided a consistent explanation of the practice and a theory of reform which could be understood by all these three groups. In fact, one may guess that it was this ability to sum up in his personality not merely the hostilities of the reformers, but also the latent ambivalence of society towards the rite, which makes Rammohun Roy a symbol of nineteenth-century reform movements. To initiate a search for the roots of his reformism in his personal life is also therefore an attempt to locate the major psychological needs behind the social forces which might have powered the rite and then rendered it anachronistic.

and Rammohun's public and private lives. Instead, I shall emphasize only some lesser known aspects of Roy's early interpersonal experiences which provide important clues to his theory of reform and to the 'inner' meaning for him of the crises of his people and his time. It was this meaning which influenced Roy's private responses to the older symbols of authority involved in the rite of sati, and his public struggle to introduce new authority symbols more congruent with the emerging psychological and cultural realities in his community. To the extent he succeeded in his historical role, it was again this meaning which cut across numerous levels and sectors of human behaviour, offsetting private history against collective self-definition and personal synthesis against a diffused collective response to environmental change.

The Logic of a Ritual

Sati, literally a virtuous wife, was the practice of widows burning themselves on the funeral pyres of their husbands (though sometimes the wives took poison or were buried alive). The rite had been prevalent among upper-caste Indians for at least two thousand years without ever becoming a standard practice.

It is not clear when and how the rite first gained a place in Indian culture. A number of studies show that widow remarriage was definitely sanctioned by ancient Hindu laws and the most venerated sacred texts were, if not actually hostile, certainly not well-disposed towards sati. The earlier law-givers, such as Manu and Yajnavalkya, had only recommended a chaste life for widows; others, such as Kautilya, allowed widows to remarry under certain circumstances. It was in the second or third century AD that sati was first recommended in *Vishnu Dharma Samhita* and it was in medieval India that the rite began to gain a new legitimacy.[2] At that time, in some small areas of the country ruled by Hindu princelings and under military, political and social pressures from the Muslim rulers of India, sati became frequent and sometimes even broke out as an epidemic. There are many popular stories about how courageous Hindu widows in the Middle Ages committed *jauhar* or mass sati after the death of their husbands in battle. However, there is also evidence that it was not entirely a matter of courage. Contrary to folklore, even in *jauhar* there was a strong element of compulsion.

Many reasons for the gradual legitimization of the rite are mentioned:

[2]A.S. Altekar, *The Position of Women in Hindu Civilization* (Banaras: Banaras Hindu University, 1938); and K.M. Kapadia, *Marriage and Family in India* (Bombay: Oxford University Press, 1958).

deliberate mistranslation of the sacred texts by the Brahmins; the difficulty of protecting women in times of war, particularly in the Middle Ages; the decline of Buddhism and its rationalist–pacifist influence; contact with some tribal and other cognate cultures which believed that the comfort of a dead man in his after-life could be ensured by burying with him his wives, jewellery, slaves and other favourite possessions.[3] Whatever be the reasons, the popularity of sati declined again after the Middle Ages. We know that by the seventeenth century the practice had become mainly voluntary and took place generally during times of war when it became difficult to protect women. In fact, by the beginning of the eighteenth century it had become a rare occurrence.

It was only towards the end of the eighteenth century and in Bengal that the rite suddenly came to acquire the popularity of a legitimate orgy.[4] Soon widows were being drugged, tied to the bodies of their dead husbands, and forced down with bamboo sticks on the burning pyres. And, this time, the practice mobilized support from many more areas of social life. For instance, on the cultural plane, the burning was invariably preceded by Kali puja and, otherwise, too, had distinctly Shakta features.[5] Again, on the political plane, the lack of self-confidence of the British colonial power and its social non-interventionism during the first phase of the Raj seemed for many a direct endorsement of the practice. In other words, to understand the reform of sati, one must first understand the gestalt of the cultural and institutional factors which might have helped popularize sati in a given region at a given time.

Let me argue the economic historian's case first. There is no doubt that the rite was partly a primitive Malthusian means of population control in famine-ridden Bengal. Previously, high mortality rates and the prohibition of widow remarriage had helped society to limit the number

---

[3]Upendra Thakur, *The History of Suicide in India* (Delhi: Munshiram Manoharlal, 1963).

[4]Detailed district-wise statistics on sati are given in Sophia D. Collet, *The Life and Letters of Raja Rammohun Roy*, edited by D.K. Biswas and P.C. Ganguli (Calcutta: Sadharon Brahmo Samaj, 1962), pp. 83–4, 200, 250. Cf. M.J. Mehta, 'The British Rule and the Practice of Sati in Gujarat', *Journal of Indian History* (August 1966), Vol. XLIV, Part II, No. 131, pp. 553–60.

[5]The word *Shakta* is the adjective derived from the noun *Shakti*, which literally means power, but usage-wise also refers to the ultimate principles of sacred maternity and femininity and to the most powerful symbols of sacred authority, the goddesses Durga and Kali. The Shakti sect of Hinduism, with its emphasis on the worship of Durga and Kali, is, in Bengal, mainly a sect of the upper castes. The pacifist Vaisnava sect, which emphasizes the worship of Krishna and his consort Radha is mainly associated with the lower castes.

of mothers to below the level of available fertile women. However, in times of scarcity, these controls became inadequate and, in times of anomie, widows at certain levels of consciousness seemed useless drags on resources—particularly amongst the upper and middle classes in which women played no direct and manifest economic role.

Eighteenth-century Bengal had both the scarcity and the anomie. After about 150 years of relatively famine-free existence, from 1770 onwards and at short intervals, large-scale scarcities challenged the traditional Bengali concept of benevolent mother deities presiding over a benevolent nature. In 1770 alone about two-fifths of all Bengalis died in a famine; most of these famines were also accompanied by major epidemics. Anomie too was widespread in the expanding urban world of Greater Calcutta, particularly among the upper caste Bengali gentry, the Bhadralok. The colonial system had generated in them a sense of rudderlessness by forcing them to maintain their traditional social dominance on almost entirely new grounds.[6] For example, the new land settlement system was displacing the landed Bhadralok aristocracy with a group of Bhadralok who had defied their caste identity to enter commerce—a profession which in Bengal was typical of the lower castes. These new landlords were merely investing in land the money they had earned from business in the cities, and they derived social status not from traditional social relations, but from British patronage. As if this was not enough, both groups of Bhadraloks found that the fast pace of monetization, by eroding caste obligations, was depriving them of the historical allegiance of artisans, the service castes and the peasantry. The various caste groups now had to work increasingly within the framework of impersonal, contractual, social relations.[7] Finally, though the new system favoured Brahminic skills for the growing tertiary sector, for the upper castes this became a competitively acquired advantage rather than an inherited asset.

So while constituting about 11 per cent of the population of Bengali Hindus, the upper castes accounted for about 55 per cent of the cases of sati, whereas the lower castes, constituting 89 per cent of Bengali Hindus,

[6]Under the new regime, they continued to own three-fourths of all estates in Bengal, dominated both politics and administration, and controlled most of the trade in the hands of Indians. On famines, their social results and normlessness, some data are available in N.K. Sinha, *The Economic History of Bengal*, Vols. I and II (Calcutta: Firma K.L. Mukhopadhyay, 1965), and R.C. Majumdar, *Glimpses of Bengal in the Nineteenth Century* (Calcutta: Firma K.L. Mukhopadhyay, 1960).

[7]N.K. Bose, *Culture and Society in India* (Bombay: Asia, 1967), pp. 358–68; Sinha, *Economic History of Bengal*, Vol. II, p. 206.

contributed about 45 per cent of the victims. This 45 per cent came mainly from the upwardly mobile, Sanskritizing sectors of the lower castes.[8] In other words, the rite was becoming popular not among the rural poor or the small peasantry, but amongst the urban *nouveaux riches* who had lost part of their allegiance to older norms and had no alternative commitments with which to fill the void.

In their simple way some Christian missionaries at the time did relate the growing anomie amongst the élite to the spread of sati. Though they also linked sati to Hindu orthodoxy, the missionaries never lost sight of the class background of sati. Marshman, for instance, felt that 'the increasing luxury of the high and middling classes, . . . and their expensive imitation of European habits' made them eager to avoid the cost of maintaining widows.[9] Rammohun Roy, too, considered economic gain to be a crucial explanation of the rite.[10]

Second, sati helped manipulate the distribution of property in a society that had rigid property rules. Under the *dayabhaga* system of Hindu law operating only in Bengal and some parts of eastern India, the right to property did not arise at the birth of a male co-sharer, but on religious efficacy. Also, a son had the right to separate or dispose of his property before partition and a widow succeeded to her husband's property on his death without a male issue even if the family was undivided.[11] This relatively liberal attitude to women in Bengal was mainly derived from the region's institutional flexibility, its non-Brahminic (mainly tribal and Buddhist) traditions and the greater emphasis which the regional culture placed on the feminine principle in the godhead.[12] All this gave

---

[8]See Rajat K. Roy, 'Introduction', in V.C. Joshi (ed.), *Rammohun Roy and the Process of Modernization in India* (New Delhi: Vikas, 1975), pp. 4–6. On Sanskritization or emulation of greater Sanskritic or Brahminic culture as a means of social mobility, see M.N. Srinivas, *Social Change in India and Other Essays* (Berkeley: University of California, 1966).

[9]One reason for this could have been that women did not play any direct part in the productive process in these sectors.

[10]He perhaps had a personal reason to see economic motives behind the ritual. While neither his father's surviving wives nor any other widow in his family had committed sati when the family was prosperous, once their fortunes started declining, things changed. Rammohun Roy's elder brother's widow burnt herself in 1811 before his eyes, it is said. This fact has been challenged, but if true, it might have established a link in his mind between economic uncertainties and the rite.

[11]P.V. Kane, *History of Dharmasastra*, Vol. III (Poona: Oriental Research Institute, 1946), pp. 558–9.

[12]S.C. Mitra, 'On the Origin and Development of the Bengal School of Hindu Law', *Law Quarterly Review*, 1905, 21, pp. 380–92; and 1906, 22, pp. 50–63; quoted and discussed in Kane, *Dharmasastra*, Vol. III, pp. 558–9.

women a legitimate right to property as wives as well as mothers who could influence the decision of their children–copartners. But these were dangerous privileges to have in a culture where survival was not easy and where there was a high chance that a widow would inherit property or use it for bargaining purposes within the family. Inducing her to commit suicide was an efficient way of checking this.[13]

Third, in families seduced away from the path of traditional virtue by the new colonial culture, sati became a means of securing social status and renown for virtue. We have already noted that the rite enjoyed some popularity among the upwardly mobile sectors of Bengali society and that they found in sati a new means of Sanskritization. Important parts of urban Bengal accepted this new means as legitimate: even when the family of the suicide was prosecuted, there was no loss of caste, infamy or disgrace; the family in fact gained in social stature and were 'backed with applause and honour'.[14] The duress exerted on the prospective sati was seen as a test of the piety of a family. Taking advantage of this social sanction, the practitioners of the rite were most ruthless with the widow who, after making the fatal decision to commit sati, later wavered.

A part of the status acquired through sati attached to the suicide herself. This was a powerful incentive in a society where humiliation and bullying were generally the widow's lot. Economic freedom for her was virtually out of the question; it could be bought only through prostitution or other such extra-social ventures. In addition, there were taboos on her attendance at festive and religious occasions and severe restrictions on food, decorative dress and adornment. Thus, the sheer misery of a widow's life partly negated the prospective suicide's fear of death. Such a future seemed even worse because of childhood prejudices and fantasies about the widow being a bad omen and an evil presence.

Fourth, a large number of Bengali Brahmins *did* claim sacred sanctions for sati; indeed, sati was seen by many observers of Indian society as a conspiracy of Brahmins.[15] It went unnoticed by most of these

[13]Interestingly, Rammohun Roy provides a more or less similar interpretation both in his famous appeal to the Governor-General and in his treatise on women's property rights in India. See *The English Works of Raja Rammohun Roy*, Vol. I. Kalidas Nag and Debojyoti Burman (eds.) (Calcutta: Sadharon Brahma Samaj, 1945–8), pp. 1–10; and Roy's letter to Mrs Woodford, ibid., Vol. IV, pp. 90–1.

[14]Rammohun Roy quoted in P.K. Sen, *Biography of a New Faith* (Calcutta: Thacker, Spink, 1950), pp. 34–5; R.C. Majumdar, 'Social Reform', in R.C. Majumdar, A.K. Majumdar and D.K. Ghose (eds.), *British Paramountcy and the Indian Renaissance*, Part II (Bombay: Bharatiya Vidya Bhavan, 1965), p. 270.

[15]For example, Thomas Bowrey, *A Geographical Account of Countries Round*

observers that the Bengali Brahmins, unlike Brahmins in some other parts of India, were not merely religious leaders and interpreters of texts, traditions and rites but major landholders and financiers who were increasingly co-opted by the colonial system. Also, they were the caste most exposed to westernization and the growing conflict between the old and the new.[16] As already noted, in the new set-up many had to maintain their traditional status on the grounds of a new set of values and not on the grounds of their older, more internally consistent, lifestyle. As a result, material and status gains were often associated with moral anxiety and some free-floating rage at adaptive problems. And they began to see all restrictions on ritualized expression of these feelings as further threats to their lifestyle. The opposition to sati constituted such a threat for them. In their desperate defence of the rite they were also trying to defend their traditional self-esteem and self-definition.[17]

But underlying these causes of sati were other causes even less amenable to conscious control and less accessible to contemporary consciousness. It is with these that this analysis is mainly concerned.

First, to reword in psychological terms what we have already said, the rite became popular in groups made psychologically marginal by their exposure to western impact. These groups felt the pressure to demonstrate, to others as well as to themselves, their ritual purity and allegiance to traditional high culture. To many, sati became an important proof of conformity to older norms at a time when these norms had become shaky within.[18] Nineteenth-century policy-makers, chroniclers and social analysts sensed this. For instance, the first Governor General of British India, Warren Hastings, attributed the increase in sati in 1821 'to the fanatic spirit roused by the divided state of feeling among the Hindus'.[19]

---

the Bay of Bengal, 1669–1679, edited by R.C. Temple (Hakluyt Society and Kraus Reprint Ltd., Neudelul Neichtenstein, Series 2), Vol. II, pp. 197–205. Rammohun himself in a general way believed in this conspiracy theory; see his *English Works*, Vol. II, pp. 43–4, 48–9.

[16]This was primarily because the colonial system needed the Brahmanic skills of reading, writing and accounting and the legitimacy which only Brahmans when co-opted by the system could give to it.

[17]A.F. Salahuddin, *Social Ideas and Social Change in Bengal, 1818–1835* (Leyden: E.J. Brill, 1965), p. 126, mentions pride and economic discontent as two possible causes of support for sati.

[18]Cf. Norman Cohn, *Europe's Inner Demons* (New York: Basic Books, 1975). Cohn argues that the European witch-hunt in the Middle Ages was a response to the fear of regression to an earlier belief system which was only partly ego-alien.

[19]Sen, *Biography of a New Faith*, pp. 34–5.

And Collet, too, in saying that the rite was prevalent among passive people and not among the 'bold and manly' type,[20] indirectly draws attention to the difference between the exposed easterners, feeling increasingly impotent ritually, and the unexposed northern and western parts of India, still mainly outside the areas of direct British rule and yet undisturbed in their traditional lifestyle. Others also noticed that there had been only one instance of the wife of a dead Indian soldier of the colonial army committing sati,[21] and that the incidence of sati was highest in the urban areas, among high and upwardly mobile castes, and in areas more exposed to western impact.[22] In other words, sati may have involved Hindu traditions, but it was not a manifestation of hard-core Hindu orthodoxy.

Second, sati expressed the culture's deepest fears of—and hatred towards—woman and womanhood. The earliest available myth about sati speaks of a Rajput wife who poisoned her husband. From this 'crime', Diodorus Siculus said in 314 BC, the 'institution took its rise'.[23] One does not know how popular the myth has been in different periods of history and in different parts of India, but it does summarize the intense fears of aggression and annihilation and deep longings for nurture and benevolent mothering that had always been associated with Indian, and particularly Bengali, concepts of womanhood.

As in most peasant cultures, the dominant image of authority in the peasant cosmology of Bengal had always been feminine. It was that of a mother goddess who was the original or basic power, *Adyashakti*, and the ultimate principle of nature and activity, *Prakriti*. The personification of this principle was Chandi, the traditional goddess of the region. Though apparently associated with only the Shakti cult, a cult in turn associated with the elite castes in Bengal, the mother goddess constituted the basic irreducible elements in Bengali cosmology.[24]

One of the most striking features of the rise in the popularity of sati

---

[20]Dispatch of 15 August 1822, quoted in Collet, p. 198.

[21]Ibid., pp. 258–9.

[22]See also J.H. Harrington, cited in K. Ingham, *Reformers in India, 1793–1833* (Cambridge: Cambridge University Press, 1956), p. 50.

[23]W.H. Carey, *The Good Old Days of Honourable John Company, Being Curious Reminiscences During the Rule of the East India Company from 1600 to 1858*, 1882 (Calcutta: Quins Books, 1964).

[24]Some of these cultural parameters have been identified by S.B. Dasgupta, *Bharater Shakti Sadhana o Shaka Sahitya* (Calcutta: Sahitya Samsad, 1960); J.C. Roy Vidyanidhi, *Puja-Parban* (Calcutta: Viswa-Bharati, 1951); Chintaharan Chakravarti, *Banglar Palparban* (Calcutta: Viswa-Bharati, 1953); and *Tantrakatha* (Calcutta: Viswa-Bharati, 1955).

was that it coincided with a gradual bifurcation of the Chandi image. Why did this coincidence occur? Why was the bifurcation necessary at that point of time? Perhaps frequent natural calamities and the new colonial culture, which constantly invalidated the older assumptions of living, created the need for a new psycho-ecological balance in which the aggressive aspect of cosmic motherhood would be better recognized. Perhaps some crucial sections of Bengali society had lost faith in the sustaining feminine principle in the environment and, in reaction, built a more powerful symbol of womanly betrayal, punishment and rage.[25]

In any case, by the end of the eighteenth century, the sacred authority image of Bengal came to be clearly defined by two co-ordinates: Durga, the demon-killing protective mother as well as the giver of food and nurture, and Kali, the unpredictable, punitive mother, till then the goddess of a few marginal groups like dacoits, thieves, thugs, prostitutes and now— increasingly and revealingly—of the exposed elites and quasi-elites of greater Calcutta, the babus.[26] Durga, an unknown goddess only a few decades earlier, now became the most popular deity and made Durga puja the most popular religious and social festival of the region. Kali became the new symbol of a treacherous cosmic mother, eager to betray and prone to aggression. She also came to be associated with almost all the other major rituals generally cited as instances of the cultural

[25]These new maternal archetypes established links with a number of second-order deities presiding over important aspects of life which were becoming sectors of stress. Annapurna of Annada, another incarnation of Durga, was the protector of crops and the soil and the giver of food. Durga's daughters, the benevolent Saraswati and the benevolent but fickle Lakshmi, were the goddesses of learning and wealth respectively. Two irascible goddesses, Olaichandi and Sheetala presided over cholera and small-pox. Shashti ruled over conception, childbirth and child-health—important functions in a community with high birth- and infant-mortality rates. Superstitions were dominated by elderly witches and the goddesses invoked in Tantra—an originally Buddhist but now Shakto ritual and magical technique (for murder, injury or enslavement from a distance) becoming popular at about this time (the first mention of *Radhatantra*, the major tantric text, was in a list of books prepared in 1777; Chakravarty, *Tantrakatha*). All these were related to the primal image of Kali. The traditional strategy of propitiating these goddesses was some form of sacrifice: human or animal, personal or group, actual or symbolic. But the most preferred sacrifice was human, as it was human sacrifice which Durga and Kali were believed to relish most (Vidyanidhi, *Puja-Parban*, pp. 10–23, 77–260). It was as if one could placate the celestial mothers by identifying with their cannibalistic selves and aggressing for the mother's causes. In sum, the Durga and Kali aspects of motherhood were not as orthogonal as they may at first sight appear.

[26]On the social and religious life of the babus of the time, see R.C. Majumdar, *Nineteenth Century Bengal*; and Binoy Ghose, *Kalkata Culture* (Calcutta: Bihar Sahitya Bhavan, 1953) pp. 91–8.

decadence of the age, and against each of which Rammohun Roy and almost every other reformer of the region fought.

It was this new psychological environment which mothered the folk theory of sati, that the husband's death was due to the wife's poor ritual performance and was her self-created fate. The theory imputed that the wife brought about the death of the man under her protection, by her weak ritual potency and by deliberately not using or failing to maintain her latent womanly ability to manipulate natural events and fate.[27] An important part of the cultural identity of women in India had always been the mythological figure of Savitri, the wife who through her tenacious piety brought her husband back from death. It was this identity which widows seemed to defy. All widows consequently seemed to be failures in propitiation and instances of homicidal wishes magically coming true.

This demonology was associated with two major rationalizations of the rite. The first was expressed in the fear that, without the authoritarian control of the husband, the widow would stray from the path of virtue; the second in the imputation that women were virtuous only because of external rewards and punishments and not because they had internalized social norms. The contemporary pro-sati literature repeatedly mentions the frailty of women, their 'subjection to passion', lack of understanding and quarrelsomeness, and their 'want of virtuous knowledge'. All three allegedly made them untrustworthy and fickle.[28]

Sati was therefore an enforced penance, a death penalty through which the widow expiated her responsibility for her husband's death. Simultaneously, it reduced the sense of guilt in those confronted with their rage against all women. Punishment by authority became, in an infantile morality, a proof of culpability.[29] It perpetuated the fantasy of feminine aggression towards the husband, bound anxiety by giving substance to vague fears of women, and contained the fear of death in a region where death struck suddenly and frequently due to what, by popular

---

[27]This was evident in the attitude towards widows in general, the various mores they had to conform to, their self-hatred and self-inflicted sufferings.

[28]See Collet, *Rammohun Roy*, pp. 92–5; also Rammohun Roy, *Granthabali*, Vol. III, Brajendranath Bandopadhyay and Sajanikanta Das (eds.) (Calcutta: Bangiya Sahitya Parishad, n.d.).

[29]On punishment as an infantile proof of guilt and as a stage or aspect of human morality, see J. Piaget, *Moral Judgement of the Child* (Glencoe: Free Press, 1948). A well-known brief review of available research on this subject is by L. Kohlberg, 'Development of Moral Character and Moral Ideology', M.L. and L.W. Hoffman (eds.), *Child Development Research* (New York: Russel and Sage Foundation, 1964), pp. 383–431.

consensus, were whimsical, feminine principles in the cosmos. On the other hand, to the extent women shared these fantasies about their ritual role and responsibility for the death of their husbands, sati was also associated with the introjection of the terrorizing maternal aspects of femininity, guilt arising from this self-image, and the tendency to use the defence of turning against one's own self in atonement.

Finally, this use of widows as scapegoats and the fear of womanhood were related to the culturally typical myths and early experiences surrounding mothering. As will be argued in a later section, a central feature of the psychological life of an Indian is his deep ambivalence towards his mother, operating within the Indian family system both as a source of close, individuating authority and as a source of uncertain, almost fickle, nurture.[30] Widows reinvoked the infantile rage towards personal mothers who always threatened to fail and towards cosmic mothers who at that point of history tended to confirm the uncertainties and 'betrayals' of the former. The 'vague rage' generated by adaptive impotence—the 'fanatic spirit roused by divided feeling' which Hastings speaks of—may have underwritten the process further.[31]

All these forces converged in the culture of the babus. Borrowing from some of the recessive aspects of Bengali folk culture and from particularized Brahminism,[32] this babu culture made a sadistic sport out of sati. And to the extent this culture was itself a product of western and modern encroachments upon the traditional lifestyle, sati was society's weirdest response to new cultural inputs and institutional innovations. In 1818 one Oakely, an administrator at Hooghly near Calcutta, tried to explain the higher incidence and growth of sati in Greater Calcutta in the following words:

It is notorious that the natives of Calcutta and its vicinity exceed all others in profligacy and immorality of conduct; and while the depraved worship of Kali, 'the idol of the drunkard and the thief', is 'scarcely to be met with in distant provinces', it abounds in the metropolis. Elsewhere, none but the most abandoned will openly confess that he is a follower of Kali. In Calcutta we find few that are not . . . . By such men, a suttee is not regarded as a religious act but

---

[30]See Section III below. For an extended treatment of the literature on the subject, see Ashis Nandy and Sudhir Kakar, 'Culture and Personality in India', in Udai Parekh (ed.), *Research in Psychology* (Bombay: Popular Prakashan, in press).

[31]On rage as a response to adaptive impotence, see E.H. Erikson, *Insight and Responsibility* (London: Faber and Faber, 1964), p. 214.

[32]This particularization of the greater Sanskritic traditions in Bengal was the other reinterpretation taking place in the community. It is, however, beyond the scope of this paper.

as a choice entertainment; and we may conclude that the vicious propensities of the Hindus in the vicinity of Calcutta are a cause of the comparative prevalence of the custom.[33]

Charles Grant, seeking clues to Hindu 'insensibility' in general and cruelty to women in particular, found them in the cruelty and licentiousness of gods, particularly Kali, the increasingly popular goddess of the Calcuttans.[34] No one noticed that the goddess in her new incarnation was neither intrinsic to the Brahminic traditions nor to its Bengali variant; nor did they know that the much maligned Kali puja was not even mentioned in the well-known Tantric texts of the region and was a new institution.[35]

Did Rammohun Roy accept the equation between sati and the content of Hindu orthodoxy? Apparently he did. It was 'the peculiar practice of Hindu idolatry which', he felt, 'more than any other pagan worship, destroys the texture of the society'.[36] That is why to him the legal prohibition of sati was not enough. By itself, it did not even seem very attractive.[37] According to him, the root of the pathology was that 'advocates of idolatry and their misguided followers . . . continue, under the form of religious devotion, to practise a system which . . . prescribes crimes of most heinous nature, which even the most savage nation would blush to commit.'[38] So, it was Hindu idolatry which had to be attacked first:

The natural inclination of the ignorant towards the worship of objects resembling their own nature, and to the external forms of rites palpable to their grosser senses . . . has rendered the generality of the Hindoo community . . . devoted to idol worship—the source of prejudice and superstition and of the total destruction of moral principle, as countenancing criminal intercourse, suicide, female murder, and human sacrifices.[39]

[33]Collet, *Rammohun Roy*, p. 85. The higher incidence of sati in the Calcutta area is borne out by published statistics. See Collet, *Rammohan Roy*, pp. 83–4. Also Majumdar, *Nineteenth Century Bengal*, p. 269.

[34]Charles Grant, 'Observations on the State of Society among the Asiatic Subjects of Great Britain, Particularly with Respect of Morals, and on the Means of Improving It', written in 1792, *Parliamentary Papers*, House of Commons, 1812–1813, *10*, Paper 282, pp. 1–112, particularly pp. 60–6.

[35]Chakravarty, *Tantrakatha*. The philosophical practice of Tantra, though Buddhist in origin, had become by this time relatively central to the Shakti cult. Popular belief considered Kali puja an essential part of it.

[36]Rammohun Roy, 1816, *English Works*, Vol. II, p. 60.

[37]Collet, *Rammohun Roy*, p. 75. It is this hesitancy, more than anything else, which has created recent doubts about Rammohun Roy's anti-sati position.

[38]Rammohun Roy, 1819, *English Works*, Vol. II, p. 23, also p. 52.

[39]Ibid., p. vii.

Thus, like his contemporaries, Roy also thought Hinduism to be the culprit. Yet obviously the causal relationship between sati and Hinduism was not so simple and perhaps it would be truer to say that it was a rather small group of exposed, marginalized men who sought in Hinduism a support for their anomic response to structural changes. The new and popular version of sati was their creation, and so was the new concept of a more terrorizing cosmic motherhood by which they sought to justify it.

The Roots of Dissent

A closer examination of Rammohun Roy's writings and personal history reveals deeper sensitivities, however. He not only linked sati to the community's mode of worship, but challenged its basis by suggesting new sex role norms and sexual stereotypes, and by showing the spurious links the practice had with Hindu traditions. The word sati is a derivative of the root *sat*, truth or goodness. The widow by dying with her husband proved that she was true to him and virtuous. Roy shifted the onus of showing fidelity and rectitude to others. While men seemed to him 'naturally weak' and 'prone to be led astray by temptations of temporary gratifications', women seemed to him to have 'firmness of mind, resolution, trustworthiness and virtue'; they were 'void of duplicity' and capable of 'leading the austere life of an ascetic'.[40]

This challenge to traditional sexual identities was to have important implications for the history of reform movements in India. During the following hundred years, nearly all such movements centered around the cause of women and the dominant models of social intervention were frequently attempts to work through the peasant society's historical ambivalence towards women.[41] Roy's reinterpretations of the older concept of womanhood and the older relationship between maleness and femininity were thus aspects of a more durable theory of social reform.[42]

The reasons for this link between Roy's model and the reforms of the next generation are not particularly obscure. The various structures

[40]Ibid., Vol. VI, p. 5; and Vol. III, pp. 87–137; and *Granthabali*, Vol. III; Collet, *Rammohan Roy*, pp. 92–5.

[41]See on the subject Ashis Nandy, 'Woman versus Womanliness', in *At the Edge of Psychology: Essays in Politics and Culture* (New Delhi: Oxford University Press, 1980), pp. 32–46.

[42]Patricia Uberoi has drawn my attention to the fact that a similar latent theory of social changes had emerged in China as a part of the May Fourth Movement (1915–20) which fought the traditional Chinese proscription of widow remarriage, and the institutional encouragement given to widows to commit suicide, particularly if dishonoured.

introduced into India by British colonialism assumed a new colonial culture which, while being compatible with traditions, would include within it new concepts of public activism and ethics, political power, interpersonal skills and professional participation. All these concepts were deeply associated with definitions of masculinity and femininity in both the greater Sanskritic culture and Bengal's folk version of Hinduism. It is to Rammohun Roy's credit that he was the first to sense this and delineate a model of reform in which a new definition of womanhood would be the central plank. This cultural sensitivity and cognitive innovation was his main contribution to the emerging culture of modern India.

The connection between the reformer in Rammohun Roy and the reform of sati brings us to his personal history, as it epitomized his society's basic problems at that point of time and to the solution which Indian society found for itself in Rammohun Roy's life and personality. In other words, it brings us to his earliest exposures to concepts of power, activism, motherhood and religiosity, his first conflicts around the interlinkages among these concepts, the distinctive sex role images to which his family sensitized him, and the early validations and invalidations in him of the typical regional myths and fantasies centering around masculinity, femininity, nurture, propitiation and defiance.

Rammohun Roy was born in 1772 in a Vaisnava Kulin Brahman family in a village about 100 miles from Calcutta. The family had been culturally atypical for at least two generations. Contemporary revenue records mention that after the death of his grandfather, his father and uncles 'did not live together as a joint family, but were divided in food, estate and interests'.[43] This complete nuclearity of the family astounds one; in eighteenth-century Bengal the joint family may not have been the norm, but it certainly was the normal ideal. Even though a majority of Hindus stayed in partly-nuclear households, the nuclearization rarely went this far among the prosperous, landed, upper castes.[44] Perhaps the Roys, being a family of urban bureaucrats, were more fully exposed to the unsettling effects of the changing political economy of eastern India than is evident on the surface.

The impact of this deviation on Rammohun Roy's early experiences was deep. However, before describing this impact, mention must be made of a few features of a typical joint household in India which, distorted by

[43]I. Singh, *Rammohan Roy*, Vol. I (Bombay, Asia, 1958).

[44]For a brief discussion of the incidence of joint families in various social strata, see M.S. Gore, *The Impact of Industrialization and Urbanization on the Aggarwal Family of Delhi Area* (Ph.D. Dissertation, Columbia University, 1961, University Microfilms, Ann Arbor), Chapter 1, pp. 2–59.

the process of nuclearization, had a direct bearing on the way Rammohun Roy conceptualized the problems of his society.

The first of these features is the tendency in an extended family to expose the growing child to a number of adult authorities and discourage him from distinguishing between 'near' and 'distant' relations amongst these authorities. The aim is to deter the growth of 'emotionally exclusive' loyalty towards one's own nuclear unit within the larger family. Within such a pattern of diffused authority and joint responsibility, the father generally plays a distant and non-committal role in relation to his children. He is neutralized as an immediate, intimate authority with a manifest and direct interest in his children. Once again, the aim is to blur the boundaries of the nuclear units.

However, the emotional restrictiveness of the father–son relationship in the joint family does not apply to mother–child intimacy.[45] In fact, the culture takes some care to see that the decisive memory trace for the individual remains the experience of the primordial intimacy with the only effective figure he has known within the family: his mother. In his relationship with other members, the son is categorized by his sex and age role. He is judged by standards which are impersonal. It is the mother who individualizes him.[46] The culture also strengthens this intimacy by 'idolizing' woman as a mother (to contain her conjugal role as wife and to stop fissures developing along the margins of nuclear units) and by devaluing wifehood (which induces her to look at her son as one who would give her status). Being necessarily the sole immediate source of power, nurture and wrath in early childhood, it is the mother who becomes the ultimate symbol of authority as well as the ultimate target of defiance.

The result is a deep ambivalence which links the concept of maternal authority to that of an undependable nurturant, prone to betray and eager to aggress.[47] In personal fantasies and cultural myths it produces a

---

[45]See P. Sratt, *Hindu Culture and Personality* (Bombay: Manaktalas, 1966). On warm non-demanding intimacy in the mother–son relationship in the early years of growth, see also G.M. Carstairs, *The Twice-Born* (Bloomington: Indiana, 1958) particularly, pp. 157–8; Dhirendra Narayan, 'Indian National Character in the Twentieth Century'; *The Annals of American Academy of Political and Social Science* (March 1967) 370, pp. 124–32; and Gore, *The Aggarwal Family*, p. 11.

[46]Ibid., p. 36. This happens also because, to regulate conjugality, a patrilineal or patrilocal society cannot easily minimize the role of the genitor. It therefore emphasizes perforce the role of the mother and underplays the role of the woman (ibid., p. 11–12). See also Margaret Cormack, *The Hindu Woman* (New York: Columbia University, 1953), pp. 150–1; Aileen D. Ross, *The Hindu Family in its Urban Setting* (Toronto: University of Toronto, 1961). pp. 101–3.

[47]For other sources and aspects of this ambivalence, see studies of the traditional Indian system of childrearing in Carstairs, *The Twice Born*, particularly pp. 152–

persistent preoccupation with maternal warmth and a persistent anxiety about motherly fickleness, aggression and counter-aggression. It also produces strong counterphobic attempts to glorify constancy in mothering and to rationalize its fluctuations as due to human frailties and aggression towards the mother or her symbols, which could be corrected by suppliance, sacrifice and restitution.[48]

The impact of these forces on the young Rammohun Roy's personality can only be guessed. For instance, it is probable that the culturally prototypical mother–son relationship might have become a source of heightened ambivalence within the nuclear household of the Roys. Both the mother and the son may have found themselves face to face in a situation where there were few structural constraints on within-family behaviour and expressive style. Again, the father might have become not merely the sole male authority and male role model within the family, but also an immediate interpersonal reality, stressing the need for a strong, intervening, paternal authority who would delineate, for himself and his sons, a clearer social identity.

Strangely, this deduced pattern neatly fits what little we know about Rammohun Roy's early interpersonal environment. Somehow both his parents appear to be exaggerated versions of traditional Indian parents, with some aspects of their personalities heavily underscored by the demands of a nuclear family.

The mother, Tarinidevi, whose turbulent relationship with her son is now accepted history, was the fervently religious daughter of a priestly family. She wielded, it is said, 'considerable influence over her husband' and was the 'real power at home'.[49] She not only 'set the general tone of family life', but directed practical affairs normally outside the prerogative of Indian women.[50] However, it is principally a certain ruthless fidelity to a cause which made Tarinidevi the most effective figure within the family. Iqbal Singh comes nearest to the maternal figure I want to invoke. He sums up Tarinidevi thus:

69; Leigh Mintern and J.T. Hitchtock, 'The Rajputs of Khalapur'; Beatrice Whiting (ed.), *Six Cultures* (New York: Wiley, 1963), pp. 203–361; Leigh Mintern and W.W. Lambert, *Mothers of Six Cultures* (New York: Wiley, 1964), pp. 230–9; and Spratt, *Hindu Culture and Personality*.

Sudhir Kakar has shown that this ambivalence is significantly deeper in Bengal than other parts of India. See his 'Aggression in Indian Society: An Analysis of Folk Tales', *Indian Journal of Psychology*, June 1974, 49(2), pp. 119–26.

[48]See some instances in Kakar, 'Aggression in Indian Society', pp. 226–7, 23–6; Carstairs, *The Twice-Born*, pp. 156–9.

[49]Collet, *Rammohun Roy*, p. 4; and Singh, *Rammohan Roy*, pp. 22–3.

[50]Singh, *Rammohan Roy*; R.C. Dutta, *Cultural Heritage of Bengal* (Calcutta: Punthi Pustak, 1962), p. 91.

... a remarkable woman but in quite a different and unconventional sense. She was ... cast in a much stronger mould than the other two wives of Ramakanta .... Whatever convictions Tarinidevi held she held strongly and with all the tenacity of a woman's will, though it is true that these convictions were not illumined by any deep understanding or moderating charity of judgement. Equally, she did not lack firmness of purpose, though, again, this firmness was not tempered by any quality of compassion and perceptiveness ....[51]

This tenacious fidelity to convictions had a history. Before marriage Tarinidevi had been a devout Shakto and, hence, not exposed to the glorification of passivity and emotional pacifism which has always been an important part of Vaisnavism all over India. After marriage she changed her allegiance—enthusiastically according to some, and with a vengeance, according to others—to her husband's denomination, 'as was expected of a good wife'.[52] Whatever be the social and familial pressures behind that apparently innocuous change, by a number of accounts it was this overnight transformation which encouraged Tarinidevi to make intense overt conformity to the family denomination the keynote of her self-image.

But rejected loyalties die harder than that. The Shakto commitment to forms and rituals, which Tarinidevi brought into the Vaisnava culture of the Roys, only forced her to model her Vaisnava self on her aggressive, ardent, anti-ascetic, Shakto identification. And the constraints of the pacifist asceticism of Vaisnavism only ensured the indirect but ruthless manner in which her persistent Shaktoism was expressed after marriage. To quote Iqbal Singh again, she had

... a hard core of intractability verging on ruthlessness she may have derived from her religious background .... They owed allegiance ... to Kali whose beauty is beyond good or evil, and carries with it, inexorably and everlastingly, the intimation of terror no less beyond good or evil.[53]

The 'hard core of intractibility verging on ruthlessness', with which Tarinidevi sought and defended her ideological purity was also reflected in her mothering. The children were drawn into her 'intricate web of ceremony and form', her 'almost neurotic attention to every minute detail of worship and observance', and her 'delirium of pieties'.[54] They had little protection in a culture where such traits were often considered aspects

[51]Singh, *Rammohan Roy*, p. 19.
[52]Ibid., p. 20; Collet, *Rammohan Roy*, p. 4.
[53]Singh, *Rammohan Roy*, p. 20.
[54]Ibid., pp. 20, 22–3.

of feminine virtue and in a family where power decisively rested with the mother.[55]

The correlation between power and fiery purism that the mother demonstrated might have carried other associations too. Many years afterwards the son was to suggest that his mother's family had shown a certain purity of avocation and fidelity to faith, which his father's family had not.

My maternal ancestors, being of the sacerdotal order by profession as well as by birth, and of a family than which none holds a higher rank in that profession, have up to the present day uniformly adhered to a life of religious observances and devotion, preferring peace and tranquillity of mind to the excitements of ambition, and all the allurements of worldly grandeur.[56]

The son may have also sensed early that power did not reside in the apparently patriarchal forms, but in the personalities that gave them substance. And the substance in this case was Tarinidevi's authoritarian ritualism which made traditions not merely a way of life but an ideology. The nuclearization of the Roy family only underwrote this pattern of dominance, and the associations among power, intervention in the real world of events, feminine identification and feminine cause.

Thus Tarinidevi was perhaps destined to become the ultimate target as well as the model of rebellion for her son. Along one axis, she was bound to generate in him a sweeping hostility towards women, towards the cultural symbols associated with mothering, and a defensive rigidity towards the mother-worshippers of Bengal. This hostility did not follow his exposure to the patriarchal elements of Christian, Buddhist and Islamic theologies; it was merely endorsed by these alternative systems.[57]

At the personal level, too, this hostility hounded modern India's first theoretician and activist for women's liberation throughout his life. No

---

[55]See a comparable situation in the childhood of a later generation Brahmo in Nandy, 'Defiance and Conformity in Science: The World of Jagadish Chandra Bose', in *Alternative Sciences* (New Delhi: Allied, in press).

[56]Roy's letter to Gordon, 1832, reprinted from *Athenaeum and Literary Gazetteer* in S.C. Chakravarti (ed.), *The Father of Modern India* (Calcutta: Rammohun Roy Centenary Committee), 1935, Vol. II, p. 119.

[57]Even in latency, he was already intolerant of the concept of a weak god subservient to a female deity. He would start crying, it is said, whenever a particular scene of the folk play *Manbhanjan* was enacted. The scene depicted Krishna, the supreme god of the Vaisnavas, placating Radha, his consort, by weeping and clasping her feet, while his peacock headgear and clothes lay rolling in the dust. Collet, *Rammohun Roy*, pp. 5–6.

one who reads about Rammohun Roy's troubled relationships with his three wives, his extra-marital peccadilloes, his long and bitter legal battle against his mother, his lonely life in a separate house away from his orthodox wives and orthodox children allegiant to their mothers, can fail to sense the depth of his rage against women. When he finally left India in 1830 to defend the proscription of sati in the British Privy Council he began his journey for the cause of Hindu women by 'forgetting' to inform his youngest wife of his departure. If one considers this to be the final evidence of Rammohun Roy's latent disdain for women, there are the questions he wrote to be put to his mother in the Calcutta High Court, after she had filed a false suit against him on behalf of her stepson:

. . . have you not instigated and prevailed on your grandson the Complainant to institute the present suit against the said Defendant, as a measure of revenge; because the said Defendant hath refused to practise the rites and ceremonies of the Hindu Religion in the manner in which you wish the same to be practised or performed? Have you not . . . estranged yourself . . . from all intercourse with the Defendant . . .? Have you not repeatedly declared . . . that there will not only be no sin but that it will be meritorious to effect the temporal ruin of the Defendant . . .? Have you not publicly declared that it will not be sinful to take away the life of a Hindoo who forsakes the idolatry and ceremonies of worship? . . . Declare solemnly on your oath, whether you do not know and believe that the present suit would not have been instituted if the Defendant had not acted in religious matters contrary to your wishes and entreaties and differently from the practices of his ancestors? Do you not in your conscience believe that you will be justified in your power to effect the ruin of the Defendant and to enable the complainant to succeed in the present suit . . .?[58]

Inevitably, this perception of a vindictive, homicidal mother led to a deep sense of hurt and anger and in turn to a haunting sense of guilt. More so because, in the final reckoning, Rammohun Roy defeated his mother decisively on every issue. He defied her religious orthodoxy, defeated her economic and familial powers, won his legal suit against her, and later on virtually denied her motherhood. In other words, the defeat he inflicted on her was total. And Tarinidevi, that proud matriarch, had to end her days humbly sweeping the steps of a temple at a well-known place of pilgrimage.

Total defeats are psychologically dangerous, but so is total victory. It was no different with Rammohun Roy:

[58]Cited in Singh, *Rammohan Roy*, pp. 80–1.

Whenever he spoke of his mother, it was with warm affection and a 'glistening eye'. The glistening eye itself was, perhaps, a screen for something too deep for tears. Behind it a more perceptive observer might well have registered the febrile pulse of a remorse for which even the most convincing intellectual essays in self justification could offer no effective therapy.[59]

Such a sense of guilt seeks large-scale rationalizations as well as large-scale reparations. I shall describe in a while how Rammohun's reformism did ultimately erect a magnificent structure of public atonement.

All this, however, does not negate the fact that, along a second axis, Tarinidevi was also bound to generate in her son a sharp awareness of the power, individuality, capacities and rights of women. I have already mentioned that Rammohun tried to reverse the traditional definitions of masculinity and femininity in his culture. These efforts were directly influenced by Roy's expanded awareness of what women were and could be. To this expansion of awareness Tarinidevi had contributed handsomely. Not merely that. When his contemporaries assess him as 'shrewd, vigilant, active, ambitious and prepossessing in his manners',[60] one is tempted to relate this image to descriptions of Tarinidevi—purposeful, authoritative and self-confident—managing the affairs of the Roys and fighting a continuous battle against all outer and inner encroachments on her new-found identity. This was a part of his self the reformer could ill afford to waste.

In fact, it was on this combination of rage, guilt and admiration that Rammohun Roy based his perception of an inverse relationship between authority images around which his community's faith was organized, and the needs of the contemporary world. Rammohun Roy had to try to topple Bengal's transcendental symbols of motherliness; and it had to be for the sake of Bengal's suffering women.

Let us now turn to the mother's lack-lustre consort and the family's grandest failure: Ramakanta Roy. Occupied with economic opportunities, profits and possibly profiteering,[61] he was in many ways a typical product as well as a representative of the Bhadralok response to new social forces. Or so it might have seemed to his son. There is some vague evidence that Ramakanta's failures as an authority figure were, for his son, the first adaptive failures of the community.

[59]Ibid., pp. 183–4.
[60]Missionary Register, Church of England, September 1816; in Singh, *Rammohan Roy*, p. 161.
[61]Ibid.; S.K. De, *Bengali Literature in the Nineteenth Century* (Calcutta: Firma K.L. Mukhopadhyay, 1962), 2nd edition, p. 503.

Ramakanta was, in the mellow and euphemistic language of an earlier generation, 'an upright and estimable man', and 'noted for his quiet and retiring disposition'.[62] This disposition, some say, was an outcome of his unhappy work experiences. He was the son of an urban bureaucrat, and had been a functionary in the Nawab's court at Murshidabad in north Bengal. It is said he was sacked for inefficiency and dishonesty a short time before Rammohun was born. It has also been suggested by chroniclers belonging to a less generous age, that the occupational failure of Ramakanta was neither singular nor unprecedented. It was 'one of a series which ended only with his death'.[63]

We do not know how far this career demonstrated to him and to his sons his ineffectiveness as an urbanite, as a member of the growing tertiary sector, and as a male authority in the family. But we know his reaction to these failures. He defended himself by an interpersonal withdrawal which was almost pathetic. He 'was often so disgusted with the treatment he received that he would neglect his affairs for a while, and retire to meditate and tell *Harinam* beads in a garden of Tulsi plants'.[64] Another biographer is more explicit. Ramakanta, he says, 'did not command any great ability or resourcefulness . . . when things did not go well . . . [he] retreated into the brittle shell of his Vaisnava devotionalism . . . .'[65] Apparently, both in the family and in the outside world, he remained 'singularly colourless, almost inchoate and lacking in clear focus, when contrasted with the granite figure of his second wife'.[66] In these, the Vaisnava idealization of passive submission and deindividualization provided him with an important consensual validation of his personal lifestyle and self-concept.

Perhaps the young Rammohun Roy was not taken in by this belated return to religion. Perhaps, at a certain level of consciousness, he connected the father's resignation of power within the family to his losing his Brahminic potency, traditionally maintained through spiritual exercises and scholarly skills.[67] There is a clue in what, many years afterwards, Rammohun Roy once said about his mother's consort:

My ancestors were Brahmins of a high order, and from time immemorial were devoted to the religious duties of their race, down to my fifth progenitor,

[62]Sivanath Shastri, 1911, quoted in Collet, *Rammohan Roy*, p. 2.
[63]For example, Singh, *Rammohan Roy*, p. 16.
[64]Collet, *Rammohun Roy*, p. 14.
[65]Singh, *Rammohan Roy*, pp. 21–2.
[66]Ibid., p. 19.
[67]Both Spratt and Castairs have suggested that the Brahmanic culture equated cerebral skills with sexual power.

who about one hundred and forty years ago gave up spiritual exercises for worldly pursuits and aggrandisement. His descendants ever since followed his example.[68]

What he meant by this description is made obvious by what he said about his mother's side of the family.

Given his retreatist style, Ramakanta did not pay much attention to his children. For them he remained a distant, detached and impersonal symbol of authority.[69] Yet the nuclear household he 'headed' and the exposures to which his family was subject demanded an altogether different style of functioning. The need for a male authority, who would show some competence in handling the contradictions within the Bhadralok lifestyle, almost certainly must have been felt by his growing sons, sensitized to exactly these needs by the family and subcultural experiences and searching for a more viable male identity. Instead, Ramakanta continued to play the traditional roles of the father as an 'intruding stranger' and as a 'castrated victim of an aggressive mother'.[70]

The distance between Ramakanta and his son produced less intimate rancour than that produced by the relationship between Tarinidevi and her son, however. Perhaps there was an awareness in both father and son that the father was fighting a battle not unlike the son's. And indeed, sharing the crisis of values in the Bengali babus, Ramakanta *was* trying to evolve a viable style of social adaptation, even if with low sensitivity and poor success. Not surprisingly, Rammohun Roy's spirited adolescent confrontations with his father always carried suggestions of mutual respect and empathy. Certainly they were free from much of the bitterness which his confrontation with the mother generated.[71] It is noteworthy that the two well-known instances of separation between the father and young son both ended with the son being accommodated. (The worldly-wise son did not opt for reconciliation in a third instance when reconciliation would have meant economic disaster for him.[72]) In adulthood too, though Rammohun Roy saw whenever tense, dejected or ill, 'the frowning features of his father rise unbidden on his imagination',[73]

---

[68]Letter to Gordon, in Chakravarty, *Tantrakatha*, p. 119.
[69]Ibid., pp. 21–2.
[70]Carstairs, *The Twice-Born*, p. 159.
[71]Rammohun cited in Singh, *Rammohan Roy*, p. 38, and Collet, *Rammohun Roy*, p. 6.
[72]Collet, *Rammohun Roy*; Singh, *Rammohan Roy*.
[73]W.J. Fox, *A Discourse on the Occasion of the Death of Raja Rammohan Roy* (London, 1833). Quoted in R. Chanda and J.K. Majumdar, *Selections from Official*

he could recount humorously, and without rancour or disrespect, his differences with his father.[74]

In sum, Ramakanta and his son found each other more acceptable antagonists than Tarinidevi and her son. To some extent at least, in spite of all the discouragement which Ramakanta's personality provided, Rammohun Roy did try to move towards the father, to establish communication with him, and to see in him a possible source of support and a possible model of social sensitivity.[75]

The Design of Reform

How did Rammohun Roy relate these early contradictions to the reform of sati? A number of suggestions can be made.

First, his earliest interpersonal experiences and conflicts had convinced him that religion was the key to the process of social change in India.[76] Piety was not Rammohun Roy's strong point and he himself was perhaps not very intensely a man of religion. If anything, he was a hard-headed man of the world, a materialist who believed religion to be an expression of man's economic and social conditions, and a hedonist in practice. There are even reasons to suspect that he held, along with what some have called his 'theistic passion', attitudes compatible with agnosticism.[77] However, Roy had seen the central role religion played in the lives of his parents and his culture. He also knew, from personal exposures, that religion could be a great divider, that it was in religion that authorities could be most intimately faced and successfully defied. And being a practical idealist, he was unwilling to sacrifice this information for the sake of any ready-made ideological package.

Letters and Documents Relating to the Life of Raja Rammohun Roy, Vol. I (1771–1830) (Calcutta: Oriental Book Agency, 1938), p. xxxiii.

[74]Collet, *Rammohun Roy*, pp. 6–7; Singh, *Rammohan Roy*, p. 38.

[75]This ability of the father to tie his son to himself 'in such a way that overt rebellion or hate was impossible' has been hypothesized to be a source of reformism. See Erikson, *Insight and Responsibility*, pp. 202–3.

[76]R.C. Majumdar, *Nineteenth Century Bengal*, p. 27, describes how in opposition to David Hare's idea of establishing a college, Rammohun pleaded for the establishment of a Brahma Sabha. Though he also took part in the propagation of western education in India, it was without rejecting the primacy of religious reform. One also remembers that Rammohun founded in 1822 an Anglo-Hindu school, being dissatisfied with the secular education provided by the Hindu College.

[77]See for instance Sumit Sarkar, 'Rammohun Roy and the Break with the Past', in Joshi, *Rammohan Ray*, pp. 46–88.

As part of this larger awareness, Rammohun Roy's first contribution to the nineteenth-century model of reform was the theory that his community's form of mother worship and the related deeper concerns with mothering and orality—expressed, as he saw it, in 'the peculiar mode of diet' that had become 'the chief part of the theory and practice of Hinduism'—constituted the crux of traditions in Bengal. In this he was a precursor of a second generation of reformers who were to make heterodoxy in food and the attitude to women the major symbols of defiance in nineteenth-century Bengal, and conformity to commensal and other oral taboos the first criterion of orthodoxy.[78]

The second theme in Rammohun's model was the equation which he made between the anomic babu lifestyle and the new content of Bengali Hinduism. His response to the religious and social situation of Bengal was a new theology and a new projective system incorporating a different set of authority images. Sati, to him, was only part of a wider syndrome. More basic was the obsessive rigidity and the deadly seriousness of rituals organized around the image of a threatening and violent mother deity. Rammohun Roy had to reject these rituals exactly as he had to reject the *Manbhanjan* play in late childhood. Both as a psychological defence and as an ideology, the cultural concept of sacred motherliness could not maintain its compatibility with the inner life of one who had faced so much maternal hostility and held in store such deep anger against his mother. The image of a powerful, irascible celestial mother—who was propitiated only when the self-castrated son identified with his ineffective father—was authentic, but had to be vehemently denied.

Invalidated by both outer and inner experiences, the Bengali pantheon became for Roy a perversity, a source of magic which did not work. But as in the case of his own mother, this rejection of cosmic mothers, too, was bound to arouse deep moral anxieties. And he had to cope with these anxieties by means of a spirited battle to protect women from men's

[78]Sivanath Shastri, 1903, *Ramtanu Lahiri o Tatkaleen Bangasamaj* (Calcutta: New Age, 1957), pp. 85–8, 101–3; Rajnarayan Basu, *Atmacharit* (Calcutta: Kuntaline, 1908); N.K. Bose, *Modern Bengal* (Calcutta: Vidyodaya, 1959), p. 48.

It should please psychoanalytically-minded readers to know that, as the pioneer of this movement and as Tarinidevi's son, Roy himself was a great gourmet. At home he ate Bengali, Mughal and western food. He drank choice wines with his European friends and to the chagrin of orthodox Calcuttans, employed a Muslim as one of his cooks. Yet such were his oral needs to defy that, when he went to England, he took a Brahmin cook with him and, at a dinner given by the directors of the East India Company in his honour in London, he turned a *pukka* Brahmin and stuck to boiled rice and water.

aggression, by fighting for their rights in different sectors of life and, trivial though it might seem, by being impersonally, but consistently and even aggressively, polite and courteous to the women he encountered in his daily life.[79]

Roy's Brahmoism incorporated both these themes.[80] First, it tried to banish the older gods from the lives of all Bengalis. Each god became to the first Brahmo a part of 'heathen mythology' and represented 'the gross errors of a puerile system of idol worship [not] becoming the dignity of human beings'.[81] He rejected Kali because in her worship 'human sacrifices, the use of wine, criminal intercourse, licentious songs are included' and 'because debauchery . . . universally forms the principal part of her followers';[82] he rejected Shiva, the submissive consort of Kali, because he was a 'destroying attribute' and a family man;[83] and he rejected Krishna because he seemed a 'debauch' and had killed his nurse-maid by sucking her blood while being breast-fed.[84] In other words, not only the themes of homicidal mother and acquiescent father, but also those of matricide and 'infanticide' had to be eliminated from the Hindu projective system. Instead, for the first time in a modern Hindu sect the concept of the deity was sought to be made patriarchal. Apparently, what Ramakanta could not do for his son, the Semiticized Brahmo concept of godhead could: it projected a paternal authority—firm, reliable, and convincing—that could be offset against the fearsome inner authority of his mother.[85]

Brahmoism also managed to give to the conjugal role of Bengali women an importance and dignity it never had before. It attacked the matriarchal status of women in the family and religion by emphasizing

[79]One does not have to be a psychologist to sense the uncertainty towards women in one who always got up from his chair when his wives entered his room, particularly when the whole world knew that the wives were on the worst of terms with Rammohun and, being aggressively orthodox, could never appreciate this formal western gesture.

[80]By 1825 Roy's religious propaganda grew into an organized faith based on the Vedas. He established a Vedanta College in that year and, finally, in 1828, the Brahmo Sabha. In 1830, Roy established a Church in Calcutta to worship in a congregational form, 'the One Eternal Unsearchable and Immutable Being who is the Author and Preserver of the Universe'. The Church deed prohibited the entry of any picture or image in the Church.

[81]*English Works*, Vol. II, p. 92.

[82]Ibid.

[83]Letter to Estlin, 1827; *English Works*, Vol. IV, p. 90; also ibid., Vol. II, p. 23.

[84]Ibid., p. 92.

[85]These imageries, however, dissociated Brahmoism from some of the basic symbols of both the greater Sanskritic culture and Bengal's folk Hinduism. Later Brahmos tried to remedy this to some extent.

their role in the world of public activities, and it sabotaged the sacred symbols and images with which Bengali women identified and sought compensation from in their narrow and constricted lives. Instead of their magical powers and magical capability of doing harm, they had in Brahmoism the justification for wielding real and direct power as individuals with the right to live their own lives.[86]

Both the themes made eminent sense to those exposed to a new set of effective, impersonal, organizational authorities—all unresponsive to acts of propitiation, sacrifice and ritual conformity. The rewards these authorities controlled were based on criteria irrelevant to anchored values: personal autonomy, achievement and initiative, denial of the fated and the ordained, shrewd competitiveness, and ambitious this-worldliness. All this could not but make apparent the latent need for a new male self-definition at the centre of which would be a new concept of authoritative masculinity. The Brahmo godhead was an attempt to meet this need and to help Rammohun Roy's private fantasies establish an inverse association with the grand myth of his culture. By toppling the absolute maternal authorities in the sphere of the sacred, he was only coping with his nuclear conflicts and trying to sabotage a tradition's symbolic core.

In this attempt the monism of *advaita* came in handy. Rammohun Roy gave a new meaning to this monism by 'misreading' Shankaracharya's ultimate objective as the revival of monotheism in India on the basis of Vedanta.[87] This was absurd because Vedanta posited an attributeless Brahmin and rejected all forms of prayer in favour of pure contemplation of God.[88] Rammohun Roy, on the other hand, actually succeeded in invoking the image of a patriarchal God, 'the author and governor of the universe'—'He, by whom the birth, existence and annihilation of the world is regulated.'[89] A recent observer, who has nothing to do with psychology or the social sciences, correctly identifies the basic imagery involved in this divine sex change:

> The very word *Upasana* employed . . . in the sense . . . of 'propitiation and worship', implies a dualistic conception of an individual's soul's longing for the divine objective . . . Rammohun's Brahma, though mentioned as 'imperceptible

[86]Ibid., Vol. I, particularly the tract on property rights of women, pp. 1–10.

[87]Rammohun Roy, quoted by R.C. Majumdar in Majumdar, Majumdar and Ghose, *British Paramountcy and Indian Renaissance*, Vol. II, p. 101.

[88]Max Muller says, 'Rammohun Roy himself, when . . . he fortified himself behind the ramparts of Veda, had no idea what the Veda really was. Vedic learning was at a low ebb in Bengal, and Rammohun Roy had never passed through a regular training in Sanskrit'. *Biographical Essays*, 20, Vol. VIII, in Sen, *A New Faith.*

[89]*English Works*, Vol. II, p. 174.

and indefinable' is a very real Brahman, who is 'the author and governor of the universe' and therefore not wholly devoid of attributes.[90]

What purpose did such a monism serve in Rammohun Roy's model of reform? The answer could be given in four parts.

First, monism has traditionally smoothened the acceptance in India of dissent, new religious cults and alternative interpretations of sacred texts, and justified them as diversities that were part of a larger transcendent unity. By giving salience to Shankara's system, Rammohun Roy not only opened a new debate amongst his contemporaries on Hinduism as a unified religious system and as a single cultural strain, but also made available for the next generation of reformers a powerful legitimacy of dissent and a tool for social intervention.[91]

Second, the Vedas and Upanishads were a sufficiently vague and complex authority to stand new interpretations. Like the fluid psychological and cultural system that Greater Calcutta had become, here too was a collection of fluid sacred authorities, on which a reformer could impose his personal meaning. In stressing an interpretive system which gave greater scope to dissent, Rammohun Roy therefore also gave centrality to texts which were best suited for plural reinterpretations.

Third, the emphasis on monism strengthened the social position of women by separating the feminine principles of nature and feminine godheads from the social role of women. Unlike in the West, where the concept of a patriarchal god has often legitimized male dominance, in India divine matriarchy burdened women with the task of coping with shared fantasies of womanly responsibility for failures of nature and nurture. Rammohun Roy's theology was an attempt to liberate Indian women from this responsibility.

Fourth, in rejecting his mother and her faith Rammohun Roy also rejected rituals and rites as the central part of Hinduism. This was basically an attack on folk Hinduism and, perhaps, a latent attempt to further Sanskritize the Hindu little cultures. In this respect at least Rammohun Roy had not misunderstood the Upanishads and his hero Shankara. All his life he pleaded for 'disinterested worship' and 'faith in God which leads to absorption', unconditionally rejecting 'rites which

---

[90]Dey, *Bengali Literature*, pp. 516–17. It is not surprising that Rammohun Roy greatly admired Luther who he felt had reinstated monotheism and toppled the idolatry practised by Catholicism. Similarly he aggressively rejected the Baptist and Anglican concepts of Trinity.

[91]See on this theme, 'The Making and Unmaking of Political Cultures in India', in Nandy, *At the Edge of Psychology*, pp. 47–69.

have future fruition for their object'.[92] It was in fact an interested worshipper, trying to sanctify the disinterested worship he himself could not offer the gods, in the hope that he would be forgiven because his own interests were not merely personal.

The fact remains, however, that Rammohun Roy's use of *advaita* was no less instrumental than his use of other religions. Perhaps only Adam, his collaborator and friend, had an inkling of it:

Rammohun Roy, I am persuaded, supports this institution [Brahmo Samaj] not because he believes in the divine authority of the Ved, but solely as an instrument for overthrowing idolatry. To be candid, . . . he uses Unitarian Christianity in the same way.[93]

We now have a better idea of which 'goddess' Roy was trying all along to overthrow and which 'god' he wanted to install in her place. To say this is not to flaunt an uncompromising psychologism. It is to recognize the fact that no reform is entirely a public event. By its very nature, it is also a private statement and Rammohun Roy's was such a statement. It is not incidental that his reform was a last compliment to his father and the final gesture of reparation to his mother. We have seen that his parents were something more than the parameters of a personal history: they also represented the contradictions of an age and a culture. The incidental fact is that Rammohun Roy's reform happened to be the only success Ramakanta ever attained and the only victory Tarinidevi ever won.

[92]Roy, Translation of *Kathopanishad*, 1818, *English Works*, Vol. III, pp. 93, 94.
[93]Quoted in Collet, *Rammohun Roy*, p. 225.

*Earlier published in Ashis Nandy, *At the Edge of Psychology: Essays in Politics and Culture* (New Delhi: Oxford University Press, 1980).

4

~~~

Final Encounter
The Politics of the Assassination of Gandhi

> Even in his death there was a magnificence and complete artistry. It was from every point of view a fitting climax to the man and to the life he had lived . . . .
>
> Jawaharlal Nehru[1]

> Godse was to Gandhi what Kamsa was to Krishna. Indivisible, even if incompatible. Arjuna never understood Krishna the way Kamsa did . . . hate is infinitely more symbiotic than love. Love dulls one's vision, hate sharpens it.
>
> T.K. Mahadevan[2]

I

EVERY POLITICAL ASSASSINATION is a joint communiqué. It is a statement which the assassin and his victim jointly work on and co-author. Sometimes the collaboration takes time to mature, sometimes it is instantaneous and totally spontaneous. But no political assassination is ever a single-handed job. Even when the killer is mentally ill and acts

[1]Quoted in Tapan Ghose, *The Gandhi Murder Trial* (New York: Asia), 1973, pp. 316–17.

[2]T.K. Mahadevan, 'Godse versus Gandhi', *The Times of India*, 12 March 1978, *Sunday Magazine*, p. 1.

alone, he in his illness represents larger historical and psychological forces which connect him to his victim.[3]

Robert Payne's biography of Mahatma Gandhi, perhaps more than any other writing on the subject, brings out this element of collaboration in the assassination of Gandhi.[4] It was an assassination, Payne seems to suggest, in which apart from Gandhi and a motley group of dedicated but clumsy assassins, crucial indirect roles were played by Gandhi's protectors in the Indian police and its intelligence branch, by the bureaucracy, and by important parts of India's political leadership including some of Gandhi's most dedicated followers.

But why was there this joint endeavour? Where did the minds and interests of so many people converge?

To answer this question I shall first define the quintessence of Gandhi's political style and then describe the psychological and social environment in India at the time of his death in January 1948.

Gandhi was neither a conservative nor a progressive. And though he had internal contradictions, he was not a fragmented, self-alienated man driven by the need to compulsively conserve the past or protect the new. Effortlessly transcending the dichotomy of orthodoxy and iconoclasm, he forged a mode of self-expression which by its apparently non-threatening simplicity reconciled the common essence of the old and the new.[5] However, in spite of his synthesizing skills, the content of the social changes he suggested, and the political activism he demanded from the Indian people, were highly subversive of the main strain of Indian, particularly Hindu, culture. Even though few intellectuals in his time thought so,[6] many conservatives who had a real stake in the old and the

---

[3]See on this theme Ashis Nandy, 'Invitation to a Beheading: A Psychologist's Guide to Assassinations in the Third World', *Quest*, November–December 1975, pp. 69–72.

[4]*The Life and Death of Mahatma Gandhi* (New York: Dutton, 1968).

[5]To effect this reconciliation, Gandhi frequently used his own contradictions and derived strength from his own inner battles against authoritarianism, his own masculine self and aggression. This also was, in the context of the dominant ethos of the Indian civilization, a major deviance. The tradition here was to use social experiences for purposes of self-enrichment, not to act out personal experience in social intervention.

[6]It is an indicator of the strength of the subliminal revolution of Gandhi that as late as in 1972, while reviewing Payne's and Erikson's books on Gandhi, a psychoanalyst mentioned as instances of Gandhi's irrationality, Gandhi's hostility to modern technology, mass education, industrialization and science. H. Robert Black, 'Review of *The Life and Death of Mahatma Gandhi* by Robert Payne and *Gandhi's Truth* by Erik H. Erikson', *Psychoanalytic Quarterly*, 1972, 41, 122–9. In about 1977, in an ecologically sensitive world discussing zero growth rates and intermediate

established sensed this subversion. As his conservative assassin was to later complain, 'All his experiments were at the expenses [sic] of the Hindus'.[7]

Particularly dangerous to the traditional authority system in India were two elements of the Gandhian political philosophy. The first was his continuous attempt to change the definitions of centre and periphery in Indian society; the second was his negation of the concepts of masculinity and femininity implicit in some Indian traditions and in the colonial situation. Both these attempted changes had important psychological components and the drama of Gandhi's death cannot be told without reference to them.

The first element can be crudely called a distinctive Gandhian theory of social justice. The theory rejected the role of the modernist, western-ized, middle-class intelligentsia as a vanguard of the proletariat. Till the advent of Gandhi, it was this gentlemanly class which dominated Indian politics and was the main voice of Indian nationalism. Gandhi, however, was always afraid that in the name of the poor and the exploited, the 'advanced-thinking', ideologically guided, middle-class intellectuals would only perpetuate their own dominance. So the first thing he tried to do was to de-intellectualize Indian politics. I should not be misunderstood: Gandhi was not against intellectuals *qua* intellectuals. He was against giving importance to intellectual activities and ideologies in a culture which believed intellection to be ritually purer and more Brahminic, and where the primacy of idea over action had a sacred sanction behind it. Therefore, anticipating Mao Tse-Tung who faced a somewhat similar literati tradition, Gandhi would not even grant the existence of pro-gressive elements within the traditionally privileged sectors of India.

As a part of the process of de-Brahminization through de-intellec-tualization, Gandhi was constantly trying to pass off many aspects of the low-status, non-Brahminic, commercial and peasant cultures in India as genuine Hinduism. While stressing the 'syntheticism' of Gandhi, one must not ignore his attempt to make certain peripheral aspects of the Hindu culture its central core, exactly the way he tried to do with Christianity in a more limited way.

To effect this cultural restructuring Gandhi evolved what for his society was a new political technology. He began emphasizing the centrality of politics and public life in an apolitical society and mobilizing the periphery

---

technologies, the fundamental criticisms of formal education ventured by educationists like Ivan Illich and Paulo Freire, and the deglamourization of much of modern science, Gandhi seems less backdated on these issues than the reviewer.

[7]Ghose, *Gandhi Murder Trial*, p. 218.

of the Hindu society, apparently for the nationalist cause so dear to the urban middle classes, but actually to remould the entire cultural stratarchy within Hinduism. It is thus that Gandhi bridged the pre-Gandhian hiatus that had arisen between mass politics and social reform movements in India.[8]

This new political technology also incidentally challenged the basis of the colonial system which rested on the assumption that the British were ruling India with the consent of the majority of Indians in the countryside, her 'martial races' and their 'natural leaders' in the Kshatriya princelings, the rajas and maharajas who owed allegiance to the British crown. Gandhi's mobilizational technique of social and political change challenged this assumption and threatened to cut the support-base of the British–Indian government.

British colonialism also predicated that the only vociferous dissenters in the colonial system were the urban middle-class babus, alienated from the real India and from the society's 'natural' leadership, and that colonial subjugation established the cultural inferiority of the Indians whose burden it was the white man's Christian duty willingly to carry. Having an acute sense of power, Gandhi accepted the first proposition as valid and took his fight against the Raj to India's villages. Concerned with the loss of self-esteem in Indians, he refused to accept that it was the Indians' responsibility to model themselves on their rulers, to be self-deprecating or defensive about their society. What at first sight seems Gandhi's obscurantism was actually his attempt to disprove the civilizing role attributed to colonialism (which at the time was closely associated with modern science, industrialism, high technology and intellectually dominant theories of progress), so that colonialism could openly become a name for racism and exploitation.

The second major element in Gandhi's philosophy was his rediscovery of womanhood as a civilizing force in human society.

Gandhi tried to give a new meaning to womanhood in a peasant culture which had lived through centuries with deep-seated conflicts and ambivalence about femininity.[9] All his life Gandhi had wanted to live down, within himself, his identification with his own outwardly powerful

---

[8]In pre-Gandhian colonial India, as is well-known, one group of modernizers pleaded for the primacy of social reform, over political freedom; another insisted that the nationalist movement should have priority over reform movements. The first group, dominating the Indian political scene in the nineteenth century, gradually gave way to the second at the beginning of this century.

[9]See Ashis Nandy, 'Woman versus Womanliness', in *At the Edge of Psychology: Essays in Politics and Culture* (New Delhi: Oxford University Press, 1980), pp. 32–46.

but essentially weak, hedonistic, semi-modernized father and to build his self-image upon his identification with his apparently weak, deeply religious, traditional but self-confident and powerful mother. Apparently his mother was the first *satyagrahi* he knew who used fasting and other forms of self-penalization to acquire and wield womanly power within the constraints of a patriarchal family. Thanks to a number of sensitive psychological studies of Gandhi, these are now reasonably well-known facts.[10] I restate them only to stress what has been always recognized in such analyses, namely, Gandhi's deep need to come to psychological terms with his mother by incorporating aspects of her femininity in his own personality.[11]

Gandhi's ambivalence towards his father was overt and his respect for his mother was total. But underlying this respect, the various studies of Gandhi's personality themselves suggest, there was—as one would expect in the case of such imputation of total goodness—a great deal of latent ambivalence towards her. And, not unpredictably, the aggressive elements of this ambivalence were associated with some degree of guilt and search for valid personal and social models of atonement.

This personal search fitted the needs of some aspects of the Indian personality too. The Indian had always feared woman as the traditional symbol of uncertain nature and unpredictable nurture, of activity, power and aggression. In consequence, he had always feared womanhood and either abnegated femininity or defensively glorified it out of all proportion.[12] As in many such cases, here too an internal psychological problem had its counterpart in cultural divisions within the Indian society. The greater Sanskritic culture tended to give less importance to woman and to value her less in comparison to the little cultures of India. Simultaneously, the colonial culture too derived its psychological strength

[10]On the frequently discussed psychological dynamics of Gandhi's childhood, particularly the identification models available to him, see Lloyd and Susanne Rudolph, *The Modernity of Tradition* (University of Chicago, 1967), Part 2; E.V. Wolfenstein, *The Revolutionary Personality* (Princeton University, 1967), pp. 73–88; and Erik H. Erikson, *Gandhi's Truth* (New York: Norton, 1969).

[11]In a recent paper Rowland Lorimer has explicitly recognized the centrality of this aspect of Gandhi. See 'A Reconsideration of the Psychological Roots of Gandhi's Truth', *Psychoanalytic Review*, 1976, 63, 191–207. An unsophisticated but touching interpretation of Gandhi from this point of view is by his grand-niece and the constant companion of his last years, Manuben. See her *Bapu—My Mother* (Ahmedabad: Navajivan, 1962).

[12]See a discussion of this in Nandy, 'Woman versus Womanliness'; and 'Sati: A Nineteenth Century Tale of Women, Violence and Protest', in this book.

from the identification of rulership with male dominance and subjecthood with feminine submissiveness.

It would therefore seem that Gandhi's innovations in this area also tended to simultaneously subvert Brahminic and Kshatriya orthodoxy and the British colonial system. He challenged the former so far as it depended upon the Indian man's fears of being polluted by woman and contaminated by her femininity; he challenged the latter in so far as it exploited man's insecurity about his masculinity and his consequent continuous potency drive.

In other words, Gandhi attacked the structure of sexual dominance as a homologue of both the colonial situation and the traditional social stratification. He rejected the British as well as the Brahminic–Kshatriya equation between manhood and dominance, between masculinity and legitimate violence, and between femininity and passive submissiveness.[13] He wanted to extend to the male identity—in both the rulers and the ruled—the revalued, partly non-Brahminic, equation between woman-hood and non-intrusive, nurturant, non-manipulative, non-violent, self-de-emphasizing 'merger' with natural and social environments.

That is, Gandhi was trying to fight colonialism by fighting the psychological equation which a patriarchy makes between masculinity and aggressive social dominance and between femininity and subjugation. To fight this battle he ingeniously combined aspects of folk Hinduism and recessive elements of Christianity to mark out a new domain of public intervention. In this domain the rulers and the ruled of India could share a new moral awareness, an awareness that the meek would not only inherit the earth but could make femininity a valued aspect of man, congruent with his overall masculinity. In other words, defiant subjecthood and passive resistance to violence—militant non-violence, as Erik Erikson calls it—became in the Gandhian world-view an indicator of moral accomplishment and superiority, in the subjects as well as in the more sensitive rulers who yielded to non-violence. Gandhi not only wanted to be a trans-sexual *mahatma* or saint in the Indian sense; he also wanted to be a bride of Christ—a St Francis of Assissi—in the Christian sense. His goal was to become an *alter ego* for his potency-seeking rulers and to align with their super-egos too. Honour, he asserted, universally lay with the victims, not the aggressors.[14] It is evidence of how much he

---

[13]See on this subject the sensitive writings of Rudolph and Rudolph, *The Modernity of Tradition*; and Erikson, *Gandhi's Truth*.

[14]It was this assumption of the universality of his political ethics which prompted

was in tune with some of the emerging though marginal strands of consciousness in the European intellectuals that at the same time that he was establishing his primacy in Indian politics, Romain Rolland was writing to his admirer Sigmund Freud, 'Victory is always more catastrophic for the vanquishers than for the vanquished.'[15]

These two basic constructions—centrality of the periphery of Indian culture and acceptance of femininity—Gandhi pronounced not through written or spoken words, a form of dissent for which there was legitimacy in the Brahminic culture. His means were large-scale mobilization, organizational activism and constant demands on the Indians for conformity to an internally consistent public ethic. These means were largely alien to the Brahminic culture which was tolerant of—and self-confident vis-à-vis—ideological dissent but became insecure when ideological dissent was supported by such low status, non-Brahminic means as active social intervention and mass politics.

In spite of erecting this elaborate and magnificent structure of dissent, Gandhi never claimed he was a revolutionary or a reformer, someone consciously reinterpreting traditional texts to justify new modes of life, as many social reformers in India had previously done. He was convinced that he was a *sanatani* Hindu, a genuine, orthodox, full-blooded Indian, not a social reformer out to alter Hinduism and Indian culture. He was, he seemed to argue, a counter-reformist, a revivalist, and a committed traditionalist.[16] According to him, he represented continuity and the Brahminic, educated, westernized middle classes represented change. He was, he claimed, the insider; the upper echelons of the Hindu society, the Brahminic cognoscenti, were the interlopers. And again, not only

---

Gandhi to give his notorious advice to the European Jews to offer non-violent, passive resistance to Hitler. But of course Gandhi was concerned with human normalities, not abnormalities. When he felt that *satyagraha* would work in the Europe of the 1930s and 1940s, he was showing greater respect for European civilization than those who have since correctly doubted his political acumen on this point. If the Nazis did not deserve Gandhi, Gandhi also did not deserve the Nazis.

It is interesting that the political groups which produced the assassin of Gandhi were open admirers of the Nazis and, at least in the early 1930s, wanted to treat the Muslims the way Hitler treated the Jews. In turn, Gandhi had for this very reason rejected these groups as totalitarian and attacked even their courage, nationalism and diligence as fascist. Pyarelal, *Mahatma Gandhi—The Last Phase, 2* (Ahmedabad: Navajivan), p. 440. Evidently Gandhi's technique failed with some varieties of Indian fascism too.

[15] D. J. Fisher, 'Sigmund Freud and Romain Rolland: The Terrestrial Animal and His Great Oceanic Friend', *American Imago*, 1976, *33*, 1–59, quote on p. 4.

[16] This is probably the explanation for his hostile comment on modern India's first social reformer, Rammohun Roy. See Stephen Hay, 'Introduction to Rammohun Roy's *A Tract against Idolatry*' (Calcutta: Firma K.L. Mukhopadhyay, 1963).

did Gandhi indulge in this 'inner speech', he went on to give it institutional forms. He mobilized the numerically preponderant non-Brahminic sectors of the Hindus, the lower strata of society, and the politically passive peripheries: the low castes and untouchables, the peasants, and villagers. Taking advantage of numbers, he began legitimizing a new collective ethic that threatened to challenge the traditional Indian concepts of individual salvation, responsibility, and action geared to the value of self-awareness; the concepts of private knowledge and self-knowledge; political non-participation and the belief that the political authorities were not central to life.

It was a remarkable achievement of Gandhi that so many sensitive intellectuals took him at his word. What the Mahatma was doing did not seem very revolutionary to them at first sight, and in fact, they were not entirely wrong. Gandhi's political innovations overtly did seem compatible with Hindu orthodoxy and there was nothing intrinsically non-Indian about his social and political theories. However, it must be remembered that like all major civilizations, the Indic included a plethora of cultural strains. The distinctive identifier of a major civilization is always the composite whole that it makes of its diverse, contradictory constituents, by giving different emphases or weights to the various norms and subcultures within it.

The danger that Gandhi posed to the greater Sanskritic tradition was exactly this. He introduced a different system of weightages and threatened to alter the basic characteristics of Indian society by making its cultural periphery its centre.

II

It is surely not accidental that Gandhi's assassin, Nathuram Vinayak Godse (1912–49), was a representative of the centre of the society that Gandhi was trying to turn into the periphery.

I want to concentrate on Godse among the conspirators who planned the assassination because, first of all, it was his finger which ultimately pulled the trigger on 30 January 1948. By his own choice and partly against the wishes of his collaborators, he killed Gandhi single-handed because he felt 'history showed that such revolutionary plots in which several persons were concerned had always been foiled, and it was only the effort of a single individual that succeeded.'[17]

---

[17]Statement of co-conspirator Vishnu R. Karkare, quoted in G.D. Khosla, 'The Crime of Nathuram Godse', *The Murder of the Mahatma* (London: Chatto and Windus, 1963), pp. 201–45. Quote on p. 230.

Godse with Narayan Apte also constituted the core of the band of conspirators. The other actors in the group were minor and 'arrived late on the scene and were unknown to each other until a few weeks before the murder. There was something strangely anonymous about them, as though they had been picked up in random.'[18] It was as if two dedicated opponents of Gandhi had mobilized the larger faceless society to eliminate Gandhi from the Indian scene.

But why Godse? I shall try to give my answer as simply as possible.

First, Godse and all his associates except one came from Maharashtra, a region where Brahminic dominance was particularly strong. He also happened to be from Poona, the unofficial capital of traditional Maharashtra and a city renowned for its old-style scholarship and for the rich, complex culture which the high-status Chitpavan or Konkanasth Brahmins had built there. Godse, himself a Chitpavan Brahmin like the other figure in the inner core of conspiracy, was by his cultural inheritance a potential opponent of Gandhi. (There had been three known unsuccessful attempts to kill Gandhi—all in Maharashtra. The first was in Poona in 1934 when Gandhi was engaged in an anti-untouchability campaign there. The second, a half-hearted one, took place in Sevagram and involved members of the Hindu Mahasabha. That was in 1944. In 1946, once again near Poona, some unknown persons tried to derail the train in which Gandhi was travelling.)[19]

The Chitpavans, traditionally belonging to the western coast of India, were one of the rare Brahmin communities in India which had a long history of valour on the battlefield. This fact gave them, in their own eyes, a certain historical superiority over the Deshasth Brahmins belonging to the plains of Maharashtra. In the absence of martial castes like Rajputs in the region, the Chitpavans could thus combine the traditional prerogatives of the priestly Brahmins and the kingly Kshatriyas. Though a few other communities, mainly the Marathas, did claim a share of the Rajput glory in the state, the social gap between the Brahmins and the non-Brahmins was one of the widest in the region, and nowhere more so than in Poona.

The Maharashtrian Brahminic élites also had a long history of struggle against the Muslim rulers of India in the seventeenth and eighteenth centuries. It is true that they were associated with powers that were essentially marauders and large parts of Hindu India too were victims

[18]Payne, *Mahatma Gandhi*, p. 612.
[19]J.C. Jain, *The Murder of Mahatma Gandhi: Prelude and Aftermath* (Bombay: Chetana, 1961), p. 45; Pyarelal, *Mahatma Gandhi*, pp. 750–1.

of their aggressiveness. But by the beginning of the twentieth century, the Maharashtrian Brahmins had reinterpreted their history in terms of the needs of Hindu nationalism. They saw themselves as the upholders of a tradition of Hindu resistance against the Muslim occupation of India. It was on this reconstructed and self-created tradition that a part of the Maharashtrian elite built up their anti-British nationalism. Like the Bengali nationalists—simultaneously, their sympathizers, ego-ideals, and admirers—they did not see themselves as morally superior individuals, non-violently—and, therefore, ethically—trying to free themselves and their British rulers from a morally inferior colonial system, as Gandhi wanted them to do. They saw themselves as the previously powerful, now weakened, competitors of the British. So terrorism directed against the Raj came naturally to them. Their aim was the redemption of their lost glory.[20]

Naturally, much of Gandhi's charisma did not extend to the Chitpavans. To the extent Gandhi rejected the Kshatriya identity by his constant emphasis on pacifism and self-control, he posed a threat to the warrior cultures of India. In addition, by constantly stressing the feminine, nurturing, non-violent aspects of men's personality, he challenged the Kshatriya male identity built on fear of woman and of the cosmic feminine principles in nature, and the no less acute fears of becoming a woman and of being polluted by woman. (In other words, he posed more or less the same kind of threat to India's martial cultures as to her priestly cultures.) Thus, given the absence of Kshatriya competition, the Maharashtrian Brahmins not only enjoyed greater status than they would have otherwise done, they incorporated—as traditional rulers, landowners, and warriors—elements of the Kshatriya identity and lived with many of the Kshatriya fears and anxieties relating to womanhood.

Nathuram Godse came from this background. So did most of his co-conspirators including his younger brother Gopal.[21]

---

[20]There was in the Maharashtrian Brahminic élites an emphasis on cynical hard-headed pure politics which was antagonistic to the essence of Gandhism. Yet Gandhi was patently beating them at their own game. He was winning over and politically organizing the numerically preponderant non-Brahminic sectors of Maharashtra itself. No wonder the cornered Brahminic élites began to regard 'Gandhi's political leadership and movement of non-violence with a strong concentrated feeling of antipathy and frustration which found expression in a sustained campaign of calumny against Gandhiji for over a quarter of a century.' Pyarelal, *Mahatma Gandhi*, 2, p. 750.

[21]There were three exceptions. One was Madanlal Pahwa, a Punjabi Hindu belonging to the Khatri or business community. He had failed the entrance examination for the Royal Indian Navy and, as a victim of the partition riots, had held a number

Gandhi's assassin was born in 1910, in a small village in the margin of the Bombay–Poona conurbation. He was the eldest son and the second child in a family of four sons and two daughters. His father was Vinayak R. Godse, a petty government official who worked in the postal department and had a transferable job which took him to small urban settlements over the years. Three sons had been born to him before Nathuram and all three had died in infancy. Both Vinayak and his wife were devoted and orthodox Brahmins and, understandably, they sought a religious solution to the problem of the survival of their new-born son. The result was the use of a time-honoured technique: Nathuram was brought up as a girl. His nose was pierced and he was made to wear a *nath* or nose-ring. It is thus that he came to acquire the name Nathuram, even though his original name was Ramachandra. Such experiences often go with a heightened religiosity and a sense of being chosen. In this instance, too, the child soon enough became a devotee of the family gods. He sang *bhajans* before the deities and, according to his family, acquired the ability to occasionally go into a trance and speak as an oracle.

Neither the burden of living a bisexual role nor the oracular religiosity, however, stood in the way of Nathuram becoming a 'strapping young man', given to physical culture and other 'masculine' pursuits. Perhaps in his culture such early experiences of socially imposed bisexuality had a clear-cut meaning and instrumentality, and it was not specially difficult to contain the diffusion of one's gender-specific self-image. Perhaps it was given in the situation that Nathuram would try to regain the lost clarity of his sexual role by becoming a model of masculinity.

Whatever the inner tensions, they did not show. By all accounts, Nathuram was a well-mannered, quiet, humble young man (unlike his flamboyant, elegant, well-placed collaborator Apte whose father was a reputed classics scholar and uncle a popular novelist; Apte himself was a science graduate with a good academic record and, in spite of his Hindu nationalism, an erstwhile holder of a king's commission in the Royal Indian Air Force and a teacher at an American mission school).

---

of odd jobs and moved from place to place. He however obviously played second fiddle in the conspiracy. Other exceptions were the South Indian servant of one of the conspirators, Shankar Kistayya, ultimately acquitted as only a marginal member of the group and Digambar Badge, who turned government approver. The conspirators included a doctor, a bookshop-owner, a small-time restaurateur-cum-municipal councillor, an army storekeeper-cum-illegal arms-merchant. That is, except for Pahwa and Kistayya, all the conspirators were middle class, educated, semi-westernized professionals and job-holders.

The facts of Nathuram's early life are borrowed mainly from Manohar Malgaonkar's *The Men who Killed Gandhi* (Delhi: Macmillan, 1978), Chapter 2.

Nathuram's quiet interpersonal style was associated with an early interest in public affairs and good works. Biographical accounts mention the help he often gave to his neighbours and the interest he took in informal social work. However, as the span of his social interests widened, his oracular abilities declined. According to his brother, by the age of sixteen he had lost his concentration and ceased to be the medium between the family deity and the family. None the less, a certain natural intellectual brightness persisted in spite of the absence of formal higher education, and so did—as a biographer puts it—a certain natural dignity. In a religious family, even a lapsed oracle cannot fail to acquire a sense of being chosen.

There is some evidence that some of these qualities became more noticeable in Nathuram after he killed Gandhi. Some who saw him in his pre-assassination days thought him poor in verbal and social skills. They were genuinely surprised by his competence and serene composure after the murder of Gandhi and the legal skill and self-confidence with which he argued his own case in English, a language he supposedly did not know well.[22] It was as if the assassination gave meaning and drive to a life which otherwise was becoming increasingly prosaic. This was perhaps the reason why Godse was eager to play out his full role as the assassin of Gandhi.[23] Until he went to the gallows, his one fear was that the Government of India, goaded by Gandhi's family and many Gandhians, might have 'pity' on him and he might have to live the rest of his life with the shame of it. He did not want an anti-climax of that kind. As he put it, 'The question of mercy is against my conscience. I have shown no mercy to the person I have killed and therefore I expect no mercy.'[24] Others who knew him in jail authenticate this attitude. 'The common feeling was that even if he were thrown out of jail and given a chance to flee, he would not have taken advantage of it.'[25]

However, there was one Brahminic trait in him which predated his encounter with Gandhi. Though he had failed to matriculate, Godse was a self-educated man with first-hand knowledge of the traditional religious

[22]Payne, *Mahatma Gandhi*, p. 616.
[23]V.G. Deshpande in Ghose, *Gandhi Murder Trial*, pp. 280–1; also Gopal Godse, *Panchavanna Kotinche Bali* (Poona: Vitasta, 1971), Chapter 6.
[24]Gopal Godse, *Gandhihatya ani Mee* (Poona: Asmita, 1967), p. 221; and Ghose, *Gandhi Murder*, p. 280. One of Nathuram's avowed purposes in killing Gandhi was to help the rulers of India break the Mahatma's spell and conduct statecraft on the basis of ruthless *realpolitik*. He thought the government's mercilessness towards him a good beginning of this. See also Nathuram's letter to G.T. Madholkar, 'Why I Shot Gandhi', *Onlooker*, 16–30 November, 1978, pp. 22–4.
[25]Godse, *Gandhihatya*, p. 306.

texts. He knew for instance the entire Bhagavad Gita by heart and had read texts such as *Patanjali Yogasutra*, *Gnyaneshwari* and *Tukaram Gatha*.[26] In addition he had a good command over written and spoken Marathi and Hindi and was widely read in history, politics, sociology and particularly in Gandhi's writings. He was also well-acquainted with the works of some of the major figures of nineteenth- and twentieth-century India, including Vivekananda, Aurobindo, Tilak and Gokhale.

Conforming to the psychologist's concept of the authoritarian man, Godse was highly respectful towards his parents, attached to conventional ideas of social status, and afraid of losing this status. While facing death, his one fear was that his execution as Gandhi's murderer might lower the social status of his parents and, in his letters to them, he sought elaborate justification from sacred texts and the Puranas to legitimize his action. He was not worried about his parents' reaction to the loss of a son.

Well-built, soft-spoken and like most Chitpavans fair-complexioned, Nathuram thus projected the image of a typical member of the traditional social élite. But there was a clear discrepancy between this image and his life story till the day of the assassination. The Godses may not actually have been poor, but they were haunted with the fear of it throughout Nathuram's younger days. So much so that at the early age of sixteen he had to open a cloth shop to earn his livelihood. This is less innocuous than it may at first seem: business was not merely considered highly demeaning for a Brahmin; in lower middle-class Brahmin families entry into business was an almost sure indicator of academic failure. To make things worse, Nathuram's shop failed and he had to turn to tailoring, traditionally an even more lowly caste profession than business.

In sum, there was an enormous gap between Nathuram's membership of a traditionally privileged sector of the Indian society on the one hand and his actual socio-economic status and experiences in adolescence on the other.

It is from this kind of background that the cadres of violent, extremist and revivalist political groups often come.[27] Not surprisingly, after a brief period in Gandhi's civil disobedience movement in 1929–30, Nathuram became at about the age of twenty an active and ardent member of the Hindu Mahasabha, a small political party, and of the Rashtriya Swayam Sevak Sangh, at that time virtually a paramilitary wing of the

[26]Ibid., p. 221.
[27]Harold D. Laswell and Daniel Lerner eds., *World Revolutionary Elites* (Cambridge: MIT, 1965); and I.L. Horowitz, 'Political Terrorism and State Power', *Journal of Political and Military Sociology*, 1973, 1, 147–57.

Mahasabha with all its key posts occupied by Maharashtrian Brahmins. Overtly both groups supported the cause of Hindu revivalism and tried to articulate the Hindu search for self-esteem. Covertly however, for the Maharashtrian Brahmins who constituted their main support base, both groups had aspects of a millennial movement which promised to reinstate the hegemony of the traditional social leadership or at least contain its humiliation. The idiom of these political groups suited Nathuram's world-view in other ways too. He was extremely religious, and he read into the sacred texts what one would expect a man from a traditional martial background to read into them. For instance in the case of the Gita, 'Unlike Gandhi he was convinced that Krishna was talking to Arjuna about real battles and not battles which take place in the soul.' Predictably, in the ardent politics of the Mahasabha he found a more legitimate expression of the Hindu search for political potency. Predictably too, he did well in the party, becoming within a few years the secretary of its Poona branch. However, he did not find the RSS militant enough, so, within a year or so, severing his links with the RSS, Godse formed a new organization, the Hindu Rashtra Dal.

In 1944, Godse purchased the newspaper *Agrani*, with the help of donations given by sympathizers, to propagate his political views. But soon the government proscribed the paper because of its fiery tone. Godse revived the paper under a new name, *Hindu Rashtra*. This time he took financial help from Narayan Apte, who became the paper's managing editor. *Hindu Rashtra* was even more violently anti-Gandhi than its predecessor and it articulated the belief popular among some sections of Indians, particularly among the Bengali and Maharashtrian middle-income, upper caste elements, that Gandhism was 'emasculating' the Hindus. However, notwithstanding its shrillness, the newspaper did not give its editor any money and he continued to be a tailor. In fact, he had to start a coaching class in tailoring to supplement his income.

Whatever else *Hindu Rashtra* did or did not, it helped crystallize some of Godse's main differences with Gandhi at the level of manifest political style.

However, it is impossible to speak about these differences without stating the many manifest similarities between the two men. Both were committed and courageous nationalists; both felt that the problem of India was basically the problem of the Hindus because they constituted the majority of Indians; and both were allegiant to the idea of an undivided free India. Both felt austerity was a necessary part of political activity. Gandhi's asceticism is well-known, but Godse too lived like a hermit. He slept on a wooden plank, using occasionally a blanket and even in the severest winter wore only a shirt. Contrary to the idea fostered by a popular Hollywood film on him, *Nine Hours to Rama*, Godse neither smoked nor drank. In fact, he took Gandhi's rejection of sexuality even further; he never married and remained a strict celibate. Like Gandhi, Godse considered himself a *sanatani* and, in deference to his own wishes, he was cremated according to *sanatani* rights. Yet, and in this respect too he resembled Gandhi; he said he believed in a casteless Hindu society and in a democratic polity. He was even in favour of Gandhi's attempts to mobilize the Indian Muslims for the nationalist cause by making some concessions to the Muslim leadership. Perhaps it was not an accident that Godse began his political career as a participant in a civil disobedience movement started by Gandhi and ended his political life with a speech from the witness stand which, in spite of being an attack on Gandhi, none the less revealed a grudging respect for what Gandhi had done for the country.

But the differences between the two men were basic. Godse was in the tradition of the westernized upper-caste elements in the tertiary sector of the Indian society who had dominated the Indian political scene in the late nineteenth and early twentieth century.[28] He was particularly impressed by the terrorist traditions of urban middle-class Bengal, Punjab and Maharashtra which, sharing the values of India's imperial rulers, conceptualized politics as a ruthlessly rational zero-sum game, in which the losses of the opponents must constantly be actively maximized. Like a 'normal' human being anywhere in the world, he considered totally irrational Gandhi's emphasis on political ethics, soul force, and the moral supremacy of the oppressed over the oppressor.

Godse's Hinduism too was essentially different from Gandhi's. To Gandhi Hinduism was a lifestyle and an open-ended system of universal ethics which could continuously integrate new inputs. He wanted to organize the Hindus as part of a geographically defined larger political community, not as a religious group. To semi-westernized Godse, unknowingly impressed by organized western Christianity and Islam and by the aggressive self-affirmation of the church and the *ulema*, the salvation of Hindus lay in giving up their synthetism and ideological openness and in being religious in the fashion of politically successful societies.

---

[28]Probably the best indicator of this was Godse's intention, virtually to the end of his days, to appeal to the Privy Council, which in 1948 was still the final court of appeal for Indians. He felt that if he could somehow take this case to England, he would get an international hearing.

He wanted Hindus to constantly organize, compete and 'self defend', to become a single community and a nation.

Finally, Godse looked at history as a chronological sequence of 'real' events. So he saw the one thousand years of domination of India by rulers who were Muslims or Christians as a humiliation of the Hindus which had to be redressed. Gandhi, in tune with mainstream Hinduism, never cared for chronologies of past events. History to him was a contemporary myth which had to be interpreted and reinterpreted in terms of contemporary needs. The long Muslim domination of India meant nothing to him; in any case defeat for him was a problem for the victor, not for the defeated.

These differences account for Godse's saying:

Gandhiji failed in his duty as the Father of the Nation. He had proved to be the Father of Pakistan. It was for this reason alone that I as a dutiful son of Mother India thought it my duty to put an end to the life of the so-called Father of the Nation who had played a very prominent part in bringing about vivisection of the country—our Motherland.[29]

But there were other historical reasons for Godse's antipathy towards Gandhi behind these fantasies of a mother who becomes a victim of rapacious intruders, a weak emasculated father who fails in his paternal duty and collaborates with the aggressors, and an allegiant mother's son who tries to redeem his masculinity by protecting the mother, by defeating the aggressors in their own game and by patricide. Let us now turn to them.

Godse's humble personal history was endorsed for him by the history of his community, particularly the encroachment which the British colonial culture was making upon the traditional self-definitions of the Chitpavans. Even before he was born, the Chitpavan—and for that matter Brahminic—domination of the Maharashtrian society had ceased to be automatic. First, they had forfeited their prerogatives as a ruling caste and they had to use their traditional Brahminic skills to compete in the alien world of colonialism to earn a part of their social status.[30] Second, the burgeoning commercial culture of metropolitan Bombay, the capital of the state, was gradually rendering peripheral the culture of Poona, opening up the stronghold of Chitpavans to a wider world and

---

[29]Godse, *Gandhihatya*, p. 228.
[30]This was a situation analogous to that of the Bengali babus. Understandably, Maharashtrian Brahmins and Bengali babus were the two subcultures to which Gandhi's charisma never fully extended.

simultaneously forcing the Chitpavans all over Maharashtra to gradually become mainly a group of lower middle-class professionals and petty government officials. Third, the Chitpavans had increasingly begun to feel the growing presence and power of the upwardly mobile sectors of the Maharashtrian Hindus such as the Marathas and Mahars, the commercial success of non-Maharashtrians like the Gujarati Banias (they included the Hindu commercial castes, to one of which Gandhi belonged, and Muslim merchant communities) and Parsees.[31] In fact, the language of commerce in Bombay was Gujarati and the language of administration under the Raj was, naturally, English. Marathi, in spite of its highly developed literary and scholarly traditions, was nowhere in the picture. Even more galling must have been the growing professional dominance in Bombay of the Gujaratis and Parsees, communities largely identified in the minds of the Maharashtrians with commerce.

So the ambivalence of the Chitpavans towards the changing social environment was deep and deeply anxiety-provoking. And the community was clearly split. A few did very well under the new dispensation; they saw the cultural advantages of the Chitpavans in the tertiary sector. Others saw British colonialism as an unmitigated evil which was eroding the Chitpavans' traditional self-definition. This ambivalence, too, was a part of Godse's heritage.

Gandhi, who started his political career in India in Godse's formative years in the 1920s, was a threat to his last antagonist in two ways. First, Gandhi was trying to make the social periphery (which, as we have seen, was a periphery first of all to the Chitpavans) a part of the political centre (which was a centre first of all to the Chitpavans). Second, while Godse was one of those who competed with the British within the same frame of discourse, Gandhi never offered political competition to either the traditional system or the 'modern' colonial establishment. Truly speaking, he competed with nobody; he was always seeking complementarities.[32]

---

[31]The Parsees in fact had gone one better. Increasingly concentrated in metropolitan Bombay, they had begun to compete successfully with the Chitpavans in exactly those areas where the Chitpavans specialized: in the professions and in government service. In fact, they had already taken fantastic strides exploiting their faster pace of westernization, their marginality to the Indian society, and their almost total identification with the British rulers. E. Kulke, *The Parsees of India* (New Delhi: Vikas, 1975).

[32]That is why his declared *gurus* included liberals like B.G. Gokhale and Rabindranath Tagore. Even his declared political heir was the westernized Nehru, who differed perhaps the most from Gandhi in lifestyle and world-view, and not Patel who had a social background similar to Gandhi and was more at home in the Indian village.

Those who speak of Gandhi either as a totally atypical Indian or as a genuine son of the soil tend to miss that what he basically offered was an alternative language of public life and an alternative set of political and social values, and he tried to actualize them as if that was the most natural thing to do. This also must have been a threat to those who wanted to offer clear resistance to the colonial system on unmixed nationalist grounds.

To come to the other major theme in Gandhi's dissent which bonded him and his assassin. Consciously or not, a recent best-seller tries simple-mindedly to provide a clue to this psychological link between Nathuram Vinayak Godse and Gandhi.[33] The book claims, on the basis of the authors' interviews with Gopal Godse, that Nathuram and his political mentor and father's namesake, Vinayak Damodar Savarkar, had had a homosexual experience. The book also seems to hint that by the time he participated in the assassination, Nathuram had become an ascetic misogynist. Finally, it adds that Apte, the 'brains' behind the assassination, was a womanizer.

All this may or may not be true. Gopal Godse has denied that he had ever mentioned his brother's homosexuality while being interviewed by the authors. Savarkar, some others claim, was a known womanizer. We know he had spent long stretches of time inside jails, often in solitary confinement, for his political activities.[34] His sexuality may have been distorted and found an outlet either in homosexuality or in promiscuity. But in either case he would have represented a heightened sensitivity to man–woman relationships and problems centering around masculinity and femininity. And whether he was involved in the conspiracy or not— the existing evidence tends to be in his favour legally, not morally[35]—he did serve as the assassins' ego ideal.[36] For many of them, the mighty elder

[33]Larry Collins and Dominique Lapierre, *Freedom at Midnight* (New Delhi: Vikas, 1976), Chapter 16.

[34]In fact, sixty-five at the time of assassination, he had already spent nearly half his life in British jails and in the penal colony in the Andamans. Notwithstanding his religious fanaticism, Savarkar was a courageous self-sacrificing nationalist. He was one of the main builders of the anti-British terrorist movement in Maharashtra and, as such, no stranger to physical violence and conspiratorial politics. He was also the mainstay of the Hindu Mahasabha, the rump of a party openly propagating a Hindu polity for India. See Dhananjay Keer, *Veer Savarkar* (Bombay: Popular Prakashan, 1966).

[35]A good impartial summary is in Payne, *Mahatma Gandhi*. For the opposite point of view, see Ghose, *Gandhi Murder Trial*; also Khosla, 'Nathuram Godse'. Justice Khosla was one of the judges who tried the assassins.

[36]It may be of interest to the more psychologically minded that three out of half-a-dozen or so aliases used by the conspirators involved the first name of Savarkar.

revolutionary was the male prototype, vigorously protesting the reduction
of the Hindus to a passive, quasi-feminine role, constantly fearing the
further encroachment of femininity on their masculine self due to the
'rapaciousness' of the Muslims and the British.

The same thing applies to Nathuram Godse. Whether he had willingly
joined Savarkar in a political and sexual bond or not, he articulated
concerns about his sexuality, often by aggressive denial of it and by his
conspicuous asceticism, often by his conflicts centering around his sexual
identification and an acute sensitivity to the definitions of masculinity
and femininity. If Collins and Lapierre have built a myth, they have
mythologized what there was in reality. Godse's political speeches and
conversations were studded with imagery which constantly reminded
the sensitive listener of the equation which Godse made between Indian
or Hindu subjugation and passive femininity. His writings were punctuated
by references to the British and Muslims as 'rapists', and Hindus as their
raped, castrated, deflowered victims.[37]

Apte, the alleged womanizer who planned the logistics of the
assassination, only strengthens this interpretation. At one plane, the
womanizer and the homosexual both articulate, through diametrically
opposite kinds of sexuality, the same sensitivities. One tries to constantly
reaffirm his masculine self and prove to himself and to others that he is
a man; the other fears woman as a sex object and is uncertain about his
masculinity. The main point is this: Godse belonged to a group which
was deeply conflicted about sexual identity and had learnt to politicize
some of these conflicts.

In sum, Godse not only represented the traditional Indian stratarchy
which Gandhi was trying to break, he was sensitized by his background
to this process of élite displacement. Similarly, he also sensed the other
coordinate of the Gandhian 'revolution': the gradual legitimacy given to
femininity as a valued aspect of Indian self-definition. This revaluation
of femininity, too, threatened to deprive the traditional élite like Godse
of two of their major scapegoats: the Muslims and the British, who had
defeated and emasculated the Hindus and made them *nirveerya* or sterile
and *napungsak* or impotent. The theory of action associated with such
scapegoating was that the Hindus would have to redeem their masculinity
by fighting and defeating the Muslims and the British. Now the new
Gandhian culture of politics had made this theory irrelevant. This
culture placed on the victims of aggression the responsibility of becoming

---

[37]See Godse, *Gandhihatya*, chapter 12, to get some idea of Nathuram's idiom;
also his letter to Madholkar.

authentic innocents, wise as the serpent to the exploitative situation, rather than pseudo-innocents colluding with the aggressors for secondary gains from the exploitative situation.[38] This self-redefinition, Gandhi seemed to argue, could not be attained by reaffirming one's masculine self—he was shrewd enough to know the might of the British empire and violence invariably associated with such reaffirmation of masculinity—but by militant non-violence, which totally refuses to recognize the defeat in violent confrontation to be defeat. No victory is complete unless the defeated accepts his defeat. The Godses had lost to the British, Gandhi seemed to argue, because they conformed to the martial values of the victors. He promised to win because he could draw upon the non-martial self of the apparent victors and create doubts about their victory in them.

So Godse was not a demented killer. Jawaharlal Nehru, soon after Gandhi's death, claimed that Godse did not know what he was doing. I contend that more than any other person Godse did know. He sensed with his entire being the threat Gandhi was to the traditional lifestyle and world-view of India. K.P. Karunakaran, a political scientist who has worked on Gandhi for a number of years, once lamented that only two persons in India had correctly assessed the power of Gandhi: Godse, who killed him, and G.D. Birla, India's biggest business tycoon, who gave him unconditional financial support in pre-independence India and reaped its benefits in post-independence India. I am afraid, at least in this one instance, the political scientist is more right than the political functionary. Nehru was wrong. Godse *did* reveal a surprisingly acute sensitivity to the changing political–psychological climate in India, by killing Gandhi. I can only add that the heightened sensitivity of Godse reflected the latent awareness of dominant sections of the Indian society of what Gandhi was doing to them. In that sense, Godse's hand was forced by the real killers of Gandhi: the anxiety-ridden, insecure, traditional elite concentrated in the urbanized, educated, partly westernized, tertiary sector whose meaning of life Gandhian politics was taking away. Gandhi often talked about the heartlessness of the Indian literati. He paid with his life for that awareness.

Ten days before his assassination, on 20 January 1948, Madanlal

---

[38]The concepts of authentic innocence and pseudo-innocence are Rollo May's. See his *Power and Innocence* (New York: Norton, 1972).

The secondary gains were of two types. Those who submitted partook of the crumbs from the colonial table. Their incentives were firstly material and secondly the psychological returns of passivity and security. Those who defied the Raj through terrorism also made secondary gains. Even in defeat they got their masculinity endorsed. They were men, it seemed to them, in a society of eunuchs.

Pahwa, one of Godse's co-conspirators, threw a bomb in a prayer meeting Gandhi was holding, and was apprehended. His intended victim pleaded with the police and the audience to have mercy on Madanlal and instead of harassing the young man, to search their own hearts.[39]

III

One final question needs to be raised: how far did Gandhi and his political heirs in the Indian government collude with the assassins?

We know Gandhi was depressed in his last days in Delhi and was fast losing interest in living.[40] The partition of India was hard on a person who had once said:

I can never be willing party to the vivisection. I would employ non-violent means to prevent it .... My whole soul rebels against the idea that Hinduism and Islam represent two antagonistic cultures and doctrines. To assent to such doctrine is for me denial of God .... If the Congress wishes to accept partition, it will be over my dead body.[41]

The primitive sadism of the pre- and post-partition Hindu–Muslim riots too had destroyed Gandhi's earlier publicly-expressed wish to live for 125 years.[42] He could see the dwindling interest and attendance at his daily prayer meetings and must have also noticed that many of those who did attend the meetings did so as a daily ritual.[43] Somehow Gandhi, as if anticipating and agreeing with the accusations Godse would later make, held himself responsible for what was happening to India and felt that God after deliberately blinding him had awakened him to his mistake.[44]

He now openly yearned for a violent death while preaching pacifism. As he became fond of telling Manuben, his grand-niece and constant companion of his last days, he now only wanted to die bravely; he felt that could turn out to be his final victory. Another time he said to her that if he were to die of an illness, he would prove himself a false Mahatma.[45]

[39] Jain, *Mahatma Gandhi*, p. 64.
[40] Brijkrishna Chandiwalla, *At the Feet of Bapu* (Ahmedabad: Navajivan, 1954), quoted in Payne, *Mahatma Gandhi*, p. 573.
[41] Jain, *Mahatma Gandhi*, p. 52.
[42] Manuben, *Bapu—My Mother*, p. 49; Pyarelal, *Mahatma Gandhi—The Last Phase*, 2 (Ahmedabad: Navajivan), p. 460.
[43] N.K. Bose, *My Days with Gandhi* (Bombay: Orient Longman), p. 250.
[44] Manuben, *Last Glimpses of Bapu* (Delhi: S.L. Agarwala, 1962), p. 81.
[45] Ibid., pp. 81, 234, 252, 297–8.

But if he was felled by an assassin and could die with Rama's name on his lips, he would prove himself a true Mahatma. Thus, it is not surprising that Gandhi's last fast at Delhi, though ostensibly directed against communal violence, was by his own admission directed against everybody.[46] His death wish found other expressions too. He now began to have forebodings of his end. He even specified, correctly as it later turned out, the religion of his future assassin and his own last words after being struck by an assassin's bullet.[47] His health, too, was fast deteriorating. In addition to ailments such as an almost chronic cough, he showed psychosomatic symptoms such as recurring giddiness and nightmares.[48]

He also became totally careless about his physical security. All his life he 'had been reckless of his own safety, and in Delhi he found abundant opportunities to place his life in danger.'[49] He was accustomed to hearing the slogan 'Death to Gandhi'.[50] Now, he seemed to be daring his detractors to act out their wish. There had been, as I have mentioned, a bomb explosion only a few days before his assassination at one of his prayer meetings, the handiwork of the same group of men who ultimately killed him. But Gandhi explicitly rejected all offers of police protection.

Those in charge of his safety too, strangely enough, did little, and this in spite of the fact that bomb-thrower Pahwa was immediately caught and was 'willing' to talk. But there was little communication between the Delhi, Bombay and Poona police. Deliberately or not, each of these police forces sabotaged the investigation. Twenty years later, the Kapur Commission of Enquiry unearthed large scale bureaucratic inefficiency and sheer lethargy in the police who had failed to pursue the clear clues they had to the existence of a dedicated band of conspirators.[51] To pass off the inefficiency and lethargy as the characteristics of individuals will not do.[52] One must consider these important and inherent characteristics

[46]Ibid., p. 114.

[47]Ibid., pp. 297–8.

[48]Payne, *Mahatma Gandhi*, pp. 550, 552.

[49]Ibid., p. 549.

[50]For example, Jain, *Mahatma Gandhi*, pp. 62–3; Pyarelal, *Mahatma Gandhi*, 2, p. 101.

[51]J.L. Kapur, *Report of the Commission of Enquiry into the Conspiracy to Murder Mahatma Gandhi*, Vols. 1–6 (New Delhi: Government of India, 1970).

[52]There is a double-bind in most antipsychologism in the arena of social interpretation. Psychological interpretation in terms of shared motives is countered by the argument that the behaviour of key individuals in a historical episode is random. Psychological interpretation in terms of individual psychodynamics is countered by the argument that the characteristics of aggregates determine all of individual behaviour.

of the culture of the modern sector of India which, in effect, colluded with the conspirators. The police officers of Delhi who later cheated and forged documents, as the Kapur Commission established, to show that the police had tried to protect Gandhi—or the police officers at Bombay and Poona, who failed to break up the conspiracy even when supplied with the names and occupations of some of the conspirators—were a part of the environment which felt menaced by Gandhi. They had worked too long for the Raj as antagonists of Gandhi, and had not been touched by his vision of a different kind of society.

The Hindu–Muslim riots which had destroyed Gandhi's will to live and turned him into a self-destructive depressive, also coloured the psychology of the investigating police, constantly exposed to the slogan of 'Let Gandhi die' during Gandhi's last 'fast unto death' to establish communal peace in Delhi. Anti-Muslim feeling was high in the predominantly Hindu police assigned to protect Gandhi. Most of them were drawn from the various Kshatriya sub-traditions or upwardly mobile social groups claiming Kshatriya status and saw Gandhi not merely as pro-Muslim but as a stereotypical model of passive Hindu submission to non-Hindu aggression. Moreover, the Indian police had already resigned from their role as secular arbiters of law. In the communal riots, the police on the subcontinent had shown itself to be particularly vulnerable to communal passions. Most policemen had supported their respective communities, and their officers had openly tolerated and colluded with the killing of people of other communities. Belonging to castes and communities which had traditionally either lived by the sword or had culturally built-in acceptance of Dionysian rules of interpersonal and public conduct, these officers must have seen in Gandhi, in the charged atmosphere of the post-Partition riots, a person identifying with a part of their feared super-ego which had been overtaken by primal impulses of violence, retribution and fear.[53]

Finally, though to his political heirs he remained a father figure, the successful completion of India's freedom struggle ending in independence had taken its toll. Statecraft and new responsibilities took up much of the time of the leaders. The chaos and near-anarchic situation in post-independence India kept them busy. If anything, they found Gandhi's style slightly anachronistic and Gandhi somewhat unmanageable.[54] For

---

[53]No wonder that Gandhi himself was suspicious of some of the police officers in charge of communal peace. See for example his comment on Inspector General Randhawa of Delhi police in Manuben, *Last Glimpses of Bapu*, pp. 170–1.

[54]To some extent, Nehru does not fit the mould. Himself never fully given to *realpolitik*, he also was never much impressed by the search for political *machismo*.

instance, Susanne Rudolph feels 'Patel . . . often wished that the Mahatma would leave him alone, especially in matters where they differed greatly— as in Hindu–Muslim relations and Patel's cold-eyed *Realpolitik* orientation'.[55] But leaving him alone was the one thing Gandhi would not do. Did Home Minister Patel's failure to protect Gandhi express his unconscious rejection of the relevance of Gandhi and his interfering style, as an important first-hand witness and a major political figure of the period, Abul Kalam Azad, seems to imply?[56] One does not know, but it is not perhaps a coincidence that the last fast of Gandhi was directed as much against violent communalism as against Nehru and Patel refusing to a hostile Pakistan its share of the funds of undivided India on grounds of *realpolitik*.

Let us not forget that Gandhi's inability to conform to the principles of *realpolitik* was one of the main reasons Godse gave for killing Gandhi. Gandhian politics, Godse said in his last speech, 'was supported by old superstitious beliefs such as the power of the soul, the inner voice, the fast, the prayer, and the purity of mind.'[57]

I felt that the Indian politics in the absence of Gandhiji would surely be practical, able to retaliate, and would be powerful with the armed forces . . . . People may even call me and dub me as devoid of any sense or foolish, but the nation would be free to follow the course founded on reason which I consider to be necessary for sound nation-building.[58]

In the course of the same speech Godse also said that Gandhi's non-violence consisted in enduring 'the blows of the aggressor without showing any resistance either by weapon or by physical force . . . . I firmly believed and believe that the non-violence of the type described above will lead the nation towards ruin.' He had an example to give, too: the 'problem of the state of Hyderabad which had been unnecessarily delayed and postponed has been rightly solved by our government by the use of armed

---

[55]'Gandhi's Lieutenants—Varieties of Followership', in P.F. Power (ed.), *The Meanings of Gandhi* (Honolulu: The University Press of Hawaii, 1971), pp. 41–58, see p. 55.

[56]A.K. Azad, *India Wins Freedom* (Bombay: Orient Longman's, 1955). It has been suggested that Patel never recovered from his sense of guilt over the whole episode and died a broken man soon afterwards. If so, he was only epitomizing the moral crisis that Gandhi wanted to precipitate in all Indians by his death. In the case of Patel, the crisis might have been further sharpened by his own alleged softness towards some of those associated with the assassination. See on this theme Gopal Godse, *Gandhihatya*, pp. 229, 237–8.

[57]Quoted in Ghose, *Gandhi Murder Trial*, p. 229.

[58]Quoted in Khosla, *Nathuram Godse*, p. 242.

force—after the demise of Gandhi. The present government of remaining India is seen taking the course of practical politics.'[59] It is an indication of how much latent support there was for this line of thinking in the country that the Government of India prevented the publication of this speech lest it might arouse widespread sympathy for the killer of Gandhi.

Perhaps the same thread of consciousness or, if you like, unconsciousness, ran through the inaction of B.G. Kher and Morarji Desai, Chief and Home Ministers respectively of the state of Bombay, where the conspiracy to kill Gandhi was hatched. They did not follow up vigorously enough the first-hand information given to them ten days before the assassination by Jagadish Chandra Jain, a professor in a college at Bombay and father-confessor of Madanlal Pahwa. Anyone reading the tragicomic exchanges between Jain on the one hand and Kher and Desai on the other cannot but be impressed by the callous, self-righteous and yet guilt-ridden ineptitude of the two politicians in this matter.[60]

Obviously the living Gandhi had already ceased to be a relevant figure for a large number of Indians. To some of them he had already begun to seem a threat to Hindu survival, a fanatical supporter of Muslims and, worse, one who rejected the principle of zero-sum game in politics. If not their conscious minds, their primitive selves were demanding his blood.

Godse reflected this desire. He was confident that millions in India (particularly Hindu women, subject to Muslim atrocities) would shed tears for his sacrifice; and he lived the months before his execution with the serene conviction that posterity would vindicate him. In his last letter to his parents he wrote that he had killed Gandhi for the same reasons for which Krishna had killed the evil King Sishupal.[61]

He was not wholly wrong in his estimate of public reactions. This is how, according to Justice Khosla, the public reacted to the killer of Gandhi after Nathuram had made his final plea as a defendant:

The audience was visibly and audibly moved. There was a deep silence when he ceased speaking. Many women were in tears and men were coughing and searching for their handkerchiefs. The silence was accentuated and made deeper by the sound of an occasional subdued sniff or a muffled cough. . . . I have . . . no doubt that had the audience of that day been constituted into a jury and entrusted with the task of deciding Godse's appeal, they would have brought in a verdict of 'not guilty' by an overwhelming majority.[62]

---

[59]Quoted in Ghose, *Gandhi Murder Trial*, pp. 228, 229.
[60]Jain, *Mahatma Gandhi*, Part 2, Chapters 1 and 5. Further details of such acts of carelessness all around could be found in Kapur Commission Report.
[61]Godse, *Gandhihatya ani Mee*, pp. 221–3.
[62]Khosla, *Nathuram Godse*, p. 243.

IV

On 30 January 1948 Nathuram Godse fired four shots at point-blank range as Gandhi was going to his evening prayer-meeting in Delhi. Before firing the shots he bowed down to Gandhi to show his respect for the services the Mahatma had rendered to the country. The killer made no attempt to run away and himself shouted for the police, even though in the stunned silence following the killing he had enough time at least to attempt an escape. As he later said, he had done his duty like Arjuna in the *Mahabharata* whom Krishna advised to kill his own relatives because they were evil.[63]

So Gandhi died, according to his own scenario, at the hands of one who was apparently a zealot, a religious fanatic, a typical assassin with a typical assassin's background: educated and intelligent, but an under-achiever; relatively young; coming from the middle class and yet from a group which was a displaced élite; and with a long record of failures. Here was a man fighting a diffused sense of self-definition with the help of a false sense of mission and trying to give through political assassination some meaning to his life.[64] One might even note, for psychologists, that there was also in Godse the authoritarian man's fear of sexuality, status seeking, idealization of parents, ideological rigidity, constriction of emotions and even some amount of what Erich Fromm would diagnose as love of death.[65]

In other ways, too, it was an archetypal assassination. Not only the background of the assassin, but everything else too fell into place. There was the hero who became the victim; the villain, motivated by values larger than him but also, at one plane, driven by fate and maniacal; and a Greek cast of characters who invited the tragedy. There were even eloquent mourners in the Nehrus, Einsteins and Shaws.

Finally, like many assassinations, this one too had as its immediate provocation something history had already passed by, namely, the partition of India in 1947. To both Gandhi and Godse partition was the greatest personal tragedy. Both blamed Gandhi for it; one sought retribution, the other expiation. Partition however was irreversible and, politically, the assassination—and the martyrdom the two antagonists sought through it—was pointless. In this sense Mahadevan is right: in the

[63]Godse, *Gandhihatya ani Mee*, pp. 46, 221.
[64]See Horowitz, *Political Terrorism and State Power*; and Ashis Nandy, 'Invitation to a Beheading'.
[65]See Fromm's *The Anatomy of Human Destructiveness* (New York: Holt, Rinehart and Winston, 1973). I have not dealt with them in this paper, but on Godse's search for self-esteem and meaning in death, see Godse, *Gandhihatya*, p. 222.

confrontation between Godse and Gandhi there could be no loser and no winner; it was like two batsmen walking into the field after the stumps had been drawn.[66]

Is this, then, the whole story? At another level, was it not also a case of the dominant traditions within a society trying to contain a force which, in the name of orthodoxy, threatened to demolish its centre, to erect instead a freer society and a new authority system using the rubble of the old? Did not Godse promise to facilitate his fellowmen's escape from this freedom that Gandhi promised? If Gandhi in his depression connived at it, he also perhaps felt—being the shrewd, practical idealist he was— that he had become somewhat of an anachronism in post-partition, independent India; and in violent death he might be more relevant to the living than he could be in life. As not a few have sensed, like Socrates and Christ before him, Gandhi knew how to use human sense of guilt creatively.

[66]Mahadevan, 'Godse versus Gandhi'.

*Earlier published in Ashis Nandy, *At the Edge of Psychology: Essays in Politics and Culture* (New Delhi: Oxford University Press, 1980).

5

~mm~

Culture, State and the
Rediscovery of Indian Politics

A SOCIETY CAN understand the relationship between its culture and its state in two ways. The first way is to look for the means by which culture can be made to contribute to the sustenance and growth of the state. The state here is seen as operating according to certain fixed, universal, sociological rules. Elements of the culture that help strengthen the state are seen as good; elements of the culture that do not help the proper functioning of the state or hinder its growth are seen as defective. A mature society, in this view, sheds or actively eliminates these defective elements, to improve both the functioning of the state and the quality of the culture.

The second way of looking at the relationship between culture and the state is to do so from the standpoint of the culture. This approach may regard the state as a protector, an internal critic or a thermostat for the culture but not as the ultimate pace-setter for the society's way of life. The state here is made to serve the needs of or contribute to the enrichment of the culture; it is never allowed to dictate terms to the culture. Even when the state is used as a critique of the culture and the culture is sought to be transformed, the final justification for the criticism and the transformation is not sought in the intrinsic logic of statecraft or in the universal laws of state formation. That justification is sought in the self-perceived needs of the culture and the people and in the moral framework used by the people.

This dichotomy between the state and the culture-oriented views of society, of course, dissolves if one uses the older idea of the state as part and parcel of culture (as obtains in many traditional societies) or if one refuses to accept the modern idea of nation-state as the only genuine version of state (as is assumed by most modern political and social analysts today). In most non-modern societies, among people who work with the older idea and not with the modern idea of the nation-state, the culture-oriented approach to state is seen as natural and the state-oriented approach as an imposition.[1] At the same time, in modern societies the nation-state-oriented approach seems natural and rational, and the culture-oriented one unnatural, irrational or primitive. The choice, therefore, boils down to one between the culture-oriented and the nation-state-oriented. Still, for the sake of simplicity, I shall use here the expression state-oriented or statist to mean the nation-state–oriented, hoping that the reader will not confuse this concept of 'statist' with that used in debates between the socialist thinkers and the liberals believing in a minimal state.

I am not considering here either the nature of the state or that of culture. These are vital issues which need to be discussed fully. For the moment I wish to avoid them because I want to do justice to the culture-oriented approach that believes that a state can destroy the civilization of which it is a part even when—forgive the anthropomorphism—the intentions of the state are 'honourable' and even when it is 'honestly' trying to improve a decaying civilization. When a state becomes ethno-cidal, the culture-oriented approach believes, the remedy does not lie merely in capturing the state, since this provides no check against the captured state becoming as ethnocidal in scope as it was before being captured.

I

For the last 150 years, westernized, middle-class Indians have learnt to look at the first approach—the one that orients the needs of the culture to the needs of the state—as the very epitome of political maturity, achievement and development. Since the nation-state system acquired its present global predominance in the nineteenth century, most political analysis in the West, too, has forgotten the alternative. And since a global science of politics became fully operational after World War II, the state-oriented attitude to culture has become the only way of looking at culture

---

[1]In traditional India, for instance, the state was clearly expected to be a part of culture and the king was expected to see himself not only a protector of *dharma* but also as a protector of multiple ways of life and a promoter of ethnic tolerance. While the *Arthashastra* may not provide a clue to this, the *puranas*, the folklore and *lokachara* do.

the world over. Nearly all the studies of political development and political culture of the 1950s and 1960s have this cultural-engineering component built into them. From Talcott Parsons, Edward Shils and David Easton to Karl Deutsch, Samuel Huntington and Lucian Pye, it is the same story. So much so that, under their influence, modern political analysts and journalists are forced to fall back on state-oriented analytic categories, even after the categories have shown poor interpretative power, as often happens when figures like M.K. Gandhi, Ayatollah Khomeini, Maulana Bhashani and Jarnail Singh Bhindranwale (to give random examples) become politically consequential.

This is part of a larger picture. Take, for instance, studies of the cultural contexts of economic growth done during the same period. The main function of culture, according to these studies, was to facilitate economic growth. Aspects of culture that stood in the way of such growth had to be ruthlessly excised. In 'stagnant' cultures, that is, in cultures which did not nurture a thriving modern economy, the engineering challenge was to rediscover or introduce cultural elements which would trigger or sustain economic growth and the spirit of the market that went with it. This was the thrust of the psychological studies of achievement motivation done by David McClelland and company, and the studies of Protestant-ethics-like elements in non-western cultures by a drove of social anthropologists. Even the tough-minded economists of the period, who did not believe in the relevance of such woolly psychological or cultural anthropological work, never faltered in their belief that a society had to give primacy to the needs of the modern economy, however defined, over the needs of culture. So did the mercenaries among them vending the materialist— read economic—interpretation of history to ensure the centrality of their dismal science in the world of social knowledge. In India, at least, I have not come across a single work of any Marxist economist of the period which challenged the basic priority of economics and sought to restore, even as a distant goal, Marx's original vision of a society freed from the bondage of economism.[2]

A similar case can be made about science. Most science-and-culture

[2]One of the first Marxist thinkers in the Third World to explicitly recognize the primacy of culture was Amilcar Cabral (1924–74). See his *Return to the Source: Selected Speeches* (New York: Monthly Review Press, 1973). He, of course, drew upon the work of Aimé Césaire and Leopold Senghor. One suspects that the African heritage of the three had something to do with their sensitivity. The distintegrating native cultures they saw around them were more threatened than threatening, something which a Mao Zedong could not say about China. In India, unfortunately, even the Marxism of classical scholars like D.D. Kosambi and D.P. Chattopadhyay has remained in essence another version of western Orientalism and colonial anthropology.

studies of the 1950s and 1960s sought to make the society safe for modern science. For this purpose, all non-modern cultures were to be retooled and made more rational or modern. Thus, scientific criticisms of culture were encouraged but cultural criticisms of science were dubbed obscurantist. Occasionally, shallow criticisms of the social relations of science were allowed—in the sense that the control over science exercised by imperialism or capitalism or by army generals was allowed to be exposed. But this was done as part of an attempt to protect the text and the core values of modern science which were seen as absolute and as the last word in human rationality. As if, somehow, the forces of violence and exploitation, after taking over much of the context of modern science, hesitated when they encountered the contents of modern science and refused to enter its sanctum sanctorum. Here, too, culture was always at the receiving end, while science kept the company of modern political and economic institutions.

We are however talking of politics at the moment, not of the witchcraft called economics or the mega-corporation called modern science. And I want to suggest that in India the primacy granted to the needs of the state—seen as a necessary part of a ruthless, global, nation-state system— is not a new idea coined in the late 1940s by the first generation of post-independence managers of the Indian polity. The primacy of the state was not the discovery of Jawaharlal Nehru or Vallabhbhai Patel, two very different persons who arrived at roughly the same statist ideology through very different personal and intellectual paths. Nor did the primacy-of-the-state theory evolve in the 1950s or the 1960s when the structural–functional models of political development and positivist-Marxist models of the state endorsed, at two ends of the political spectrum, its primacy. The new model merely re-legitimized what had been brewing for more than a hundred years in India and, perhaps, for more than three hundred years in Europe.

The statist model first came to India in the nineteenth century, in the second phase of colonialism, when a more reactive, self-defensive Hinduism began to take shape in response to the consolidation of social theories that saw colonialism as a civilizing influence and as a pathway from feudalism to modern statehood.[3] It was towards the middle of the

[3]For a discussion of the political consciousness which characterized this phase of colonial politics, and its persistence within the culture of Indian politics as an important strain, see Ashis Nandy, 'The Making and Unmaking of Political Cultures of India', in *At the Edge of Psychology: Essays in Politics and Culture* (New Delhi:

nineteenth century that a series of dedicated Hindu religious and social reformers first mooted the idea that what Hinduism lacked was the primacy which most forms of post-medieval, western Christianity granted to the state. Even Islam, they felt, had a built-in space for such primacy. The Hindus did not. That was why, in their view, the Hindus were having it so bad. The sorrow of that generation of reformers was that the Hindu seemed an animal peculiarly hostile and insensitive to the subtleties of the nation-state system; their hope was that the hostility and insensitivity could be corrected through proper cultural and social engineering. This the religious reformers tried to do through a revision of the Hindu personality and way of life.

This effort, because it came as part of a defence of Hinduism, hid the fact that this was the first influential indigenous form of the primacy-of-the-state thesis advanced in India. The thesis, for the first time, brought modern statism within Hinduism, in the sense that the Hindu state of the future was not to be the Hindu polity of the past but a centralized, modern nation-state with a Brahminic idiom. Suresh Sharma's recent paper on V.D. Savarkar neatly sums up the spirit of this particular form of Hindu nationalism and the political form it later had to take. It is a measure of the cultural tragedy which colonialism was for India that even a person like Savarkar, after spending nearly forty years in intense, often violent, anti-colonial struggle and suffering for it, had ultimately to turn intellectually and culturally collaborationist, purportedly to save the Hindus from Islamic domination with the help of the culturally and politically more 'advanced' British.[4]

The earlier generation of reformers, in what can be called the first phase of British colonialism, had pleaded for greater political participation

---

Oxford University Press, 1980), pp. 47–69; and *The Intimate Enemy: Loss and Recovery of Self under Colonialism* (New Delhi: Oxford University Press, 1983).

[4]Savarkar was a product of Marathi nationalism, which sought legitimacy by developing the European-style idea of a common culture, will, and a fixed territory with 'natural' boundaries. Enrico Fasana, 'Deshabhakta: The Leaders of Italian Independence Movement in the Eyes of Marathi Nationalists', *Asian and African Studies*, 1994, 3(2), pp. 152–75. Also, Suresh Sharma, 'Savarkar's Quest for a Modern Hindu Consolidation: The Framework of Validation', in D.L. Sheth and Ashis Nandy (eds.), *Hindu Visions of a Desirable Society: Heritage, Challenge and Redefinitions* (forthcoming). Bankimchandra Chattopadhyay (1838–94) was probably the first well-known theoretician of the state-oriented approach in India. I say 'probably' because he stated his position indirectly, often through his literary and theological works or through commentaries on the works of others. Sudipta Kaviraj suggests that Bhudev Mukhopadhyaya (1827–94), a less known contemporary of Bankimchandra, was the first to explicitly accept and plead for a modern nation-state in India.

of Indians and also for greater state intervention in the society. But there were externally imposed limits to their enthusiasm; they did not stress the absolute primacy of the state, partly because the state was not theirs and partly because even their British rulers had not yet shown any great ideological commitment to the state system they were running. The state for the first generation of British rulers was mainly a means of making money, not a means of cultural engineering. These rulers feared and respected Indian culture, which they tried not to disturb as long as it did not stand in the way of their money-making. Moreover, the Raj occupied a relatively small part of the subcontinent and certainly did not give the impression of being the paramount power in the country. Indians pressurizing their British rulers to intervene in Indian society could not internalize a highly activist or an awesomely grand image of the state.[5]

Nonetheless, the first generation of social reformers had provided the base on which the second generation of reformers built their adoration for the modern idea of the nation-state and their suspicion of all grass-roots politics. Certainly, these latter reformers did not put any premium on participatory politics, which they accepted theoretically only as a vague, populist possibility. Even when they spoke of mass politics as desirable, they saw it as something that had to come later—after the Hindu had been morally and educationally uplifted and after he had learnt to take on modern responsibilities.[6] This shielded them from the awareness that they were unwilling or incapable of mobilizing ordinary Indians for basic political changes, including full participation in the anti-imperial struggle.

The votaries of a Hindu nation-state, thinking that they were pleading for a Hindu polity, were also mostly unaware that the nation-state system was one of the more recent innovations in human civilization and that it had come into being only about two hundred years earlier in Europe, in the mid-seventeenth century. They chose to see it as one of the eternal verities of humankind. Naturally, they diagnosed Hindu inadequacy in state-oriented politics as the result of a major defect in the Hindu

---

[5]There was also probably a feeling among Indians that there should be limits to which a colonial state should be involved by its subjects in the matter of social reform. Consider, for instance, the ambivalence of Rammohun Roy (1772–1833), who worked aggressively for the abolition of the practice of sati but who doubted the wisdom of a state-imposed ban on it.

[6]Aurobindo Ghose (1872–1950) in his revolutionary years, when he was under the influence of Mazzini, was a good example of such romantic populism. The hero of Saratchandra Chattopadhyay's novel *Pather Dabi*, Sabyasachi, is a faithful idealization of this approach to political participation. The pathological possibilities of the approach have been explored in some detail in Rabindranath Tagore's novels *Gora, The Home and the World* and *Char Adhyay*.

personality and culture, which had to be reformed as the first step to political freedom. (The British in India, for their own reasons, endorsed this priority of the cultural over the political enthusiastically.) Many of these social reformers, inappropriately called Hindu revivalists, were later to have much sympathy for the anti-British terrorist movements. But that sympathy was not accompanied by any passion for wider political participation of the people. Indeed, they were always a little afraid of the majority of Hindus who lived in the 500,000 Indian villages. Hindu *rashtra*, yes; but not with the full participation of all the Hindu *praja*, at least not with that of the *praja* as they were, and certainly not with the participation of all Hindus in the short run. The conspiratorial style of the terrorists was handy here since it automatically restricted mass participation in politics. Even the constant invocation of the Hindu past by the revivalists—the practice which gave them their distinctive name—was a criticism of living Hindus. It was a compensatory act. It hid the revivalists' admiration for the West and for western Christianity and middle-eastern Islam, seen as martial and valorous, and it hid the desperate search for the same qualities in the Hindu past. The political consequence of this admiration for the conquerors of the Hindus was the continuous attempt by many to re-educate the 'politically immature', anarchic, living Hindus, so that the latter could rediscover their lost western and Islamic values and play their proper role in the global system of nation-states. Swami Vivekananda, when he envisioned a new race of Vedantic Hindus who would build a western society in India, was only being true to the primacy-of-the-state thesis.[7]

I am arguing that the nineteenth-century characters whom modern Indians have learnt to call revivalists were never truly anti-West or anti-Islam. They were only anti-British and anti-Muslim in the Indian context. Their ideal, in important respects, was western Christianity or West Asian Islam. And as for their concept of the state, it was perfectly modern. If anything, they were fundamentally and ferociously anti-Hindu.[8] The only good Hindu to them was the Hindu who was dead, that is, the imagined Hindu who had lived a few thousand years ago. They wanted to enter the world scene with an engineered Hindu who, but for his ideological commitment to classical Hinduism, would be a western man, a man who would accept the rules of the game called the nation-state system and

[7]It was the same statist vision of India which explains Sister Nivedita's (1867–1911) discomfort with Ananda Coomaraswamy (1877–1947) whom she considered too conservative.

[8]This has been discussed in Nandy, *The Intimate Enemy*. See also 'The Twilight of Certitudes', pp. 61–82.

who could not be shortchanged either by the westerner or by the Muslim.

It was this heritage on which both the mainstream liberal and the official Marxist ideologies in India were to later build. Strange though it may sound to many, there *was* a cultural continuity between the early primacy accorded to the state and the strand of consciousness which was later to seek legitimacy in popular modern theories of the state in India. Both liberals and official Marxists like to trace their origins to the earlier integrationist tradition of social reform, the one beginning with Rammohun Roy (1772–1833) and more or less ending with Rabindranath Tagore (1861–1940) and Gopal Krishna Gokhale (1866–1915). This ignores the checks within the ideological frame of these pioneers. Rammohun Roy, for instance, was a modernizer, but he located the origins of the problems of Hindu personality and culture in the colonial situation and not in Hindu traditions. He believed that the pathologies of Hinduism he was fighting could be found only around the institutional structures introduced by British rule and, therefore, his own religious reforms and the new Hindu sect he established were directed only at 'exposed' Hindus, not at parts of the society untouched by colonialism. As he himself put it:

From a careful survey and observation of the people and inhabitants of various parts of the country, and in every condition of life, I am of the opinion that the peasants and villagers who reside at a distance from large towns and head stations and courts of law, are as innocent, temperate and moral in their conduct as the people of any country whatsoever; and the further I proceed towards the North and West [away from British India], the greater the honesty, simplicity and independence of character I meet with.[9]

In his own crude, unsure way Roy did try to protect the architectonics of Indian culture. He did not want Indian culture to be integrated into the modern world; he wanted modernity to be integrated into Indian culture. His modern admirers have chosen to forget the checks within him—weak though the checks were. They have built him up as the father of modern India and as a mindless admirer of everything western.

Thus, as far as the role of the nation-state in the Indian civilization is concerned, Indian modernists as well as radicals have drawn upon the

---

[9]For example, Rammohun Roy, 'Additional Queries Respecting the Condition of India', in Kalidas Nag and Debajyoti Burman (eds.), *The English Works* (Calcutta: Sadharan Brahmo Samaj, 1947), Part III, pp. 63–8; see especially pp. 64–5. Cf. Gandhi's critique of the railways and lawyers in *Hind Swaraj*, in *Collected Works of Mahatma Gandhi* (Delhi: Publications Division, Government of India, 1963), Vol. 4, pp. 81–208.

ideological framework first popularized by Hindu nationalism. It was in their model that the modern nation-state first became an absolute value and acquired absolute primacy over the needs of the Indian civilization./

II

Yet, there has always been in India during the last 150 years another intellectual current that has looked differently at the needs of the society. This current sees state-oriented politics as a means of criticizing Indian culture, even as a means of renegotiating traditional social relationships, but it refuses to see such politics as the *raison d'être* of Indian civilization. However, though the majority of Indians may have always lived with such a concept of politics, for modern India the concept has survived only as part of an intellectual underground since the middle of the nineteenth century.

It was only under the influence of Gandhi that this current temporarily acquired a certain self-consciousness and political dominance. Gandhi has been often called an anarchist. To the extent that he suspected and fought state power and refused to grant it the primary role in guiding or controlling political and social change, he *was* close to anarchism. Also, while leading a freedom struggle against a foreign power, he could get away with his antipathy to the state. This situation could not last beyond a point. His very success dug the grave of his ideology; his anti-statist political thought quickly went into recession after Independence. The demands of statecraft in a newly-independent nation were such that national leaders not only began to look with suspicion at the Gandhian emphasis on cultural traditions, they also began to encourage political interpretations of Gandhi which fitted him into the state-oriented frame of politics, neutralizing or ignoring his culture-oriented self as irrelevant saintliness or eccentricity. On this ideological issue, they were in perfect agreement with Gandhi's assassin Nathuram Godse, an avowed statist. It was no accident that Godse, though called an ultra-conservative, felt threatened not by modernists like Jawaharlal Nehru, but by Gandhi.[10]

It is only now that this recessive strain of consciousness is again coming into its own in the works of a number of young and not-so-young scholars—traditionalists, counter-modernists, post-Mao Marxists,

[10]Ashis Nandy, 'Final Encounter: The Politics of the Assassination of Gandhi', in this book; and 'Godse Killed Gandhi?', *Resurgence*, January–February 1983 (96), pp. 28–9.

anarchists and neo-Gandhians. Evidently, an open polity has its own logic. At the peripheries of the modern Indian polity itself, the demand for fuller democratic participation by people who carry the heavy 'burden' of their non-modern culture is becoming an important component of the political idiom.

This consciousness has been endorsed by a political reality that has two facets: (a) an increasingly oppressive state-machine that constantly imperils the survival and ways of life of those Indians it has marginalized and (b) the growing efforts of these marginalized sections to interpret their predicament in terms alien to the modern world and to the state-centred culture of scholarship.[11] There is enough evidence for us to believe that this strain of consciousness may begin to set the pace of public consciousness in India in the coming decades and the following section is written as a guide and a warning for those pragmatic spirits and hard-boiled modernists of both the right and the left who might have to close ranks to fight this new menace to the modern Indian nation-state.

The first element in this odd strain, the strain that views the needs of a civilization as primary, is the belief that a civilization must use the state as an instrument and not become an instrument of the state. This of course also means that the Indian state should be reformed before Indian civilization can be reformed. It does not argue out cultural reforms or even cultural revolutions. But the needs of the state do not determine such interventions. The idea that a civilization can be destroyed or changed beyond recognition reportedly for its own survival in the jungle of the nation-state system is given up here. At the same time, the culture-oriented approach believes that if there is need either for a cultural revolution or for modest cultural changes in this society, it should begin in decultured Anglo-India and then, if necessary, end in its externed parts (to translate into English the concept of *bahiskrit samaj* used by Sunil Sahasrabudhey).[12] Culture, in this approach, is the world-view of the oppressed and it must have precedence over the world-view of the dominant, even when the

---

[11]The attempt to grapple with this reality has revived Gandhian social theory in India, mostly among people who reject the orthodox Gandhism of many of the direct disciples of Gandhi. The revival has as little to do with the personal life and the personal successes or failures of Gandhi as Marx's life and his successes and failures have to do with Marx's thought today. Modern Indians naturally like to give credit for the revival either to 'Hindu woolly-headedness' or to the false consciousness generated by 'romantic propagandists' like Richard Attenborough.

[12]Sunil Sahasrabudhey, 'Towards a New Theory', *Seminar*, May 1982 (273), pp. 19–23; and 'On Alien Political Categories', *Gandhi Marg*, Feb. 1983, 4(11), pp. 896–901. Sahasrabudhey is one of the few serious Marxists in India who have self-consciously built into their models indigenous cultural categories.

latter claims to represent universal, cumulative rationality and sanctions the very latest theory of oppression.

Second, this approach believes that a cultural tradition represents the accumulated wisdom of a people—empirical and rational in its architechtonics, though not in every detail. It does not automatically become obsolete as a consequence of the growth of modern science or technology. In fact, a complex culture has its own ethnic science and technology which are sought to be destroyed by modern science and technology with the help of state power and in the name of the obsolescence of traditional knowledge-systems and lifestyles.[13] The non-statists believe that the traditions are under attack today because the people today are under attack. As classical liberalism and czarist Marxism have both by now shown their bankruptcy, many liberals and socialists have increasingly fallen upon the use of concepts like cultural lag and false consciousness to explain away all resistance to the oppression that comes in the guise of modern science and development. The primacy-of-culture approach fears that more and more models of social engineering will be generated in the modern sector which would demand from the people greater and greater sacrifices in the name of the state and in the name of state-sponsored development and state-owned science and technology. The culture-oriented approach believes that when the lowest of the low in India are exhorted to shed their 'irrational', 'unscientific', anti-developmental traditions by the official rationalists, the exhortation is a hidden appeal to them to soften their resistance to the oppressive features of the modern political economy in India.[14]

[13]In the context of Indian traditions of science and technology, this point has been made indirectly but painstakingly by Dharampal, *Indian Science and Technology in the Eighteenth Century: Some Contemporary European Accounts* (New Delhi: Impex India, 1971); and directly and passionately by Claude Alvares, *Homo Faber: Technology and Culture in India, China and the West* (New Delhi: Allied, 1979). See also Shiv Visvanathan, 'The Annals of a Laboratory State'; and Vandana Shiva, 'Reductionist Science as Epistemic Violence', in Ashis Nandy (ed.), *Science, Hegemony and Violence: A Requiem for Modernity* (Tokyo: U.N. University Press; New Delhi: Oxford University Press, 1988), pp. 257–88; and Claude Alvares, *Science, Development and Violence: The Twilight of Modernity* (New Delhi: Oxford University Press, 1991).

[14]On development as it looks from outside the modern world, some of the clearest statements are in Claude Alvares, 'Deadly Development', *Development Forum*, October 1983, 9(7); and *Science, Development and Violence*; also see the Special Issue on Survival, *Lokayan Bulletin*, 1985, 3 (4/5); Madhya Pradesh Lokayan and Lokhit Samiti, Singrauli, *Vikas ki Kimat* (Ahmedabad: Setu, 1985); Arturo Escobar, *Encountering Development: The Making and the Unmaking of the Third World* (Princeton: Princeton University Press, 1995); Vinod Raina, Aditi Chowdhury and Sumit Chowdhury (eds.), *The Dispossessed: Victims of Development in Asia* (Hong

Third, the culture-oriented approach presumes that culture is a dialectic between the classical and the folk, the past and the present, the dead and the living. Modern states, on the other hand, emphasize the classical and the frozen-in-time, so as to museumize culture and make it harmless. Here, too, the modernists endorse the revivalists who believe in time-travel to the past, the Orientalists to whom culture is either a distant object of study or a projection of their own cultural needs, and the deculturized to whom culture is what one sees on the stage or in the gallery. Such attitudes to culture go with a devaluation of the folk which is reduced to the artistic and musical self-expression of tribes and language groups. Ethnic arts and ethnic music then become, like ethnic food, new indicators of the social status of the rich and the powerful. Correspondingly, new areas of expertise open up in the modern sector such as ethnomuseology and ethnomusicology. And cultural anthropology then takes over the responsibility of making this truncated concept of culture communicable in the language of professional anthropology, to give the concept a bogus absolute legitimacy in the name of cultural relativism.

Culture in the present context covers, apart from 'high culture', indigenous knowledge, including indigenous theories of science, education and social change. The defence of culture, according to those who stress cultural survival, is also the defence of these native theories. The defence must challenge the basic hierarchy of cultures, the evolutionist theory of progress, and the historical awareness with which the modern mind works.[15] This radical departure from the Englightenment vision the modern admirers of native cultures will never accept.

Fourth, the culture-oriented approach tries to demystify the traditional reason of the state: national security. It does not deny the importance of collective security, even though the statists feel that anyone who is not a statist jeopardizes such security. However, the culture-oriented

Kong: Arena, 1997). Also see 'Culture, Voice and Development', in this book; 'Development and Violence', in *The Romance of the State and the Fate of Dissent in the Tropics* (New Delhi: Oxford University Press, 2003), pp. 171–81.

[15]In the Indian context such a point of view was aggressively advanced by Gandhi. See the pioneering essay of A.K. Saran, 'Gandhi and the Concept of Politics', *Gandhi Marg*, 1980, 1(1), pp. 675–726. Also Thomas Pantham, 'Thinking with Mahatma Gandhi: Beyond Liberal Democracy', *Political Theory*, 1983, 2(2), pp. 165–88; and Ashis Nandy, 'From Outside the Imperium: Gandhi's Cultural Critique of the "West" ', in *Traditions, Tyranny and Utopias: Essays in the Politics of Awareness* (New Delhi: Oxford University Press, 1987), pp. 127–62.

approach believes that national security can become disjunctive with people's security and may even become a threat to the latter.[16] Some of those who take culture seriously fear that India is fast becoming a national-security state with an ever-expanding definition of security which threatens democratic governance within the country as well as the security of India's neighbours, who are parts of Indian civilization.[17]

The culture-sensitive approach to Indian politics seeks to demystify the two newer reasons of state: conventional development and mainsteam science (including technology). It believes that new forces of oppression have been unleashed in Indian society in the name of these new reasons of state and the new legitimacies they have created. Those for the primacy of culture believe that these three reasons of state—security, development and modern science—are creating internal colonies, new hierarchies and recipient cultures among the people, so that a small élite can live off both economic and psychosocial surpluses extracted from the people as part of the process of modernization.[18] Modernization, the argument goes, has not fallen into wrong hands; built into it are certain forms of domination and violence. The concept of the expert or the revolutionary

[16]For instance, Giri Deshingkar, 'Civilization Concerns', *Seminar*, December 1980, (256), pp. 12–17; and 'People's Security versus National Security', *Seminar*, December 1982, (280), pp. 28–30.

[17]For instance, Bharat Wariavwallah, 'Indira's India: A National Security State?', *Round Table*, July 1983, pp. 274–85; and 'Personality, Domestic Political Institutions and Foreign Policy', in Ram Joshi (ed.), *Congress in Indian Politics: A Centenary Perspective* (Bombay: Popular Prakashan, 1975), pp. 245–69; also Deshingkar, 'People's Security versus National Security'.

[18]For some culture-sensitive Indian intellectuals, the only valid definition of conventional development is the one given by Afsaneh Eghbal in the context of Africa in her 'L'état contre L'ethnicité—Une Nouvelle Arme: Le Developpement Exclusion', *IFDA Dossier*, July–August 1983 (36), pp. 17–29:

Development is a structure in which a centralized power, in the form of a young sovereign state, formally negotiates international funds for rural populations representing ethnicity . . . no external aid, in the field of development, can relate directly to ethnic groups caught in the problematique of survival. All aid is first absorbed and often plundered by state power.

The Indian critic of development will however further generalize the principle and affirm that it holds for internal resources, too. A good summary description of the process of development in India from this point of view is in Alvares, 'Deadly Development'. For a theoretically alert description of the political context within which such developmental pathologies emerge, see Rajni Kothari, 'The Crisis of the Moderate State and the Decline of Democracy', in Peter Lyon and James Manor (eds.) *Transfer and Transformation: Political Institutions in the New Commonwealth* (Leicester: Leicester University Press, 1983), pp. 29–47.

vanguard is part of the same story or, as it looks to the non-moderns, part of the same conspiracy.[19]

It is a feature of the recipient culture which is to be created through the modern state system, that the superstitions of the rich and the powerful are given less emphasis than the superstitions of the poor and lowly. This is the inescapable logic of development and scientific rationality today. Only the young, the 'immature' and the powerless are left to attack the superstitions of the powerful. (For instance, the belief popularized by the two post-World War II superpowers that national security requires the capacity to kill all living beings of the world thirty times over, as if once is not good enough; the belief of our rulers that every society will one day reach the level of prosperity of the modern West, as if the earth had that kind of resources; or the faith of our science bosses that the expansion of TV or nuclear energy would strengthen development without setting up a centralized political control system.) The so-called mature scientists, the ultra-rational liberals and professional progressives are kept busy attacking superstitions such as astrology because these are the small-scale enterprises of ill-bred, native entrepreneurs, not the trillion-dollar enterprise which the arms trade, cosmetics and pet-food industries are. It is part of the same game to emphasize the unequal economic exchanges between the East and the West and under-emphasize the unequal cultural exchanges between the two, which has already made the modern western man the ideal of the official culture of India. The culture-oriented activists believe that the latter form of unequal exchange is more dangerous because it gives legitimacy to the 'proper' dissenters wanting to lead the masses to a utopia which is but an edited version of the modern West. The first step in the creation of this new set of élites for the future is the destruction of the confidence of the people in their own systems of knowledge and ways of life, so that they become recipients both materially and non-materially.[20]

Fifth, faith in the primacy of culture over the state does not mean the absence of a theory of state. It connotes another kind of a theory of the state, a theory rooted in the non-modern understanding of modernity

---

[19]A proper critique of the rhetoric of revolution has not yet emerged in India. Revolution could be considered, in certain contexts, a reason of a shadow state, the state which would come into being after the present one is captured by middle-class, urbane, upper-caste revolutionaries. The sacrifices that revolutionaries demand serve, in this sense, the class interests of the shadow rulers of a shadow state. However, a critique of statism and a non-modern awareness of culture has just begun to take shape at the peripheries of the Marxist movement in India.

[20]Ashis Nandy, 'A Counter-Statement on Humanistic Temper', *Mainstream*, 10 October 1982, and *Deccan Herald*, 18 October 1981.

and in a worm's-eye view of the imperial structures and categories that go with modernity. It can also be called an outsider's theory of statist politics. (I have said earlier that this approach does give a role to the state as a protector, an internal critic and thermostat for the culture.) However, it is an undying superstition of our times that only the moderns can handle the complexities or negotiate the jungle of international politics, ensure internal and external security, maintain national integration and inter-communal peace. It is a part of the superstition to believe that politics is exclusively the politics organized around the state and the prerogative of the self-declared professional politicians.[21]

The theories of the state used by outsiders—by those who take the cultural approach seriously—differ in important respects from the dominant theories of political modernization. It is the use of such alternative theories which accounts for the allegations of irrationality or false consciousness made against these outsiders. These theories look bottom up towards the modern sector of India and they are therefore not palatable to the political élite or the counter-élite dreaming of capturing the state in the future. Such non-modern theories of the state have no commitment to the ideas of one language, one religion or one culture for India; nor do they think that such linguistic, religious or cultural unification advances the cause of the Indian people. Unlike the modernists and Hindu revivalists, those viewing Indian politics from outside the framework of the nation-state system believe it possible for a state to represent a confederation of cultures, including a multiplicity of religions

---

[21]I must again emphasize that the culture-oriented approach to the state stands for greater democratic participation and, thus, for more politics, not less. It wants to pursue the logic of an open polity to its end, to widen the compass of democratic politics. On other hand, state-oriented politics, in societies where there are living non-modern traditions, have often shown the tendency to throttle democratic institutions the moment participation by the underprivileged crosses a certain threshold.

I should also emphasize that non-statist politics is not the same as non-party politics. However, the two can sometimes overlap. The new interest in non-party politics is not the same which inspired some of the earlier writers on the subject such as M.N. Roy and J.P. Narain. The new interest, however, builds upon the old. For a sample of recent writings on the non-party political processes in India, see D.L. Sheth, 'Grass-roots Stirrings and the Future of Politics', *Alternatives*, 1983, 9(1), pp. 1–24; and some of the papers in Harsh Sethi and Smitu Kothari (eds.), *The Non-Party Political Process: Uncertain Alternatives* (Delhi: UNRISD and Lokayan, 1983), pp. 18–46, mimeo. On the issue of culture and authoritarianism in India, particularly on how authoritarianism often rears its head in such societies as part of an effort to contain the nonmodern political cultures of the peripheries, see Ashis Nandy, 'Adorno in India: Revisiting the Psychology of Fascism', in *At the Edge of Psychology*, pp. 99–111; and 'Political Consciousness', *Seminar*, 1980, (248), pp. 18–21.

and languages. To each of these cultures, other cultures are an internal opposition rather than an external enemy. Thus, for instance, true to the traditions of Hinduism, many of these outsiders believe that all Indians are definitionally Hindus, crypto-Hindus or Hinduized; it sees the modern meaning of the exclusivist concept 'Hindu' as a foreign imposition and as anti-Hindu. The culture-oriented do have a commitment to India as a single political entity, mainly because it helps Indian civilization to resist the suffocating embrace of the global nation-state system and the homogenizing thrust of the culture of the modern West. But they are willing to withdraw this commitment if statist forces begin to dismantle the civilization to make it a proper modern nation-state and a modern culture, that is, if India is sought to be fully de-Indianized for the sake of a powerful Indian nation-state. This does not imply any innocence about the nature of the global system. It indicates a refusal to accept the games nations play and an awareness that the problem of internal colonialism in India is part of the global structure of dominance.

Sixth, as should be obvious from the foregoing, the cultural approach draws a distinction between political participation and participation in state-oriented politics—between *lokniti* and *rajniti*, as some following Jayaprakash Narain put it—and it stresses the former. This is the kind of participation that tries to bring all sections of a society within politics without bringing all aspects of the society within the scope of the state. To those stressing such participation, the politics of the nation-state is only part of the story and democratization must have priority over system legitimacy. Alas, this also means that the non-state actors refuse to accept the need for democracy as secondary to the need for a strong state. In recent years, this approach to politics has spawned a vigorous human-rights movement in India which is trying to make democratic participation more real to the lowest of the low.[22]

To the statists, this other kind of political participation is a danger signal. It looks extra-systemic and non-institutionalized—the kind of participation that the well-trained political scientist, if brought up on Samuel Huntington et al., has learnt to identify as a sure indicator of political decay—a situation where political participation outstrips system legitimacy.[23] No wonder, that many of those militantly allegiant

---

[22]See the *PUCL Bulletin and Vigilindia* for an idea of the scope and concerns of various such groups, of which the better-known examples are, of course, the People's Union of Civil Liberties, People's Union of Democratic Rights, and Citizens for Democracy.

[23]Evidently, liberal democracy in a multi-ethnic society has built-in limits on its own commitment to democracy. See Kothari, 'Crisis of the Moderate State'.

to the Indian state would prefer to see the peripheries and the bottom of this society either remain apolitical or, if the latter are already in politics, systematically depoliticized.[24]

In other words, the culture-oriented approach takes the concept of open society seriously. It knows that the glib talk of culture often hides Third-World despotism. Indeed, the approach takes the principles of democratic governance to their logical conclusion by refusing to accept the definition of civic culture vended by those in control of the state. Culture, this approach affirms, lies primarily with the people. Next door in Pakistan, the army rulers could have found no consolation in the new culturist point of view which is emerging in many traditional societies and, particularly, in this subcontinent. Nor could the Ayatollah of Iran in his late-life incarnation as an Islamic Dracula. Their Islam is a state-controlled set of slogans and gimmicks; it had little to do with Islamic culture, for such a culture can be identified only through open democratic processes. Hopefully, a culture-sensitive polity in India will not stop at mechanical electoral representation of atomized individuals or secularized classes; it will extend representation also to the myriad ways of life in the hope that in the twenty-first century Indian democracy will reflect something of the uniqueness of this civilization, too, and pursue the principle of 'freedom with dignity' as a basic human need.

III

Finally, I must borrow two terms from the contemporary philosophy of science to explain the link between the world-view which swears by the primacy of the state and that which swears by the primacy of culture. The former thinks it has an explanation of the latter. The statists see the emphasis on culture as a product of the frustrations of those who have been displaced from their traditional moorings by the force of modernity. More, not less, modernity is seen as the antidote for the insane, anti-scientific world-view of the disgruntled, culture-drunk, uprooted non-moderns. This is the tired crisis-of-change thesis. The latter world-view believes that alternative paradigms of knowledge—whether they come from updated Indian traditions or from powerful postmodern theories of the state—cannot be legitimized by categories generated by the presently

---

[24]Such depoliticization may come through the increasing criminalization of politics or from the apathy brought about by the failure of the political opposition to the basic social problems. Both can be found in India today.

dominant paradigms of political analysis. There is a fundamental and irreconcilable incommensurability between the two sets of paradigms. This is one instance, this world-view claims, where no genuine common language or dialogue is possible. However, the non-moderns do believe that it is possible for parts of the modern vision to survive in another incarnation, as a subset of a post-modern, and simultaneously more rooted Indian vision—somewhat in the way the Newtonian world-view survives in the Einsteinian world. With the growing cultural self-confidence of Indian intellectuals and informed activists, it is possible that the modern West will be seen by a significant number of Indians the way Gandhi used to see it; as part of a larger native frame—valuable in many ways, but also dangerous by virtue of its ability to become cancerous.

It is known that when one attempts to explain the Newtonian world-view in Einsteinian terms, elements of it such as 'mass' and 'velocity' retard rather than facilitate communication. This is because the concepts supposedly common to the two world-views are rooted in different theories and, thus have different meanings. (This is the well-known meaning-variation argument in post-Popperian philosophy of science.) In the context of the issues we are discussing, concepts such as rationality, empirical data, mathematization and experimental verification provide no bridge between the state-oriented and the culture-oriented world-views. Nor do concepts like history, injustice, patriotism or dissent. No sentiment-laden lecture by the nation-security chap on how much he loves his culture is going to appease the activist working among tribals to protect their lifestyle. Nor will the copious tears shed by the ultra-modern, rationalist scientist for the Indian villager move the person to whom the superstitions of the rich (such as the billion-dollar con-games involving anti-diarrhoeal drugs, so-called health-food products like Horlicks and Bournvita, or mostly unnecessary surgeries such as tonsillectomy, removal of impacted molar and Caesarean section) are more dangerous than the pathetic antics of the small-time pavement palmist, being pursued by urban rationalists for conning someone out of a few rupees (somewhat in the manner in which village lunatics are pursued by stone-throwing teenagers while greater lunatics are allowed to become national leaders or war heroes). If you speak to culture-oriented Indians about the superstitions of the witch doctors or *mantravadi*s, they will shrug their shoulders and walk away. They are more concerned about the irrational search for permanent youth that helps the annual cosmetics bill of American women outstrip the combined budgets of all the African countries put together. They are more worried about the superstitious fear—of being left behind by other nations that prompted the Indian Sixth Five-Year Plan to invest more than Rs 9000 million in only the R&D for space and nuclear programmes when the corresponding figure in the case of education was Rs 1.2 million.[25]

The two sides—the statists and the culturists—speak entirely different languages. It is the unmanageable crisis of one world-view—in this case that of the nation-state-oriented modernity which has prodded some to switch sides, in some cases willingly, in others unwillingly. Call this defection another kind of political realism or call it an act of faith. I like to call it the latter; after all, faith does move mountains.

[25]Dhirendra Sharma, *India's Nuclear Estate* (New Delhi: Lancers, 1983), p. 141.

*This essay was delivered as the Rajiv Bambavale Lecture at the Indian Institute of Technology, New Delhi, 1983.

6

The Twilight of Certitudes
Secularism, Hindu Nationalism and Other Masks of Deculturation

WHAT FOLLOWS IS basically a series of propositions. It is not meant for academics grappling with the issue of ethnic and religious violence as a cognitive puzzle, but for concerned intellectuals and grass-roots activists trying, in the language of Gustavo Esteva, to 'regenerate people's space'.[1] Its aim is three fold: (*a*) to systematize some of the available insights into the problem of ethnic and communal violence in South Asia, particularly India, from the point of view of those who do not see communalism and secularism as sworn enemies but as the disowned doubles of each other; (*b*) to acknowledge, as part of the same exercise, that Hindu nationalism, like other such ethno-nationalisms, is not an 'extreme' form of Hinduism but a modern creed which seeks, on behalf of the global nation-state system, to retool Hinduism into a national ideology and the Hindus into a 'proper' nationality; and (*c*) to hint at an approach to religious tolerance in a democratic polity that is not dismissive towards the ways of life, idioms and modes of informal social and political analyses of the citizens even when they happen to be unacquainted with—or inhospitable to—the ideology of secularism.

I must make one qualification at the beginning. This is the third in a series of papers on secularism, in which one of my main concerns has been to examine the political and cultural–psychological viability of the

[1]Gustavo Esteva, 'Regenerating People's Space', *Alternatives*, 1987, 12(1), pp. 125–52.

ideology of secularism and to argue that its fragile status in South Asian politics is culturally 'natural' but not an unmitigated disaster. For there are other, probably more potent and resilient ideas within the repertory of cultures and religions of the region that could ensure religious and ethnic co-survival, if not creative inter-faith encounters. Few among the scores of academic responses to the papers—some of them hysterically hostile—have cared to argue or examine that part of the story, which I once foolishly thought would be of interest even to dedicated secularists. They were more disturbed by my attempts to identify the spatial and temporal location or limits of the ideology of secularism. Evidently, for some academics, the ideology of secularism is prior to the goals it is supposed to serve. Much less provoked were those who had some direct exposure to religious or ethnic strife either as human rights activists, first-hand observers or victims, for whom the papers were written in the first place. For even when uncomfortable with M.K. Gandhi's belief that 'politics divorced from religion becomes debasing',[2] they seemed to intuitively gauge the power of Raimundo Panikkar's pithy formulation: 'The separation between religion and politics is lethal and their identification suicidal'.[3]

The Paradox of Secularism

Secularism as an ideology can thrive only in a society that is predominantly non-secular. Once a society begins to get secularized— or once the people begin to feel that their society is getting cleansed of religion and ideas of transcendence—the political status of secularism changes.[4] In such a society, people become anxiously aware of living in an increasingly desacralized world, and start searching for faiths to give meaning to their life and to retain the illusion of being part of a traditional community. If faiths are in decline, they begin to search for ideologies linked to faiths, in an effort to return to forms of a traditional moral community that would negate or defy the world in which they live. If

[2]M.K. Gandhi, in Raghavan Iyer (ed.), *The Moral and Political Writings of Mahatma Gandhi* (Oxford: Clarendon Press, 1986), p. 374.

[3]Raimundo Panikkar, 'The Challenge of Modernity', *India International Centre Quarterly*, Spring–Summer 1993, 20(1/2), pp. 183–92; see p. 189.

[4]The decline of faith I am speaking of has its rough counterpart in the erosion of beliefs surveyed in a somewhat different context by Mattei Dogan, 'Decline of Religious Beliefs in Western Europe', *International Social Science Journal*, 1995, 47(3), pp. 405–17; and Ronald Inglehart, 'Changing Values, Economic Development and Political Change', ibid., pp. 379–403. See also Ronald Inglehart, *Culture Shift in Advanced Societies* (Princeton: Princeton University Press, 1991).

and when they find such ideologies, they cling to them defensively—'with the desperate ardour of a lover trying to converse life back into a finished love', in the language of Sara Suleri. What sometimes happens to communities can also happen to sections of a community or to individuals. Thus, in recent years, many expatriate South Asians in the West have become more aggressively traditional, culturally exclusive and chauvinistic. As their cherished world becomes more difficult to sustain, as their children and they themselves begin to show symptoms of getting integrated in their adopted land, they become more protective about what they think are their faiths and cultures.

The enthusiasm of some states to aggressively impose secularism on the people sharpens these fears of deracination. Already sensitive about the erosion of faith, many citizens are particularly provoked by a secularizing agenda imposed from the top, for that agenda invariably carries with it in this era a touch of contempt for believers. Such secularism is:

[E]ssentially a religious ideology, not based on any scientifically demonstrable propositions. . . . It is the religion of a divinized human rationality of a particular kind, making critical rationality the final arbiter. This religious ideology is then imposed on our children in schools—from which all other religions are proscribed. . . . This religion spread in the UK and the USA for two generations. Sunday schools were established. Catechisms of the new religion were published. With the rise of Nazism and the Second World War it fizzled out, and merged with modern liberalism, which is also the religion of the new civilization now sweeping Europe. . . . Secularism creates communal conflict because it brutally attacks religious identity, while pretending to be tolerant of all religions.[5]

When Indian public life was overwhelmingly non-modern, secularism as an ideology had a chance. For the area of the sacred looked intact and safe, and secularism looked like a balancing principle and a form of legitimate dissent. Even many believing citizens described themselves as secular, to keep up with the times and because secularism sounded like something vaguely good. Now that the secularization of Indian polity has gone far, the scope of secularism as a creed has declined. Signs of secularization are now everywhere; one does not have to make a case

[5]Paulos Mar Gregorios, 'Speaking of Tolerance and Intolerance', *Indian International Centre Quarterly*, Spring 1995, 22(1), pp. 22–34; see pp. 24–5, 27. On the contempt for believers that lies at the heart of secularism and the capacity this contempt has to legitimize western dominance over all traditional societies, see Ziauddin Sardar and Merryl Wyn Davies, *Distorted Imagination: Lessons from the Rushdie Affair* (London: Grey Seal, and Kuala Lumpur: Berita, 1990).

for it. Instead, there has grown the fear that secularization has gone too far, that the decline in public morality in the country is due to the all-round decline in religious sensibilities. Many distorted or perverted versions of religion circulating in modern or semi-modern India owe their origins to this perception of the triumph of secularization rather than to the persistence of traditions.

As part of the same process, many 'non-secular' ideologies and movements have become more secular in style and content. They do try to look religious, for the sake of their constituency, but they can pursue political power in a secularized polity only through secular politics, secular organization and secular planning. They increasingly resemble the jet-setting gurus and *sadhus* who, while criticizing the 'crass materialism of the West', have to use at every step western technology, western media and western disciples to stay in business. A popular way of recognizing this in India is to affirm that politicians misuse religion. But that affirmation usually fails to acknowledge that only a person or a group at least partly repudiating the sanctity of religion can 'misuse' religion or 'use' it only instrumentally.[6] In this sense, the Bharatiya Janata Party and the Shiv Sena, though called fundamentalist, are two of the most secular parties in India, for they represent most faithfully the loss of piety and cultural self-doubts that have come to characterize a section of urban, modernizing India. While other parties observe, even if by default, some limits to their instrumental use of religion, there seems to be no such restraint in the BJP or the Shiv Sena. The people these parties mobilize may sometimes be driven by piety—in the Shiv Sena's case even that is doubtful—but their leaders value that piety only as a part of their political weaponry.

Even religious riots or pogroms are secularized in South Asia. They are organized the way a rally or strike is organized in a competitive, democratic polity and, usually, for the same reasons—to bring down a regime or discredit a chief minister here or to help an election campaign

---

[6]The great European witch-hunt, it has frequently been pointed out, peaked not during the period when European Christendom and the Church were secure, but when modernity had weakened their bases. Speaking of the belief in witches in the sixteenth and seventeenth centuries, H.R. Trevor-Roper says, 'It was not, as the prophets of progress might suppose, a lingering ancient superstition, only waiting to dissolve. It was a new explosive force, constantly and fearfully expanding with the passage of time.' H.R. Tevor-Roper, 'The European Witch-Craze in the Sixteenth and Seventeenth Centuries', in *The European Witch-Hunt in the Sixteenth and Seventeenth Centuries and Other Essays* (New York: Harper, 1967), pp. 90–192. See also Norman Cohn, *Europe's Inner Demons* (New York: Basic, 1975).

or a faction there. Some political parties in India today have 'professionals' who specialize in such violence and, like true professionals, do an expert job of it. Often these professionals, though belonging to antagonistic religious or ethnic communities, maintain excellent personal, social and political relationships with each other. Fanaticism, they appear to believe, is for the hoi polloi, not for serious politicians playing the game of ethnic politics.[7] It is not difficult today to find out the rate at which riots of various kinds can be bought, how political protection can be obtained for the rioters and how, after a riot, political advantage can be taken of it.

There is even a vague consensus among important sections of politicians, the bureaucracy and the law-and-order machinery on how such specialists should be treated. Despite hundreds of witnesses and detailed information, hardly anyone has ever been prosecuted for complicity or participation in riots in India or, for that matter, in the whole of South Asia. The anti-Sikh riot in Delhi in 1984 provides dramatic evidence of such a consensus. Though over 3000 Sikhs were killed in the three-day pogrom in India's capital, for over fifteen years its instigators and active participants have not only escaped prosecution but have risen high in the political hierarchy. At least two have been in the Union cabinet and another three have been Congress party MPs from the capital. It does not need much political acumen to predict that more or less the same fate awaits the self-declared instigators and perpetrators of the anti-Muslim violence in Bombay in January 1993 and in Gujarat in March 2002.

On the other hand, though by now human-rights activists and students of communal violence have supplied enough data to show that riots are

---

[7]In the context of the films of Woody Allen, Barbara Schapiro speaks of the 'clever, manipulative technique by which Allen attempts to control his critics by demonstrating an awareness of his own potential weaknesses . . . . The character displays awareness of his problem while in the very act of demonstrating the problem, and that self-awareness, of course, creates the humour.' Barbara Schapiro, 'Woody Allen's Search for Self', *Journal of Popular Culture*, Spring 1986, 18, pp. 47–62. I am speaking here of an analogous process which produces, instead of humour, tragedy for millions.

However, there is some scope for irony, if not humour, within such tragedies. Recently, when Brijbhushan Sharan Singh, an MP of the Bharatiya Janata Party (BJP), the most powerful political front of the Hindu nationalist formations, was accused of harbouring criminals with terrorist connections and protecting them from the law, the criminals turned out to be associates of the notorious don of Bombay's underworld, Dawood Ibrahim. Likewise when the former BJP President Lal Krishna Advani was accused of being involved in criminal money-laundering, the main source of payments to him was said to be one Ameerbhai. The party has established its secular credentials the hard way!

organized, they have rarely pushed this point to its logical conclusion. Riots *have* to be organized because ordinary citizens—the 'illiterate', 'superstitious' South Asians, uncritically allegiant to their primordial identities—are not easy to arouse to participate in riots. To achieve that end, one needs detailed planning and hard work. It is not easy to convert ordinary citizens into fire-spitting fanatics or killers; they may not be epitomes of virtue, but they are not given to blood-curdling Satanism either—not even when lofty modern values like history, state and nationalism are invoked.[8] South Asian loves and hates, being often community-based, are small-scale. In the case of communal violence, the most one can accuse them of is a certain uncritical openness to the rumours floated before riots, which help them make peace with their conscience and their inability to resist the violence.

Yet, they do resist. Each riot produces instances of bravery shown by persons who protect their neighbours at immense risk to their own lives and that of their families.[9] Often entire families and communities participate in the decision to resist. There is no empirical basis whatever to explain away this courage as a function of individual personality while, at the same time, seeing the violence it opposes as a cultural product. In South Asia as much as in Nazi Germany, those who resist such violence at the ground level derive their framework from their religious faith.[10] I have been hearing since my childhood literally hundreds of caustic accounts of the victims of the great Partition riots—about their suffering in 1946–7. In most cases, the experiences have made them bitterly anti-Muslim, anti-Sikh or anti-Hindu. Despite the bitterness, however, most accounts include a story of someone from the other community who helped the family. The loves and hates of everyday life, within which usually are fitted ethnic and religious prejudices and stereotypes, may be small-scale but they are not always petty.

[8]Probably the rational–legal values of an individualized, mass society have not yet made inroads into the interstices of the South Asian personality and the values and faiths most South Asians live with cannot be mobilized too easily for collective action cutting across sects or denominations. Urbanization and massification is changing this profile, but the changes so far affect only a minority.

[9]For instance, Tariq Hasan, 'How Does it Matter Who is the Victim?', *The Times of India*, 3 April 1995. See also, Ashis Nandy, Shikha Trivedy, Shail Mayaram and Achyut Yagnik, *Creating a Nationality: The Ramjanmabhumi Movement and Fear of the Self* (New Delhi: Oxford University Press, 1995).

[10]Cf. Eva Fogelman, 'Victims, Perpetrators, Bystanders, and Rescuers in the Face of Genocide and its Aftermath', in Charles B. Strozier and Michael Flynn (eds.), *Genocide, War and Human Survival* (New York: Rowman and Littlefield, 1996), pp. 87–98; see pp. 91–2.

The resistance is stronger where communities have not splintered into atomized individuals. Not only do riots take place more frequently in the cities, but also they are harder to organize in villages. The village community is breaking down all over the world, but it has not broken down entirely in South Asia. Even the smaller towns in South Asia have often escaped massification. It is no accident that, despite the claim of some Hindu nationalists that more than 350,000 Hindus had already died fighting for the liberation of the birthplace of Rama, Ramjanmabhumi, during the previous 400 years, the residents of Ayodhya themselves lived in reasonable amity till the late 1980s. The Sangh Parivar sensed this; till the mid-1980s, the case for demolishing the Babri mosque at Ayodhya was not taken up by any of the noted Hindu nationalists, from V.D. Savarkar, Balkrishna Munje and Keshav Hedgewar to Bal Thackeray, Lal Krishna Advani and Murli Manohar Joshi. The Babri mosque was turned into a political issue only after India's urban middle class attained a certain size and India's modernization reached a certain stage.[11]

The first serious riot in the sacred city of Ayodhya took place on 6–7 December 1992. For seven years, despite all efforts to mobilize the locals for a riot, no riot had taken place.[12] This time, it was organized by outsiders and executed in many cases by non-Hindi-speaking rioters with whom the local Hindus could not communicate. These outsiders were not traditional villagers, but urbanized, semi-educated, partly westernized men and, less frequently, women. They broke more than a hundred places of worship of the Muslims in the city to celebrate the 'fall' of the unprotected Babri mosque.[13]

In the final reckoning, the demolition of the Babri mosque in 1992 was proof that the secularization of India has gone along predictable lines.

The Politics of Secularism

Over the last fifty years or so, the concept of secularism has had a good run. It has served, within the small but expanding modern sector in India, as an important public value and as an indicator of one's commitment to the protection of minorities. Now the concept has begun to deliver

---

[11]Nandy et al., *Creating a Nationality*.

[12]In the case of both Kashmir and Punjab, despite the bitterness produced by the militants and the agencies of the state and despite some determined efforts to precipitate riots, there has been no communal riot till now.

[13]Nandy et al., *Creating a Nationality*.

less and less. By most imaginable criteria, institutionalized secularism has failed. Communal riots have grown more than tenfold and have now begun to spread outside the perimeters of modern and semi-modern India.[14] In the meanwhile, the ruling culture of India, predominantly modern and secular, has lost much of its faith in—and access to—the traditional social and psychological checks against communal violence. In this respect, one is tempted to compare the political status of secularism with that of modern medicine in India. Traditionally Indians used a number of indigenous healing systems, and did so with a certain confidence and scepticism. These systems were seen as mixed bags; they sometimes worked, sometimes not. But they were not total systems; they did not demand full allegiance and they left one with enough autonomy to experiment with other systems, including the modern ones. Slowly well-meaning reformers broke the confidence of their ignorant compatriots in such native superstitions. In the second half of the nineteenth century, modern medicine was introduced into India with great fanfare. It was introduced usually with the backing of the state and sometimes with the backing of the coercive apparatus of the state, not merely as a superior science but also as a cure for the irrational faith of the natives in traditional systems of healing.[15] People were constantly bombarded with the message that the older systems were bogus or, at best, inefficient; that they should, therefore, shift to the modern, 'truly universal' system of medicine.

Once the confidence of a sizeable section of Indians in the older, more easily accessible healing systems was destroyed, the inevitable happened. Most of those who converted to modern medicine found it prohibitively costly, more exclusive, often inhuman and alienating. They also found out that their proselytizers had other priorities than to give them easy access to modern medicine. In the meanwhile, the converts had lost some of their faith in the traditional systems of healing. Many of the practitioners of the traditional systems, too, had lost confidence in their vocation and had begun to pass themselves off as deviant practitioners of modern medicine; they had begun to copy allopaths in style and, more stealthily, in practice.

Similarly, the concept of secularism was introduced into South Asian

[14]Ibid., ch. 1.
[15]See for instance Frédérique Apffel-Marglin, 'Smallpox in Two Systems of Knowledge', in Frédérique Apffel-Marglin and Stephen A. Marglin (eds.), *Dominating Knowledge: Development, Culture and Resistance* (Oxford: Clarendon Press, 1990), pp. 145–84.

public life by a clutch of social reformers, intellectuals and public figures—
seduced or brainwashed by the ethnocidal, colonial theories of social
evolution and history—to subvert and discredit the traditional ideas of
inter-religious understanding and tolerance. These traditions had allowed
the thousands—yes, literally thousands—of communities living in the
subcontinent to co-survive in reasonable neighbourliness for centuries.
The co-survival was not perfect; it was certainly not painless. Often
there were violent clashes among communities, as is likely in any 'mixed
neighbourhood'. But the violence never involved such large aggregates or
generic categories as Hindus, Muslims, Sikhs, Tamils, or Sinhalas. Conflicts
were localized and sectored, and were almost invariably seen as cutting
across religious boundaries, for such boundaries were mostly fuzzy.[16] More
important, both conflict and resolution were explained and negotiated
in languages that were reasonably transparent to a majority of the people
living in the region.[17] To the reformers, thinkers and politicians—brought
up on the colonial state's classification of Indians into broad European-
style religious categories—this 'living past' was an anachronism, an
embarrassment and a sure prescription for ethnic and religious strife. To
them, some of the clashes between sects, denominations or ethnic groups
in earlier centuries began to look in retrospect like clashes between entire
religious communities. Simultaneously, the categories that sustained
such interreligious adaptations or tolerance—or, to put it modestly,
the categories that contained communal animosities within tolerable
limits—were systematically devalued, attacked, and ridiculed as parts

[16]See Kumar Suresh Singh, *People of India: An Introduction* (New Delhi: The
Anthropological Survey of India, 1992), Vol. 1, part of a voluminous and authoritative
survey which almost incidentally shows that even in the 1990s, nearly 50 years after
the Hindu–Muslim divide has become the most dangerous cleavage in the
subcontinent, of the 2800 odd communities identified as Hindu and Muslim, more
than 400 cannot be identified as exclusively Hindu or Muslim. There are probably
something like 600 such communities which live, not with multiculturalism without,
but with multiculturalism within in South Asia. In a personal communication Singh
estimates that the proportion of such fuzzy-bordered communities had been much
higher in earlier times. For a fascinating case study, see Frédérique Apffel Marglin,
'On Pirs and Pandits', *Manushi: A Journal about Women and Society*, 1995 (91), pp.
17–26. Also, Shail Mayaram, 'Representing the Hindu–Muslim Civilizational
Encounter: The Mahabharata of Community of Muslims', Jaipur: Institute of
Development Studies, 1996; and 'Ethnic Co-existence in Ajmer', Project on Culture
and Identity, Colombo, Centre for Ethnic Studies and Delhi, Committee for Cultural
Choices, 1995.

[17]Ashis Nandy, 'Time Travel to Another Self: Searching for the Alternative
Cosmopolitanism of Cochin', *Japanese Journal of Political Science*, 2000, 1(2), pp.
295–327.

of an enormous structure of irrationality and self-deceit, and as sure markers of an atavistic, retrogressive way of life.

In place of these categories, the concept of secularism was pushed as *the* remedy for all religious conflicts and fanaticism, something that would do away with the constant religious violence and bloodletting that had reportedly characterized the region from time immemorial. 'Reportedly' because no one produced an iota of empirical evidence to show that such conflicts had existed on a large scale and involved religious communities as they are presently defined.[18] That did not cramp the style of well-educated South Asian liberals and progressives. They seemed convinced that the data did not exist because their societies were ahistorical; had a proper scientific, objective history existed, it would have shown that pre-modern South Asia had been a snake-pit of religious bigotry and blood lust.

That innocent social–evolutionist reading today lies in tatters. Yet, the dominance of the ideology of secularism in the public discourse on religious amity and ethnic plurality in India continues. Why? Why do even the Hindu nationalists uphold not religion but genuine secularism (as opposed to what they call the pseudo-secularism of their political enemies)? Above all, who gets what from secularism and why? Any attempt to even raise this question triggers deep anxieties; it seems to touch something terribly raw in the Indian bourgeoisie. As if secularism was a sacred trans-historical concept, free from all restraints of space and time, and any exploration of its spatial and temporal limits was a reminder of one's own mortality. As if those disturbed by the questions knew the answers, but did not wish to be reminded of them. I shall risk political incorrectness here and obstinately turn to these very questions.

First, once institutionalized as an official ideology, the concept of secularism helps identify and set up modernized Indians as a principle of rationality in an otherwise irrational society and gives them, seemingly deservedly, a disproportionate access to state power. After all, they are the ones who have reportedly freed themselves from ethnic and religious prejudices and stereotypes; they are the ones who can even be generous and decide who among the majority of Indians who do not use the idiom of secularism are nevertheless 'objectively' secular. Secularism for them

---

[18]For a concise, if non-committal coverage of this part of the story, see C.A. Bailey, 'The Pre-History of "Communalism"? Religious Conflict in India, 1700–1860', *Modern Asian Studies*, 1985, 19(2), pp. 177–203.

is often a principle of exclusion. It marks out a class that speaks the language of the state, either in conformity or in dissent. At this plane, secularism is emblematic of a person or group willing to accept two corollaries of the ideology of the Indian state: the assumption that those who do not speak the language of secularism are unfit for full citizenship, and the belief that those who speak it have the sole right to determine what true democratic principles, governance and religious tolerance are.[19] The main function of the ideology of secularism here is to shift the locus of initiative from the citizens to a specialist group that uses a special language.

To be more generous to this sector and those mentoring them in the mainstream global culture of scholarship, secularism has become mainly modern India's way of 'understanding' the religious tolerance that survives outside modern India. It has become a concept that names the inexplicable and, to that extent, makes it more explicable. Its necessity depends on modern India's loss of touch with Indian traditions and loss of confidence in the traditional codes of religious tolerance that constitute an alternative vantage ground for political intervention in a democratic polity. Hence the modern Indian's fear of the void that the collapse of the concept of secularism might produce.

Many secularists are secular on ideological or moral grounds. They consider their ideology to be compatible with radical or leftist political doctrines and seem oblivious of its colonial connections and class bias. Evidently, class analysis for them, unlike charity, does not begin at home. Some of them have personally fought for religious and ethnic minorities, but now face the fact that, with the spread of participatory mass politics, they are being reduced to a small minority among the very section within which they expected to have maximum support—the westernizing, media-exposed, urban middle classes. They can neither give up their faith in secularism, because that would mean disowning an important part of their self-definition, nor can they shake off the awareness that it is doomed, at least in ground-level politics.[20] Such politics is already getting too secularized to be able to sustain secularism as a popular ideology.

Second, the ideology of secularism not merely fits the culture of the Indian state, it invites the state to use its coercive might to actualize the

[19]An apparently harmless but chilling example of this attitude is Sumanta Bannerji, 'Sangh Parivar and Democratic Rights', *Economic and Political Weekly*, 1993, 28(34), pp. 1715–18.
[20]For a profile of westernizing, media-exposed urban India as the site of rivalry between secularists and Hindu nationalists, see Nandy et al., *Creating a Nationality*.

model of social engineering the ideology projects. Secularism and statism in India have gone hand in hand—perhaps the main reason why Hindu nationalism, statist to its core, has not given up the language of secularism.[21] The goal of both is to retool the ordinary citizen so that he or she, though given democratic rights, would not exercise the rights except within the political limits set by South Asia's westernizing élite, constituting the steel-frame of the region's wog empires. Secularism too, has its class affiliations; it too, has much to do with who gets what and when in a polity. Tariq Banuri compares the dominant position of the ego in Freudian psychology with the dominant position of the nation-state in contemporary ideas of political development.[22] To complete his evocative metaphor, one must view secularism as a crucial defence of the ego.

Banuri's metaphor also supplied a clue to the fanaticism of many secularists in India, eager to fight the cause of secularism to the last Muslim, Christian, or Sikh. It is their version of a passionate commitment to interests or, if you like, irrational commitment to rationality (a typical nineteenth- and twentieth-century psychopathology in which allegiance to an ideology outweighs the welfare of the targeted beneficiaries of the ideology). Such romantic realism is the underside of what Banuri calls 'the overly enthusiastic pursuit of national integration'.[23] Though carrying the white man's burden after the demise of empires in the subcontinent, these secularists seem particularly unhappy at the South Asian failure to internalize the psychological traits and social skills congruent with the ideology of secularism. Underlying the unhappiness, however, is a certain glee at the persistence of religious belligerency. It

---

[21]Theologian Jyoti Sahi claims that both the modern state and secularism owe their origins to the Judaeo-Christian world-view and secularism particularly has no theological status outside Christianity. 'Monotheism has created its own understanding of the state and its relation to the nation . . . . The concept of a nation-state based on a religious identity derives from a Judaeo-Christian background, but now has been adopted by other faith systems, giving rise to a very new idea like a Hindu nation-state . . . . The concept of a secular state has also come from a Christian debate on the relation of church to State . . . . Hinduism and Buddhism have never discussed or defined this kind of distinction; in fact the sacred and the profane are interwoven . . . . Even in Islam there is no clear distinction drawn between the sacred and profane, or religious and secular.' Jyoti Sahi, 'Response to Asghar Ali Engineer's "Imaging and Imagining Religious Symbolism in Mass Media"', Paper presented at the conference on Globalization of Mass Media: Consequences for Indian Cultural Values, United Theological College, Bangalore, 29 June–1 July 1998.

[22]Tariq Banuri, 'Official Nationalism, Ethnic Conflict and Collective Violence', (Islamabad: Sustainable Development Policy Institute, 1993), p. 8.

[23]Ibid.

is proof that the average South Asian's internship to qualify for full citizenship is not yet complete and it justifies further postponement of the day when the plebeians would be allowed to 'legitimately' claim their full democratic rights and exercise the power of numbers.

The third reason for the survival of secularism as an important ideological strain in Indian public life is for some reason even less accessible to political analysts, journalists and thinkers. Though the culturally rootless constitute a small, if audible, section of the population, to many of them, secularism is not just a way of communicating with the modern world but also with compatriots trying to enter that world. These neophytes do not have much to do with the European associations and cultural baggage of the term 'secularism'. But they have stretched the meaning of the term for their own purposes and adapted it in such a fashion that it manages to communicate something to others who have to cope, however unwillingly, with Indian realities.[24] They seem satisfied that such secularism allows one to break the social barriers set up by castes, sects and communities, and helps one to converse not only with the political and social élite, but also with the metropolitan intellectuals and professionals. Secularism for them is a marker of cosmopolitanism. Many Indian politicians—when they pay lip service to the standard, universal concept of secularism—have one eye on the response of the national media, the other on their clever competitors who have profited from the secular idiom.

Finally, there are the self-avowed 'genuine secularists'—political actors and ideologues who have an instrumental concept of secularism. They see secularism partly as a means of mounting an attack on the traditional secularists and partly as a justification for majoritarian politics. (The limited appeal that this majoritarianism has to an urban, deracinated minority can be a frustrating experience and this frustration probably contributes significantly to organized attack on constructed 'others' in South Asia.) These are the people who often use, participate in, or provoke communal frenzy, not on grounds of faith but on grounds of secular political cost calculations. Occasionally, in place of political

[24]I am afraid that much of the recent academic defence of secularism, however elegantly formulated, is totally irrelevant to South Asian political life from this point of view. See, for instance, Akeel Bilgrami, *Secularism, Nationalism and Modernity* (New Delhi: Rajiv Gandhi Institute for Contemporary Studies, 1995), paper no. 29, pp. 1–29; and Amartya Sen, 'Secularism and its Discontents', in Kaushik Basu and Sanjay Subramanyam (eds.), *Unravelling the Nation: Sectarian Conflict and India's Secular Identity* (New Delhi: Penguin, 1996), pp. 11–43. It is a pity that the academic viability of many ideas in the mainstream global culture of universities does not ensure their political survival in the tropics.

expediency, they are motivated by political ideology and that ideology may *appear* to be based on faith. But on closer scrutiny it turns out to be only a secularized version of faith or arbitrarily chosen elements of faith packaged as a political ideology.[25] I accept the self-definition of the genuine secularists simply because their world *is* entirely secular. They use religion rationally, dispassionately and instrumentally, untouched by any theory of transcendence. They genuinely cannot or do not grant any intrinsic sanctity to the faith of even their own followers.

At one time, secularism did have something to contribute to Indian public life. That context presumed a low level of politicization, a personalized, impassioned quality in collective violence, its expression and execution.[26] As ethnic and religious violence has become more impersonal, organized, rational, and calculative,[27] it has come to represent, to rework my own

[25]There has been some discomfort about the distinction between faith and ideology I have drawn in this and other papers on the subject. As should have been obvious from the context, my use of the concept of ideology is not Marxian or Mannheimian but conventional social–psychological and cultural–anthropological. However, I now find that at least one respected scholar–activist and a historian of religion has arrived at the same dichotomy, starting from altogether different concerns. Abdolkarim Soroush claims that 'Islam, or any other religion, will become totalitarian if it is made into an ideology, because that is the nature of ideologies.' Quoted in *Communalism Combat*, October 1997, (37), p. 24. A similar distinction informs Julius J. Lipner, *Brahmabandhab Upadhyay: The Life and Thought of a Revolutionary* (New Delhi: Oxford University Press, 1999). The relevance of the distinction to contemporary India is reflected in, for instance, Pratap Bhanu Mehta, 'Hollow Hinduism: The VHP's Self-Defeating Vision', *The Times of India*, 18 February 1999, and Sukla Sen et al., 'Savarkar Memorial' (letter to the editor), *Economic and Political Weekly*, 26 December 1998, p. 3286.
I should clarify here that, following the conventions of contemporary social psychology, I make no assumption regarding the truth or falsity of the consciousness that underlies faith or ideology. I am merely underscoring the psychological organizational principles of two distinct forms of consciousness, one of which includes a theory of transcendence, while the other does not or is not supposed to. The distinction echoes the differences in emotive tone of most collective violence in our times and the more hate-filled religious violence that marked earlier centuries. Ethnic cleansing carries the psychological stamp of the modern farmer's attitude towards pest control rather than that of a crusade or *jihad* (see below). This is a difference to which others also, notably Hannah Arendt and Robert J. Lifton, have drawn our attention. See also 'Introduction: Science as a Reason of State', in Ashis Nandy (ed.), *Science, Hegemony and Violence: A Requiem for Modernity* (Tokyo: UN University Press and New Delhi: Oxford University Press, 1990), pp. 1–16.
[26]See Ashis Nandy, 'The Politics of Secularism and the Recovery of Religious Tolerance', *Alternatives*, 1998, 13(3), pp. 177–94. See especially the table on p. 189.
[27]According to Zygmunt Bauman, 'The most shattering of lessons deriving from the analysis of the twisted road to Auschwitz' is that—in the last resort—*the choice of physical extermination as the right means to the task of* Entferung *was a product*

cliché, more a pathology of rationality than that of irrationality. As part of the same process, the ideology of secularism too has become ethnocidal and dependent on the mercies of those controlling or hoping to control the state. It has become chronically susceptible to being co-opted or hijacked by the politically ambitious. Simultaneously, religion as the cultural foundation for the existence of South Asian communities has increasingly become a marker of the weak, the poor, and the rustic.

As a result, modern India, which sets the tone of the culture of the Indian state, now fears religion. That fear of religion, part of a more pervasive fear of the people and of democracy (which empowers the majority of Indians who are believers), has thrown up the various ready-made, packaged forms of faith for alienated South Asians—Banuri calls them Paki-Saxons—who populate urban, modernized South Asia.[28] For that feared, invisible majority, on the other hand, the religious way of life continues to have an intrinsic legitimacy. That majority seems to believe, with Hans-Georg Gadamer, that 'the real force of morals . . . is based on tradition. They are freely taken over but by no means created by a free insight grounded on reasons'.[29] If that religious way of life cannot find normal play in public life, it finds distorted expression in fundamentalism, revivalism and xenophobia. That which is only a matter of Machiavellian politics at the top does sometimes acquire at the ground level the characteristics of a *satyagraha*, a *dharma yuddha* or a *jihad*.

---

of routine bureaucratic procedures: means–ends, calculus, budget balancing, universal rule application . . . . The "Final Solution" did not clash at any stage with the rational pursuit of efficient, optimal goal-implementation. On the contrary, *it arose out of a genuinely rational concern, and it was generated by bureaucracy true to its form and purpose.*' Quoted in Akbar S. Ahmed, 'Ethnic Cleansing: A Metaphor for Our Time', *Ethnic and Racial Studies*, 1995, 18(1), pp. 1–25; see p. 4. Italics in the original.

[28]These packaged forms go with various circus-tamed versions of religion, meant for easy consumption. In India, these versions are bookish, high-cultural, pan-Indian, and go well with modern cults, political skullduggery, and fashionable, jet-setting gurus—both within India and among the decultured, uprooted, expatriate Indians and Indophiles in the West. Those given to this modern version of religion find all other spiritual experiences low-brow, corrupted and, thus, meaningless, uncontrollable and fearsome. That fear of religion of the uncontrollable kind (to which the majority of Indians of all faiths give their allegiance) is part of the fear of the vernacular, the democratic, and the plural. It is the fear that the majority of Indians are religious in a way that is not centrally controllable and does not constitute a 'proper' religion in contemporary times.

[29]Hans-Georg Gadamer, quoted in Arindam Chakrabarti, 'Rationality in Indian Philosophy', Lecture given at the Devahuti-Damodar Library, 13 July 1996, mimeo, p. 15. Of course, neither Gadamer nor Chakrabarti seems aware that this is also a typical Gandhian formulation.

I do not mean to identify secularism as a witches' brew in South Asia. Perhaps in parts of the region where political participation has not outstripped the legitimacy of the nation-state, secularism still has a political role, exactly as it had a creative role to play in India in the early years of Independence. But its major implications are now ethnocidal and statist, and it cedes—in fact, lovingly hands over—the entire domain of religion, in societies organized around religion, to the genuine secularists—the ones who deal in, vend or use as a political technology secularized, packaged versions of faith. Secularism today is threatening to become a successful conspiracy against the minorities.

Is secularism doomed to political impotency in the Southern world where historicization of consciousness and individuation are not complete? What is the fate of secularists who are dedicated crusaders for communal peace and minority rights? There is no reliable answer to the questions but some secularists, I suspect, *will* survive the vicissitudes of South Asian politics. They are the ones in whom there is no easy, cheerful assumption that one day they would abolish categories such as Hindus, Muslims, Buddhists, and Sikhs, including their myriad subdivisions, and have the luxury of working with newly-synthesized categories such as Indians, Sri Lankans or Pakistanis. They do what they do—by way of defending the human and cultural rights of the minorities—not so much as a well-considered, ideological, and cognitive choice, but as a moral reaction set off by a vague sense of rebellion against the injustice and cruelty inflicted on fellow citizens. The social evolutionary project sits lightly on such secularists. They do not really expect the world to be fully secularized over time. Nor do they expect the 'rationality' of modern science to gradually supplant the 'irrationality' of religion. (Somewhat like Sigmund Freud who, propelled simultaneously by the optimism of the Enlightenment and a tragic vision of life, hoped that the human ego would gradually win over more and more territory from the id, without fully giving up the belief that the dialectic between the two was an eternal one. I am sure Banuri will accept this qualification of his metaphor.)

It is not much of an inheritance. However, I like to believe that that inheritance is not trivial either, for it has something to do both with the very core of our humanness and the key civilizational categories that distinguish this part of the world. It cannot be written off as ethically pointless or politically futile.

I have said that the huge majority of South Asians know neither the literal meaning of the word 'secularism' nor its connotative meaning

derived from the separation of the state from the church in post-medieval
Europe; and, sadly, in an open polity, the choice of this majority matters.
I have also pointed out that most properly educated Indians love to believe
that life in precolonial India was nasty, brutish and short; that communal
violence was a daily affair till the imperial state forcibly imposed some
order on the warring savages. Strangely, many secular South Asians are
not comfortable with that 'history' either. They feel compelled to remind
us, often in maudlin detail, how gloriously syncretic India was before
religious fanaticism and scheming politicians spoilt it all.[30] Only they
do not stop to ask if that syncretism was based on secularism or on
some version of 'primitive proto-secularism' and if those who did so well
without the ideology need it now.

These secularists seem oblivious that mass politics in an open polity
demands an accessible political idiom, even when that idiom seems crude
and unbecoming of the dignity of a modern state or looks like a hidden
plea to return to the country's brutal, shabby past. That is why, at times
of communal and ethnic violence, when the state machinery and the
newspaper-reading middle classes keep on harping on the codes of
secularism, at the ground level, where survival is at stake, the traditional
codes of tolerance are the ones that matter, however moth-eaten they
may otherwise look.[31]

Finally, I should like to venture two formulations. First, religion as
the foundation of social life is true for mainly the weak, the poor and
the rural. Modern India, which sets the tone of the culture of the Indian
state, fears that kind of religion. Second, the opposite of religious and
ethnic intolerance is not secularism but religious and ethnic tolerance.
Secularism is merely one way of ensuring that tolerance. However, in
societies where most citizens have been uprooted from traditional lifestyles, secularism *can* become the counterpoint of religious chauvinism,
because both begin to contest for the allegiance of the decultured, the
atomized and the massified. In other societies, religious fanaticism mainly
contests the tolerance that is part of religious traditions themselves.

That is why in South Asia secularism can mostly be the faith of—and
be of use to—the culturally dispossessed and the politically rootless. In
favourable circumstances, it can make sense even to the massified in the
growing metropolitan slums, but never to the majority living its life with
rather tenuous links with the culture of the nation-state. True, when such
a concept of secularism is made profitable by the state and the élite—

---

[30]For a random example, see the superbly executed television series made by
Saeed Naqvi and shown on Doordarshan between 1992 and 1994.
[31]Nandy et al., *Creating a Nationality.*

that is, if lip-service to the concept pays rich enough dividends—many begin to use it, not in its pristine sense but as an easy, non-controversial synonym for religious tolerance. If such a reward system functions long enough in a society, political institutions may even begin to protect the view that religion is essentially a drag on civil society. The primary function of secularism then becomes management of the fear of religion and the religious.

To function thus, the ideology of secularism must presume the existence of an individual who clearly defines his or her religious allegiance according to available census classifications and does not confuse religion with sect, caste, family traditions, *dharma*, culture, rituals and *deshachara* or local customs. That is, the ideology presumes a relatively clear, well-bounded self-definition compatible with the post–seventeenth-century ideal of the individual, comfortable in an impersonal, contractual-relations-dominated society. There is nothing terribly wrong with such a presumption and many people might in fact wish to live in such an individualistic society, seeing in it the scope for true freedom. Only, they have to take into account two political developments, working at cross purposes.

On the one hand, the majority, impervious to the charms of the official ideology of secularism, has now *some* access to political power. And with quickening politicization in this part of the world and large-scale efforts to empower newer sections of people by parties and movements of various kinds, this access is likely to increase. So, the contradiction between the ideology of secularism and the democratic process is likely to sharpen further in the future. To be implemented, the secularist project may then have to depend even more on the coercive power of the state. Not merely to keep in check the enemies of secularism, but also to thought-police history (through the production of official histories, history textbooks, time capsules, and other such sundry tricks of the trade to which both India's intellectual left and the liberals are privy).[32] This should not be much of a shock to the Indian secularist. Secularism has always had a statist connection, even in the West, and most South Asian, especially Indian, secularists are confirmed statists. As the legitimacy of the state as a moral presence in society declines, this state connection may produce new stresses within the ideology of secularism.

On the other hand, there is now a powerful force that may find meaning

---

[32]That is partly the reason why even the Bharatiya Janata Party, being ideologically committed to unqualified statism, is unable to shed the idiom. It has to define its position as loyalty to 'true' secularism, in opposition to what it calls the 'pseudo-secularism' of other parties dependent on minority vote banks.

in the secularist world-view. Modern India—by which I mean the westernized, media-exposed India, enslaved by the urban–industrial vision—is no longer a small, insignificant oasis in a large, predominantly rural, tradition-bound society. One-fourth of India is a lot of India. In absolute terms, modern India is itself a society nearly four times the size of its erstwhile colonial master, Britain. It is—to spite Thomas Macaulay, that intrepid, romantic ideologue of the Raj—no longer a buffer between the rulers and the ruled. Modern India is the world's fourth largest country in itself.

This India does have sufficient exposure to the ideology of the state to be able to internalize the concept of secularism and sections of it are willing to go to any length to ensure that the concept is not questioned. But that by itself is not particularly surprising. There are a number of Indians now who are willing to sacrifice the unmanageable, chaotic, real-life Indians for the sake of the idea of India. They are miserable that while Indian democracy allows them to choose a new set of political leaders every five years, it does not allow them to choose, once in a while, the right kind of people to populate the country. Instead, they have to do with the same impossible mass of a billion Indians—uneducable, disorganized, squabbling and, above all, multiplying like bedbugs. For in the Indianness of Indians who are getting empowered lies, according to many learned scholars, the root cause of all the major problems of the country.

Hindu Nationalism and the Future of Hinduism

When a secularizing society throws up its own versions of religion, extremist or otherwise, to cater to the changing psychological and cultural needs of the citizenry, what is the link between these versions and the faith that serves as their inspiration? The relationship between Hindutva, the encompassing ideology that inspires all Hindu nationalist movements in India, and Hinduism provides the semblance of an answer.

Speaking pessimistically, Hindutva will be the end of Hinduism. Hinduism is what most Indians still live by. Hindutva is a response of the mainly Brahminic, middle-class, urban, westernizing Indians to their uprooting, cultural and geographical. According to V.D. Savarkar, the openly agnostic, westernized nationalist who coined the term, Hindutva is not only the means of Hinduizing the polity but also of militarizing the effeminate, disorganized Hindu. It is a critique of—and an answer to the critique—of Hinduism, as most Indians know the faith and an attempt to protect, within Hinduism, the flanks of a minority consciousness—

including the fears and anxieties—that the democratic process threatens to marginalize.[33]

Though I have stressed earlier the pathology of rationality that characterizes this minority consciousness, there is also in it an element of incontinent rage. It is the rage of Indians who have decultured themselves, seduced by the promises of modernity, and who now feel abandoned. With the demise of imperialism, Indian modernism—especially that sub-category of it that goes by the name of development—has failed to keep these promises. Hence the paradoxical stature of Hindutva; it is simultaneously an expression of status anxiety and a claim to legitimacy. At one plane, it is a *savarna purana* that the lower-middle class ventures while trying to break into the upper echelons of modern India; at another, it is an expression of the fear that they may be pushed into the ranks of the urban proletariat by the upper classes, not on grounds of substance, but 'style'. The 'pseudo-secularists' represent for them the ambition; the Muslims (in India, consisting mostly of communities of artisans getting proletarianized) the fear. Hence, the hatred for both.

It is as part of the same story that Hindutva represents in popular, mass-cultural form some of the basic tenets of the world-view associated with secularism and the secular construction of the Muslim. Built on the principles of religious reform movements in the colonial period, Hindutva cannot but see Hinduism as inferior to the Semitic creeds—monolithic, well-organized, and capable of being a sustaining ideology for an imperious state. And, being a mass-cultural ideology, it *can* do to

[33]This critique of Hinduism, often masquerading as a personological critique of the Hindus, is central to Hindutva. For a useful discussion of this part of the story, see Chaturvedi Badrinath, *Dharma, India and the World Order: Twenty Essays* (New Delhi: Centre for Policy Research, 1991). A flavour of the intellectual and cultural climate that produced Hindutva can be had from Dhananjay Keer, *Veer Savarkar* (Bombay: Popular Prakashan, 1966). For a succinct comment on the Rashtriya Swayamsevak Sangh as a lower-middle-class, political expression of the ideology of Hindutva and its relationship with Hinduism, see Parsa Venkateshwar Rao Jr, 'The Real RSS: Not Hindu, Cultural or Nationalist', *The Times of India*, 8 July 1998.

The line drawn between Hinduism and Hindutva is visible at the ground level, when communal violence spreads to or breaks out in rural India, where communities have not yet fully broken down and where the ideology of Hindutva faces resistance from everyday Hinduism. Some have academic objections to such a separation, but I doubt if those who offer such resistance would worry about that. They will draw sustenance either from the 'low-brow' Hinduism of everyday life (see for instance, Marglin, 'On Pirs and Pandits'; and Mayaram, 'Representing the Hindu–Muslim Civilizational Encounter') or from even some of the pillars of Brahminic/classical orthodoxy, such as Shankaracharya Chandrasekharendra Saraswati Swami, *Hindu Dharma: The Universal Way of Life* (Bombay: Bharatiya Vidya Bhavan, 1996).

Hinduism what the secularists have always wanted to do to it. Hindutva at this plane is a creed which, if it succeeds, might end up making Nepal the world's largest Hindu country. Hinduism will then survive not as a faith of the majority of Indians, but in pockets, cut off from the majority who will claim to live by it—perhaps directly in Bali, indirectly in Thai, Sri Lankan and Tibetan Buddhism and, to the chagrin of many Hindu nationalists, in South Asian and Southeast Asian Islam. The votaries of Hindutva will celebrate that death of Hinduism. For they have all along felt embarrassed and humiliated by Hinduism as it is. Hence, the pathetic, counterphobic emphasis in Hindutva on the pride that Hindus must feel in being Hindus. Hindutva *is* meant for those whose Hinduism has worn off. It *is* a ware meant for the supermarket of global mass culture where all religions are available in their consumable forms, neatly packaged for buyers. Predictably, its most devoted consumers can be found among the expatriate Hindus of the world.

I go back once again to the important question that many years ago H.R. Trevor-Roper raised in the context of the great European witch-hunt: did the inquisitors discover a new 'heresy' beneath the faith of the heretics or did they invent it?[34] He reached the conclusion that, on the whole, the witch-craze did not grow out of the social and religious processes operating in medieval Europe; it 'grew by its own momentum' from within modernizing Europe.[35] The growth of Hindutva has depended heavily upon invented heresies that are organized around themes that have no place in Hindu theology: the modern state, nationalism and national identity. It has borrowed almost nothing from existing Hindu theology in its construction of the non-Hindus; it has followed its own trajectory in the matter. This is another crucial difference between Hindutva and Hinduism. It is a pity that, to some extent, the same can be said about some of the more fanatical opponents of Hindutva in the modern sector, too. That fanaticism comes from a tacit recognition that, beneath the skin, they are each other's doubles. Only, while the ideologues of Hindutva have already found Indian analogues of *The Protocols of the Elders of Zion*, some opponents of Hindutva are still desperately looking for them.[36]

---

[34]Trevor-Roper, *The European Witch-Craze*, pp. 115–27.

[35]Ibid., p. 119.

[36]For a while, they found it in M.S. Golwalkar's book, *We or Our Nationhood Defined* (Nagpur: Bharat Publications, 1939). Things became a little convoluted when his disciples disowned it and claimed that Golwalkar, too, had disowned it. That was not what self-respecting fascists were expected to do and it was considered almost a betrayal by important sections of the Indian Left.

Speaking optimistically, Hindu nationalism has its territorial limits. It cannot spread easily beyond the boundaries of urban, westernizing India. Nor can it easily penetrate those parts of India where Hinduism is more resilient and Hindus are less prone to project on to Muslims the feared, unacceptable parts of their self. Hindutva cannot survive where the citizens have not been massified and come to speak only the language of the state.

To those who live in Hinduism, Hindutva is one of those pathologies that periodically afflict a faith. Hinduism has, over the centuries, handled many such pathologies; it still retains the capacity, they feel, perhaps over-optimistically, to handle one more. It will, they hope, consume Hindutva once a sizeable section of the modernized Hindus finds an alternative psychological defence against the encroaching forces of the market, the state, and the urban–industrial vision.

Whether one is a pessimist or optimist, the choices are clear. They do not lie either in a glib secularism talking the language of the state or in pre-war versions of nationalism seeking to corner the various forms of increasingly popular ethnic nationalism breaking out all over South Asia. It lies in alliance with forces that have risen in rebellion against the social forces and the ideology of dominance that have spawned Hindutva in the first place. As the world built by nineteenth-century imperialism collapses around us, Hindutva, too, may die a natural death. But, then, many things that die in colder climes in the course of a single winter survive in the tropics for years. Stalinism has survived better in India than even in the Soviet Union and so probably will imperialism's lost child, Hindutva. Maybe its death will not be as natural as that of some other ideologies. Maybe post-Gandhian Hinduism—combined with a moderate, modest and, what Ali Mazrui calls, ecumenical state—will have to take advantage of the democratic process to help Hindutva die a slightly unnatural death. Perhaps that euthanasia will be called politics.

*Earlier versions of this essay have been published in *Alternatives* and *Postcolonial Studies*.

7

A Report on the Present State of Health of the Gods and Goddesses in South Asia

Great Pan is not dead;
he simply emigrated
   to India.
Here, the gods roam freely,
disguised as snakes or monkeys. . . .
It is a sin to shove a book aside
   with your foot,
A sin to slam books down
   hard on a table, . . .
You must learn how to turn the pages gently
Without disturbing Sarasvati,
Without offending the tree
From whose wood the paper was made.

—Sujata Bhatt, 'A Different History' (1993)

SOME YEARS AGO, in the city of Bombay, a young Muslim playwright wrote and staged a play that had gods—Hindu gods and goddesses—as major characters. Such plays are not uncommon in India; some would say they are all too common. This one included gods and goddesses who were heroic, grand, scheming and comical. This provoked not the audience but a formation of Hindu nationalists, particularly the Hindu Mahasabha, which had for long been a spent political force in Bombay, the city being dominated by another more powerful Hindu nationalist formation, the Shiv Sena.

It is doubtful if those who claimed they had been provoked were actually provoked. It is more likely that a pretence of being offended was deployed to precipitate an incident which made their political presence felt. Vikram Savarkar of the Hindu Mahasabha—a grandson of Vinayak Damodar Savarkar (1883–1966), the non-believing father of Hindu nationalism who thoughtfully gifted South Asia the concept of Hindutva—organized a demonstration in front of the theatre where the play was being staged. The demonstrators caught hold of the playwright and threatened to lynch him. Ultimately, they forced the writer to bow down and touch Savarkar's feet, to apologize for writing the play. The humiliation of the young playwright was complete; it was duly photographed and published in newspapers and news magazines.

Though Savarkar later claimed that Hinduism had won, for he had not allowed a Muslim to do what Muslims had not allowed Hindus to do with Islam's symbols of the sacred, at least some Hindus felt that, on this occasion Hindutva may have won, but Hinduism had lost. It had lost because a tradition at least fifteen hundred years old was sought to be dismantled. During these fifteen hundred years, a crucial identifier of Hinduism—as a religion, a culture and a way of life—has been the particular style of interaction humans have had with gods and goddesses. Deities in everyday Hinduism, from the heavily Brahminic to the aggressively non-Brahminic, are not entities outside everyday life, nor do they preside over life from the outside; they constitute a significant part of it. Their presence is telescoped not only into one's transcendental self but, to use Alan Roland's tripartite division, also into one's familial and individualized selves and even into one's most flippant, comic, naughty moments.[1] Gods are beyond and above humans but they are, paradoxically, not outside the human fraternity.[2] You can adore or love them, you can disown or attack them, you can make them butts of wit and sarcasm. Savarkar, not being literate in matters of faith and pitiably picking up ideas from the culture of Anglo-India to turn Hinduism into a 'proper'

---

[1]Alan Roland, *In Search of Self in India and Japan: Toward a Cross-Cultural Psychology* (Princeton, NJ: Princeton University Press, 1988).

[2]As a distinguished, expatriate ethnomusicologist, oblivious of the new, city-sleek 'defenders of Hinduism' has recently put it, '. . . the Gods and Goddesses are neither remote nor really frightening or incomprehensible, as in many other religions. Their adventures are real enough for us to empathise with them, and what makes for this feeling of reality is that they not only maintain lofty principles but also have some of our own weaknesses and feelings.' Nazir Ali Jairazbhoy, *Hi-Tech Shiva and Other Apocryphal Stories: An Academic Allegory* (Van Nuys, CA: Apsara Media, 1999), pp. viii–ix. See also Surabhi Sheth, 'Self and Reality', in D.L. Sheth and Ashis Nandy (eds.), *The Future of Hinduism*, forthcoming.

religion from an inchoate pagan faith, was only ensuring the humiliating defeat of Hinduism as it is known to most Hindus.

Since about the middle of the nineteenth century, perhaps beginning from the 1820s, there has been a deep embarrassment and discontent with the lived experience of Hinduism, the experience that, paradoxically, the young Muslim playwright, Savarkar's victim, represented. Vikram Savarkar is only the last within a galaxy of people—Hindus, non-Hindus, Indians, non-Indians—who have felt uncomfortable with the overpopulated Indian pantheon, its richly textured, pagan personalities, its unpredictability, variety and all too human foibles. For nearly a hundred and fifty years, we have seen a concerted, systematic effort to either eliminate these gods and goddesses from Indian life or tame them and make them behave. I am saying 'Indian' and not 'Hindu' self-consciously, for these gods and goddesses not only populate the Hindu world but regularly visit, and occasionally poach on, territories outside it. They are not strangers outside India either.[3] By indirectly participating in the effort to retool or gentrify them, Savarkar was only following the tradition of Baptist evangelists like William Carey and Joshua Marshman and rationalist religious and social reformers such as Rammohun Roy and Dayanand Saraswati in nineteenth-century India. They all felt that the country's main problem was its idolatry, and the rather poor personal quality of its gods and goddesses. These reformers wanted Indians to get rid of their superfluous deities and either live in a fully secularized, sanitized world in which rationality and scientific truth would prevail or, alternatively, set up a regular monotheistic God, as 'proper' Christians and Muslims had done. Vikram Savarkar was attacking in the playwright a part of his self that was no longer acceptable, but not easy to disown either.

Early attacks on the gods and goddesses by the various Hindu reform movements, from the Brahmo Samaj to the Arya Samaj, have been dutifully picked up by formations that were till recently at the periphery of Indian politics, such as those that centre around Hindutva. Today, overwhelmed

---

[3]In Malaysia and Indonesia, for instance, they critically influence the mythic life of a majority of the people. Under the influence of Islamic revivalism, there are in Malaysia now stray attempts to purify Malaysian Islam and demands that the Malaysian sultans, who constitute a ruling council, drop the parts of their titles that are 'Hindu' or obvious remnants of pre-Islamic traditions. However, the sultans seem reluctant to do so, for a part of their legitimacy in a predominantly Muslim community is linked to their ritual status. Gods and goddesses can survive in odd places. See for instance Dilip Padgaonkar, 'Kuch Kuch Hota Hai in Indonesia', *The Times of India*, 30 January 2000.

by the experience of the Ramjanmabhumi movement and the destruction of the Babri mosque at Ayodhya in 1992, we no longer care to read the entire Hindutva literature produced over the last seventy-five years. We think we know what they have to say. If all nationalist thought is the same, as Ernest Gellner believed, Hindu nationalist thought cannot be any different, we are sure.[4] However if you read the literature of Hindutva, you will find in it a systematic, consistent and often direct attack on Hindu gods and goddesses. Most stalwarts of Hindutva have not been interested in Hindu religion and have said so openly. Their tolerance towards the rituals and myths of their faith have been even lower. Many of them have come to Hindutva as a reaction to everyday, vernacular Hinduism.

This rejection is a direct product of nineteenth-century Indian modernity and its models of the ideal Hindu as a Vedantic European or, for that matter, Vedantic Muslim. That is why till recently, in no *shakha* or branch of the Rashtriya Swayamsevak Sangh (RSS) could there be any icon of any deity except Bharatmata, Mother India. The Ramjanmabhumi temple is the first temple for which the RSS has shed a tear, or shown any concern. And that concern, to judge by their participation in worship or rituals at the temple, seems skin-deep.

In 1990–1, I interviewed at great length the chief priest of the Ramjanmabhumi temple, a remarkably courageous, ecumenical man of religion who was murdered soon after the mosque was demolished. He said that, during the previous seven years of the movement in support of the temple, no major political leader of the movement had cared to worship at the temple, except one who had had a puja done without herself visiting the temple. At this point I should tell my favourite, probably apocryphal, story about the devotion to Ram of Hindu nationalists. Once, in course of his only visit to an RSS shakha, Mohandas Karamchand Gandhi reportedly looked around and found, on the walls of the shakha, portraits of some of the famous martial heroes of Hindutva, such as Shivaji and Rana Pratap. Being a devotee of Ram, Gandhi naturally asked, 'Why have you not put up a portrait of Ram as well?' Those were not the days of the Ramjanmabhumi movement and the RSS leader showing him around said, 'No, that we cannot do. Ram is too effeminate to serve our purpose.'

I am not going to speak about a style of relating to gods and goddesses which invites one to fight their causes while caring nothing for them. I am going to speak about gods and goddesses who inhabit the world we

[4]Ernest Gellner, *Nations and Nationalism* (Ithaca: Cornell University Press, 1983), p. 124.

live in, sometimes as house guests, sometimes as our neighbour's headache, sometimes even as private ghosts without whom we think we can live in greater peace. The literary theorist D.R. Nagaraj accused me of writing on these things as an outsider. 'You come to the gods and goddesses as an intellectual, academically,' he said. I often felt like telling him that though I did not want to come to them, they forced me. There is an inevitable logic through which these obstreperous deities infect our lives, pervade it, even invade and take it over, independently of our likes and dislikes. Like most other South Asians, belonging to a whole range of faiths, I have no choice in the matter.

For even within persons, communities, cults, sects, and religions that deny gods and goddesses, there persist relationships more typical of religions with a surfeit of gods and goddesses. Gods and goddesses may survive as potentialities even in the most austerely monotheistic, anti-idolatrous faiths. They are not permitted into the main hall, but they are there, just outside the door, constantly threatening to enter the main hall uninvited—as in some of the best-known Indonesian mosques, where the entrance doors and boundary walls are guarded or manned by Hindu or Buddhist gods and goddesses. The reverse also holds true. Some gods and goddesses do have a special symbolic place for anti-polytheism. Lord Thirupathi, nowadays the presiding deity of India's high politics and entertainment industry, reportedly has a Muslim son-in-law whose temple is right within the Lord's campus. And Sabarimala, one of the more potent deities in south India, is also known for his Muslim friend.

Even in starkly monotheistic religions, gods and goddesses are waiting just outside the doors of consciousness. Most of the anger against *The Satanic Verses* was inspired by the gratuitous insults that Rushdie heaped on some of Islam's revered figures, but part of it might also have been a response to the latent fear that the banished might return. The non-Islamic or pre-Islamic forms of consciousness that the book unwittingly invokes may or may not threaten 'mainstream' Islam, but they perhaps haunt many Islamic communities in those parts of the world where such forms are, as I remarked, no longer one's distant, superseded past. Thanks to colonial constructions of 'true' Islam in the nineteenth century, this past often seems an immediate, destabilizing temptation in the neighbourhood. It is probably no accident that the main agitation against the *The Satanic Verses* took place in countries like Iran, Pakistan, and India, and among expatriate Indians and Pakistanis in Britain.

Shamoon Lokhandwala mentions a medieval religious composition of western Indian Muslims that depicts Prophet Muhammad as the last of the ten avataras and which served as a sacred text of these Muslims.[5] But even in the more austerely monotheistic versions of Islam, gods and goddesses may survive as aspects or qualities of God, as in the ninety-nine names of Allah. Even in Judaism, despite the faith's hard monotheistic core, the dialogical relationship between God and humans in everyday life has many of the features of pantheistic faiths. In this relationship, much sarcasm, wit, accusations of partiality and injustice, light-hearted banter and sharp criticisms of divine dispensation—of the kind that Vikram Savarkar did not relish—are all common. These are neither seen as blasphemous nor as detracting from the majesty of the divine. Such dialogues can be found in old Judaic folk-tales, in the work of contemporary Jewish writers, and even in extreme conditions such as the recorded reactions of Jewish victims in Nazi concentration camps. Theological monotheism is not foolproof protection against theophily or attempts to fraternize with the sacred.

In South Asia, such dialogical relationships with divinity sometimes acquire oracular grandeur. I must repeat here a story that philosopher Ramchandra Gandhi has made famous.[6] As he tells it, the famous religious leader and social reformer Vivekananda (1863–1902), while on a visit to Kashmir, went to a temple of the goddess Kali and asked her what many self-conscious westernized Hindus must have begun asking since the nineteenth century—why had she tolerated so much vandalism and the destruction of temples. Vivekananda heard in his heart the reply of the great mother goddess: 'Do you protect me or do I protect you?' Even the most fearsome deities in South Asia have, I like to believe, a double responsibility which they must balance—they have to protect both their devotees and the humanity of their devotees. The human responses that gods and goddesses give to human predicaments may also be responses to the limited human ability to give or accept human answers grounded in secular reasons and secular morality. These responses may be another kind of self-excavation represented by visions within the devotee, where questions and answers are both latent in his inner self. In a cosmology dependent on gods and goddesses, this is a moral self-affirmation that can be simultaneously a rational argument.

A this-worldly articulation of the same process can be found in the Indian politician's perpetual fascination with astrology, palmistry, *yajnas*

[5]Shamoon T. Lokhandwala, 'Indian Islam: Composite Culture and Integration', *New Quest*, March–April 1985 (50), pp. 87–101.
[6]Ramchandra Gandhi, *Sita's Kitchen: A Testimony of Faith and Enquiry* (New Delhi: Wiley Eastern, 1994), p. 10.

or sacrificial rituals, and *tantra*. Prime Minister Indira Gandhi, for instance, undertook a series of pilgrimages during her last years. (She overdid it, some spitefully say, because her arithmetic was poor.) I have never heard of a politician, either in her party or in the opposition, who underestimated her rational, cost-calculating, political self. Nobody believed she would passively manage fate by such pilgrimages. She went to the pilgrimages but retained her sharp, wily, ruthless political self. The issue of 'agency' in such matters is important but not simple. The heavens, though continuous with everyday life on earth, expect nobody to be passively dependent on them. They refuse to deliver results or confirm the belief that 'agency' has been transferred to the right quarters. This compact is fully understood by all the parties involved.[7]

Nothing shows this better than the art and science of astrology. Astrology is most popular in four sectors of South Asia: business (especially if it involves speculative ventures), spectator sports, the film world, and politics. However, I have never heard anyone claiming that successful business people of the region depend on astrology to solve their problems in the stock market. They do business to the best of their knowledge and understanding, *and* then take the help of astrologers, *tantrik*s and temple priests to negotiate terms with gods and goddesses. As if there was a vague awareness that astrology could be another way of asking questions, the answers to which might be known but needed to be endorsed by superhuman specialists.[8] Thus, when despite elaborate rituals and consultations with astrologers, roughly 80 per cent of the nearly 500 commercial films annually produced in India bomb at the box office, film producers and directors do not give up their belief in astrology. They blame failure on their own imperfect reading of the future, and on flawed ritual performance (which is another way of acknowledging one's faulty reasoning). Presumably, modernity will now make sure that psychotherapists occupy the space astrologers and priests, backed by gods and goddesses, now occupy. It will be in many ways a less colourful cultural life, but that is a different story.

When gods and goddesses enter human life in South Asia, they contaminate it not in the way the modern, sophisticated, urbane believer fears they will. Nor do they do so the way the rationalist thinks the idea

[7]For a more detailed discussion, see Ashis Nandy, *The Tao of Cricket: On Games of Destiny and the Destiny of Games* (New Delhi: Penguin, 1989), ch. 1.

[8]This part of the story is entirely missed by those who read all recourse to astrology as the denial of free will. For a recent example, see Peter R. deSouza, 'Astrology and the Indian State', *The Times of India*, 19 July 1996.

of God contaminates the lives of devotees. They enter human life to provide a quasi-human, sacral presence, to balance the powerful forces of desacralization in human relationships, vocations and perceptions of nature. This familiarity has bred not contempt, as the Vikram Savarkars of the world suspect, but a certain self-confidence vis-à-vis deities. Gods and humans are not distant from each other; human beings can, if they try hard enough, approximate gods. They can even aspire to be more powerful and venerable than gods. *Tapas*, penance of various kinds, and sometimes even the benediction of one god, wisely or foolishly given, can give one superhuman, godly powers. First, spirituality is partly a gift of mortality; it is associated more with mortals than with gods, who are usually seen to possess a streak of hedonism. The persistent asceticism of Shiva is an exception rather than the rule. Second, defying Vivekananda, some gods can also be vulnerable and require the help of humans to fight demons or other gods.

That is, the human inferiority to gods is not absolute; no wide chasm separates the goals and motivations of gods and humans. Indeed, the difference between immortal humans and gods occasionally becomes notional. For the classicists, this proposition is not difficult to swallow because, of the seven immortals mentioned in the Puranas (Ashvathama, Bali, Vyasa, Hanumana, Kripa, Vibhishana and Parashurama), none, except perhaps Hanumana, can claim divine status.[9] There *is* continuity between the divine and the earthly; the chasm between gods and humans in South Asia is narrow or shifting. At times, some gods might even be less effective, potent or pious than humans.

Maybe that is the reason why allegiance to a deity is often personalised and looks like a bilateral contract or a secret intimacy between two unequal but sovereign individuals. This allegiance may often have little to do with one's faith—manifestly. Anybody who knows something about the great sarod players, Alauddin Khan and Ali Akbar Khan, will also know that both have been great devotees of goddess Saraswati. Yet, they have simultaneously been devout Muslims, and proudly so. That

[9]Though I have recently found out that, in Sri Lanka, there is at least one temple where Vibhishana is worshipped. Of the seven immortals (*Ashvathama Balir Vyaso Hanumanascha Vibhishanah Kripah Parashuramascha saptaite chiranjivinah*), Ashvathama is the best known, and, until some decades ago, one could hear claims once in a while that he had been seen still moving around with a wound on his forehead, usually at the foothills of the Himalaya. I have never been able to decipher the fondness for the hills in this tragic *puranic* character.

Despite the unenviable state of *puranic* immortals, immortality has been a major fantasy in Indian cultural life. Indian alchemy has been more concerned with the search for an elixir of life, less with the transmutation of base metal into gold.

devotion to Islam and Islamic piety does not require them to reject their personal goddess or *isthadevi* who presides over the most important area of their life, musical creativity. Alauddin Khan once composed a new *raga* called Madanmanjari. As its name indicates, the *raga* immediately invokes Krishna and Vaishnava culture. When someone took the courage to ask the Ustad why he had used such a blatantly Hindu name, the Ustad, I am told, was surprised. 'Is it Hindu? I composed it in honour of my wife Madina Begum,' he is supposed to have said. What looked blatantly Hindu to some can look to others a marker of Islam devotion. The piety of neither is disturbed.

While studying the Ramjanmabhumi movement, we found a hillock at Ayodhya, venerated both by local Hindus and Muslims. The Hindus considered it to be the discarded part of the sacred *Gandhamadan* of Ramayana, which Hanumana had foolishly carried, unable to locate the magical drug Vishalyakarani that he was told to find on the hill for the treatment of Lakshmana's war wounds. The Muslims associated the same hillock with Hazrat Shish and considered it a remnant of Noah's ark, discarded of all places at Ayodhya after the great deluge.

When gods and goddesses invade our personal life or enter it as our guests, when we give them our personal allegiance, they may or may not have much to do, apparently, with the generic faiths we profess. The theologian and painter Jyoti Shahi once reported a survey carried out in Madras where, according to official census, 1 per cent of the people are Christian. This survey found that about 10 per cent of the population identified Jesus Christ as their personal god or *isthadevata*. Such data warn us not to be taken in by what some politicians, acting as vendors of piety, and some experts on ethnic violence, tell us about the geography of faiths. The Indic civilization has been there slightly longer than the Hindutva-peddlers and the Indologists have been, and it may well survive its well-wishers. The more continuous traditions of this civilization may reassert themselves in our public life. A majority of people in South Asia know how to handle the gods and goddesses, their own and that of others. The gods and goddesses, on the other hand, not only live with each other, they also invite us to live with their plural world.

Years ago, while studying the psychological landscape of western colonialism in South Asia, I checked some nineteenth-century documents on Calcutta, because Calcutta is where it all began. Not being a historian, many of the documents surprised me. For instance, certain scrappy details of British households showed that they had a large retinue of servants and retainers, including often a Brahmin priest who did puja in the house. Many British houses also had small temples which the Brahmin retainers took care of. Apparently, these householders went to Church on Sundays but found nothing inconsistent in the puja at home.[10] The standard reading, I guess, would be that the Indian wives or concubines of such Britishers—the Suez Canal was not yet dug and most had Indian spouses—required this facility. However, something else might also have been involved. For the East India Company itself owned 'shares' in at least two temples. During important religious festivals, the army band went and played at these temples and the musketeers of the Company fired volleys in the air to celebrate the occasion. In return, the Company was given a share of donations made to the temples. It also seems that many individual British residents in India, while proclaiming disbelief in the special spiritual skills of Brahmins and attacking them as charlatans, were at the same time scared stiff by their possible magical abilities. At least some British householders maintained temples at their homes not because they were lapsed Christians or crypto-Hindus, but because they were afraid of local gods and Brahmins and did not want to antagonize them. This was their idea of buying an insurance policy in matters of the sacred. The apparently sharp theological distinctions between some religions may, in specific cultural contexts, observe the logic of complementary self-organization.

I have come to suspect that theistic worlds in South Asia observe a series of principles of mediation in their relationships with each other. These mediations ensure continuity and compatibility, but also a degree of anxiety, hostility and violence, though not perhaps distance or incomprehension. Whether the protagonists are Bosnian Muslims and Serbs in East Europe, or Hutus and Tutsis in Africa, or Hindus and Muslims in South Asia, fractured familiarity can breed contempt and venomous, genocidal passions; more so in a context of imminent massification, threatening cultural identities.

A respected Pakistani political analyst and journalist once claimed that the ultimate fear in many Pakistanis was that, if they come too

---

[10]What arouses anxiety in modern Indians does not apparently do so in societies where the élite has not lost its cultural self-confidence. I am told that it has become fashionable in recent years for young Japanese couples to get married in picturesque European churches. They get married there according to Christian rites and the marriages are perfectly acceptable in Japan, legally and socially. Has this openness something to do with the eight million gods in Shinto cosmology?

close to India, they would be fitted in the Hindu social order, mostly in the lower orders of the caste hierarchy. India and Pakistan have separated fifty years ago; there is hardly any Hindu left in Pakistan. Most Pakistanis have not even seen a single Hindu in their life; they have seen Hindus only in films and on television. Why then this anxiety? My Pakistani friend himself seemed perplexed, but insisted that there *was* this lurking fear in Pakistan that Hinduism was not something outside, but a vector within. Probably, living in two complementary worlds—of legends, folk-tales, rituals, marriage rites, music, craft, traditions and, even, some of the same superstitions, fears, gods and demons—also has its costs. Perhaps many of the anti-idolatrous faiths in South Asia—they include many Hindu sects—are not merely negations of the sphere of gods and goddesses, but also constitute a system of internal checks and balances. Perhaps out gods and goddesses also need such checks.

When another faith provides such a counterpoint or balancing principle, it no longer remains an alien faith or someone else's faith. You do not have to open an inter-faith or intercultural dialogue with such a faith, to conform to contemporary sensitivities. The dialogue already exists, waiting to be joined. Islam, for instance, by the very fact that it denies gods and goddesses, provides in South Asia a different kind of meaning-system that becomes accessible to people who want to defy the world of gods and goddesses while living within it. So, even a threat of becoming a part of the Islamic order and disowning the Hindu pantheon, by, say, an oppressed Dalit, becomes a particular way of interacting with the pantheon. Islam in South Asia may mean going outside the sphere of gods and goddesses, but it may also mean renegotiating terms and conditions with one's traditional gods and goddesses.

It can even mean renegotiating the social status of communities sharing an overlapping structure of sacredness. Many of the most famous temples of Ayodhya, the pilgrimage centre that has become a symbol of religious intolerance in South Asia today, were built with the help of land grants and tax exemptions given by the Shia Nawabs of Avadh in precolonial days. By being patrons of Ram temples, they were making a statement both on their positions vis-à-vis the Ramanandis who dominated the sacred city, and the Sunnis, who constituted an important component of the Muslim community there. Likewise, B.R. Ambedkar, the Dalit leader and the author of India's Constitution, when he decided to convert to Buddhism along with a sizeable section of his followers, did so after much deliberation. It was not standard Therawada Buddhism, with its abundance of deities, that Ambedkar chose, but a more austere Buddhism that, by being close to Islam and Christianity would represent a sharper disjunction with Hinduism. By his conversion he was making a statement to the Hindu world.[11]

A more intense form of such interrelationship is the South Asian version of multiculturalism which does not remain a cultural artefact, but gets telescoped into the self of the individual. Kumar Suresh Singh's survey of Indian communities shows that hundreds of communities in India can be classified as having more than one 'religion'. (It is doubtful if these believers see themselves as having multiple religious identities; they define their Hinduism or Islam or Christianity in such a way that the symbols of sacredness of another faith acquire specific theological, cultural and familial status.) Thus, there are 116 communities that are both Hindu and Christian; at least 35 communities that are both Hindu and Muslim. Sant Fateh Singh, who fought for the cause of Khalistan, was said to be a convert from Islam and a part of his family, I am told, remains Muslim, exactly as a part of the family of Guru Nanak, the founder of Sikhism, remains Hindu. L.K. Advani, a leader of what is reputed to be one of the world's largest fundamentalist formations, is probably the only one of his ilk to have publicly proclaimed that, in his personal religious sensitivities, he is closer to Sikhism than to the religion he fights for, Hinduism. M.A. Jinnah, the founder of Pakistan, which separated from India on grounds of religion, belonged to a Muslim community that, to many 'thoroughbred' Muslims, still looks more Hindu than many Hindu communities. When he spoke of the Hindus and Muslims of South Asia being two nations by virtue of their faith and lifestyle, one wonders if he was not compensating for being part of a community that many Gujarati Hindus and Jains did not even include among the Muslims till a few decades ago. In all these instances, I am not talking of recent converts retaining traces of their older faiths; I am speaking of identities that appear to encompass more than one faith, culturally *and* theologically.

Such pluralism has its cost. The Meos, too, while being devout Muslims, trace their ancestry from the Mahabharatic clans and also often have Mahabharatic names.[12] Only in recent years, after being victims in a series of communal riots that have taken place since the days of

---

[11]That ultimately things did not go the way Ambedkar thought they would go, and that he himself had to end up as a part of the Buddhist–Hindu pantheon of the Dalits, is, of course, a different story.

[12]Shail Mayaram, *Resisting Regimes: Myth, Memory and the Shaping of a Muslim Identity* (New Delhi: Oxford University Press, 1997); and 'Representing the Hindu-Muslim Civilisational Encounter: The Mahabharata of Community of Muslims' (Jaipur: Institute of Development Studies, 1996), unpublished ms.

Partition, have they begun to feel that they can no longer live in two houses, that they will have to choose. And some of them have chosen to be Muslim in the sense in which the Tabligh and the Jamaat-e-Islami define Islam. Apart from their own tradition of Islam, that is the only other Islam available to them in contemporary India. Similarly, in the re-conversion programmes being run by the Vishwa Hindu Parishad clandestinely, the aim is to introduce non-Hindus into the Hindu fold as so many low-status mimics of a shallow, neo-Brahminic Hinduism, because that is the only Hinduism the evangelists themselves know. This is a modern tragedy that we have not yet sensed and it affects hundreds of communities all over the region today: Muslims, Hindus, Christians, Sikhs, Buddhists. I think South Asia will be poorer if its rich, intricate tapestry of faiths gets destroyed through neglect or shrinks into six or seven standard, mutually exclusive faiths because, in the contemporary world, only such standard faiths enjoy respectability and political clout. It will simultaneously impoverish Hinduism, Islam, and the other South Asian faiths.

I have said at the beginning that South Asian gods and goddesses, like their Hellenic counterparts, can sometimes be found on the wrong side of morality or law. The Puranas and the *upakathas* are full of instances of how loyalty to and the instrumental use of certain gods and goddesses can destroy a person or a community. The *vamachari* tradition is old in South Asia, and there are deities that have a special relationship with deviant social groups. Years ago, while studying the nineteenth-century epidemic of sati in Bengal, I found out that the popular public worship of Kali (*sarvajānin* puja) became an important socio-religious festival in eastern India only towards the end of the eighteenth century. Previously Kali—the fierce, violent, dark goddess of popular imagination—had been primarily the goddess of marginal groups such as robbers and thieves, and some incarnations of her were associated with certain dangerous diseases.[13] These gave her an ambivalent status. Now, along with Durga, she emerged as one of Bengal's two presiding deities from the great traditional mother goddess of the region, Chandi. After the great famine

---

[13]Some folk-tales presume Olaichandi, who presided over cholera for instance, to be a thinly disguised incarnation of Kali. Her Islamic edition was Olaibibi. Often, in a village or town, if Olaibibi was seen as more potent, the Hindus also went to her and vice versa. Exactly as many Muslims in Dhaka go to the Dhakeshwari temple for specific forms of protection or blessings. Dhakeshwari, some believe, still protects people from serious accidents and few among them want to take the risk of testing the truth of this—not even in an Islamic society.

of 1772 killed off nearly a third of Bengal and the colonial political economy caused massive cultural dislocations, Kali continued as the goddess of marginal groups, becoming for instance the presiding goddess of the thugs ravaging the countryside and pilgrimage routes. But she also acquired a new connection. She gradually became the chosen deity of the anomic, culturally uprooted, urban, upwardly mobile, upper castes in Greater Calcutta and areas heavily influenced by the British presence, where a new political economy and urban culture were ensuring the collapse of traditional social norms. Durga became a more benevolent incarnation of Chandi and gradually emerged as the most important deity in Bengal. This changing cartography of gods and goddesses, who can be benevolent but are also associated with the extra-social, the amoral and the criminal, gives an altogether different set of insights into cultural changes. It profiles the anxieties, fears, and hopes of a society that neither a desiccated, formal study of theology and high culture yields, nor any ethnography of the better-known deities.

To give another example, in 1994, during the last episode of plague in India, I discovered that, while there were goddesses for cholera and smallpox in large parts of India there was probably no popular goddess for plague except in Karnataka. I wondered why the goddess, Pilague-amma, found her congenial abode only in that state, and why she had that Anglicised name, as if she was a newcomer to India. Could it be that plague was a pestilence that did not arouse crippling anxieties in most parts of India? Could it be a pestilence with which most Indians did not have to wrestle psychologically, except perhaps in western coastal towns in contact with merchant ships coming from West Asia, Africa and Europe? I do not know. Perhaps there *are* goddesses corresponding to Pilague-amma in southern Gujarat and in Konkan; only I have not had the privilege of their *darshan* yet. Once again, the geography of popular religion gives one a clue to the reasons why plague in India has not triggered the imageries and passions it has in Europe since medieval times and why Indians have never fathomed the anxieties that incidents of plague in India arouse in other parts of the world.

This brings us to a central feature of South Asian concepts of divinity: the intimate relationship between gods and goddesses on the one hand, and demons, *rakshasas* and ogres on the other. The *suras* and the *asuras*, the *adityas* and the *daityas*, the *devas* and the *danavas*, are all dialectically interrelated; gods and goddesses cannot survive or be imagined—they are not even complete—without their counterparts among the demons.

The divine pantheon—populated by the good and the bad, the targets of right-handed worship and those associated with left-handedness, *vamachara*—is part of a larger cosmic order. The gods and goddesses are integrally related to the anti-gods or demons. No theory of violence, no metaphysics of evil in this part of the world, is complete unless it takes into account this relationship. The fuzzy boundaries of South Asian concepts of evil, the temporal and spatial limitations of the concept of *papa* (that distinguish it from the more 'intense' Judaeo-Christian concept of sin, which is more sharply defined but, paradoxically, expected to transcend space and time more easily), and the tolerance of diverse moral universes can be read as reflecting the inextricability of the ideas of the good, the divine and the godly from those of the evil, the desacralised and the ungodly. Appropriately, the mother of the gods and goddesses in mythic India, Aditi, is a sister of the mother of the demons, Diti, and in story after story there is an intricate, personalized, ambivalent relationship between gods and demons. Even Ravana, the fearsome Brahmarakshasa, the worst kind of rakshasa, is intertwined with Rama in the cosmic order as two approaches to the same divinity. Circumstances and accidents separate the approaches and only in death is the contradiction resolved. By dying at the hands of Rama, an incarnation of Vishnu, Ravana reaches his personal god, Vishnu.[14] Even the gift of the great Indian thinkers, writers, and painters to sometimes turn gods into villains and demons into heroes, and the ability of the less Sanskritized sectors to erect temples to persons as ungodly as Duryodhana or as demonic as Hidimba, carry a message. Devotees at such temples do not see them as temples of evil. Nor are such devotees parts of any cabal, eager to fulfil secret ambitions through ritualized Satanism (though that can happen on occasions). Rather, the worshippers seem to have an alternative idea of divinity in which Duryodhana has a place that in more respectable versions of the Mahabharata, his popular cousins monopolize.

These permeable borders between gods and demons, between the definitions of what is sacred in everyday life and what is not, are a major source of social tolerance and of the tacit awareness that the evil excluded from the self cannot be entirely projected outwards. For such projected evil remains only apparently outside, at a safe distance from the self. Indeed, the godliness one acknowledges and the ungodliness one is forced

---

[14]So the great act of rebellion of Michael Madhusudan Dutt (1824–73), his epic *Meghnadbadh Kavya*, which makes a hero out of Ravana and a villain out of Rama, as in some of the earlier dissenting pre-modern Ramayans, was after all not as disjunctive with the original as Dutt might have thought. I think I now know why, despite being taught like all Bengalis to hero-worship Dutt, I could still enjoy my grandmother's conventional version of the Ramayana.

to acknowledge are ordered as two sets of potentialities. They supply the culture's distinctive theories of violence and oppression. The politics of confrontation does not go far in India because, as an aging radical activist told me some years ago, 'the people are like that!'

But people are like that because there is a cosmology to back them up. That cosmology textures and configures the good and the evil differently. These configurations—and the moral ambiguity that can go with it—deeply offended even a compassionate observer like Albert Schweitzer. Schweitzer believed that such a cosmology was morally flawed because it did not clearly separate good and evil. He felt that some forms of social intervention and altruism were just not possible in such a frame of morality.[15] Maybe he was right. But that limitation also ensures that some forms of violence, based on the absolutization of differences, are not easy to precipitate in South Asia. In the long run, all attempts to draw conclusive, non-equivocal lines between the insiders and the outsiders, between the godly and the ungodly, seem eventually doomed in the region. Even during the fearsome communal violence during the partitioning of British India, the killings were often interspersed by resistance and mutual help that crossed religious borders, for these borders were never frozen.

Can this interpretation be read as an instance of camouflaged cultural nationalism? 'Why have all the avataras been born in India, nowhere else?', an academic once asked me aggressively. Answers to such questions can only be as clear—or vague—as a culture insists on giving. According to many versions of popular Hinduism there are roughly 330 million gods and some of their avataras might have been born elsewhere in the world. At least one important one, I know, was born in Nepal, at Lumbini. A proper census of these 330 million gods and goddesses and their countless incarnations is still awaited.

Such questions are also partly answered everyday by some of the apparent accidents of history, such as the existence of a city called Ayodhya in Thailand. Thai Ayodhya is not only sacred, it is rather unlikely that the Thais will concede it to be a copy of the Indian Ayodhya. Exactly as Tamilians are unlikely to concede that Madurai is only a derivative of Mathura. However, once you historicize Rama, once you locate his birthplace at a particular Ayodhya at a particular point of time, either to territorialize his claim to a temple or to oppose it, you automatically

[15]Albert Schweitzer, *Indian Thought and its Development* (New York: Beacon, 1959).

deny or diminish the sacredness of the other Ayodhya and, while you may establish Rama as a historical figure or national hero, you cannot sustain his status as a god who, as a god, has to exist *today*. If Rama *was*, he is no Rama. If Rama *is*, only then is he Rama. That is the paradox in which one gets caught when one accepts the language of the Hindutva-hawkers and the secular fundamentalists.

There is also the question D.R. Nagaraj raised about the status relations between the Brahminic and the non-Brahminic deities. Nirmal Kumar Bose wrote years ago about the South Asian stratarchy of gods, based on the caste system.[16] And M.N. Srinivas grappled with the same issue more than thirty years ago, though as a problem of ethnographic *versus* textual reality. Srinivas had found during his fieldwork that it was not unusual for the learned to attribute qualities to a deity that others did not; that even in the case of Sanskritic deities, the qualities associated with them in the Vedas and the Puranas were not often relevant in the field.[17] This sanctions a distinctive politics of cultures, perhaps even some play in matters of spirituality. First, the higher the status of a deity, the less directly helpful and relevant in everyday life he or she usually is.[18] Thus, Indra, the king of gods, has a high status in the pantheon but his potency as a god relevant to our day-to-day existence is not particularly high, at least not in our times; likewise with Brahma, creator of the universe and senior-most in the pantheon. Hindu temples within the precincts of most Buddhist temples in Sri Lanka tell the same story. Devotees see the Buddhist divinity as too austere and otherworldly; for everyday purposes they prefer to deal with more amenable, lower-ranked Hindu deities. The stratarchy balances the Brahminic and the non-Brahminic, the greater Sanskritic and the local, the Buddhist and the Hindu.[19]

One's manifest loyalty to a deity, too, may not say much about the powers one imputes to the deity. Thirty-five years ago, when I joined a psychoanalytic research centre and clinic at Ahmedabad, most of the

[16]Nirmal Kumar Bose, *Culture and Society in India* (New Delhi: Asia, 1967).

[17]M.N. Srinivas, 'A Brief Note on Ayyappa, the South Indian Deity', in K.M. Kapadia (ed.), *Professor Ghurye Felicitation Volume* (Bombay: Popular Book Depot, 1954), pp. 238–43.

[18]This also seems to indirectly emerge from Veena Das, 'The Mythological Film and its Framework of Meaning: An Analysis of Jai Santoshi Ma', *India International Centre Quarterly*, 1981, 9(1), pp. 43–56. There is a glimpse into the politics of the language the gods speak in 'Lingua Franca of Tamil Gods: Sanskrit or Tamil', *The Statesman*, 11 November 1990. Predictably, the Hindu nationalists have taken up the cause of Sanskrit.

[19]Appropriately enough, Simhala chauvinists have begun to interpret this expression of mutuality as an instance of contamination of Buddhism by Hinduism.

patients who came to the clinic were upper-caste Gujarati Vaishnavas. Ahmedabad itself was then an identifiably Vaishnava city, a sharp contrast to my native Calcutta. My teacher, the psychoanalyst Shiv Kumar Mitra, however, pointed out to me that the Vaishnava style overlay a clear Shakto substratum, with its usual bevy of powerful mother goddesses. When confronted with serious illness of a financial crisis, many residents of Ahmedabad rushed to these goddesses. Popular temples, in normal times, were not necessarily the same as temples popular at times of crisis. It was as if Ahmedabad recognized that goddesses could not only be more powerful than gods, but also a corrective to the secular status of women.

There can also be a hierarchy of godliness patterned by lifecycle. Some gods are more divine as children than as adults. Krishna, the king in the Mahabharata, is a god all right, but not a god of the same stature as he is as the child-god Balakrishna of the Bhagavata. Exactly as the status of the temple of Bhadrakali at Ahmedabad tells us something about the status of women in Gujarati society, the status of Balakrishna is a statement on childhood in India.[20] Likewise, Rama as a raja may have one set of devotees; Rama as an avatara of Vishnu has another. While working at Ayodhya in 1990–2, I was surprised to find a section of the priests there convinced that the Ramjanmabhumi movement was a Shaivite plot to take over the pilgrimage centre. With the whole of India on fire on the Ramjanmabhumi issue, some priests insisted that the movement was a political ploy to defeat not the Muslims, but the Vaishnavas. A few openly expressed their displeasure that the leaders of the movement, especially the firebrand Shaivite *sannyasins* like Uma Bharati and Ritambhara, talked of Rama primarily as a king.

If there are checks and balances within the pantheon in terms of power, interpersonal relations, status, morality and their following, there are human checks, too, against gods and goddesses. This is so, not only in the form of pious men, women and children with unblemished records of penance whose spiritual powers make gods tremble, but also in the form of heroic, epical, if flawed figures and ordinary folk who take up a position against mighty gods on moral grounds. Karna's defiance of fate and his disarming by Indra, Chand Saudagar's defiance of the goddess Chandi and her jealous revenge against him and his family, are instances. Parents in Mithila even today reportedly refuse to allow their

[20]Interested readers may look up Ashis Nandy, *The Intimate Enemy: Loss and Recovery of Self under Colonialism* (New Delhi: Oxford University Press, 1983); 'Politics of Childhood', in *Traditions, Tyranny and Utopia: Essays in the Politics of Awareness* (New Delhi: Oxford University Press, 1987), pp. 56–76.

daughters to marry someone from Ayodhya, however eligible the prospective bridegroom (because of the ill-treatment of Sita by Rama and the residents of Ayodhya). The practice has lasted for centuries and may outlast the Hindu nationalist politicians shouting themselves hoarse about Rama being a national hero or affirming the unity and homogeneity of the Hindu nation. I am sure there are devotees of Rama who support the Ramjanmabhumi movement and vote for Hindu nationalists, yet would not like their daughters to marry someone from Ayodhya. Is this refusal only comic folk superstition, or is there in this obstinacy an embedded comment on the limits of the spiritual and moral status of Rama—or, for that matter, gods and goddesses in general? Do we have access to the complexity of such discriminations and loyalties?

Finally, the matter of birth and death of gods and goddesses. New gods and goddesses are regularly born in South Asia.[21] Despite their theoretical immortality they also die frequently. They die not of illness or accidents but out of forgetfulness or deliberate erasure. These diseases are not uniquely South Asian; they are becoming epidemic the world over. Iconoclasm has killed fewer gods than have erasure or reconfigurations of memory. Certainly, evangelical Christianity between the sixteenth and the nineteenth centuries could not, despite its best efforts, manage to finish off gods and goddesses—coming from a Christian family, I know how much my family lived with them while aggressively denying that they did. And mine was not an atypical Christian family.[22] My father's Christ, in retrospect, was remarkably Vaishnava. Official Christianity need not be the last word on Christianity, which Gandhi recognized in his wry comment that Christianity was a good religion before it went to Europe. There are Christian sects and denominations that have made systematic *theological* deals with vernacular concepts of divinity. At a pinch, most religions probably know how to live with each other; it is probably the turn of some of the religious to re-learn how to live with each other.

While gods and goddesses *are* mainly responsible to their devotees, not to outsiders scrutinizing them 'scientifically', even for such outsiders

---

[21]Veena Das gives a fascinating account of the birth of a god sired by commercial cinema; see Das, 'Jai Santoshi Ma'. Such entry into the pantheon can even be quite enduring. Only a few weeks ago, writing this essay, I chanced upon a temple at Madangir, New Delhi, which, to spite Das, claimed to be an ancient Santoshi Ma temple, *Prachin Santoshi Mata Mandir*.

[22]Probably, gods have another kind of incarnation, not captured in any avatara theory. As we know, many of the European Christian saints, in their Latin American incarnations, bear clear imprints of pre-Christian Aztec deities. Even the figure of Christ has been transformed into a Meso-American one, far removed from the standardized figure of Christ in European Christendom.

they often faithfully hold in trust, on behalf of future generations, parts of their selves that devotees disown and would like to jettison. Gods and goddesses do get born, they live and die; their birth, life and death record not only what they are but also what we are. The historian of popular religion Michio Araki claims that the premodern Japan we know is not the Japan that encountered the West in Meiji times, for Japan only theoretically escaped colonization. With two great civilizations, India and China, succumbing to European powers in the neighbourhood, Japan had always lived with the fear of being colonized. This has forced Japan to redefine even its traditions and its past. Araki adds that clues to what Japan was before the western encounter and before it retooled its self-definition cannot be found in available histories of Japan but in its popular religion.

Not being a believer, I have come to gods and goddesses through politics, mainly through the politics of knowledge and democratic participation. I am all too aware that the world of gods and goddesses with which we are acquainted will not die soon. For our gods and goddesses, like Vivekananda's Kali, can take care of themselves. However, there are other worlds of gods and goddesses that are facing extinction. These gods and goddesses are exiting the world stage silently, without any fanfare, lament or scholarly obituary.

Some years ago I studied India's first environmental activist, Kapil Bhattacharjea (1904–89), who opposed the Damodar Valley Corporation (DVC), the multipurpose project of dams, hydel plants and irrigation systems modelled on the Tennessee Valley Authority (TVA). I arrived at the usual story—that when the DVC was built in the 1950s and 1960s, hundreds of thousands of people were uprooted, a majority of them tribals. They were given paltry compensation and told to settle elsewhere. And as usually happened during those tumultuous times in a newly born nation-state pathetically trying to catch up with the West, these displaced people went and quietly settled elsewhere, lost touch with their past, their inherited skills and environmental sensitivities (the ecology of resettlement area being usually different). Mostly belonging to the non-monetized section of the Indian economy, they also quickly spent the money they received as compensation on alcohol and fictitious land deals. Soon they became like any other uprooted community, migrant labourers working in small industrial units or landless agricultural labourers.[23] They were some of the earliest members of that growing community—

[23] Ashis Nandy, 'The Range and Limits of Dissent: Kapil Bhattacharjea's Critique of the DVC', see chapter 15 in this book.

an estimated sixty-odd million Indians whom development has uprooted during the last fifty years. This is more than three times the number of people displaced during the Partition riots in 1946–8. People have not forgotten the sixteen million displaced by Partition but they have forgotten these sixty million. A large proportion of the displaced are tribals and Dalits; one-third of India's entire tribal population has been uprooted in the last fifty years and 15 per cent of our tribes have been fully uprooted.[24] The gods and goddesses of these vanishing communities who face, silently and invisibly, threats of extinction, are those that have made me aware of a divine species which, unlike Vivekananda's Kali, requires something in addition to devotion. There are also communities that, after centuries of oppression, have begun to undervalue or forget their gods and goddesses, so that they can redefine themselves as only a group of oppressed poor, operating from a clean cultural slate.[25] I believe that all these gods and goddesses—as 'living' biographies of threatened cultures, as symbols of their resilence and resistance against the juggernaut of mega-development—deserve something more than standard, rationalist, dismissive ethnographies or archaeologies. We owe something not only to them and their humble devotees, but also to our own moral selves. For no intervention in society, politics and culture becomes moral because we cannot at the moment think of an alternative to it.

[24]Smitu Kothari estimates that of the 60 million aboriginal tribals in India belonging to some 212 tribes, 15 per cent have been displaced by development projects. Smitu Kothari, 'Theorising Culture, Nature and Democracy in India' (Delhi: Lokayan, 1993), ms. Other estimates are as high as 33 per cent.

[25]Many Dalit communities in contemporary India are good examples of such deculturation. In response, some sensitive Dalit writers have made a conscious effort to rediscover and defend Dalit cultural traditions. See for instance, D.R. Nagaraj, 'From Political Rage to Cultural Affirmation: Notes on the Kannada Dalit Poet-Activist Siddalingaiah', *India International Centre Quarterly*, Winter 1994, 21(4), pp. 15–26.

*Earlier published in *Manushi*, March–April (99) 1997.

PART II

Politics of Self

8

The Illegitimacy of Nationalism
Rabindranath Tagore and the
Politics of Self

The Ideology

Nationalism versus Patriotism

DURING THE LAST hundred and fifty years, Afro-Asian reformers and
thinkers have tried to reconcile three basic sets of contradictions or
oppositions: that between the East and the West; that between tradition
and modernity; and that between the past and the present. For some,
the contradictions overlap; for others, they are orthogonal. To many,
traditions and the past seem synonymous; to others, surrounded by
tradition, they are very much a part of the present, politically cornered
but nonetheless alive and kicking. To some, the East is by definition
traditional; to others, important aspects of eastern traditions seem more
compatible with the modern western personality and culture.

The attempts to reconcile these contradictions have produced many
modes of negotiating the three sets. For contemporary India, the ultimate
prototypes for such modes have been provided by two persons: Mohandas
Karamchand Gandhi (1869–1948) and Rabindranath Tagore (1861–1941).
Each deeply respected the other—Tagore was the first person to call
Gandhi a *mahatma*, Gandhi was the first to call Tagore *gurudev*—and
they shared many basic values. However, they differed significantly in
their world-views. These differences, often articulated publicly and with
some bitterness, can be traced to the ways in which they handled the
three sets of oppositions. To Tagore, the oppositions could best be handled

within the format of India's 'high' culture, within her classical Sanskritic traditions, leavened on the one hand by elements of European classicism, including aspects of the European Renaissance, and on the other by India's own diverse folk or little traditions. In his world, modernity had a place. To Gandhi, on the other hand, resolution of the contradictions was possible primarily within the little traditions of India and the West, with occasional inputs from Indian and western classicism, but almost entirely outside modernity. Consequently, there were often sharp debates in public as well as private discomfort about what the other represented politically.

When closely examined, however, these differences turn out to be a matter of emphasis. Few Indians have used the folk within the classical more creatively than Tagore. And few Indians have used the classical within the format of the non-classical more effectively than Gandhi. Also, despite being a modernist, Tagore began to make less and less sense to the modern world in his lifetime. He ended as a critic of the modern West and, by implication, of modernity. Gandhi, despite being a counter-modernist, re-emerged for the moderns as a major critic of modernity whose defence of traditions carried the intimations of a postmodern consciousness. It should also be recognized that the two appreciated, and were fascinated by, each other's enterprise, and between them they offered post-independence India a spectrum of choices in the matter of coping with India's diverse pasts and linking them to her future. However, on the whole, we can stick to our proposition that Tagore sought to resolve these contradictions at the level of high culture, Gandhi at the level of the 'low'. It is fitting that independent India's first prime minister claimed to be an heir to both traditions. Being a practised politician, Jawaharlal Nehru was aware that a durable basis of political legitimacy could be built only by simultaneously drawing upon both.

In one area, however, Tagore and Gandhi's endeavours overlapped and ideologically reinforced each other. Both recognized the need for a 'national' ideology of India as a means of cultural survival and both recognized that, for the same reason, India would either have to make a break with the post-medieval western concept of nationalism or give the concept a new content.[1] As a result, for Tagore, nationalism itself became

---

[1]An excellent introduction to the ideological content of Indian nationalism as it developed in the second half of the nineteenth century, is provided in Partha Chatterjee, *Nationalist Thought and the Colonial World: A Derivative Discourse?* (London: Zed, 1986). On the social basis of Indian nationalism, the most useful work remains A.R. Desai, *Social Background of Indian Nationalism* (Bombay: Popular Prakashan, 1946).

gradually illegitimate; for Gandhi, nationalism began to include a critique of nationalism. For both, over time, the Indian freedom movement ceased to be an expression of only nationalist consolidation; it came to acquire a new stature as a symbol of the universal struggle for political justice and cultural dignity. It was as if they recognized unself-critical Indian nationalism to be primarily a response to western imperialism and, like all such responses, shaped by what it was responding to. Such a version of nationalism could not but be limited by its time and its origin.

This fear of nationalism in the two most influential theorists of Indianness of our times was not an expression of the easy internationalism that became popular among the Indian middle classes in the interwar years, thanks to the intellectual bridgeheads already established in the country by some schools of liberalism and radicalism. In both Tagore and Gandhi, the fear of nationalism grew out of their experience of the record of anti-imperialism in India, and their attempt to link their concepts of Indianness with their understanding of a world where the language of progress had already established complete dominance. They did not want their society to be caught in a situation where the idea of the Indian nation would supersede that of the Indian civilization, and where the actual ways of life of Indians would be assessed solely in terms of the needs of an imaginary nation-state called India. They did not want the Indic civilization and lifestyle, to protect which the idea of the nation-state had supposedly been imported, to become pliable targets of social engineering guided by a theory of progress which, years later, made the economist Joan Robinson remark that the only thing that was worse than being colonized was not being colonized.

This essay explores, mainly through an analysis of the three explicitly political novels Tagore wrote, the political passions and philosophical awareness which pushed him towards a dissident concept of national ideology. This concept could survive for a while as an ideological strand in India's political culture, thanks to Gandhi's leadership of the national movement. But the dissent was doomed. For in this ideology, of patriotism rather than of nationalism, there was a built-in critique of nationalism and refusal to recognize the nation-state as the organizing principle of the Indian civilization and as the last word in the country's political life.

In examining this critique, the essay follows Tagore in his intellectual and emotional journey from the Hindu nationalism of his youth and the Brahminic-liberal humanism of his adulthood to the more radical, anti-statist, almost Gandhian social criticism of his last years. It was a journey made by one who had been a builder of modern consciousness in India, one who ended up—against his own instincts, as we shall see—almost a counter-modernist critic of the imperial West.

Tagore's 'Nationalism'

Humayun Kabir claims that the principles of non-alignment and federalism were Tagore's contributions to Indian foreign policy and the Indian Constitution, respectively.[2] He was the first great Indian, according to Kabir, who defied the Eurocentrism introduced by colonialism into India and revived India's ancient ties with Asia and Africa. As for federalism, Kabir says, it was Tagore who had first declared, towards the beginning of this century, that 'if God had so wished, he could have made all Indians speak one language . . . the unity of India has been and shall always be a unity in diversity.'[3]

Neither non-alignment nor federalism are solely Tagore's contributions to the culture of Indian politics. Both principles have been supported by Indian traditions, by a galaxy of influential anti-imperialist Indian political thinkers, and by the process of participatory politics in a multi-ethnic society. But few gave non-alignment and federalism greater legitimacy than Tagore did within the modern sector, for not even Gandhi could ram down the throat of the Indian literati his particular awareness of Indian traditions as Tagore did. Any modern Indian who claims that nationalism and the principles of the nation-state are universal has to take, willy-nilly, a position against both Gandhi and Tagore. And taking a position against the latter is often more painful. Gandhi was an outsider to modern India, Tagore an insider. Tagore participated in shaping the modern consciousness in India; his voice counted. When Jawaharlal Nehru claimed that he had two *gurus*—Gandhi and Tagore—what he left unsaid was that the former was his political *guru*, the latter the intellectual. In rejecting Tagore, one rejects an important part of the modern consciousness in India.

Nationalism against Civilization

What was Tagore's starting point in the matter of nationalism? In his brief, well-argued—though at places uncomfortably purple—book on nationalism, he distinguishes between government by kings and human races (his term for civilizations) and government by nations (his term for nation-states). He believes that 'government by the Nation is neither

[2]Humayun Kabir, 'Tagore was no Obscurantist', *Calcutta Municipal Gazette*, 1961, Tagore Birth Centenary Number, pp. 122–5.
[3]Ibid., p. 125.

British nor anything else; it is an applied science.'[4] It is universal, impersonal, and for that reason completely effective.[5]

Before the Nation came to rule over us (under British colonial rule) we had other governments which were foreign, and these, like all governments, had some elements of the machine in them. But the difference between them and the government by the Nation is like the difference between the handloom and the powerloom. In the products of the handloom the magic of man's living fingers finds its expression, and its hum harmonizes with the music of life. But the powerloom is relentlessly lifeless and accurate and monotonous in its production.[6]

Tagore admits that India's former governments were 'woefully lacking in many advantages of the modern governments'. However, they were not nation-states—'their texture was loosely woven, leaving gaps through which our own life sent its threads and imposed its designs.'[7] Squarely confronting the popular belief in the backwardness of pre-colonial India, Tagore says,

I am quite sure in those days we had things that were extremely distasteful to us. But we know that when we walk barefooted upon ground strewn with gravel, our feet come gradually to adjust themselves to the caprices of the inhospitable earth; while if the tiniest particle of gravel finds its lodgment inside our shoes we can never forget and forgive its intrusion. And these shoes are the government by the Nation—it is tight, it regulates our steps with a closed-up system, within which our feet have only the slightest liberty to make their own adjustments. Therefore, when you produce statistics to compare the number of gravels which our feet had to encounter in the former days with the paucity in the present regime, they hardly touch the real points . . . . The Nation of the West forges its iron chains of organization which are the most relentless and unbreakable that have ever been manufactured in the whole history of man.[8]

Does this relate only to colonial India? Will the analysis hold true even for an independent society ruled by its own nation-state? Tagore answers these questions, too. He says, to his non-Indian audience:

Not merely the subject races, but you who live under the delusion that you are free, are every day sacrificing your freedom and humanity to this fetish of nationalism . . . . It is no consolation to us to know that the weakening of

[4]Rabindranath Tagore, *Nationalism* (1917) (reprint, Madras: Macmillan, 1985), p. 10.
[5]Ibid.
[6]Ibid.
[7]Ibid., p. 14.
[8]Ibid., pp. 15–16.

humanity from which the present age is suffering is not limited to the subject races, and that its ravages are even more radical because insidious and voluntary in peoples who are hypnotized into believing that they are free.[9]

He recognizes that the standard advice to India will be: 'Form yourself into a nation, and resist this encroachment of the Nation.'[10] He rejects the advice because it assumes that human salvation lies in the 'dead rhythm of wheels and counterwheels' and on 'mutual protection, based on a conspiracy of fear'.[11] Instead, he looks back to what he sees as the real tradition of India, which is to work for 'an adjustment of races, to acknowledge the real differences between them, and yet seek some basis of unity.'[12] The basis for this tradition has been built in India at the social level, not the political, through saints like Nanak, Kabir, and Chaitanya. It is this solution—unity through acknowledgement of differences— that India has to offer to the world.[13] Tagore believes that India 'has never had a real sense of nationalism' and it would do India 'no good to compete with western civilization in its own field.'[14] India's ideals have evolved through her own history and if she desires to compete in political nationalism with other countries, it would be like Switzerland trying to compete with England in building a navy.[15]

Yet the educated Indian was trying 'to absorb some lessons from history contrary to the lessons of their ancestors'. To Tagore it was part of a larger problem: the entire East was 'attempting to take into itself a history, which [was] not the outcome of its own living.'[16] India, he believed, would have to pause and think before buying the more dazzling, transient products of contemporary history and paying for them by selling its own inheritance.[17]

The author of India's national anthem, one who had so deeply influenced Indian nationalism through his poetry, songs and active political participation, was outspoken in his views. Years earlier, he had spoken of nationalism as a *bhougalik apadevata*, a geographical demon, and

[9]Ibid., p. 18.
[10]Ibid., pp. 18–19.
[11]Ibid., p. 59.
[12]Ibid.
[13]Ibid., p. 64.
[14]Ibid.
[15]Ibid., p. 65.
[16]Ibid., p. 64.
[17]Ibid., p. 65.

Shantiniketan, his alternative university, as a temple dedicated to exorcise the demon.[18] He now declared even more directly that he was 'against the general idea of all nations.' For nationalism had become 'a great menace'.[19] Tagore recognized the sanctity of the anti-colonial movement and the futility of the method of 'begging' for 'scraps' used by the early Indian National Congress, at the time a liberal institution. But he also rejected the ideals of the 'extremists' which were based on western history.[20] Tagore sought a political freedom which would not be only the freedom to be powerful, for he knew,

Those people who have got their political freedom are not necessarily free, they are merely powerful. The passions which are unbridled in them are creating huge organizations of slavery in the disguise of freedom.[21]

Strong words indeed; spoken at a time when the spirit of nationalism had already made a place for itself in the Indian public consciousness and when some like Sri Aurobindo (1872–1950) had already located their nationalist passions in a theory of transcendence that made sense to many Indians:

Nationalism is an *avatar* (incarnation of divinity) and cannot be slain. Nationalism is a divinely appointed *shakti* of the Eternal and must do its god-given work before it returns to the bosom of the Universal Energy from which it came.[22]

Tagore was probably encouraged by the entry into Indian politics of a person who openly declared that his nationalism was 'intense internationalism', that it was 'not exclusive' because it recognized the eternal truth '*sic utere tuo ut alienum non laedas*'.[23] This new entrant, Mohandas Karamchand Gandhi, was not afraid to say, even if it meant disowning one important strand of anti-imperialism in India, 'Violent nationalism, otherwise known as imperialism, is the curse. Non-violent nationalism is a necessary condition of corporate or civilized life.'[24] And

---

[18] Letter to Jagadananda Roy, quoted in Seema Bandopadhyaya, *Rabindrasangite Swadeshchetana* (Calcutta: National Book Agency, 1986), p. 22.

[19] Tagore, *Nationalism*, pp. 66–7.

[20] Ibid., p. 68.

[21] Ibid., p. 73.

[22] Sri Aurobindo, 'The Life of Nationalism', in *On Nationalism, First Series* (Pondicherry: Sri Aurobindo Ashram, 1965), pp. 33–9; see p. 39.

[23] M.K. Gandhi, *Collected Works* (New Delhi: Publications Division, Government of India, 1969), Vol. 32, p. 45; and *Collected Works*, 1971, Vol. 45, p. 343.

[24] Gandhi, *Collected Works*, Vol. 25, p. 369.

the Indian freedom movement, therefore, was 'India's contribution to peace'.[25]

The Novels

The Home and the World

Against the stated political ideology of Tagore, we shall now examine the three explicitly political novels he wrote, treating them as vital psychological and cultural clues to his concept of politics and his political selfhood. We shall do so with the awareness that some of his other novels—for instance two early works, *Bouthakuranir Hat* and *Rajarshi*—also have clear political messages;[26] the vicissitudes of power and the corruption brought about by it were amongst Tagore's favourite themes. However, the novels analysed here are ones which give a central place to the political debates taking place in India over the methods of the Swadeshi movement and social reform in general.

Of the three novels, *Gora* is technically closest to the nineteenth-century idea of a proper novel. But it has the worst English translation of the three and almost invariably disappoints the English-speaking reader. There have, however, been excellent translations of the novel into the Indian languages and its reputation and influence are built on them. *Gora* was written in 1909, when the poet was forty-eight.[27] It was Tagore's sixth novel, counting his unfinished first novel, *Karuna*.

The second novel considered here is *Ghare-Baire*, available in English as *The Home and the World*.[28] Published in 1916, it was Tagore's eighth novel. The third is *Char Adhyay*, translated slightly more competently into English as *Four Chapters*.[29] It was Tagore's thirteenth and last novel. When published in 1934, it immediately sparked off a first-class public controversy because of its theme.

[25]Ibid., Vol. 48, pp. 226–7.

[26]Rabindranath Tagore, *Bouthakuranir Hat* and *Rajarshi*, in *Rabindra-Rachanabali* (reprint, Calcutta: Vishwabharati, 1988), Vol. I, pp. 607–98, 703–83.

[27]Rabindranath Tagore, *Gora*, in *Rabindra-Rachanabali* (reprint, Calcutta: West Bengal Government, 1961), Vol. 9, pp. 1–350. English tr. Anon. (Calcutta: Macmillan, 1924, reprint 1965). All quotations are from the English translation.

[28]Rabindranath Tagore, *Ghare-Baire*, in *Rabindra-Rachanabali* (Calcutta: West Bengal Government, 1961), Vol. 9, pp. 405–550. English tr. S.N. Tagore, *The Home and the World* (Madras: Macmillan, 1919). All quotations are from the English translation.

[29]Rabindranath Tagore, *Char Adhyay*, in *Rabindra-Rachanabali* (Calcutta: Viswabharati, 1986), Vol. 7, pp. 375–418. To bear comparison with the quotations from *Pather Dabi*, all quotations have been translated from the Bengali version.

As we shall see, Tagore's political concerns in the three novels were roughly the same; they did not change over the twenty-five years of his life that the writing of the three novels spanned. This analysis therefore will not follow the historical order in which a problem that is primarily political-psychological in *Gora* becomes predominantly political–sociological in *Ghare-Baire* and political–ethical in *Char Adhyay*. Instead, the analysis imposes a psychological sequence on the historical order by tracing the political sociology of *Ghare-Baire* and the problem of political ethics in *Char Adhyay* to the political psychology of *Gora*.

Bimala's Choice

The story of *Ghare-Baire* is simply told. Bimala is a highly intelligent, fiery girl whose very name conveys both everyday plainness and transcendent power. She marries into a rich, aristocratic family proud of the beauty of its women and equally of its dissipated, self-destructive men. However, her husband Nikhilesh or Nikhil, she finds out, has broken with family tradition. Not only has he married in her a girl who is not beautiful; he is a well-educated, modern man, given to scholarship and social work.

Bimala's main support in Nikhil's family turns out to be his grandmother, who adores Nikhil and believes Bimala provides an auspicious presence in the house. The grandmother is the one who vehemently defends Nikhil when he founds a bank to give easy, unsecured loans to poor peasants in his area, and loses a fortune through it. She considers it a small price to pay for Nikhil's refusal to be drawn into the 'normal' lifestyle of the men of his family.

Nikhil adores his wife who is happily absorbed in her domestic life, but has other ambitions for her. A liberal humanist, he wants her to enter the modern world by learning the English language and English manners and he engages an English governess, Miss Gilby, to instruct her. Gradually, Bimala gains acquaintance with the outer world through Miss Gilby who virtually becomes a member of the household.

There are also two widowed sisters-in-law of Nikhil in the household—in the English version only one of the characters is retained—who provide the counterpoint to Bimala. They are uneducated and petty-minded, but Nikhil does not seem concerned with their education or exposure to the world. To some readers, though, they may emerge as self-willed women outside the control of the hero, what Bimala herself might have become, had she been less sensitive, impassioned, or alert.

It is the era of the Swadeshi movement, and one day a friend of Nikhil's, Sandip, comes to the house. Sandip, true to his name, is a fiery nationalist leader. Nikhil has been supporting him financially, much against his wife's wishes. Bimala had seen Sandip's splendid features in photographs but has never quite liked him, feeling that he lacked character, that 'too much of base alloy had gone into (the) making' of his handsome face and 'the light in his eyes somehow did not shine true.' However, when Bimala hears him speak in public she is thrilled, and inspired by his ideas; he appears like a conqueror of Bengal who deserved 'the consecration of a woman's benediction'.[30] For the first time Bimala feels unhappy at not being 'surpassingly beautiful', since she wants Indian men to 'realize the country's goddess in its womanhood'. Above all, she wants Sandip to find the *shakti* or divine power of the motherland manifest in her.[31] She invites him to dinner at home.

Over dinner, Bimala and Sandip discuss the national movement. Sandip makes a show of being impressed by her and invites her to rise above her diffidence and become 'the Queen Bee' of the movement. He promises that his associates would rally around her, that she would be their centre as well as inspiration.[32] As for himself, he is more direct: 'The blessing of the country must be voiced by its goddess.'[33]

Bimala is carried away by all this. She starts meeting Sandip regularly and Sandip begins to consult her on every aspect of the nationalist movement. As Bimala recounts it,

I who was plain before had suddenly become beautiful. I who before had been of no account now felt in myself all the splendour of Bengal itself . . . . My relations with all the world underwent a change. Sandip babu made it clear how all the country was in need of me.[34]

This change acquires for Bimala transcendental features. She would later remember the experience in almost mystical terms—'Divine strength had come to me, it was something which I had never felt before, which was beyond myself.'[35] Sandip nurses her new-found sense of magical power and is quick to establish an equation between his political mission and the 'natural' politics of women, as opposed to the socially-learned politics of men.

In the heart of a woman Truth takes flesh and blood. Woman knows how to be cruel . . . . It is our women who will save the country . . . . Men can only think,

[30]Tagore, *The Home and the World*, p. 34.
[31]Ibid., p. 24.
[32]Ibid., p. 37.
[33]Ibid., p. 26.
[34]Ibid., p. 43.
[35]Ibid.

but you women have a way of understanding without thinking. Woman was created out of God's own fancy. Man, he had to hammer into shape.[36]

Bimala now goes all-out to help Sandip in his work, neglecting her husband, home and friends. She even 'takes' from the household money to give to the movement. Her love for Sandip has, however, a tragic end; Bimala loses both the home and the world, for Sandip runs away once large-scale violence, instigated by his speeches, breaks out and he is shown to be merely a shallow and callous manipulator; and Nikhil dies trying to quell the violence born of Sandip's version of nationalism. The angry, bitter outburst of one of Nikhil's sisters-in-law at his death reveals the deeper conviction of the family: it is a death brought about by Bimala, by her cannibalistic impulses.

It also becomes clear that the tragedy is not merely a personal one, for the social divide brought about by nationalism is more permanent than the political movement it spawns. Bimala's identification with the country becomes a literal one; the destruction of her home and her world foreshadows the destruction of the society.

The story of *Ghare-Baire* is told through the first-person narratives of the three main characters. But there is no Roshomon effect; it is the same story, fleshed out by all three in their own ways. The aim is to reveal differences in personality through differences in perspective, not the plural nature of reality itself. The issues and personalities of the main protagonists do not change from narrative to narrative. There is, in effect, a single, straight narrative from the point of view of Bimala, symbolizing Bengal, who is shown confronting the choice between two forms of patriotism. Though the background is the Swadeshi movement, in which Tagore himself had actively participated and for which he had written some of his finest poetry and songs, the novel's message is clear: nationalism has enormous hidden costs. To make this point, the British remain a shadowy presence in the novel, which is essentially an exploration of the Indian consciousness as it confronts, grapples with, and resists the colonial experience. The author splits this consciousness into two parts: one finds expression in the contrast between the hero and the villain, the other in the conflicts within the heroine.

As for the contrast between the hero and the villain, one gradually learns from the narrative that the aristocratic landowner Nikhil is no less a patriot than the demagogue Sandip. But Nikhil's patriotism is not as dazzling or strained as his friend's. Sandip believes that God is manifest in one's own country and it must be worshipped. Nikhil believes

[36]Ibid., pp. 31, 43–4.

that, in that case, God must be manifest in other countries, too, and there is no scope for hatred of them. He believes that countries which live by oppressing others have to answer for it; their history has not yet ended.[37] Sandip and, under his spell Bimala, hold that one has the right to be humanly covetous on behalf of one's country, while Nikhil feels that as a human one should avoid projecting individual evil into the self-definition of a country. To Sandip, Nikhil's position is staid, unimaginative and unfeeling;[38] to Nikhil, Sandip's nationalism is only another form of covetous self love.[39] It is easy to guess which ideology wins in the short run: Sandip becomes a successful political leader who invades and overruns Nikhil's family life.

Bimala's first instincts were right. Sandip *is* inauthentic, both as a patriot and as a lover. He is only a professional politician. Bimala's love for him, however, is genuine, though it is of a special kind. Though there is a physical component to it, the love is not entirely blind infatuation: she is shrewd enough to sense Sandip's shallowness but considers it her patriotic duty to ignore it. Fired by the spirit of nationalism and a search for freedom which demands no deep political vision and partly stems from the defiant idealism of youth, Bimala finds in Sandip both a heroic role model and a love-object which she cannot break away from.

Nikhil, in contrast, is low-key and unheroic both as a lover and patriot, and he is outshone by Sandip's flamboyance till a tragic, irreversible sequence of political, social, and personal events reveals his true heroism to Bimala.

Bimala, therefore, is the link between the two forms of patriotism the men represent. Not only is she the symbol for which Sandip and Nikhil fight, but her personality incorporates the contesting selves of the two protagonists and becomes the battlefield on which the two forms of patriotism fight for supremacy. In this inner battle, Nikhil's form of patriotism eventually wins, but at enormous social and personal cost.

There is another, less consequential, link between the protagonists: Amulya, an idealistic young student, with whom Bimala has a special relationship. Amulya works closely with Sandip and as a result, finds out quite early Sandip's instrumental concept of patriotism. Caught between his affection and respect for Bimala and his awareness of what Sandip is, Amulya turns out to be the real victim of Bimala's politics, and Bimala knows this. His death at the end of the story foreshadows Tagore's later anxiety about the nature of the violence let loose by nationalism.

[37]Ibid., pp. 28–9.
[38]Ibid., p. 29.
[39]Ibid., p. 35.

The violence, a full-fledged Hindu–Muslim riot, is the inevitable corollary of Sandip's nationalism, Tagore suggests. The riot that kills Nikhil—his fate is left unclear in the novel, though in Satyajit Ray's film he dies—is set off by the ruin that poor Muslim traders face due to the nationalist attempts to boycott foreign goods immediately and unconditionally.

The violence is a natural by-product of the strategy of mobilization employed by Sandip and his enthusiastic followers. Such a mobilization requires, Tagore implies, symbols embedded in an exclusivist cultural–religious idiom. *Ghare-Baire* does not say why it should be so, but there are hints that, for Tagore, this form of populism combines mob politics with *realpolitik*. It is this combination which Tagore holds responsible for the growth of communalism, nor religious differences, not even the representation of these differences in the political arena. Sandip precipitates a communal conflagration not merely by refusing to accommodate the interests of the Muslims as a community, and by imposing on them glaringly unequal suffering and unequal sacrifice for the nationalist cause, but also by depending on a form of political stridency which requires primeval sentiments to be mobilized and acted out.

One remarkable aspect of the novel is Tagore's brief but prescient reconstruction of the process by which a communal divide takes place in Nikhil's world. As Tagore tells the story, the image of the Mussalman in Bengali upper-caste Hindu minds emerges as that of a primal force, representing untempered, unmediated, 'primitive' impulses. However, Mussalmans are also part of the 'natural' scene in Bengal and are in communion with similar primordial forces within Hinduism which, by common consent, have to be contained. Thus, beef-eating among Muslims is balanced by buffalo-sacrifice among the predominantly *shakto*, upper-caste Hindus of the area. But once Sandip's nationalism reaches down to find roots in the primordial, to give nationalism a base in the deepest of passions, it induces a similar regression in Muslims. On Nikhil's estate, Muslims who had more or less given up eating beef turn to it now on ideological grounds. To them, too, religion becomes less a faith or a way of life than an ideology.[40]

Lukacs' Choice

How incommunicable such an approach to anti-colonialism can sometimes be is best evidenced by Georg Lukacs' caustic review, published in

[40]Ibid., pp. 156–9. For further discussion of the split between religion-as-ideology and religion-as-faith, see Ashis Nandy, 'The Politics of Secularism and the Recovery of Religious Tolerance', *Alternatives*, 1988, 13(3), pp. 171–94.

1922, of *The Home and the World*.[41] It is true that the novel in translation fails to convey the subtlety of the original and Tagore's magical power
over words, notably his poetic use of prose. Also, Tagore comes off in
the English version as moralistic and 'consciously attitudinizing' in his
narrative.[42] Yet one suspects that behind Lukacs' critical judgement there
are specific political barriers erected by the European critical consciousness which Tagore could not penetrate. Lukacs, given his Eurocentric
Marxism, would find it difficult to admit the extent to which his critical
apparatus was designed to maintain a hegemonic cultural discourse. For,
if Lukacs is right and Tagore cannot but fail to communicate with
Europe, Satyajit Ray's reasonably faithful film version of *The Home and
the World* should make little sense to the modern world fifty years after
the novel was first written. Yet, Ray's work does not raise doubts about
Tagore's anti-imperialism either in India or in Europe.

Lukacs notes with great sarcasm that Tagore's hero is an aristocrat.
He ignores that Nikhil, even if by default, stands with a religious minority
which is also the poorest section of the society, and confronts boldly a
middle-class-dominated, avowedly majoritarian formation that, modelling
itself on India's colonial rulers, is dismissive towards the peripheries of
the society. Lukacs says:

Tagore himself is—as imaginative writer and as thinker—a wholly insignificant
figure. His creative powers are non-existent; his characters pale stereotypes;
his stories threadbare and uninteresting; and his sensibility is meagre,
insubstantial . . . .
The intellectual conflict in the novel is concerned with the use of violence . . . .
The hypothesis is that India is an oppressed, enslaved country, yet Mr Tagore
shows no interest in this question . . . .
. . . . A pamphlet—and one resorting to the lowest tools of libel—is what
Tagore's novel is, in spite of its tediousness and want of spirit.
This stance represents nothing less than the *ideology of the eternal
subjection of India* . . . .
This propagandistic, demagogically one-sided stance renders the novel
completely worthless from the artistic angle . . . .
But Tagore's creative powers do not stretch to a decent pamphlet . . . . The

[41]Georg Lukacs, 'Tagore's Gandhi Novel: Review of Rabindranath Tagore, *The
Home and the World*', in *Reviews and Articles*, tr. Peter Palmer (London: Merlin,
1983), pp. 8–11.
[42]Kalyan K. Chatterjee, 'Lukacs on Tagore: Ideology and Literary Criticism',
Indian Literature, 1988, 31(3), pp. 153–60; see p. 158. This paper is a fascinating attempt
to place Tagore's novel within its cultural context and to separate the novel as a socio-
political document from its more time-and-space-bound stylistic elements.

'spiritual' aspects of his story, separated from the nuggets of Indian wisdom into which it is tricked out, is a petty bourgeois yarn of the shoddiest kind . . . (his) 'wisdom' was put at the intellectual service of the British police.[43]

Lukacs gives a number of reasons for his distaste for the novel. Three of them are obvious. First, Tagore raises the issue of violence in the context of nationalism and ventures a moral—according to Lukacs, spiritual—critique of the anti-colonial struggle. Second, Tagore glorifies conventionality, family life and one-sidedly turns the nationalist leader Sandip into a 'romantic adventurer'. The extent of Lukacs' knowledge of Indian politics can be gauged from his belief that Sandip is a caricature of Gandhi. For some strange reason, this alleged attack on Gandhi goes against Tagore, because Lukacs seems naïvely unaware that he has neatly displaced on to Tagore the Comintern's evaluation of Gandhi ventured two years earlier in September 1920, at its First Congress in Moscow. That evaluation (which Lukacs did not contest), states: 'Tendencies like Gandhism, thoroughly imbued with religious conceptions, idealize the most backward and economically most reactionary forms of social life, preach passivity and repudiate the class struggle, and in the process of the development of the revolution become transformed into an openly reactionary force.'[44] Third, Lukacs thinks that Tagore has failed to write a proper novel with detailed development of characters. The characters in *Ghare-Baire* are almost caricatures, the plot is a trivial one and the tone partisan.

Ghare-Baire is a nineteenth-century novel, written in a nineteenth-century style. It is only chronologically a product of this century. The novel's English translation, whatever its other demerits, is fortunately not designed to introduce somewhat provincial European intellectuals to the plural traditions of the Indian freedom movement and the debates within it. Lukacs, having read *The Home and the World* second- or third-hand and living in what he believed to be the middle kingdom of world literature, is naturally willing to believe that, to Tagore, Gandhi in the form of Sandip is the rabble-rouser, seducing India in the form of Bimala from a gentle colonial figure, Nikhil, who is keen to introduce her to the modern world.

As we shall see, Tagore provides a slightly more nuanced approach to the interconnected problems of violence, anti-imperialism and nationalism. But to understand where Lukacs goes wrong, we must look beyond

[43]Ibid., pp. 8–11.
[44]Quoted in Chatterjee, 'Lukacs on Tagore', p. 156.

his Eurocentrism and his absolute faith in his culture's critical apparatus, into the nature of the enterprise which Tagore's political novels are.

The concept of the novel entered South Asian societies in the nineteenth century as part of the colonial experience. There are many descriptions of this process of assimilation, which first took place in eastern India. The process itself is not particularly relevant to our concerns, though its end-products are. The genre quickly became popular and entered the interstices of the Indian literary world; Bankimchandra Chattopadhyay (1838–94) was already India's first established novelist when the novel as a literary form entered other Asian and African societies.

Bankimchandra was influenced by a number of English novelists. Of them, for some reason, he found Walter Scott to be the most congenial. Many contemporary critics were to call Bankim the Scott of India. Yet Bankim's concerns and world-view were fundamentally different; he only borrowed from Scott something of his narrative method.[45] These influences and the subsequent popularity of the novel form in India should not blind one to the sophisticated narrative traditions that predated the novel in the region and which, once the genre was established, entered it as if through the back door. *Upanyasa*, the Bengali term for the novel, itself indicates that the novel was expected partly to serve the purposes of—and to seek legitimacy and sustenance from—the older tradition of *upakathas*, fairy-story-like narratives surviving in the public memory, often as morality tales. This tradition is alive in *Ghare-Baire* and it dominates *Char Adhyay* in many ways.

At first, the novel served as a residual category for many South Asian thinkers. Individual novelists gave it a more personalized form, before such liberties became common in Europe: after all, the reason for the popularity of the novel form in South Asia was its ability to take up issues and themes that were peripheral to traditional forms of literature. For instance, the novel could be directly used, Indian writers found out, for political, polemical, and satirical purposes. Tagore himself used it mostly as an extended short story. Once he had written his early novels— *Gora* being one of them—he chose to move from the prose form of a conventional novel to a poeticized form more suited to allegorical tales of the kind which were to appear on the English and French literary scene much later. In the Indian context, one could say that he started writing contemporary *upakathas* or Puranas rather than *upanyasas*.

---

[45]For an analysis of some of these concerns, see Sudipta Kaviraj's as-yet, untitled work on Bankimchandra Chattopadhyay (New Delhi: Nehru Memorial Museum and Library, 1988), mimeo.

This specific cultural experience with the novel was alien to Lukacs to whom the categories of literary criticism could not but be universal, which in his case meant exclusively European. Hence his two devastating errors of political judgement which no Indian social analyst can ignore, for the errors arise from an ethnocentrism that verges on racism.

The first of these errors is a ludicrous one and only someone like Lukacs could have made it. The 'villain' in *Ghare-Baire* is not a caricature of Gandhi. (Gandhi was hardly a part of the Indian political scene when Sandip was created in 1915–16. Tagore had observed from a distance Gandhi's South African *satyagraha*, and the two had met in March 1915; this limited acquaintance made him an admirer of Gandhi. His reservations about important aspects of Gandhi's politics and counter-modernism came later.) Sandip is, if anything, anti-Gandhi and criticism of him is an oblique defence of Gandhian politics before such a politics had taken shape, besides being a bitter criticism of sectarian Hindu nationalism, which at the time was a powerful component of Indian anti-imperialism. Creating a character like Sandip at that time would actually have deeply offended many Bengali revolutionaries who would have seen in him an attack on their own ideology, as well as character.

Second, *Ghare-Baire* offers a critique of nationalism but also a perspective on the form anti-imperialism should take in a multi-ethnic, multi-religious society where a colonial political economy encourages the growth of a complex set of dependencies. In such a society, the politically and economically weak and the culturally less westernized might be sometimes more dependent on the colonial system than the privileged and the enculturated. The novel suggests that a nationalism which steam-rollers society into making a uniform stand against colonialism, ignoring the unequal sacrifices imposed thereby on the poorer and the weaker, will tear apart the social fabric of the country, even if it helps to formally decolonize the country.

Lukacs does, however, get the title of his review right. *Ghare-Baire* is Tagore's Gandhi novel. It anticipates the low-key, unheroic, consensual nationalism which Gandhi wanted a multi-ethnic society like India to follow. For it was on such a consensus that Gandhi sought to build his more complex critique of the West and the western—that is, modern—civilization.

The Politics of New Violence

Char Adhyay begins by recognizing that the propagation of violent revolt against colonialism in India was an 'appropriate' transition to the violence associated with the modern scientific world-view—from the language of sacrifice and feud that a traditional society uses, to the language of vivisection or scientized violence.[46] From the time of the Boer war Tagore had been sensitive to the growing role of violence in human affairs. Some of his poems in *Naivedya*, published in 1901, reflect that sensitivity. One even knows that when he wrote *Char Adhyay*, Tagore had already become aware of the new forms of violence let loose on the world by modern technology. In the travelogue *Parasye*, based on his experiences on the way to Iran in 1932, he had commented on the special form of sanitized violence increasingly available in the modern world, thanks to the discovery of new means of 'distant violence' such as aerial bombing. Such forms reified not merely the individual humanity of their targets but also the reality of violence itself.[47]

Colonialism had a special role to play in the growth and legitimation of this sanitized violence, both as a source of such violence and as a system that encouraged its victims to mimic the style of violence practised by their oppressors. Colonialism, after all, was not merely the product of a theory of progress that hierarchized races, cultures, and civilizations; it was also a by-product of the Baconian theory of objective, scientific, 'true' knowledge which strictly partitioned off the observer from the observed, the subject from the object of knowledge, the enlightened agents of history from the passive ahistorical laity, the rational from the non-rational.[48] For the theory of progress grounded the right to rule oneself not so much in democratic principles as in the ability to run a modern nation-state objectively, rationally or scientifically—all defined according to the Baconian world-view.

The underlying evolutionist assumptions of colonialism did not leave the colonized cultures untouched. Many living in these cultures sensed that they were victims of a world-view which saw the alien human beings inhabiting Africa, Asia, and South America as closer to nature and therefore, given the growing objectification of nature, as things. In turn, many of these victims began to reinterpret their alien rulers and to see them, through a complex process of identification with the aggressor, as

[46]The first part of this section is almost entirely based on a part of Veena Das and Ashis Nandy, 'Violence, Victimhood and the Language of Silence', *Contributions to Indian Sociology*, 1985, 19, pp. 177–95.

[47]Rabindranath Tagore, '*Parasye*', *Rabindra-Rachanabali* (Calcutta: West Bengal Government, 1961), Vol. 10, pp. 747–802; see pp. 749–56. For a discussion of the cultural context in which the awareness of the new scientized violence emerged, see Ashis Nandy, 'Science, Authoritarianism and Violence: On the Scope and Limits of Isolation Outside the Clinic', in *Traditions, Tyranny, and Utopias* (New Delhi: Oxford University Press, 1987; reprint, 1992), pp. 95–126.

[48]Ashis Nandy, *The Intimate Enemy: Loss and Recovery of Self under Colonialism* (New Delhi: Oxford University Press, 1983; reprint, 1992).

closer to things. Among the first to diagnose this process and to identify the new language of violence emerging in the Indian political culture was Tagore, by then an admirer of Gandhi even though he had already rejected important aspects of the Gandhian world-view.

When in 1934 Tagore wrote *Char Adhyay*, one of his slighter novels according to most critics, he chose to set it even more explicitly within a political context. This novel, too, grapples with the dual encounter between East and West, and between politics and ethics, against a colonial background. However, unlike *Ghare-Baire*, *Char Adhyay* specifically introduces and deals with the changing nature of violence in contemporary politics. For it was written after World War I, the Nazi takeover in Germany, and the growing violence in Indian public life despite the by then predominant presence of Gandhi.

Through the development of characters rather than the plot, and the depiction of the characters' inner struggle, Tagore's own critique of terrorist violence is set out. The preface to *Char Adhyay* states that the inspiration for the novel was the life of Brahmabandhab Upadhyay (1861–1907), a Catholic theologian and Vedantist scholar, editor, social worker and nationalist revolutionary, who had been a pioneer in the use of terror as a political weapon. Tagore, according to the preface, was attracted by the personality as well as work of Upadhyay, who was one of the first critics to recognize his literary worth. The preface then goes on to describe Upadhyay's last visit to Tagore:

At the time I had not met him for a long time. I thought, having sensed my difference with him on the method (*pranali*) of the nationalist movement, he had become hostile and contemptuous towards me.

. . . . In those days of blinding madness, one day when I was sitting alone in a third floor room at Jorasanko, suddenly came Upadhyay. In our conversation we recapitulated some of the issues we had discussed earlier. After the chat he bid me goodbye and got up. He went up to the door, turned towards me and stood. Then said, 'Rabibabu, I have fallen very low.' After this he did not wait any longer. I clearly understood that it was only to say these heart-rending words that he had come in the first place. But by then he had been caught in the web of his actions (*karmajal*), there was no means of escape.

That was my last meeting and last words with him.

At the beginning of the novel this event needed to be recounted.[49]

Following the outcry over the novel in Bengali nationalist circles who were still fired by the ideal of a violent revolution led by a few exemplary revolutionaries, Tagore withdrew the preface from later editions and

[49]Suddhasatva Bosu, *Rabindranather Char Adhyay* (Calcutta: Bharati Publications, 1979), pp. 6–7.

claimed that the novel was mainly a love story. It does seem, however, that whatever Tagore may have thought later, at the time of writing he was more concerned with the exploration of the inner world of political extremists and especially the loss of self in Atin, a young revolutionary caught in the violence. Despite this concern though, the characters in the novel remain primarily symbols or mouthpieces rather than complex many-faceted persons.

Ela's Choice

Char Adhyay is the story of a group of Bengali revolutionaries who are under pressure from the colonial police. Early in the novel we are told that informers have begun to take an unusual interest in some members of the group who outwardly lead a conventional, apolitical life. As the pressure mounts, not only does the group begin to disintegrate, so do its members. Under stress, the psychological and moral costs of living the life of a terrorist are bared and the cultural rootlessness of the movement is underscored. So that what begins as a struggle for freedom becomes, by the end of the story, an invitation to a new form of bondage.

The story of *Char Adhyay* revolves around three persons: Indranath, a revolutionary leader; Atindra or Atin, scion of an impoverished aristocratic family and a young recruit to the revolutionary cause; and Ela, an attractive girl who is also a member of Indranath's group and in love with Atin. The plot is simple: it is woven around the course of Ela and Atin's relationship. Attracted by Ela, Atin joins the revolutionary group led by Indranath, a revolutionary trained in Europe, a brilliant student of science and languages and also skilled at armed and unarmed combat. But Indranath's most striking trait is a dispassionate, fully scientific, ruthless, commitment to what can only be called instrumental rationality. Under Indranath's tutelage, Atin becomes competent at his revolutionary tasks but also begins to lose his humanity. Atin's love for Ela provides him with a partial escape from this dehumanization, but the situation is complicated by the fact that though Ela takes the initiative in establishing a relationship with him, she refuses to marry him because of her vow to remain a celibate in the service of the country.

Finally, Ela herself becomes a liability to the group. The task of eliminating her falls on Atin, and in a moving last chapter, there is a confrontation between Atin and Ela. Both are aware that the meeting must end in Ela's execution. Ela is a willing victim; she refuses the anaesthesia that Atin offers her not only because she wants to die fully self-aware but because to die at Atin's hand has an erotic significance for her. Further, she has a sense of guilt over Atin's penury and devastated health. Though roughly of the same age, she had occasionally claimed to be older than him and felt responsible for him.

For Atin this is the final revelation that he has fallen from his own distinctive *svadharma* (code of conduct) and *svabhava* (individual specificity). He recognizes that Ela is willing to be sacrificed not because she accepts the meaning given to it by Indranath's modern nationalism but because of a privatized meaning, derived from her relationship with him, Atin.

It is necessary to describe briefly the structure of the novel. The four chapters which give the novel its title are preceded by a prologue, which is purely narrative. It gives us the life-history of Ela, and we learn that she has had an unhappy childhood, seeing throughout her early years her mother tyrannizing over her submissive father, a professor of psychology. Later, in her uncle's home, she found a similar situation: her aunt turned out to be petty, jealous, and narrow-minded. These experiences left Ela with a distaste for marriage and encouraged her to live the life of an independent woman.

This life story is not provided for other characters in the novel. It is as if Tagore had again chosen to make his heroine the battleground where different political ideologies and moralities were being tested out and as if Ela, as a woman and symbol of her society, needed to be given more substance than the various competing social engineers.

Each of the four chapters begins with a brief narrative that provides the context for the dialogues that follow. The narrator, rather like a cameraman, records a series of nearly static interpersonal situations. The first chapter is in the form of a dialogue between Ela and Indranath in a cafe, from which the reader gathers that Indranath takes pride in using his followers as instruments for furthering the nationalist cause. He repeatedly uses the language of sacrifice and compares himself to Krishna, who advised Arjuna to kill his kinsmen in the service of *kshatradharma*, the warrior's code of conduct. Yet the difference between the two is also established by Indranath's clinical attitude toward his own followers. Ela is obviously recruited for her ability to attract young men like Atin to the revolutionary group.

The second chapter establishes the growing attraction between Ela and Atin through a conversation that takes place in Ela's bedroom. Though Ela admits she loves Atin, she refuses to marry him for she has vowed to remain celibate. In the third chapter Ela goes to Atin's hideout and sees the utter penury to which he has been reduced. She offers then to marry him but it is a futile reparative gesture from a puppet attempting to be an autonomous being. In the final chapter Atin goes to Ela's home to execute her. As the two converse, Atin reflects upon the journey he has completed to reach this stage in his life. Again, the characters reveal themselves through their conversation; nothing is allowed to intervene between the characters and the reader, as if the experiential reality of violence could be understood only through an intellectual discourse.

It is obvious from the above that Tagore allotted the personal traits of Upadhyay to both Indranath and Atin. Indranath is the theologian of the new violence and the Gita is his bible. He is the *mantradata*, the giver of *mantra*, in Tagore's words. The transformation of self and the inner experience of violence is projected on to Atin. At this plane, Indranath as the prototype of Upadhyay and Atin as his disciple are caught in an ambivalent relationship. Indranath senses Atin's imperfect commitment to nationalism; Atin discovers Indranath's betrayal of his civilization. Yet, neither can disown the other, for each is the other's double.[50]

The author makes clear that Indranath's training of Atin—who is not fully amenable to the training, being not only a revolutionary, but a poet, and a lover too—also represents a ruthless training of Indranath's own self; and that Ela's death signifies not only the final destruction of Atin's selfhood but also the final defeat and fall of Indranath. Through this defeat and fall Tagore tries to convey something of the meaning of Upadhyay's anguished reference to his having fallen very low.

The fact that the novel begins with the story of Ela's life suggests two points. First, it is into Ela's world that Indranath and Atin are to enter and not the other way round. Second, Atin comes face to face with his own loss of humanity only as it may be registered with regard to Ela, recalling the confession of Upadhyay to the poet himself. In the final encounter Atin describes himself as *svadharma-bhrasta* (fallen from his own *dharma*) and *svabhavachyuta* (fallen from natural inclination). His own relation to Indranath, his revolutionary leader and teacher, is movingly summarized:

The theoretician (*mantradata*) said, 'All of you collectively tug at a thick rope (of the juggernaut) closing your eyes—this is your only work.' Thousands of boys began doing so. Many fell under the wheels, many were maimed for life. Suddenly the theory changed; the order came to pull in a reverse direction. The chariot (*ratha*) turned the other way. Those whose bones were broken (as a result) could not be put back to health. The invalids were swept away into the dust heaps on

[50]I have in mind here the clinical picture drawn by the likes of Otto Rank. See his *The Double: A Psychoanalytic Study* (tr. and ed.) H. Tucker, Jr. (University of North Carolina Press, 1971).

the roadside. The faith in one's own strength was destroyed so fully that everyone proudly agreed to mould oneself after the official ideal of the robot. When in response to the strings pulled by the leader everyone began to dance the same dance, strangely enough everyone thought it to be a dance of power. The moment the puppeteer loosened his strings, thousands became superfluous.[51]

The question that remains to be asked is whether, in Tagore's view, violence always led to loss of self or whether there was something specific in the way in which violence was used in the freedom movement in Bengal that was under criticism. One has to remember that the concept of necessary and legitimate violence was present in Indian society; that legitimate violence *was* linked to the notion of sacrificial renunciation.[52] It is no accident that *dharmayuddha* and *yajnayuddha* (just war or war as sacrifice) were the operative concepts borrowed from the Gita. Much of the available folklore on just wars also counterpoises the fight for *dharma* against the fight for gain. One must fight to the last for a just cause, they seem to say, regardless of the strategy or victory. Were the revolutionaries continuing this tradition of legitimate violence or had they in fact reversed it?

It does seem that Tagore had sensed the basic difference between sacrificial violence and the new political violence which made instrumental use of people. Sacrificial violence is justified only if it involves self-sacrifice, that is, if sacrifice *to* god is balanced by sacrifice *of* god,[53] and this necessarily demands the consent of those sacrificed within the meaning-world of the sacrifice. Sacrifice loses its sanctity if awareness of the subjectivity, both of those who are compelled to be victims and of those others who identify themselves with them in the community, is lost. As Indranath trains himself to become 'ruthless', 'impersonal', and

---

[51]Tagore, *Char Adhyay*, p. 398. The tacit assumption here is that the theory of dissent developed by the likes of Indranath represents the internalization of the new language of the state that the colonial power has brought into India's political discourse. It also emphasizes the control and technological manipulation of subject populations and the total impersonalization of the public realm.

It would be interesting to compare the discourse on violent resistance in *Char Adhyay* with both Bankimchandra Chattopadhyay's *Anandamath* and Saratchandra Chattopadhyay's *Pather Dabi* which are partly the ideological counterparts of Tagore's novel. *Pather Dabi* tries to bypass the issue of 'thingification'—as Aimé Césaire calls it in his *Discourse on Colonialism* (New York: Monthly Review Press, 1972)—by either legitimizing counter-violence as resistance or by using the language of feud. Saratchandra in this respect might be read as Indranath's self-justification outside the bounds of *Char Adhyay*. However, as we shall see below, the heroine of *Pather Dabi* defies its author to reproblematize the issue.

[52]Das and Nandy, 'Violence, Victimhood and the Language of Silence'.

[53]Veena Das, 'The Language of Sacrifice', *Man* (n.s.), 1983, *18*, pp. 445–62.

'scientific', it becomes necessary for him to snap the emotional link between him and his followers, now being used as so many puppets. He has to manipulate the inner world of his followers and empty it of moral autonomy.

Franz Fanon's defence of exorcism through violence was that the only way victims could recover their subjectivity was by 'objectifying', in their turn, the violent oppressors. Tagore, on the other hand, seems to have been persuaded that a ruthless, clinical theology of violence must inevitably lead to a loss of self and of signification. To him, the continuity with the language of the Gita, used so frequently by Indian votaries of the new violence, only masked a discontinuity in concepts. In this respect, *Char Adhyay* represented a break in the structure of ideas within which violence was being understood in India. The novel recognized that the consciousness and political culture of the Indian people were being irreversibly altered by new modes of resistance which took the world-view of the colonizers for granted; that the revolutionaries' ability to find legitimacy for their actions in ancient texts only showed that real disjunctions in consciousness could often be hidden by the use of traditional language.

Bharati's Choice

Char Adhyay includes an impassioned critique of Indranath's politics, but not a full critique of his personality. Though Tagore hints at the possibility of such a critique, he does not make Indranath a rounded, flesh-and-blood character—it is only Ela, the heroine, who has the nuances of her personality delineated and to some extent contextualized. So, to get an idea of how Indranath as a type may have fitted into the political culture of the Bengal of the time and Tagore's implicit assessment of that culture, I shall have to go outside Tagore's world and re-enter it through a well-known nationalist novel of the post-Swadeshi period, *Pather Dabi*.[54] Written by Saratchandra Chattopadhyay (1876–1938), by far the most popular novelist India has produced and a major influence on Indian middle-class consciousness during the first half of the twentieth century, *Pather Dabi* was published in 1926, eight years before *Char Adhyay*, and was almost immediately banned by the British Indian government. The first edition of *Pather Dabi*, though, was entirely sold out in less than a week, before the police could move in to pick up the copies. The ban was lifted in 1939, a year after the author's death.

Saratchandra requested Tagore to join in the widespread protest

[54]Saratchandra Chattopadhyay, *Pather Dabi*, in Sukumar Sen (ed.), *Sarat Sahitya Samagra* (Calcutta: Ananda Publishers, 1986), pp. 1130–266.

against the ban. The poet refused, not on the grounds of political ideology, an issue he deftly bypassed, but on the grounds of Saratchandra's undoubted literary gifts. He wrote:

. . . . What a writer like you tells in the form of a story will have permanent influence . . . . From immature boys and girls to the elderly, all will come under its influence. Under the circumstances, if the English did not stop the circulation of your book, it would have shown their total contempt and ignorance about your literary powers and your status in this country.[55]

Tagore, however, gratuitously chose to add that, everything considered, the British regime was, comparatively, the most tolerant regime in the world. Saratchandra was furious. In his response, which he did not finally send or publish, he asserted that if the regime had the right to ban the book, the subjugated Indian had at least the right to protest.[56]

After the publication of *Pather Dabi*, its hero Savyasachi quickly became the ideal of many Bengali freedom-fighters. A number of memoirs of post-Swadeshi freedom-fighters mention how they took enormous risks and sometimes faced police prosecution to possess or even read the novel and how greatly they admired Savyasachi. It is against this background that one must take note of the remarkable similarities between him and Indranath, including the similarity in names. Savyasachi is another name of Arjuna; Indranath means, among other things, one whose lord or father is Indra. It can therefore also mean Arjuna. Anyone interested in literary sleuthing would be tempted to hypothesize that the character of Indranath was inspired by Savyasachi and was an attempt to develop—and define the limits of—some aspects of Savyasachi's self-definition. These are the aspects widely admired in the modernized sections of the non-western world as markers of political rationality and the ideal political personality.

Savyasachi is a Bengali Brahmin who brings to his Kshatriya vocation the full power of Brahminic cerebral potency. As a Bengali police officer pursuing Savyasachi says, with sardonic respect, Savyasachi is a *mahapurush*, a great man, who has rebelled against the king and deserves to be called *svanamadhanya*, a person true to his name. Not merely is he ambidexterous, all his ten senses, *dashendriya*, are equally powerful. A superb shot, he can swim across torrential tropical rivers

[55]Sarojmohan Mitra, *Saratsahitye Samajchetana* (Calcutta: Granthalaya, 1981), pp. 153–4.
[56]Ibid., p. 154. The bitterness was deep and persistent. See Saratchandra Chattopadhyay's letters to Radharani Debi, 10 October 1927, and to Umapradas Mukhopadhyay, 10 Bhadra 1334 (1927), reproduced in Gopalchandra Roy, *Saratchandrer Patrabali* (Calcutta: Bharati, 1986), pp. 291–3, 320.

and simultaneously take on half-a-dozen policemen in single combat.[57] He is a master of disguise, too.

These abilities are matched by his mental powers. Savyasachi knows at least ten languages (at one point he claims that he 'knows' all the languages of the world) and he has been educated (like all good Indian, middle-class ultra-nationalists) in Europe and North America. He is a man of dazzling virtuosity and versatility. He has studied medicine in Germany, engineering in France, law in England and an unmentioned discipline in the United States.[58] The reader may remember that Indranath, too, lived in Europe for many years and studied science there. Equipped with excellent testimonials from his European professors, Indranath has taught French, German, botany, and geology, and is also a trained doctor, besides being an expert at armed and unarmed combat.[59] And Savyasachi, too, despite being an agnostic, seeks support for his work from the Gita.

Savyasachi's attainments were not chosen at random. Among those who contributed to Saratchandra's conceptualization of his hero were well-known, gifted revolutionaries like Jatindranath Mukherjee (1879–1915), Jadugopal Mukherjee (1886–1976), Rashbehari Bose (1886–1945), M.N. Roy (1887–1954), Bhupendranath Dutta (1880–1961), Taraknath Das (1884–1958), and Satish Chandra Chakravarti (1889–1968).[60] Thus the combination of extraordinary physical strength and courage and the capacity to be forgiving and caring came from Jatindranath; the skill at disguise from Jadugopal; organizational ability, particularly the ability to build international networks, from Bose and Roy; western education from Dutta and Das; and ambidexterousness from Chakravarti.[61] There were indirect influences from figures such as Aurobindo, though it is pretty obvious from the narratives that both Saratchandra and Tagore had sensed the break that had already taken place between the transcendental theories of nationalism ventured by the likes of Aurobindo and the new, secularized nationalism increasingly backed by a theory of 'scientized violence'. Within that new nationalism, even the Gita had acquired a paradoxical status; it had become a cultural sanction for the primacy of desacralized nationalist politics and for the separation of politics from morality. (The text of course had a completely different set of meanings in Gandhian politics.)

[57]Chattopadhyay, *Pather Dabi*, pp. 1149–74.
[58]Ibid., p. 1149.
[59]Tagore, *Char Adhyay*, pp. 381, 385.
[60]Saratchandra Chattopadhyay, quoted in Mitra, *Sarastsahitye Samajchetana*, p. 155.
[61]Ibid.

With Savyasachi's wide repertoire of skills go other 'attainments' which aroused deep ambivalence in his creator. Savyasachi is 'passionless like a stone' and callous.[62] Through single-minded, rigorous training, he has acquired extraordinary control over every part of his body and mind.[63] This is the kind of control which Indranath, too, so conspicuously displays.

We . . . have given up kindness and charity, otherwise we would have hated ourselves for being sentimental. This is what Sri Krishna has taught Arjun. Do not be cruel but, when duty is involved, be ruthless . . . . My nature is impersonal . . . . I accept with the illusionless mind of a scientist that one who is will die . . . . If one seeks to do one's duty out of anger, one is more likely to do that which is not one's duty.[64]

As Savyasachi puts it,

. . . I am a revolutionary. I have no attachment, no mercy, no sense of nurture— both sins and good deeds are nonsense to me. India's freedom is my only goal, only *sadhana* . . . except for it in this life I have nothing nowhere.[65]

Predictably, Savyasachi is a secular rationalist. To him all traditions are lies, 'primitive superstitions'; the human race has no greater enemy than them.[66] This faith gives his calculations about human life and sacrifice almost mathematical precision. With all this apparent objectivity and rationalism, however, the precision includes an erotic fascination with violence. Savyasachi believes that the sins of man-made suffering can only be washed away by the blood of its rebellious victims.[67] For him, the poison in the heart of the victimized is the real capital of revolution, the base on which he would have to build his rebellion. All talk of peace, he declares, is mere rhetoric and a conspiracy of the exploiters.[68]

Savyasachi, therefore, is psychologically and culturally ambidexterous, too. He is equally accomplished as Kshatriya and as Brahmin, he has internalized both the East and the West, and he is at home both with modern instrumental rationality and the primitive, passionate love for his motherland that drives him from country to country 'like a wild animal'. In addition, he oscillates between fulfilling the traditional Bengali concept of the ideal person and the modern European concept of the ideal person he has chosen for himself.

[62]Chattopadhyay, *Pather Dabi*, p. 1172.
[63]Ibid., pp. 1223, 1232–3.
[64]Tagore, *Char Adhyay*, pp. 385, 388–9.
[65]Chattopadhay, *Pather Dabi*, p. 1234.
[66]Ibid., p. 1249.
[67]Ibid., pp. 1232–3.
[68]Ibid., p. 1233.

But, within all this, there is a schism: Savyasachi's world-view is hyper-masculine. In political ideology, strategies, and in the stereotypes he has of his own Bengali community, he is openly potency-driven. At the same time, he cannot fully disown those personality traits that rebel against his self-definition. These contradictory pulls imbue him with some of the qualities of Saratchandra's other heroes, who are always conspicuously androgynous. It is as if Savyasachi were hiding this other bipolarity—his ability to be almost maternal in some situations, defying his own overly masculinized concept of the ideal male. The dynamics of this self-defiance, which Tagore chose to ignore, unfolds in the course of Savyasachi's interpersonal experiences narrated in the novel.

The story of *Pather Dabi* is set entirely in Burma, at that time a part of British India. It revolves around Apurba, a young, orthodox, middle-class Bengali Brahmin who comes to Rangoon to work as a petty official in a Dutch company. Apurba is the son of a district magistrate under the Raj, and has a Master's degree in science. He confesses to being a physical coward, has a touch of misogyny born of fears of pollution, and is a docile colonial subject, a maudlin, conventional mother's boy. He is accompanied by a Brahmin cook-bearer, Tiwari, who is as cowardly and fearful of the whites as Apurba is. In Rangoon, they come to know Bharati, the daughter of a Bengali Brahmin woman who defied her family to marry an aggressive, boorish, hard-drinking south Indian Christian. Apurba's first encounter with Bharati is unpleasant, but they draw close to each other when Bharati nurses Tiwari through an attack of small-pox.

Meanwhile, Apurba becomes friendly with a spirited Maharashtrian Brahmin called Ramdas Talvarkar. Through Talvarkar and Bharati, Apurba is introduced to a nationalist secret society called Pather Dabi (literally, The Demand of the Road) and its leader, Savyasachi, whom everyone in the group calls 'Doctor'. The president of the Rangoon branch of Pather Dabi is Sumitra, an intelligent, self-assured, attractive woman, half-Jewish and half-Bengali-Brahmin, whom Savyasachi has rescued from 'a life of indignity'. Sumitra is in love with Savyasachi.

After a while, Apurba's courage fails him and he informs on the secret society. He is captured by members of the society and condemned to death. Partly from pity and partly for Bharati's sake, Savyasachi spares Apurba's life, against the wishes of the majority of the group. Savyasachi then has to repair the damage done by Apurba's betrayal and deal with at least one member who finds in Savyasachi's kindness towards Apurba a new excuse for liquidating Savyasachi himself. The novel ends on a melancholy but dramatic note, with the revolutionary leaving Rangoon on a stormy night to rebuild his shattered organization in Asia.

Much of the second half of *Pather Dabi* consists of long conversations between Bharati and Savyasachi, following Savyasachi's magnanimous gesture to Apurba. From these conversation, one comes to suspect towards the end that the author's identification with his hero is not total, that he identifies partly with Bharati whose world-view is at variance with her leader's.

While a cursory reading of the novel reveals the similarities between Savyasachi and Indranath, one must read it more carefully to notice the differences. For these are based on qualities that enter the narrative despite the author's obvious sympathy with his hero. Saratchandra shares much of Savyasachi's political wisdom, such as his diagnosis of 'Europe's world-engulfing hunger from which no weak nation has ever been able to protect itself'; the belief, obviously borrowed from nineteenth-century European radicalism, that 'peasants never risk life for ideas, for they do not want freedom, they want peace—the peace of the incompetent and the impotent'; and the conviction that it is wrong to believe that 'lies need to be created while truth is permanent and uncreated' because 'truth is constantly recreated by mankind, for truth also lives and dies.'[69] Saratchandra even makes his hero mouth a defence of the Bengali middle classes as a creative and potentially revolutionary formation,[70] as if to compensate for the negative portrayal of Apurba's personality.

But once again—one is tempted to say, despite himself—the author introduces into the novel another form of patriotism. This is a patriotism which his hero self-consciously rejects but at times unwittingly lives out. It has two main elements.

First, Savyasachi does not turn out to have as clear-cut a personality and ideology as he appears to have at first. His ambivalence towards Bengal and the Bengalis, for example, is deep. He believes that Bengalis are cowardly and selfish but also confidently states that, of all the languages in the world, Bengali is the sweetest.[71] As for his instrumental rationality and the primacy he gives to the goal of freedom, he acknowledges at one place, 'Independence is not the end of independence. *Dharma*, peace,

[69]Ibid., pp. 1239, 1241, 1247.
[70]Ibid., p. 1261.
[71]Ibid., pp. 1248–9.

poetry—these are even greater. It is for their unique development that one needs independence.'[72]

Second, the novel subtly suggests that Savyasachi's *dharma* is actually *apatdharma*, codes of conduct that can be followed in exceptional circumstances, in this instance in a situation where his motherland is being violated and he, as a freedom fighter and dutiful son of India, has to live in a liminal world inhabited by marginal individuals. Almost all the characters of *Pather Dabi* are from or live on the periphery of Bengali middle-class Brahminism. Even their secret society, though it extends over much of Asia, is poorly linked with the mainstream of Indian political activity. Savyasachi claims he has chosen Burma as the headquarters of *Pather Dabi* because women in Burma are freer and he expects women to make his revolution.[73] Yet the role of the Burmese ends with that statement. The novel has no notable local character. The cultural and physical characteristics of Burma, usually the latter, merely act as the backdrop for a clutch of marginal Bengalis and their few non-Bengali associates playing out their political and historical roles. The writer's final warning to his own hero, delivered through Bharati talking in her sleep, is thus of significance.

You are a superman; for you my respect, adoration and affection will ever remain immovable. But I shall never accept your intellectual judgement (*vicharbuddhi*). Let freedom come to our country through your hands, but never give the immoral the shape of the moral . . . . If you give necessity the highest priority and thus create for the weak-hearted the impression that *adharma* is *dharma*, your sorrow will never end.[74]

This could be Ela speaking to Indranath, not in her sleep but in her most alert, self-conscious moments. And we are left with the question: could Bharati repeat her criticism of her hero when fully awake? Perhaps what Tagore says directly in *Char Adhyay*, Saratchandra can only say indirectly, almost despite himself in *Pather Dabi*. Yet, the continuity cannot be ignored. In both cases, the authors express their moral doubts through their heroines and assume that their heroes have compromised, at least partly, with the forces of *adharma* and impersonal, instrumental violence.

In other words, resisting his actual political ideology, Saratchandra's identification with his hero is less than complete, and his differences with

---

[72]Ibid., p. 1237.
[73]Ibid., p. 1221.
[74]Ibid., p. 1251.

Tagore less sharp than the poet might have cared to admit. Saratchandra *was* an ardent nationalist, he *did* write *Pather Dabi* as a political act, and he *did* conceive of Savyasachi as a national hero. But a narrative in the hands of a creative writer acquires an impulse and momentum of its own. Saratchandra's novel acquires this autonomy through the author's residual identification with Bharati.

Tagore all but misses this identification when modelling Indrajit on Savyasachi. He makes an anti-hero of Savyasachi in the form of Indranath. The 'ruthless, firm-hearted, fearless, unpitying' revolutionary of *Pather Dabi* becomes in *Char Adhyay* something more—a passionless, calculating industrialist of violence, to whom violence is a matter of assembly-line deaths, geared to the production of political results.[75] At this plane, Tagore is less than sensitive to the subtleties of Saratchandra's response to the problem of scientized violence. At another plane, however, Tagore's creative self, too, acquires an autonomy of its own. It senses his colleague's latent identification with his half-caste, crypto-Gandhian heroine. Bharati's political philosophy finds voice and her moral anxieties concrete shape in *Char Adhyay*'s Ela.

Loss and Recovery of Self

That which is mainly a matter of social choice in *Ghare-Baire*—between two political ideologies represented by two different persons with distinct personalities—becomes primarily a problem of inner choice in *Gora*. The continuity between Bimala and Gora is maintained in *Char Adhyay* through Ela, for whom morality and politics—also moral and political action, the private and the public, and the home and the world—gradually become inseparable. At this plane, the three characters can be seen as extensions of each other and the novels constitute a single narrative, one continuing story of a divided self in which two antagonistic social forces are represented by two persons, who first constitute a latent (Nikhil and Sandip), then a manifest double (Atin and Indranath), and finally a split self (Gora).

However, there are clear breaks in the narrative. The choice for Bimala and the reader of *Ghare-Baire*—as Lukacs points out—is made easier because of Sandip's flawed character. In *Char Adhyay*, too, Atin faces internal choices which are almost entirely moral and, for some reason, deliberately located in a two-dimensional fairy-tale world. It is not surprising that once Tagore withdrew his preface from later editions of

[75]Ibid., p. 1257.

the novel, *Char Adhyay* could quickly be absorbed into the mainstream of Bengali literature as a mythic statement on political morality, far less controversial and questionable than Tagore intended it to be.

In *Gora*, the choice, which remains political, takes a psychological form. Whereas in *Ghare-Baire* the conflict over political morality is shown to be external to the two main antagonists, who remain close to ideal-typical representations, *Gora*, like *Char Adhyay*, projects the problem of public morality into the personality of Gora himself, into his self-definition. The moral and apolitical contradictions are almost entirely within him; it is Gora who learns to evaluate or pass judgement on himself. Here there is no Indranath to share the blame. As we shall see, even those who side with Gora's political super-ego cannot share his pain as he works through his older political–psychological self to acquire a new moral vision.

The characters in the novel play out their roles against the background of an ideological debate which makes no sense to the non-Bengali reader or to Bengalis of later generations. This debate, between orthodox Hinduism and the Brahmo reform movement, gradually turns out to be more than an intellectual encounter between two sects or faiths. Shorn of its denominational meaning, it is seen to be a clash between two structures of consciousness. By the end of the novel, the author virtually repudiates the manifest planes of Hinduism and Brahmoism along which he places the characters at the beginning; he now places the characters along the two orthogonal structures of consciousness, serving as two latent, political–ethical planes in Indian public life.

Gora's Choice

Though written during the period of the Swadeshi movement, *Gora* is set at the fag end of the 1870s. The chief protagonist is a young, passionate, but scholarly social reformer who has turned ultra-Hindu, and believes that the humiliation of being colonized can only be overcome by a tough protectiveness towards everything indigenous. Gora is familiar with the common arguments against his position and he has well-thought-out, powerful counter-arguments. Thus, when he decides to bathe at Triveni, it is not in search of purity or piety; he knows there will be pilgrims there; he will have to shed his diffidence and stand with the common people.[76] As he says, 'When the whole world has forsaken India and heaps insults upon her, I for my part wish to share her seat of dishonour—this caste-

[76]Tagore, *Gora*, p. 29.

ridden, this superstitious, this idolatrous India of mine.'[77] In this respect, Gora has a touch of Swami Vivekananda (1863–1902) and Sister Nivedita in him:

Those who *you* call illiterate are those to whose party *I* belong. What *you* call superstition, that is *my* faith . . . . Reform? . . . . More important than reform are love and respect. Reform will come of itself from within after we are an united people . . . .[78]

. . . . The goddess of my worship does not come to me enshrined in beauty. I see her where there is poverty and famine, pain and insult.[79]

Predictably, Gora is not apologetic about being oriented to the past. He believes that one kills the past by talking about it as if it were dead and gone.[80]

His exclusivism pushes Gora towards a strain of nationalism that was not then a political force in India. Originally inspired by the 'nativism' of Bankimchandra Chattopadhyaya and Vivekananda, this strain only became a significant political movement after the partition of Bengal in 1905. However, it was already showing signs of its future shape. As it grew into a movement, it brazenly embraced western concepts of the nation, state, statecraft, technology, and history as the unavoidable universals of contemporary politics. This reactive westernization subsumed under the western category of nationalism—he called it the internalization of western history—prompted Tagore to avoid grappling with the issue of imperialism directly and instead to focus on the two conflicting forms of response to imperialism.

The novel is organized around a series of events that constitute an attack on Gora's nationalism and self-definition. These events goad him to search for more authentic forms of patriotism and faith, grounded in a more authentic self. In the course of the search, Gora's inner divide comes to acquire a sharpness greater than that in some of the real-life characters on whom he might have been modelled. But there are continuities, too. They bridge the divide and make his personality change

[77]Ibid., p. 267.
[78]Ibid., pp. 50–1.
[79]Ibid., p. 71. A critic has suggested on the basis of biographical details that the inspiration for the character of Gora, for much of his life, an Indian ultra-nationalist of Irish origin, was primarily Nivedita. Bimanbehari Majumdar, *The Heroines of Tagore: A Study in the Transformation of Indian Society, 1875–1941* (Calcutta: Firma K.L. Mukhopadhyay, 1968), p. 225.
[80]Ibid., p. 88.

believable. The most important of these continuities is Gora's initial reluctance to mimic the West. 'If we have the mistaken notion', he says at one place, 'that because the English are strong we can never become strong unless we become exactly like them, then that impossibility will never be achieved, for by mere imitation we shall eventually be neither one thing nor the other.'[81] On this belief is built Gora's self-discovery towards the end of the novel.

Gora is the son of a retired government official who, in retirement and after living a rather naughty life, has turned to orthodoxy with a vengeance. Anandamayi, his superbly composed, insightful wife, has a matter-of-fact, pragmatic morality which helps her negotiate both the fiery Gora and her other son Mahim, who is perfectly 'normal' and, hence, 'realistic' and cynical. Anandamayi's primary concern, though, is the 'abnormal', idealistic Gora, and her life is organized around him. Unlike her husband, Anandamayi is at peace with tradition and therefore more open to cultural differences and dissent. There are hints that her liberal vision stems from her deep roots in tradition. We are told that her father died in her infancy; she was brought up by her grandfather, a pandit at Varanasi.

The novel begins with Binay, Gora's friend, accidentally meeting a reformist Brahmo family headed by a philosophical, ideologically open, doting father, Pareshchandra Bhattacharya, known as Pareshbabu. Pareshbabu's reformism is 'natural' and derives more from his personal morality and spiritual sensitivity than from any ideology. However, though Paresh dominates his family morally, his comically-Anglicized wife Baradasundari dominates its political thinking. Barada is as particular about maintaining the purity of Brahmoism as Gora is of Hinduism.

Gora resents the encounter between Binay and Pareshbabu's family. He fears that his friend will be influenced by the family and lose his ideological purity. He has no inkling that the main attraction the family has for Binay is its ability to satisfy his growing rebelliousness against Gora's idea of India as 'negation incarnate'.[82] As it happens, Gora himself is gradually sucked into Paresh's social orbit, if only for occasional testy exchanges with the family and their prim, self-certain guests, including a pillar of Brahmo orthodoxy, Haranbabu. So it is in front of Gora's unbelieving eyes that Binay ultimately falls in love with a daughter of the family, Lalita.

[81]Ibid., p. 102.
[82]Ibid., p. 30.

A spirited, defiant girl with a mind of her own, Lalita is jealous of Binay's emotional dependence on Gora. An accident suddenly alters the context of this grudge. Lalita wants to avoid taking part in a dramatic performance organized by her mother in honour of an English commissioner who has sentenced Gora to imprisonment a few days earlier for championing the cause of oppressed villagers. She precipitates a first-class scandal by running away from home and joining Binay on his journey back to Calcutta. Binay now finds his allegiance to Gora's ideology pitted against Lalita's direct moral reaction to the injustice done to him.

Meanwhile, Gora's concept of India is severely shaken by his experiences in rural Bengal and, particularly, from his encounter with the resistance offered by a predominantly Muslim village. Especially impressive to him is the more open Hinduism of the village barber who lives in solidarity with the Muslims rather than with their Hindu oppressors.

Ultimately, Gora himself gets emotionally involved with another girl of the Brahmo family, Sucharita, an adopted daughter of Pareshbabu. At one time, 'the fact that there were women in India hardly entered Gora's mind'; now he makes 'a new discovery of this truth through Sucharita . . .' and this shakes him.[83] He comes to regard Sucharita not as a special individual, but as a special idea, a representation of Indian womanhood.[84] He becomes aware that women do not merely symbolize the motherland; they are the motherland and it is the indifference to the humiliation of women-as-motherland which explains the Indian male's insecurity about his loss of manhood.[85] Gora is now torn between the attraction he feels for Sucharita—at first, he is unable to own up his love for her—and his political–religious ideology. More so since, to go by Pareshbabu's reading, 'Gora is too high-handed. . . . The simple and assured peace which clothes the thought and word and deed of those who are the bearers of truth, [is] not one of Gora's possessions . . . .'[86]

The dénouement—a rather contrived one—comes when Gora finds out that he himself, though he has tried to live the life of a pure, ascetic Brahmin, is actually the orphaned child of an Irish couple, abandoned during the Sepoy Mutiny in 1857. He is reduced overnight to an untouchable and a non-Indian. Traumatic though it is, the revelation does not, however, destroy Gora as a person. Instead, he acquires the courage to

---

[83]Ibid., p. 271.
[84]Ibid., p. 272.
[85]Ibid., pp. 272–3.
[86]Ibid., p. 89.

confront the fact that Pareshbabu's religious consciousness is superior
to his and so is Anandamayi's practical morality. Once he has acquired
this awareness, his first symbolic act is to own up the Christian—and
hence presumably untouchable—domestic help, Lachmi, who was once
his nurse-maid.

Although the novel is roughly twice the length of *Ghare-Baire* and *Char
Adhyay*, its plot is not particularly complex. However, the characters in
Gora are more fully developed than in *Char Adhyay*, and the ideological
confrontations in it are filigreed with detail. Indeed, one can make out
a case that the basic theme of *Gora* is the changes in personality and
ideology that are brought about by interpersonal and cognitive encounters.
Tagore's own political ideology, his ideas of 'true' patriotism and desirable
modes of social change, enter the narrative less directly and aggressively
than in the other two novels. Gora at the end is not a mere vehicle of
Tagore's political philosophy.

Central to the narrative is Gora's patriotism. When it finds expression
in nationalism, this patriotism has a number of distinct features. First,
Gora has no awareness that his nationalism, his idea that Hindus should
become a single homogeneous nation,[87] is borrowed from the West; and
that therefore it has no cultural roots. When he goes to a village as a
political and social activist, he encounters another form of political
community, culturally more rooted in the moral codes of the civilization.
The experience does not free him from his ideology; it merely plants
some doubts in his mind. Only towards the end does Gora discover that
his nationalism and cultural exclusivism are reactions to his own uncertain
cultural moorings and are, therefore, doubly purist.

Second, Gora's nationalism reifies the idea of the nation. Those
forming a part of the Indian nation or serving as the beneficiaries of
nationalist ideology have some sanctity for him but, ideologically, they
are political and cultural abstractions. It is only much later that the reality
of rural Bengal—the oppression and violence it contains—confronts
him with a choice between the empiricism of life and that of books.
This ability of nationalism (as of any theory) to reify its prospective
beneficiaries—that is, the citizens of the nation that it idealizes—is a
constant theme in Tagore's work; in *Gora* he explores its consequences
in contemporary politics for the first time.

Third, Gora's nationalism assumes that the indigenous is intrinsically
and fundamentally different from the exogenous and that the Indian

[87]Ibid., p. 294.

or Hindu self can be fully defended on its own terms. So even Hindu catholicity and tolerance become arguments to prove the catholicity and tolerance of a superior civilization. Gora's parentage is used by Tagore as the ultimate symbolic proof that such a concept of national identity is itself exogenous and violates the fundamental principles of Indianness and Hinduism.

One should note that in 1909, when he wrote *Gora*, Tagore was already trying to move away from the conventional structure of the western novel, introducing elements from the Indian epic tradition into it. We have seen how this approach also led Tagore to write *Char Adhyay* almost in the form of a fairy tale. *Gora* allows one a glimpse of the other side of the coin—of some of the possible reasons for the success of the new form in India: the novel can explore aspects of the self in ways that are simultaneously psychological, moral, and spiritual.

Gora's changing concept of nationalism is a consequence of the changing contours of his self-knowledge, acquired through a painful process of self-confrontation. The secret of his birth does not clinch the issue. The reader knows the secret, Gora does not, and when it comes out at the end, it only gives a certain poignancy to the self-awareness that has already been arrived at.

Four persons play crucial roles in this self-confrontation—Binay, Paresh, Anandamayi, and Sucharita. Of the four, Paresh provides the metaphysical and moral fulcrum for the story and is the main agent of change in Gora's personality. But it is Anandamayi who emerges as the most powerful presence in the narrative. Forced to choose between the India of Gora and India as Anandamayi, Gora's closest friend and double, Binay, chooses Anandamayi. The choice is 'passive' and 'intuitive'. Later, Gora himself makes the same choice more self-consciously when he senses that Anandamayi represents in her womanliness the spirit of India more truly than his pure, disinfected, masculine version of Indianness and Hinduism.

One guesses that Anandamayi is the prototype of the character that in the later novels develops into the splintered personalities of Bimala and Ela. It is Anandamayi's authenticity that is being engineered, by Sandip in one instance and Indranath in another, in the cause of nationalism. This engineering seeks to break down the barrier between the private and the public by giving absolute priority to conjugality over maternity, and erects a new barrier between the home and the world: one which does not permit feminine values in the domestic space to invade or spill over into public life. To ensure that the maternal selves of Bimala and Ela are not entirely overshadowed by their conjugal selves or sexuality, Tagore introduces in *Ghare-Baire* and *Char Adhyay* the characters of Amulya and Akhil.[88] They underscore the continuity between Anandamayi, Bimala and Ela and the threat to the authenticity and authority of the feminine self which serves as an organizing principle of the Indic civilization.

The other central issue in *Gora* is that of purity, both as a cultural value and as an aspect of personal morality. Gora starts with a fixed concept of pure Hinduism and tries to be true to it. To him, Pareshbabu's family is contaminated and Anandamayi compromised. By the end of the novel, Gora's original concept of purity has disintegrated and he sees Paresh and Anandamayi as more truly pure than his own father and Haranbabu. Paradoxically, Paresh and Anandamayi acquire this new status in Gora's eyes by their willingness to sacrifice their purity to reaffirm a moral universe which Gora finds that, despite all his efforts, he cannot disown.

That shared moral universe, Tagore suggests, is a universal one and, if Anandamayi can so effortlessly make it her own and defend it, it is in continuity with Indian traditions. What Paresh has acquired through self-discipline, Anandamayi has acquired through everyday womanliness, by being herself. This is what Bimala in *Ghare-Baire* tragically fails to recognize. It is also what Ela in *Char Adhyay* refuses to acknowledge till the end, once again with tragic consequences. Bimala and Ela, under the influence of Sandip and Indranath, are as much *svabhavachyuta* as Atin is, for they try to become equals in a man's world by choosing values derived from that world. Their personal tragedies come from the pursuit of values embedded in the masculinized world of nationalism and nation-state—from what could be called the principle of egalitarian patriarchy—rather than from any genuine reaffirmation of feminine values.

To locate the moral fulcrum in femininity in this fashion is to repudiate the aggressively phallo-centric, 'fierce self-idolatory of nation-worship' (of which Indranath represents the sophisticated form and Sandip a more street-smart version) and 'the colourless vagueness of cosmopolitanism' (depicted in *Gora* through the pathetically comic imitative modernity of Baradasundari).[89] India's history, Tagore believed, was the 'history of continual social adjustment and not that of organized power for defence and aggression.'[90] Hence, when voluntary and self-imposed, such masculine nationalism in India can be even more devastating.[91]

Of the three novels discussed here, *Gora* is the only one to end on a

---

[88]Suddhasatva Bosu, *Rabindranather Char Adhyay* (Calcutta: Bharati Publications, 1979), p. 36.

[89]Rabindranath Tagore, *Nationalism* (reprint, Madras: Macmillan, 1985), p. 2.

[90]Ibid.

[91]Ibid.

happy note. It was as if, after establishing the illegitimate birth of Hindu nationalism, Tagore could afford to allow his hero to live with himself. The new awareness of his origins and his 'genetic untouchability' saves Gora from his narrow nationalism and brings him closer to his mother and, by implication, motherland. It was as if a self overly well-defined and exclusive could not, by definition, be an authentic Indian self capable of serious relationships with other Indians and Indianness. Once the point was made, Tagore's other political novels followed; they were the logical corollary of the political psychology of *Gora*.

Kipling's Choice

To understand the politics of self in *Gora* more fully, it may be useful briefly to compare its hero with that of Rudyard Kipling's well-known and influential novel, *Kim*.[92] I shall attempt the comparison here keeping in mind a recent paper by Kalyan Kumar Chatterjee,[93] where Gora is seen not as an Indian who is finally shown to have alien roots but as an outsider who has come to stay as an insider.

Kim was published in 1901, nine years before *Gora*, and was an immediate success. It is possible that Tagore had at least heard of the major concerns of *Kim*. Even if he had not, his own novel provides a counterpart to Kipling's. Both deal with the loss and recovery of selves, and the anxieties and pain associated with that.

Kipling's novel, at first sight consistent with his other work, turns out to have some unique features. Kipling had been away from India for about a decade when he wrote *Kim*, and his painful, tense ambivalence towards the country and its inhabitants had partly worn off by the time it was completed. The novel has an uncharacteristic mellowness and an evocative, nostalgic tone, as if it was an attempt to capture the fleeting spirit of eternal India as reflected in her contemporary absurdities and social contradictions. These qualities do not fully fit the Kipling one is familiar with, who usually shows such sensitivity only when dealing with the flora and fauna of India, for instance in the *Jungle Books*, not when dealing with the human beings who inhabit the country's hot and dusty plains. Some critics have recognized this break with the past. One has called *Kim* Kipling's valedictory address to India and the most genuine interpretation of everyday Indian life written by an Englishman.[94]

---

[92]Rudyard Kipling, *Kim* (reprint, New York: Dell, 1974).

[93]Kalyan Kumar Chatterjee, 'Incognitos and Secret Sharers: Patterns of Identity, Tagore, Kipling and Foster', *Indian Literature*, May–June 1989, no. 131, pp. 11–130.

[94]K. Bhaskara Rao, *Rudyard Kipling's India* (Norman: University of Oklahoma Press, 1967).

The hero, Kim, is a white child lost in the wilderness of urban India, cruelly tanned by the Indian sun and speaking an Indian tongue. Kim's parents, like Gora's, were Irish,[95] but are now dead and Kim lives like any other Indian street child in Lahore. The novel describes how he recaptures his 'true' identity through a series of adventures which link him to the colonial government and make him a protector of its security interests. The story begins at the Lahore Museum, which is presided over by an English curator modelled on Kipling's father, where Kim accidentally meets a 'strange' Tibetan Lama on a pilgrimage. Kim befriends the otherworldly, lovable Lama and becomes his disciple or *chela*.

Much of the novel consists of a description of the adventurous journey the two undertake along the Grand Trunk Road. In the course of it, they meet a variety of people and Kim gets more enmeshed in unravelling and resisting a conspiracy against the Raj. In this unravelling and resistance, Kim's Indian self comes in handy. He can lie like an Oriental and all hours of the day are the same to him, he can give and take bribes like any Asiatic, and he can passive-aggressively ensure his own and his *guru*'s survival. Thus, he begs skilfully, exploits the superstitions of the natives to negotiate difficult social situations, and even—V.S. Naipaul would enjoy this—chews *paan* and spits on the floor of the compartment he is travelling in to blend with his environment.[96]

Gradually it becomes clear to the reader that Kim and the Lama constitute not merely a social but also a psychological dyad. They serve as each other's double and, in the process, come to symbolize forces larger than themselves. They are bound together by their latent common Other—the India which the Lama has transcended and which Kim uses instrumentally as a camouflage. To put it simplistically, Kim represents Kipling's self as it might have been, a self which can suspend its suspicion of the diversity, rawness and violence of India mixed with the country's seductive, androgynous charm. The Lama, on the other hand, is what one critic calls 'the triumphant achievement of an anti-self' by Kipling, so powerful that it becomes the 'touchstone for everything else'.[97] The

[95]The psychological significance of being of Irish blood in a British–Indian relationship remains underexplored in fiction as well as social analysis. *Ex facie* Irishness represented a form of liminality. It marked out a westernness which seemed culturally more accessible, being non-dominant and non-mainstream; it marked out a territoriality which seemed to be a co-victim of British imperialism; and carried associations with a form of Christianity, Catholicism, which was obviously not the religion of the empire and which was explicitly more open to the cultural styles and traditional religious beliefs of Indians (see pp. 202–3 below).

[96]Kipling, *Kim*, pp. 27, 30–1, 36.

[97]Mark Kinkead Weeks, quoted in Lord Birkenhead, *Rudyard Kipling* (London: Weidenfeld and Nicolson, 1978), p. 222.

Lama in his childlike otherworldliness is a negation of everything Kipling politically stands for. The character was for Kipling a once-in-a-lifetime break with his painfully-constructed imperial self.

Kim can be read as an interplay of the two selves, a play in which neither wins; both are finally subjugated to a third self serving the conventional state. But, in the meanwhile, the novel provides a moving justification for the two abrogated selves—one located in Kipling's lost past, and the other in the disowned present of the Orient. It is this empathy with the defeated which makes *Kim* different from the majority of Kipling's works. Kipling was never to show the same cultural and psychological sensitivity or the same moral courage again. He was a person who feared identifying with victims, especially when they defied authority, and he always found some sanction for authorized violence. Elsewhere I have associated this fear with Kipling's deeper fear of looking within, of baring his latent awareness of what he actually was—an insecure bicultural whose sources of creativity lay in his biculturality rather than in his unicultural self. For this was artificially constructed with the help of current theories of progress and social Darwinism to avoid facing the moral demand to identify with the subjugated and the weak.[98]

In the boy Kim can be found Kipling as he appeared to many of his fellow Anglo-Saxons in India—ill-mannered, under-socialized, unruly and, even, overly tanned.[99] Like Gora, Kim comes from the outside to become part of the Indian world. What marginalizes him in Anglo-India brands him as an insider for Indian society. What could be a handicap in a 'civilized' society is an asset in the 'native quarters of Lahore'. He can merge with the Indian environment easily and with uninhibited grace.

Gora, on the other hand, comes in like a storm into a conventional Bengali family and manages to lay bare not merely his own but also his family's latent contradictions and hypocrisy. He is the mythical Englishman who, as Tagore had written in 1898, had been sent by destiny as an envoy 'to burst through our rickety door and enter into the very interior of our house.'[100] Despite being brought up as an Indian, Gora's character retains elements of his western self, physical as well as psychological. He 'roars' when he speaks, is needlessly assertive, and he lives in a world which does not admit any shade of grey.

Whereas Gora's voice and assertiveness give the lie to his copper-coloured skin, and set him apart in Indian society, Kim's sensitivity to

[98]Nandy, *The Intimate Enemy*, pp. 35–9, 64–73.
[99]Birkenhead, *Kipling*, pp. 62–3.
[100]Rabindranath Tagore, quoted in Chatterjee, 'Incognitos and Secret Sharers', p. 113.

the local scene reflects the consciousness of an insider. Unlike Gora, Kim does not have to affirm his Indianness as a psychological defence; he uses it naturally as part of his social armour. He is what Kipling could have been or felt he had been in his earlier life.

Underlying these differences is a deeper parallel. Tagore in *Gora* tries to integrate a part of his Indian self modelled on the western man; Kipling in *Kim* tries to own up the Indian part of his western self. The struggle is more intense and painful in Kipling. He has to grapple with his fears of Indianness which he can neither own up nor jettison; he clings to his English selfhood with a desperation which his overdone commitment to the Raj and notions of racial superiority cannot hide.[101]

Hence the dramatically different endings of the two novels. In *Gora* the hero acquires a wider self-definition where his western self is not disowned but finds a place in a larger philosophy of life:

The significant note here is of re-birth. At the very moment of being caught in a limbo, of having nowhere to go, he (Gora) finds a new habitation through a new baptism. At the same time as Hindu sanctums closed their doors against him, the vast country with its diversity is thrown open before him for a new quest, a new career, a new victory possibly.[102]

In *Kim*, there is no rebirth. Its Mowgli-like hero already has an everyday philosophy of life that embeds him in his culture. At the end, Kipling does provide a bureaucratic link with the Raj for Kim, but that is a somewhat contrived ending shaped by Kipling's private anxieties and his inner need to give an acceptable meaning and legitimacy to Kim's Indian self. In what must be one of the great anti-climaxes of literature, Kim narrows down his self-definition to become a member of the security services of the empire. He has to become an outsider to his own cultural self to be acceptable to the world of his creator.[103]

---

[101]Nandy, *The Intimate Enemy*. See also Edmund Wilson, 'The Kipling that Nobody Read', in Andrew Rutherford (ed.), *Kipling's Mind and Art* (Stanford University Press, 1964), pp. 17–69.

[102]Chatterji, 'Incognitos and Secret Sharers', p. 118.

[103]Angus Wilson seeks to explain away this narrowing of self by arguing that the regime or state to which Kim gives his allegiance protects the innocence of both Kim and the Lama. 'The two higher values in the book—the richness and variety of Indian life and the divine and spiritual idiocy of the Lama—can only be preserved from destruction by anarchic chaos or from despotic tyranny by that [British] rule.' Angus Wilson, *The Strange Ride of Rudyard Kipling, His Life and Works* (London: Secker and Warburg, 1977), p. 130. Wilson fails to notice that Kim's acute sense of survival and repertoire of defensive skills come from his Indian self and the Lama is protected not so much by the Raj as by Kim. Wilson himself remarks four paragraphs earlier,

The Politics of Dissent

Let us pause for a moment and take stock. All three of Tagore's novels deal with the fragility and resilience of political authority and the birth, survival, and death of moral dissent. All show how the division between the public and the private—and, by implication, the secular and non-secular—domains of morality are not ultimately sustainable. The subversion of morality in the public sphere after a while distorts primary human relationships and the very core of one's cultural selfhood.

What gives the three novels their complexity—and their politics of self its depth—is the author's plural concepts of authority and dissent. Political authority for Tagore has three distinct strands. There are the standardized, routine structures of authority, a new set of claimants to authority trying to usurp the moral space created by the rebellious victims of the first set, and a third category, cutting across these two, consisting of those committed to their traditions and to the victims as living, suffering, real human beings rather than as categories in an abstract ideology of dissent. The third set carries the seeds of a genuine rebellion in the future, against the oppressive aspects of the past and an intolerable present. For it includes those in deeper touch with traditions who are, for that very reason, more open to the new and the exogenous. Nikhil's grandmother, Gora's mother and Pareshbabu exemplify the inner strengths of the Indian tradition far better than those aggressively defending the tradition.

The existing structure of authority against which rebellion begins, is weak, compromising, doomed to defeat. The claimants to authority are arrogant, totalizing, efficiently violent, and confident in their new-found power and legitimacy derived from history. It is as if, after demystifying the power of a coercive paternal authority—Indian social orthodoxy on the one hand, and the illegitimate colonial power on the other—one was suddenly confronted with a new fraternal counter-authority claiming total allegiance on the grounds that the other rebels were neither adequately oppositional nor versed in the intricacies of dissent.[104] Tagore's own attack is directed mainly against this new counter-authority. He feels that the moral bankruptcy of the establishment, native as well as foreign, has already been revealed and need not be re-emphasized.

Kim 'unites the knowingness, the cunning, the humour and the appeal of the Dodger, with the gentleness and goodness of Oliver Twist, a seemingly impossible task' (ibid., p. 129).

[104]Cf. Erik Erikson, 'The Legend of Hitler's Childhood', in *Childhood and Society* (New York: Norton, 1961), 2nd ed., ch. 9.

Of the two powers in recession, social orthodoxy and colonialism, the latter remains mostly in the wings. An occasional English magistrate, police officer or informer are all that there is by way of a direct encounter with the Raj. But the presence of colonialism is everywhere felt and it shapes the narrative at every stage. Each major contradiction in the novels involves the entry of western ideas of the nation-state, history, and progress, into the Indian lifestyle, as a means of reorganizing the culture's self-definition. These ideas set the terms of political discourse even among Indians. This success of colonialism is matched by the ambitions of a nationalism which, after faithfully swallowing the colonial world-view hook, line, and sinker, is willing to sacrifice Indians at the altar of a brand-new, imported, progressivist history of the Indian nation-state in the making.

In contrast, the hollow paternal authorities representing Hindu social orthodoxy, who might have set the tone for the heroes of *Ghare-Baire* and *Char Adhyay*, are all dead and their self-destructive, feudal traditions are easy to break. More difficult it is to defy the new breed of robust dissenters who fight these decrepit, collapsing authorities on the one hand, and British imperialism on the other. Both Sandip and Indranath find Indian orthodoxy insufficiently rebellious against the Raj but, in an Oedipal twist, they are themselves tied to their target, the colonial authorities. This is not merely on account of their general conceptual grid but also through the specific theory of political morality and scientized violence borrowed from modern Europe. Ultimately, the followers of Sandip and Indranath get caught in the same trap. Politics, they discover, can be liberating, but it can also mask a form of self-deception that helps hide less obvious bondage.

Nikhil, who rebels against the first set of authorities, social orthodoxy and colonialism, also rebels against the second. But he comes to realize that the second battle, the one against the emerging counter-authorities, will have to be fought out primarily in the minds of the victims. For him the battleground turns out to be both the local community and his wife. Bimala reaches the same intellectual position, but only after a tortuous and self-destructive journey.

Likewise, Ela sees through the empty power of her domineering mother and the self-castration of her academic father soon enough. She creates for herself an independent professional existence outside her unhappy parental home with relative ease. But the moral totalism of Indranath turns out to be both alluring and suffocating. Atin, like Nikhil, finds it easy to despise the meaningless luxury of his aristocratic family home, but is unable to fight Indranath's authority and its fatal charm, and that inability destroys him. Ultimately Indranath, the brilliant self-possessed strategist, loses the battle for Ela's mind to Atin, the weak self-doubting poet. But the victory is more Ela's than Atin's, for it is she who breaks Indranath's spell, he cannot.

In *Gora*, this new authority is internalized; it is part of the hero's fractured self. He sees through the emptiness of his father's authority and his return to faith in his old age. It is more painful for Gora to disown his self-imposed nationalism and the psychological defences that go with it. That nationalism colonizes his self more successfully than any imperial power could have done. This victory of nationalism, Tagore implies, is ultimately a victory of the West over Indian civilization.

A final word. The apparent robustness of Sandip, Indranath, and the Hindu nationalist in Gora derives from their denial of aspects of their culture and self that are identified with effeminacy, especially maternity. The strongest resistance to them, too, finally comes from women; they are the psychological barricade that the culture puts up to protect its *svadharma*. Hence, when women conform or collaborate, they become mere caricatures of conformity and collaboration. Baradasundari is only the most absurd of such caricatures.

Of the women who resist the contesting ideologies of conventionality, collaboration and defensive neo-conservatism, it is Anandamayi whose resistance is the deepest and most 'natural'. She fathoms the inauthenticity of Gora's nationalism from the beginning, while Bimala, despite her initial scepticism about Sandip as a person, is disillusioned with him and his ideology only when destruction has already stared her in the face. Ela lacks even that initial doubt. Both become aware of the psychopathology of nationalism through their relationships with the two men they love. In Tagore's world, motherliness questions the dominant consciousness and resists it more radically and effectively than does conjugality. Hence, when Gora goes through his climactic transformation to arrive at a political position that anticipates the Gandhian world-view in significant ways, his first reconciliation is with his mother and his childhood nurse.

That resistance is the obverse of the seductive unstated claim of nationalism that it is a tested Oedipal remedy—against the anxieties aroused by an indigenous paternal authority, who is perceived to be impotent. Nationalism offers the hope that, by adopting aspects of an exogenous authority that has already laid bare the impotency of the indigenous authority, it is possible to defeat both forms of authority. These aspects include a clearly territorialized concept of the nation-state as the first identifier of a people, a sharp sense of history that reconstructs the past as a unilinear narrative or unfolding of an amoral cross-national zero-sum game, and a theory of progress that sanctions the increasing impersonalization of violence as a mode of cultural self-engineering and self-preservation. The male ancestors of Nikhil and Atin, and even Gora's father, despite their dissipated lifestyle that suggests sexual promiscuity, invoke anxieties about self-castration and social retreat. Nationalism sets up against them rebel claimants to authority who convey a different, more potent cosmopolitan image of male authority. Sandip, Indranath, and the nationalist self of Gora are violent intrusions into the Indian cultural scene. These claimants act out their imperial paternity, both in rebellion and in conformity. All are caught in a painful Oedipal situation intensified by the presence of two sets of paternal authority, one eastern, the other western. As against them, the biculturality of Nikhil and the 'reborn' Gora represents a new mode of cultural continuity. They have been through and emerged relatively intact from the humiliation of the colonial experience; and the even greater humiliation of fighting colonialism with the help of methods and ideologies imported through the colonial connection.

The Lives

Brahmabandhab Upadhyay: Tagore's Political Double

The three novels can be read in many ways. We have read them as a testament of Tagore's political beliefs. We can also read them as a record of Tagore's attempt to grapple with his ambivalence toward the complex, melodramatic personality of Brahmabandhab Upadhyay (1861–1907), a contemporary who served as Tagore's other self in matters of nationalist politics. In the process, I shall explore the form of patriotism which Tagore finally endorsed, superficially opposed to the one Upadhyay upheld but actually in alliance with what Tagore saw as the other self of Upadhyay.

Brahmabandhab Upadhyay was one of the most colourful figures of late nineteenth-century India. Tagore found him 'spirited, fearless, self-sacrificing . . . and extraordinarily gifted', and recognized that it was in *Sandhya*, a journal founded and edited by Upadhyay, that 'the first subtle hints of the beginnings of terrorism in Bengal appeared.'[105] Tagore may

---

[105]Rabindranath Tagore, quoted in Suddhasatva Bosu, *Rabindranather Char Adhyay* (Calcutta: Bharati Publications, 1979), pp. 6–7. Julius Lipner argues that contrary to Tagore's belief, Upadhyay never explicitly advocated violence as the means of expelling the British from India but on occasion came close to doing so. It is, of course, not important whether Upadhyay really said what Tagore thought he was saying, but whether Tagore read Upadhyay's political writings in a particular way.

have sensed that these 'beginnings' were not an accidental by-product of Upadhyay's politics but the direct result of Upadhyay's efforts to work through some of the inner conflicts with which Tagore himself had struggled for much of his life.

Brahmabandhab was born the same year Tagore was, 1861, in a village called Khanyan, thirty-five miles north of Calcutta, in Hooghly district. He was the youngest of three brothers. His real name was Bhavanicharan Bandopadhyay; at home he was called Bhedo. It was a high-status Kulin Brahmin family, proudly Shakto. One marker of Kulin status was hypergamy. Bhavani's great-grandfather, Madanmohan Bandopadhyay, had as a matter of fact established his Kulinhood the hard way, by marrying fifty-four times.

Madanmohan's son, Bhavani's grandfather Harachandra, was said to be opposed to polygamy, for he had considerately married only twice. Perhaps this had something to do with the fact that Harachandra was the first in the family to be exposed to the expanding world of British India and the opportunities it presented to educated, upper-caste Bengalis. He was a police inspector working with Sleeman to eliminate thuggee. Bhavani's father Debicharan, a less colourful upholder of the family tradition, was also a police inspector and had a transferable job which took him to all parts of India. We presume that he was as much a pillar of the Raj as his father had been.

Details of Bhavani's childhood and family are scanty. We know next to nothing about his brothers and nothing about his relationship with them. We know that his mother died when he was less than a year old and that he was brought up by his grandmother, Chandramoni. Though an orthodox Brahmin, Chandramoni had travelled in India, thanks to her husband's job as Sleeman's assistant. She introduced to Bhavani not only the vividness of his cultural traditions but also something of her own disjunctive experiences. Despite being a 'formidable' presence in the household, Chandramoni was particularly fond of her motherless grandson and often protected him from the ire of her stern, disciplinarian son. Despite the tact of Bhavani's biographer, Brahmachari Animananda, Debicharan comes through as an 'autocrat' and 'a man with an iron will' who faithfully followed the imported Victorian adage of never sparing the rod and spoiling his son.[106] However, Debicharan was often not at

---

Julius Lipner, 'A Case-Study in "Hindu Catholicism": Brahmabandhab Upadhyay (1861–1907)', *Zeitschrift fur Missionswissenschaft und Religionswissenschaft*, January 1988, pp. 33–54.

[106]Brahmachari Animananda, *The Blade: Life and Work of Brahmabandhab Upadhyay* (Calcutta: Roy and Son, n.d., estimated 1940), pp. 10–11.

home and it was Chandramoni who defined much of Bhavani's early social environment for him. Animananda sums up his guru's early interpersonal world as follows:

There, right under his nose, were two cultures . . . . Inside the house too it was not all the old system . . . in Chandramoni . . . lived all the spirit of affectionate self-sacrifice that belonged to old *Bharat*. It is on her lap that he learned the language of the Bengali village. She was the source of the sparkling touches, the beautiful homely expressions that brightened domestic topics in the *Sandhya*. She it was who gave him an eye for things Indian,—the mossy tank, the trees, shrill birds, and the sacred river Sarasvati . . . . Her pious devotions, her sacred stories, her very life was an embodiment of the old Hindu ideal; Bhavani would never forget it.[107]

The family deity of the Bandopadhyays was the goddess Kali. 'This could not have been', Julius Lipner points out, 'the mild, sensuous figure the sage Ramakrishna popularized later in Bengal, but the awesome deity current in popular devotion—of frightful countenance, terrible to her enemies but beneficent to her devotees.'[108] Many years later, Lipner adds, Upadhyay would invoke 'Kali-the-Terrible' in graphic Bengali, 'as the mediatrix of India's freedom'[109]—perhaps to legitimize the violent, sacrificial element he sought to introduce into Indian nationalism. It was to remain a major cultural innovation in Indian nationalism, an innovation which built upon Bankimchandra's more nuanced invocation of Bengal's dominant mother deities, to provide the symbolic and paradigmatic frame for the invocation of the sacredness of mother India.

Bhavani's early education in a village school probably only confirmed his interpersonal stereotypes. In the school, discipline was strict and physical punishment common. There was only a single teacher; decades later, Bhavani was bitter enough to remember him as Pitambara the Lame and to call him 'a veritable *yama-raj*', God of Death.[110] Bhavani probably suffered more than other students from the culture of his school, for he was a particularly rebellious boy. The fact that he was an excellent student did not help much. One is left with the impression that, between them, Debicharan and Pitambara succeeded in shaping for Bhavani the concept of a terrorizing male authority.

At the age of thirteen, Bhavani had his sacred-thread ceremony and within a year he also took a vow not to eat meat or fish and not to taste

---

[107]Ibid., pp. 9–10.
[108]Lipner, 'Hindu Catholicism', p. 38.
[109]Ibid.
[110]Ibid.

alcohol. It was a strange vow to take in a Shakto family and one can only hazard the guess that young Bhavani chose unconsciously to identify with his widowed grandmother rather than with the men in the family; that he already felt some discomfort with the lifestyle associated in his mind with his male elders and was trying to move closer to the mix of the old and the new his grandmother represented. Also, Bhavani's mother Radhakumari might have been a Vaishnava. At least Lipner guesses so from her name.[111] Her faith might have underscored the association young Bhavani could have sensed between being abstemious and moving away from the available male role models in the family.

In keeping with his new ascetic commitments, the adolescent Bhavani also took to physical culture and traditional learning with a vengeance. He joined an indigenous gymnasium, *akhada*, to learn wrestling, picked up ju-jitsu, and became a favourite student of the well-known wrestler, Ambika Guha. Bhavani also turned out to be an excellent cricketer. As for traditional learning, he joined a Sanskrit school, *tol*, to study Sanskritic texts from the famous pandits of Bhatpara. According to one of his biographers, at this age Bhavani also showed qualities of leadership.[112]

Bhavani was not unhappy when, at about this time, his father was transferred to Chinsura, a small city west of Calcutta, where he was admitted to a less oppressive school. But he did even better when, after another transfer, he was sent to a school at Hooghly. There he became a great favourite of Robert Thwaytes, the school's English principal, and Yajnesvara Ghose, the headmaster. When Debicharan was transferred yet again, Bhavani was admitted to the General Assembly Institution which, despite its odd name, was a well-known school in Calcutta. Vivekananda, then known as Narendranath Datta, was his class-fellow.

These rapid moves exposed Bhavani to the invigorating atmosphere of the late-nineteenth century urban culture of the Bengali babus, many of them trying to bring about major changes in their traditional way of life in response to the colonial impact. The stirrings of Indian nationalism which were visible by the mid-1840s had now acquired momentum. By the 1860s, metropolitan Calcutta and the surrounding areas were seething with new ideas about—and experiments with—lifestyles, faiths and ideologies.

There was one expression in particular of this adventure of ideas and reformist zeal which acquired a special meaning in Bhavani's life. His uncle, Kalicharan Banerjea (1847–1907) had become a convert to

---

[111]Lipner, 'Hindu Catholicism', p. 38.
[112]Animananda, *The Blade*, p. 11.

Christianity when Bhavani was three, and was something of a pillar of the Bengali Christian community. Kalicharan was an educationist, political thinker, and close associate of liberals and nationalist leaders like Surendranath Banerjea (1848–1925) and Ananda Mohan Bose (1847–1906).[113] Though his conversion had shaken the family, social links with him were not severed; he used to visit Khanyan at weekends. During his visits, he helped Bhavani with his lessons and told him stories from the Mahabharata, which quickly became a favourite with the boy. From the accounts available, one suspects that it was Kalicharan who, of all the father-figures Bhavani encountered in his early life, maintained some continuity with Chandramoni's magical world of maternal nurture. One wonders if, through his uncle, Christianity too did not get identified for the young boy as a possible link to that world.

The attraction of Christianity for young, well-placed, upper-caste reformist Hindus in Bengal had many aspects which we need not go into here. However, in the context of Upadhyay's life, the comments of Bhupendranath Dutta (1880–1961)—who knew Upadhyay and his family well, was himself a respected freedom fighter of the Swadeshi era, and a believer in the use of violence in the anti-imperialist struggle—are particularly relevant. He diagnoses the attraction of Christianity in late nineteenth-century Bengal to be the result of the all-too-manifest glamour and power of western civilization. This glamour and power dazzled many young Indians exposed to the modern sector and Christian missionaries often rubbed this in. They 'equated the new western civilization with Christianity to establish the superiority of their civilization and religion. . . . Consequently, seeing the poor state of their own religion and race, many Hindus were attracted to Christianity . . . .'[114]

We shall have to come back to this issue in the context of Bhavani's life, but should mention here that by the time Kalicharan embraced Christianity, Christian missions in India had developed two sharply contrasted attitudes to Indian culture: one was 'strongly evangelical in tone, viewed human nature as utterly corrupted by the Fall', and was uncompromisingly confrontational towards Hinduism and Indian traditions; the other, more conciliatory, refused to condemn non-Christian religions *a priori* and, therefore, was less keen on proselytization and more open

---

[113]Kalicharan Bandopadhyay also played an interesting role in Gandhi's life. See Mohandas K. Gandhi, *The Message of Jesus Christ* (reprint, Bombay: Bharatiya Vidya Bhavan, 1986), p. 9.

[114]Bhupendranath Dutta, 'Bhumika', in Haridas Mukhopadhyay and Uma Mukhopadhyay, *Upadhyay Brahmabandhaba* (Calcutta: Firma K.L. Mukhopadhyay, 1961), pp. v–xix.

to Hindu categories.[115] Broadly speaking, the first attitude was mainly associated with the Protestants, especially the Baptists, the second with the Catholics.[116] There were unexpected consequences: from the time of Rammohun Roy, the urban upper-caste Bengalis regarded Protestantism as a protest against the amoral hedonism emerging among the babus exposed to colonial rule, while Catholicism was regarded as a culturally more tolerant—and thus less critical—faith. Strange though it may seem in retrospect, this made Catholicism less attractive to the social critics and reformists among the babus who were searching for new bases for social criticism and for new uses of aspects of western culture in India. The number of urban *bhadralok* who turned to Catholicism remained small. We shall return to this point.

At the age of fifteen, Bhavanicharan completed his schooling and was admitted to the Hooghly Mohsin College. The next phase of his life is best described in a delightfully witty, tongue-in-cheek autobiographical essay written by him many years later and, in the next few paragraphs, I shall broadly follow that essay in narrating his story.

The life of a regular student could hold Bhavani only for a year or so (1876–7). Impressed by the nationalist fervour of some of his uncle Kalicharan's mentors, mainly Surendranath Banerjea, he decided to devote all his time to the freedom struggle. Beyond a point, however, the constitutionalist approach of the liberal nationalists failed to satisfy him. It struck him as ineffective, futile posturing. Though he was deeply moved by the public lectures of Banerjea and Ananda Mohan Bose and was later to compare his condition at the time to that of the *gopis* after they had heard Krishna's flute,[117] Bhavani was also influenced by his grandmother's caustic comment: 'Lectures have finished the country.'[118] At the same time, the idea of the ascetic warrior that had become a part of *bhadralok* folklore since the publication of Bankimchandra's *Anandamath*, was re-emerging in Bhavani's imagination as a practical proposition, probably sanctified by his reading of *Gita* as a political text. Finally, a year later, he decided to give up his studies and join the army of the Maharaja of Gwalior to learn *yuddhavidya*, the science of war. (He also attempted to join the British Indian army so as to fight the Zulus, through a step-uncle of his who worked for the commissioner of

[115]Lipner, 'Hindu Catholicism', p. 37.
[116]Ibid.
[117]Animananda, *The Blade*, p. 13.
[118]Brahmabandhab Upadhyay, '*Amar Bharat Uddhar*', *Swaraj*, 26 May and 2 June 1907. For an English translation of this essay I have mainly depended on the extracts translated in Animananda's *The Blade*, pp. 13–22.

recruitment. The uncle did not want his nephew to choose such a risky job; he made sure that the application was shelved on the grounds of Bhavani being a minor.)

Bhavani set off for Gwalior with ten rupees in his pocket, the money for two months' college fees. Three of his friends who joined him were roughly in the same financial state. As a result, the journey turned out to be particularly eventful. They managed to travel up to Etawah in western Uttar Pradesh by train, but Gwalior was another seventy-two miles away. They finally walked it.

The adventure did not last long, for there were three families looking for them. The boys were soon found and brought back to Calcutta. This time Bhavani was put into another college, the Metropolitan Institute, where Surendranath Banerjea himself taught English. But not even the privilege of studying under one of his political idols helped and Bhavani went into a kind of depression for a while, and it appears, even took to drugs.

But he was not one to remain in this condition for long—within a year he had give up taking drugs. His romance with Gwalior was not yet over; the city still beckoned the prospective revolutionary. Soon Bhavani ran away from home again, this time on his own. He was now eighteen and had the princely sum of thirty rupees with him. On it, he reached Gwalior via Agra and Dholepur and even had a dietary adventure on the way. He had turned vegetarian but, on the way to Gwalior, in his enthusiasm to prove himself truly a member of a martial race, he broke his vow and ate meat at the home of a Bengali family. He even persuaded himself that he had enjoyed his return to meat-eating as part of his return to a martial lifestyle, *kshatradharma*.[119] Like many other social reformers and political leaders of his time, Bhavanicharan believed that there was a direct relationship between the cultural practices of the British and their political success; that if Indians could somehow model themselves on the British, political success would automatically follow. And like Vivekananda and unlike Gandhi, he never quite grew out of the belief.

But the Gwalior army remained an unattainable dream, though for an altogether different reason this time. On arriving at Gwalior, Bhavani first took to teaching English to make a living—he had been an excellent student of English in his school days—and then found the courage to go and meet an elderly general of the Scindia army and tell him straight out, 'Make me a soldier.' The general was, as his interlocutor was to recount many years later, a remarkably impressive, kindly, calm and humble man

[119]Ibid., p. 19.

whom Bhavani immediately respected. He patiently explained to the young nationalist the state of affairs in British protectorates, pointing out that though he was called a general, he did not have any power at all. Even more painful to Bhavani was the reason the general gave for his loss of power. Apparently, once, during exercises, the maharaja and the general were heading two opposing forces. Some English guests were also present. When the maharaja felt hungry, he ordered a path to be cleared for breakfast to be brought in; the general sent word that meals would not be given safe conduct. The maharaja, given his priorities, quickly acknowledged defeat and the relationship between the two soured.[120] After hearing this story, Bhavani could no longer avoid facing the fact that the Scindia of Gwalior was already a toothless vassal of British India. He came back heartbroken to Calcutta in 1880–1.

As with many of his contemporaries, Bhavani's martial nationalism was parallelled by his religious quest. For a while he did odd jobs at a couple of places and went, somewhat aimlessly, on one pilgrimage after another. He also drew close to the mystic philosopher—teacher Ramakrishna Paramhamsa (1836–86) and to Keshabchandra Sen (1838–84) of the Nababidhan Brahmo Samaj, who led at the time one of the most prominent social reform movements in India. By the end of 1881 Bhavani had become a devotee of Sen whom he now considered the greatest Indian of his time.[121] He even enthusiastically joined Sen's Bible classes. Though he met the seer Ramakrishna through Sen and admired him greatly, he remained primarily Sen's disciple. It was through Sen and his uncle Kalicharan that Upadhyay began to move towards Christianity.

When Sen died in 1884 Bhavani found his successor, Pratap Chunder Majumdar, impressive as well as inspiring. As a result, in 1887 Bhavani became a Brahmo and formally joined the Nababidhan movement. Meanwhile there was another development. In 1883 a few graduate students of Calcutta University had established a discussion group called the Eagle's Nest which Bhavani had joined as a teacher of Sanskrit. Among the founders of the Nest was a young Sindhi student, Hiranand, later to become famous as Sadhu Hiranand. After obtaining his BA from Calcutta University, Hiranand had returned to Sind, and in 1888, he asked Bhavani to help him in running a school he had founded in Hyderabad, Sind. Bhavani agreed and joined the school as a teacher of Sanskrit.

By all accounts, Bhavani was extremely popular with his students. Certainly he was an uncommon classics teacher at a time when teachers

---

[120]Ibid., p. 22.
[121]Mukhopadhyay and Mukhopadhyay, *Upadhyay Brahmabandhab*, p. 15.

of Sanskrit were stereotyped as being totally cut off from the contemporary world. He played cricket and football with the students, swam,
went kite-flying with them, and was as much their friend as their teacher.
In addition, he delivered public lectures, worked as a Brahmo missionary,
and even officiated at a Brahmo wedding. His integration into the local
community was apparently complete. Animananda goes so far as to
describe him in Sind as an influential Sindhi among Sindhis.[122]

By now it must be fairly obvious that Bhavani's relationship with his
peers always tended to be happier than that with male authorities: the
traces of his relationship with Debicharan were probably not dead in
him. Now that Bhavani was acquiring the trappings of authority himself,
he may have taken special care to see that he remained the first-among-
peers rather than become a feared authority.

It must have appeared to many of his well-wishers that at last Bhavani
was a happily settled man. They were soon to be proved wrong. He was
a person constantly searching, a person for whom a stable external
environment only brought into the open new questions and unknown
inner passions. This time it was the sudden illness of his father, who had
been transferred to Multan in west Punjab that provided the occasion.
Bhavani rushed to Multan and nursed him devotedly, but Debicharan
died.

It was while nursing his sick father that Bhavani read Joseph Faadi
Bruno's *Catholic Faith* which exposed him to a new world. He had
always been interested in Christianity; the Brahmoism Keshabchandra
represented was itself heavily influenced by Christianity. According to
Animananda, 'Bhavani had been attached to Jesus Christ from his early
boyhood. He looked upon him as a personal friend.'[123] Now the exposure
to Bruno pushed Bhavani onto a more adventurous religious path. He
had encountered what to him must have seemed a version of Christianity
unconnected with the Raj and more open to the Indian style of spirituality.
He was not unduly perturbed by the Catholic connection with imperialism
in Africa and South America.

Hiranand, who had some indication of the way his friend's mind was
working, wrote to Bhavani's elder brother, warning him of Bhavani's
intentions, and was asked to dissuade Bhavani from becoming a Christian. Bhavani dutifully agreed to postpone his conversion by a fortnight.
But the die was cast. After the fortnight was over, on 26 February 1891,
he joined the Protestant church in which his uncle Kalicharan was

[122]Animananda, *The Blade*, p. 33.
[123]Ibid., p. 31.

already an important figure. Six months later, on 1 September, he became a Catholic and moved to Karachi.

During his ten years in Sind, Bhavani was successful as a social worker and he took an active interest in a number of religious traditions. Prominent among them were Sikhism and Islam, particularly the Islamic tradition of Latif. It was in Karachi in 1893 that Bhavani adopted the name Brahmabandhab Upadhyay, a name which invokes the informal title 'Brahmananda' given to his hero Keshabchandra Sen by his admirers, and also hints both at Bhavani's Brahminic origins and his lifelong efforts to establish a less hierarchical relationship with the patriarchal theistic authority common to both Brahmoism and Christianity.

The name also invoked that part of his hereditary vocation which never failed to excite him—teaching.

I have adopted the life of Bhikshu (i.e. mendicant) Sannyasi. The practice prevalent in our country is to adopt a new name along with the adoption of a religious life. Accordingly, I have adopted a new name. My family surname is Vandya (i.e. praised) Upadhyay (i.e. teacher, lit. sub-teacher), and my baptismal name is Brahmabandhu (Theophilus). I have abandoned that first portion of my family surname, because I am a disciple of Jesus Christ, the Man of Sorrows, the Despised Man. So my new name is Upadhyay Brahmabandhu.[124]

Later, as it was felt that 'Brahmabandhu' could be considered not adequately respectful, a slight change was made in the last name without altering its meaning.[125] More confident of himself now, in 1894 Upadhyay started *Sofia*, a Catholic journal, wanting to make it not merely a mouthpiece of Catholicism but a journal that would cover comparative, critical theology and attempt to search for truth. He also declared that politics would not be discussed in the journal.[126]

It must be obvious by now that Upadhyay had cast himself in the heroic mould and his experiences in Sind had not allowed him much chance to prove himself. The only half-chance that came his way was late in 1896 when Annie Besant (1847–1933) came to Karachi and Upadhyay was drawn into a public debate with her on, of all things, the nature of God. A public debate has a logic of its own: the fireworks and excitement generated by two learned, well-motivated, but highly-charged and self-righteous persons could not but lead to each being convinced that he or

[124]Editorial in *Sofia*, December 1894, quoted in Lipner, 'Hindu Catholicism', p. 43.

[125]Ibid.

[126]*Sophia*, January 1894, pp. 1–2, quoted in Mukhopadhyay and Mukhopadhyay, *Upadhyay Brahmabandhab*, p. 34.

she had won the debate. The last word on the subject, though, was certainly said by Mrs Besant and it must have hurt the thirty-five-year old, saffron-clad Catholic. On 14 December 1896, she wrote to him:

Dear Sir . . . I trust that some day you also may feel that God is an object of adoration rather than a subject for debate, and that He is better served by truth and good-will than by the stirring up of strife.[127]

What Paresh says about Gora applied as much to Upadhyay: simple, assured peace of mind was not one of his possessions. But Mrs Besant's admonition might have gone home. When plague broke out in Karachi in January 1897, Upadhyay and his disciples, with extraordinary courage and dedication, nursed the abandoned, plague-stricken poor of Karachi; they lived amongst them and cooked for them. One of his devoted disciples, Daulatsing Ramsingh, died of the plague; it was a miracle that in Upadhyay's circle the toll was so slight.

Despite his own beliefs Upadhyay's Catholicism was in fact a unique statement of faith which he hoped would become part of the Indian culture. On the basis of his study of the neo-Thomists and others, he seemed to take the position that while Hinduism was a natural religion, Christianity was a supernatural one and hence one could simultaneously be both Hindu and Christian. That is, an Indian could be a Christian without needing to renounce or vilify Hinduism or deculturizing himself. A religion that seeks to go beyond reason, he argued, destroys its own basis when it attacks a religion based on nature and reason such as Hinduism. One suspects that Upadhyay wanted to remain a Hindu as far as everyday practices were concerned and make Catholicism the vehicle for his personal spiritual quest, perhaps with Jesus Christ as his *ishthadevata* or personal god.[128] But he was clear in his mind about his religious beliefs: 'Let us be called by any name. We mean to peach the reconcilation of all religions in Christ whom we believe to be perfectly divine and perfectly human.'[129]

---

[127] Annie Besant, quoted in Animananda, *The Blade*, p. 4.

[128] Lipner, 'Hindu Catholicism'. For a discussion of the environment within which this response arose, see Julius Lipner, 'A Modern Indian Christian Response', in H.G. Goward (ed.), *Modern Indian Responses to Religious Pluralism* (The State University of New York Press, 1987), pp. 291–314.

It seems that while Upadhyay's theology has had a direct impact on the Indian church only recently, his basic philosophical position established a continuity with Indian practices, *lokachara*, early enough. I learn from Jyoti Shahi that in Madras the proportion of those who accept Christ as their *isthadevata* is more than five times the proportion of Christians.

[129] Animananda, *The Blade*, p. 39.

Also, the politics of culture always remained a latent passion of Upadhyay's. Even his definition of his new-found faith was contaminated by this passion:

> By birth we are Hindus and shall remain *Hindus* till death . . . . But as *dvija* (twice-born) by virtue of our sacramental rebirth, we are *Catholic*: we are Hindus as far as our physical and mental constitution is concerned, but in regard to our immortal souls we are Catholics. We are Hindu-Catholics.[130]

Such a view of the relationship between Hinduism and Christianity contrasted strongly with the confrontational style of the missionaries of the period and, even more important, with the attitude of Bengali converts to Christianity. One of the main attractions of Christianity for upper-caste Bengalis was the uncompromising hostility shown to Hindu traditions by most missionaries, specially the Protestant denominations chief of whom were the Baptists. Since the days of Rammohun Roy, the Bengali youth had been searching for faiths and ideologies which would take a clear position on the growing hedonism and anomie among the urban Bengalis brought about by the large-scale social disruptions caused by the colonial political economy. Many of these rebels saw no possibility of Hinduism being reformed from within. Catholicism often seemed to such youth, despite the efforts of a number of Catholic missionaries, to be 'soft' on rituals, icons, a plurality of gods, and worldly pleasures. The severity of Protestantism with its sternly monotheistic beliefs and puritan ethic seemed to offer a more appropriate remedy for the social problems of the Bengali middle classes.

The Catholic Church of the time, perhaps sensitive to the same issue, was unlikely to be sympathetic towards Brahmabandhab's venture, especially since there was a heavy dose of Vedanta in Brahmabandhab's version of Christianity. The Church soon stopped the circulation of *Sofia* among Catholics and the journal had to close down in 1900. When Brahmabandhab restarted *Sofia* as a monthly, the Church again expressed its displeasure with some vehemence, for the journal now had a clear political line. The journal finally closed the same year.

It was while editing *Sofia* that Upadhyay first acknowledged the presence of Tagore as a major literary figure in the world. In 1901, as the co-founder and editor of the *Twentieth Century*, one of the first things he did was publish an appreciative review of a book of Tagore's. Tagore

---

[130]Brahmabandhab Upadhyay, in *Sophia*, July 1898. Quoted in Chaturvedi Badrinath, *Dharma, India and the World Order: Twenty Essays* (New Delhi: Centre for Policy Research, 1991).

remarks in the preface to *Char Adhyay* that that was the first 'unhesitant' critical praise he had ever received. At about this time Tagore started his rural university at Shantiniketan, and in this he sought the help of his new-found friend who had earlier experimented with similar educational ideas.

Upadhyay did help Tagore but did not stay at Shantiniketan for long. He moved to Calcutta and became an ardent preacher of Vedanta and, in his new incarnation, a passionate apologist of the *varnashrama dharma*, the caste codes. He also undertook a trip to England in 1902–3 to lecture on Hindu philosophy and society. His childhood friend, Vivekananda, had just died and partly the inspiration to spread the philosophy of Vedanta in the West came from Vivekananda's earlier success there. At one time Upadhyay had criticized Vivekananda and his version of the Vedanta; now, deeply moved by Vivekananda's death, he took upon himself his friend's unfinished task, at least partly motivated by what he saw as his friend's real mission: *firingijaivrata*, literally 'the rite of conquering the whites'.[131]

Upadhyay started for England with twenty-seven rupees in his pocket. He was later to describe the visit in his typically self-deprecating manner as an attempt to get from the fair-skinned the same applause that he had received in Calcutta, Bombay and Madras.[132] He was more than successful. Both at Oxford and Cambridge his lectures were highly thought of and Cambridge University not only requested him to recommend a traditional Vedantic scholar as a lecturer at the University but also to find the money to finance a chair in Vedantic studies. However, Upadhyay himself disliked what he saw of the western lifestyle—its rampant consumerism, its self-interest based competitiveness and, above all, its 'liberated' women.

Upadhyay's reaction to the western woman was, to say the least, surprising. He had a Brahmo past and was still a Christian. Both these religious movements had eagerly taken up in Bengal the cause of women. Perhaps, as a *brahmachari* and *sannyasi*, having struggled long with his sexuality, he found the man–woman relationship in England overly eroticized and, hence, painfully anxiety-provoking. Perhaps he missed in England the manner in which both Brahmoism and Christianity in nineteenth-century Bengal linked the cause of women and sexual

---

[131]Mukhopadhyay and Mukhopadhyay, *Upadhyay Brahmabandhab*, pp. 75–6. In later life, Lipner says ('Hindu Catholicism', p. 48), Upadhyay used the pejorative term *Firingi* for the European.

[132]Mukhopadhyay and Mukhopadhyay, *Upadhyay Brahmabandhab*, p. 78.

puritanism. He did write on what he described as the English over-concern with *prakriti* (the common Sanskrit and Bengali word for women as well as nature, including human nature), and the English inability to understand the Hindu ideals of *nivritti* or abstinence, and *nishkama* or desireless autonomy from *prakriti*. He was probably already unwittingly moving towards the position that Gandhi was to formalize later as an attempt to transcend patriarchy through celibacy.[133]

On his return from England in 1904, Upadhyay started a new daily in Bengali, called the *Sandhya*. When Bengal was partitioned in 1905, *Sandhya* was at the forefront of the struggle against partition and its policy became increasingly supportive of the idea of violent resistance to British rule. It is said that at this time he repeatedly faced and was deeply hurt by the hostility of some Hindu nationalists partly because of his Brahmo and Protestant past but primarily because he was still a practising Catholic. To finally allay their misgivings, Upadhyay performed *prayaschitta* (penitential rite or penance) under the *mitakshara* system of social codes to become a Hindu again. According to his Christian disciple Rebachand, Pandit Panchanan Tarkaratna gave Upadhyay the *vidhan* or injunction for this form of penance. But even before he had performed the rite, Bhupendranath Dutta says, Upadhyay had begun to move towards Hinduism, somewhat in the manner in which the Spanish nationalist El Cid had moved towards Christianity.[134]

In 1907, Upadhyay started a weekly to supplement *Sandhya*. Among other things, the weekly attempted to discover the native culture of the Aryans and attack Nordism in its various guises, particularly its aesthetics. Even a cursory look at Upadhyay's writings of the time makes it clear that he was moving towards a total rejection of the West and a redefinition of the Indian self in such clear-cut, well-bounded, native terms that it could not but lead to the idea of violent resistance and terrorism to drive the British out of India. When Dutta told him in 1907 of an instance of passive resistance by the early Christians, Upadhyay told him straightaway, 'That will not do for us.'[135]

Predictably, Upadhyay was soon picked up and tried for sedition. He refused to appear in court, saying:

[133]Brahmabandhab Upadhyay, '*Bilat-Jatri Sannyasir Chithi*', 1906, quoted in Mukhopadhyay and Mukhopadhyay, *Upadhyay Brahmabandhab*, pp. 82–4; also see Pat Caplan, 'Celibacy as a Solution? Mahatma Gandhi and *Brahmacharya*', in Pat Caplan (ed.), *The Cultural Construction of Sexuality* (London: Tavistock, 1987), pp. 271–95.
[134]Dutta, 'Bhumika', pp. xiii–xiv, xvii.
[135]Ibid., p. xvii.

I do not want to take part in the trial because I do not believe that in carrying out my humble share of the God-appointed mission of Swaraj I am in any way accountable to the alien people who happen to rule over us.[136]

While the trial was on, Upadhyay suddenly fell ill and was taken to the Campbell Medical College, Calcutta, where, on account of a tetanus infection after a hernia operation, he died in pain on 27 October 1907.

The hospital authorities, perhaps because they were government officials, did not even wait for his relatives and friends to come and take the body; it was put out in the street, in the sun, outside the hospital.[137] But his admirers by now were legion; they picked up the body and, spontaneously forming a procession in which about 10,000 persons participated, took it to the cremation grounds.

The British–Indian press could hardly hide their relief at Upadhyay's death. The Indians were heartbroken. Many talked of his death as *ichchha-mrityu*, self-chosen death, to avoid being tried by the British.

My brief account of Brahmabandhab Upadhyay's life cannot begin to convey its drama and passions. (Fortunately, there are a few biographies which do some justice to him, particularly the ones by Swami Animananda and Haridas and Uma Mukhopadhyay.[138]) However, I hope I have conveyed some of its richness and complexity, and shown how, since he represented some of the major streams of the nationalist and social reform movements, debates or exchanges over these were not a matter of external encounters for him but became internal confrontations.

In coping with social and political cross-currents as inner vectors Upadhyay was not unique. His friend Vivekananda's brief life was equally stormy, dramatic, and characterized by deep internal contradictions.[139] Similarly, the Gujarati poet, Narmadashanker Lalshanker Dave (1833–86),

[136]Brahmabandhab Upadhyay, quoted in Jogeshchandra Bagal, *National Biography* (New Delhi: Government of India, 1974), Vol. 4, pp. 372–4.

[137]Dutta, 'Bhumika', p. xiv.

[138]The latter also includes a fascinating foreword by Bhupendranath Datta. We have already used them in this account. Julius Lipner and George Gispert-Sauch are working on a new anthology of Upadhyay's writings which promises to deal with the unique world-view and theology Upadhyay developed. Lipner's two published papers, which we have also used in this account, provide an excellent introduction to Upadhyay's life and work and the reasons which have made him a cult figure for contemporary Christian theologians in India.

[139]Sudhir Kakar, *The Inner World: Childhood and Society in India* (New Delhi: Oxford University Press, 1979; reprint, 1981), pp. 160–81; Krishna Prakash Gupta, 'The Role-Playing of a Religious Tradition: Vivekananda's Reconstruction of Hinduism', in D.L. Sheth and Ashis Nandy (eds.), *The Hindu Vision: Heritage, Challenge and Redefinitions* (New Delhi: Sage, forthcoming).

known as Narmad, had, unknown to Upadhyay, internalized and then given flamboyant, personalized expression to the public issues of his time.[140] However, the social currents in Bengal in Upadhyay's time were more sharply opposed and, as we have already seen, Upadhyay was prone to seek his solutions to private and public problems in a heroic and extravagant fashion. This made his shifts of belief and vocation all the more spectacular and his failures, as Tagore might have put it, more heart-rending. This was fit material for a novelist and Tagore did not waste it.

In all three political novels, Upadhyay is the model for the hero as well as the 'villain'; in two of them, *Char Adhyay* and *Gora*, the heroes, being anti-heroes, can also be seen as the villains. It is possible to contend that Sandip's distorted personality cannot possibly represent Upadhyay's but it is equally possible to answer that, to Tagore, Sandip was the inevitable pathological end-product of the political forces released by the likes of Upadhyay in his later life, and should be construed as Upadhyay's brain child. Nikhil, on the other hand, could be read as the socially creative other self of Upadhyay or as Rabindranath himself, identifying with the earlier, pre-Swadeshi self of Upadhyay. There is little scope for debate about the other two novels. In both, the social conflicts around culture and selfhood are presented in a poignant fashion and, as part of the exercise, nationalism itself is analysed with a ruthlessness which only a self-confident theorist and builder of Indian self-definition like Tagore could have the courage to do. Had they been written by anyone else, all three novels would have seemed collaborationist to Indians, as at least one of them seemed to Lukacs. (Though a part of Tagore's self-confidence, as we shall suggest below, might have been powered by the morally discomforting awareness that he had within himself something of both Sandip and the earlier Gora.)

Authority and Defiance: The Artist as Autobiographer

What attracted the romantic, anti-imperialist poet to the heroic nationalist revolutionary? This question is only a variation of one which neither Tagore nor we have posed directly in connection with his three political novels: what attracted Atin to Indranath and Binay to Gora? Or, even more pertinently, what bonded Nikhil to Sandip? Nikhil, after all, knew Sandip well and sensed the seductive pull he might exert over Bimala. Where did innocence end and collusion begin?

Part of the answer can be gleaned from the complex story of Tagore's

---

[140]Navalram Lakshmiram Pandeya, *Kavijivan*, (ed.) Mohanbhai Shankarbhai Patel (Ahmedabad: Gujarat Vidyapeeth, 1955); Gulabdas Broker, *Narmadashankar* (New Delhi: Sahitya Academy, 1977).

life, and from his personality as it intermeshed with Upadhyay's. That is a subject too vast for the scope of this essay, but I shall nevertheless permit myself a brief digression on Tagore's early exposure to various forms of social and political authority, with the help of Tagore's two autobiographical works, *Jivansmriti* and *Chhelebela*. I shall suggest that Tagore's relationship with authorities in his childhood was never as conflicted as Upadhyay's and, more crucially, that Tagore often sensed the fragility and transience of such authorities. His rebelliousness, therefore, was tempered as well as deepened by a stronger sense of filial responsibility and personal efficaciousness.

It is as well to remember that the poet himself had little time for biographies and historical empiricism. According to him, a life history has no relevance to a poet's life or selfhood. In 1901 he reviewed a two-volume work on Alfred Tennyson, produced by Tennyson's son, and stated in the review that a poet does not compose his own life the way he composes poetry.[141] Unlike the biographies of *karmaviras*, successful social activists who intervene in life to re-define it and thus lend a touch of poetry and greatness to their own lives, the life of a poet may consist of trivial and routine details.[142] While curious about the lives of the poets of ancient India, he is therefore not unhappy that there is no biography of any of them. 'No one will accept as history the stories that are current about Valmiki. But we feel that they constitute the observed reality about the poet.'[143] Defying this warning however, we shall try to enter the personal life of Tagore, not to define him by the 'hard' realities of his early life, but to set a context to his construction of his own past as it interacted with his times.

There were remarkable differences between the life-experiences of Rabindranath Tagore and Bhavanicharan Bandopadhyay turned Brahmabandhab Upadhyay. Tagore was born in the same year Bhavani was, at Calcutta, thirty-five miles away from the village where Bhavani spent his early years. He too was the youngest child of his parents. Here the similarities end, for Tagore was born into an aristocratic, wealthy, Brahmo family, already well-known for its contribution to the political, economic and cultural life of India. His grandfather, Dwarakanath Tagore (1794–1846), was considered one of the greatest Indians of the nineteenth century. A close associate of the scholar, social reformer and religious

---

[141]Rabindranath Tagore, '*Kavijivani*', in *Rabindra-Rachanabali*, Vol. 4, pp. 688–90.

[142]Ibid., p. 688.

[143]Ibid., p. 689.

leader, Rammohun Roy (1772–1833), and one of the first to embrace Brahmoism, Dwarakanath started life as an official of the British East India Company and ended as a successful entrepreneur, a pioneer in the mining industry, shipping and banking in India, and as a noted social reformer.

Socially at ease with the British community in India, Dwarakanath remained, despite his reformist zeal, a pillar of Bengali society till the end of his life. He was in the forefront of the movement against the practice of *sati* and worked throughout his adult life for the spread of western education, especially the modern system of medicine, in India. Like his hero, Rammohun Roy, he spent his last days in England and died in Surrey.[144]

Dwarakanath's son and Rabindranath's father, Debendranath Tagore (1817–1905), suffered huge financial losses. But the loss was compensated by his enormous stature as a pious man and a social reformer. Debendranath became an ascetic early in life—to judge by his fascinating autobiography, mainly as a reaction to his father's hedonism—and remained so deeply involved in spiritual pursuits that he came to be known in later life as a *maharshi*, a great seer.[145] Such was his commitment that even Benjamin Franklin's 'worldly-wise' religiosity, otherwise clearly impregnated with puritan ethics, disturbed him by its worldliness.[146] Asceticism, however, did not interfere with Debendranath's organizational skills and it was he who did the most to give a sustainable structure to the Brahmo Samaj movement. Even after Keshabchandra Sen (who was to fire the imagination of the young Bhavani) parted company with him in 1864, Debendranath continued to head a major faction of the Brahmos.

By the 1870s, the Tagores were even more heavily influenced by western intellectual traditions and social mores. There was obviously some legitimacy for this bicultural existence in urban, upper-caste Bengali society; it must have met a widely-felt social need. The babus perhaps sensed that such experiments in bicultural living were important and, contrary to popular belief, they did not view the Tagores' western ways

---

[144]The Tagores were *Pirali* Brahmins with a lower status than ordinary Brahmins. Two generations earlier, a forefather had reportedly accepted meat from a Muslim and invited the censure of the community. This marginality, it can be argued, made them fit candidates for new vocations and ventures which would allow them to redeem their lost social status. And the new political economy in eastern India, introduced by the Raj, opened up such a possibility for them.

[145]Debendranath Tagore, *Atmajivani*.

[146]Rabindranath Tagore, '*Jivansmriti*', *Rabindra-Rachanabali*, Vol. 10, pp. 3–125; see p. 45.

as an attack on native society. Certainly the Tagores, despite their cultural and religious heterodoxy, dominated the Bengali cultural scene for about one hundred years, not only in the world of literature, music and the fine arts, but also in fashions and lifestyle. They remained till the 1940s the most important of the families trying to set the standards by which urban upper-caste Bengalis decided what should or should not be borrowed from the culture of their rulers, and what could or could not constitute the necessary new forms of pan-Indian contemporaneity. (There is no better illustration of this than the now-dominant style of wearing the sari which the Tagore women evolved. Influenced by the traditional Bengali and some south Indian ways of wearing a sari, the new style evolved by the Tagores quickly became for most urban Indians the formal, pan-Indian, 'traditional' Bengali way of tying the sari. The only comparable 'invention of tradition' I can think of is the Gandhian *charkha*, which was a version of the traditional *charkha* developed by an urban Parsi technician with Gandhi's encouragement.)

Rabindranath claims in his autobiography—and most knowledgeable Bengalis would agree with him—that though his family adopted many western practices or *prathas*, the Tagore always retained their pride in their own country.[147] This pride found expression in a somewhat adolescent, romantic defiance of the British authorities, which the authorities were mature enough not to take seriously or attempt to suppress. In *Jivansmriti* Tagore comments, with a mixture of sarcasm, self-deprecation, and admiration for the finesse of the colonial power, that no one had written to the London *Times* complaining about the casual attitude of the British–Indian government to the arrogance of a defiant young poet and the danger he posed to the Raj.[148]

Tagore relates in *Jivansmriti* how he attended a number of adventurous secret meetings organized by his cousin Jyotirindranath Tagore or Jyoti. These were held, appropriately enough, in an abandoned house in a Calcutta lane. The only thing dangerous about the meetings was their secrecy.[149] Tagore constructs the moral of the story thus:

Courage may be comforting or discomforting but it always invokes respect; a way must be kept open in any state for the expression of heroism. In the absence

[147]Ibid., p. 66.
[148]Ibid., p. 67.
[149]Ibid.

of such an opening, it finds expression in peculiar ways and its consequences become unthinkable.[150]

Rabindranath perspicaciously adds that if the government had suspected real danger, the farce would have become a tragedy.[151] He goes on to describe Jyoti's introduction of a rather comic form of national dress that was a cross between *dhoti* and pyjama, and his attempts to establish an indigenous match-box factory and a textile mill. Both were fiascos and it was only the entry of a couple of realistic, 'sane' persons into the group that brought it down to earth.[152] But not before Tagore had internalized the image of Jyotirindranath as a possible model for a patriotic hero—romantic, to the extent of being comically so, but also courageous, moral and supportive. Almost, one is tempted to add, an early prototype of Nikhil in *Ghare-Baire*.

Jyoti and his kind may not have left a mark on the political history of Indian nationalism, but they did provide for Tagore another model of patriotism. In this model, patriotism had touches of aristocratic amateurishness, of a game that was serious, but not serious enough to be turned into a combat with no scope for chivalry, romance, or fun. The casual comments in Abanindranath Tagore's autobiography on Jyoti's nationalism endorse Rabindranath's memories in every important respect, besides indicating why, to the Tagores, the tense nationalistic spirit of the post-Swadeshi period was to seem a betrayal of the youthful innocence and authenticity of truly Indian nationalism.[153]

In Abanindranath's reconstruction of the spirit of that nationalism, there was no intense pain or conflict, no gory heroism; there were only lovable successes and forgivable failures. Rabindranath led the younger Tagores into adventurous business ventures which invariably failed, reaffirmations of Bengali culture, dress and language which sometimes succeeded, and into the collection of funds for nationalist work through organizing processions and demonstrations which, whether they were successful or not, ended as noisy, festive events. Few feared such nationalism, certainly not the whites. Abanindranath even recounts one episode where some English residents of Calcutta waved their hats and shouted nationalist slogans like 'Bande Mataram'. When Abanindranath's

---

[150]Ibid.
[151]Ibid.
[152]Ibid., pp. 68–9.
[153]Abanindranath Tagore and Rani Chanda, *Gharoa* (Calcutta: Visvabharati, 1971).

mother took to the *charkha*, a Mr Havell (presumably the principal of the Government Art College, Calcutta) imported a *charkha* from England for her.[154]

'One's memories of one's life', Tagore says at the beginning of *Jivansmriti*, 'is not the same as the history of one's own life'; 'the invisible artist who draws one's life on one's memory paints a picture and is not interested in a mirror image.'[155] If the story of one's life is not the same as a life history or a formal autobiography, if such a story is ultimately a matter of creative fantasy, it should bear a relationship with one's literary works and perhaps even with the organizing principles of one's creative imagination. We shall briefly introduce here only one of the threads of continuity running through Rabindranath's story of his own life, his political novels, and his complex ambivalence towards Upadhyay's nationalist politics. This continuity is the nature of the male authority Rabindranath encountered in his early years, the means he developed to cope with it, and the strengths and weaknesses which eventually informed his concept of a political leader. The discovery of Jyoti as a model might not have been an accident.

Rabindranath's father, we learn from *Jivansmriti*, was frequently away from home during the poet's childhood. At home, Debendranath's authority was unquestioned; when he was absent, a huge staff of servants constituted the immediate authority for the young Rabindranath. His mother, with her large brood of children, always remained for him something of a distant source of love and care.

The urban, upper middle-class Bengali world had already developed in Calcutta a culture which was to play a significant social role over the next hundred years. This culture gave servants an important place in child-rearing and pre-adolescent socialization, a function that survived till after the end of World War II. One important aspect of the function was the disciplinary powers the servants exercised over the children, perhaps as a partial compensation for the monetization of their work culture and social relationships with employers. Holding such authority over the children was probably a mutually acceptable means of reaffirming the non-contractual nature of social relations between employer and employee. In *Jivansmriti*, Rabindranath calls the system *bhrityarajak tantra*, and compares its presiding authorities with the slave dynasty which had ruled India in medieval times.[156]

---

[154]Ibid. See especially pp. 24–34.
[155]Ibid., p. 5.
[156]Ibid., pp. 16–17. Cf. the role of the servants in the life of another great Calcuttan,

Certainly in Tagore's family, to judge by a number of memoirs, the servants wielded enormous authority.[157] They supervised the food, dress and play of the children and their power, though only a delegated one, seemed to the children quite awesome. It was this second-order, fragile but oppressive immediate authority that Tagore first learnt to negotiate in life. He quickly found out that while physical punishment was frequently given, it could, with some adroitness be avoided. For if a child preferred to have simpler (and cheaper) snacks than the parents had provided for, it allowed the servants to make money on the children's food. If a servant was addicted to opium and, needing extra nourishment, did not press the children unduly to drink their milk, a child very soon learnt—as Rabindranath did—to make a fuss about drinking milk.[158]

This created space for manoeuvre went with a latent perception of the feebleness of the servants' hold over them. The final authority vested in the adult members of the family, who were a varied lot, mostly unconcerned with the children's day-to-day life, and lived in their own world, a world to which the children had only limited access.[159] Certainly nowhere in Rabindranath's childhood memories does one find the tense, passionate bitterness towards authority that is revealed in Upadhyay's reconstruction of his childhood. Both in *Jivansmriti* and *Chhelebela*, there are references to oppressively strict schools and unimaginative teachers but the happier memories of affectionate, highly creative authorities soften them and convert them into half-serious half-comic experiences. At least

---

a physicist turned plant physiologist, Jagadis Chandra Bose (1857–1937), in Ashis Nandy, 'Defiance and Conformity in Science: The World of Jagadis Chandra Bose', in *Alternative Sciences: Creativity and Authenticity in Two Indian Scientists* (revised edition, New Delhi: Oxford University Press, 1993), Part 2.

In later life, in one of his most moving short stories, Tagore was to reverse the relationship he describes with such wit in *Jivansmriti*. See Rabindranath Tagore, '*Khoka-babur Pratyavartan*', *Rabindra-Rachanabali*, Vol. 8, pp. 514–9. The story indicates that underlying the tense relationship between servants and children of the Tagore family lay an awareness of the loyalty, affection and, what Takie Lebra calls self-other exchange which bound the two sides together. See note 157 below.

[157]See for instance the two classic general descriptions of the Tagore family environment in Tagore and Chanda, *Gharoa*; and *Jorasankor Dhare* (Calcutta: Visvabharati, 1960). Cf., for instance, Takie S. Lebra, 'Socialization of Aristocratic Children by Commoners: Recalled Experiences of the Hereditary Elite in Modern Japan', *Cultural Anthropology*, in press; and 'Migawari: The Cultural idiom of Self-Other Exchange in Japan'; presented at the International Conference on Perceptions of Self in China, India and Japan, Honolulu, 14–18 August 1989. Interestingly, Lebra presumes her observations, very similar to ones available about the Tagore family, to be unique to Japan.

[158]*Jivansmriti*, pp. 16–17.

[159]Tagore, *Gharoa*, pp. 103–4.

the two autobiographical accounts suggest that Debendranath never seriously interfered with Rabindranath's autonomy, not even when assertion of that autonomy involved defiance of Debendranath's tastes and opinions.[160] The only thing Debendranath seemed uncompromising about was cold baths; Rabindranath says that even at Dalhousie, the Himalayan hill resort, he had to bathe in icy water.[161]

While young Rabindranath was discovering for himself the secret of controlling his immediate authorities, his family was introducing him to the secret of new forms of dissent from the established and the authoritative. In this, Jyotirindranath again played an important part. Jyoti was the first to offer young Rabindranath not merely a model of dissent but also a model of male authority which was both ardently patriotic and gifted with an intense capacity for artistic expression together with a style of creativity which borrowed uninhibitedly from both the East and the West. Rabindranath says:

In studying literature, in the cultivation of the arts, from childhood onwards, my main support was Jyotidada . . . . I uninhibitedly joined him in discussions of things emotional and cognitive; he did not ignore me as a mere child.
   He gave me a certain large-sized freedom; in his company I lost my inner inhibitions. Nobody else would have dared to give that kind of freedom . . . . If I had not been freed from fetters at the time, I would have been crippled for the rest of my life.[162]

It was Jyoti who was the formative influence in developing Rabindranath's basic ambivalence towards the idea of social evolution and human engineering. Discussing the role Jyoti played in his life Rabindranath says:

The powerful always seek to limit freedom by talking of the misuse of freedom, but freedom cannot be called freedom unless one has the right to misuse it . . . . Only Jyotidada, without any inhibition and through all good and evil, has pushed me towards my self-realization . . . . From this experience I have learnt to fear the menace of the good-that-comes-in-the-form-of-improving-others more than evil itself.[163]

There have been many rumours about Rabindranath's love for, or even affair with, Jyoti's wife, Kadambari Devi. The rumours, even if they

[160]Ibid., p. 47.
[161]Ibid.
[162]Ibid., p 61.
[163]Ibid.

have no basis, serve to underscore the intense relationship Rabindranath had with his sister-in-law. If it was Jyoti who introduced Rabindranath to the world of politics and the arts, she was the first of the Tagores and their family friends to recognize Rabindranath's immense creative talent. Certainly she was the first to give the young Rabindranath, deeply unsure of his writing, confidence in himself.

Kadambari Devi killed herself a few months after Rabindranath's marriage. The suicide probably had more to do with Jyoti and his association with the world of the theatre than with Rabindranath, but it was nevertheless a trauma for the young poet. He was certainly haunted till the end of his life by painful memories of one who represented a mix of protective care, and the spirit of intellectual adventure and social commitment. In his seventies, when he took to painting, the face of Kadambari Debi became a leitmotif in his work. It is probably no accident that in some of his important novels, including *Ghare-Baire*, there are situations where wives guiltily recognize that they have fallen in love with talented, spirited poetic figures—men who were sometimes inspired, like the young Rabindranath, by passionate, violent forms of nationalism— thus betraying the trust of their less flamboyant husbands who were equally noble, public-spirited, courageous beings.[164] In Tagore's novels, such husbands are often men who are open to other cultures, and their affirmation of Indianness is often affirmation of a more catholic form of cultural selfhood. Jyoti might have provided the inspiration for Nikhil and it is easy to interpret Nikhil and Sandip as being two aspects of Brahmabandhab; but at another plane both Nikhil and Sandip can be read as aspects of Rabindranath himself, with the 'guilty' self 'villainized' and projected counter-phobically into Sandip.

Jivansmriti underscores another sharp contrast between the life experiences of Upadhyay and Rabindranath Tagore. To Tagore, thanks to his early exposure to the West, the West was never a forbidding presence.[165] He perceived the social and cultural diversity of the West, including the poor, the humble and idealistic. In *Jivansmriti* he remembers his Latin teacher in England—shy, badly-dressed, undernourished, prematurely old, and vulnerable.[166] He remembers his English school as a place where he was the subject of friendly curiosity and where his fellow-students would often shyly push apples and oranges into his pocket and run away.[167]

[164]See especially Rabindranath Tagore, 'Nastanir', in *Rabindra-Rachanabali*, Vol. 9, pp. 337–70. Also accessible in film form as Satyajit Ray's classic film *Charulata*.
[165]Tagore, '*Jivansmriti*', see particularly pp. 73–88.
[166]Ibid., p. 75.
[167]Ibid., p. 74.

He was also exposed early in his stay to the less-than-imperial self of an England brutalized by the industrial revolution. In his second letter from England he mentioned, with a clear touch of disgust, the dirty, pathologically violent, subhuman existence of the lower classes in England.[168] He noticed the cultural barrenness of everyday life in England as well as the inferior position of women and the empty lives they led.[169] It was unlikely that he would ever be in awe of England: to him the country would be like any other, a mix of good and evil. Tagore, like Gandhi, could not but feel that there was an acceptable, in fact, a lovable West, and that this other West was waiting to be rediscovered.

In comparison, Tagore's sensitivity to the India beyond Bengal is somewhat obtuse. His description of his days at Ahmedabad is culturally empty, and though the city inspired him to write one of his finest stories, *Kshudita Pashan*, the inspiration came primarily from the palace in which his elder brother, an official of the Raj, stayed. There is nothing of Gujarat in the story. Likewise, the little cultures of the Himalaya are hardly noticed in the *Jivansmriti*, even though he writes with great feeling about his days at Dalhousie. The closest Rabindranth comes to acknowledging the other traditions of India is when he mentions his father's participation in the singing of *gurvani* at the Golden Temple in Amritsar.[170]

Here, too, one notices the contrast with Upadhyay, who—despite his deep commitment to the greater Sanskritic culture, and his occasional crude harangues against the little cultures of India—was deeply influenced by his experiences in Gwalior and Sind. Tagore's catholicity, on the other hand, had little place for the little cultures of India outside eastern India; he presumably identified them as minor local variations of the greater Sanskritic tradition. On the whole, however, for both Tagore and Upadhyay—or for that matter almost all the major political and intellectual actors of their age—Vedantic Hinduism was the real core of Hinduism and the basis of all social and political activism. Few were sensitive to the élitism and defensiveness implicit in such Vedanticism. It was only after the entry of Gandhi into Indian public life that a new awareness arose of the politics of cultures which was turning the little cultures of India into the society's last line of defence against the colonizing West. They became a major source of resistance against what Tagore identified as the pathologies of nationalism and the organized violence

---

[168]Rabindranath Tagore, 'Europe-*Pravasir Patra*', in *Rabindra-Rachanabali*, Vol. 10, pp. 242–6.

[169]Ibid.

[170]Tagore, '*Jivansmriti*', p. 43.

increasingly associated with the modernization of India. Gandhi was willing to build upon the contradiction between the nationalism which entered India as an imperial category and the nationalism which sprang out of democratic aspirations, hoping that the latter would some day supersede the former. For the former had established clear links with the classical tradition and the Brahminic order, the latter with the non-canonical and the local. The Mahatma might not have shared Tagore's hostility to the very idea of nationalism but he did share the poet's moral concerns.

Presumably they were the same moral concerns that moved Upadhyay. Or so at least Tagore believed when he described his last encounter with his revolutionary friend a short while before he died in 1907. To the extent Tagore saw Upadhyay as rooted in his culture, he also saw him as sharing his concerns with resisting the scientization and impersonalization of violence in the name of nationalism. At the least, the poet must have presumed, there was a painful and intense struggle within the revolutionary to reconcile his culture with his own political methodology.

The encounter between the two derived its moral tension and tragic grandeur from Tagore's faith that Upadhyay in his authenticity could not but rebel against the other Upadhyay who gave priority to nationalist allegiance over cultural selfhood.

Underlying the tension was, however, Tagore's deep ambivalence towards Upadhyay as a nationalist actor. The ambivalence was generated by something more than the purely moral concerns we have spelt out. We have already hinted that during his younger, Hindu *mela* days, Tagore had agreed with many elements of Upadhyay's culturally exclusivist ideology. Tagore's image of India at that stage, at least one commentator has noticed, excluded not merely Muslims and Christians but also the low-brow pagan India of the epics.[171] We have already noted that Tagore's sensitivity to the little cultures of India was less than impressive. As late as 1902, Tagore wrote authoritatively that the Brahmavidyalya at Shantiniketan would not allow anything which went against the Hindu society;[172] his concept of Hinduism at that time was not as Catholic as it was to become later.

It is even possible to argue that for Tagore, before the turn of the

[171]Surajit Dasgupta, '*Desh o Dharma Prasange Rabindrachetanar Vivartan*', in Premendra Mitra and Amyakumar Majumdar (eds.), *Rabindra Prasanga* (Calcutta: Baitanik, 1976), pp. 36–40.
[172]Ibid., p. 38.

century, only a Brahminic India could be India.[173] It was after 1905 that he became open to an inclusive concept of India, and capable of writing the three political novels we have analysed in this essay.

To this second Tagore, Upadhyay was a psychological threat. At one time, Upadhyay had summed up for Tagore Indian attempts to resolve the contradictions between East and West, and between Hindu and non-Hindu. Upadhyay had achieved in personal terms what Tagore was only now struggling to do. Yet, for reasons which were not very clear, Upadhyay was not merely willing to retreat—from inclusiveness and tolerance to exclusivism and intolerance—he seemed on the verge of acting out his new-found ideology. What must have disturbed Tagore even more was his realization that it was not a new ideology; Upadhyay was merely reverting to Tagore's earlier nationalist stance, which the poet had—perhaps painfully—transcended.

Conclusion

The Larger Crisis

Many of my observations on Tagore's attitude to nationalism may sound strange to Indians whose own nationalism has been significantly shaped by Tagore and his creative works. Many former freedom fighters recall how they faced police violence during the freedom movement singing Tagore songs. Jogendranath Gupta mentions how in 1906 the aging freedom fighter Bipin Chandra Pal once caught hold of the horse of a Superintendent Kemp, at the head of a baton-wielding police posse, and tremulously sang these lines from a Tagore song:

> The more they tighten their knots
> The weaker will our knots be . . . .[174]

What is the nature of this consciousness to which Tagore was trying to give shape, while rejecting nationalism?

One obvious answer would be that Tagore rejected the idea of nationalism but practised anti-imperialist politics all his life. But this only leads to the further question: how did he arrive at this position at a time when nationalism, patriotism and anti-imperialism were a single concept for most Indians? One suggestion, already given, was that to Tagore, Indian

---

[173]Ibid., pp. 37–9.

[174]Jogendranath Gupta, 'Rabindranath o Swadeshi Andolan', in *Rabindra Shatabarshiki Smarak Grantha*, Calcutta Municipal Gazette, 1961, pp. 35–41.

unity was primarily a social fact, not a political agenda. From the days of the ninth Hindu Mela in 1875, when at the age of fourteen he was first exposed to public life, to the day he resigned his knighthood in protest against the Jallianwalla Bagh massacre in 1919, Tagore refused to grant primacy to politics even while sometimes participating in politics. Here lay his basic difference with Gandhi, to whom politics was a means of testing the ethics appropriate to our times and was therefore crucial to one's moral life. Everyone did not have to be an active politician, but everyone, Gandhi felt, had to work within a framework in which politics had a special place.

What linked the two was, however, their continuing attempts to reaffirm a moral universe within which one's politics and social ideology could be located. This is a concept of politics which had begun to recede a little more than two hundred years ago. For the global system of nation-states—which, according to Tagore, had made a science out of statecraft—did not recognize any link between politics and morality, unless morality was willing to articulate itself as a political force, so that it could not be ignored as a significant presence in political calculation. Gandhi understood this and was perfectly willing to politicize his moral stance, though on moral grounds, not political. He was willing to live, to borrow an expression from Arnold Toynbee's tribute to him, in 'the slum of politics'. Tagore respected Gandhi's world-view up to a point but lived in a different world.

A central theme in Tagore's reaffirmation of a moral universe was a universalism that denied moral and cultural relativism and endorsed a large, plural concept of India. He said so directly:

Because we have missed the character of India as one related to the whole world, we have in our action and thought given a description of India which is narrow and faded; that description has given primacy to our calculativeness, out of which nothing great can be created.[175]

This universalism of Tagore was not an entirely new contribution to Indian politics. (The terms Arabindo Poddar and some others use to describe the concept of patriotism that underpins this universalism are apt: *Bharatchinta* or *swadeshchinta*, literally 'thinking about or concern with India or one's own country'. Both terms convey the idea of patriotism without nationalism.) From the very beginning of the growth of Indian 'nationalism', there had been a conscious effort on the part of many Indian social reformers and political activists to develop a *Bharatchinta* which

[175]Arabindo Poddar, '*Rabindranather Bharatchinta*', *Calcutta Municipal Gazette*, Tagore Birth Centenary Number, 1961, pp. 86–9.

would project a self-definition transcending the geographical barriers of India. The first serious political thinker of modern India, Rammohun Roy, had refused to view the problems of India in isolation from the world, and this tradition was even more alive in Tagore's time. Despite occasional attempts to base Indian nationalism on unalloyed self-interest, 'pure' nationalism had never been able to mobilize even the Indian middle classes fully. Indian nationalism still vaguely reflected, in however distorted a form, what could be called the ultimate civilizational ambition of India: to be the cultural epitome of the world and to redefine or convert all passionate self–other debates into self–self debates.

In Tagore's case, this ambition was sharpened by his attempt to locate the problem of India in the crisis of the global civilization. He was to diagnose this crisis in a moving testament he published on his 80th birthday, a few weeks before his death.[176] It is an appropriate text with which to end this essay.

In the testament Tagore points out that India has always been open to other civilizations and particularly to Europe, since a unique conjunction of events had fastened India's fate to England's history in their struggle for national freedom, Indian faith in the English people was not completely extinguished.[177] Not merely the declamations of Burke and Macaulay, but the poetry of Shakespeare and Byron, and the English openness to political refugees from other countries contributed to the survival of this faith.[178] Tagore mentions that, as a boy in England, he had heard John Bright speak and his 'large-hearted, radical liberalism' had left such a deep impression on him that it had not faded even at the age of 80. He mentions that since the *sadachara* of Manu (the concept corresponding to civilization in Sanskrit), appeared to many young Indians of that time to have degenerated into a 'socialized tyranny' of 'set codes of conduct', they had preferred the ideal of 'civilization' represented by the English term.[179]

Slowly, however, came a 'painful parting of ways' and disillusion. Tagore began to discover 'how easily those who accepted the highest truths of civilization disowned them with impunity whenever questions of national self-interest were involved.'[180]

---

[176]Rabindranath Tagore, *Crisis in Civilization* (Bombay: International Book House, 1941).
[177]Ibid., p. 2.
[178]Ibid.
[179]Ibid., pp. 2–3.
[180]Ibid., p. 4.

There came a time when perforce I had to snatch myself away from mere appreciation of literature . . . . I began to realize that perhaps in no other modern state was there such a hopeless dearth of the most elementary needs of existence. And yet it was this country whose resources had fed for so long the wealth and magnificence of the British people. While I was lost in the contemplation of the world of civilization, I could never have remotely imagined that the great ideals of humanity would end in such ruthless travesty. But today a glaring example of it stares me in the face in the utter and contemptuous indifference of a so-called civilized race to the well-being of scores of Indian people.[181]

This political awareness brought about Tagore's 'gradual loss of faith in the claims of the European nations to civilization.'[182]

The spirit of violence which perhaps lay dormant in the psychology of the West, has at last roused itself and desecrates the spirit of man. I had at one time believed that the springs of civilization would issue out of the heart of Europe, but today when I am about to quit the world that hope has gone bankrupt altogether . . . .

As I look around I see the crumbling ruins of a proud civilization. And yet I shall not commit the grievous sin of losing faith in Man. I would rather look forward to the opening of a new chapter in history . . . .[183]

Perhaps this was merely the rambling despair of an elderly pacifist confronted with two world wars within his lifetime. Or perhaps Tagore had come full circle to Gandhi's position that Indian nationalism as well as universalism had to be built on a critique of the modern West. We only know that this indictment of the West was the context within which Tagore sought to locate his new politics.

On the other hand, it is doubtful if he had much hope of Indian nationalism either. Once he had dreamt, like Gandhi, that India's national self-definition would some day provide a critique of western nationalism, that Indian civilization with its demonstrated capacity to live with and creatively use contradictions and inconsistencies would produce a 'national' ideology that would transcend nationalism. However, even before his death, nationalism in India proved itself to be not only more universal but also more resilient than it had been thought. Today, fifty years after Tagore's death and forty years after Gandhi's, their version of patriotism has almost ceased to exist, even in India, and for most modern Indians this is not a matter of sorrow but of pride. Only a few Indians, who have begun to sense the decline of the present global system of nation-states, perceive that the decline of that distinctive tradition of

[181]Ibid., pp. 4–5.
[182]Ibid., p. 8.
[183]Ibid., pp. 10–11.

political self-awareness means the loss of an alternative basis for human and political orders.

Writing of nationalist thought, Ernest Gellner comments that the precise doctrines of nationalist thinkers

are hardly worth analyzing. This is because we seem to be in the presence of a phenomenon which springs directly and inevitably from basic changes in our shared social condition, from changes in the overall relation between society, culture and polity. The precise appearance and local form of this phenomenon no doubt depends a very great deal on local circumstances which deserve study; but I doubt whether the nuances of nationalist doctrine played much part in modifying these circumstances.[184]

Maybe Gellner is right. But the question still remains: how were Tagore or, for that matter, Gandhi able to defy the universal sociology of nationalism? And how were they able to institutionalize their scepticism of the clenched-teeth European version of nationalism in the Indian national movement itself? Was there something in Indian culture, as Tagore believed, which allowed such play, even if it was only a temporary phase?

This essay has not answered these questions adequately. Yet, to round off the picture and to add to the part-answers, I shall briefly consider here the possibility that questions about nationalism can be posed on an altogether different plane. On that plane, cultural and psychological issues are less inconsequential and human ingenuity is more significant. To give random examples, attempts to pose the question thus have been made by Erik Erikson in his study of Adolf Hilter's younger years; Sudhir Kakar in his study of Swami Vivekananda's childhood; Susanne and Lloyd Rudolph and Victor Wolfenstein in their essays on Gandhi.[185] In this way of looking at nationalism, individual thinkers and their thoughts become crucial in ways which Gellner may not approve of.

A simple-minded book formulates the issue plainly: Richard A. Koenigsberg argues in *The Psychoanalysis of Racism, Revolution and Nationalism* that faith in the absolute reality of the nation is constituted of three interrelated core fantasies: the fantasy of the nation as a suffering

---

[184]Ernest Gellner, *Nations and Nationalism* (Ithaca: Cornell University Press, 1983), p. 124.

[185]Erik Erikson, *Childhood and Society*; Susanne Rudolph and Lloyd Rudolph, *The Modernity of Tradition: Political Development in India* (Chicago University Press, 1967); Kakar, *The Inner World*, pp. 160–81; E. Victor Wolfenstein, *The Revolutionary Personality* (Princeton University Press, 1967).

mother, the fantasy of the nation as omnipotent mother, and that of the nation as a projection of infantile narcissism.[186] The wish to save the nation is the 'projective equivalent of the wish to restore the omnipotence of the mother',[187] Koenigsberg argues, and he goes on to use, among others, the example of Sri Aurobindo's invocation of the mother:

Insofar as the nation is experienced by the nationalist as a projection of the omnipotent mother, the nationalist tends to feel that, as long as he is contained within the boundaries of the nation, he shall be shielded from the external world: the nation shall act as a 'buffer', standing between the individual and the harshness of reality . . . .[188]

It is this projection which helps the religious impulse to find expression in the ideology of nationalism.

Koenigsberg is supported in the Indian context, and specifically in the case of Aurobindo, by others suggesting a roughly similar interpretation.[189] But something more might have been involved for persons like Gandhi and Tagore. They saw themselves as belonging to a civilization that refused to view politics only as a secularized arena of human initiative. While associating the country with maternity and sacredness, they insisted that the association imposed a responsibility on the individual to maintain that sacredness. Certainly in both there was not only a built-in critique of nationalism but also that of the social and cultural realities of the nation. It is significant that Gandhi, who dismissed Catherine Mayo's racist criticism of India in *Mother India* as a drain inspector's report, nevertheless advised every Indian to read the book.[190]

Thus, at one plane, Tagore may be read as a perfect instance of Koenigsberg's thesis; his uninhibited use of the symbolism of the country-as-mother in many of his patriotic songs and poems gives them intense emotional vibrancy. However, this symbolism of the country as mother also invokes something of a peasant's or tribe's traditional, ecologically sensitive, ego-syntonic fantasy of a nurturing mother who can any moment turn less benevolent. The omnipotence of the mother is recognized

[186]Richard A. Koenigsberg, *The Psychoanalysis of Racism, Revolution and Nationalism* (New York: The Library of Social Science, 1977), p. 2.
[187]Ibid., p. 6.
[188]Ibid., pp. 8–9.
[189]Philip Spratt, *Hindu Culture and Personality* (Bombay: Manaktalas, 1966); on Aurobindo see specially Nandy, *The Intimate Enemy*, pp. 85–100.
[190]Catherine Mayo, *Mother India* (New York: Blue Ribbon Books, 1927).

but feared; it is not romanticized or defensively glorified. Nor is it used merely as a means of restoring one's infantile narcissism through identification with a nation, as probably happens in societies that have clearly broken away from or repressed or lost touch—through disasters like large-scale uprooting—with their pre-modern pasts.

So while Tagore wrote with great sensitivity and felicity about the nation as suffering mother, he also took a position against nationalism. Even the national anthems he wrote (he posthumously flouted the first canon of exclusivist nationalism by authoring the national anthems of two independent nation-states which are not always on the best of terms and one of which is the only Islamic state ever to have a national anthem written by a non-Muslim) are remarkably free of any parochialism. They celebrate the contemplation of the Earth Mother in one case and the ruler of the hearts of the people on the other. But then, perhaps only in South Asia would they be chosen as national anthems.

One should not underestimate the hostility Tagore's concept of nationalism aroused in the expanding middle-class culture of Indian politics. The modern India, I have already indicated, has never been happy with Tagore's idea of patriotism. For instance, controversy has dogged the national anthem, *Janaganamana*, and claims have occasionally been made that the song was written in honour of King George V when he visited India. There is a particularly touching letter of Tagore to the literary critic Pulinbihari Sen that expresses the poet's distress on that score, for Tagore *did* sense that many Indians, unable directly to question his patriotism, were focusing on the supposed origins of the song. In the letter to Sen, written in 1937, Tagore says,

You have asked if I have written the song *Janaganamana* for any particular occasion. I can sense that the question has arisen in your mind because of the controversy in some circles of the country about the song . . . . I am responding to your letter not to stoke the fire of the controversy but to satisfy your curiosity . . . .

. . . . That year arrangements were being made for the arrival of the emperor of India. A friend of mine well-established in the government made an earnest request to me to compose a song of victory (*jayagana*) for the emperor. I was shocked and with the shock there rose in me anger, too. In a strong reaction, I announced in the song *Janaganamana* the victory of that creator of India's destiny (*bharatabhagyavidhata*), who is the eternal charioteer (*chira sarathi*) of travellers walking eon after eon on the uneven road of declines and ascents (*patana abhyudaya bandhur-panthay yuga-yuga dhabita yatri*), a charioteer who knows the heart of the people and can show them the way (*antarayami patha parichayaka*). That that eternal charioteer of human fate (*yugayugantarer manavabhagyarathachalaka*) could not be the fifth, sixth or any George even the loyalist friend of mine understood. For however firm he might have been in his loyalty, he did not lack intelligence . . . .[191]

Tagore never defended himself publicly over this issue:

I should only insult myself if I care to answer those who consider me capable of such unbounded stupidity as to sing in praise of George the Fourth or George the Fifth as the Eternal Charioteer leading the pilgrims on their journey through countless ages of the timeless history of mankind.[192]

But he was bitter about the controversy all the same, for he knew that it was a no-win situation. He could never satisfy his detractors, as their accusations did not stem from genuine suspicions about the origins of the song but were partly a product of middle-class dissatisfaction with the 'insufficient nationalism' the song expressed, and partly a response to what seemed to them to be Tagore's own 'peculiar' version of patriotism. To the chagrin of Tagore's critics, his version of patriotism rejected the violence propagated by terrorists and revolutionaries, it rejected the concept of a single-ethnic Hindu *rashtra* as anti-Indian, and even anti-Hindu, and it dismissed the idea of the nation-state as being the main actor in Indian political life. His critics guessed correctly that *Janaganamana* could only be the anthem of a state rooted in the Indian civilization, not of an Indian nation-state trying to be the heir to the British–Indian empire. They also probably sensed that *Janaganamana* was possibly the poet's attempt to moderate his earlier deep allegiance to *Bande Mataram* because of the fierce associations the latter had acquired in the course of the growth of post-Swadeshi extremism.

There might even have been some guilty recognition on Tagore's part that, despite his long record of anti-imperialist activity and his attempts to shape the Indian cultural resistance to imperialism, he *had* for a long time avoided the responsibility of providing a developed cultural critique of the modern West. In the name of cultural syncretism, he had chosen to believe that knowledge and creativity could be neatly separated from political passions and interests, that he had pushed the line that while knowledge and the arts were universal, politics was parochial. Blinkered

[191]Rabindranath Tagore, Letter to Pulinbihari Sen, 10 November 1937, quoted by Chinmohan Sehanabis, in '*Janaganamana Adhinayaka Sangita Prasange Rabindranath*', *Parichay*, May–June 1986, pp. 20–2.

[192]Rabindranath Tagore, Letter of 29 March 1939. Quoted in Prabodhchandra Sen, *India's National Anthem* (Calcutta: Visvabharati, 1972), p. 7. Sen's book covers the whole controversy reasonably thoroughly.

by that belief, he had even accepted a knighthood from the British government soon after he won the Nobel Prize in literature, presumably on the grounds that it was a reward for artistic achievement, not political loyalty. (Tagore's acceptance of the knighthood saddened many freedom fighters. Saratchandra Chattopadhyay mentions that Chittaranjan Das [1870–1925], a respected leader of the freedom struggle, broke down on hearing that Tagore had accepted the award.[193] People like Das were mollified only when Tagore returned the knighthood in 1919.) I have already suggested that, exposed to the tumultuous events of the 1920s and 1930s, Tagore later began to move towards somewhat different concepts of creativity, intellectual responsibility and universalism. They were no longer located in a facile synthesis of India's civilizational categories and the values of the Enlightenment but in an awareness of the global politics of cultures. As he put it in a letter to Amal Home soon after the Jallianwalla episode, 'We also needed this [the massacre] to get out of our illusions.'[194]

Under the circumstances, Tagore could do little beyond accept philosophically the stray criticism of *Janaganamana*. Towards the end of his letter to Sen, he says with a touch of resignation, 'In this connection I remember an advice of Bhagwan Manu which goes, "treat honour like poison, accusations like nectar."'[195]

Fortunately for Tagore, middle-class, modernized Indian never was nor is it now the whole of India.[196] The public space created by him and, even more, by Mohandas Karamchand Gandhi for a distinctive Indian concept of a public realm and state was never fully occupied by the nascent Indian nation-state. Some of their concerns have returned after about half a century, to haunt Indian nationalists and statists from time to time.

This is a story of divided selves, in confrontation and in dialogue. It has been told at three planes: ideological, mythic and biographical. The story tells how British colonialism in India released cultural forces which

---

[193]Mitra, *Saratsahitye Samajchetana*, p. 110.

[194]Ibid., p. 109.

[195]Tagore, quoted in Sehanabis, '*Janaganamana Adhinayaka Sangita Prasange*', p. 22.

[196]The only opinion survey of the three possibilities for India's national anthem was conducted in Bombay. The results of the survey show that while on some criteria *Bandemataram* was found a superior anthem, the respondents rated *Janaganamana* to have the strongest 'national characteristics' (Sen, *India's National Anthem*, pp. 55–7). Tagore did not live to see the survey. *Janaganamana* remained the last patriotic song he wrote, although he lived thirty years longer.

fractured the personality of every sensitive exposed Indian and set up the West as a crucial vector within the Indian self. The endorsement that was earlier available to the Indian self from the precolonial culture of public life was thus irrevocably lost.

Nationalism, being a direct product of the western past and thus an imported category, was caught in this inner tension. It consolidated the western presence on the cultural plane, while it nurtured the rebellion against the West on the political plane. This schism led to further conflicts. In a small minority, nationalism triggered off a resistance to itself. This minority distinguished nationalism from anti-imperialism and patriotism; for them it was an imposition, an attempt to mould the Indian concept of the public realm to the requirement of standardized western categories. They sensed that Indian nationalism did not merely mean internalization of an alien history, it was also an exteriorization of India's inner conflicts triggered by the colonial political economy.

Was the separation of nationalism from both patriotism and anti-imperialism viable in India? Was it a viable alternative for any Third World society which had been a victim of the West?

This question has not been answered here. Which does not mean that the alternative to nationalism which Tagore and Gandhi hinted at was too ephemeral or fragile to withstand the turbulence of mass politics. It means that they foresaw some of the problems that are now emerging in the political culture of nation-state in both the West and the East. Perhaps the time has come to take stock of the costs of the nation-state system and the nationalism that sustains it. Such stocktaking may not alter the past but it may lead towards a redefinition of the concept and functions of the state, at least in this part of the globe.

Many years ago, at the time of World War I, a person as manifestly apolitical as Sigmund Freud claimed that the state had forbidden to the individual the practice of 'wrong-doing' not because of a desire to abolish it but because of a desire to monopolize it. Gandhi and Tagore may never have read Freud, but they pushed this awareness into the political culture of India. That the awareness did not survive the harsh realities of international relations and the early stages of nation-building and state-formation in the Southern world has no bearing on the viability of their dissent. And we, at the end of the twentieth century, may be in a position to affirm that eighteenth- and early nineteenth-century Europe did not say the last word on the subject. Time may still vindicate the vision of the two dissenters.

*Earlier published in 1994 (New Delhi: Oxford University Press).

9

—∿—

The Fantastic India–Pakistan Battle

Or the Future of the Past in South Asia

India's Pakistan

WHEN THE BANGLADESH war created a new state to the east of India in 1971, it ended Pakistan's unique status as a country in two parts, separated by one thousand miles of hostile India. Before the war, the late Sisir Gupta, scholar and hard-eyed Indian diplomat, used to claim that the crisis of Pakistan's identity was mirrored in the inability of Pakistani children to even draw the map of their country without drawing India.[1] Twenty-five years after the event, Indians have now proved the cultural unity of the subcontinent by successfully redefining their country in such terms that even adult Indians cannot define India without involving Pakistan in that self-definition.

Pakistan has a history and a geography. Beyond them, shaping India's

---

[1] Lest this sounds like the rambling of a prejudiced Indian diplomat, I quote what a Pakistani intellectual has to say on the subject towards the end of 1998: 'Over the last half a century, government after government has groped for a consensus on our identity, but to no avail. . . . Pakistan's dilemma since it came into being has been that we have forever tried to establish our legitimacy as a nation-state, and in this endless quest, we have forced ourselves to undergo countless constitutional contortions. . . . The one common thread in these different attempts to define a national identity and to establish Pakistan's legitimacy has been a consistently anti-Indian stand. Indeed, it is almost as though we could only be accepted through our "un-Indianness." Also if we aren't totally different from the Indians, why did we create Pakisstan?' Irfan Hussain, 'The Two-Nation Shadow', *The Asian Age,* 31 October 1998.

imagination of her neighbour in elemental ways, is the myth of Pakistan. This myth transcends Pakistan's empirical and geopolitical status. It cannot be subsumed under rubrics such as defence studies, class analysis, political history, and development economics. That mythic Pakistan is not even made in Pakistan. It originates in India and dominates India's public life, though it is also sometimes exported or smuggled into Pakistan. When it enters Pakistan, it becomes a deadly bond between the two countries. For the myth is not obediently mythic; it shapes behaviour and policy. People die and kill for it. To use a cliché, if the Pakistani state does not conform to the myth, some Indians will certainly invent a new nation-state to do so.

Pakistan is the name of a country to the north-west of India, carved out of the Muslim majority provinces of British India. It has survived for nearly fifty years, to intermittently haunt the Indian state and army. About twenty-five years ago Pakistan shrunk to less than half its original size, when Bangladesh was born. India played an important part in that shrinkage. But few Indians believe that the bisection taught Pakistan any lesson or reduced its power an iota. Pakistan, they believe, is exactly what it was when it started life as a new nation. Most Indians, therefore, react to Pakistan as if it was the Pakistan of 1947.

For the Indian state, therefore, Pakistan has retained its parity and remained a genuine counter-player. Few Indian state functionaries think of Pakistan as anything but superior to India in its ability to make mischief or subvert neighbouring states. This is no mean achievement, given that Pakistan is one-eighth the size of India, that even after spending nearly 6 per cent of its GDP on defence—as compared to India's 2.5 per cent[2]— its army is about one-third the size of the Indian army, that the country has its own ethnic problems and separatist movements, and Pakistanis seem more unsure about Pakistan's sustainability than Indians are about India's.

Even for many highly educated, urbane, middle-class Indians, what matters is that Pakistan is full of Muslims, most of them from north-west India and belonging to the 'martial races'. India's north-west includes Punjab and that makes it worse. Secularism is all right, even commendable, but rationality demands that one recognizes Muslims to be hot-headed, tough, masculine, anti-democratic and prone to fundamentalism. More

[2]The figures on defence expenditures are official figures and taken from *The Times of India*, 31 March 1995. Unofficial figures are naturally higher. According to the UNICEF Regional Office for South Asia, Pakistan and India have spent 25.1 per cent and 14.4 per cent respectively of their annual budgets on defence during 1995–6.

so if they happen to be from the north. One must handle them firmly to protect progress and democracy and to ensure that they get stewed in the global melting pot to become atomized, law-abiding citizens of a proper modern state!

At this plane, Pakistan is what India does not want to be; indeed, it is what India's modern élite would hate to be. This bonding in hate, fifty years after the division of India into two nation-states, is growing. As India becomes more of a modern nation-state, Pakistan for it becomes both a double and the final rejected self. The next-door neighbour now arouses deep anxieties not merely in Hindu nationalist formations like the Rashtriya Swayamsevak Sangh, the Bharatiya Janata Party and the Shiv Sena, but also in Indian liberals and leftists. For them, too, Pakistan is the ultimate symbol of irrationality and fanaticism.

Jawaharlal Nehru, we are told, expected Pakistan to collapse within months in 1947. A theocratic state, he thought, could not survive in the contemporary world. (Pakistan always looks a theocratic state to the Indian élite, never as a nation-state created by its modernizing middle classes, working with a vague pan-Islamic fervour or an instrumental concept of Islam.) Pakistan, Nehru's reading of world history presumably went, had to be an aberration in history, brought about by a few ambitious nuts who had successfully mobilized the atavistic sentiments of a section of some South Asians. Strictly speaking, the reading is no different from that of the young historian Ayesha Jalal or the respected jurist H.M. Seervai.[3] Only Nehru believed that the stupidity and ambition were concentrated in the leaders of the Muslim League; the other two believe that these qualities were concentrated in the Indian National Congress.

Nation-states in our times, however, have been sturdy entities. In the present world system, they have a logic that transcends the naive social evolutionism of Nehru. Pakistan has survived not only as an 'unreasonably' stable nation-state, to trust the Indian policy makers and the leaders of India's main political parties, it has survived to become the equal of India. Today the two national security states stand face to face, more equal that ever. For India's efforts to prove, once for all, its military superiority by exploding a 'peaceful' nuclear device in 1973, has misfired. Pakistan in its unending search for parity, has acquired nuclear capability to neutralize India's one-up manship. This new parity, gifted to Pakistan by India's super-patriots and the international arms bazaar, is going to

[3] Ayesha Jalal, *The Sole Spokesman: Jinnah, the Muslim League and the Demand for Pakistan* (Cambridge: Cambridge University Press, 1985); H.M. Seervai, *Partition of India,* 2nd ed. (Bombay, N. M. Tripathi, 1994).

be a permanent fixture, neutralizing the three-to-one superiority India reportedly has in conventional arms.

Is this cultivated nuclear equality unintended? Or does the Indian nation-state, to complete its self-definition, need a powerful, hostile Pakistan as its hated but valued double? Or is the fantasized Pakistan an essential technology, for modern Indians, to complete the conversion of the Indian civilization to a standard, nineteenth-century nation-state?[4] From where has Pakistan got this magical strength to take on a country eight times its size? Do Indians secretly believe what General Yahya Khan openly claimed—that each Pakistani soldier is equal to ten Indian? Is it all a matter of American military aid and the Indian state's softness, the ignominy that Professor Gunnar Myrdal so compassionately diagnosed in the 1960s and left the Indian élite to live with?[5]

One part of the answer lies in the shared memories of Pakistan's separation from India. These memories prompt every modern Indian to mutter under his or her breath about Pakistan: 'There goes, but for the grace of God, India.' But with it also goes the wistful belief that they should have been little more like the Pakistanis, at least in international relations and cricket.

That ambivalence comes from two pivotal imageries: First, Pakistan is seen as a product of the conspiracy between India's erstwhile British rulers pursuing a 'divide and rule' policy and the religion-based parties in the region.[6] Pakistan at this plane is seen as an illegitimate child of the West. The 'killer instinct' imputed to it comes partly from this. A bastard of the West is, everything said, half-western and has to be better in wily statecraft than the natives.

That Islam is a Semitic creed and that most Pakistanis are Punjabis

---

[4]These questions have as their underside others: Does an analogous process work in the case of Islamic civilization and Pakistani state? Is statist nationalism itself an attempt to reduce complex, rich cultural and religious experiences to manageable political realities within the standardized format of the contemporary global nation-state system? Is this attempt a product of the increasing incomprehensibility and fear of these experiences to the politically powerful modernized, massified sectors of South Asian societies? These questions may not have priority in the research agenda of the South Asian diaspora, both outside and within South Asia, but they cannot but haunt the intellectuals who live with and in South Asian realities. They know that the answers will have to be simultaneously cultural–psychological and political.

[5]Gunnar Myrdal, *The Asian Drama: Inquiry into the Poverty of Nations* (London: Penguin, 1968).

[6]According to one estimate, actually only 16 per cent of the subcontinental Muslims voted for Pakistan. Mani Shankar Aiyer, *Pakistan Papers* (New Delhi: UBS Publishers, 1994), pp. 91–8. However, a majority of the subcontinent's westernised Muslim élite certainly sympathized with the idea.

feed this imagery. The West might be phobic about Islam and Pakistanis may be suspicious of the West but, for modern Indians, Pakistan cannot but remain a natural ally of the West. They love to see Islam, even South Asian Islam, as closer to European Christianity than to Hinduism. Every modern reform movement in Hinduism, from Brahmoism to Arya Samaj, has tried to make Hinduism more Semitic and incorporate within it elements of Islam.[7] And Punjabis, as is well known on both sides of the border, are pushy, martial, avaricious, and amoral at the same time. A country full of Muslims is bad enough, but a country full of Punjabi Muslims can only be considered a conspiracy against decent politics.

Hence the frequent inability of the Indian rulers to distinguish the Pakistani people—theoretically, misguided Indians who made a wrong choice in 1947—from the Pakistani government, led by a series of military or, as it looks from this side of the border, theocratic regimes.[8] The Pakistani disinclination to be ruled by the army or by the *mullahs* can be taken seriously by all countries in the world except India. Hence, few Indians have seriously surveyed the political support-base of Islamic parties and formations in Pakistan, their electoral performance, and the resistance they have faced. The success of Islamic fundamentalism in Pakistan is taken for granted.

Second, Pakistan has to be a successful conspirator against India, because religion, culture and state in Pakistan are seen to constitute a symbiotic triad. The symbiosis explains, to the satisfaction of many

[7]My favourite quote is from Rammohun Roy (1772–1833), by common consent the father of modern India: '. . . I have observed with respect to distant cousins, sprung from the same family, and living in the same district, when one branch of the family had been converted to Mussulmanism, that those of the Muhammadan branch living in a freer manner, were distinguished by greater bodily activity and capacity for exertion, than those of the other branch which had adhered to the Hindoo mode of life.' Rammohun Roy, 'Additional Queries Respecting the Condition of India', *The English Works* (Calcutta: Sadharon Brahmo Samaj, 1947), Part 3, pp. 63–8; see p. 63. For this 'deformity' Roy held Hindu vegetarianism culpable, which in turn he traced to 'religious prejudices' and 'want of bodily exertion and industry' brought about by a hot climate and a fertile land (ibid.).

A major cultural paradox of contemporary India is how Hindu nationalism, often considered an illegitimate child of the nineteenth-century religious reform movements, has turned against Islam, not as an alien other but as disowned part of one's own self.

[8]The ordinary Indians seem to do better in this respect. According to the only survey in India available on the subject in *The Times of India,* in January 1996, after years of effort by the Hindu nationalist parties to blur the line between the Pakistani regime and the subcontinental Muslim communities, a majority of the respondents clearly distinguished between the Pakistani citizens and the Pakistani state.

Indians, Pakistan's fanaticism and the superhuman efficiency of its state. This symbiosis has been a goal of modern Indians since the last century and they feel they have not succeeded in it, thanks to the obstinate inertia of the ordinary Hindus and the 'soft', non-martial, fuzzy-ended 'effeminacy' their religion inculcates in them.[9] Therefore, the omniscience imputed to the agencies of the Pakistani state is matched by the innocence attributed to their Indian counterparts.[10] The Pakistani Army's intelligence wing, the Inter-Services Intelligence, for instance, has acquired in India a mythic stature as a villain that puts to shame the boisterous villains in the popular Bombay films. In comparison, the Indian intelligence agency, the Research and Analysis Wing, is perceived as a set of bungling, politics-afflicted innocents controlled by civilians. Everything said, the staff in the ISI are seen as trained by the CIA; those in RAW are seen as either home-spun or trained by the miserable NKVD.

The obverse of that perception is the constant demand for more masculine, tough statecraft from the Indians and pleas to match the militarization of the Pakistani society by building a garrison state in India. The fear of separatism everywhere, the tendency to see all demands for decentralization as a conspiracy against Indian unity, the panicky response to criticisms of state violence by human rights groups—they all are indicators of a concept of a state critically shaped by Pakistan. So much so that it is possible to visualize a time when the Indian state will only mirror the Pakistani-state-as-fantasized-by-the-Indian-élite.

Pakistan is many things to many people. But the mythic Pakistan I am talking about is, above all, a definer of Indianness. It is a means of self-analysis and self-intervention. If Mother India can be put on an analytic couch, the enterprising psychoanalyst who does so will not miss her schizoid personality and the mix of paranoia and admiration with which some of her selves look at each other. That one of these selves is identified with Pakistan is now part of South Asia's psychological landscape. In the dynamics of that self lie crucial clues to the nature of the Indian nation-state.

[9]Many years ago, while working on the assassination of Mohandas Karamchand Gandhi, I found to my utter astonishment that Hindu nationalist literature was the harshest not on Islam and the Muslims, but on the Hindus. Swami Vivekananda (1866–1902) who pleaded for a Vedantic brain and Islamic body as the stuff of his vision of the future India, was only slightly less explicit.

[10]This has its obverse in the innocence attributed to the ordinary, 'lion-hearted but dumb' Muslim masses to protect whom Pakistan is supposed to have been brought into being. More about that later.

Pakistan's India

Pakistan's India, the image of India Pakistan lives with, is also mostly Pakistan's own. It has almost nothing to do with what India is or might have been. It tells us what Pakistan is, feels it should be, or could have been.

Pakistan's India has two selves. The source of one is the official ideology of the Pakistani state; official Pakistan likes to believe it to be the only India that counts. The other is a disowned India; even Pakistani ideologues carry it in their veins, though many of them would deny that vehemently. That disowned India is also a mythic entity that defines Pakistan's boundaries and origins, loves and hates, past and future, its very core.

The official India of Pakistan—the India that looks like a pure product of Pakistani propaganda to many—is actually a desperate defence against facing the unofficial India that Pakistanis carry within themselves. That unofficial India contaminates and subverts Pakistan every day. It subverts not in the way the many Pakistanis fear being subverted—through political deceit or treachery or through the armed might of its larger neighbour—but in the way Sigmund Freud talked of the return of the unconscious to subvert our self-image as rational, normal, sane human beings.

No wily Indian politician scheming to destroy Pakistan could do worse. For the most the clever, *dhoti*-clad Indian politician can do is to try to wreck Pakistan through inspired statecraft and military adventure, against both of which Pakistan has built excellent defences in the last fifty years. Whereas the latent India that haunts Pakistan has no devious political leader to guide its destiny and no army to back it up. It is entirely a home-made Pakistani product.

That haunting, strangely seductive India Pakistanis cannot share with any other country; they have to fight that apparition alone. Paradoxically, they can sometimes share it with Indians, who also have now begun to live with a home-made ghost called Pakistan.

The manifest India of Pakistan—to judge by Pakistan's official ideology, mainstream historical scholarship, school and college texts, and the language of propaganda used by Pakistani media—has some clear features. I state them in the form of three propositions. First, India is led by a westernized, highly professional, upper-caste, Hindu élite who, taking advantage of their early modernization, began to dominate the subcontinent, much before the simple, lion-hearted, Kiplinesque Gungadins—also known as the South Asian Muslims—woke up to it.[11]

---

[11]Syed Ahmad Khan was arguably the first one to wake up to this. See Shan Mohammad (ed.), *Writings and Speeches of Sir Syed Ahmad Khan* (Bombay:

The élite even had, the self-construction of Pakistan goes, subtly changed the rules of the game in the 1920s under the leadership of the likes of M.K. Gandhi—by introducing symbols and idiom from the Hindu world-view and by refusing to grant Muslims parity with the Hindus, which the Muslims deserved for being the subcontinent's largest minority and erstwhile rulers. It was thus that the Hindu élite ensconced in the Indian National Congress prepared the ground for the creation of Pakistan. For Pakistan, according to the underside of its official history, is the only country in the world to have come into being reluctantly—as a response to the chicanery of the Hindu élite of undivided India. An authentic anti-imperialist and an important leader of the Congress, Mohammad Ali Jinnah, saw through the game, left the party, and decided to lead the Pakistan movement. Being a westernized professional lawyer, and a Gujarati Bania to boot, Jinnah could be a perfect foil for the other Gujarati Bania who was going places with his bogus slogans of non-violence, soul force and moral politics, his unending fasts and tiresome counter-modernism.

Defeated in its own game, the Hindu upper-caste élite gulped the idea of partition of India as a political ploy but continued to have designs on the infant Pakistani state. Not only during the 1971 war but subsequently too, India has been entirely responsible for Pakistan's ethnic problems. In addition, what the Brahminic élite could not do to the bulk of Indian Muslims in pre-Partition days, it has now done to India's supine Muslim minority and, for that matter, to all other minorities.

Second, Pakistan is an Islamic state and an Islamic state should not, Pakistan believes, be preoccupied with its Indian past, pre-Islamic or otherwise. For over-concern with that past can only detract from one's Islamic heritage and the solidarity of the Muslims that constitutes the Pakistani nation-state. Pakistan's history should begin neither with the Indus valley civilization nor with the entry of Islam into India at a time when India's ruling élite was still predominantly Hindu, that is, when Islam in India was not backed by state power. Pakistan's history must begin with the West Asian invaders of India who not only gave Indian Islam a new political and military edge, but also brought along with them a huge majority of the ancestors of the South Asian Muslims. The South Asian Muslims, therefore, are basically an exogenous ruling élite who have found in Pakistan a social and political status appropriate to their

Nachiketa, 1972). For a fascinating, recent exploration of official history in Pakistan and its often-comic contradictions, see Ayesha Jalal, 'Conjuring Pakistan: History as Official Imagining', *International Journal of Middle East Studies*, 1995, 27, pp. 73–89.

true self. It is this status that India's Hindu rulers grudge. The Muslims who do not fit this self-image are irrelevant and can be safely forgotten.

Not only the distant past but much of India's anti-colonial struggle—except probably the rebellion in 1857—is irrelevant to Pakistan, for the struggle sought to bypass the Indian Muslims. Many Hindu leaders of the struggle, the ideologues of Pakistan believe, were dedicated enemies of the Muslims because they wanted to inherit the mantle of the Raj in its entirety, even though representing only the sectional interests of the Hindus.

Third, Muslims and other minorities in present-day India are not only oppressed, the leaders they have thrown up are servitors of the Hindu élite who rule India with an iron hand. Official Pakistan believes that the stridency towards Pakistan displayed by many Muslim leaders of India can be traced to their political ambitions; they want to be more loyal than the king to India's Hindu state, for reasons of personal greed or ambition.

Of course, Pakistan, the declared home of South Asian Muslims, will not like to accept all the Muslims in India, even if they were willing to migrate. For that would be the end of Pakistan.[12] On the other hand, the fact that both India and Bangladesh have as large number of Muslims as Pakistan is a statistical artefact for many Pakistanis. For them, the Muslims stay in India under duress and Bangladesh is merely an Indian concoction and a trickery of history. The Indian Muslims are poor and oppressed, though their Islam is no worse than that of Pakistan; the Bangladeshi Muslims are not only poor; they are fish-eating, Bengali-speaking, non-martial, quasi-Muslims whose numerical strength is a Malthusian artefact. Ideally, India should be officially a Hindu state and the Indian rulers should shed the pretence of running a multi-ethnic state, to justify *ex post facto* the creation of Pakistan. For Pakistan still desperately craves to represent the interests of all South Asian Muslims, including the Muslims of India and Bangladesh. The size and political clout of India's Muslim community discomfits Pakistan's rulers. Because granting intrinsic legitimacy to the politics of Indian Muslims—and that of the Bangladeshi Muslims—means recognizing that Pakistan is only one among the three major players in the region's Muslim politics and involves seeking sanction from the Muslims of India and Bangladesh before making claims in the name of Islam in this part of the world.

---

[12]For the last twenty-five years, Pakistan has refused to accept as immigrants even non-Bengali Muslims, ideologically fully committed to Pakistan, who have been left behind in Bangladesh.

Underlying these components in the official ideology of the Pakistani state—which already makes Pakistan an atypical ideological state in that it depends so heavily on India to define itself—is the unofficial culture of the Pakistani state. That unofficial culture involves India in an entirely different way.

First, Pakistan was built as a home of South Asian Muslims, against the proposal for a multi-ethnic society that looked, rightly or wrongly, to most of the subcontinent's westernized Muslim élite, like a plan to create a majoritarian nation-state dominated by the Hindus. Anti-Hindu sentiments therefore have to be an ingredient of the ideology of Pakistan. Pakistan, however, is a nation-state and, like all nation-states, uncomfortable with the demands of an ideological state. (For instance, it likes to be in good terms with Nepal. The fear of big brother India brings them together but, for both, it is not a happy exposure. Pakistanis discover a Hindu state with whom they are forced to be friendly; the Nepalese, living in the world's only Hindu kingdom, discover a peculiar ally which claims to hate a central plank of Nepal's cultural self.)

Also, thanks to the large-scale violence in 1946–7 and the separation of Bangladesh, anti-Hindu themes have increasingly become an odd, anachronistic presence in Pakistan's national ideology. Many young Pakistanis, who have not even seen many Hindus, do not find the themes evocative, despite being brought up on a steady diet of anti-Hindu texts. That only increases the stridency and bitterness in official Pakistan, for it has come to feel in recent years that the younger generation in Pakistan is not adequately patriotic or aware of the sacrifices made for Pakistan by the older generation of Pakistanis.

Second, everyone in Pakistan suspects, even those who claim otherwise, that a huge majority of the South Asian Muslims have no genuine claim to West Asian ancestry. Their forefathers were converted from Hinduism or Buddhism and their 'peripheral' Islam is not a learnt behaviour but an inherited culture.[13] The real fear is of drowning in the morass called Hindu cultural order as other religions and even prophetic creeds have sometimes done or being fitted within its hierarchical order, from which

---

[13]Ziauddin Sardar says, '[In South Asia] All Muslims were, somewhere in the past, actually Hindus, or, at best, hybrid Hindus having one parent who was Hindu. The Muslim hatred of Hindus is actually the hatred of what they have rejected in their genealogical history. The Hindu hatred of Muslims is a direct result of this betrayal—a betrayal reinforced by the partition of India and creation of Pakistan.' Ziauddin Sardar, 'On Serpents, Inevitability and the South Asian Imagination', *Futures*, November 1992, 24(10), pp. 942–9; see p. 946.

Islam has often been an escape for important sections of South Asians.[14] This fear might or might not have been vaguely strengthened by certain similarities between Hinduism and pre-Islamic Arab faiths that Islam fought in its earliest years.

Third, by conceptualizing Hinduism as a negation of Islam, the Pakistani state is forced to take a position on South Asian Islam, which has interacted over the centuries with other faiths, especially Hinduism, influencing them and being influenced by them. South Asian Islam cannot but look to the ideologues of Pakistan a deviant, half-baked form of Islam that has strayed from the straight, narrow path of 'authentic' Islam practised in West Asia. The very distinctiveness of South Asian Islam, cultural and social, is seen as its liability, as the final proof that it has been influenced by Hinduism and Buddhism. Virtually every Islamic reform movement in South and Southeast Asia has vended the idea of *a* genuine Islam and the myriad tropical varieties of Islam as essentially flawed. Gradually the largest Muslim communities in the world—Indonesia, India, Bangladesh, Pakistan and Malaysia, which among themselves constitute a decisive majority of the global Islamic community—have been reclassified during the last hundred years as the abodes of peripheral Islam where dumb apprentice-believers of Islam perpetually wait to be retooled into textbook versions of Muslims.

Fearful of the egalitarian thrust of Islam and its emphasis on an unmediated relationship between the believer and divinity, this particular form of reformism has also led to the development of an ornate structure of theological justifications for authoritarian regimes that ambitious despots find very soothing. Pakistan's India is an adjunct to this set of justifications. Pakistanis may not like it, but their India comes closest to the India of the Hindu nationalists. What the Pakistani élite imagine India to be, the Hindu nationalist want India to be. In the India that these dedicated enemies have co-authored, there is the same pathetic masculinity strivings, the same uncritical acceptance of the principles of the modern state and nationality, the same contempt towards the ordinary citizen and ordinary believers.

There is, however, one important difference. The criteria used by official Pakistan to conjure up its India are, by the standard of the Hindu

---

[14]It is an indicator of the remarkable hold of the Indian caste system in the subcontinent that instead of owning up the Hindu origins of a majority of the Muslims of the subcontinent and thus emphasizing the emancipatory role of Islam, most Islamicist movements in the region have emphasized their exogenous origins and further underlined a social hierarchy within Islam which corresponds to the hierarchy within Hinduism.

nationalists, almost entirely Hindu. Whereas the criteria used by the Hindu nationalists to define their ideal India are, as paradoxically, close to the ones the ideologues of Pakistan consider truly Islamic. Both sets include elements with which the westernized middle classes in South Asia feel at home.

Fourth, Pakistan wants India to leave it alone and accept the partition of India, but Pakistan cannot accept as genuine an India that leaves it alone and accepts partition. India, to qualify as India for Pakistanis, must interfere in and try to subvert the Pakistani state. For Pakistan needs India to be its hostile but prized audience which, after trying out all its dirty tricks, will have to admit someday that Pakistan has made it, that Pakistan is not the failure that the Pakistanis themselves secretly suspect it to be. That acceptance by India and, by implication, the Hindus is even more important for the ideologues of Pakistan than what the common run of Pakistani citizens think of Pakistan. For, everything said, India is the exiled self of Pakistan, by exteriorising and territorializing which Pakistan has built its identity and it remains, fifty years after its creation, the final measure of the worth of Pakistan.

The Future of the Past

This story is not concerned with history; it is concerned with the future of 'reconstructed' pasts, with the myths that frame the fate of South Asia as it enters the twenty-first century. It is actually a story which has many of the ingredients that constitute an epic—a cast of millions, memories of wars and an exodus that have taken the toll of someone near to virtually everyone, and anger over lost or stolen patrimonies. Above all, to please literary theorist D.R. Nagaraj's concept of an epic, it has two antagonistic sides that are intimately related to each other through kinship and shared but often-disowned memories—like the Pandavas and the Kauravas in the Mahabharata. The only concession made to contemporary times is that both sides believe themselves to be the wronged Pandavas and other side to be the ungodly Kauravas; yet each is convinced, as upholders of virtue, that they must retain a clandestine Kaurava self to ensure final victory of justice and truth.

Nation-states in South Asia, Ziauddin Sardar argues, are fictitious entities. Indian and Pakistani nationalism, too, is 'an artefact: a fabrication that is treated and enforced as though of the natural universe.'[15] But millions have been uprooted and much blood has already been shed

[15]Sardar, 'On Serpents, Inevitability and the South Asian Imagination', p. 944.

for these entities. Fictions do kill in our times. What gives poignancy to that suffering is that all of it might have been a waste, though it might have consolidated two nation-states and satisfied a lost generation brought up to view the nation-state as *the* key to survival in the contemporary world.

Much of the ethnic violence—particularly the venom that has come to characterize it in India, Pakistan and Sri Lanka—has sprung not from any distance among communities or from clashing civilizations, but from proximity and fear of one's disowned selves. As in the cases of the Hutus and the Tutsis, the Bosnians and the Serbs, South Asian ethnic and religious violence, too, can be identified as a classic instance of what Sigmund Freud might have called a desperate, panicky 'turning against the self' as a means of exorcizing the feared Other. That attempted exorcism, even at the cost of self-annihilation, is becoming in South Asia the marker of a nihilistic affirmation of one's cultural selfhood. Strangely, that affirmation has come at a time when cultures are under attack not from one's neighbours but from more impersonal forces of global cultural unification and the loss of the life-support systems that once sustained traditional identities.

This is tragic, for there are signs that the coming century may belong not to the nation-states or to public consciousness built around nation-states, but to other kinds of aggregates organized around cultures and civilizations, including those previously marginalized. These aggregates will face formidable challenges from other non-state actors, such as multinational corporations and transnational economic institutions, but these corporations and institutions will have even less to do with the present order of nation-states. South Asia among all the regions of the world seems least prepared to face that situation. I remember economist Rahman Sobhan once predicting that the seven states in the region will walk like so many ghosts in the global corridors of power with none interested either in their plight or mutual bickering.

It is one of the clichés of contemporary sociology of science that, in modern science, major new discoveries or changes in cosmology are brought about not by empirical data or spectacular changes of heart in important scientists moved by reason, but by the death and retirement of the older generation of scientists. As we near the end of this particularly violent century, perhaps we should pin our hopes on an younger generation of South Asians less conditioned or brainwashed by the nineteenth-century European world-view and its obsessive preoccupation with the state. They will, I am confident, look at the organizational principles of their societies less blinkered by nineteenth-century western scholarship and rediscover that the South Asian societies are woven not around the state, but around their plural cultures and pluri-cultural identities. They will also discover, if I might use that paradoxical expression for a region that has not yet been massified, the grandeur of the humble, everyday life of their peoples and their little cultures. It is unlikely that I shall live to see that day, but I am consoled by the thought that I belong to a generation of South Asian scholars whose demise can only hasten the end of the present phase of self-hatred and attempts to live out some other culture's history.

*Delivered as the Keynote Address at the Symposium on Rethinking South Asia, organized by the Department of Political Science, University of Hawaii, at Honolulu on 9–10 April 1996, this paper commemorates the fiftieth anniversary of the independence of India and Pakistan. An earlier version of it was published in *Emergences,* 1995–6, Special issue no. 7–8; and *Futures,* October 1997. I am grateful to D. R. Nagaraj and the participants in the symposium for their comments and suggestions.

10

Satyajit Ray's Secret Guide to
Exquisite Murders
*Creativity, Social Criticism, and the
Partitioning of the Self*

I

MANY YEARS AGO, in the 1940s and 1950s in Calcutta, I read some of the science fiction of H.G. Wells (1866–1946). I had then just crossed the boundaries of childhood. On reading Wells, I remember being especially impressed by *The Time Machine* (1895), *The Island of Dr Moreau* (1896), *The Invisible Man* (1897), and *The War of the Worlds* (1898). The last two novels I read in Bengali, my English being still somewhat uncertain.

While all four novels intrigued me, two did something more; they jolted me out of conventionality. They made me aware that everyone in the world did not look at science the way my school teachers and parents did, or said they did. The criticism of science in *The Invisible Man* and *The Island of Dr Moreau* was so direct and impassioned that it could not be ignored even by a teenager being constantly exposed to the then new slogans about scientific rationality, being vended systematically by India's brand-new, youthful prime minister.

It was therefore a surprise when, more than a decade later, I began to read Wells on history and society. For I discovered that there was not a whiff of the criticism of modern science that I had confronted in my teens in his novels; there were criticisms only of the social relations of modern science. When Wells wrote on the political sociology of science self-consciously, as for instance in his *Outline of History* (1920), he was prim, predictable, and just like some of my teachers and relatives. This was disappointing at the time but also consoling in strange ways, for his criticisms of science *had* shaken me.

Everyone tries to forget one's childhood heroes. Mine were going out of fashion right before my eyes during my adolescence. Wells, like George Bernard Shaw (1856–1950), Bertrand Russell (1872–1970) and Aldous Huxley (1894–1963), was yielding place to the new heroes of the times. Before long, I was keeping the company of others. I had nearly forgotten the two Wells until, many years later, I discovered that one of the other heroes of my teens, Arthur Conan Doyle (1859–1930), was a practising spiritualist and theosophist. Here was a major writer of crime fiction— whose hero Sherlock Holmes had done so much to sell the idea of induction, empiricism, and value-neutral, dispassionate, rational knowledge to us in our teens—and he turned out to be, in his other incarnation, a direct negation of all the right values.[1]

I was to remember both Wells and Conan Doyle yet again when, two decades later, I read some of Salman Rushdie's non-fiction soon after reading his *Midnight's Children* and *Shame*.[2] When I read *Midnight's Children*, I had not even heard of Rushdie. Parts of the novel, therefore, came to me as a revelation. Few had written about the Indian middle-class consciousness of our times with such sensitivity. The middle classes Saratchandra Chattopadhyay (1878–1938) wrote about with such deep understanding were no longer there, and few had sensed the new pot-pourri of multicultural life of the middle-class Indian of the 1960s and 1970s. Before Rushdie, even fewer had tried to capture the interplay among the popular, the folk, and the nascent pan-Indian mass culture in urban India, creating new contradictions and absurdities for millions. Only a handful of writers have matched the insight with which Rushdie speaks in *Midnight's Children* of elements of the new popular culture in urban India, such as Bombay films and professional wrestling bouts, entering the interstices of the middle-class world-view. Rushdie's novel recognizes the inner dynamics of India's upper-middle-brow metropolitanism better than almost anyone else's—the fragments of self derived from the parochial, the local and the cosmopolitan; the peculiar, shallow mix of East and West which defines many western-educated Indians; a cauldron of emotions bubbling with the profound, the comic, and the trivial in a startling amalgamation.

---

[1] For a discussion of this issue, see Ashis Nandy, *The Tao of Cricket: On Games of Destiny and the Destiny of Games* (New Delhi: Viking and Penguin, 1989), ch. 1.

[2] Salman Rushdie, *Midnight's Children* (London: Pan, 1982); and *Shame* (Calcutta: Rupa, 1982).

Rushdie's formal social and political comments are a direct negation of these sensitivities. They have all the 'right' values in a predictable social–democratic format, but, on the whole, what he has to say in his non-fiction is cliché-ridden and pathetically dependent on categories derived from the popular Anglo-Saxon philosophy of the inter-war years. Rushdie's social and political comments could well be what Jawaharlal Nehru might have said about the public realm today if he were recalled in a séance by an enterprising medium. And when Rushdie writes on public issues in non-fictional form, he seems even to lack Nehru's grandfatherly charm. He speaks in a tone that may be very comforting to the ageing Left, but that is not even good radical chic, being at least thirty years out of date.[3]

Nothing reveals the insensitivity of the self-declared political sociologist Rushdie, compared to the novelist Rushdie, better than his article on Mohandas Karamchand Gandhi (1869–1948), written soon after Richard Attenborough's blockbuster *Gandhi* was released and had captured the imagination of film-goers, if not of film critics.[4] Rushdie's essay is ostensibly on the film, but it also tells a lot about his understanding of the subject of the film. Rushdie's Gandhi is a slippery partisan of things medieval—a shrewd, if not slimy politician who could be forgotten but for his tremendous capacity to mobilize public sentiments for irrational, primordial causes. Implicitly, it is a Gandhi who was responsible for the partition of India on religious grounds, a better-edited version of that spokesman for Muslim atavism, Mohammad Ali Jinnah (1876–1948). Rushdie's Gandhi is not even the ultimate social base of the bicultural, alienated Nehru but the political equal of the future prime minister of India, debating crucial issues with the young, modernist social reformer and hero of India's middle classes.

Not being a Gandhian, Rushdie's criticism of Gandhi did not disturb me. What did disturb me was my discovery of Rushdie as the last serious disciple of the late Professor Harold Lasky and Rajani Palme Dutt, and

---

[3]Though Rushdie is Bombay-born, in his adult life he may have been in closer touch with Pakistan. And his social and political naïveté may have something to do with the Pakistani connection; I have noticed this touching, unqualified Nehruism in many Pakistani intellectuals. I suspect that certain social and cultural processes were short-circuited in Pakistan by the country's obtuse military rulers and what was a natural and necessary phase in Indian politics has become an unfulfilled dream in Pakistan. Perhaps Pakistanis need Nehru more today than Indians do. I say this not in empathy with the unthinking though understandable anti-Nehru posturing of many Indian intellectuals, but in the belief that Nehru's humane, 'progressivist' concept of the public realm once had an important role to play in Indian politics but has been, alas, badly mauled by time and almost entirely co-opted by India's ruling élite.

[4]Salman Rushdie, 'Gandhi: How and Why the British are Continuing to Distort our History', *The Telegraph*, 5 June 1983.

the shocked recognition that this lost child of the 1930s was behind the creation of *Midnight's Children*. Later, it was to help me understand better the reaction of the Islamic world to his *Satanic Verses*, but the discovery, when I first made it, was somewhat disheartening.

After reading Rushdie, I was back to the curious case of H.G. Wells and the vague awareness it had spawned in me years ago—about the ability of the highly creative to partition their selves, disconcertingly but effectively. Effectively, because by now I had begun to suspect that this partitioning was something Wells and Rushdie had to do to protect their creative insights—their painfully dredged-out, less accessible self— from being destroyed by their 'normal', 'sane', rational self. It was as if they sensed that their conventionalities would overwhelm their deeper but vulnerable insights into the changing nature of the human predica- ment, unless they took care to defend that conventionality morally in another sphere of life, a sphere in which 'pure cognition' and 'rationality' dominated.

Perhaps psychoanalysis tells only part of the story. The conditions under which human passions get less contaminated by interests than do human cognition have remained an understudied aspect of personality theory. As a result, the pathologies of irrationality today are more vividly recognized than the pathologies of rationality and intellect. Perhaps the trend began not with Sigmund Freud but with the crystallization of the culture of Galilean Europe—with Francis Bacon (1561–1626) himself. After all, over the last three hundred years, only a few thinkers such as William Blake, John Ruskin, Joseph Conrad, Hannah Arendt, and Herbert Marcuse in the western world have paid some attention to the pathologies of rationality, though it has continued to be a major concern of many non-western thinkers, Gandhi being the most conspicuous recent example. The great minds of Europe after the Enlightenment—from Giovanni Vico to Karl Marx to Sigmund Freud—have all been more keen to unravel the pathologies of human irrationality.

Both Wells and Rushdie, professed champions of western modernity and the Enlightenment, demonstrate in their own ways the perils of this intellectual imbalance. To make my point in a more roundabout way (after all, that is what scholarship is all about) I shall now discuss the same process in more detail in the case of a highly creative, contemporary Indian film-maker, Satyajit Ray.

II

Satyajit Ray was born into a well-known family of littérateurs and social reformers in 1921. It was originally a Kayastha family that had probably come from Bihar to settle at Nadia in western Bengal in medieval times. Since the sixteenth century, the Rays also had an East Bengali connection through their estates in Mymensingh, now in Bangladesh. They had acquired the surname Ray (originally Rai, a Mughal title) when an ancestor held office under the Mughals. Previously, they had been known as Deos and then Debs. Unlike the majority of Bengali Kayasthas who are Śāktos, the Rays were Vaiṣṇavas.[5]

By the time Satyajit was born, the Rays were already an important presence in Calcutta's social and intellectual life. Satyajit's grandfather, Upendrakishore Raychowdhury (1863–1915), had renounced orthodox Hinduism and embraced Brahmoism early in his life, as an act of social defiance and a statement of commitment to social reform. He had joined the Sadharan Brahmo Samaj, the most radical of the Brahmo sects, and married into a well-known family of Brahmo social reformers. Upendrakishore's father-in-law, Dwarkanath Ganguli, was one of the founders of Sadharan Brahmo Samaj, and Dwarkanath's wife and Upendrakishore's stepmother-in-law, Kadambini Ganguli, was the first woman graduate in the British empire, South Asia's first modern woman doctor and a delegate to the fifth session of the Indian National Congress. Despite these connections, however, Upendrakishore managed, in life as well as in death, to avoid being typed as an abrasive activist. He was primarily known as a famous writer of children's literature, a printer and publisher.

Upendrakishore's eldest son and Satyajit's father, Sukumar Ray (1887–1923), has been described by many as India's greatest writer of children's stories and verses in modern times. He began to publish from the age of nine, specializing in writing nonsense verse. Apart from Gijubhai of Gujarat, one cannot think of another major Indian writer during the past hundred years whose fame depended so entirely on writing for children. Sukumar was also a talented printing technologist, illustrator, actor, and the editor of Bengal's finest children's magazine *Sandes*, which had been founded by Upendrakishore.[6]

There were other eminent persons in the family, too. Sukumar's cousin, Leela Majumdar, was a gifted humorist and writer of children's fiction; so was Sukhalata Rao, Sukumar's elder sister. Upendrakishore's brother Sharadaranjan pioneered the game of cricket in eastern India; another

---

[5]On the psychological correlates of Śākto and Vaiṣṇava cults, see a brief discussion in Nandy, *Alternative Sciences: Creativity and Authenticity in Two Indian Scientists*, 2nd edition (New Delhi: Oxford University Press, 1995), part 2.

[6]The most elegant and charming invocation of Sukumar Ray as a person is in Leela Majumdar, *Sukumar Ray* (Calcutta: Mitra o Ghose, 1969).

brother, Kuladaranjan, was a recognized artist. Kuladaranjan and his younger brother Pramadaranjan translated into Bengali popular English science fiction and crime thrillers for children.

On the whole, the family had a special relationship with children's literature, art, and theatre—having written and published for children for so long, it turned that specialization into a family tradition. Each member of the family had to support the weight of the tradition and, simultaneously, affirm his or her own distinctive style of creativity. This balance was in turn influenced by the ideological tilt of the family; by the time Satyajit was born, the family culture had become, through the Brahmo connection with late Victorian culture, aggressively rationalist, anti-hedonistic, and, despite their nationalism, Anglophile. The Rays were proud of their British connection, of the fact that many of them were trained in England, and that they played the civilizing role demanded of them by the modern institutions introduced by the Raj into the country.[7]

The problem of harmonizing these diverse strains was, however, complicated for young Satyajit by Sukumar's tragic death at the age of 36, when his only child was less than two years old. Sukumar died of *kālājvar*, literally black fever. At that time it was a fatal disease that, like tuberculosis in Victorian England, had acquired a special meaning for some sections of Bengalis. *Kālājvar* carried the contradictory associations of pastoral life and the new threats to it, the growing chasm between city and village, the lurking fear of the abandoned countryside, taken over by the darker forces of nature and thus no longer hospitable or nurtural, as well as associations of fatalism, melancholia, and self-destruction. When offset against Sukumar's robust humour and zest for life, the disease must have had a strange, ominous, tragic significance. Its impact was certainly magnified by the family's awareness that Sukumar's impending death would also mean the end of the family's publishing business and lead to their financial decline. They were not wrong; the business folded up soon after Sukumar died, and the family's fortunes fell sharply.

A joint family protects its children from the full impact of such bereavement. In Satyajit's case, for instance, there were his uncles and cousins to cushion the loss of his father.[8] It is likely that for Satyajit his

[7]The ideological bias was reflected in Ray's youthful indifference to and perhaps contempt for Indian cinema, music and painting. Till his college days his tastes were completely western. His sojourn at Shantiniketan, where he went on his mother's insistence, reluctantly leaving his beloved Calcutta, changed his attitude radically. Partha Basu, '*Garpār theke Shantiniketan*', *Anandalok*, 9 May 1992, pp. 16–21; esp. p. 21.

[8]Ibid., p. 17.

father survived in his memory mainly as a mythic, larger-than-life figure, serving both as a prototype of charismatic but distant male authority, and as a figure that was vaguely vulnerable and fragile. The theme of a childlike gifted adult in whom loneliness masquerading as search for privacy combined with obsessive preoccupation with creative work would later on be an important one for his son both in his life and his work.[9]

Satyajit naturally grew up close to his young widowed mother, an impressive, firm, self-disciplined woman and a good singer. Suprava constituted not only his first and immediate model of care and adulthood but also of power and resilient authority. Indeed, one critic has hinted that she was for her only son also an authoritative symbol of purity and expiation through widowhood that was to recur in his work in two different guises—as a nurtural mother who invests in her son her all (as in *Aparajito*) and as a seductive, eroticized presence, fighting against and finally yielding to the demands of her 'lost' conjugal self (as in *Aranyer Din Rātri*).[10]

In addition, Suprava might have become an immediate, 'real' authority for her young son and even have been for him a sturdier, more tenacious, nuanced, and acceptable target of ambivalence. He may have been spared the sharper edges of Oedipal tussles in a crypto-Victorian family in the tropics, not the problems of authority common in a culture with a marked substratum of matriarchy. Many years afterwards, he remarked:

In my moves I have brought in a certain detachment in the women. I like to think of women as lonely, unattached and self-absorbed. I can understand the power and the beauty of women easily. I think women have more power of mind.[11]

But that power of mind was not isolated from feelings:

Many among the women around us keep us alive emotionally.... The qualities in women that I admire most are intelligence, grace and sophistication. Much of the beauty of women is captured in their patience and tolerance.... In some areas, men are much more fragile than women. In those areas only women can protect men.[12]

[9]Aparna Sen, '*Purano Ātāp*', *Sananda*, 15 May 1992, 6(21), pp. 63–7; esp. pp. 63–4.

[10]Ranjan Bandopadhyay, *Viṣaya Satyajit* (Calcutta: Navana, 1988), p. 39. Bandopadhyay reads the second image differently. He sees in it Ray's inability to discover in his widowed characters the stern, sanitized standards set by his own mother. Satyajit Ray, *Aparajito* (Calcutta: Epic Films, 1956), story: Bibhutibhushan Bandopadhyay; and *Aranyer Din Rātri* (Calcutta: Nepal and Ashim Datta, 1970), story: Sunil Gangopadhyay.

[11]Ibid., p. 32.

[12]Ranjan Bandopadhyay, '*Satyajiter Chabir Nārīrā*', *Anandalok*, 9 May 1992, pp. 92–5; see pp. 93, 95.

In sum, one guesses that the family culture and mythologies underpinning it were to shape Satyajit's life and work through four dominant themes. First, the Ray family encompassed and summarized within itself the cataclysmic changes that had taken place in the social world of the Bengalis over the previous 150 years. Marie Seton and Chidananda Dasgupta have summarized these changes and shown how the Rays represented as well as responded to the changes and turned them into distinctive strains—and sources of creativity—within the family.[15] Indeed, the very fact that the family had arrived at a large frame of reference, within which could be located these representations and responses, brought the family traditions close to being a world-view that could not be easily defied but within which there was some scope for dissent.

Second, since the end of the nineteenth century the family had consistently been in the forefront of social change in Bengal and faced the consequences of it. The emphasis on humour and children's literature, and the self-confident style most of them cultivated, often obscured the fact that they were part of a small minority and perhaps even felt isolated and beleaguered. When Seton speaks of the combination of 'sensitivity' and 'imperviousness' in Satyajit the film-maker, one is tempted to relate it to the experience of the Rays over the previous hundred years, to the peculiar mix of respect, love, social distance, and defiance with which the family had learned to live.[14]

Also, it was a dissenting family, and in that dissent the ideology of modernity had played a major part. The ideology justified their non-conformism and gave meaning to their 'odd', occasionally 'eccentric', experimental careers. The Rays had reason to be grateful for the process of westernization in Indian society and to post-Renaissance Europe for the distinctive style of creativity they evolved.

Third, their Brahmo faith—a quasi-puritanic protest against the hedonism of the babus of Greater Calcutta, in turn triggered by the disorienting and violent entry of the colonial political economy into eastern India—gave a sharp edge to moral issues, especially those that involved sexual norms and the channelling of violence in society. In a culture that was traditionally not greatly inhibited in the matter of heterosexual relationships, this quasi-puritanic strain was, paradoxically, not an indicator of conformity but of dissent.

As part of this attempt to reinstate a moral universe, emphasis on

[13]Marie Seton, *Portrait of a Director: Satyajit Ray* (London: Dennis Dobson, 1971), chs. 2–3; Chidananda Dasgupta, *The Cinema of Satyajit Ray* (New Delhi: Vikas, 1980), pp. 1–14.

[14]Seton, *Satyajit Ray*, p. 64.

the public role of women and on the problems of women was something more than a matter of ideology for the Rays; the emphasis represented an unselfconscious, probably latent, attempt to rediscover one's relationship with a culture that included an identifiable substratum of matriarchy and with a society that, in facing the alienation and anomie produced by the colonial intrusion, had begun to wreak vengeance on women, seeing in them symbols of continuity with a capricious maternal principle in the cosmos that had begun to falter and sometimes failed altogether.[15]

Finally, as a result of this configuration of cultural and psychological strains, there persisted in the Rays an inner tension between unfettered imagination and disciplined rationality, perhaps even a tendency to live at two planes, which they could not fully reconcile. The imaginativeness was primarily reserved for what they wrote, drew, and fantasized for children; the rationality for organized intervention in society and for defining their social responsibility in an adult world in which children, too, were part of one's trust.

III

Because you believe in the indivisibility of life, you seem to me to be the most Indian of all film directors.[16]

Against these details of Ray's background and early life, I shall now attempt a capsuled reading of his creativity and the controlled split and divisibility of self the creativity presupposes, hoping that my reading will also have something to say about the relationship between popular culture and high or classical culture in South Asia.

Satyajit Ray lived simultaneously in the East and the West and operated at two levels. As a film-maker, which is what Ray at his best was, he was a classicist; his style was classical, even though heavily influenced by post-World War II neo-realism. In the context of the Apu trilogy, Dasgupta defines this classicism as follows:

The depth of feeling which Ray creates . . ., all his fragile and ineffable evocations of beauty and mortality, are contained firmly within the story framework and expressed with the utmost economy . . . .

---

[15]For an analysis of this process, see Ashis Nandy, 'Sati: A Nineteenth Century Tale of Women, Violence and Protest', in *At the Edge of Psychology: Essays in Politics and Culture* (New Delhi: Oxford University Press, 1980), pp. 1–31.

[16]Ranjan Bandopadhyay, open letter to Satyajit Ray, quoted in Bandopadhyay, *Visaya Satyajit*, p. 10.

Ray's own stories are even more tightly constructed, to the point of being over-structured.[17]

As a person, however, Ray lived in the pre-war, bicultural world of Rabindranath Tagore that had a touch of Edwardian England. 'Ray's classicism like so much else in his outlook is derived from Tagore', for 'it was in Tagore that the restless reformism of the "Bengal Renaissance", of the East and West, had found its equilibrium'.[18] The ideological basis of that equilibrium was, to a significant extent, constituted by the values of the Enlightenment—scientific rationality, uncritical acceptance of the theory of progress, and secularism being the most conspicuous among them—and aspects of Indian high culture. Among the latter were certain readings of Vedānta and the Upaniṣads, once aggressively pushed by the Brahmo Samaj in Bengal and the Prarthana Samaj in west India. These readings were monistic—many would say monotheistic—and puritanic in scope and rationalist in orientation. To this mix of West and East, some of the nineteenth-century social reformers of India, including Ray's Brahmo forebears, gave respectability.

The 'Tagorean synthesis', as Dasgupta names it, had, however, its own strengths and weaknesses: 'At its best, . . . it resulted in the emergence of noble images of character; at its worst, it was hypocritical, a little puritan, a little afraid of Freud. It was never suited to the depiction of life in the raw.'[19]

The passions that drove the Bengali social reformers of the last century have long since subsided, but they do survive as an intellectual and cultural underside of modern consciousness in Bengal. Understandably, in this world, neither the mass culture of the post-World War II West nor Indian folk or popular culture has any say. An exception is made for some elements of Bengali non-classical culture, but that is probably an accidental by-product of personal socialization in most instances.

As part of the same cultural–psychological baggage, Ray was not satisfied with being a mere film director. He saw himself as a Renaissance man in the tradition of the great Calcuttans of the last century, and his movies are witness of this self-definition. Like Charles Chaplin and Orson Welles he was more than a director. He usually wrote the scripts and the music for his films, and, reportedly, at least one cameraman, Subrata Mitra, left his unit on the grounds that Ray only technically hired

[17]Dasgupta, *The Cinema*, pp. 65–6.
[18]Ibid., p. 68.
[19]Ibid., p. 69.

cameramen for his films, for he was primarily his own cameraman. Ray also wrote the stories for a number of his films.

Apart from the cinema, Ray had a number of other interests—he was a famous art designer and editor of a highly respected children's magazine. He was best known, however, as a writer of immensely successful crime thrillers and science fiction. He did try to maintain a distinction between the two genres but frequently did not succeed. Much of his science fiction, too, revolves around crime, and violence remains the central concern of both genres. During the last two decades of his life, Ray published nearly thirty books of popular fiction, two of which he also turned into successful films.[20]

Though his popular fiction was apparently meant for children, Bengalis of all ages adored Ray's thrillers and science fiction and eagerly waited for the next adventures of the young private detective Pradosh C. Mitter alias Feluda—the anglicization of the surname is Ray's—and Professor Trilokeśvar Śanku—some of whose western friends affectionately call him Shanks—a researcher–inventor who looks like Professor Calculus of the Tin Tin series and lives alone in a small town near Calcutta, while keeping in touch with the best scientific minds in the world.

For those acquainted with late nineteenth-century thrillers and science fiction, Feluda is the more predictable of the two characters. He is a young professional detective who works in tandem with his teenage cousin, Tapeś. Tapeś, unlike Dr Watson in the Sherlock Holmes stories, is bright and observant; nonetheless, he acts as a foil to Felu because of his Watson-like inability to fathom the master's analyses and game plans. His pet name, 'Topse', reminds the Bengali reader of *topse* fish, known for its perplexed and blank look. There is a third person in the team, the famous thriller-writer Lalmohan Ganguli, better known by his pen name Jatayu, who provides comic relief of the Dr Watson variety. However, it is not Jatayu but young Topse who narrates the Feluda stories, often making snide comments on Jatayu's style of narration in his highly popular crime thrillers. The events usually take place within India, though one story has been set in Kathmandu and another in England.

Professor Śanku's diary—recovered by chance from a crater left by the eccentric professor when he took off in a home-made space rocket—is the basis for the Śanku stories. Śanku is a peculiar familiar-but-strange surname. It is usually a shortened form of Śankara in Bengal but unknown as a surname. The name gives Ray's hero a region- and caste-less identity,

[20]Ray's popular fiction also includes some brilliant stories that cannot be classified as science fiction or tales of detection. I have not taken them into account in this essay except tangentially.

somewhat in the manner of the conventional hero of popular Bombay commercial films, who is rarely given a surname. The diary was written in a magic notebook that was fireproof, elastic and chameleon-like in its ability to change colour. Each Śanku story is a long extract from the diary.

Prima facie Śanku is a more original character than Felu, for he resurrects a romantic model of the creative scientist who has nothing to do with the practising research scientists of today. He is a lonely researcher who works in laboratory in his own home in Giridi, a small insignificant town on the Bengal–Bihar border that has for decades served as a summer resort for Bengali babus. His loneliness is mitigated by his cat, Newton, his very human robot with a very Bengali name, Vidhuśekhar and his devoted servant Prahlād, who is courageous but foolish, given to the kind of 'simple faith' which prompts him to read the Ramayana while travelling on a space rocket. Śanku is a physicist, but he conveys the impression of being a gifted amateur in a number of other sciences also. His discoveries and inventions span a wide range of disciplines—from archaeology to chemistry, from weapons research to biology, and from computer science to botany. He even builds an interplanetary rocket in his backyard and discovers a drug, miracurall, which miraculously cures all illnesses except the common cold (though in one story it cures colds too). As one would expect, Śanku loves to work alone.[21] However, his work and inventions bring him in touch with a wide variety of people from all over the world. So, unlike Feluda's adventures, Śanku's take place in different continents.

For the psychologically minded reader, both genres deal with all-male worlds, though the 'homoerotic' impulses in them are differently patterned. In the crime stories, by making the elderly novelist a comic figure and the assistant a cousin, Ray leaves little scope for explicitly sexual spoofs of the kind that have dogged the Sherlock Holmes stories in recent decades. In his science fiction, the homoeroticism has been given a Hegelian master–slave dimension. It is playfully done but there is in it just the hint of sado-masochistic content which is, in turn, legitimized by a conventional theory of progress and Baconian scientific rationality. Thus, in the stories there are instances of Śanku harassing Prahlad by means of some newly invented drug or contraption, not in spite but in fun. We shall come back to this.

The Bengali middle classes may respect the film-maker Satyajit Ray but they love the popular-fiction writer Ray. The writer Ray reminds them

---

[21]These personal details of Śanku are scattered in a number of stories, most prominently in Satyajit Ray, '*Byomyātrir Diary*', *Professor Śanku* (Calcutta: n.d.), pp. 9–38.

of his father, Bengal's most loved humorist and writer of nonsense verse, and his grandfather, Bengal's most popular writer of fairy-tales in this century.

In response to the respect and the love, Ray partitioned his self into two neat compartments. Into one he fitted his 'classical' ventures—the feature films he had made over a period of three decades. Into the other he fitted his popular, low-brow ventures—his thrillers and tales of mystery, adventure, and violence.

The first category has a number of identifiable features. The most prominent of them is the centrality given to women and his use of women as windows to some of the core social problems of his society and his times. This place given to women's issues is not unique to Ray. From Rammohun Roy (1772–1833), who made the cause of women central to his platform of social reform in the first decades of the nineteenth century to Gandhi, who saw the role of women as vital to his movement for winning political freedom for India and for expanding the sector of freedom for all humanity, nearly all great thinkers and social reformers in India have viewed womanhood as the arena where the moral consciousness of the Indic civilization has to be re-contextualized in response to the new social forces emerging on the Indian scene.[22]

This is equally true of the creative writers who have influenced Bengali social life. From Bankimchandra Chattopadhyay (1838–94) to Rabindranath Tagore and Saratchandra Chattopadhyay (1876–1938) the great Bengali writers have been consistently concerned with the problems of women and used them to mirror the crises of Indian society. (I deliberately avoid using here the examples of women reformers and writers, lest their attempts to make the problems of women central to the society look interest-based and sectoral.)

In Ray's case, however, both these strands of awareness have been further underscored by the experiences of his family. No wonder he saw himself as heir to the nineteenth-century Bengali 'Renaissance' and, though some scholars now find the term inadequate and misleading in the context of Bengal, the term and its progressivist implications did not lose their shine for Ray. For he lived intellectually and morally in the pre-war world of Tagore.[23] To Ray, the continuity between the problems of women and the crisis of the Indian society seemed obvious and inevitable.

---

[22]This issue is discussed in some detail in Ashis Nandy, 'Woman versus Womanliness: An Essay in Cultural and Political Psychology', in Nandy, *At the Edge of Psychology*, pp. 32–46.

[23]Even Ray's favourite actor, Soumitra Chatterji, who often played the hero in his films, looks remarkably like the young Tagore (Dasgupta, *The Cinema*, p. 71).

And women constitute a formidable maternal as well as conjugal presence in his important films. Even in those where there are few women characters—for instance, *Parash Pathar, Jalsaghar* and *Goopi Gyne Bagha Byne*—the issues of gender and potency enter the scene indirectly and constitute a salient theme.[24]

In Ray's world femininity is not merely an important principle, it is given added power by telescoping into all situations of conjugality a clear touch of maternity. Here Ray is in the company of the great myth-makers of late nineteenth- and early twentieth-century Bengal, and also perhaps of the great Indian myth-makers of all time.

The second major feature of Ray's movies is exclusion of the sentimental and dramatic. Ray loved to tell a story in his films; he does not provide a political or philosophical text. He considered movies that do away with a proper story-line self-indulgent. On the other hand, he would take great care not to overload his films with events, to have too dense a plot, or to assume too partisan a tone. One critic repeatedly speaks of Ray's *parimitibodh*, sense of restraint, and considers this restraint part of Ray's personality.[25] Another has gone so far as to say:

Ray is not naturally drawn towards contradictions in mental make-up . . . . The grace in Ray's films often comes from the way he approaches confrontations, averts actions, decisions, events. Where he tries to be direct, the result is often ineffective or jarring.[26]

Even *Charulata* and *Ghare Baire*, moves that stick closely to the novels on which they are based, de-dramatize their originals to some extent.[27]

The fear of being melodramatic or maudlin that dogs many contemporary creative writers in Bengal is partly a reaction to the somewhat maudlin world of Saratchandra Chattopadhyay, who dominated Indian middle-class consciousness in the inter-war years. Ray is no Ernest Hemingway or Bertolt Brecht (two random examples of western authors who made tough-minded detachment their hallmark), but even when he deals with a subject as cataclysmic as the Bengal famine of the early

---

[24]Satyajit Ray, *Parash Pathar* (Calcutta: L.B. Films International, 1957), story: Parasuram; *Jalsaghar* (Calcutta: Satyajit Ray Productions, 1958), story: Tarashankar Bandopadhyay; and *Goopi Gyne Bagha Byne* (Calcutta: Purnima Pictures, 1969), story: Upendrakishore Raychaudhuri.

[25]Bandopadhyay, *Viṣaya Satyajit*, p. 13.

[26]Dasgupta, *The Cinema*, pp. 70, 80–1.

[27]Satyajit Ray, *Charulata* (Calcutta: R.D. Bansal, 1964), story: Rabindranath Tagore; and *Ghare Baire* (Calcutta: NFDC, 1984), story: Rabindranath Tagore.

1940s, he makes a special effort not to be emotionally too involved with his subject. As a result, when *Ashani Sanket* was released, some of his critics accused him of producing a pretty picture postcard on a subject as grim as famine.[28] They interpreted his somewhat detached gaze as an indicator of inadequate social commitment.

Partly, however, this *parimitibodh* and 'distance' come from the fact that Ray usually avoided dealing with subjects with which he was directly acquainted.[29] By underplaying the stress and anomie of urban India, by concentrating on rural India about which he knew little, Ray had paradoxically acquired a comprehensive, dispassionate view of the gamut of macroscopic changes to which his family had been an important witness. He saw it whole, Dasgupta says, because he saw it from a distance.[30] There were obvious deep, unresolved passions behind his restraint; however, the demands made on him for direct, impassioned social commitment only cramped his style. He was never able to match the creativity of his first decade as a director, when his cinematic voice was soft and his commitments understated.

Third, despite his emphasis on femininity, Ray's films are characterized by a low-key, almost hesitant, treatment of sex. As a recent assessment puts it:

In nearly every film where a frank treatment might have been appropriate, a natural barrier to intimacy has existed. In *The Goddess* it was Doyamoyee's reluctance, in *Charulata* Amal's, in *Kapurush* Amitava's, in *Days and Nights in the Forest* Sanjoy's (although intercourse between Hari and the tribal girl is suggested), in *The Chess Players* Mirza's, and in *Pikoo* the mother's (though semi-nakedness is shown because the film was being made for French television).[31]

This avoidance of sexuality is matched by an avoidance of overt conflict.

In *Charulata*, intensity of love is expressed without the lovers even holding hands; there is a rather impulsive, rather brotherly, embrace, but it contributes only a minor note in the tension created between the two. The fascinating scene of the memory game in *Aranyer Din Ratri*, together with the walks, the interplay and repetition of themes, creates a musical statement in which the seduction scenes are only the fortissimos, not raucous even in violence.[32]

[28]Satyajit Ray, *Ashani Sanket* (Calcutta: Sarbani Bhattacharya, 1973), story: Bibhutibhushan Bandopadhyay.

[29]Bandopadhyay, *Viṣaya Satyajit*, p. 19.

[30]Dasgupta, *The Cinema*, pp. 43–4.

[31]Andrew Robinson, 'Ray's View of the World', *The Telegraph*, 3 December 1989, pp. 6–9.

[32]Dasgupta, *The Cinema*, p. 81.

Dasgupta recognizes in the context of *Apur Sansar* that Ray's ambition, given his anti-hedonistic Brahmo heritage, is nothing less than to redress the overemphasis on conjugality at the expense of maternity and to re-emphasize love in its all-embracing sense:

Apu and Aparna's love for each other is only another aspect of Sarvajaya's love for her children or theirs for their aunt or father—a comprehensive all-pervasive, non-sexual love which has seldom been celebrated in the cinema with such purity.[33]

The first time Ray showed a couple kissing in his films was in *Ghare Baire*, made in the mid-1980s; even when he made an avowedly adventure film such as *Abhijan*, he took care to avoid showing extreme violence.[34] Many have attributed this restraint to his Brahmo puritanic upbringing; others have seen in it a compromise with conventionality and an inability to 'let go'. Ray himself is clear on the subject:

People do not seem to bother about what you say as long as you say it in a sufficiently oblique and unconventional manner—and the normal-looking film is at a discount . . . . I don't imply that all the new European film makers are without talent, but I do seriously doubt if they could continue to make a living without the very liberal exploitation of sex that their code seems to permit.[35]

Certainly in Ray's world sex enters stealthily and fearfully, whether he is dealing with conjugality directly or with eroticized maternity (as in *Charulata*). Similarly with violence. It enters Ray's world as something that is sinister by virtue of what it implies or what it can be, rather than by what it is. Often the violence is not physical but involves injuries to a person's or a group's dignity, self-definition, or way of life. For instance, *Abhijan*, *Pratidwandi* and *Seemabaddha*, particularly the first two, offer ample scope for disturbing, if not spectacular, violence.[36] The temptation is consciously avoided. Even in the two movies Ray has made out of his own crime thrillers, overt violence is minimal.

To begin with, this restraint may have been Ray's attempt to mark off his work from the Indian and western commercial films and create a specific audience for his kind of cinema. He pioneered art films in

---

[33]Ibid., p. 22. Satyajit Ray, *Apur Sansar* (Calcutta: Satyajit Ray Productions, 1959), story: Bibhutibhushan Bandopadhyay.

[34]Satyajit Ray, *Abhijan* (Calcutta: Abhijatrik, 1962), story: Tarashankar Bandopadhyay.

[35]Satyajit Ray, quoted in Dasgupta, *The Cinema*, p. 67.

[36]Satyajit Ray, *Pratidwandi* (Calcutta: Nepal and Ashim Datta, 1970), story: Sunil Gangopadhyay; and *Seemabaddha* (Calcutta: Bharat Samsher Rana, 1971), story: Sunil Gangopadhyay.

India; he did not have a ready audience at least for his early works. Later, such restraint became part of his style.

Some of these features extend into Ray's fiction. But there are important distinctions in the way they appear in their low- or middle-brow incarnations, primarily designed to amuse children.

First, Ray's popular fiction is set in a nearly all-male world. If Ray's cinema tends to shrink from the details of man–woman relations,[37] the tendency is even more apparent in his fiction. Women enter this world rarely and as subordinate presences, much as they do in classical Victorian thrillers, in Arthur Conan Doyle's and G.K. Chesterton's works. The deeper relationships, whether of love or hate, are invariably between men. Not only is the device of pairing the sleuth with a somewhat obtuse imperfect man of science imported from Victorian England for the Feluda stories, even Ray's science fiction introduces a similar doubling: Professor Śanku has an innocent, loyal servant on whom he tries out his ideas. Occasionally, Śanku goes farther than Holmes; the scientist literally tests some of his new inventions on his servant Prahlād. To make this inoffensive, there are the 'mitigating' aspects of the relationship—Śanku's paternal concern for the welfare and 'upliftment' of Prahlād, Prahlād's poor intelligence and 'distorted' awareness of the world (which places him in an intermediate category between his master, representing scientific rationality and professional expertise, and the 'things' his master has mastered), and the load of the inferior culture Prahlād carries by virtue of being embedded in the local and parochial. Together they ensure that his subjecthood is complete and Ray has no self-doubt about it.

Second, Ray's popular fiction places much emphasis on scientific rationality which is identified entirely with Baconian inductionism and empiricism. The stories usually posit a clear-cut division between the cognitive on the one hand, and the affective and normative on the other, and here again Ray's direct inspiration is the Victorian crime thriller. The underlying assumption in both cases is that objective reality lies hidden behind manifest reality, and the detective, using superior techniques and unencumbered scientific rationality—that is, by disjuncting cognition from affect—tears the mask off false innocence. The detective, thus, not

---

[37]Bandopadhyay, *Viṣaya Satyajit*, p. 25. It seems that Ray once confided to writer Sunil Gangopadhyay that he was not comfortable creating women characters. Gangopadhyay thinks that that might be the reason why Ray liked to write for children and not for adults. Memorial meeting on Satyajit Ray, organized by the Sahitya Akademi at the India International Centre, New Delhi, 15 May 1992.

merely reveals the objective reality underneath, but ensures that authentic, informed innocence reasserts itself socially. As I have discussed the psychological profile of such thrillers in more detail elsewhere, I shall leave this issue at that.[38]

Third, Ray's detective stories and science fiction are two forms of adventure story. But his idea of adventure has a geographical content. Many of his stories assume that while crime is universal both in theory and practice, science is universal more in theory than in practice. The criminals in Ray's stories of detection are home-brewed; in his science fiction, they are usually whites with German names or what the South Africans once used to identify as honorary whites.[39]

The reasoning seems to be as follows. To do 'great science', as the moderns define it, one has constantly to rub shoulders with western scientists, for creative science is primarily a western pursuit. Naturally, Śanku's status in the world of science can only be established through his jet-setting participation in the 'global' community of first-class scientists, a community that is predominantly white. Śanku's Indianisms, his home in a small town (not too far from a metropolis, though), his family traditions (his father was a well-known Ayurvedi and great-grandfather a *sannyāsī* who renounced the world at the tender age of sixteen), and his occasional *khādi*-clad associate Nakurbabu's openness to things such as telepathy and clairvoyance, and the contradiction between his self-image as a pure scientist and his actual life lived out as a brilliant practising technologist and inventor—they are all hitched to his global hierarchy of scientists. If, however, the hierarchy is accepted, its obverse, too, has to be stipulated: the great scientific frauds and the great scientist-psychopaths, like the great creative scientists and the great scientist-savants, must also come mainly from the West.

Fourth, many elements of the commercial Bengali and Hindi movie, the exclusion of which negatively define Ray's concept of good cinema, are introduced in his popular fiction. Not only do magical elements return in the guise of superscience to play an important part in his science fiction, so does the element of predictability in his crime stories. One knows for instance that Śanku as well as Felu will negotiate all crises in style and emerge intact. It is the content of the style—the events through which the

[38]Nandy, *The Tao of Cricket*, Ch. 1.
[39]Of the twenty-one villains in the Śanku stories, only two are Indian. Most of the villains are immoral scientists misusing their scientific talent. See the excellent 'guide' to these stories in Anish Deb, 'Professor Śanku', *Ānandamelā*, Satyajit Ray Special No., 13 May 1992, pp. 15–31.

style unfolds—that are less than predictable for readers. And to ensure this unpredictability, there is an emphasis on dramatic events—and an avoidance of details—that would be unthinkable of the film-maker Ray. In this respect, the popular writings of Ray fit in with the dominant frame of popular cinema in India.[40] Within that frame, the search of both the popular film-maker and the viewer is not for the entirely unpredictable, the original or the unique, but for a new configuration of the familiar, updated in terms of contemporary experience and therefore found novel.[41]

In this configuration, there is hardly any semblance of the patient, leisurely—some would say laboured—development of character and setting one finds in Ray's serious movies. As in popular Bombay films, the narratives in Ray's popular fiction are built almost wholly around a structure of fast-moving events. The characters are revealed, to the extent they are, through the drama of the events.

Fifth, one suspects that Ray's identification with his scientist-hero and detective-hero is at least partly powered by his self-image as a Renaissance man, straddling the disjunctive cultures of the humanities and science to defy the likes of C.P. Snow. The identification is located in a self-definition on which three generations of Rays and modern Bengalis have worked diligently for nearly a century. It also seems to be powered at the personality level by a certain insecure narcissism of a once highly protected child who has been the carrier of his mother's hopes, ambitions, and feelings of insecurity, and who has internalized the image of a male authority that is overwhelming as well as vulnerable.

The result is again an uneven distribution of certain qualities between Ray's films and his popular fiction. There are in his films reflections of what appear to be conspicuous forms of anxiety-binding strategies—enormously detailed technical work and workmanship and a search for complete dominance or control over the entire technical process of film-making. In popular fiction, however, his commitment to the world-view of science is romanticized. Specially in his science fiction, the events on which he builds his stories often reveal an openness to experiences (such as paranormality and extra-sensory perceptions of various kinds) that might be taboo to the other Ray. Ideologically, he may be more closed in his popular works, methodologically he is much less encumbered. Even a

---

[40]Ray himself has contrasted the enormous 'respect given to detail' in traditional Indian art with the 'poverty of detail' in Indian cinema. According to him, all great artists except the abstract ones are set apart by their emphasis on detail. Satyajit Ray, '*Detail Samparke Du'cār Kathā*', *Viṣaya Calaccitra* (Calcutta: Ananda Publishers, 1976), pp. 26–9.

[41]See 'An Intelligent Critic's Guide to Indian Cinema', above.

casual reader quickly finds out that Ray is not a perfectionist in his popular writings: he is less careful about his workmanship and his imagination is less controlled.

Finally, there is a distinctive quality of violence in Ray's popular works. It is immediate, concrete, and personalized. It is often physical, though carefully sanitized. This difference can be traced to the different ways Ray treats evil in the two genres. In his films, the source of evil is usually diffused and not easily identifiable (a feature Ray fails to maintain in his lesser films) and the carriers of evil do not stray beyond the reach of humanity and morality. They are driven by uncontrollable forces and motivations. As in many traditional Indian epics, Ray gives his audience a choice between reading his 'villains' as villains and reading them as twisted figures bent by life.

The focus and concreteness of evil in Ray's lesser work come from characters which are guided—as in the works of Conan Doyle and other Victorian writers of crime thrillers—by a scientific rationality that is untouched by any insight into social ethics. The villains are only villains; they are openly guided by amoral passions and self-serving greed backed by a value-neutral science. The clash is usually between two kinds of reason—the self-interest-backed psychopathic reason of the criminal and the socially acceptable moral reasoning of the sleuth. (Actually, the criminal expertise of the sleuth is also amoral; only the sleuth as a person is governed by conventional social morality.)

All three features make Ray the producer of popular fiction complementary to Ray the film-maker. And in this respect, he is not unique. All the persons we have mentioned in this essay show similar relationships between their partitioned selves. Thus, the Wells of science fiction is not conceivable without the Wells of *The Outline of History* (which is, of course, a history of western civilization, even though it is written in the innocent belief that it is a global history which does full justice to the non-western world). The Conan Doyle of the Sherlock Holmes stories neatly complements Conan Doyle the theosophist; and the Rushdie of *Midnight's Children* is possible only because there is the other Rushdie, the brain-child of the easy theories of progress of the 1930s.

Is this complementarity a matter of *ex post facto* search for order, the artificial imposition of a deterministic theory of aesthetics on these authors? Possibly not. Psychologically, the Ray of the Apu trilogy, *Devi* (1960) and *Ghare Baire* seems to have been made possible by Ray the tame, uncritical believer in the emancipatory and educative role of Enlightenment values. In this respect, the complementary is not merely aesthetic; it is personological. By writing for children and by upholding the conventional Victorian norms as the embodiment of Englightenment values—thus intervening in child-rearing and education to inculcate, institutionalize, and perpetuate these values—Ray does appear to make peace with his social conscience. He can then be more daringly 'free associative' and give controlled expression to his less socialized, less tamed, less 'educated', more intuitive self in his serious cinematic work. It is Ray's way of making peace with himself and using the integrative capacities at the disposal of his self.[42]

Such forms of partitioning, one suspects, come more easily to the South Asian, traditionally accustomed to live in many cultures and, in fact, in many worlds. This alternative is available, of course, to creative writers in the modern West but they have to search more self-consciously for internal consistency in their work. Perhaps that is why, in Wells' case, the more well-thought-out cognitive ventures are conventional and conformist, whereas in someone like Ray, the more serious and carefully thought-out ventures are more imaginative and less constrained by values derived from the dominant culture. Wells is more conventional in history, Ray in fiction, which, for him, is a 'freer' medium than cinema.

Note that Rushdie, too, driven by his internalization of the West, tries in his non-fiction to be allegiant to Enlightenment values, to win through such conformity the freedom to be more careless about these values in serious fiction. In the West, you can be playful only in fiction, not in science, not even in scientized social analysis. When Rushdie self-consciously tries his hand at serious social analysis through playful fiction, as in *Satanic Verses*, it ends in disaster.[43] He loses almost entirely the targets of his reform, who feel humiliated and provoked by his style of social analysis and intervention.[44]

One may also note that in Wells' serious novels, such as *Ann Veronica* and *Tono-Bungay*, the political and social ideology of the author intrudes to shape the narrative more perceptibly than it does in Ray's work. Wells is more influenced by his ideas of scientific history and rationality in serious literature; Ray, in popular fiction. It is a minor paradox that both

---

[42]On ego strength being a crucial personality factor in the highly creative, see for instance, Frank Barron, 'The Psychology of Creativity', in *New Directions in Psychology II* (New York: Holt, Rinehart and Winston, 1965), pp. 1–134.

[43]Salman Rushdie, *Satanic Verses* (New York: Viking, 1988).

[44]See, for instance, an impressive analysis of the responses to *Satanic Verses* among the Muslims in B.C. Parekh, 'Between Holy Text and Moral Void', *New Statesman*, 24 March 1989, pp. 29–33.

emerge as better social analysts when they cease to be self-consciously socially scientific and socially relevant.

Some of these comments apply to another tormented, internally split writer, Rudyard Kipling (1865–1936). He, too, came close to partitioning his self in his works in the manner we have described, but failed to contain his highly conventional, imperial values when writing even his more creative, intellectually daring novels. As Edmund Wilson points out, it is something of an anti-climax that in *Kim*, which comes close to being one of the great novels of our times and one of the most sensitive ever written about India—Bernard Cohn calls it the best fictional ethnography of India—the hero, after all his encounters with the mysteries of nature and human nature and after all his encounters with an alternative world-view and an alternative vision of human potentialities (represented in the novel by the kaleidoscope of India's cultural diversity and by the haunting figure of the Lama respectively), ultimately decides to become a servitor of the Raj.[45]

The two Satyajit Rays are not in watertight compartments. There is an occasional leak. He made charming films based on two of his own thrillers, and once wrote a script for a science fiction movie, *The Alien*, on which two Hollywood blockbusters, *ET* and *Close Encounters of the Third Kind* were reportedly based.[46] Likewise, some of the early Professor Śanku stories, such as the charmingly Gothic '*Professor Śanku o Robu*', do have

[45]Edmund Wilson, 'The Kipling that Nobody Read', in Andrew Rutherford (ed.), *Kipling's Mind and Art* (Stanford: Stanford University Press, 1964), pp. 17–69.

[46]Amrit Rai, 'Satyajit Ray: A Rare Creative Genius', paper presented at the memorial meeting on Satyajit Ray, 15 May 1992, mimeo. Rai's unwitting source was writer Arthur C. Clarke who wanted Ray to sue the producers of the two Hollywood films.

The main attraction of Ray's script for Hollywood film-makers might have been its positive attitude to the unknown, the strange, and the other-worldly. For Hollywood, the alien has traditionally been an evil and hostile presence, a source of fear. For it, the prototypical science fiction movie is *The War of the Worlds*. For Ray, the strange is a self-enriching and self-expanding experience.

This belief colours not merely Ray's science fiction but his fantasy life in general. His last film, *Agnantuk* (Calcutta: NFDC, 1991, story: Satyajit Ray) can be read as a moving effort by its maker to reaffirm this faith. In it, Ray defies the conventions of his own thought and his self-definition as a chosen carrier of the European Enlightenment in India even more dramatically than he usually does in his more ambitious movies. The defiance comes through a painful process of self-transcendence and self-negation; he has to set up a formidable anti-self in the form of a truant anthropologist who rejects all progressivist definitions of civilization and gracefully lives out his faith.

a latent critique of science built into them.[47] However, here I am not talking of such self-conscious bridges but of the subtler communication and 'division of labour' between the two selves. Thus, what we have identified as an understatement of violence in Ray's cinema often becomes a form of sanitized violence in his popular fiction. Professor Śanku's discovery, the anihilin gun, is as its name indicates a weapon that not only kills instantly but does so cleanly, smokelessly, and soundlessly. It vaporizes its target, leaving no messy blood-drenched body or injured victim to be taken care of.

However, the seepage is usually in the other direction. The identification with the ordinary person confronting life incompetently but nobly—as in *Aparajito, Apur Sansar, Mahanagar, Abhijan* or even *Parash Pathar*—does enter the world of the other Ray.[48] It even acquires a touch of romantic grandeur in a story such as '*Bankubābur Bandhu*', cast in the mould of science fiction, about a harassed schoolteacher who is the constant butt of the crude humour of a village landlord and his cronies. The teacher acquires a new sense of dignity and self-confidence when he accidentally encounters and befriends extraterrestrial beings in the village woods. Technology here puts one in touch with things larger than oneself and with an awareness that positivist knowledge knows nothing about.[49]

Notwithstanding such leaks or exchanges, there are reasonably clear principles by which the selves are separated. We have already hinted at the presence of three of the principles. First, the second self is primarily a pedagogic self. (Though the public stereotype about the selves is exactly the reverse—the film-maker Ray is seen as being serious, the popular writer Ray as fun.) It may be true that 'in Ray's stories there is no crude attempt to provide a moral',[50] but the Brahmo concept of what is good for children informs much of Ray's crime thrillers and science fiction indirectly. Ray's aunt, Sukhalata Rao, another gifted writer of children's literature, once started a brief controversy in Bengal by arguing that ghost stories should not be written, for they were bad for the character—read moral development—of children.[51] Others may not have taken Sukhalata's

[47]Satyajit Ray, '*Professor Śanku o Robu*', in *Professor Śankur Kandakārkhānā* (Calcutta: Ananda Publishers, 1970), pp. 1–18.

[48]Satyajit Ray, *Mahanagar* (Calcutta: R.D. Bansal, 1963), story: Narendranath Mitra.

[49]Satyajit Ray, '*Bankubabur Bandhu*', *Ek Dozen Gappa* (Calcutta: Ananda Publishers, 1970), pp. 17–28. For a fascinating discussion of the theme of lower-middle-class, humble persons living a life of imagination or in touch with things larger than themselves, see Sen, '*Purono Ālāp*', pp. 63–4.

[50]Bandopadhyay, *Viṣaya Satyajit*, p. 52.

[51]Buddhadev Bose, '*Bhuter Bhaya*' (1932), *Racanāsamgraha* (Calcutta: Granthalay, 1982), 5, pp. 466–72.

advice seriously but her nephew has, for though Ray *has* written ghost stories and often brilliantly, his popular fiction always has a series of unstated morals and is guided by an implicit concept of 'healthy pastime' or 'healthy fun', parallels to which can only be found in some writings on cricket produced in Victorian England and in Lord Baden-Powell's concept of the Boy Scouts movement.

Second, the second Ray is distinguished by a 'masculine' concern—the term is not entirely appropriate—with the world of machines, power, intrusive or invasive curiosity, competition for priorities and dominance, combined with an often astonishing insensitivity to nature, including human nature. As if Ray's concern in his popular fiction was nothing more than telling a story in which his hero would solve a proper criminal puzzle. All subtleties of characterization are seen as diverting from a good, strong narrative line. The androgynous sensitivities of Ray, so evident in cinema, seem to give way to a romanticized, two-dimensional, materialistic, phallocentric world where puzzle-solving and a certain toughness predominate. I use the word 'romanticized' advisedly, for the element of romance does not run counter to the materialism and the tough, positivist view of the world. Rather, Ray works with a romantic vision of materialism and positivism with which many non-western ideologues of scientific rationality feel comfortable and which was first popularized in India in the nineteenth century by the babus of Calcutta. There is a perfect and innocent continuity between Father Eugène Lafont's physics classes at St Xavier's College and Mahendralal Sarkar's science movement in *fin de siècle* Calcutta, and the dreary enthusiasm for modern science shown by many like Ray in post-independence India, blissfully unaware of the altered social relations of science in the country.

Third, readers may have noticed that, in the partitioning of the self, the values and concepts associated with the European Enlightenment have a special role to play. Among these values are scientific rationality; the idea of dispassionate, impersonal, falsifiable knowledge, obtainable through a scientific method strictly defined by positivist criteria; the idea of expertise, represented by the experimental scientist and the private detective-as-a-professional-criminologist; and a wholly instrumental concept of knowledge that allows one to see true knowledge as value-neutral, usable either for good or for evil. Ray's crime thrillers and science fiction pay homage to these values.

Ray's message in cinema is profoundly different. We have already described it. It is that message which makes his films, to borrow an expression from Ronald Laing, an experience of experience.

IV

A creative person can be at times a sounder critic of himself than his critics are. There are at least three stories by Ray, all formally classifiable as science fiction, that try to capture the tragedy of the creative person in a conformist society. In all three, but particularly in '*Āryaśekharer Janma o Mṛtyu*', Ray depicts how the creative are forced to opt for survival at the cost of creativity because, in the environment in which they live, the extra-normal is no different from the abnormal and both are repressed by the society to protect and restore the domain of normality.[52] All three stories carry the latent message that creativity is often destroyed because the creative fail or refuse to internalize the social need to repress the strange and the mysterious in them. For instance, in '*Āryaśekharer Janma o Mṛtyu*', the saddest and most direct of the three, the hero, a child prodigy in mathematics, first loses his gifts and then dies because he is uncompromising in his scientific curiosity and recklessly confronts his staid, unimaginative father with his socially daring 'scientific theory'. When dying, in pain and perhaps with an awareness of the futility of it all, it is only his mother that he remembers.

That is about all I can say. We have no direct clue as to whether Ray saw himself as a survivor who had made realistic compromises, or as an uncompromising rebel who nurtured a latent fear of being destroyed by his surroundings, or, more likely, as one who had in him elements of both. Ray's stories, usually pitched in a low key, do not seem to address themselves to other questions that dog the steps of psychologists researching creativity: Which way do the ego defences of a creative person operate? In what kind of work can the creative 'leg go'? Where does he or she tighten the reins of imagination?

No clear answers to these questions emerge from Ray's life story either. The only additional comment I can make on the subject sounds, therefore, so naïvely Freudian and speculative to my own ears that I shall have to ask the reader to take it as entirely tentative.

Creativity—to the extent that it involves the interplay of the conscious and unconscious, the regressive and the ego-integrative, the rational and non-rational or irrational—must at some point encounter the creative person's own moral self. Behind this clinical platitude lies the fact that over the last three hundred years the structure of morality in the dominant

---

[52]Bandopadhyay, *Viṣaya Satyajit*, pp. 53–4; Satyajit Ray, '*Āryaśekharer Janma o Mṛtyu*', *Tin Rakam* (Calcutta: Kathamala, n.d.), pp. 9–24. See also '*Professor Śanku o Khokā*', *Professor Śanku* (Calcutta: Newscript, 1987), pp. 169–90.

culture of the world has gradually come to include a number of Baconian values: a specific form of rationality, a specific concept of knowledge, and a specific set of methods to live by that rationality and to generate that knowledge. In the dominant global culture today, these, too, are part of our socialized—one may say, oversocialized—self and an aspect of the demands of the modern super-ego. Whoever does not know that while all selves are equal, some selves are more equal than others.

As a consequence, it appears that creativity has begun to demand from the creative person both defiance of conventional morality and also some conspicuous conformity to an aspect of morality which is not overtly conventional. To meet this demand, the creative person sometimes creates a kind of shadow self which is perfectly compatible with dominant social ideals and one's oversocialized self, but wears successfully the garb of unconventionality. This shadow self allows freer play to one's undersocialized self, having greater access to the primitive, the non-rational and the intuitive.

The partitioning of the self we have seen in Ray and others is, it seems to me, part of this larger dynamic. It allows greater play to the internalized aspects of social processes which would otherwise have been irreconcilable. Some manage to do this partitioning painlessly, others painfully; some do it with self-conscious finesse, others clumsily and unselfconsciously. But in each case, they pose a challenge to the students of creativity to crack the code of this shadowy self and decipher the writer's language of communication with the other self as a crucial component of the creative process.

This issue of communication often becomes part of a larger politics of cultures, too. The reader may have noticed that, in the case of Wells and Rushdie, their imaginal products are less encumbered by the authors' prim theories of life; with Ray, it is the lighter works that are more encumbered. Is this accidental? What about the fact that in all three cases, time and the changing concepts of social knowledge have shown that their concepts of reliable, valid, scientific social knowledge were less reliable and valid than they might have thought? Does not the very fact that these two questions can be asked today have something to tell us about the changing landscape of the intellectual world?

I shall leave the reader with these questions, in the belief that all questions cannot—and should not—be answered by those who raise them.

---

*Published earlier in Ashis Nandy, *The Savage Freud and Other Essays on Possible and Retrievable Selves* (New Delhi: Oxford University Press, 1995).

Politics of Knowledge

11

Science, Authoritarianism and Culture
On the Scope and Limits of Isolation outside the Clinic

M.N. ROY WAS always certain that he was fighting for the modern world. He was openly anti-traditional and openly a rationalist who sought to transcend his culture. But is this the whole truth about him? Does commitment to one's culture have to be explicit and aggressive? Could it not be implicit and unconscious? When Roy as a young revolutionary, escaping from the colonial police, changed his name from Narendra Nath to Manabendra Nath, was it only carelessness that he retained in his new name the meaning of the old? Or was it a clue to his deeper awareness of the need to recognize continuities and traditions? In his later life when he used the concept of cultural renaissance, did he mean what he said or did he have only a naissance in mind?

One discipline's trivia are always another discipline's life-blood. I venture the guess that Roy here was unwittingly hinting at a psychological process which has often been inaccessible to the modern experience, namely the affirmation of traditions and cultural continuities in the face of the homogeneity that the modern world imposes in the name of universalism. Is such affirmation a pathology, a shared irrationality or a nostalgia which an old society must overcome to enter the contemporary world? I shall try to amplify here one possible answer to this question, exploring in the process one aspect of the linkage between modern science, authoritarianism and culture.

I

Every age has its prototypical violence. The violence of our age is based not so much on religious fanaticism or tribal blood feuds, as on secular, objective, dispassionate pursuit of personal and collective interests. Every age also probably has a cut-off point when the self-awareness of the age catches up with the organizing principles of the age, when for the first time the shared public consciousness begins to own up or rediscover— often through works of art or speculative thought—what the seers or the lunatics had been saying beyond the earshot of the 'sane', 'normal', 'rational' beings who dominate the public discourse of the time.

Thus, it was the mindless blood-letting of the First World War which created a new awareness of an old psychopathology of our times. As the range of human violence and the role of science in that violence began to weigh on the social conscience, a number of European intellectuals woke up at about this time to the dangerous human ability to separate ideas from feelings and to pursue ideas without being burdened by feelings. With the advantage of hindsight, one could trace the cultural sanction for this ability to changes in European cosmology in the sixteenth and seventeenth centuries. It was then that the anthropomorphic world-view began to give way to a mechanomorphic view of nature and society. It was then that what psychoanalysts may call a projective science—a science heavily dependent on the psychological capacity to project into the outer world the scientist's inner feelings and panpsychic fantasies— began to give way to a new concern with objective impersonal pictures of nature and society as the goal of knowledge and as an indicator of progress. But it was the First World War which for the first time shook the popular faith in perpetual progress through increasingly objective science. And as all other traditions of science were moribund in the West and some of them were living in the East, the war, also for the first time, led to a serious, self-conscious effort to involve the East in Europe's self-doubts.

Sigmund Freud first gave a name to this splitting of cognition and affect. He called it isolation. He described it as an ego defence, a psychological mechanism that helped the human mind to cope with unacceptable or ego-alien inner impulses and external threats. According to Freud, the individual sometimes isolated an event, idea or an act by cauterizing it emotionally and by preventing it from becoming a part of his significant experience. The event, idea or the act was not forgotten; it was reincorporated into consciousness after being deprived of its affect.[1] This did not, Freud granted, really free ideas or actions from feelings. It merely replaced conscious associations by unconscious ones and displaced the affect to other ideas or events. (Freud also noted the heavy use of isolation in the character disorder called obsession–compulsion. The connection, by itself, may not seem important but it acquires a different meaning if we remember that some psychological works have referred to the obsessive–compulsive associations of modern authoritarianism. I shall come back to this.)

Later, two second-generation psychoanalysts, Anna Freud and Otto Fenichel, were to define isolation more formally. Here is Fenichel on the subject, in his well-known textbook:

> The most important special case of this defence mechanism is the isolation of an idea from the emotional cathexis (load of feelings) that originally was connected with it . . . . In discussing the most exciting events, the patient remains calm but may then develop at quite another point an incomprehensible emotion, without being aware of the fact that the emotion has been displaced . . . .
>
> The normal prototype is the process of logical thinking, which actually consists of the continued elimination of affective associations in the interest of objectivity . . . . Compulsion neurotics, in their isolation activities, behave like caricatures of normal thinkers . . . they always desire order, routine, system.[2]

Such a definition, however clinical or sterilized it may sound to its author, already verges on social criticism. It admits that order, routine and system are not absolute values, that an over-commitment to them could be an illness. It also implies that objectivity, and the separation of the observer from the observed, is not an unmixed blessing; sometimes it can hide fearsome passions.

Psychoanalysis was not alone. At about the same time that the young discipline was forging the concept of isolation, the surrealist manifestos of André Breton and his associates were rejecting conventional rationality and indirectly attacking the growing use of isolation in modern life. Salvador Dali, for instance, 'absurdized' in his art and life exactly this psychopathology. His watches which melted and his machines which were part-human were but instances where the lost affect was made to re-enter social perceptions, to shock or to enchant. Some years afterwards George Orwell was scandalized when the middle-aged Dali put into his

---

[1]Sigmund Freud, *Inhibitions, Symptoms and Anxiety* (1926), Standard Edition, Vol. 20 (London: Hogarth, 1959).

[2]Otto Fenichel, *The Psychoanalytic Theory of Neurosis* (New York: Norton, 1945), p. 156.

memoirs, with obvious relish, the following incident which took place when Dali was six years old:

While crossing the hall I caught sight of my little three-year-old sister crawling unobtrusively through a doorway. I stopped, hesitated a second, then gave her a terrible kick in the head, as though it had been a ball, and continued running, carried away with a 'delirious joy' induced by this savage act.[3]

Orwell correctly guessed that Dali's pathology tied up with the pathology of a period and quoted a rhyme popular around 1912 to make his point:

> Poor little Willy is crying so sore,
> A sad little boy is he,
> For he's broken his little sister's neck
> And he'll have no jam for tea.[4]

As if to prove Orwell right, Dali's autobiography became a best-seller.

Within a decade or two, a number of movements in literature and the arts caught up with the same pathology, often brilliantly though rarely self-consciously. Thus, many of the comic devices of Bertolt Brecht can be read as attempts to tear away the mask which isolation allows the industrial society to wear. When one laughs with Brecht, one also laughs at the subversion of the defence of isolation. Under the structure of isolation lies, Brecht seems to say, psychopathic hypocrisy or sheer self-deceit. Those who have seen or read his *Mr Puntilla* (1940) will know that it is the story of a businessman whose personality is split. He is a heartless calculating machine when sober; humane and lovable when drunk. When sober, pathological isolation is the main feature of his personality. When drunk, the feelings he dissociates from ideas and actions re-emerge uncensored and get reattached to his ideas and actions. That this happens only when he is drunk is, of course, Brecht's final comment on the psychopathology of modern society.

Another instance from the popular arts could be Charles Chaplin's *Monsieur Verdoux* (1947), a black comedy set against the collapse of values in inter-war Europe. The movie makes subtle use as well as criticism of the mechanism of isolation. It tells the story of a lovable psychopath who marries and then charmingly kills his wives for money. Chaplin offsets

---

[3]Quoted in George Orwell, 'Benefit of Clergy: Some Notes on Salvador Dali' (1944), in *Decline of the English Murder* (Harmondsworth: Penguin, 1965), pp. 20–30.

[4]From Harry Graham's *Ruthless Rhymes for Heartless Homes*, quoted in Orwell, 'Benefit of Clergy', p. 29.

this isolation against the larger isolation taking place in the European society and against the isolation that the movie induces in viewers. As we isolate the acts of murder from the emotions they should arouse, we laugh at Chaplin's murders and sympathize with his hero, who does on a small scale what societies do on a grander scale.[5]

Chaplin's folk philosophy found its clearest expression in Orwell's essay on the use of the English language to sterilize thinking and to cover up violence and cruelty:[6]

In our time, political speech and writing are largely the defence of the indefensible. Things like the continuance of British rule in India, the Russian purges and deportations, the dropping of the atom bombs on Japan, can indeed be defended, but only by arguments which are too brutal for most people to face . . . . Thus political language has to consist largely of euphemism, question-begging and sheer cloudy vagueness. Defenceless villages are bombarded from the air, the inhabitants driven out into the countryside, the cattle machinegunned, the huts set on fire with incendiary bullets: this is called *pacification*. Millions of peasants are robbed of their farms and set trudging along the roads with no more than they can carry: this is called *transfer of population* or *rectification of frontiers*. People are imprisoned for years without trial, or shot in the back of the neck or sent to die of scurvy in Arctic lumber camps: this is called *elimination of unreliable elements*.[7]

Orwell wrote this in the mid-1940s. Around the same time, basing themselves on two major empirical studies done from Freudian and Marxist vantage grounds, some scholars began to mention the over-use of isolation by the fascist personality. Erich Fromm described the authoritarian person not only as sado-masochistic but as having a mechanical, rigid mode of thinking characterized by isolation. Fascism, he said, thrived on the objectification of persons and groups.[8] Theodor Adorno and his associates, too, wrote about the 'empty, schematic, administrative fields' in the mind of the fascist and about the constriction of his inner life.[9] The fascist, they said, partitioned his personality into more or less closed compartments. He had a narrow emotional range

[5]More recent examples of successful attempts to create black comedies on the basis of the human capacity to isolate are Stanley Kubrick's *Dr Strangelove* and *A Clockwork Orange*. Incidentally, black comedy as a genre is nearly absent in Indian and other non-modern creative traditions. It is probably a modern innovation.

[6]George Orwell, 'Politics and the English Language' (1946), in *Inside the Whale and Other Essays* (Harmondsworth: Penguin, 1957), pp. 143–57.

[7]Ibid., p. 153.

[8]Erich Fromm, *Escape from Freedom* (New York: Holt, 1941).

[9]T.W. Adorno, Else Frenkel-Brunswick, D. Levinson and N. Sanford, *The Authoritarian Personality* (New York: Norton, 1950).

and he rejected emotional richness, intuitions and the softer side of life. He admired organization and their formal hierarchies and he sought security in isolating hierarchical structures.[10]

If all this seems overly psychological, there were scholars who traced the institutional roots of European Fascism to the separation of ideas from feelings, and of the rational from the irrational. Friedrich Meinecke, for instance, located the origins of National Socialism in the ancient 'bipolarity extending throughout life of the Western Man' between the utilitarian which was stressed and the spiritual which was suppressed, to the excessive emphasis on the 'calculating intelligence', and to a Machiavellian rebirth which transformed Machiavellianism from a trait of the aristocracy to that of the middle classes and, later on, the masses.[11] Alexander and Margarete Mitscherlich's psychological profile of post-war Germany fits the pattern:

The most important collectively practiced defense is to withdraw cathectic energies from all processes related to enthusiasm for the Third Reich, idealization of the Führer and his doctrine, and, of course, actual criminal acts . . . . The community of those who had lost their ideal 'leader', the representative of a commonly shared ego ideal, managed to avoid self-devaluation by breaking all affective bridges linking them to the immediate past . . . . Had it not been counteracted by these defense mechanisms—of denial, isolation, transformation into the opposite, and above all withdrawal of interest and affect, that is to say of rendering memories of the whole period of the Third Reich devoid of feeling—a condition of extreme melancholia would have been inevitable for a large number of people in postwar Germany . . . .[12]

Hannah Arendt was to later contribute to the same awareness with her portrait of Adolf Eichmann, a plain-thinking, non-ideological, hard-working bureaucratic killer who saw his genocidal responsibility as a problem of efficiency, organization and objective planning.[13] Arendt recognized that Eichmann was the ultimate product of the modern world,

[10]All these traits were seen as aspects of the obsessive–compulsive personality of the fascist. I have already mentioned that in his earlier formulation of the problem Freud had posited a close bond between isolation and obsession–compulsion.

[11]Friedrich Meinecke, *The German Catastrophe: Reflections and Recollections*, trans. Sidney B. Fay (Cambridge, Mass.: Harvard University, 1950), pp. 37, 51. Cited in Renzo De Felice, *Interpretations of Fascism*, trans. Brenda H. Evrett (Cambridge, Mass.: Harvard University, 1977), pp. 15–17.

[12]Alexander Mitscherlich and Margarete Mitscherlich, 'The Inability to Mourn', in Robert J. Lifton and Eric Olson (eds.), *Explorations in Psychohistory: The Wellfleet Papers* (New York: Simon and Schuster, 1974), pp. 257–70; se pp. 264, 266, 268–9.

[13]Hannah Arendt, *Eichmann in Jerusalem* (New York: Viking, 1963).

not because he established a new track-record in monstrosity but because he typified the evil that grew out of everyday isolation rather than from the satanism which comes from unbridled passions. (Appropriately enough, the great majority of his victims too were 'utterly unable to comprehend what had happened to them . . . . They had no consistent philosophy which could protect their integrity as human beings, which could give the strength to make a stand . . . . They had obeyed the law handed down by the ruling classes, without ever questioning its wisdom.'[14] Evidently, in Eichmann's industry of death, mechanical, bureaucratic acceptance faced a mechanical, bureaucratic death machine.)

Thus, since the 1920s, sensitive minds were warning us about the dangers of affectless sanitized cognition, about what Robert Pirsig calls 'a noncoalescence between reason and feeling'.[15] And, by the early 1950s it was clear to many that fascism was the typical psychopathology of the modern world, for it merely took to logical conclusions what was central to modernity, namely the ability to partition away human cognition and pursue this cognition unbridled by emotional or moral constraints.

II

Only one area of modern life escaped the full impact of the critique of isolation: modern science. There were reasons for this. Modern science was structured isolation. The values of objectivity, rationality, value-neutrality and inter-subjectivity were definitionally the values of the modern scientific world-view. And these values *did* heavily draw upon the human capacity to isolate. Moreover, there was a latent awareness in the society that science was, at times, isolation at its best and at its most exciting, that somehow the abstractive and generalizing capacities of science were closely related to the process of isolation. Theodore Kroeber, a relatively unknown psychologist, once perspicaciously described objectivity as a coping mechanism, which was the healthy counterpart of the defence of isolation.[16] Science as a personal search for truth and as a means of human self-realization seemed to be a form of this creative

---

[14]Bruno Bettelheim, *Surviving and Other Essays* (New York: Knopf, 1979), pp. 56–7.

[15]Robert Pirsig, *Zen and the Art of Motorcycle Maintenance* (London: Corgi, 1976), p. 162.

[16]T. Kroeber, 'The Coping Function of Ego Mechanisms', in R.W. White (ed.), *The Study of Lives* (New York: Atherton, 1963), pp. 178–98.

objectivity. It did not seem that isolating to many. The attacks of the artists, writers and the fashionable mystics, in contrast, were bound to wash off as eccentric responses to the creative isolation of modern science.

Moreover, a part of the attack on science was diverted to technology. As the dehumanizing and mechanomorphic aspects of technology became obvious after the First World War, there emerged the view that questions of ethics applied mainly to technology, not to science. This was certainly the argument of the major social critics who shaped the popular response to science. Take for instance the two literary figures who helped to bring us up in the first half of this century: George Bernard Shaw and H.G. Wells. Shaw wrote savage indictments of modern technology in *Major Barbara* and *The Doctor's Dilemma*. But he also wrote fiery tracts pleading for more modern scientific management of societies. Wells's science fiction could be read as a trenchant critique of a science contaminated by human greed and violence. (*The Island of Dr Moreau* and its vivisectional horrors, one may argue, were distant in only geographical terms; psychologically they were right in the midst of the modern world.) Yet, when it came to social problems, Wells became a votary of scientism.

One of the most poignant examples of such ambivalence was Betrand Russell, amongst the first to sense the full destructive power of modern science and technology. In his *Icarus*, an essay on the future of science, as well as in a number of other works, Russell touched upon the relationships between authoritarian control, science and technology, and the instrumental use of isolated rationality. As a corrective, he wanted both reason and love, not isolated reason.[17] Yet, in his system, reason had an intrinsic legitimacy; love did not. Love had to be reasoned love; reason did not have to be feeling reason. He wanted love *and* reason, not love *in* reason.

At least two millennia before modern psychology was born, the *Kaushitaki Upanishad* advised one to try to understand the speaker behind the spoken word and the doer behind the deed.[18] And I hazard the crude *ad hominem* argument that Russell's own life provides clues to the disjunction between ideas and feelings that his philosophy endorsed. His emotional relationships showed that he never sensed the subtle exploitation in a two-person situation where one operated according to

[17]See the 'Prologue' in Bertrand Russell, *Autobiography* (London: Unwin Paperback, 1975), p. 10.
[18]'Kaushitaki Upanishad', translated with comments by Prafullakanta Basu, in *Upanishad*, Vol. 2, (ed.) Sitanath Tattwabhushan, trans. and commentary by Maheshchandra Vedanta-Ratna, and Prafullakanta Basu (Calcutta: Haraf, 1976); 2nd (ed.), pp. 511–77; see pp. 563–4.

the principle of rational love and the other had faith in reasons of heart. He never imagined that what Freud might have called a rational transference could become—with its built-in bias for impersonal, negotiable, part-object relationships—an instrument of oppression. The simple, non-intellectual biography of Russell by his daughter Katherine Tait recognizes this. It unwittingly reveals how Russell's own children rebelled against the oppression of rational love. Katherine herself found religion and missionarism, both as a means of de-isolating and as a means of defying her aggressively atheistic father; and her brother found madness, of a kind which usually has the split between ideas and feelings as its main symptom.[19] It is Mrs Tait's naïve comment in the context of her brother's illness which turns out to be *intellectually* the most challenging; she in effect wishes that her father had been more influenced by the open-ended, easily criticizable, more holistic and less scientific psychology of Sigmund Freud than by the positivist, progressive and ultra-scientific system of J.B. Watson.

Implicit in such torn creative minds of this century's Europe was the belief that while the context of modern science and its applications were faulty, the text of science was liberating. In fact, as diagnosed by the modernists, the problem was that the objectivity of science had not yet fully informed the social uses of science. That is, while the scientifically minded had used isolation, they had not isolated deeply and widely enough; feelings still dominated many sectors of human life, and these sectors were waiting to be liberated by the further growth of the scientific temper.

Some years ago Gerald Holton, one of those optimists who are not embarrassed to seek security by surrendering more fully to the forces which cause the insecurity in the first place, declaimed:

While we may intuitively feel that the choice is unpleasant, it is perhaps not necessarily so paradoxical as it seems. A number of social or physical systems offer models in which stability, when disrupted by the introduction of a new factor, can be reestablished at some level only by increasing the role of the new factor even further.[20]

Predictably, a majority of natural scientists toed this line. Not so predictably, many social analysts, too, chipped in with the same analysis. They valiantly tried to solve the social problems of science by promoting

[19]Katherine Tait, *My Father Bertrand Russell* (New York: Harcourt, Brace, 1975), pp. 62–4.
[20]'Introduction', in Gerald Holton (ed.), *Science and Culture: A Study of Cohesive and Disjunctive Forces* (Boston: Beacon, 1965), p. x.

more science. The new credo was: the context or text of modern science is universal and amoral but its social context is often parochial, value-loaded and evil. Individual scientists, too, can sometimes be self-interested, hypocritical or opinionated. Change the social relations of science and you will have finally an ethically pristine, fully liberating, modern science.

Entire schools of thought have by now grown up on this staple diet, and the Ernest Nagels and Peter Medawars have even tried to build an entire dietetics on it. As such ideas and their political power are widely known, I shall not discuss them further. Instead, I shall draw attention to the new generation of ordinary citizens and consumers of science who have been so well brought up on the principle of the purity of scientific text, that they, even when practising homeopathy or palmistry or even when growing a sacred tuft of hair or going on a pilgrimage, have to justify themselves on scientific grounds. Among the Third World élites today, such uncritical acceptance of science as the absolute standard of validation is now more common than the Asian flu.

This growing body of uncritical supporters of science operate with the same folk philosophy with which, according to Bruno Bettelheim, apolitical victims often face oppression in 'extreme situations'. Used to being obedient to the scientific establishment, they dare not oppose the ruling ideology. Each inhumanity imposed or legitimized by science is seen as a mistake of the system which could be corrected from within it.[21]

III

Today, in the last quarter of the twentieth century, another response is conceivable. Older, tired and wiser, we can now take courage to affirm that the main civilizational problem is not with irrational, self-contradicting superstitions but with the ways of thinking associated with the modern concept of rationality; that modern science has already built a structure of near-total isolation where human beings themselves—including all their suffering and moral experience—have been objectified as things and processes, to be vivisected, manipulated or corrected. According to his view, the irrationality of rationality—as Herbert Marcuse might have described the pathology—in organized normal science—as Thomas Kuhn might have described the system—is no longer a mere slogan. It is threatening to take over all of human life, including every interstice of culture and every form of individuality. We now have

[21]Bettelheim, *Surviving.*

scientific training in modern sports and recreations; our everyday social relations and social activism are more and more guided by pseudo-sciences like management and social work and by pseudo-technologies like transactional analysis and T groups. Our future is being conceptualized and shaped by the modern witchcraft called the science of economics. If we do not love such a future, scientific child-rearing and scientific pedagogy are waiting to cure us of such false values, and the various schools of scientific psychotherapy are ever-ready to certify us as dangerous neurotics. Another set of modern witch-doctors has taken over the responsibility of making even the revolutionaries among us scientific. In fact, the scientific study of poverty has become more important than poverty itself. Even in bed, our performance is now judged according to the objective criteria of some highly scientific, how-to-do-it manuals on sex.

Such a process has continuously justified our ability to freeze or fix a subject for study and to place it at a distance to evaluate. Those acquainted with Bettelheim's account of human beings facing arbitrary torture and murder will know why I have used the word 'distance' here. Distancing is a psychological device which both the victim and his oppressor have to use, one to ward off the reality of his fate and the other to reduce his victim into an object.[22]

It is the second use which is pertinent to my argument here. It is the use which prompts Aimé Césaire to write the quaint formula: 'colonization = thingification'.[23] In its extreme form such objectification becomes necrophilia, the passion to kill so as to freeze, place at a distance, and love.[24]

The warning against the rationality from which the objectification derives is best given in the words of Fromm:

Logical thought is not rational if it is merely logical . . . . (Paranoid thinking is characterized by the fact that it can be completely logical . . . . Logic does not exclude madness.) On the other hand, not only thinking but also emotions can be rational . . . .

Reason flows from the blending of rational thought and feeling. If the two functions are torn apart, thinking deteriorates into schizoid intellectual activity, and feeling deteriorates into neurotic life-damaging passions.

[22]Ibid., Part I.
[23]Aimé Césaire, *Discourse on Colonialism*, trans. Joan Pinkham (New York: Monthly Review Press, 1972), p. 21.
[24]Erich Fromm, *Anatomy of Human Destructiveness* (Connecticut: Fawcett, 1973). See also George Devereux, *From Anxiety to Method in the Behavioural Sciences* (The Hague: Mouton, 1967).

The split between thought and affect leads to a sickness, to a low-grade chronic schizophrenia, from which the new man of the technotronic age begins to suffer . . . . There are low-grade chronic forms of psychoses which can be shared by millions of people.[25]

Fromm here endorses, with the help of nosological entities similar to the ones I have used, the social analyses which nervously view a growing number of societies getting structurally and morally reorganized to meet the needs of organized science. He in the process unwittingly provides another reason why criticisms of modern science from within the scientific world-view cannot go very far.

The importance of the other position which insists that the social problems created by modern science cannot be handled within the culture of modern science, has also grown because the idea of more science to cure the ills of science seems especially to enthuse normal scientists and the political spokesmen of the scientific estate. It is now obvious that the slogan of internal criticism and the search for the hair of the dog to cure dog-bite serve the interests of the scientists rather well, for they delegitimize criticisms from the outside and suggest that while the scientific world-view cannot be judged by other world-views, the other world-views can be judged and indeed should be judged by science.[26]

To give a well-known example, Paul Feyerabend, no lover of astrology himself, examines at one place a joint statement by 186 modern scientists, eighteen of them Nobel-laureates, against astrology.[27] He shows that none of the 186 had studied astrology before attacking it. Some of them, when contacted by journalists, were unashamed that they knew nothing about astrology. Their statement shows the same ignorance of the relevant findings of modern science. That of course did not stop them from passing judgement. Not only were they unwilling to apply their scientific method to judge the claims of a competing system, they did not stop to ask why they needed 186 signatures and not one, if the arguments were so good and so conclusive.

One is tempted to argue that the 186 signatures were necessary mainly to deny the principle of reciprocity. They were meant to deny the counter-claim that, if modern science claims the right to criticize other systems,

[25]Erich Fromm, *The Revolution of Hope: Toward a Humanized Technology* (New York: Harper and Row, 1974), pp. 42–3.

[26]I have discussed this issue in more detail in 'Science in Utopia: Equity, Plurality and Openness', *India International Centre Quarterly*, 1983, 10(1), pp. 47–59.

[27]Paul Feyerabend, 'The Strange Case of Astrology', *Science in a Free Society* (London: NLB, 1978), pp. 91–6.

it should give the right to criticize science if not to other systems at least to its own victims, that it should grant that a part of the ethical restraint on modern science may now have to come from outside science, from the totality of human experience confronting science.

Any idea of external control on science, however, sounds like a denial of free thought to many. Discredited by the clumsy, sometimes tragic battle waged against science by the medieval church, the idea of external control seems dangerous even now, when science rules the world. But could it be that the church in its obscurantism was expressing its fears of a system of knowledge freed from the restraints of ethics and social conscience, however faulty that ethics and however rigid that conscience? The answer may be less unfriendly to the church today when modern science is a part of the global establishment, when most faiths have become defensive and all organized faiths are seeking endorsement from science. Today the issue is: which pathology has become more unsafe for human survival, that of scientific rationality or that of its 'irrational' subjects?

IV

The problem I am posing is, I hope, clearer. I am suggesting that when the world of uncritical traditions faced the first onslaught of organized modernity, the principle and practice of isolation played a major role in it. Modern science at that stage was a creative, and modern authoritarianism a pathological, possibility of the ability to isolate. Gradually, over-isolating, fully organized modern science has become another pathological correlate of the demise of traditions and the erosion of cultures, the false claims of the rationalists, scientific socialists and Hobbesian liberals notwithstanding.

The earlier creativity of modern science, which came from the role of science as a mode of dissent and a means of demystification, was actually a negative force. It paradoxically depended upon the philosophical pull and the political power of traditions. Once this power collapsed due to the onslaught of modern science itself, modern science was bound to become, first, a rebel without a cause and then, gradually, a new orthodoxy. No authority can be more dangerous than the one which was once a rebel and does not know that it is no longer so.

The moral that emerges is that modern science can no longer be an ally *against* authoritarianism. Today it has an in-built tendency to be an ally *of* authoritarianism. We must now look elsewhere in the society to find support for democratic values.

Why has something which began as a movement of protest become part of the Establishment? Why do the moderns continue to view science as a cornered voice of dissent fighting powerful opponents when it all too visibly owns the world? Why do even the radical critics of society exercise restraint when criticizing science?

Any answer to these questions must begin with the admission that modern science is both a social institution and a search for new meanings and aesthetics. During its first two centuries, it was the second aspect of modern science which predominated. In Europe till the eighteenth century the scientist was claiming the right to search for another truth and adopt another mode of reaching it. But that philosophical quest was a hangover from the days of classical science and the scientists recovered from it soon enough to produce, by the end of the nineteenth century, a formidable organization and strong links with that other child of seventeenth-century Europe, the modern nation-state system. In another five decades, the scientist has become the main author of the Establishment cosmology. He is now the orthodoxy; he is now the Establishment. So much so that to perceive him still as a weak, unorganized fighter against authority can spell disaster for all of us.

When science was primarily a philosophical venture, it allowed for more plurality. In the days of organized science there is little scope for a scientist to protect his individuality as a scientist. Over-organized science has managed to do the impossible: it has become a market-place and a vested interest at the same time. It has an organizational logic independent of the creativity of the individual scientist but dependent on—and subserving—his material interests. Thus, there is an inner incentive for the scientists—for even the most creative among them—to orient their creativity to the dominant culture of science. The scientist can fully encash his creativity in the market-place of science only if he plays according to the existing organizational rules of modern science and, better still, if he remains unconscious of the rules in the fashion of what Georg Lukacs calls the silent species.[28]

This depoliticization is camouflaged by a special brand of pseudo-politics. The normal scientist, who could be defined as the practitioner of Thomas Kuhn's normal science, is expected to be politically involved, but he is expected to operate *as if* the pathology of modern science lay only in its context. He can shout himself hoarse over nuclear armaments—as a pacifist, a liberal or as a Marxist—but he cannot say that violence

[28]Georg Lukacs, 'The Twin Crisis', in San Juan, Jr. (ed.), *Marxism and Human Liberation* (New York: Delta, 1973), p. 316.

lies at the heart of modern science. He may speak of the origin of science in superstitions, prejudices and myths; he can speak of the persistence of these in the individual scientist; but he cannot speak of their persistence in the text of science. In other words, there is now a standard officially-sponsored model of political dissent for the scientists. If a normal scientist follows that model, science rewards him handsomely, otherwise he is valued not as an eccentric professor but as a lunatic who has missed his professional bus. It is this cultural twist which has pre-empted basic internal criticism in science.

This point can be made in another way. The culture of modern science gives a special role to the scientist in defining the concerns of science, whether these concerns be textual or contextual. But it encourages him to shirk all responsibility if something goes wrong with the concerns. That responsibility is passed on to other citizens. Thus, the scientist gets the credit for the constructive discoveries of science, not for the destructive ones. Indeed, his training encourages him to either criticize science only in terms of its context ('Nothing is wrong with nuclear research; the politicians and the generals are the ones who misuse it and produce nuclear arms') or reduce all contextual problems to textual ones ('If science threatens an ecological disaster, do not seek woolly social or political solutions; seek scientific ones, for science can always solve the problems it has created').

This is the other way the culture of science is structured by ego-defence like isolation and denial, and controlled by a small number of two-dimensional scientists who, unlike the political élites, have exempted themselves from criticisms, checks and competition. The bureaucratic violence that results is endorsed by the total socialization of the individual through modern child-rearing, education and mass media. The scientists decide the use of science in society; the lay person considers such control proper. Increasingly, scientists exercise their power with the enthusiastic approval, in fact on the demand of a section of the society. Both sides view the suffering inflicted by or in the name of science as a needed sacrifice for the advancement of human rationality and social progress.

The traditional cultures, not being driven by the principles of absolute internal consistency and parsimony, did allow the individual to create a place for himself in a plural structure of authority. In such cultures the individual always had some play vis-à-vis the institutions he worked with. For instance, a guru could be a false consciousness to many but, traditionally, one man's guru was always another man's anti-guru. Such fragmentation of the world of gurus was presumed by every disciple of every guru. So there were at least varieties of false consciousness competing for the allegiance of the believers. Such multiplicity is not granted by modern science which, because it presumes universal norms and unitary truths, must reject all gurus, and claim religious allegiance to one truth and one form of liberation. So you have faith but faith without the different forms of godmen, revelations and prophets which enriched the traditional religions.

Finally, the four pluralities science disarmingly accepts. In each case, there is an implicit but irrevocable principle of hierarchy as well as a totalist vision of social consciousness. First, there is classical science, by which one means pre-modern western science, seen as a heroic, but an earlier, romantic and inferior stage in the evolution of true knowledge, the final stage of which is presumed to be modern western science. In this hierarchy classical science is fitted in as a museum-piece, not as an alternative view of nature and humanness.

Second, there are the ethnosciences, the non-modern, non-western traditions of science which are seen as semi-scientific reservoirs from which modern science may have to pick up insights and practices, rejecting the rest as so much mythology and magic. The borrowing by modern medicine of reserpine from Ayurveda does not imply any respect for the philosophy or the structure of Ayurveda; it shows a pragmatic openness towards some specific findings of Ayurveda. It is the respect we show an alert child who by chance spots a misplaced railway ticket which the elders should have spotted in the first place but, through a series of accidents and oversights, did not.

Third, there is the internal plurality of competing scientific theories. It, too, has no intrinsic legitimacy. If science has more than one explanation of a phenomenon, the expectation is that only one of them will finally win and establish its hegemony; otherwise a new theory will emerge and supplant all the competing theories. Usually, of course, there is one dominant theory in existence; this is held by the scientists in the fashion of, to use Kuhn again, a totalizing dogma.

The fourth plurality, too, is internal. Scientists grant legitimacy to the divide between what J.R. Ravetz calls the mature and the immature sciences.[29] Though theoretically any kind of science can be immature, in practice the social sciences are so classified, mainly because of their paradigm-surplus nature. For all paradigm-scarce disciplines are definitionally mature following Kuhn. This is despite the critical power the human sciences sometimes derive from their paradigm-surplus nature

---

[29]J.R. Ravetz, *Scientific Knowledge and its Social Problems* (Harmondsworth: Penguin, 1973), pp. 156–9.

and from their ability to offer wider social choices as well as openness of vision.[30] The main function of this concept of maturity is to avoid having critical social sensitivity close to the heart of science.

The pluralities of science, therefore, are no pluralities at all. They may be necessary for the progress of modern science but to participate in or manage such a culture of science requires something more than the qualities imputed to the stereotypical scientist; they require a complex of psychological skills most frequently found in the authoritarian personality, either as part of a search for 'authoritarian domination' or as an expression of 'authoritarian submission'.

V

I have said that modern science was once a movement of dissent. It then pluralized the world of ideas. I have said that it is now the centre-piece of the Establishment cosmology and can function neither as an instrument of basic criticism nor as an expression of scepticism—its philosophical hallmarks at one time. I have also said that modern science, at its best, was once a creative response to a particular psychological problem, the pathological response to which later turned out to be modern authoritarianism. I am now suggesting that modern science, which began as a creative adjunct to the post-medieval world and as an alternative to modern authoritarianism, has itself acquired many of the psychological features of the latter. In fact, in its ability to legitimize a vivisectional posture towards all living beings and non-living nature, modern science is now moving towards acquiring the absolute narcissism of a new, passionless Caligula.

Modern science began by giving a dissenting meaning to the man–nature relation. It was not merely another ideology claiming that other ideologies were false or inferior; it was another view of the human condition which sought to make all ideologies redundant. (The end-of-ideology argument, so popular a decade ago, can be seen as a projection of the triumph of this anti-ideology in human mind and society.) In its earliest form, modern science disturbed the older world image not so much by being unconditionally true, but by introducing a new style of demystification which subverted parts of the European tradition that had become stale, self-justifying and inconsistent with experience. This is why when specific scientific theories were falsified and reduced to the

[30]The problem of pluralities has also been discussed in Nandy, 'Science in Utopia'.

status of myths by the growth of modern science, it did not lead to any great jubilation among the believers, not even when the falsified theories dealt with matters of theological concern. The believers sensed that modern science had offered a way of looking at things which was partly independent of the changing content of modern science. They sensed that one could not escape the critical gaze of modern science by taking advantage of the changes within it.

However, like some of the schools of social criticism it directly or indirectly spawned, modern science too developed features which were to help it, as a critical tradition, to demand and get uncritical support. Not only did modern science gradually develop a rigid, unidirectional mode of demystification which saw all such other modes as subsidiary or peripheral, it began to see all alternatives to its mode of demystification as conspiracies against human good. This was backed up by a self-justifying tough-mindedness.[31] What was first a quality of consciousness was now institutionalized and concretized as a 'thing' and as an independent reality, in fact the only reality.

First, there was the concretization of concepts. Rationality, for instance, was once an attribute of thinking. It became a concrete body of knowledge and a set of methods of knowing. Adjectives thus became nouns and the psychological became the crypto-physical under the influence of an anti-intraceptiveness which, in another context, was later found to be closely associated with modern authoritarianism.

Second, the worlds of nature and, later on, human nature came gradually to mean the worlds of the sciences of nature and of human nature. This is not the old argument about science cornering culture, though that argument, too, has some power. I am speaking of the operationalism which reduces reality to the reality accessible to the methods of science, and then reconstructs the 'whole' reality—of nature, persons or cultures—by extrapolating from that operational reality. The dangers of such concretization—and the isolating, part-object relations it promotes—are especially obvious in the human sciences. In psychology, for instance, intelligence tests are no longer seen as imperfectly operationalizing intelligence; intelligence is now what the intelligence tests measure. A strategy of research has come to define the whole of the reality of human intellect.

I am often told that this is a price we must pay for the growth of science, and once the infant science of psychology matures, it should be

---

[31]The word has been borrowed from modern psychology which uses it to distinguish indirectly the more scientific from the less, and the better from the worse.

able to handle the complexities of human nature. I am not so sure. The rewards of operationalism and that of the control it gives over individuals and groups are enormous. And once it is institutionalized in a society, it acquires more and more autonomy. The means gradually begin to define the goals and ultimately become the goals. In another context, Freud might have called this an instance of process pleasure—the pleasure which should be associated with an instinctual goal but is displaced on to the process of reaching the goal.

Finally, within the scientific estate there is the pressure on objectivity to move closer to objectification due to the constant stress on the subject–object dichotomy. In the modern knowledge systems, this dichotomy is seen as a major pathway to power through knowledge and to knowledge through isolation.[32] This has necessarily led to a further endorsement of mechanomorphism. The old European concept of the world machine included the idea of God the clock-maker which, retrogressive though it may sound to modern ears, did provide a check on the potential for isolated cognition implied in the idea of the world as a machine. The new secularized concept of the world machine represents a desacralized mechanomorphism which admits no limit on itself. Behaviourists like J.B. Watson and B.F. Skinner have only taken to its logical conclusion this process of objectification. How far they derive their legitimacy from the promise of scientific control over human fate is obvious from the fact that behaviourism remains the official ideology of both the orthodox modernism of the West and the critical modernism of Soviet Marxism.

Any mention of the duality of the observer and the observed prompts a section of scientists and philosophers of science to mention particle physics, Werner Heisenberg or microbiology. And then some social scientists join them with Freud's concepts of transference and counter-transference or the structuralist concept of the savage mind. As if these concepts defined the mainstream culture of modern science or disturbed the poise of the normal scientist pursuing his normal science! I do not think it an overstatement to say that the culture of normal science, as we know it, will collapse if it gives up the division between the observer and the observed or the hierarchy between the scientists and the laity.

Once again we are close to what some psychologists have identified as a basic feature of political authoritarianism: all-round objectification and the idea of a leadership supposedly representing both the true interests

---

[32]Gregory Bateson is one of the many who have suggested that the objectivity of experience is a typically Occidental view of the world. See his *Mind and Nature: A Necessary Unity* (Toronto: Bantam, 1980), pp. 33–4.

of the masses and the superior understanding of those interests. Political authoritarianism *has* to see the citizen as a subject whose subjecthood is no different from that imposed on the laity by science. The sometimes harmless distance between the scientist and his subject becomes in politics the chasm between a self-declared élite—the 'revolutionary vanguard' in some theories of progress—and their increasingly voiceless objects of manipulation: the reportedly immature masses, underdeveloped, primitive, and carrying the heavy baggage of false consciousness. Seen thus, the culture of modern science is part of a more general theory of imposed secular salvation, the other special case of which is modern authoritarianism.

It is therefore not a paradox of our times that to contain modern science many are falling back on what has been one of the main targets of modern science during the last three hundred years—cultural traditions. It is part of the attempt to protect the plurality of human consciousness and provide a critique of science from outside. In so far as the various in-house criticisms of modern science have not defied modernity and in so far as modern science is inextricable from the modern consciousness, in many societies one is forced to fall back on the traditional world-views. At least the latter have tried to protect, at the margins of the 'civilized' world, the crucial insight that the battle against isolation is joined when one gives up the concept of a fully autonomous observable and opts for the dyad of the observer and the observed as the basic unit of analysis. A number of non-modern systems of thought have sought freedom and understanding in the deliberate search for a continuity between the observer and the observed, in cross-identifications and empathy. Here, for example, is Toshihiko Izutsu speaking of Islam:

The problem of the unique form of subject–object relationship is discussed in Islam as the problem of *ittihad al-alim wa-al-ma' lum*, i.e. the 'unification of the knower and the known'. Whatever may happen to be the object of knowledge, the highest degree of knowledge is always achieved when the knower, the human subject, becomes completely unified and identified with the object, so much so that there remains no differentiation between the two. For differentiation or distinction means distance, and distance in cognitive relationship means ignorance.[33]

True, the traditional philosophies generally place such unity of the knower and the known outside everyday life, which these philosophies

---

[33]Toshihiko Izutsu, *The Concept and Reality of Existence* (Tokyo: The Keio Institute of Culture and Linguistic Studies, 1971), p. 5.

often see as unavoidably dualistic. Nonetheless, the awareness of such possibilities delimits the role of modern science and helps one to see it as only a finite system of knowledge and as a corrective to an overly projective world-view. Such delimitation in turn allows the peripheries of the world to use their traditions as a legitimate vantage ground for social criticism.

This, however, only brings us to another question: what kinds of tradition can be used as tools of criticism and what kinds are open to criticism? Apparently, the answer to this question is known. One knows the kind of tradition which renaissance science criticized and the reasons thereof. The moderns never tire of remembering the isolating, heartless, frozen aspects of traditions which Galilean science attacked. Modern Indians, too, never fail to remind themselves that the last two hundred years of Indian life have been a continuous struggle against not merely the colonizing West but also the negative aspects of Indian traditions. Even the counter-modernists grant that cultural traditions can become ritualized, self-justificatory and a means of perpetuating institutionalized violence. They grant that traditions, too, may push one to isolate their contents. It is probably in the nature of any complex cultural system to seek self-perpetuation through isolation. After all, according to Freud, the main role of rituals is to isolate, and a culture is hardly conceivable without its own quota of rituals.[34]

This is only another way of saying that no culture can survive on a staple diet of passions. Nothing can be as dead as last year's passions. A culture must constantly persevere, if that is the word, to survive on an appropriate mix of non-heroic self-definition and ritualization of everyday life.

Let us not, however, minimize the complexity of the problem. Choosing the right traditions is not a matter of choosing from among the discrete elements of a culture. A culture is not a grocery store, with each customer a free purchaser and each purchase an independent purchase. A culture is an interconnected whole with some strong interconnections and some weak; a culture has some odd, unpredictable, ill-understood bonds with those who live by it, use it or even disown it. Within it, you have some options only if you exercise others, and the options exist only if yet others are not exercised. The choice of traditions I am speaking of involves the identification, within a tradition, of the capacity for self-renewal through heterodoxy, plurality and dissent. It involves the

[34]Freud, *Inhibitions, Symptoms and Anxiety.*

capacity in a culture to be open-ended, self-analytic and self-aware without being overly self-conscious.[35] There are traditions, or at least constructions of traditions which, even when you introduce crucial changes into them, are not threatened. These traditions can give meanings to the changes in terms of categories internal to them. Because they have sub-traditions which operate as baselines for social criticism, they are accustomed to converting external criticisms into internal ones. On the other hand, there are traditions which are so fragile or so consistent internally that the removal of a single plank may mean total collapse. In neither case can one mechanically apply the principle of choice.

Fortunately, cultures are usually more open and self-critical than their interpreters. In the first half of this century, Ananda Kentish Coomaraswamy wrote his brilliant critique of the modern civilization. He contrasted this civilization with the traditional vision of man— humane, contemplative and just. He thus took to an elegant conclusion the critique initiated by Thomas Carlyle, John Ruskin, William Blake and Leo Tolstoy on the one hand and a galaxy of non-western thinkers on the other. However, even if one grants that everyone has the right to project a utopia into the past, Coomaraswamy's tradition remains homogeneous and undifferentiated from the point of view of man-made suffering. His defence of the charming theory of sati, for example, never takes into account its victims, the women who often died without the benefit of the theory. By refusing to consider this mundane issue, Coomaraswamy's traditionalism ceases to be critical, however open it might be metaphysically to the idea of self-criticism and self-renewal. Such traditionalism reactively demystifies modernity to remystify traditions.[36] It also promotes isolation, even if in a much less dangerous form than did Dr Josef Mengele and Shiro Ishii under the banner of science.

Likewise, one may concur with Coomaraswamy that the untouchables

---

[35]Apart from my obvious indebtedness to the critical tradition, I have in mind here the meaning of 'analysis' that emerges from the works of Philip Rieff on Freudian ethics. See especially his *The Triumph of the Therapeutic: The Uses of Faith after Freud* (New York: Harper, 1968). Such a meaning in some ways ties up with the concept of criticism as used throughout this paper. Though neo-Freudian and neo-Marxian in origin, the concept does have some degree of cross-cultural validity. It certainly ties up with the critical uses to which some forms of *advaita*, especially the theory of *maya*, could be put. Also relevant in this context is the work of one who may seem a strange bed-fellow, Karl Popper. See his 'Towards a Rational Theory of Tradition', *in Conjectures and Refutations: The Growth of Scientific Knowledge* (London: Routledge and Kegan Paul, 1972), pp. 120–35.

[36]See 'Evaluating Utopias' in this volume.

in traditional India were better off than the proletariat in the industrial societies. But this could be an empty statement to those victimized by the caste system today. When many untouchables opt for proletarianization in contemporary India, is their choice merely a function of faulty self-knowledge? Can we draw a clear line between the experts on traditions and the laity, and declare the latter's knowledge, feelings and values irrelevant to the understanding of traditions? Are we not then replicating nineteenth-century colonial anthropologists and historians who stratified persons, races and cultures into the producers and the consumers of knowledge, into those who were historians to the world and those who were objects of history? I am afraid Coomaraswamy's traditionalism, despite being holistic by design, does not allow a creative, critical use of modernity within traditions. This never happens with the living traditions which Coomaraswamy theoretically supports. The Ramayana and the Mahabharata, for instance, take into account the modern consciousness in the form of the personality types represented by some demons (*danavas, daityas, rakshasas* and *asuras*), and some anti-heroes such as Karna. These types are rejected; but they are first considered seriously, given due respect and used as critiques of the types favoured.

An excellent example of the critical use of modernity within tradition is the two hundred years of the recent past of Indian society from Rammohun Roy to Gandhi. Throughout the period, continuous and sometimes successful efforts were made to make the modern world a meaningful!—and manageable—part of Indian experience. Even the parallel negative past of modern India—from Radhakanto Deb, who opposed Rammohun Roy, to Nathuram Godse, who killed Gandhi—can be read as an unsuccessful effort to arrive at a creative use of modernity. That such efforts did not always succeed or that they often led to dangerous visions should not blind us to the seriousness of the efforts. Deb opposed the abolition of *sati* by the British, but was a pioneer in women's education. Godse was an ultra-Hindu, but the Hinduism he fought for was more modern than Gandhi's. A part of Coomaraswamy's problem arises from his emphasis on the classical at the expense of the folk and on the 'pure' at the expense of the 'hybrid' and the 'dirty'. Perhaps if he had not had that odd middle name, if he had not had to disown his mixed origin and bicultural consciousness, or live away from his tradition for so long with such enormous knowledge of it, he might have defended Indian culture less uncritically.

Today, with the renewed interest in cultural visions, one has to be aware that commitment to traditions, too, can objectify by drawing a line between a culture and those who live by that culture, by setting up some as the true interpreters of a culture and the others as falsifiers, and by trying to defend the core of a culture from its periphery. Such uncritical commitment tends to undervalue the folk as opposed to the classical, the contextual as opposed to the textual, the reinterpreted as opposed to the professionally interpreted, and the subsequent or 'interpolated' as opposed to the earlier or the 'original'. As in science, so in culture. A closed system tends to become a vested interest, sometimes in the name of openness.

Some of the models of Hinduism produced during the last one hundred and fifty years neatly exemplify the consequences of such one-sidedness. They glorify Hinduism but tend to look down upon the Hindu. Thus, Swami Vivekananda's traditionalism defended the texts and symbols of Hinduism fully but sought to improve the Hindus by giving Hinduism an institutional structure borrowed from western Christianity. Though he attacked some of the westernized reformers of Hinduism, he also sought to create, by his own admission, a western society of Vedantic Hindus to pay back the imperial West in its own coin.[37]

Vivekananda, like Bankimchandra Chatterji before him and Bal Gangadhar Tilak after, sought to blend with Hinduism elements of positivism, socialism, nationalism and masculine Christianity, including the Protestant work ethic. This spirit of synthesis has played, for better or for worse, a significant role in Indian politics for nearly one hundred years.[38] The other versions of Hindu nationalism have been cruder; they have devalued the living Hindu and sought to improve his character and potency, to turn him into a proper counterplayer—often a mirror image— of the conquering westerner and the 'potency-driven' Muslim. In its self-hatred, Hindu nationalism has wanted to rewrite Hinduism as a 'proper' religion, as well-organized and well-bounded as organized Christianity and Islam. The ordinary Hindu probably senses the threat to his survival posed by such cultural engineering; politically, Hindu nationalism had been reduced to an urban, semi-modern, middle-class phenomenon.[39]

[37] Ashis Nandy, *The Intimate Enemy: Loss and Recovery of Self under Colonialism* (New Delhi: Oxford University Press, 1983), chapter 1.

[38] Ibid.; also 'The Making and Unmaking of Political Cultures in India', in my *At the Edge of Psychology: Essays in Politics and Culture* (New Delhi: Oxford University Press, 1980), pp. 47–69.

[39] A pathetic expression of this ideology was Nathuram V. Godse, the assassin of M.K. Gandhi. For an analysis of the clash between two forms of Hinduism protesting differently against colonialism, see Ashis Nandy, 'The Final Encounter: The Politics of the Assassination of Gandhi', *At the Edge of Psychology*, pp. 70–98; and 'Godse Killed Gandhi?', *Resurgence*, January–February 1983, (96), pp. 28–9.

The psychogenesis of such nationalism has been explored in depth ˙ in Rabindranath Tagore's novel *Gora*, which tells the story of an ultra-Hindu who turns out, at the end of the novel, to be the abandoned child of an Irish couple. An accident of life history here symbolizes a deeper cultural equation: the more doubtful one's roots, the more desperate one's search for security in exclusion and in boundaries. Gora, however, proves himself more authentic than those he symbolizes. At the end of the novel he opts for the wisdom of a more inclusive consciousness, not as a compromise but as a superior form of Hinduism.

Tagore here is hinting at another kind of tradition which is reflective as well as self-critical, which does not reject or bypass the experience of modernity but encapsules and digests it. Such a tradition refuses to give primacy to the needs of pure cognition at the expense of totality of consciousness and it refuses to sanction total redefinition of itself in response to defeat or humiliation. It of course rejects imitation, but it goes beyond that and rejects, as a path to self-esteem, the compulsive rejection of other cultures and fights the compulsion to be only the other culture. Even in defeat, it retains its authenticity, though it incorporates the experience of defeat as relevant.

Not being a Gandhian, I can say without any apologia that Gandhi represented such a concept of critical traditionalism aggressively. (Tagore recognized this, and though he had reservations about many aspects of Gandhism, it was the Gandhian theory of nationalism which he found least offensive.) Not being a Maoist, I can afford to say, now that the semi-educated peasant is no longer in fashion, that in some of his incarnations he probably had an inkling of what was involved in such rootedness. He attacked Confucianism, but, often against himself, he sought to fit Marxism within Chinese culture rather than the other way round.

Not being a Marxist, I shall only hesitantly say that Marx himself was often a prisoner of nineteenth-century scientism and the petty ethnocentrism it underwrote. In spite of his seminal contribution to the demystification of the industrial society, he had no clue to the role modern science had played in legitimizing such a society and in the repression of other cultures and societies.[40] (And if one is not sensitive to the way science has provided a model of domination in our times, one cannot be sensitive to the way the non-modern cultures can provide a baseline for social criticism.) A faithful product of Enlightenment, Marx acquitted science

[40]A third-generation Marxist like Jürgen Habermas has done better in this respect. See his 'Science and Technology as Ideology', in *Toward a Rational Society* (London: Heinemann, 1977), pp. 81–122.

and put it outside history, locating the source of human exploitativeness solely in the sphere of political economy. It is thus that his theory kept the door open for scientific social engineering based on objectification of persons and groups. That is why Stalin is not an accidental entry in the history of Marxism. He remains a brain-child of Marx, even if, when considered in the context of Marx's overall vision, an illegitimate one.[41]

The critical traditionalism I am talking about does not have to see modern science as alien to it, even though it may see it as alienating. It sees modern science as part of a new cognitive order which can be occasionally used for critical purposes within the earlier traditions. Such traditionalism uncompromisingly criticizes isolation and the over-concern with objectivity, but it never denies the creative possibilities of limited objectivity.

Wisdom recognizes continuities as much as change; it recognizes optimality and the limits of applicability of concepts and character-traits. As in the clinic, so in the culture. Ultimately, intelligence and knowledge are poor—in fact, dangerous—substitutes for intellect and wisdom.

VI

I might be able to make my point better by recalling a brief, apparently trivial, episode in the life of M.N. Roy. It is said that once when he was ill during his last days, Roy insisted that his wife Ellen wear, while nursing him, a red-bordered white sari as his mother used to do in his childhood. Others have disputed the veracity of the story. Being rationalists, they evidently see the irrationality of any rationalist as dangerous spicy gossip. That a person may not choose to work with objectivity in all situations seems to them not merely vulgar; it is a fall from humanness itself.

But should objectivity work in all cases? I like to believe that when Roy reportedly 'fell' from his rationalism by seeking a symbolic reaffirmation of his private concept of motherhood and mothering, he was actually admitting the continuities in the symbols of nature and *caritas*. Perhaps against his will, he admitted some of the undying concerns of his culture and the subtler modes of cultural communication among human beings who are ready to 'listen'. That is, he accepted the limitations of the conventional concept of rationality and tried to be true to the full meaning

---

[41]See on this subject Leszek Kolakowski, 'Marxist Roots of Stalinism', and Mihailo Marcovic, 'Stalinism and Marxism', in Robert C. Tucker (ed.), *Stalinism: Essays in Historical Interpretation* (New York: Norton, 1977), pp. 283–319. On the roots of technocratic Marxism in the positivist Marx, see Albrecht Wellmer, *Critical Theory of Society* (New York: Herder and Herder, 1971).

of his own faith—that human reason and morality expressed the harmony of the cosmos.[42] That is why Roy wanted from his wife not only professional nursing and the institution called medical after-care, but wanted these hard realities to be given meaning with the help of the traditional symbols, and the feelings and aesthetics associated with them. He was recognizing the mysteries called maternity and wifeliness, and accepting Thomas Mann's maxim that 'It is love, not reason, which is stronger than death.' He was de-isolating.

I want to believe that this disputed episode in Roy's life is true. To admit such an episode is to admit that Roy was, through his apparent irrationality, expressing his superior intellect and his superior wisdom, if not a higher form of rationality itself.

---

[42]M.N. Roy, *Reason, Romanticism and Revolution*, Vol. 2 (Calcutta: Renaissance, 1955), p. 301.

*Published earlier in Ashis Nandy, *Traditions, Tyranny, and Utopias: Essays in the Politics of Awareness* (New Delhi: Oxford University Press, 1987).

12

Culture, Voice and Development
A Primer for the Unsuspecting

> It took twenty years for two billion people to define themselves
> as underdeveloped.
>
> Ivan Illich
> quoted by A. Escobar from a documentary

> Development, as in Third World Development, is a debauched
> word, a whore of a word. Its users can't look you in the face ....
> It is an empty word which can be filled by any user to conceal
> any intention, a Trojan horse of a word. It implies that what is
> done to people by those more powerful than themselves is their
> fate, their potential, their fault.
>
> Leonard Frank
> in 'The Development Game'

The Meaning of Culture

IN THE GLOBAL public discourse of our times, 'culture' has become an
amoeba word. It can take any shape and convey any meaning—from
high fashion to obscurantism, from entertainment to class status. Even
within cultural anthropology, a discipline self-consciously engaged in the
scientific study of culture, there are now dozens of meanings of the word
'culture'. Usually however, when the articulate middle classes and the
mass media in Third-World societies talk of culture, they have its two
predominant meanings in mind. And, however text-bookish and cliché-

ridden they may sound, any discussion of culture and development must grapple with these meanings. Meanings today are a form of politics, too.

Culture as Resource

The first meaning of culture comes into play when we go to an art exhibition, stage performance or museum, having in mind a concrete, packaged, distinctive, public expression of a community's artistic self. The meaning presumes that this self can be seen, appreciated and studied by both insiders and outsiders, usually as a leisure-time activity but sometimes, as in the case of public performers and art critics, as a profession. When it becomes a profession and when a professional from a developed society begins to take interest in the artistic and cultural resources of an 'underdeveloped' society, it of course no longer remains a purely artistic performance or art criticism; it becomes ethnomusicology, ethnomuseology or expertise in ethnic arts.

In this meaning, culture is first separated from everyday life and viewed as a form of cultivation or entertainment or as a sum of serious expressive forms. It is then reincorporated into everyday life on the basis of a new set of justifications. These justifications may come in various incarnations. In literature, for instance, they can range all the way from the so-called morally or politically elevating role of art to the critical role of art in some mid-Victorian theories of art-as-a-criticism-of-life to the various neo-puritanic theories of socialist realism.

The justifications often go with an organizational structure which sustains culture as a well-demarcated, circumscribed, social system or area of life, somewhat in the manner in which the political system in a society is sustained. There can be politics in every sphere of life—in education, family, sports, and in arts and culture—but there is nevertheless something clearly marked out and identifiable called a political system. In the same way, culture can be everywhere but the moderns refer to something more specific and concrete when they talk of culture or the domain of culture.

Such demarcations almost automatically disjunct critical aspects of culture from the way of life that sustains it. They are predicated on the assumption that the artist as a producer of culture must self-consciously take a social or political stand, for art itself is not *by definition* social criticism or an alternative form of realism. It has to be used as such. Thus, in India during the last hundred and fifty years, influenced by the main currents of modern thought, some of the country's great national leaders and social reformers have tried to reconcile culture and society mainly at this plane, often showing scant sensitivity to the springs of their own creativity and to the long-term relevance of their own works in their culture. They have viewed art as a means of social criticism and political intervention at the crudest of levels.

Thus, the gifted Bengali writer Saratchandra Chattopadhyay (1876–1938), who can be said to have brought up at least three generations of middle-class Indians and taught them how to think about the problems of their society, considered his novel *Pather Dabi* (1926) a good and relevant cultural product because it was a nationalist novel. (The novel is concerned with a slice of the life of a Bengali revolutionary, and clearly mirrors the author's sympathy for the violent anti-imperialist movement against the British in the early twentieth century.) Many of his readers thought so, too, and the British–Indian colonial regime tried to prove both parties right by dutifully banning the book. However, it is possible to argue that the author's less ambitious story *Mahesh* (1934) had a more long-term relevance to India's destiny because the author in the story may have been less self-consciously political but more subversive of the metropolitan culture on which was predicated the civilizational mission of western colonialism in Asia. In *Mahesh*, he is not trying to be a political activist or socially relevant; he is merely trying to give expression to the experienced suffering of a people deprived of their voice. He does so, almost unwittingly, through an analysis of the politics of culture reflected in the futile, anthropomorphic love of a poor Muslim peasant for his cow, which is only technically not sacred for him. If the colonial bureaucracy had been shrewd enough, it would have banned the story rather than the novel, for a culture of politics is usually built on the critical consciousness reflected in stories such as *Mahesh* rather than on the middle-class nationalism preached in novels such as *Pather Dabi*.

I give this example not to make the facile point that an author's evaluation of his own work may go wrong, but to emphasize two aspects of the concept of culture as a resource. First, that culture as a well-thought-out, socially-useful mode of self-expression may sometimes limit cultural criticism and creative intervention in politics and society. Second, that this demand for social usefulness arises from a concept of culture which disjuncts it from life and then reincorporates it into life on the basis of a new set of principles.

Predictably, modern nation-states and modern mass societies usually find this meaning of culture most acceptable. By separating culture from everyday life and concretizing it—and thus allowing the urban–industrial world to turn it into a consumable commodity—this meaning helps bring a culture within the ambit of the modern market, makes it more manipulable from the point of view of the modern state, and depoliticizes the idea of culture (to the extent that while this meaning does not dissuade one from seeing culture as a possible political instrument, it refuses to acknowledge that culture may be a subversive presence in society).

Culture as Lifestyle

The second meaning of culture is less influential. It is borrowed from anthropology and is a recent acquisition of many Asian and African intellectuals. Now, even in anthropology there are a number of important meanings of the word 'culture', as every textbook of cultural anthropology in its first chapter says. However, the meaning that has entered the public lexicon in the Southern world (where, according to Fiodor Dostoevsky, the subjects of the anthropologists live) from the world of anthropology (where the anthropologists themselves have to survive) is the one in which culture refers to the organizing principles of a way of life or a tradition of social living.

Anthropologists stress two methodological points as crucial markers of their discipline: that a culture must be described with the help of native or emic categories (that is, those internal to the culture) and that a culture must be assumed to be by-and-large self-justifying. The latter of course is the well-known principle of cultural relativism. Such relativism, to be fair, justifies not so much individual cultural practices as larger cultural designs, though it also tries to give empathetic interpretations of the former and tends to underwrite the belief that cultures can be criticized only from inside.

As it happens, social life is rarely self-consistent; anthropology itself has had a long, colourful colonial connection, and its emphasis on native categories and the principle of cultural relativism have often coexisted with attempts to classify cultures as primitive and modern, simple and complex, ahistorical and historical, little and great, and so on. These attempts usually have a social evolutionist thrust and they do often manage to hierarchize cultures for popular consumption and for social and political engineering.

Even when anthropologists have consciously eschewed such evolutionism—by learning, adopting, using or giving transcultural meaning to the categories of a culture—they have introduced a new brand of expertise into the global scene. This expertise consists of a new bilingualism that seeks to displace the bilingualism of the natives who learn or are forced to operate within the same bicultural space. After an anthropologist has entered a cultural space, the native's bilingualism—usually an offshoot of attempts to grapple with aggressive modernity in an *ad hoc*, pragmatic, and even comical fashion—begins to look less authentically native, even to those revaluing native categories. Over a period of time, the anthropologist's voice may even become the official, audible voice of a culture protesting against all encroachments on it and that voice may marginalize or silence its 'unofficial', 'low-brow' native versions.

Culture as Resistance

There is, however, a third meaning of culture, even less well-known and influential—culture as simultaneously a form of political resistance and the 'language' in which such resistance is articulated.

From Mohandas Karamchand Gandhi to Amilcar Cabral, a galaxy of politically sensitive thinkers and activists have given shape to this meaning of culture.[1] Since 1850 or so in South Asia, many have used this meaning of culture unselfconsciously, without being aware of its ideological possibilities. Thus, for instance, the reaffirmation of Indian culture under the colonial dispensation was often at the same time a protest against political domination, a means of challenging the legitimacy of the domination, and a defiance of the language of domination. Examples range all the way from the spontaneous rebellions of the Santhals in east India in the nineteenth century to Gandhian satyagraha in the twentieth, from the anti-colonial struggles of the Khudai Khidmatgars among the Pathans of north-west India to the more recent Chipko movement in Garhwal in northern India.[2]

---

[1]For instance, M.K. Gandhi, *Hind Swaraj*, in *Collected Works of Mahatma Gandhi* (Delhi: Publications Division, Government of India, 1963), Vol. 4, pp. 81–208; Amilcar Cabral, *Return to the Source* (New York and London: Monthly Review Press, 1973). Among the few contemporary scholars to recognize this politically crucial role of culture are Henry Reynolds, *The Other Side of the Frontier: Aboriginal Resistance to the European Invasion of Australia* (Harmondsworth: Penguin, 1982); Peter Worsley, *The Three Worlds: Culture and World Development* (Chicago: University of Chicago Press, 1984); Gustavo Esteva and Madhu Suri Prakash, *Grassroots Post-Modernism: Remaking the Soil of Cultures* (London: Zed Books, 1998); and Frédérique Apffel-Marglin with Pratec (eds.), *The Spirit of Regeneration: Andean Culture Confronting Western Notions of Development* (London: Zed Books, 1998).

[2]M.K. Gandhi, *Sarvodaya*, ed. Bharatan Kumarappa (Ahmedabad: Navajivan Publishing House, 1954); Dharampal, *Civil Disobedience and Indian Traditions, with Some Early Nineteenth Century Documents* (Varanasi: Sarva Seva Sangh Prakashan, 1971); Khan Abdul Ghaffar Khan, *My Life and Struggle: Autobiography of Badshah Khan* (New Delhi: Hind Pocketbooks, n.d.); Sundarlal Bahuguna, 'People's Response to Ecological Crisis in the Hill Areas', in Jayanta Bandopadhyay et al. (eds.), *India's Environment: Crisis and Responses* (Dehradun: Natraj, 1985),

Today, this meaning of culture is an uncomfortable reminder to the privileged of the Third World that the victims of history in these parts of the globe do not merely carry with them the experience of man-made suffering, that these victims also have a language in which to express their pain and a theory of domination by which to explain their predicament, and this language and this theory may exclude their self-proclaimed vanguards, protectors and often even their own westernized leaders and well-wishers.

This exclusion is particularly painful to the moderns. One characteristic of the Enlightenment world-view underpinning modernity is the stipulation that all dissent from modernity, to qualify as worthwhile, must be expressed in a language consistent with modernity, particularly with the demands of historical consciousness, the theory of progress, and scientific rationality. Culture in the third sense rejects this stipulation and the assumption that the future shape of all human consciousness was decided once for all in seventeenth-century Europe.

Culture in the present sense, thus, is not only the language of resistance; it is itself resistance. It is resistance especially to the oppression which comes packaged as a 'historical necessity', often under the names of such worthy causes as scientific history, technological growth, national security, and/or development.[3] In the second part of this essay I shall turn to that part of the story.

Culture, Victimhood and Voice

Every intervention in the world of culture must be located in the matrix defined by these three meanings of culture. Many working with the first two meanings of culture are perplexed by the hostility towards them of those working with the third. Yet, such hostility is inevitable. To those whom culture is a form of resistance, a person who spends his or her entire life patronizing, promoting or studying culture is not *ipso facto* a protector of culture if he or she has no sensitivity to the new forces of vandalism which have been let loose in many societies by unrestrained urban–industrial growth and mega-technology. The patron must prove

---

pp. 217–26; and Jayanta Bandopadhyay and Vandana Shiva, 'The Chipko Movement: India's Civilizational Response to the Forest Crisis', presented at the U.N. University Conference on 'The Ganga Himalaya Problem', New Paltz, New York, 4–11 April 1986; Tanika Sarkar, 'Jitu Santal's Movement in Malda, 1924–1932: A Study in Tribal Protest', in Ranjit Guha (ed.), *Subaltern Studies IV: Writings on South Asian History and Society* (New Delhi: Oxford University Press, 1985), pp. 136–64.

[3]See 'Culture, State and the Rediscovery of Indian Politics', in this volume.

his or her credentials by being sceptical towards that part of the national and global ideology which is wedded to the urban–industrial vision and is implicitly anti-cultural. Likewise, a person studying a tribal culture or tribal art does not automatically become a 'culturalist' in the third sense. To qualify, he or she must show some sensitivity to the politics of cultures and the politics of cultural survival.

Secondly, the protagonists of the third meaning are aware that not only can life sometimes be a criticism of cultures, culture, too, can sometimes be a criticism of life, that the unintended dialectic between the two forms of criticism define the basic choices many Afro-Asian intellectuals face today. The main question in matters of culture to them, therefore, is: should one criticize local cultures to strengthen the global nation-state system and the modern sector in the non-modern world? Or should one use culture as a baseline to criticize the nation-state system and the resource-intensive principles of modern living in the non-modern societies? The answer depends on which pathology one diagnoses as more fearsome in the Southern societies at this point of time—that of culture or that of modernity?

Predictably, the third meaning of culture usually goes with the belief that it is the state sector, located in the modernized parts of Asian and African societies, which suffer from the more vulgar forms of normlessness, and one must seek to restore the normal dialectic of public life in these societies by putting greater and, perhaps, an overdone emphasis on culture-as-protest. Those using culture in the third sense admit that culture-as-protest may sometimes be the 'false consciousness' of the resister whose voice has been taken away and on whom a 'violent silence' has been imposed. After all, the cultural decadence of the defeated is also a fact of life.[4] But those subscribing to the third meaning insist on using the language of this 'false consciousness' because it restores or, at least, revalues the voice of the victims and does not force the latter to express their experiences of suffering in a more 'cultivated' way or through their better-informed well-wishers.

Indeed, many using the third meaning flaunt the fact that culture is partly non-rational and non-material, for the simple reason that the experience of suffering cannot but be subjective. Culture today, according to them, is mainly the victim's version of the truth and this truth recognizes that in the world in which we live, domination and exploitation are

---

[4]For example, Collin M. Turnbull, *Mountain People* (London: Pan, 1976); Ashis Nandy, 'Sati: A Nineteenth Century Tale of Women, Violence and Protest', in *At the Edge of Psychology: Essays in Politics and Culture* (New Delhi: Oxford University Press, 1980), pp. 1–31.

increasingly by-products of pathological forms of rationality and ultra-materialism, not of irrationality and idealism. Development, according to some, has become a crucial plank of the first kind of pathology.

Those who consider the languages of modern science and history to be the only languages left for global communication may find this position insensitive to the violence and exploitation that come in the guise of cultural traditions. But to those whom culture is a form of resistance, neither scientific rationality nor historical consciousness seems particularly emancipatory any more. To them, however oppressive cultures might have been in the past, it is only by incorporating important aspects of modernity—for instance, the social–evolutionist and racist implications of pre-war biology and the absolute instrumental rationality of post-war technology—that a few cultures have managed to enter the big league of human violence and greed. All this not because cultures are automatically less contaminated by human violence, but because in a world dominated by the language of modernity, human ingenuity has found new sources of legitimacy for social injustice in the dominant language of global communication. Whatever might have been their uses in the past, the languages of the defeated civilizations have become less relevant to the powerful and the rich for the purposes of legitimating dominance. Hence also probably the attraction these languages hold for many social and political activists the world over.

Development, Science and Colonialism

Development has come into the Southern world as an analogue of two processes: modern science, wedded to evolutionism and the theory of progress; and modern colonialism, seeking legitimacy in a new civilizing mission.

Development is not merely a process having historical parallels with the growth of science and colonialism, both of which reached their apogee in the nineteenth century. It is an idea contextualized by the ideological frame within which the social changes that we retrospectively call development took place between the seventeenth and nineteenth centuries in the European societies. The ideology of development has come to faithfully mirror the key ideas of the colonial world-view and Baconian philosophy of science, as many in the South have come to experience these ideas, either as beneficiaries or as victims.[5] The origins of development may be in the Judaeo-Christian world-view, in the sense

---

[5]Claude Alvares, *Science, Development and Violence: The Twilight of Modernity* (New Delhi: Oxford University Press, 1992).

that development has shown a historical correlation with the emergence of Protestantism, especially of the Calvinist variety. But the idea of development is grounded in a concept of science that promises not only absolute human mastery over nature (including human nature) but even human omniscience, and in an edited version of the idea of the white man's burden vis-à-vis those living with 'Oriental despotism' and the 'idiocy of rural life' in the backwaters of Asia and Africa.[6]

From science, development has inherited the belief that it is possible to go on increasing the power of human beings over the non-human cosmos, for the world has enough resources to meet not only all human needs but also all human greed. For the ideology of development, this non-human cosmos now includes also the 'subhuman' cosmos—that part of the living earth which can be, for the greater glory of science and the needs of objectivity, ascribed the status of non-living things.[7] From colonialism, development has inherited the idea of a hierarchical ordering of living and non-living beings and the belief that those who are on the higher rungs of history have their right as well as the responsibility to shape the ways of life and the life chances of those on the lower. Even Albert Schweitzer innocently claimed, on behalf of the European civilization, that the Africans were his brothers all right but younger brothers. The basic assumption here is that the developed world has the automatic right and unavoidable obligation to set the pace for the underdeveloped, for what the developed are today, the underdeveloped will become tomorrow, either through their skills in imitation (euphemistically called diffusion of innovations or transfer of technology) or through the generosity of the wealthy and powerful (euphemistically called aid).

The justification for this hierarchy is sought in the analogies drawn between underdevelopment, insanity, immaturity and irrationality, within a conceptual grid that crystallized out as a by-product of the Enlightenment and was neatly picked up by western colonialism and science.[8] The relationships can be crudely summarized as follows:

---

[6]For a discussion of the evolutionist underpinnings of the mainstream concept of development, see Ashis Nandy, 'The Idea of Development: The Experience of Modern Psychology as a Cautionary Tale and as an Allegory', in Carlos Mallmann and Oscar Nudler (eds.), *Human Development in its Social Context: A Collective Exploration* (London: Holder and Stoughton, 1986), pp. 248–61.

[7]See for example, Shiv Visvanathan, 'From the Annals of the Laboratory State', in Ashis Nandy (ed.), *Science, Hegemony and Violence: A Requiem to Modernity*. (New Delhi: Oxford University Press, 1989), pp. 257–88.

[8]For more details, see Nandy, 'The Idea of Development'.

development: underdevelopment::
sanity (normality): insanity (abnormality)::
maturity (adulthood): immaturity (childhood)::
rationality: irrationality

At this plane, development, modern science and colonialism are not parallel processes, but mutually potentiating forces defining a common domain of consciousness.[9] There is no difference between the way the development experts look at the objects of social engineering, the professional scientists look at the laity, and the colonial powers once laid claim to define the welfare—and in fact, even the concept of welfare—of their subjects. Together they have thrown up a new idea of the social élite who, as secular high priests of the various theories of progress, have faithfully replicated some aspects of European Christendom's passionate fear of the heathens waiting outside the walls to subvert civilization.

Developmentalism

Against this background I shall now examine the four responses to developmentalism that have emerged in recent years, the first visible cracks in the ideology, and the first intellectual and political signs of a post-development era. I do so with full awareness of the power and pull of the ideology of development. The ideology still enthuses the majority of the westernized middle classes and intellectuals in the South. A large majority of the states in the South, too, continue to legitimize themselves in the language of development, even though these states have developed nothing much except themselves and their coercive might.

The first response embraces the conventional idea of development to affirm that modernization is not westernization, and development being modernization, is not western. George Aseniero calls this the response of a new breed of Leibnitzians who believe that we are presently living in the best of all possible worlds and for whom the idea of progress has not yet lost its shine.[10] The developmentalism of these dedicated neo-Leibnitzians does not even have the critical edge of earlier theories of progress, which being the products of a more self-confident age in Europe

---

[9] A detailed discussion of these themes is in the essays in Nandy, *Science, Hegemony and Violence*; and Alvares, *Science, Development and Violence*.

[10] George Aseniero, 'A Reflection on Developmentalism: From Development to Transformation', in Herb Addo et al., *Development as Social Transformation: Reflections on the Global Problematique* (London: Hodder and Stoughton, and the U.N. University, 1985), pp. 48–55.

and North America, allowed at least some criticism of the existing global order.[11]

The response goes with the belief that development, like modern science, has a universal text. If it occasionally shows signs of change when transported over space and time, it is because its core text adjusts to historical and cultural contexts. Such adjustments are, however, more political than intellectual. That is, they are compromises imposed on the universal text of development by sectional interests in a society. Intellectually, the principles of such adjustment can be derived from other parts of the text of development. So, such adjustments or alterations strengthen, not weaken, the paradigm of development in the long run.

It follows that development is the fate of all societies. Some societies may hold up the onward march of history for a short time, but ultimately every society will have to develop through a series of more or less fixed stages. The best that an underdeveloped society can do is to prepare itself to pay the cost of development in as short a time as possible, for everything said, development cannot come free and the countries which are developed have all paid the cost some time or the other during their history.

The response involves two other implicit assumptions. First, the social costs of development cannot be equitably and justly distributed. Unfortunately but inevitably, the weaker sections of a society pay a disproportionately heavy cost for development. However, this should be considered an unavoidable sacrifice imposed on them by world-historical forces. The pain can be reduced by building into development some version of a principle of redistributive justice, but the principle cannot and should not be absolutized; otherwise it goes against the long-term interests of the victims themselves. Second, all societies can be accommodated in the developed world at some future date, for modern science will release unforeseen productive capacities (such as unlimited fusion energy) over the next few decades. In the meanwhile, every society must try to beat the others to enter and/or remain in the big league at all costs.

Critical Developmentalism

The second response assumes development to be a perfectly healthy concept distorted by the political, social and cultural forces shaping or contextualizing it. Accordingly, the pathologies of development are presumed to be by-products that can be fought, even in the god-forsaken Third World, through correct political, economic or cultural engineering— to minimize if not eliminate the costs of development to the poor and

[11]Ibid., p. 71.

the powerless. If the problem with development is not its text but the imperfections of societies trying to develop, development can be turned into a relatively painless process for the society's underprivileged if the society is retooled, the assumption goes.

This response admits that in some societies external forces, such as the rapacity of the First World and global capitalism, have linked up with internal forces of inquity and injustice, but it assumes that this link can be snapped.

Implicit in this response is also the assumption that development is only a means of increasing the productive capacity of a society. In the final analysis there cannot be any resource constraint in a technologically-creative and socially-just society. It follows that the nineteenth-century world-view, including the liberal and the socialist visions, needs no extensive revision, for the major pathologies of development—such as unbridled consumerism, ecological insensitivity, and the crudities of middle-class mass culture—will be automatically corrected once the state is captured by progressive forces serving as a vanguard of the people.

Alternative Development

The third response faults the dominant concept of development for being dismissive towards the distincitve cultural configurations of human potentialities and for absolutizing the experience of the developed world as a universal pathway to a monolithic human future. This response seeks to redefine development, to include in it conceptual modules borrowed from a wide range of sources—from humanistic psychology, studies of human creativity and human potentiality, to holistic ecology and Gandhian praxis. The aim is to liberate development from its economistic and historicist straitjacket, and to relocate it in a non-positivist, more open philosophical grid.

The response grants that the costs of development are intrinsic to development and admits that it is impossible to avoid the sufferings caused by development among the poor and the powerless without substantially modifying the idea of development. The response seeks to make development more culture-sensitive and culture-specific and to resocialize the development community to this new definition.[12] The thriving on-going grassroots movements and intellectual currents like sustainable

[12]Random examples are Johan Galtung, *The True Worlds: A Transnational Perspective* (New York: Free Press, 1980); Henryk Skolimowsky, *Eco-Philosophy* (London: Marion Boyars, 1981); and Ramashray Roy and R.K. Srivastava, *Dialogues on Development: Individual, Society and Political Order* (New Delhi: Sage Publications, 1986).

development, eco-development, indigenous, national or ethno-development are all instances of the third response to the five-decades-long experience of development. They have all enriched themselves from the attempts which began in the 1970s to widen the scope of development to include within it, in addition to economic growth, variables such as social and political development, information expansion, and scientific and technological growth. The growing literature on alternative development has even reconceptualized the needs which development should meet or serve and the institutional fabric within which such needs can be met.

Because this response presumes that development has to be culturally rooted, non-economistic, holistic, and ecologically sensitive, it is politically close to the fourth response described below. However, the third response does have a built-in space for the concept of development, even though the concept is relocated in voluntarism and alternative lifestyles.

Beyond Development

Finally, there is the response to development that believes, partly in reaction to the global experience with development since the 1950s, that the concept as well as the process of development are fundamentally flawed and, therefore, irretrievable. 'Development stinks', says Gustavo Esteva,[13] because whether defined in conventional or in unconventional terms, whether viewed as a concept or as a social process, it is fundamentally incompatible with social justice, human rights, autonomy and cultural survival. Development in all its forms is contaminated by its origin in the structure of repression implicit in the social sensitivities produced by colonial exploitation and by the systematic scientization and desacralization of life and living nature.

This response goes with the belief that, whereas the older forms of violence and oppression have weakened due to the growth of modern consciousness and institutions, new justifications for dominance and exploitation have been built out of contemporary key words like national security, individualism, secular statecraft, socialism, scientific and technological growth, and development, at least some of which could be once considered emancipatory. Exactly as organized religion and nationalism could once be used for justifying violence and injustice, development, too, can be used to justify the imposition of unequal sacrifices by impersonal

---

[13]Gustavo Esteva, 'Regenerating People's Space', *Alternatives*, 1987, 12(1), pp. 125–52; see pp. 135, 137.

agencies like the market and the state on the weak, and to extract the usual surplus from the usual sources. Seen thus, what is happening to the life-support systems and cultures of the victims of development today is not too different from what happened to the victims of colonialism in the nineteenth century and what has been happening to the victims of modern science and technology in the twentieth century.

Obviously, this response goes with the belief that development is incompatible with democratic governance; that it has much in common with modern authoritarianism and tends to legitimize police states, as has been repeatedly shown by virtually all the states which have developed dramatically during this century. From imperial Japan to the Shah's Iran, from army-ruled Pakistan, Thailand, Taiwan, the Philippines and Brazil to Singapore and South Korea under 'controlled democracy', it has been the same story. It is the story of what Herb Feith so appropriately calls 'repressive developmentalist regimes' trying to sell their developmental performance as a substitute for democratic politics. Even societies which have tried to work out more humane forms of development, such as India and Sri Lanka, have fallen prey to the lure of 'pure' development in recent years and have become increasingly willing to pay the social and political costs of such purity.[14] These societies are now more prone to ignore the rights of their minorities and dissenters and more dependent on the coercive power of the state to cope with the unpleasant political by-products of development, such as the protests of the uprooted, the disinherited, and the marginalized.

This fourth response insists that when development becomes incompatible with cultural traditions, the latter should have priority over the former. Not because such traditions are ever perfect but because they are close to the ways of real-life people and are more accessible to and more restrained by participatory politics and the democratic process. Those looking beyond development believe that a culture, especially when it is non-modern, has no business to become a handmaiden of development nor does it have any responsibility to alter its priorities to accommodate development. Development is merely one way of changing a society; it should not be allowed to hegemonize the idea of social change. There have been other pathways to a desirable society before the idea of development entered the world stage and humankind is quite capable of conceptualizing new, post-developmental modes of social change in the

---

[14]A more detailed discussion of this theme is in 'Development and Violence', in *The Romance of the State and the Fate of Dissent in the Tropics* (New Delhi: Oxford University Press, 2003), pp. 171–81.

future; there is no reason for every society to compulsorily pass through the stage of development before moving into the post-development world of the future.

A Cultural Critique of Development

The four responses show that there is now a heightened awareness of something being wrong with the state of development. Even those who think of development only in terms of the first two responses are no longer fully convinced that only misguided radical activists, fanatic environmentalists and dyed-in-the-wool obscurantists are resisting development.

Those associated with the last two responses are the ones more sensitive to the relationship between development and culture. There *is* a concern with culture even among those who read development as a universal text. After all, they have often studied what they consider to be the common flaws in the cultures of the South impeding development and their basic premises. But that concern is primarily the concern of cultural engineers, to whom culture is something that facilitates or retards the 'secondary modernization' of the Third World.[15] To these engineers, the major non-western civilizations are like continents of darkness waiting to be broken into the modern world; they are not terribly unhappy that many of the smaller non-modern cultures are fractured today or are crumbling. Strong believers in nineteenth-century Europe's world image, these partisans of development are waiting for the emergence of a single, homogeneous, fully-developed world, with a touch of cultural diversity thrown in for the sake of entertainment or variety.

The third and fourth responses to development are the ones that have provoked serious enquiries into the relationship between development and culture. From the third response have emerged the outlines of theories of development grounded in cultural definitions of a good life and global well-being, and ideas of development that explicitly take into account the constraints on resource use, and the ideas of commons that grow out

---

[15]The major developmental schools of this genre in the post-war era have mainly drawn upon the Parsonian world-view. Some random examples are D.C. McClelland, *The Achieving Society* (New York: Van Nostrand, 1961); Everett C. Hagen, *On the Theory of Social Change* (Homewood, Ill.: Dorsey, 1963); Alex Inkeles and D.H. Smith, *Becoming Modern: Individual Change in Six Developing Countries* (London: Heinemann, 1974). For a good assessment of the literature relating to this theme in political sociology, see Leonard Binder, 'The Natural History of Development Theory', *Comparative Studies in Society and History*, January 1986, 28(1), pp. 3–33.

of cultural traditions.[16] However, these theories and ideas, though they have enriched the understanding of development, often have little to say about the way the modern nation-state in non-modern cultures presides over the oppressive aspects of development. Not that the theories of alternative development do not have a critique of the mainstream theories of state, but the critique rarely extends to the modern concept of the nation-state and to the way the global nation-state system reduces all experiments with alternative development to the status of peripheral, dissenting voices or esoterica—in effect, into forms of ornamental dissent, by tolerating which one establishes one's democratic credentials.

Two other features of development limit the theories and ideas thrown up by the third and fourth responses. First, development, when it revalues aspects of culture traditionally latent or peripheral, usually ends up by underwriting the psychological demands of modernity—hard this-worldly individualism, unrestrained achievement needs, aggressive competitiveness, priority of productivity principle over the expressive ones, acceptance of a mechanomorphic view of nature, and so on. These traits were not unknown to the non-modern cultures in pre-developmental times. However, there were elaborate cultural checks on the expression of the traits. The idea of development has produced, probably for the first time, a philosophical baggage that unconditionally endorses these traits and institutionally balances the Baconian and Hobbesian impulses. The balancing is done through a carefully built reward–punishment system, the key monitors for which are the market, the state, and the media.

By removing all restraints on these traits, the idea of development has not, as is commonly believed, turned the spiritual East materialistic, but it has destroyed the delicate balance between the soft materialism of everyday life and the hard materialism that ignores the fate of the life-support systems dependent on a naturalistic, often-unstated environmentalism that undergirds many cultures.

Put simply, development does not annihilate cultures; it merely exploits cultures to strengthen itself. That is why, once the idea of development has been internalized by a culture, the internal contradictions produced by development within the society begin to work in favour of

[16]For instance Sulak Sivaraksa, 'Buddhism and Development', in Mallmann and Nudler, *Human Development*, pp. 233–47; W. Lambert Gardiner, 'On Turning Development Inside Out or (Better) On Not Turning Development Outside-In in the First Place', ibid., pp. 63–90. For a good summary of the literature on alternative development, see Bjorn Hettne, *Development Theory and the Third World* (Stockholm: Sarec, 1982).

the process of development and systematic cultural self-destruction. Defying the growing intellectual fascination for different cultural styles of development, development in the real world has everywhere shown the same social patterning. It has proved itself to be a powerful unifying process in the contemporary world, one which taps some of the basic human motives and aspirations. At this plane, and perhaps only at this plane, the universalist assumptions of the mainstream development theories seem to have a secure foundation in human experience. Only, this universalism ignores the fact that these motives and aspirations were ones that some of the major civilizations of the world had carefully kept under check. The checks were as 'universal' as the predispositions they checked. Let me give an example.

Ethology and comparative psychology suggest that both co-operation and competition are universal human traits. But it was by overstressing co-operation that many traditional cultures kept in check human competitiveness. Dissenting sects and subcultures within these cultures admitted the deep psychological roots of competition; they were not propelled by any 'innocent' faith that competition could be totally eliminated. But often they also had the institutional awareness that cooperation, not competition, needed to be over-emphasized for cooperation to have a reasonable run in human affairs.[17]

Operating from within extremely narrow philosophical visions, many modern knowledge-systems have read such one-sided emphasis on certain traits as either hypocritical or näive. These systems have no clue to the reasons why, once the idea of development enters a society and the traditional checks on competition and other allied virtues like individualism and consumerism are removed, development begins to reproduce its universal pattern faithfully. As Dennis O' Rourke's moving documentaries suggest, in the short run, development may show some tolerance of cultures, ideologically it may even be committed to such

---

[17]See Deviprasad Chattopadhyaya, *Lokayata: A Study in Ancient Indian Materialism* (New Delhi: People's Publishing House, 1973); D.D. Kosambi, *Myth and Reality: Studies in the Formation of Indian Culture* (Bombay: Popular Prakashan, 1962). Recently, while exploring the culture of Victorian cricket, now the national game of a number of ex-colonial societies, I came across a description of the game in a South Pacific island. While elsewhere in the world the game is becoming more brazenly competitive, in this island's version of cricket, a match between rival tribes has to serve as a substitute for traditional inter-tribal competition and/or feud and— here lies its distinctiveness—has always to end without a winner or loser. I invite the reader to ponder if this illustrates Polynesian insensitivity to human competitiveness or a higher-order sensitivity to the power of human competitiveness and the need to contain it.

tolerance, but in the long run development cannot but turn ethnocidal.[18]

Second, despite the efforts of environmentalists and others concerned with the survival of cultures, development introduces into a society a new hierarchy of knowledge. Sometimes for a short while some of the traditional knowledge-systems may enjoy symbolically a high status in a developing society—traditional medicine in Maoist China and Islamic jurisprudence in army-ruled Pakistan, for instance—but in the long run, all the incentives are realigned to knowledge compatible with development. So, even though in the short run the various systems of knowledge—traditional and modern—may seem to be peacefully coexistent, in the long run, the older ecology of knowledge is destroyed. Not merely because the modern systems and those allegiant to them are intrinsically intolerant of other systems operating from fundamentally different premises, but also because, in a developing society, knowledge commensurate with development acquires dominance as well as prestige, and such knowledge begins to ignore or corner knowledge irreverent or extraneous to development. Wherever development has come, positivist science and mega-technology have come, too. So have ideas of the absolute priority of the human over non-human living nature, the impersonal over the personal, the experimental over the experiential, the productive over the expressive, and the monetized over the non-monetized. In the context of India, Francis Zimmermann has spoken of the counter-systems within a system of knowledge which reproduce competing and/or incommensurable systems of knowledge as a check against the destruction of any of the systems. The experience of a number of cultures shows that, in the long run, many majestic but politically-undefended systems of knowledge end up as transient counter-systems within the dominant modern systems of knowledge.

In other words, in non-western societies trying to develop—actually, it is doubtful if societies try to develop, mostly their regimes and élites do—the positive sciences have broken out of the limited sphere within which they were housed in earlier times and have established close links with the state sector and the middle-class consciousness that sustains the culture of the state. Against such sciences, the various fashionable non-positivist critiques of positivism, the various movements for intermediate technology and for a socially-responsible science have proved to be minor irritants. Despite such criticisms and movements, these sciences, using the coercive might of the state, have occupied much

---

[18]Dennis O'Rourke, *Yap—How Did They Know We'd Like TV?* (documentary film, 1980); and *The Shark-Callers of Kontu* (documentary film, 1982).

of the available political space. Simultaneously, modern science in general has become the organizing principle and ultimate standard of knowledge and has begun to dominate the spirit of the society; those who cannot organize their experiences into standard formats accessible to modern science and positivist consciousness—usually they are the marginals and dissenters—suffer the most from what can be called 'developmental terrorism'.

Development as a State of Mind

Like war, development, too, begins in the minds of men. If it has to be altered or jettisoned, that, too, must begin in the minds of men. But once development is institutionalized in a society, like war, again, it becomes nearly impossible to exorcise it. It becomes a form of rationality, and begins to cannibalize alternative forms of social intervention. So that the remedies for the ills of development are increasingly seen to lie either in more development or in an edited version of development. That is why development may have begun as one particular form of social change among many but has become an identifiable way of life that must, by its very nature, help other ways of life incompatible with it to die a natural or unnatural death. This is the trap in which the developmentalists and much of the development community are now caught.

In this world of development, officially there can be no legitimate dissent. For the idea of dissent imputes some minimal sanity and good faith to those who differ from the establishment, whereas the official language of development makes no such imputation to those who differ from the core concepts of development and to those who do not grant any moral status to the advocates of development. Unofficially, there *are* dissenters in the world of development, but they are usually dissenters only to themselves. They speak a different language and their voice has no audibility in the public realm. Often, when they belong to small tribes of dissenting communities, they die out before being able to speak out, in oblivion and in silence. When they survive, they do so at the margins of their society, oscillating between fears of extinction and what Nikos Papastergiadis calls the 'violence of silence'.[19]

These dissenters—not the small group of intellectuals who have traditionally opposed development, but the victims of development— have tried often to speak to us through their representatives. However,

[19]On the issue of voice and audibility, an excellent statement is Werner Herzog's *Where the Green Ants Dream* (feature film, 1984).

these representatives, liberals or radicals, have usually represented only those aspects of the victimhood which make sense to the modern world—stark material deprivation or destitution, absence of modern health care, physical dislocation, loss of employment, et cetera. The representatives have had little patience with the victims' ways of life—for instance, physical dislocations leading to the loss of psycho-ecological balance, loss of employment leading to a loss of vocation and art forms and lifestyle, and destitution leading to the denial of even the traditional dignity of poverty.

As a result, the voices of the victims have become even more mute and their links with those who fight for them are weakening by the day. Their sorrows and sufferings are represented in reified, economic terms in international fora and in academic debates in the development community. And, in a reversal of the concept of reification, they become the victims of a hard materialism and a form of concretization that presume all economic complaints to be more real than all meta-economic complaints. Above all, they become the victims of systems of modern knowledge which take away from them, the victims, even their right to interpret their own plight in their own terms.

The politics of development begins with attempts to delink the problems of these victims from their interpreters, representatives, and well-wishers within the development community, and, then, empowering both the victims and their categories and theories.

*This essay was written for a Japanese volume, Yoshikaju Sakamoto (ed.), *The Changing Structure of World Politics* (Tokyo: Iwanami Shoten, 1991).

13

Towards an Alternative Politics of Psychology

SCIENTIFIC CHANGES ARE generally plotted along two axes. On the first axis are plotted changes in the structure of scientific knowledge. Such changes are seen as cumulative, universal and thus 'true', legitimate and valid. On the second axis are plotted changes in the culture of science, especially the shifting concept of science as a social activity. These changes are seen as non-cumulative, contentious and non-rational. Though they are seen as important, there still persists a vague feeling that they are an intrusion into the sphere of orderly scientific knowledge.

Such dichotomy between the text and context of science has worked well until quite recently. But it is now showing signs of breaking down. First of all, the coming-of-age of the social sciences has encouraged them to discount the nineteenth-century public image of the natural sciences. Imitative, self-hating and reductionist, the new sciences have nevertheless picked up from where medieval theology gave up. They have challenged the idea of science as a system of perfectly rational knowledge, separated from the imperfections of politics, culture and ethics. For the first time in human history a part of science itself, in the form of social sciences, has begun to argue that science is not a fully autonomous, rational, affectless pursuit; it too has its myths, magic and rituals, not merely in its culture as a context, but also in its core as a part of its text.

Second, the modern world's two open-eyed death-dances with the help of 'high' technology in this century—particularly that glorious achievement which allegedly made the scientists 'know sin'—have been a great teacher. The fear of a limitless science they aroused has given a special meaning to the accumulated mass of data on scientific creativity and scientific functioning which show that there is not only a 'republic of science' but that the republic is part of a larger political and cultural order.

It is this loss of purity and innocence of science as a knowledge system which provides a new baseline for discussing the politics of contemporary psychology, particularly the prospects the science has of breaking away from its present culture. It also opens up the possibility of visualizing an alternative framework of scientific ethics based on a new political concept of the relationships between the psychologist and his work and between the psychologist and his subjects.

'Crisis' is an overworked term. Every generation believes itself to be in a crisis, coping with the problems thoughtlessly bequeathed to it by the earlier generation and tirelessly working for the betterment of the next. If however I am permitted use of the word 'crisis' to describe the predicament of modern psychology, I would like to define it in terms of a basic dilemma.

It is only in this century that 'psychological man' has truly come into his own. This is the age which has seen, on the one hand, what Philip Rieff has called 'the triumph of the therapeutic' and on the other, both a sharpened consciousness of consciousness and a full-blown consciousness of false consciousness. The falseness of conventional conceptions of false consciousness, too, has become more and more evident. We work now with what somebody has, in a different context, called 'the double falsity of consciousness'. Yet, at the same time, it is in this century that we have seen the climax of the process of mechanization of inanimate and animate nature, and ultimately of man himself, which started in the West in the seventeenth century. As a part of these twin processes, modern psychology has de-psychologized humanity in the age of psychological man. It has popularized a concept of the person which is for the most part mechanomorphic, two-dimensional and anti-psychological. In other words, what psychology has given with one, it has taken away with the other.

This could be put in another way. Our age has given the science of psychology a new political power by placing it at the centre of human life in society. The science has become one of the standards by which the quality of our lives is being valued or criticized. But our age has also made us aware of the way psychology has often been in league with the forces of cruelty, exploitation, and authoritarianism by taking for granted the endorsing of everyday incarnations of the 'banal evil' of our times and by creating new hierarchies, hegemonies, and subjecthoods in the psychologia itself to make the science adjust to the modern world as it exists. It is my contention that the search for a new ethic of psychology cannot begin unless the link between these two processes, one contextual and one intra-disciplinary, is clearly perceived. The subjecthood that psychology promotes is inextricably a part of the politics of the science of psychology. The republic of psychology, in turn, is an extension of the role of the science in an inequitable, oligopolistic world of organized knowledge. I shall try to spell out here the implications of this reading of the politics of psychology. Such a reading will not, by itself, alter our vision of the future of the discipline. But as every psychotherapist intuitively knows, an imperfect interpretation, too, has its uses. Sensitizing a person or a group to the possibilities of looking within can itself be therapeutic and creative. Perhaps that which is true of a person or a group is not wholly untrue of a science.

My task is facilitated by the fact that psychology is one modern science that has a sub-tradition of self-exploration, however apolitically that self-exploration might have been defined until now. Though the science also has a developed capacity to 'manage' dissent by co-opting all dissent into the mainstream as so many new sub-disciplines within psychology, it is better equipped than many other sciences to cope with the new awareness that threatens the dominant culture of world science. After all, modern psychology was one of the first human sciences—the other being Marxist political economy—to unwittingly reject the split between the observer and the observed and to use the observer/observed dyad as its basic unit of analysis. The whole of modern psychology, it is true, did not participate in that early breakthrough. But much before particle physics made the use of such a unit fashionable, and certainly before structural anthropologists began to speak of the 'savage mind' as a double or a mirror—that is, before a serious onslaught on the mechanomorphic, Newtonian world-view came to be mounted—the depth-psychological model of therapeutic transaction implicitly defied dichotomy between the subject and the object. I am here not considering the psychological traditions of non-western civilizations that have never strayed from the vision that the knower is inextricably a part of the known and vice versa. I am here speaking of psychoanalysis and certain other schools of thought, like existential psychology, as I read them from outside the world of western psychology.

To make my point, I shall briefly describe two postulates common to some of the traditional psychologies and to the therapeutic tradition pioneered by Freud. The first postulate is that the therapeutic situation is the epitome of all human intervention in personality, society and culture; the therapist is to therapy what the researcher is to research and the activist is to social intervention. If it involves subjects and objects, each situation of knowledge *is*—add the word 'symbolically' or 'analogically' if we wish to sound scientific and non-mystical—simultaneously all situations of human interaction. Responsibility therefore is always total for anyone trying to know. Sri Aurobindo, the Indian mystic, used to speak of his intervention in Stalingrad and in the Battle of Britain through his yoga during the Second World War. It could be seen as a comic-strip delusion of grandeur or as a symbolic reaffirmation of the organic unity of the universe. On one plane Aurobindo's 'insanity' was not very different from the link many establish between what Jean-Paul Sartre said in a Paris café and what happened in the marshes of Vietnam. It was this equation between the microscopic and the macroscopic which implicitly coloured much of Freud's work on human civilization and its discontents. It also coloured his position on the continuity between mental health and ill-health. Some well-meaning ego psychoanalysts and humanistic psychologists insist that Freud depended overly on the pathological or the clinical to build his general theory of mind. Their criticism is flawed by an insensitivity to the civilizational thrust of Freud's work. The pathology in the clinic *had* to reflect the pathology of the 'normal' world. It is only on the basis of such an assumption that psychoanalysis, against Freud's injunction, could serve as a world-view and a philosophy for many.

The second assumption, too, can be stated in terms of the experience of psychoanalytic psychology. It is actually a further development of the first principle. From the point of view of the 'savage', the *reductio* of the ethic of psychoanalysis can also be written as:

Therapist : counter-transference :: patient : transference

The patient, in other words, is isomorphic to the therapist in that the processes of transference and counter-transference constitute a single process split by an extraneous factor—the acquired ability to 'work through' in the case of the counter-transference of the therapist, and the future possibility of acquiring this ability in the case of the transference of the patient. Intervention, the model says, is always self-intervention; alloplasticity always involves an element of autoplasticity. Thus, there is not only a continuity between health and ill-health, but also between the patient and the healer. The therapeutic situation is always corrupted—and enriched—by the interacting experiences, ideologies and inner struggles of the participants. As he helps the patient to regain health, the therapist, too, moves towards his own health. The therapist does not arrive fully healthy or finished from his training. Nor is his goal the identification of a clientele, even for the sake of a 'client-centred' therapy. Rather, it is assumed that in making any interpretation, the interpreter has to come to terms with himself through his work. To the extent the interpretation reflects the interpreter, it is autobiographical and self-exploratory. It represents a shared experience rather than an impersonal contract artificially personalized for the sake of functional gains. It generates a new language of bilaterality rather than decodifying a private language in terms of the public categories of a profession.

The vision has another implication which can be teased out of the recent 'anti-psychiatric' works on madness and culture. To the extent that the therapist co-constructs the patient's environment, he bears responsibility for the patient's patienthood. The suffering of the patient is produced, as well as defined, by his environment, which in turn is a construction in which the patient and the therapist participate. Responsibility in this sense, too, is always shared by the patient and the therapist, the subject and the researcher, and by civilizations that have been 'sick' and civilizations that have specialized in seeing other civilizations as patients to be healed or counselled. What the patient is, the argument goes, cannot be separated from what the therapist is. If the patient's illness is definitionally linked to the therapist's health, it becomes the therapist's illness too. In this reading of the discipline of psychology, there are no victors so long as there are victims. Subjecthood is shared and health, too, is indivisible.

I am trying to argue that psychology has neglected the humane implications of some of its own traditions and that of the living traditions of non-modern psychologies. It has developed a disciplinary culture that recognizes 'contamination' but spends its entire effort on purifying research from this contamination, exactly as it recognizes that the laboratory differs from real life but, instead of thinking of the laboratory as another enriching experience, seeks to remove the difference between the laboratory and life. Yet, this is one contamination that could have been used creatively to discover a clue to the way some persons and cultures must be defined as the known (or as the knowable) for others to be defined as the knowers, exactly as some persons and cultures must be defined as mentally unhealthy in order that others can be defined as healthy. The organized attempt to bypass this issue has eroded the psychologist's ability to study the 'experience of experience' (an ability which, according to R.D. Laing, makes psychology the science of science) and it has made the psychologist captive to the intellectually and ethically sterile idea of an absolute disjunction between the researcher and his subject, and between the healer and his patient. Moreover, as the researchers and the healers predominantly belong to particular cultures and polities, this inability has parochialized psychology and promoted as features of the dominant 'eupsychia'—Abraham Maslow's expression for a psychological Utopia—the psychological characteristics of the privileged, the successful and the powerful.

To reinstate the idea of a community between the observer and the observed as the basic unit of analysis in psychology and the idea of a shared, global responsibility (a sub-category of the idea of oneness of experience and of the universe, as some Vedantists and Sufis view it), we shall have to make two other postulates or assumptions. Both follow from the two assumptions discussed above. These new assumptions, or at least one of them, may seem hackneyed to readers brought up on a staple diet of radical sociology of knowledge, but they do define for me the baseline of all psychology worth the name.

The first assumption is that political psychology is not the name of a sub-discipline or a circumscribed domain of knowledge where politics and psychology intersect. Every psychology is political and each psychological theory is a political statement. The second is that there are many psychologies and the ruling culture of psychology, being controlled by modern psychology, is hostile to such a view of psychologia.

The first assumption parallels Harold Lasswell's concept that politics is not merely the name of a social sub-system but also a quality or form of social relationship. It denies that an apolitical psychology is possible. It affirms that each science reflects not merely a set of scientific norms but also a set of political preferences. This is, of course, another way of saying that all attempts to resist the entry of alternative political values in psychology, by raising the slogan of value-neutrality, are attempts to promote one kind of politics of science at the cost of others. A science that defines itself as value-free can be democratic only to the extent that it does not have to accommodate a science that is value-laden by design; a science that has built-in values and defines all science as normative has the scope (whether or not actualized), to see even ultra-scientific fraternity. After all, the openly normative sciences, by their own principles, must see the value-free sciences as indirectly expressing a different set of values. (This of course raises the question of whether non-modern psychologies can truly stand up to modern psychology with its anti-democratic concept of science and its missionary zeal. The question parallels two old questions: should democratic rights be given to the anti-democrats?

And can there be a coexistence of faiths when some are proselytizing and others are not? The answer this time, too, has to be the same; it is the fate of some creeds to be tolerant of the intolerant in order to retain their identity.)

The first assumption, by now familiar to most social scientists, is an uneasy one to make for many psychologists. The entire literature on the political sociology of science has been bypassed by modern psychology and despite all its self-exploratory traditions, the assumption may still seem like a compromise with scientific sanity to many psychologists. Though most psychologists recognize the social context of science, in practice they see large parts of their disciplinary text as functionally autonomous. They certainly show little awareness that many of the ethical problems of their science are political in nature and that one of the main challenges facing them today is to produce a new politics of psychology.

The second assumption implies that so-called modern psychology is no less an ethnopsychology than the 'primitive', traditional, local or folk psychologies; it is only another traditional psychology that has managed politically to corner the other traditions of psychology with the help of a new theory of progress. From B.F. Skinner's utopia beyond freedom and dignity through the more positivist readings of psychoanalysis to the strident political psychology of some of the radical schools trying to 'conscientize' the underdogs and retool the ahistorical cultures, modern psychology has served as the ethnopsychology of a small part of the world and peddled itself as a universal psychology on the basis of the political, economic and cultural dominance of precisely that part. Someone once defined language as a dialect with political, economic and military power. It is possible to see modern psychology as a language in this sense.

I hasten to clarify that these remarks do not constitute a new plea for a more culturally relative psychology. They are a plea for a more plural culture of world psychology and for the coexistence of numerous universal psychologies produced both within and outside the known world of knowledge. I am suggesting that psychology need not be the name of a game in which universal models generated by modern psychology are applied to different cultures, with or without theoretical modifications, to cope with 'deviant' or 'odd' data sets. I am suggesting that it is possible to see each culture of psychology as an aspect of a world-view that is no less universal than modern psychology. Each cross-cultural setting thus becomes an interface between at least two ethnopsychologies—one of them likely to be local, rooted in the indigenous lifestyle, implicit, and usable as a critique of the imported; the other likely to be imported, explicit and, at its best, usable as a critique of the native one. It is a confrontation between two competing universal psychologies, both equally culture-bound but not often equally powerful. In such a view there is a place for modern psychology, even outside the modern world. That place, however, is limited.

The last argument can be formulated a little differently if our focus is on the person. One pay-off of seeing psychology as a confederation of ethnic psychologies is to view each psychological phenomenon or process as an experience, interpretable in terms of an encounter of the ethnopsychology of the subject and the ethnopsychology of the interpreter, and to see this encounter as generating its own set of concepts and an ideographic 'model' that may or may not be usable in other situations. The role of a psychological theory here becomes that of a critical catalyst (in both senses of the term 'critical') in a series of interpretive models.

In both formulations, this view circumvents the inner contradiction of those who claim that a value-free psychology is not possible and, in the same breath, accuse western psychologists of ethnocentrism for articulating western values. I am arguing that there are actually two models of handling ethnicity in psychology. One in which we cleanse the science of all forms of ethnicity; the other in which we tolerate and, in fact, cherish such ethnicity, and promote mutual criticism and dialogue. In the first case, there is always the danger of the so-called secular domain of science becoming a masked expression of a particular form of ethnicity. In the second case, that danger is mitigated because the goal is politically to balance each ethnicity by developing a culture of checks and counter-checks. It is my contention that the creative possibilities of the first concept of ethnicity in science has by now been almost fully exhausted and that it is time for us to explore the creative possibilities of the second conception of ethnicity.

To understand why such a 'retrogressive' model of tolerance of ethnicity is necessary, a word here about the kinds of political awareness often used as bulwarks against the ethnocidal and inequitable aspects of modern psychology.

One way in which the problem of ethnic 'contamination' of modern psychology has been handled is through external criticism of the science. Mostly such criticism has been levelled from the vantage point of one of the major ideological components of modernity (generally the critical modernity of some forms of radicalism or the conformist modernity of some aspects of liberalism); the other way has been to work towards an internal criticism or professional self-correction, as in cross-cultural and humanistic psychologies. Both forms of criticism have shown major limitations.

As for the former, most schools of radical psychology are heavily committed to some version or another of the doctrine of progress. Their evolutionism forces them to ignore the basic politics of cultures and to contribute handsomely to the existing patterns of cultural and intellectual dominance, often while fighting the overt economic and political hegemony of classes, societies and nation-states. By positing a new person and a new culture in the future, and by placing the ahistorical, non-modern societies farthest from those ideals, what such radicalism gives in the form of sensitivity to the socio-economic exploitation of parts of the world, it takes away by usurping a hegemonic role in the life of mind as a phalanx of an advanced consciousness. It, too, reduces the psychologies of the rest of the world to second-class citizenship, even in the world of future knowledge and in the non-exploitative Utopias of the future. It does so (*a*) by positing a science that is apolitical in its content and faulty only in its context, and (*b*) by identifying all criticism of the two central myths of our times—science and history—as counter-revolutionary conspiracy. The core of this tradition of external criticism is an idea of the person-in-society that is caught in a historical play of villains and victims. According to the radical script, only the second-rate versions of the play are available in the provincial repertoires of the ahistorical societies. The assassination of the characters of persons and societies is written into the charter of such a radicalism and there can be no appeal against its ultimate verdict, based on a specialist knowledge of the 'science' of history. The concept of Oriental despotism is the ultimate example of its typical analytic tools.

On the other hand, the idea of contractual, competitive individuality in some forms of liberalism, when combined with the technological world-view of nineteenth-century science, has proved to be a deadly coinage. It seeks to reduce every psychological insight into a saleable, packaged, consumption item, purchasable at the shop-counter of the psychologist as a patented cure for loneliness, inefficiency, boredom, sadness, violence, stupidity—anything which is maladjustive to mainstream modern consciousness. We avoid the politics of knowledge, the argument goes, if we focus on the practical and try to solve small, real-life problems instead of running after the mirage of a holistic psychology. This anti-metaphysics is not a matter of innocent pragmatism. It is a systematic effort to discourage questions about the basic features of modern psychology and to legitimize the forces of the status quo through a manipulative, applied psychology geared to an instrumental view of individuals, groups and cultures.

One plank of such liberalism is the theory of modernization, now dying a slow death in social psychology. The theory has relativized many of its micro-theories with the help of empirical work all over the globe. But it has absolutized the social goals of the Enlightenment as the last word in human visions of a desirable society. The history of Utopias has come to an end and so have, reportedly, alternative civilizational visions of the future. Thus, the principle of cultural relativism has become part of a game in which modern psychological discourse is deepened, not by alternative world-views but by cross-cultural data. These data are then fitted into a hierarchy of value systems and seen in an evolutionary perspective. Psychological resistances to economic development, modern science and 'high' technology, to participation in western political institutions and in the nation-state system, and even resistances to the growth of a respectable revolutionary consciousness become proper subjects of research, and it is implicitly assumed that, while the non-western psychologists would produce data on and micro-theories for their own societies, the psychologists in the First World would have to have the responsibility of producing theories appropriate not only for their own corner but for the world as a whole.

Caught in this ethical grid, the modern psychologist has remained insensitive to the oppression of the unilinear, diachronic models of social change and scientific growth. He has ignored the oppression of the idea of history and the consequent crises of those cultures that have borne the brunt of the 'scientific' history of a few select societies seeking to subvert all visions of a desirable society except their own. Psychological studies of ethnocentrism show no awareness that one can be partial not only to one's national culture but also to one's national history. It is probably in human nature to use strange cultures or alien histories as psychological dystopias. Whatever the reason, the modern psychologist has shown no concern for the struggle for cultural survival of the perpetual 'subjects' of psychology, of those who seek liberation from the stranglehold of modern history and modern science themselves. Nor is he aware that this battle for survival is also a battle for survival of a variety of classical and folk psychologies, of, in fact, psychology in its full ethnic richness.

Finally, something is held in common by both conventional Marxist and liberal concepts of a science of mind. Modern psychology has never clearly separated science and technology, nor has it given science any intrinsic legitimacy as a philosophical criticism of the existing world and everyday life. The psychologist's scientism is mostly simple-minded technologism. Like the post-Galilean natural scientists, the psychologist too has sought legitimacy in theories of doing, not being. This has further bound the discipline to the dominant culture of science—to competition, achievement, productivity and control over man and nature. Psychology has gradually become a bastion of non-critical pragmatism.

Thus, the psychologist has often sought to identify himself with the educationally backward, the economically underdeveloped or the politically powerless. But he has rarely questioned the conceptions of education, intellect, development, maturity, and national interest. He has bought his concepts wholesale from other social scientists and tried to weld them into a managerial construction of human consciousness. If this seems an unfair criticism of a 'normal science', let us not forget that hundreds of departments of psychology the world over are trying to live out these meanings of their discipline, while their subjects are discovering in the psychological correlates of uncritically examined variables like development, education, population control and management, new forms of institutionalized violence, ethnocide and exploitation. Take, for instance, the way correlates have often been used as causal explanations in social psychology. Because economic backwardness is mostly non-western, the large mass of research on psychological aspects of economic growth in the 1950s and 1960s only dutifully confirmed that backwardness was a result of the non-westernness of individuals and cultures. Apart from being circular, this reasoning neglected that backwardness was often the flip side of the state of 'advancement' and that the structural basis of such advancement could not be sustained without backwardness in large parts of the globe. The studies ignored that a great part of the human race might have been cussedly resisting the loving embrace of an economic system which they know to be oppressive as well as totalizing.

Similarly, one of the morals of the now-dying IQ debate for me is that it would not have mattered if Cyril Burt had been an honest researcher. Intelligence testing had already done what it had set out to do: banish the traditional concepts of intellect, make intelligence an instrument and an adjunct to conventional socio-economic status, and hegemonize the concept of intelligence by applying the slogan 'intelligence is what intelligence tests measure'. The consequences had ultimately to be independent of the personal ethics of IQ researchers like Sir Cyril. The psychologist's idea of intelligence could not fight the fact that, along the dimensions valued by the powerful and the privileged, the powerless and the underprivileged perform poorly. If we construct and validate our

own measures of our favourite being-states and processes, with reference
to performance within structures we ourselves have set up or dominate,
and then go about assessing the rest of world according to these measures,
the results cannot be otherwise. But then, it should also not surprise us if,
to the rest of the world, the measurement looks less like science and more
like a conspiracy.

The stratagem of internal criticism has a different thrust. I have already
indirectly discussed it in my remarks on non-critical cultural relativism
which constitutes the ethical core of conventional cross-cultural psychology or, for that matter, humanistic psychology. Only one more point
remains to be made. Such relativism was originally a response to the
indiscriminate universalism that mirrored the parochial cultures in which
the social sciences had grown. And it was supposed to correct the bias of
the first generation of social scientists, often drawn from among Christian missionaries and colonial bureaucrats. But political processes are
made of more resilient stuff than conceptual innovations in the social
sciences. And the idea of cultural relativism was soon co-opted by that
particularism which the relativism was supposed to fight. Even in their
more sophisticated versions, most cross-cultural and humanistic psychologies see modern psychology as a transcultural reservoir of knowledge
and other psychologies as its handicapped cohorts waiting to be interpreted by and integrated with the world of modern psychology. The other
psychologies thus become, definitionally, mixed bags of good and bad
insights and good and bad data. The good in them are to be swallowed
by modern psychology, the bad rejected. Neither cross-cultural nor
humanistic psychology, despite the best of intentions, can grant alternative psychologies the right to integrate within the latter what they see as
the best of modern psychology and to reject the bad.

The implication of seeing the non-modern psychologies as sacks of
isolated insights or data is that these insights and data can then be used to
ornament, strengthen or alter the micro-theories of modern psychology.
The basic paradigms and culture of modern psychology remain untouched
and are, in fact, carefully adapted to new empirical facts. What changes
over time are the microtheories, not the architectonics of modern
psychology. Yet, as I have said, what is particularist about the latter is not
merely its data or sub-theories but also its postulates about the nature of
science and about the human situation from which scientific knowledge
emerges.

All this may seem like a frontal attack on modern psychology. Actually,
it is an attempt to make the trite point that imperfect societies produce

imperfect psychologies, even when such psychologies are avowedly radical or cross-cultural. And that imperfection colours not only the data and the theories but also the conception of psychology as a science. Even concept of knowledge is imperfect, coming as it does from another imperfect culture. All I can claim for this critique is that it does not see any given psychology as the end-state of an evolutionary process of scientific growth; it sees the discipline as a confederation of mutually tolerant and mutually critical cultures of understanding and studying the human mind. I only hope that such a view—and it is an avowedly political view—grapples at least indirectly with a problem that cultural relativism has never taken seriously: how to sustain within the culture of psychology a critical tradition while not denying cultural and normative plurality.

By now it should be obvious that I do not see the future of psychology as a paradigm-scarce discipline which, according to Thomas Kuhn, would be an indicator of its maturity as a science. I cherish its paradigm-surplus status as an indicator of its strength, a reflection of its simultaneous rootedness in a number of philosophical systems. Psychology to me is vital for a future dialogue of philosophies, world-views and civilizations. I do not expect the science to increase human choices through improved psycho-techniques or greater control over the human environment; I expect it to widen human choices by enriching self-awareness and by exploring varieties of social experience.

This means that the task of the psychologist today is not only to widen the spatial and temporal scope of the discipline but also to examine the meanings, experiences and values associated with different psychological systems. Unless the second task is recognized, modern psychology will only manage to bring newer cultural areas and larger time spans within its scope; it will further marginalize other traditions of psychology. That way lies homogenization.

The alternative I am suggesting might also give a new dignity to those parts of psychology that concern themselves with society. Traditionally, social psychology has accepted obsequiously the lexicon of other modern sciences. Often it has set up crudely measured 'non-psychological' dependent variables and then studied the psychological correlates of the variables. Acceptance of an urban–industrial environment and an impersonal, contractual work situation thus becomes the criteria of maturity as well as progress as in the work of Alex Inkeles and his associates; per capita income or the consumption of electricity or steel becomes the prime measure of the economic growth of a nation, as in David C. McClelland's work with the achievement motive; academic performance within a doubtful educational system validates the measures of intelligence for a whole generation of IQ-testers; and a two-party system or a Westminster-style parliamentary democracy becomes the measure of political development or democratization for another generation of political psychologists. This, we are then told, is what operationalism is all about.

Such uncritical acceptance of the categories used by the other social sciences has bound psychology to some of the most retrograde ideas in political and social philosophy. It has produced a science of mind which not merely discourages any debate on issues such as the meanings of growth, development, intelligence, democracy and health but it also ignores the psychological contexts that set up these variables as valued qualities and give them their meanings.

Health of people and societies, I repeat, is indivisible. As the dominant schools of psychology have collaborated in dismantling alternatives to the post-Enlightenment West, as they have helped destroy the autonomy, freedom and self-respect of the barbarians, these schools have themselves sunk deeper into the morass of a disciplinary culture characterized by over-organization, hyper-competitiveness, ritualism and anti-intraceptiveness. The wages of sin for one, says Irish Murdoch paraphrasing Plato, is the kind of person one becomes. As the psychologists have embraced technocracy, part–object relations and some forms of anti-psychologism as parts of their code, they have settled down into a fragmented, dull professionalism and converted their science into an industry. Their over-allegiance to 'normal' science has ousted most possibilities of 'revolutionary' science. That is the inner logic of all dominance and of all attempts to secure one's autonomy by abridging the autonomy of others. No wonder that the ontological problems of modern psychology are exactly along those planes on which modern psychology has tried to marginalize alternative traditions of psychology as non-scientific, overtly philosophical, non-utilitarian, non-predictive and non-productive.

The search for a humane psychology never ends. What looks like a morally desirable psychology to one generation, looks like a disguise for subtle forms of dominance, oppression and institutionalized suffering to the next. This could be read as an indicator of human fickleness and as a weakness of psychology; it could be read as an indicator of the social sensitivity and sense of survival of psychology as a social science and as a philosophy. I prefer the second formulation. It is the strength of the science that every generation of psychologists must discover the scope and limits of their science in terms of the explicit and implicit utopias they live with. They are, after all, dealing with human consciousness.

Thus, the ethical issues I have raised here should also be dead in a few years' time. That does not mean that political problems of psychology would end. That means that a new critical awareness will look for a new set of norms for psychology and tear the mask off this defence of ethno-psychology. That will not be a great loss for me. Unlike the modern critical traditions of Vico, Herder, Nietzsche, Marx, and Freud, the ancient critical traditions of Madhyamika do allow for unending criticism and for criticisms of criticisms.

*Earlier published in *International Social Science Journal* 35(2) 1983.

14

~~~

The Savage Freud
The First Non-Western Psychoanalyst and the Politics of Secret Selves in Colonial India

OF THE NINETEENTH-CENTURY European schools of thought that have shaped our self-definition in this century, the two most influential 'in-house' critiques of the modern West are those offered by Marxism and psychoanalysis. Both are deeply ambivalent towards their culture or origin. They seek to bare the normative and institutional anomalies of the Enlightenment and to demystify the bourgeois culture that has inherited the anomalies, but they do so in terms of the values of the Enlightenment itself. This is what makes the schools internal, rather than external critiques of the modern West.

The other aspect of this ambivalence is the tendency of both schools to own up their cultural roots by building into their theoretical frames aggressive Eurocentric critiques of non-western cultures. For both, the primitive world, especially the Orient, is an anachronistic presence and represents an earlier stage of cultural order that social evolution has rendered obsolete. Through this second criticism, that of the non-West, the schools pay homage to their first target of criticism, the West, and atone for being dissenting children of the Enlightenment.

Both schools, it is true, have their self-doubts, expressed through their lurking nostalgia towards the very cultures they try to relegate to the dustbin of history or the wastepaper basket of the clinic. Apart from the fascination the Orient exercised over their founders—the Orient viewed as a victim of imperial Europe or as an anthropological field populated by the 'natural', the antiquated, and the exotic—both schools have produced ideas such as those of primitive communism and regression at the service of ego as latent reparative gestures, to correct for or work through the arrogant social evolutionism that structures their theories of progress. It is the obverse of Albert Schweitzer's famous reparative gesture towards the West, to disabuse all those who thought that his medical mission to Africa was a homage to human dignity or an atonement for colonial violence. The African was his brother, the intrepid missionary agreed, but a younger brother.

When Marxism and psychoanalysis were imported into the savage world in the high noon of imperialism, this racial arrogance was not obvious to their native converts. For the main attraction of these schools of thought in the tropics was their bidirectional criticism—of the contemporary European society *and* of the savage world. Afro-Asian scholars and activists found these schools excellent instruments of self-criticism. In fact, when it came to the native way of life, such scholars and activists rejected or undervalued ideas that softened the critical thrust of the two schools. Thus, psychoanalysts such as Carl Jung, who were especially open to the Indian world-view, found few adherents in India; Marxist scholars such as Ernst Bloch, who sought to establish a continuity between the Marxist vision and the older religious world-views, never enjoyed a vogue in non-European societies organized around religion. Such 'returns to tradition' were considered legitimate attempts to enrich social criticism in the modern West, not in societies bogged down in tradition.

Marxism was to have a more lasting impact on intellectual and political life in the South than psychoanalysis, which, after an early flurry of activity in a few societies—after as it were a late spring lasting about two decades—gradually became peripheral to the culture of public life in the South. Was this because Marxism became a political movement in Asia and Africa at a time when politics was about to become the most important sector of these societies? Or were there other reasons that had to do with the culture of psychoanalysis, such as the torn personalities of those who tended it in its new habitat and the persisting indigenous theories of the mind that, like a chronic illness, resisted western remedies prescribed for the problems of living in Asian and African backwaters?

This essay pursues the second set of questions. It does so by focusing on the cultural meanings psychoanalysis acquired in its early years in India where it first established a bridgehead in the 1920s. The essay examines these meanings through the prism of the personal experiences, intellectual concerns, and metapysychology of the first non-western psychoanalyst, Girindrasekhar Bose (1886–1953), who pioneered the discipline in India.

Bose began trying out psychoanalytic concepts and methods in his clinical practice towards the end of the 1910s when, following the partition of Bengal in 1905, the Swadeshi movement had become a significant political presence; and he founded the Indian Psychoanalytic Society in 1921, when the non-cooperation movement had started and Gandhi had become the leader of India's freedom struggle. Both these political events had their cultural counterparts, such as renewed efforts to revalue indigenous systems of knowledge and growing awareness that the West's intellectual domination depended greatly on the philosophy of science and analytic categories popularized by the European culture of knowledge.

Psychoanalysis in its early years reflected these changes in India's intellectual climate. The discipline came to represent something more than a therapeutic technique that could be adapted to the mental health problems of India's burgeoning, partly decultured, urban bourgeoisie, even though that is how Bose often viewed it, especially when writing for his international audience. Psychoanalysis also had to serve as a new instrument of social criticism, as a means of demystifying aspects of Indian culture that seemed anachronistic or pathological to the articulate middle classes, and as a dissenting western school of thought that could be turned against the West itself.

The following story tells how Bose's unique response to Freud's theories was shaped by the psychological contradictions that had arisen in Indian culture due to the colonial impact and by the cultural contradictions within psychoanalysis itself. As a result, the usual encounter between an ancient culture with its distinctive culture of science and an exogenous science with its own distinctive culture fractured the self-definitions not only of Bose but of many others involved in similar enterprises. At the same time, the encounter initiated a play of secret selves which widened as well as narrowed the interpretations of both Indian culture and the culture of psychoanalysis. The story suggests that the more speculative, political, cultural–critical aspects of the young science—its disreputable 'secret self'—gave greater 'play' to non-western psychoanalysis in the early years and might even have given it a stronger creative 'push' under another kind of political–intellectual dispensation.

Part One: The Psychology of Morality

I Śarvilaka's Gita

In ancient Magadha in eastern India, there lived a powerful, learned, highly respected, rich Brahmin called Śarvilaka. Disciples came to him from distant lands and his house resonated with the recital of and discussions on sacred texts.

Śarvilaka had a gifted son called Puṇḍarīka. Though young, Puṇḍarīka had already mastered the religious texts. When Puṇḍarīka reached the age of sixteen, Śarvilaka told him, 'Son, today is an auspicious day. Fast for the entire day and maintain your purity by following the right practices. At 2 o'clock tonight, when the moonless night begins, I shall initiate you into our *kaulika prathā* or family custom. From evening onwards stay in seclusion and meditate.'

At 2 AM Puṇḍarīka was still reciting the name of God when, suddenly, the doors of his room opened. In the faint light of a lamp, he saw a huge man entering the room. The intruder wore a loin-cloth, his body shone with oil, and he held an axe on each shoulder. With a shock Puṇḍarīka recognized that the stranger was his father. Śarvilaka said, 'Son, do not be afraid. The time for your initiation has come. Come, dress yourself like me, take one of these axes, and follow me.' Puṇḍarīka followed as if mesmerized.

Through a maze of streets, Śarvilaka led his son to the highway connecting Magadha to Varanasi and stood under a banyan tree. He then said, 'Puṇḍarīka stand quietly in the dark, so that nobody can see you.' Puṇḍarīka stood trembling with fear, shock, and the strain of the long walk.

A rich merchant was travelling from the palace of Magadha to Varanasi in a horse-drawn carriage. He was carrying with him 10,000 gold coins. The route being dangerous, he had eight armed guards escorting the vehicle. As soon as the carriage reached the banyan tree, Śarvilaka attacked it with a mighty roar. In the faint light, he looked even more fearsome. The driver and guards immediately ran off. Śarvilaka decapitated the merchant with his axe, picked up the heavy bag containing the gold coins on his shoulders, and came back to the banyan tree. Puṇḍarīka by then was shaking with terror; his axe had fallen from his hand. Śarvilaka picked up the axe and led Puṇḍarīka by the hand towards home. He then pushed his son into his room and latched the door from outside.

After a long while, Puṇḍarīka regained some of his composure. By now, his mind was churning with contempt, anger and hurt. He decided not to stay at his father's home for even one moment. In this state of high tension, he fell asleep. When he woke up in the morning, he found the sun's rays shining into his room. His father was standing near the bed, his usual serene self, wearing his usual dress. For a moment Puṇḍarīka felt that his memories of the previous night were part of a nightmare. But his own oily body and loin-cloth showed otherwise. Śarvilaka broke the silence to say, 'Son, do not be unnecessarily perturbed. Nothing has happened which should cause you heartburning.' Puṇḍarīka said, 'I don't want to stay in your house even for a moment.' His father responded, 'You are not in the right state of mind because you haven't eaten or slept properly, and you are tense. Have a bath, eat and rest. Then I shall tell you about our family custom. If after hearing me out you still want to leave, I shall not stop you.'

Sarvilaka returned in the afternoon and had a long conversation with his son. He first narrated how the family had followed the same *kaulika pratha* from the time of the Mahabharata and how he himself was initiated into the custom by his father. He said he knew he seemed a hypocrite, robber and murderer to his son. But he also had faith in his son's intellect and knowledge of the sacred texts. Sarvilaka then went on to justify every act of his by the tenets of the Gita, for he felt that Pundarīka's moral anxieties were similar to those of Arjuna before the battle of Kurukṣetra; they were born of *moha*, attachment. Arjuna, too, had felt like living on alms rather than killing his own relatives for material gain.

Sarvilaka's arguments were sophisticated and they could be summed up by three broad propositions. First Sarvilaka agreed, he did not openly talk of his *kulācāra* (family practices) because he feared public censure and harassment. He followed *lokācāra* (customary practices) by day and *kulācāra* at night. As a result, he now appeared to be a hypocrite to his own son. Yet no one could survive in the world by being totally truthful. All human beings were weak to a degree; to defend themselves they had to lie. Even Lord Kṛṣṇa had to hide his intentions when he killed the demon Jarāsandha. Otherwise, too, untruth was of divine origin. The creator of the universe had equipped some of his creatures with the capacity to lie and cheat; even animals like lions and tigers resorted to stealth when stalking their prey. Human beings were too insignificant a species to invent on their own the idea of falsehood.

Second, everyone was to some extent a robber. When one ate fruit, one deprived the trees of their fruit or perhaps animals of their lives. Living itself meant living off other lives. Moreover, God had not sent anyone to earth with property or riches. One won worldly success by depriving others. *Vasundharā vīrabhogyā*—the earth was for the enjoyment of the brave.

Third, one had to overcome the fear of being called a murderer. Arjuna feared the epithet when the battle of Kurukṣetra was imminent and the correct response to that fear, Sarvilaka felt, was best given in Kṛṣṇa's sermon to Arjuna in the Gita. The oppressor and the victim, the Gita said, were both unreal because *ātman* (soul) was the sole reality and it was indestructible—*na hantā na hanyate*. None should rue the loss of a destructible, transient body. The prosperous merchant killed on the road to Varanasi was aged and yet attached to his worldly goods. The destruction of his body had actually done him good. If Śarvilaka had forsaken his *kuladharma* or family's code of conduct to spare the traveller, that would have been far more sinful. Human beings were mere agents of divinity—*nimittamātra*.

Puṇḍarīka listened to this discourse with rapt attention. The doubts and contradictions in his mind rapidly dissolved. At the end of the discourse, he touched his father's feet to pledge undying loyalty to their family custom.

With this story of homicide, secret selves, a seductive 'immoral' father, his vulnerable 'moral' son, and their final Oedipal compact after an aborted rebellion, the world's first non-western psychoanalyst, Girindrasekhar Bose, begins in 1931 his interpretation of the Gita in the pages of *Pravāsī*, the influential Bengali journal of the pre-independence years.[1] Bose was already a famous psychiatrist and had founded the Indian Psychoanalytic Society. By the time he began his work on the Gita, he had been exposed to psychoanalysis for nearly two decades. Yet there are odd anomalies. Though it has been called 'perhaps his most significant work' and a pioneering attempt 'to correlate Hindu philosophy to western psychology',[2] the interpretation is more social–philosophical than psychoanalytic. Though Bose claims to be motivated by psychological curiosity rather than religious faith,[3] in many places psychology enters the interpretation almost inadvertently, even diffidently.

Was Śarvilaka's interpretation of the Gita correct? Did the Gita permit him the interpretation he offered? And if he was wrong, on what grounds was his interpretation flawed? What were the real meanings of the *ślokas* Śarvilaka cited? Bose interprets the Gita in response to these questions.[4] In a society where texts survive as living texts mainly through

---

[1]Girindrasekhar Bose, 'Gita', *Pravasi*, 1931, *31*, Part 2(1), pp. 9–16.

[2]Jagdish Bhatia, 'Pioneer Who Explored the Psyche of India', *Far Eastern Economic Review*, 13 August 1987.

[3]Bose, 'Gita', p. 15.

[4]Ibid., p. 13. Bose's commentary is based on the following principles he enunciates in the opening paragraphs of his work on the Gita: 'Wherever more than one meaning of a *śloka* is possible, the simpler and more easily comprehensible meaning is taken. Gita, it is presumed, is meant for the ordinary people and the author of Gita did not lack the skill to write lucidly.'

'If an interpretation of a *śloka* contradicts other *ślokas*, it is rejected. So are all internally inconsistent interpretations. Also rejected are all supernatural meanings. As a general principle, the commentary also tries to be imperial and non-sectarian.' Ibid., p. 15.

interpretation and reinterpretation, Bose could create a space for his new science of interpretation only by enunciating and demonstrating its principles. Yet he ventures his interpretation of the Gita without any open reference to a psychoanalytic concept.

To find out how Bose relates his interpretation to his own theories of consciousness, especially psychoanalysis, we shall therefore have to go to some of his other writings. Before we do that, however, we should be aware of the broad outlines of the personal and social background he brought into psychoanalysis. For we must remember that while the story of Śarvilaka affirms the emergence of a new exegetic voice, that of an Indian psychoanalyst, it also enforces on Bose strange silences. It remains unexplained why Bose has nothing to say about the passive resolution of the Oedipal encounter that takes place in the story or about the inverted relationship between a weak son personifying his father's manifest moral self and a powerful father personifying moral seduction and the amoral rationality latent in the son. Was Bose's psychoanalysis a negation of Puṇḍarīka's weak, transient rebellion against a strong, amoral, paternal authority? Did that defiance of defiance make Bose's cognitive venture an ethical statement? Why does Bose refuse to consider the possibility that Śarvilaka's secret self, the one that his son finally owns up, represents unmediated primitive impulses of the kind that psychoanalysis subsumes under the category of the id? Is it because there is in Śarvilaka a complex structure of rationalization, including an element of controlled, dispassionate violence, that defies the conventional definition of the id and the primary processes?

Nor does Bose explain why his partiality for Puṇḍarīka's early Oedipal dissent is justified not in the language of the ego but that of the super-ego, whereas Puṇḍarīka's moral seduction by Śarvilaka is cast not in the language of the super-ego but that of the ego. It was as if the triumph of the therapeutic in South Asia heralded not so much a new bridgehead of the ego in the realm of the id as an empowerment of the super-ego through an abridgement of the sphere of the unencumbered, psychopathic ego. The rest of this essay can be read as an attempt to work out the full implications of these abstract and somewhat opaque formulations.

II *The Rediscovery*

Girindrasekhar Bose was probably born on 30 January 1886, the youngest of four sons and five daughters. He often described to his students and trainees, with great relish, two details about his early years: first, he was a breech baby. As he loved to put it, he was born feet first, holding his head high. He paid dearly for the privilege; injury at birth left him with one foot slightly shorter than the other. Second, he was breast-fed till he was five. Defying psychoanalytic wisdom, Bose claimed that the prolonged breast-feeding had not heightened his oral dependency needs; rather it had contributed to his psychological well-being and optimism.

The Boses came from Nadia in West Bengal. Girindrasekhar's father Chandrasekhar had worked for an English landlord early in his life, but was the Maharaja of Darbhanga's Diwan when his youngest son was born. As a result, the son spent most of his formative years outside Bengal, in north Bihar. His childhood memories of Bihar occasionally emerged in later years in the form of rustic wisdom laced with wit, and provided a part-comic but robust counterpoint to urbane babus in his works of fantasy.

Chandrasekhar conformed to the Bengali urban élite's ideal of a gentleman: he was known for his managerial efficiency, financial probity, and Vedantic scholarship. By the time he reached middle age, the Boses were established as a rather successful Kayastha family—respected, prosperous, and committed to learning. Chandrasekhar himself, however, despite his social status, was regarded with some ambivalence by the local Brahmins on account of his attempts to break into traditional scholarship. That might explain why the family, despite their orthodoxy, moved in the social world of reformist Brahmos after they moved to Calcutta. Many actually mistook the Boses for Brahmos. That did not improve matters much; the Brahmos now began to make fun of the orthodox ways of the Boses, especially their faith in gurus, *purohitas, kuladevatās, iṣṭadevīs,* etc.

Chandrasekhar's first two wives had died young. A daughter by his first wife had also died early. In middle age, he remarried yet again, this time a young girl 22 years younger than him called Lakshmimani, who bore him all his nine surviving children. If Chandrasekhar was a scholar, Lakshmimani had imagination. Superbly well read, especially in the *purāṇas,* she was also a poetess who had a lively intellectual curiosity. The two provided for their children a potent intellectual atmosphere, enlivened by stories from the Ramayana and the Mahabharata. Two of Chandrasekhar's sons were to become well-known writers. Rajsekhar, the most successful of the siblings, became famous as a satirist, classical scholar, translator, grammarian and, perhaps reflecting Chandrasekhar's range of interests, an applied chemist and industrial manager. He was also an early patron of the Indian Psychoanalytic Society; the first psychoanalytic clinic in South Asia, probably the first in the non-western world, was established on a piece of land donated by him.

Of the siblings, Rajsekhar remained the closest to Girindrasekhar. His literary work resembled in style the self-articulation Girindrasekhar assumed in his scientific discourse. There was a combination of rigour and robust directness, on the one hand, and a dependence on the idiom of the epics and the philosophical visions of the classical Sanskritic heritage, on the other. Both brothers strove for the nearly-unattainable—an austere, rationalist discourse that would reflect the moral urgency and poetry of the classics. Both, one suspects, were searching for culturally rooted moral codes appropriate for their times, away from the puritanic moralism of the reformist Brahmo and the defensiveness of the orthodox Hindu.

We know little else about Girindrasekhar Bose's childhood. Though a psychoanalyst, he showed a certain reticence about his own personal life, born partly from a sense of defensive privacy and partly from an indifference to history. Even his own comments about himself, of the kind I mentioned earlier, were off-the-cuff, casual ones; they served mainly as capsuled, psychoanalytic witticisms. They were also gulped down as such by his students, trainees, and admirers. As a result, even today, an enterprising clinician cannot easily produce a psychoanalytic case history of the Southern world's first psychoanalyst. The reader will have noticed that one cannot be absolutely certain even about the exact date of Bose's birth. By way of a life history, one is mainly left with the memories of a few surviving contemporaries and the biographical notes of some of his students and trainees, notably those of psychoanalyst Tarun Chandra Sinha, his closest associate.[5] In addition, there are the outlines of Bose's educational career, which followed a course somewhat resembling that of his chosen guru, Sigmund Freud.

According to Sinha, Chandrasekhar was a 'true' father who exercised 'full authority and control'.[6] He was a strict disciplinarian and a conservative who conformed to family traditions 'fairly rigidly'.[7] Though Sinha hastens to add that Chandrasekhar was no autocrat, as if apprehensive that he was hinting at a classical Oedipal situation, something of the father's style rubbed off on the son. Girindrasekhar, it seems, was domineering even as a child and he enjoyed exercising his authority.[8] This was probably tolerated by the family because of his physical handicap and his fragile health, caused by an attack of blood dysentery in the first year of his life. The child despot was taken to school in a palanquin, we are told.[9]

[5]Tarun Chandra Sinha, 'A Short Life Sketch of Girindrasekhar Bose', *Samiksha*, Bose Special No., (ed.) Nagendranath Dey, 1954, pp. 62–74.
[6]Ibid., p. 62.
[7]Ibid.
[8]Ibid.
[9]Ibid.

Girindrasekhar's early schooling took place in Darbhanga. As a result he had a good command of Hindi. He was also well-versed in Sanskrit, thanks to his father. However, Girindrasekhar later claimed, in some Bengali essays, that his knowledge of the language was inadequate and that he depended on the help of traditional Sanskrit scholars in his serious work. (Perhaps he felt intimidated by Rajsekhar's superb Sanskrit and highly creative use of Hindi.) We also know that Girindrasekhar was a handsome, self-confident child despite his physical handicap, and was, perhaps because of the handicap, protected by and close to his mother. This self-confidence must have been an asset when, having been brought up in an environment alien to the world of Bengali babus, he later entered Calcutta's intellectual life.

In 1904, at the age of seventeen, Girindrasekhar was married off to Indumati, a girl of ten. They had two daughters, one born in 1908, the other four years later. From the beginning, it seems, Bose kept family life separate from his academic life. The former was private, the latter public. Except on a few rare occasions, Bose's students and trainees never had a glimpse of his family; many of them never ever met or even saw his wife or daughters. This may or may not have anything to do with his attitude to women. His brother and ego-ideal, Rajsekhar, who was a bachelor, maintained a similar, if not stricter, separation between his private and public lives.

After finishing school, Girindrasekhar joined the Presidency College, Calcutta's foremost educational institution and intellectual hub, where he studied chemistry, a discipline that was Rajsekhar's vocation, too. After graduating in 1905, Girindrasekhar joined the Medical College in Calcutta. At about this time his father retired and the entire family moved to Calcutta, purchasing a house in north Calcutta (14 Parsibagan Street), and settled down there. The house was to become famous afterwards as a citadel of psychoanalysis in India. In 1910 Girindrasekhar got his medical degree and started private practice.

Bose's earliest passion was yoga and a focus of scholarly curiosity in his teens was Patañjali's *Yogasūtra*. Bose's nephew Bijayketu Bose, a psychoanalyst himself, believes that his uncle was basically searching at this point of time for supernatural or magical powers, *alaukika kṣamatā*.[10] Later on, at the age of fourteen or so, Bose developed a keen interest in

[10]Psychoanalyst Bhupen Desai believes that an analogous search for magical powers explains the choice of psychoanalysis as a career by many Indians. Desai says that he himself was motivated by the search for omniscience and gives the examples of others whose unconscious goals were similar.

magic and hypnotism, and became an amateur magician and hypnotist. This was not particularly uncommon in Calcutta at the time. Many middle-class Bengalis had begun to take an interest in these pursuits, perhaps attracted by their liminal status. In Bose's case, if we accept his nephew's interpretation, there was also a direct continuity between the choice of magic as a vehicle of self-expression and the earlier search for magical powers.

Bose made a success of this venture. While still a medical student, he gave occasional public performances, and even won a prize for an original article in a journal of magic. He went still further with hypnosis. Encouraged by some of his teachers, he used hypnotic therapy with partial success in cases of insomnia, nausea in pregnancy, and, more dramatically, in an instance of cardiac asthma. This was while he was still an adolescent (1902–7). Later, when he came to know more about psychoanalysis, he did not entirely give up hypnotism in deference to the psychoanalytic belief in the absolute superiority of free association.[11] He retained, as part of his analytic technique, hypnotic suggestion as an occasional therapeutic tool. He even made good use of the differences between two types of hypnosis: the father-type and the mother-type. One was didactic; the other persuasion-based.[12]

After taking his medical degree, Bose quickly established himself as a general practitioner, and became within a decade one of Calcutta's leading doctors with a large private practice. When in 1926–7 he decided to restrict his general practice and concentrate on cases of mental illness, he was barely forty.[13]

Bose's fascination with Freud's new science began with casual encounters. Though he might have heard of psychoanalysis as early as 1905–6, his interest in it was first stimulated around 1909 by articles published in various periodicals. At the time only Brill's translation of a selection of Freud's papers was available in English. (Bose began to learn German only in his middle years.) The preface to *Concept of Repression* suggests that Bose, when he started psychoanalytic work, had not even

[11]See a brief discussion of Bose's long-term interest in hypnosis later in this essay.

[12]The classification was borrowed from Sandor Ferenczi. See Girindrasekhar Bose, *Concept of Repression* (Calcutta: Sri Gauranga Press, 1921, and London: Kegan Paul, Trench, Troubner and Co., 1921), pp. 140–1.

[13]This account of Bijayketu Bose is not consistent with Sinha's claim that Bose had to undergo financial hardships in his early years as a doctor. Perhaps Sinha had in mind the fact that when Bose concentrated on psychiatry, his average income declined dramatically to about Rs 100 a month. Sinha, 'A Short Life Sketch', p. 64.

read Brill.[14] The preface, in fact, reveals that some of the concepts Bose thought he had developed he found had already been developed by Freud when translations of Freud began to reach India after the World War ended in 1918. He was not defensive about the discovery; he accepted the superiority of the psychoanalytic concepts and began to use them in his work. He was actually better off in this respect than his more famous Tamil contemporary, the untutored mathematical genius, Srinivasa Ramanujan (1887–1920). A large proportion of Ramanujan's discoveries later turned out to be rediscoveries; he had to reconcile himself to being an immortal in the world of mathematics on the basis of the remainder.

Over the next five years, three more translations of Freud's books were published: *The Three Lectures on Sexuality* (1910), the lectures at the Clark University in the United States, published as *Five Lectures on Psychoanalysis* (1910), and the *Interpretation of Dreams* (1913). By that time Bose was committed to the new science. One suspects from the sequence of events that the reasons for his decision to switch from conventional psychiatry were not purely intellectual ones, that he gave his allegiance to Freud even before he had read him systematically. Something in the framework and concerns of psychoanalysis had deeply touched the young doctor. The strange, new-fangled ideas of the controversial Viennese physician *did* have something to say about Bose's own world.

Bose's 'conversion' did not signify much to his community, for few people in India had heard of Freud. Rabindranath Tagore (1861–1940) relates in a letter that a Bengali admirer of Freud, while speaking to Tagore about psychoanalysis, consistently pronounced 'Freud' as if it rhymed with 'fruit'. Bose, however, found in Freud a kindred soul and saw immense possibilities in psychoanalysis. He eagerly read everything available on the subject and began to apply the method in his psychiatric work; he appears to have been satisfied with the results. At any rate, given his background and the intellectual position he had been moving towards before discovering psychoanalysis, he did not have to make too many modifications in his therapeutic style.

Bose's new passion heightened his curiosity about the discipline of psychology in general. From his early years, he had been an orderly person and, in many respects, a perfectionist. Once his interest in psychology was aroused, he began to feel handicapped by his limited knowledge of abnormal psychology. Whatever he knew was derived from the

[14]Bose, *Concept of Repression*, pp. v–viii.

undergraduate courses in medicine he had attended, inadequate grounding for a practitioner especially interested in the theory and practice of psychiatry.

When the Calcutta University opened a new department of psychology in 1915, Bose enrolled as a student, and got his Master's degree in two years, once again doing well in the examinations. He was immediately appointed a lecturer in the department. One of the first things he did was make courses in psychoanalysis compulsory for all students of psychology, making the department one of the first academic establishments in the world to do so.[15] He was then thirty-one.

After four years, Bose completed his doctoral thesis which was published as the *Concept of Repression*.[16] Though fascinating in many ways, it is a clumsy work, made still clumsier by Bose's awkward and cluttered English. Despite this, it was well received. The thesis was reportedly dictated to a stenographer in a week, in response to a bet taken with a fellow member of the Utkendra Samiti or Eccentric Club that Bose and some of his friends had founded at his Parsibagan residence. His friends had ragged him, claiming that his disregard for degrees and formal qualifications was a pose, meant to hide his incapacity to get a doctorate.[17] Bose's dissertation was to remain the only doctoral thesis in psychology completed in an Indian university during the 1920s, and this further underwrote the pre-eminence of psychoanalysis in Indian academic psychology. Perhaps in no other country was psychoanalysis to register such easy dominance as in India.

When his thesis was published, Girindrasekhar sent a copy of the book to Freud. It bore the inscription: 'From a warm admirer of your theory and science'. Freud was pleasantly surprised and wrote back almost immediately. The old dissenter was not used to easy acceptance; he was genuinely intrigued that in far-off India psychoanalysis should have met with so much interest and recognition so early in its career. Thus began an intermittent correspondence between the two which lasted nearly two decades.[18] Bose never met Freud. Going to the West for an education and 'proper' recognition of one's worth was popular among the westernized élites of colonial India and this irritated Bose. Despite an invitation from

[15]Christiane Hartnack, 'Psychoanalysis and Colonialism in British India', Ph.D. dissertation, Berlin, Freie Universität, 1988, p. 85.

[16]Bose, *Concept of Repression*.

[17]Sinha, 'A Short Life Sketch', p. 64.

[18]Sigmund Freud to Girindrasekhar Bose, 29 May 1921, in 'Correspondence regarding Psychoanalysis', *Samiksha*, 1956, *10*, pp. 104–10, 155–66.

his guru, he refused to go abroad because that would be 'more of a fashion than need'.[19] There were also, according to Ernest Jones who invited Bose to Europe several times, Bose's numerous duties in India and 'perhaps a certain shyness'.[20]

In 1922, barely three years after the British Psychoanalytic Society was formed, Bose founded the Indian Psychoanalytic Society in Calcutta at his own residence. Of the fifteen founding members of the group, nine were college lecturers of psychology and philosophy, five were doctors, and one a business executive who also happened to be a generous patron of the Society. Of the thirteen Indian members, twelve were upper-caste Bengalis; the two remaining members were whites. The social origin of the thirteenth Indian member is not apparent from his name. Of the five doctors, two were British, one a relatively nondescript doctor in the colonial health service. The other was Owen A.R. Berkeley-Hill (1879–1944), also a member of the health service but already famous as the psychiatrist who had made the Ranchi Mental Hospital one of the best known in the East. Berkeley-Hill's name is inextricably linked to the history of modern psychiatry and psychoanalysis in India, and he epitomized in many ways some of the central problems in the culture of the two disciplines in South Asia. He was the first westerner to attempt a psychoanalytic study of the Hindu modal personality and the first westerner to use psychoanalysis as a form of cultural critique in India. A word on him will provide a counterpoint to Bose's philosophy of knowledge.

Berkeley-Hill was no ordinary migratory bird in India. Son of a wealthy and famous English physician, he was educated at Rugby, Göttingen, the University of Nancy, and Oxford, from where he received his medical degree. Berkeley-Hill entered the Indian Medical Service in 1907 and, except for a four-year stretch during World War I, spent the rest of his life in India, complaining all the while about living conditions in the colony. He married a Hindu, despite his preoccupation with the distorted personality and culture of the Hindus. The marriage and its Eurasian offspring were an almost certain indicator, during the period we are talking about, both of social defiance and uncertain social status among the whites. Neither defiance nor uncertainty was lacking in Berkeley-Hill. Christiane Hartnack points out that in Berkeley-Hill's autobiography,

---

[19]Bhatia, 'Pioneer'. Also Freud to Bose, 1 March 1922, 'Correspondence', *Samiksha*, 1956, *10*, p. 108.

[20]Ernest Jones, 'Foreword', *Samiksha*, 1954, Bose Sp. No., p. 1.

which includes an open discussion of his premarital sex life and ends with 'a detailed description of the character and look of his horses, there is less mention of his wife than of [his] extra-marital affairs.'[21]

Perhaps as a result of his liminal stature, Berkeley-Hill showed in many of his papers an aggressive psychoanalysism. Given his fractured self, simultaneously repelled and seduced by imperial England and Brahminic India, this analysism took necessarily a particular form. As befitted an Edwardian gentleman educated at an English public school and Oxford, he showed a deep concern with the vicissitudes of anal eroticism and found in its patterning among the Hindus *the* clue to their cultural pathology and moral depravity. He passed judgment on their character, on behalf of all other cultures, in the following words:

It is not unlikely that the strange antipathy that is felt for the Hindus by most, if indeed not all, the races of the world is nothing more than an expression of an unconscious feeling of antagonism brought about by some of the peculiarities of the manifestations of anal eroticism as met with among the Hindus. It is certainly a fact that wherever the Hindu may go, no matter whether it be in Asia, Africa or Europe, he is to the inhabitants of that country a veritable Dr Fell. We must therefore assume that this obscure but nevertheless very real dislike which is shared by all races of mankind for the Hindu, must, from its very nature, have its roots in some deeply buried source of feeling. Books on India teem with references to this singular 'otherness', if I may use the term, of the Hindu as compared, for instance, with the Muslim or Christian Indian.[22]

On the basis of the theoretical work of his mentor, Ernest Jones, Berkeley-Hill then goes on to identify, rather charmingly and with the confidence of one advancing a dispassionate scientific thesis, the two effects of anal eroticism.[23] The valuable qualities thrown up by anal eroticism are:

individualism, determination, persistence, love of order and power of organization, competency, reliability and thoroughness, generosity, the bent towards art and good taste, the capacity for unusual tenderness, and the general ability to deal with concrete objects of the material world.[24]

[21]Hartnack, 'Psychoanalysis and Colonialism', pp. 28–9. Most of the biographical material on Berkeley-Hill used in this paper is from Hartnack's comprehensive work on the shadow cast by colonialism on the work of the first psychoanalysts in India.

[22]Owen A.R. Berkeley-Hill, 'The Anal-Erotic Factor in the Religion, Philosophy and Character of the Hindus', in *Collected Papers* (Calcutta: The Book Co., 1933), pp. 75–112; first published in the *International Journal of Psycho-Analysis*, 1921, 2, pp. 306–38.

[23]Ibid., p. 107.

[24]Ibid., pp. 108–9.

The despicable ones are the obverse of the above:

incapacity for happiness, irritability and bad temper, hypochondria, miserliness, meanness and pettyness, slow-mindedness and proneness to bore, the bent for tyrannising and dictating and obstinacy.[25]

Predictably, the Hindus suffered from a 'metapsychosis' featuring the second set of traits. On the other hand, 'the character traits of the English people as a whole belong for the greater part to the first of the two groups distinguished by Ernest Jones.'[26]

Berkeley-Hill's views were, however, not as one-sided as these extracts from his papers suggest or as Hartnack would have us believe. On occasion, his defiance overcame his social insecurities and he could be remarkably incisive in his cultural analysis. Nearly twenty-five years before James Baldwin made such ideas a part of American folklore, Berkeley-Hill suggested that colour prejudice among the whites sprang from a deep fear of the perceived greater potency of the blacks and from the fear that the whites would lose their womenfolk to the blacks.[27]

The aggressive psychoanalysism was, however, the dominant tone. Like Kipling's imperialist stance, it reads today like an exaggerated gesture of allegiance by a marginal man to the culture of the ruling community, though at one time it must have appeared to be a pungent exercise in social criticism and demystification. Berkeley-Hill, like Kipling, was both fascinated and repelled by India, and the fascination was more painful to bear. It cut him off from his own kind and tainted him as culturally impure. His writings make it obvious that to him India was a living negation of the Victorian ideal of a moral self, and the seductive appeal of Indian culture had to be fiercely resisted.

For Berkeley-Hill to pursue the cultural–critical aspect of psychoanalysis to its logical conclusion would have meant taking a political position against a part of himself and against the social evolutionism that underpinned Victorian morality and sanctioned colonialism. He could not afford to own up that responsibility. He had to defend himself by turning the tools of his new-found critical apparatus against the Indian culture itself, both with a vengeance and an immense effort of will, the way Kipling had earlier turned against that part of himself which constituted his Indianness.[28]

[25]Ibid.
[26]Ibid., p. 111.
[27]Berkeley-Hill, 'The "Colour Question" from a Psychoanalytic Standpoint' (1923), *Collected Papers*, pp. 139–48.
[28]For a brief sketch of Kipling from this point of view, see Ashis Nandy, *The*

Berkeley-Hill began his personal analysis at London with the well-known Welsh psychoanalyst, Ernest Jones, and he probably completed his training with Bose at Calcutta. Along with his lesser-known compatriot Claud Dangar Daly, another protégé of Jones and subsequently an analysand of Freud and Ferenczi, Berkeley-Hill defined for his generation of psychoanalysts the domain of psychoanalytic studies of modal personality or national character in India.[29] We have already told a part of that story. The political psychology of that pioneering effort—especially the links between psychoanalysis, colonialism, and the culture of science in the inter-war years—is neatly summed up in Christiane Hartnack's verdict on the two British psychoanalysts. After analysing their work and interpretive styles, she concludes:

There is an unquestionable tendency in both writers to find in psychoanalysis a new scientific tool for getting a grip on problems of public order that were getting out of control. . . . This explicitly political appropriation of psychoanalytic theory . . . coincided in the 'twenties and 'thirties with the first successes of the newly formed Indian independence movement. In line with European thought at the time, Berkeley-Hill and Daly conceptualized a moral hierarchy with white men at the top and dependent people, women, infants, so-called primitives, and neurotics at or near the bottom.[30]

Thus,

Berkeley-Hill's and Daly's writings on Indians had in common that they . . . both failed to note any achievement or positive aspect of the Indian culture . . . . Both men identified themselves fully with British colonialism. For them, Indians were a source of threat and had thus to be combatted, and resistance had to be smashed not only on a military but also on a cultural level. Unlike Orwell, who left colonial India in order not to cope with the dual identity of a colonial bureaucrat by day and a questioning and critical human being by night, Daly and Berkeley-Hill worked to . . . contribute to a properly functioning colonial world.

Contemporary psychoanalytical thought offered them models to legitimize their . . . separation from Indians. If one was not a British (i.e., Christian) adult healthy male, one was in trouble . . . . Victorian women, Anglo-Indians, Irish,

---

Intimate Enemy: Loss and Recovery of Self under Colonialism (New Delhi: Oxford University Press, 1983).

[29]For example, Owen A.R. Berkeley-Hill, 'A Report of Two Cases Successfully Treated by Psychoanalysis', *The Indian Medical Gazette*, 1913, 48, pp. 97–9; and 'The Psychology of the Anus', ibid., pp. 301–3; also 'The Anal Erotic Factor'. One wonders after reading the last paper if its diagnosis was not partly influenced by Berkeley-Hill's long personal acquaintance with Bose. Also Claud Dangar Daly, 'Hindu-Mythologie und Kastrationkomplex', tr. Peter Mandelsohn, *Image*, 1927, 13, pp. 145–98.

[30]Hartnack, 'Psychoanalysis and Colonialism', p. 5.

Moselms, children, sick and old people could to some extent still be accepted, as there were some common denominators between them and the British ideal. But women who did not obey the Victorian mores, mentally disturbed British subjects, Hindus and people of colour . . . were not only perceived as entirely different and thus inferior, but were also considered to be dangerous. They were not only in the majority, but there was the potential of hysteria, violence, revolution, sexual seduction and other supposedly irrational acts, which would be difficult to control. Therefore, it was the 'white man's burden' to keep them under surveillance . . . .[31]

One should not be too harsh on the two well-meaning, simple-hearted practitioners of the young science of psychoanalytic psychiatry when the dominant culture of the now fully grown science has not done much better and when all around them the two could find even Indians lovingly embracing the same overall perspective. It is fairly obvious that both British psychoanalysts were strictly allegiant to a transfer-of-technology model that had already become popular on the Indian scene and would remain paramount in Indian intellectual life four decades after formal decolonization. Berkeley-Hill and Daly, like many before them and after, saw psychoanalysis as a state-of-the-art therapeutic device and hoped to introduce it with minor modifications into India as a partial cure for the worst affliction Indians suffered from—Indianness. The exclusive universality imputed to most systems of modern scientific knowledge was a function, then as now, of the political privileges such a transfer created for specific individuals and groups.

With hindsight, is it fair to ask if the early Indian analysts were adequately aware that they were caught in a colonial grid of knowledge? Did they sense that analytic responsibility in the hot and dusty tropics had to own up a new political responsibility? They both did not and did.

Manifestly, they did not react at all to the colonial psychology of Berkeley-Hill and Daly. To the first generation of Indian psychoanalysts, such politically loaded cultural interpretations were not uncommon and they blended with the dominant tone of the humanities and social sciences at Indian universities; Berkeley-Hill and Daly would not have appeared particularly vicious or scathing. Also, the Indians attracted to analysis were themselves searching for new modes of social criticism that would make sense to their community; they were themselves given to provocative and arrogant psychoanalytic summary trials of the Indian culture and personality. To them their British colleagues were probably merely two

[31]Ibid., p. 73.

slightly overenthusiastic white associates of Bose having their fling at the psychoanalysis of Indian culture. After all, in Bose's circle their formal status though high was not formidable.

But psychoanalysts, too, have their unconscious. During the early years of the Indian Psychoanalytic Society, one member of the Society did an imaginary portrait of Freud, not having seen the master nor even a photograph of him. This portrait, a near-perfect test of projection, was, appropriately enough, gifted to Freud. Freud was pleased, but complained in a letter that he looked a perfect Englishman in the portrait.[32] None pointed out to the ageing patriarch the analytic implications of his casual remark and the political tragedy that lay unarticulated in it.

Some questions, however, still remain unanswered. Were Berkeley-Hill and Daly merely tropical extensions of the arrogantly international, 'universal' culture of knowledge of which psychoanalysis was trying to be a part? Or were they adapting to the stress induced by the colonial situation with the help of existing psychoanalytic categories and by seeking sanction from the acceptance of psychoanalysis by some 'learned Hindus', as Freud described them?[33] Were Bose's attempts to locate psychoanalysis in the Vedantic tradition and giving it a distinct non-progressivist language an unintended response to the colonial psychoanalysis of his two white colleagues and the social evolutionism implicit in the dominant culture of psychoanalysis?[34] Is it coincidental that some methodological comments in his *Purāṇa Praveśa* read like a direct response to Berkeley-Hill's interpretive style? Was it significant that both British psychoanalysts had a record of mental illness and therapy under Jones? Were they both 'infected' with the hard-boiled social evolutionism and positivism of Jones and the 'imperious', 'opinionated', 'spiteful' aspects of his self?[35] Did they pick up from Jones his fear of ideas, metaphysics and, above all, the fear of a reading of psychoanalysis that would allow one to turn the discipline upon itself? Or was the problem deeper and did it begin with Freud himself? I shall attempt an indirect answer to a few of these questions later in this essay.

[32]Sigmund Freud to Lou Andreas-Salome, 13 March 1922, in Ernest Pfeiffer (ed.), *Sigmund Freud and Lou Andreas-Salome Letters*, trs. W. Robson-Scott and E. Robson Scott (New York: Harcourt, Brace and Jovanovich, 1972), p. 114, quoted in Hartnack, *Psychoanalysis and Colonialism*, p. 1. One wonders if this is the same portrait that the well-known illustrator Jatindra Kumar Sen did of Freud.

[33]Ibid.

[34]Bose claimed to be a Vedantic, even though he reportedly helped his wife in her *pujā* or worship, Sinha, 'A Short Life Sketch', p. 69.

[35]Paul Roazen, *Freud and His Followers* (London: Allen Lane, 1976), pp. 345–6.

Berkeley-Hill and Daly did not define entirely the culture of psychoanalysis in India. Other psychoanalysts were also to leave their mark on the history of psychiatry and psychology, though in different ways. Tarun Chandra Sinha was one of the pioneers of psychoanalytic anthropology in India; Haripada Maiti and Pars Ram were to be associated with the founding of major institutions of psychoanalysis and psychology at Patna, Ahmedabad and Lahore; Bhupen Desai contributed handsomely to the growth of psychoanalysis in Bombay; Suhrit C. Mitra and S.K. Bose became central to the growth of professional psychology in the country. Two of the most important pioneering figures in the Indian social sciences and humanities were also in the psychoanalytic movement: Nirmal Kumar Bose, in later life the doyen of social anthropology in the country, and Debiprasad Chattopadhyay, who was to make signal contributions to the philosophy and history of science in India. Others like Rangin Halder and Sarasilal Sarkar made crucial inputs into Bengali cultural life. Many of them were not merely Bose's students, the imprint of Bose's intellectual and clinical concerns carried over into their work, including some of the limitations of Bose's distinctive style of psychoanalysis. Of his students and trainees, Sinha, who had had psychological problems and had been Bose's analysand, was to prove particularly dynamic organizationally. He used his therapeutic experience creatively to become a talented psychoanalyst and a gifted institution-builder, enabling psychoanalysis to be a continuing presence in Bengali social life after Bose's death.

Through Freud and Ernest Jones, then the president of the International Psychoanalytic Association, the Indian Society soon got affiliated to the international brotherhood of psychoanalysis. And Bose joined two others, Freud himself and August Aichhorn, as one of the only three psychoanalysts ever to be recognized as psychoanalysts on the basis of his self-analyses. Bose remained president of the Indian Psychoanalytic Society till his death in 1953.

It is not easy to judge Bose's contribution as the founding father of the Indian Psychoanalytic Society. One gets differing assessments of him as an ideologue, organizational man and as a person. Some say he was indiscriminate in his admissions policy and overly eager to spread psychoanlaysis to all corners of India. Others point out that he never had many trainees, and that many dropped out in any case. However, there are two things about which one can be more certain.

First, the formal requirements of psychoanalysis were often diluted for organizational and logistic reasons in India, so that the technical aspects of psychoanalysis remained underdeveloped. This may not have been entirely a tragedy. The under-emphasis on technique allowed psychoanalysis to retain the potentiality (never actually realized) of becoming something more than an Indian subsidiary of a multinational professional corporation.

Second, as a pioneer in matters of the mind and as an organizational innovator, Bose showed remarkable ideological tolerance. He was a difficult person and, according to one of his students, a relatively self-contained man of knowledge. It is doubtful if for him psychoanalysis was an ideological movement with a core of inviolable dogma. He used to say, an associate remembers, that psychoanalysis was a medical system like ayurveda or homeopathy; it worked with some people, while other systems worked better with others. Others mention that Bose never pushed psychoanalysis with his students of psychology and his own psychological theories with his analytic trainees or colleagues.

This non-ideological stance was mirrored in Bose's politics, or non-politics. Psychoanalysis became established in India at politically tumultuous times, when Gandhi was emerging as the new leader of the anti-imperialist movement, displacing both moderate and extremist leaders. Among those being threatened by such displacement and facing political demise were the entire old leadership of Bengal, with their base mainly among the Hindu middle classes and the cities. Before their very eyes politics had become mass politics, bypassing them to reach into India's sleepy villages. Even in the metropolitan cities, the political atmosphere was no longer what it had been only five years earlier. Though there is some controversy among those who knew Bose about his response to Gandhi, he probably did believe that Gandhi represented the 'well-sublimated', rational, healthy personality.[36] Otherwise, but for a vague patriotism, Bose remained quite apolitical throughout his life. Even that patriotism was, according to some, methodologically open. He was never particularly enamoured of political movements or the nitty-gritty of politics.

This apolitical attitude might have underwritten the low salience of

---

[36]Debiprasad Chattopadhyay believes that Bose was a *nisthāvāna* or loyal Gandhian; others like Bijayketu Bose and Charuchandra Bhattacharya strongly disagree. An indirect but important clue to Girindrasekhar's attitude to Gandhi is in Rajsekhar Bose's futuristic, comic fantasy, '*Gāmāṇus Jātir Kathā*', in *Galpakalpa* (Calcutta: M.C. Sarkar, 1950), pp. 1–19. The fantasy lends indirect support to Chattopadhyay, rather than to Bose and Bhattacharya. On the other hand, Bhupen Desai himself a Gandhian and from a family of Gandhian freedom fighters that has made major sacrifices for the Gandhian cause, remembers the touch of sarcasm with which Bose once talked about Gandhian asceticism. Desai believes that Bose, though he admired Gandhi, rejected the Gandhian attitudes to sexuality and the *varna* system.

the cultural–critical aspects of the new science in India, but it allowed Bose to hold the loyalty of a wide variety of young enthusiasts belonging to diverse ideological strains, ranging from Indra Sen, one of the first transpersonal psychologists of our times and later on a prominent mystic at the Pondicherry Ashram, to Debiprasad Chattopadhyay, then a budding radical philosopher of science, apart from being a practising psychoanalyst. The latter, however, did have to bear Bose's aggressive interpretation of the Oedipal roots of Marxism.[37] Probably Bose's belief that psychoanalysis was primarily a method helped him to be ideologically open; he expected methods to have limitations and to be controversial. (Apparently the Indian Psychoanalytic Society failed to retain its intellectual catholicity after Bose's death. Chattopadhyay was excommunicated soon after his mentor died as his Bengali book, *Freud Prasange*, an early Marxist interpretation influenced by the likes of John Somerville and Joseph Needham, was found too critical of Freud, though it was less so than many works produced later by pillars of the psychoanalytic establishment. *Freud Prasange* paid handsome tribute to Freud's method and accepted it fully but faulted the master on his philosophical assumptions. The tribute did not help Chattopadhyay; he was expelled all the same. After Bose's death, a stylistic similarity appears to have developed between the psychoanalytic movements in India and the West. Both shared the same internal contradiction when it came to dissent—limited theoretical tolerance with unlimited organizational intolerance.)

It says something about Bose's organizational skills that, unlike its western counterparts, the Indian Psychoanalytic Society quickly acquired a sound financial base. Once when the parent body was in financial trouble, the Indian branch sent it some money as a contribution. It is not known how his friend Berkeley-Hill reacted to such evidence of organizational ability, whether he attributed the trait to Bose's deviation from Hindu culture through self-analysis or to the persistence in him of Hindu anal-erotic style.

Bose himself, however, changed in the process of becoming a psycho-anlayst and institutionalizing the new discipline, at least according to his wife. From being an 'energetic' and 'jolly' person he became a 'thoughtful'

---

[37]Chattopadhyay recounts his debate with Bose on the subject. It seems he once asked Bose why, if Bose was so keen on an Oedipal explanation of communism and the indigenous 'terrorist' movement, he exempted Gandhi from it, even though Gandhi also had risen against authority. Bose's reply was that Gandhi had been effective because of his rationality and his cool, dispassionate, efficacious politics. This conversation seemingly confutes Bijayketu Bose's belief in the methodological openness of his uncle's politics.

one.[38] He also, it appears, had different styles of management for the Indian Psychoanalytic Society and the Department of Applied Psychology of the Calcutta University, which he had headed since it was established in 1937. In the Society he was easy and egalitarian; in the university more paternalistic, socially withdrawn, and unwilling to share power. When Sinha says in his biographical note that Bose was considered stingy, impersonal and aloof, he was probably speaking of Bose in the university setting.[39] Some who knew him in the university find similarities between his style and that of his friends J.C. Bose, whom we have already mentioned, and P.C. Mahalanobis (1893–1972), the pioneer of modern statistics and development planning.

However, it was not the Society or the Department which ensured the early success of psychoanalysis in the metropolitan culture of India. It was Bose's own intellectual presence and, later, that of some of his talented students and admirers such as Tarun Chandra Sinha, Haripada Maiti, Pars Ram, Rangin Halder, and Indra Sen. Bose's own intellectual range was formidable: he was chemist, Sanskritist, historian of ideas, experimental psychologist, doctor, teacher, artist, translator, and man of letters. In addition he wrote scholarly commentaries on sacred texts and was the author of a highly popular children's tale, *Lāl Kālo*, which included some lively poems and a drawing that could have adorned a Gothic horror story.[40] His very personality attracted some of the better young minds of metropolitan India. (Bose had a ready Freudian explanation of the careerism which did not allow the brightest of the Bengali youth, with a few exceptions, to come to psychoanalysis.)

This intellectual presence was underscored when the Indian Psychoanalytic Society belatedly brought out its journal, *Samiksha*, in 1947. The journal was an immediate success and its early days were the last few golden years of Indian psychoanalysis. Apart from Indians, the contributors included Geiza Roheim, David Rapaport, Clara Thompson, George Devereaux, Edmund Bergler, K.R. Eissler, Jules Masserman, and Fritz Wittels. Moving evidence of how seriously the journal was taken is a contribution by James Clark Moloney, who wrote from aboard a warship approaching Okinawa before one of the climactic battles of World War II.[41]

---

[38]Sinha, 'A Short Life Sketch', p. 68.

[39]Ibid.

[40]Girindrasekhar Bose, *Lāl Kālo* (Calcutta: Indian Associated Publishing Co., 1956).

[41]James Clark Moloney, 'The Biospheric Aspects of Japanese Death by Suicide'; *Samiksha*, 1949, 3, pp. 104–24.

Bose was a gifted therapist, too, effecting cures that were nothing less than spectacular. His writings give the impression that he was overly didactic, in the sense in which the same expression is used by some of Erich Fromm's erstwhile colleagues to describe Fromm's therapeutic style. Such directness is said to have been not entirely alien to Freud's own therapeutic style, either.[42] It has also been said that Bose reinvoked the *guru-śiṣya* relationship in his analytic encounters.[43] Perhaps he did, but the result was dramatic therapeutic successes. As a result, by the time he was in his late forties, he had become for the urban Indian a legendary doctor of the mind.

This directness, however, also introduced into Indian psychoanalysis a theoretical twist. Therapy was viewed primarily as a cognitive venture, involving the acquisition of knowledge or information, and only second-arily as a matter of rearrangement or reinterpretation of emotions. His success as a therapist suggests that he may have deviated from this view in practice, but the view did influence and, according to some, lowered the standard of analytic training in India.

As a person, Bose was, like many successful clinicians, a bundle of contradictions. Since many of those who knew him belonged to the fraternity of psychoanalysts, he also comes off as a depot of neurotic symptoms. Some remember his pronounced orality—his love for food, cooking and the spoken word; his language skills; and his emphasis on the core fantasy of the split mother, what Sudhir Kakar calls the 'hegemonic myth' of Indian culture. Others remember Bose's long struggle with the hypertension that finally killed him. (The concern with the fantasy of the split mother has proved particularly resilient. From Berkeley-Hill, Daly, Philip Spratt and G. Morris Carstairs, to John Hitchcock, Leigh Mintern, Monisha Roy, Susan Wadley, Kakar, and Alan Roland—a wide range of social scientists influenced by psychoanalysis, including this writer, have returned to the myth with the feeling of making a new and important discovery.[44] They have been strengthened in their belief by a

---

[42]Marie Jahoda, *Freud and the Dilemmas of Psychology* (London: Hogarth, 1977), p. 10.

[43]Sudhir Kakar, 'Stories from Indian Psychoanalysis: Context and Text', in James W. Stigler, Richard A. Shweder, and Gilbert Herdts (eds.), *Cultural Psychology* (New York: Cambridge University, 1990), pp. 427–45. On the *guru-śiṣya* relationship as a possible model for therapeutic work, the best-known paper is J.S. Neki's 'Guru-Chela Relationship: The Possibility of a Therapeutic Paradigm', *American Journal of Orthopsychiatry*, 1973, 43, pp. 755–66.

[44]Berkeley-Hill, 'The "Colour Question"'; Claud D. Daly, 'Hindu Treatise on Kali', *Samiksha*, 1947 1(2), pp. 191–6; Philip Spratt, *Hindu Culture and Personality* (Bombay: Manaktalas, 1966); G. Morris Carstairs, *The Twice Born: Study of a Community*

galaxy of Indian writers and artists, myth-makers in general, who have regularly reinvoked the fantasy of a partitioned mother in their creative works and autobigoraphies.)[45]

Most remember Bose's obsessive–compulsive ways—the meticulous records, the orderly minutes, the spotlessly white, immaculately starched Bengali dress that was virtually his uniform, the frugality and—as with many nineteenth-century Indians exposed to the western concept of time and seeking to over-correct for the perceived Indian overemphasis on 'timelessness'—the fanatic devotion to punctuality. The frugality was of a special kind; it went with much wasteful expenditure to ensure order and cleanliness. For his small family he had a retinue of twelve to fourteen domestic servants and his wardrobe included, one student claims, at least eighty dhotis. His orderliness influenced his taste in music: he liked *dhrupada* with its austere, orderly, rigid frame and not the flamboyant *khayāl* with its greater emphasis on fluidity and imagination.[46] He recognized these traits in himself; he once bluntly told his trainee Desai, 'I am obsessive–compulsive'.

Whether the orderliness interfered with his own creativity or not, he retained a sharp sensitivity throughout his life to the obsessive–compulsive traits of his students and analysands. Remarkable stories are told about how he would leave coins scattered about on his desk and draw diagnostic conclusions from the way some of his visitors and students handled them. Indian psychoanalysis inherited this sensitivity; some of the most fascinating work on individual cases and cultural patterns in India centres around the analysis of the same psychopathology.

Others remember livelier scenes. Debiprasad Chattopadhyay remembers Bose washing with an antiseptic lotion the goat to be eaten at his

---

of High-Caste Hindus (London: Hogarth, 1957); J. Hitchcock and Leigh Mintern, 'The Rajputs of Khalapur', in Beatrice Whitting (ed.), *Six Cultures* (New York: John Wiley, 1963), pp. 203–361; Monisha Roy, *Bengali Woman* (Chicago: University of Chicago, 1975); Susan Wadley, *Shakti: Power in the Conceptual Structure of Karimpur Religion* (Chicago: University of Chicago, 1975); Sudhir Kakar, *The Inner World: A Psychoanalytic Study of Childhood and Society in India* (New Delhi: Oxford University Press, 1978); Alan Roland, *In Search of Self in India and Japan: Toward a Cross-Cultural Psychology* (Princeton, N.J.: Princeton University, 1988); Ashis Nandy, *At the Edge of Psychology: Essays in Politics and Creativity and Authenticity in Two Indian Scientists* (New Delhi: Oxford University Press, 1995).

[45]Kakar has recently related this myth to the difference between Bose and Freud on gender psychology. Bose believed that the acceptance of the maternal-feminine component by Indian males in themselves made them less prone to castration anxiety and hence psychologically healthier. Sudhir Kakar, *Intimate Relations: Exploring Indian Sexuality* (New Delhi: Viking, 1989), ch. 7.

[46]Sinha, 'A Short Life Sketch', pp. 68–9.

daughter's wedding. Charuchandra Bhattacharya remembers how he
went, armed with a stop-watch, from Bose's home to the Howrah railway
station on two successive days, once without and once with luggage, as
a rehearsal for Bose's planned train journey the following day. Desai
remembers Bose saying once that for his holidays at Deoghar in Bihar,
he had calculated beforehand all the possible expenses, including that of
the wear and tear of his car tyres. Many speak of the twelve goats that
Bose purchased for his nephew Bijayketu's marriage feast being fed on
gram to make their meat more tender. Though he planned the marriage
and marriage reception with meticulous care, he could not attend the
actual ceremony, because he had to go to bed at his usual hour, at exactly
8 PM. All this contributed to the myth.

There might have been a weightier reason, too, for Bose's emergence as
an important cultural figure in Bengal. Bose turned to psychoanalysis
at a time when the traditional social relationships that took care of most
of the everyday problems of living—the neuroses and less acute forms
of psychosis—were breaking down in urban India. These relationships
and the world-view that informed them were being replaced by a new
network of social relationships sanctioning a new set of 'superstitions'—
constructions of mental illness derived from remnants of traditional ideas
of lunacy and available scraps of modern psychiatric knowledge. The
first victims of this change were the psychologically afflicted; they were
no longer seen as aberrant individuals deserving a place within the family
and the community, but as diseased and potentially dangerous waste
products of the society. As Bijayketu Bose puts it, the shock-absorbing
capacities of the society had declined considerably at the time. And as a
Michel Foucault or a Ronald Laing might have said, the dialogue between
sanity and insanity had broken down; the society was now dominated by
a monologue of sanity.

Girindrasekhar Bose took it upon himself to attack these perceptions
and to offer the mentally ill a more humane treatment and voice. In 1933,
he established India's first psychiatric out-patient clinic in Calcutta's
Carmichael Medical College and Hospital. In 1948, on the initiative of
Sinha and partly financed by Rajsekhar Bose, the Indian Psychoanalytic
Society established a hospital and research centre at Calcutta's Lumbini
Park. In 1949, Bose founded a school for small children organized on
psychoanalytic lines.

A word on the early impact of psychoanalysis on urban India in
contrast to that on Europe and North America, may be appropriate at
this point. Freud's explosive emergence on the European intellectual scene

had shattered the Victorian world image. The image, as Carl Jung once pointed out, was not merely a feature of Anglo-Saxon societies but of much of Protestant Europe, though on the continent 'it never received such an appropriate epithet'. Along with that image went a concept of bourgeois respectability built on attempts to artificially keep alive through repression a set of anaemic ideals. These ideals were, Jung felt, remnants of the collective ideals of the Middle Ages, badly damaged by the French Enlightenment.[47]

When Freud challenged this respectability, he seemed to flout the basic tenets of social decency and challenge the moral universe of nineteenth-century Europe that framed and 'stabilized' everyday culture after the disruptions and uprooting brought about by the industrial revolution. In this stabilization, along with the concepts of the nation-state and progress, a central role had been played by the concept of scientific rationality, viewed as a tool of knowledge and power but serving in fact as a moral fulcrum. The concept might have been thrown up by the Enlightenment but ensured now, independently, a certain moral continuity and social sanction. By invoking this concept of rationality and hitching it to the newly dominant philosophy of individualism, Freud sought to legitimize a new concept of self that would accommodate a rediscovered, previously disowned underside of the self—a 'more real self' operating according to principles the 'apparent self' knew nothing about or rejected as immoral.[48] The Victorians could neither ignore nor swallow them.

Freud's ideas were much less controversial in India. He might have viewed himself as one of those who disturbed the sleep of the world, but he did not disturb many Indians even in their waking hours. Only small sections of the Indian middle classes had deeply internalized Victorian moral codes. Even fewer were exposed to the Victorian social norms relating to sexuality—among them, objections to psychoanalysis were often strong and impassioned. Many of them saw Bose's love for psychoanalysis as a moral betrayal and the content of psychoanalysis as dirty. (For instance, one well-known Bengali writer, Saradindu Bandopadhyay, in one of his plays compared the Freudian to a pig enjoying itself in a sewer. And Debiprasad Chattopadhyay's father stopped sending money to Debiprasad when he found that his college-going son had purchased Freud's works with this money. Such hostility

[47]G.G. Jung. 'Sigmund Freud in His Historical Setting', in Frank Cioffi (ed.), *Freud: Modern Judgement* (London: Macmillan, 1973), pp. 49–56; see pp. 49–50.

[48]Cf. Roland, *In Search of Self*, esp. chs. 1 and 2, for insights into the comparative impact of psychoanalysis in India, Japan, and the West.

was not widespread. Only a Marxist outfit named after Ivan Pavlov kept up the barrage till the late 1950s by rejecting psychoanalysis as being bourgeois and pornographic.)

Otherwise, Indian academics did not find Freud's ideas particularly wicked. Psychoanalysis might not have made much headway in India as a discipline, but the opposition to it could hardly be called frenzied. Most Indians, perhaps even most Indian psychoanalysts, would have been perplexed by Freud's famous statement to Jung on their way to Clark University as their ship approached New York harbour in 1909, 'They don't realize we're bringing them the plague'.[49] Why this indifference?

The easy answer is that there was both a casual unconcern with the content of the discipline and a widely felt need for an updated, reasonably holistic theory of mental illness in urban India. The need was strong enough for many to ignore the actual content of psychoanalysis. While this might on the whole be true, there is also a less pleasant answer. The bourgeois respectability that Freud attacked and which paradoxically defined him—the way industrial capitalism defines trade unionism—came to colonial India as part of the West's cultural baggage, interwined with other forms of respectability. But these other forms—colonialism itself, secularization, scientism, individualism and impersonalization of social relationships are four examples that immediately come to mind—were rarely targets of the social criticism psychoanalysis offered in the Southern world. As a result, psychoanalysis was bound gradually to look like another tame professional enterprise, another of those many new sciences being imported by westernized Indians, rather than as a critical, subversive presence. For a discipline that was 'double-edged'—both a means of exploring the human mind and a means of avoiding such exploration—this could not but lead to loss of selfhood.[50] Let me spell out the first and easier answer here because it relates directly to Bose's life. I shall return to the second answer at the end.

It was from Bengal that the British empire had started expanding after the Battle of Plassey in 1757. Bengal was the region where colonial intrusion was the deepest and the most disruptive in South Asia. Calcutta was not only the capital of British India, it was the second largest city in the empire and probably the liveliest marketplace of ideas from the East and the West in the world. Already some modern institutions—such as those providing western education and law—had entered the interstices of Bengali society and created a flourishing westernized middle class

[49]Douglas Kirsner, 'Is there a Future for American Psychoanalysis?', *The Psychoanalytic Review*, 1990, 77, pp. 176–200, see p. 197.
[50]Ibid.

that sustained a variety of cultural forms, neither exclusively western nor Indian. From theatre to food, from family dynamics to sports, and from dress to style of scholarship, every area of middle-class life in Bengal carried the imprint of the West.

Living in two worlds is never easy, and the new middle class in Bengal had lived for decades with deculturation, the breakdown of older social ties, and disruption of traditional morality. In response to these, the class had even produced a series of highly creative social thinkers and reformers who sought to design new world-views and new moral visions for fellow-Indians.

As it happened, none of these reformers had directly addressed the psychological problems thrown up by the breakdown of social ties and cultural uprooting. There had been indirect efforts to grapple with such problems in literature, social criticism and theology; there were even the rudiments of new social and political theories sensitive to them. But there was as yet no new theory of consciousness, no new culturally rooted, self-assured theory of modern individuality and subjectivity. Modern Bengal and for that matter urban India, were waiting for a theory of personality and selfhood to explain the psychological forces by which they were being buffeted.

This was the need Bose attempted to meet with the help of psychoanalysis. There might also have been a vague awareness in him that the sectoral, one-dimensional approach of the various schools of conventional academic psychology could not really cope with the psychological problems of Indian society or establish a durable link with Indian traditions. Psychoanalysis with its complex, holistic approach to the human personality—with its invocation of the person as a thinking, feeling, driven individual—at least allowed one to reinterpret its interpretations and to adapt them to the complexities of Indian society. To turn the discipline on itself, psychoanalysis could allow itself to be used as a projective medium for parts of Indian society, while being simultaneously used as a critique of that society.

It was this possibility of the young discipline that Bose exploited, and it was this possibility that gave it its early start in India. Even Freud, no stranger to theoretical speculations, was impressed by the vivacity and intellectual power of the first Indian psychoanalyst and recognized the Indian's philosophical acumen. On receiving *Concept of Repression*, he wrote:

It was a great and pleasant surprise that the first book on a psychoanalytic subject which came to us from that part of the world should display so good a knowledge of psychoanalysis, so deep an insight into its difficulties and so much deep going original thought . . . [the author] is aiming at a philosophical evolution . . . of our crude, practical concepts, and I can only wish psychoanalysis should soon reach up to the level to which he [Bose] strives to raise it.[51]

Of course, there was a touch of politics in Freud's enthusiasm and, later, that of Ernest Jones, who reviewed Bose's book in the *International Journal of Psychoanalysis*.[52] Both were happy to see psychoanalysis spread to India when it was still beleaguered in Europe and North America. Hence also Freud's emphasis, in a letter to Lou Andreas-Salome, on the fact that most members of the newly founded Indian Psychoanalytic Society were 'learned Hindus', not white expatriates or semi-literate native dilettantes.[53] Its cultivated Indian converts gave psychoanalysis, apart from ethnic colour, the semblance of cross-cultural validity.

However, there might also have been in Freud's and Jones's views a mix of awe and ambivalence that Bose spanned so effortlessly the worlds of psychoanalysis, philosophy, and cultural tradition. Certainly Jones, nurtured in the heady atmosphere of Anglo-Saxon positivism, might have found Bose's speculative bent of mind a bit of a trial. Jones needed, he himself said, 'the sense of security which the pursuit of truth gives'— in this instance, the certitudes produced by science—and he lived in an intellectual atmosphere in which Bertrand Russell was soon to call J.B. Watson the greatest scientist after Aristotle and compare the ultra-behaviourist with Charles Darwin.[54] For Jones, as for James Strachey, even Freud's cultural origins were an 'eccentricity' rather than a 'living factor in his life' and all religions were superstitions.[55] But then, Jones also had a more mundane reason to tolerate Bose's flirtation with philosophy. In another few years, he would want to make the British Society the regulating psychoanalytic body for the British empire, with the societies in the colonies functioning as subordinate groups. Bose's support in this venture might have been seen as vital.[56]

Freud, on the other hand, was brought up in an intellectual culture in which the pedagogic split between philosophy and science had not ossified. It was typical of the 'temperamental differences' between Jones

[51]Freud to Bose, 20 February 1922, in 'Correspondence', *10*, p. 108.

[52]Ernest Jones, 'Review of *Concept of Repression*', *International Journal of Psychoanalysis*, 1921, 2, p. 453.

[53]Freud to Andreas-Salome, p. 1.

[54]Ernest Jones, *Free Associations: Memories of a Psychoanalyst* (London: Hogarth, 1959), p. 63; also David Cohen, *J.B. Watson—The Founder of Behaviourism: A Biography* (London: Routledge, 1979).

[55]Roazen, *Freud and His Followers*, p. 347.

[56]Ibid., p. 346.

and Freud, Roazen says, 'that whereas the former feared religion's anti-naturalism, the latter was more afraid of the dangers of medicine's scientific materialism'.[57] Freud could not but be intrigued by Bose's daring. Though he claimed to steer clear of philosophy, Freud was nevertheless impressed by it; it was with some difficulty that he kept his interest in metapsychology in check.[58]

Neither this support from Freud nor its precocious growth and cultural distinctiveness saved Indian psychoanalysis from exhaustion within a few decades. So much so that Alan Roland has recently asked why psychoanalysis developed so early in India, and why it has not grown there as it has, for instance, in America or even France since the late 1960s.[59] Roland gives the answer at two planes. He notes the ease with which a theory of the unconscious can be integrated within a culture demanding 'extraordinary interpersonal sensitivity' from those living in extended families and other traditional groupings as well as the 'highly particularistic emphasis on a person's development through the combination of their qualities (*guṇas*), power (*śakti*), effects of familial and individual actions (*karma*), and attachments (*samaskāras*) carried over from past lives'.[60] Roland's answer to the second part of the question is socio-cultural and it supplements what has already been said about the non-controversial impact of psychoanalysis on Indian society. Comparing India with the western developed societies, Roland speaks of the 'deconversion' that has taken place from the belief systems and symbols of the traditional communities in the West and of the shift to a culturally less integrated society that shares only the symbols of science and where each individual must create his world-view of symbols and meaning.[61] The individual has been thrown back upon himself or herself in the West; not in India.

In other words, the factors which gave vibrancy to psychoanalysis in its early years in India may also have handicapped it as a vocation. The individuation that has taken place in the West remains in India the characteristic of a small proportion of the society. Psychoanalysis as a therapeutic technique in such circumstances has to remain a matter of cognitive choice; it cannot resonate with the private search for

[57]Ibid., pp. 354–5. Roazen bases himself on a letter of Ernest Jones to Sigmund Freud, 10 January 1933 (Jones Archives).
[58]On Freud's ambivalent attempts to distance himself from philosophy, see Section IV of this paper below.
[59]Roland, *In Search of Self*, p. 57.
[60]Ibid.
[61]Ibid., p. 58.

self-definition or a theory of life for the majority of Indians. In a paper on the early years of psychoanalysis, Kakar says: 'Cut off from the thrust and parry of debate, controversy and ferment of the psychoanalytic centres in Europe, dependent upon not easily available books and journals for outside intellectual sustenance, Indian psychoanalysis was nurtured through its infancy primarily by the enthusiasm and intellectual passion of its progenitor.'[62]

Probably it was. Probably, for the same reason, psychoanalysis in India never grew spectacularly as a clinical discipline. In a culture in which complex, often ornate, theories of consciousness of both right- and left-handed kinds were an important component, psychoanalysis had neither enough philosophical punch as a theory of the person. It neither threatened to supersede all other theories of the person, nor did it carry a strong enough impress of the evil and the smutty (in a society that treated the *Kāmasūtra* as a sacred text) to become the subject of a highly charged moral debate on the nature of the human mind. Psychoanalysis rather quietly became the best-known school of western psychology in India, controversial but not particularly live politically.

Christiane Hartnack says that 'the reception of psychoanalysis in British India varied from outright rejections of Freud's concepts as inappropriate for Indian conditions to unquestioned transfers.'[63] Actually, the 'outright rejections' here means in most cases nothing more dramatic than a certain unconcern. Only a few pages later, Hartnack is surprised at the public response to Rangin Halder's paper on the Oedipus complex in Rabindranath Tagore's poetry:

Halder's attempt[s] to demystify the writings of this celebrity, the first Indian Nobel prize winner, who was seen as a kind of national hero in his country, do not seem to have caused any negative reaction from the Bengali side.[64]

So much so that Halder presented the same paper a few years later to a wider audience at the Indian Science Congress—this time in English.

One reason for such 'tolerance' was public ignorance about Bose's world-view. Bose was not popularly known to the urban middle classes of India as a psychoanalyst, though that is usually what he called himself. Most Indians knew him as a doctor of the mind. They were relatively

---

[62]Kakar, *Stories from Indian Psychoanalysis.*
[63]Hartnack, 'Psychoanalysis and Colonialism', p. 151.
[64]Ibid., pp. 161–2.

unconcerned (*udāsīna* is the expression Bijayketu uses) about psycho-analysis. Girindrasekhar himself, as we shall see below, may have been obsessive about many things, but not about the purity of psychoana-lytic concepts, their philosophical roots in western thought, or about the therapetuic tradition being built in Europe by the Freudian move-ment. Nor did he stress that psychoanalysis was unique as a school of psychology.

Was psychoanalysis, then, merely an artefact in urban India's attempts to explore its own soul? Was it severely refracted through and, hence, incidental to Bose's personal quest for selfhood as a healer? That, too, is doubtful. It says something about the science that Bose, already ex-posed to a wide range of eastern and western options—from Patañjali's *Yogasūtra* to academic psychiatry to behaviourism and experimental psychology—should have chosen to call himself a psychoanalyst. Some-where, at some plane, the discipline's concerns and implicit social–critical thrust had crossed the boundaries of culture, though not in the sense in which its Viennese founder's Eurocentric world-view would have it.

On the other hand, one must hasten to add that Freud's Eurocentrism, too, had its in-built checks. The most conspicuous of them was his con-cern with the future of psychoanalysis. He did want the discipline to cross cultural barriers and become a truly international movement; when faced with a choice, therefore, the old war-horse did try to create a space for Bose's concerns within the mainstream of psychoanalysis. Perhaps in the case of Bose he was spared some of the anxieties that dogged his relationships with his European followers. Certainly in his treatment of Bose's work there was no reflection of the 'tragic flaw' in Freud's person-ality to which Peter Rudnytsky has again recently drawn our attention.[65] But that tolerance of Bose by the founding father of psychoanalysis had its own limits:

After corresponding with Bose and confronting his publications, . . . Freud could no longer easily defend his claims for the universality of his concepts. Confronted with Bose's deviant theory, Freud considered working aspects of Bose's concepts into his system. He evidently intended to functionalize Bose's contribution like some kind of intellectual raw material, and to incorporate them into his own theory, not realizing that these were based on an entirely different conceptual system.[66]

[65]Peter L. Rudnytsky, 'A Psychoanalytic Weltanschauung', *The Psychoanalytic Quarterly*, 1992, 79, pp. 289–305.
[66]Hartnack, 'Psychoanalysis and Colonialism', p. 192.

Part Two: The Morality of Psychology

III *The Relegitimation*

The compliment from Freud notwithstanding, Bose's English papers on
the range and concerns of psychology, especially psychoanalysis, lack
something of the philosophical imagination and elegance of his Bengali
papers on the same subject. The reasons for this are not clear. Perhaps he
was less at ease in English than in Bengali, being more self-conscious and
aware of an international audience when he wrote in English. It is even
possible that in Bengali he could more openly reconcile Indian classical
traditions and the science of psychoanalysis, not as two distinct cognitive
orders but as two aspects of his own self. Thus, while 'The Aim and Scope
of Psychology' (1932) and 'A New Theory of Mental Life' (1933) are
both competent and fresh, one misses in them the touches of theoretical
daring born of cultural self-confidence that one finds in some of his
Bengali papers.[67]

Both papers introduce the reader to the broad disciplinary framework
within which he, the first non-western psychoanalyst, worked and the
conceptual boundaries of his depth psychology. 'The Aim and the Scope'
specifically seeks to create a legitimate place for psychology in the world
of knowledge by anticipating and resisting attacks on the infant discipline
on three fronts. First, the paper rejects as invalid the behaviourist approach
in psychology, for behaviourists deny the existence of mind on the grounds
that mind cannot be perceived without the intervention of matter. Bose
considers the denial analogous to a physicist's rejection of the existence
of matter on the grounds that matter cannot be 'seen' without the
intervention of mind.[68] Second, the paper tries to reclaim from physiology
terrain that rightfully belongs to psychology. Bose rejects attempts to
reduce psychology to the functioning of the brain and the nervous system:
using the same arguments, one could then claim endocrinology was a
branch of psychology. If changes in psychological states follow changes
in the brain, glandular changes also follow from psychological changes.
The paper obviously does not suffer from the positivist modesty which
sometimes afflicted Freud. It does not even hint that in some distant future
psychology would in effect become the biology of the mind.[69] Finally,

[67]Girindrasekhar Bose, 'The Aim and Scope of Psychology', *Indian Journal of
Psychology*, July–Aug. 1932, 9, pp. 11–29; and 'A New Theory of Mental Life', *Indian
Journal of Psychology*, 1933, 10, pp. 37–157.

[68]Bose, 'The Aim and Scope', p. 13.

[69]Ibid., p. 14.

the paper takes on 'the oldest claimant to the psychological terrain', philosophy. Here Bose is more tolerant, given his own bent of mind, and he makes his point with qualifications. 'I am quite willing to admit that philosophical studies afford an excellent discipline to the science students but I cannot understand why it should be tacked on to psychology alone and not to any other science such as physics.'[70]

The second paper recapitulates Girindrasekhar's once-popular theory of pan-psychic psychophysical parallelism, first propounded in *Concept of Repression*. Now entirely forgotten, the theory was at one time taken seriously in many circles. It also subtly influenced the course of his friend Jagadis Chandra Bose's vitalistic biophysics, which took the world of knowledge by storm in the inter-war years.[71] The theory has parallels with Freud's belief in his student days that 'the physiological processes of the brain and the psychological processes of the mind were not parallel and causally linked but, rather, were identical. They were one and the same thing apprehended by the scientist in two different ways: through external observation in the natural sciences and through inner perception in psychological investigation.'[72] 'A New Theory' is unlikely to impress even a sympathetic psychologist reading it in the 1990s; it is likely to interest only the historians of science. For though it is the work of a psychologist well-versed in and committed to the non-dualist Vedantic tradition, it can be read as only a plea for a dualist psychology rooted in the Vedanta. The dualism, however, is a qualified one; it is set within the frame of a non-dualist vision and idiom.

In sum, while neither of the two papers reveals Bose's hand fully, both show that, unlike Freud and some of the early analysts, Bose made no attempt to underplay the philosophical and social meaning of the new science. Nor did he share Freud's belief that psychoanalytic therapy 'would be overtaken within half a century by biochemical therapies'.[73] On the contrary, he was not hesitant about making large claims for his discipline. 'We can look forward to the day', he grandly says at the end of 'The Aim and Scope', 'when Psychology [note the capital] will establish itself as our guide, friend and philosopher in all human affairs, and will be looked upon as the greatest of sciences.'[74]

[70]Ibid., p. 16.
[71]See Nandy, *Alternative Sciences*, Part II.
[72]William J. McGrawth, *Freud's Discovery of Psychoanalysis: The Politics of Hysteria* (Ithaca and London: Cornell University Press, 1986), p. 18.
[73]*Psychoanalysis and Faith: The Letters of Sigmund Freud and Oscar Pfister* (London: Hogarth, 1963), quoted in Jahoda, *Freud and the Dilemmas*, p. 10.
[74]Bose, 'The Aim and Scope', p. 29.

In Bengali, Girindrasekhar Bose wrote voluminously and with enormous intellectual energy. (Most of these writings are now out of print and not easily available; some of his essays and important letters are lost.) The most remarkable feature of his Bengali writings is that, when on India's sacred texts and epics, they were often surprisingly unencumbered by his disciplinary faith. Thus, his *Purāṇa Praveśa*, a three-hundred-page tome on the Indian epics, is mainly a meticulous—some may say Teutonic—study of genealogy, a chronological dynastic history of the *purāṇas*, not a study of fantasies or defences.[75] There are, however, in the book fascinating comments on the politics of scholarship and the responsibility imposed on Indian commentators on the *purāṇas*. We shall touch on this later. Similarly, there is the low-key presence of psychoanalysis in his commentary on the Gita, as we have already noted. All this 'restraint' was observed at a time when the analysis of myths and religious texts had already become, thanks to Freud himself and to younger psychoanalysts like Ernest Jones and Geiza Roheim, an important and fashionable part of psychoanalysis and even in distant India some had experimented with such analysis.

However, Bose did write a few perceptive essays in Bengali which help to link his reading of Indian culture to the Freudian theory of mental life. Unlike Berkeley-Hill and others who followed him, in these essays Bose did not use psychoanalysis solely to demystify Indian culture and everyday life or to bare the pathologies of western middle-class culture in the colonies. He also used Indian cultural categories to domesticate psychoanalysis for Indians. From this point of view, his two most important papers are: '*Sattva, Rajaḥ, Tamaḥ*' and '*Mānuṣer Mana*', both written in Bengali and published in 1930.[76] Some of the ideas in the essays were later included in his English works but they lacked the same directness. The first essay offers an understanding and justification of psychological knowledge in native terms, leading up to the Freudian tenet that the ego should ultimately supplant or supersede the id. The second extends the argument further and defines psychology as a science of persons, a personology, as Henry A. Murray might have described the venture.

Both papers depend on Indian classical texts and on a particular reading of India's past. The second dependence has however to be gleaned

---

[75]Girindrasekhar Bose, *Purāṇa Praveśa* (Calcutta: M.C. Sarkar, 1934).
[76]Girindrasekhar Bose, '*Sattva, Rajaḥ, Tamaḥ*', *Pravāsī*, 1930, 30, part 2(1), pp. 1–5; Girindrasekhar Bose, '*Mānuṣer Mana*', *Pravāsī*, Āsād 1337 (1930), 30, part 1(3), pp. 339–53.

from Bose's other Bengali writings. Thus, from *Purāṇa Praveśa*, also written in 1933 though only published the following year, we come to know of Bose's conviction that foreign—read western—historians of India are bound to be partial. They cannot be fair to the Indian texts because they think of themselves as a superior race. To expect an impartial history of India from the *videśīs* or foreigners is, Bose says, the same as expecting the British to protect Indian self-interests in politics.[77] Bose tries to correct for such racist interpretations by proposing that the *purāṇas* are supported both by reason and empirical data.[78] There is no need to study the history of these epics, for they themselves are the Indian equivalent of history.[79]

Then, responding as it were to Berkeley-Hill, Bose mentions the two kinds of exaggeration to which Hindus are allegedly given: the fantastic exaggerations in the *purāṇas* (*atiranjana*) and the exaggeration of the past achievements of their culture. As for the former, Bose believes that the stylized exaggerations of the *purāṇas* can be handled through *atyukti vicāra*, analysis of overstatement. It is a question of appropriate and empathetic reading of texts. Bose's response to the second issue is more political. He traces the hostility of western scholars to things Indian to two main causes. First, Indians, unlike the ancient Babylonians or Egyptians, have survived to flaunt their glorious past against their inglorious present status as colonial subjects.[80] This cannot but infuriate many westerners. Second, western scholars project into the Indian situation the enmity between Church and State existing in Europe. This makes them hostile to Hinduism and virulently anti-Brahminic.[81] Under such circumstances, given that the organizing principle of Indian culture has always been religion, any serious consideration of India's past cultural achievements is bound to look like an exaggeration.

'Sattva, Rajaḥ, Tamaḥ' discusses *guṇas* (traits, attributes or qualities) in *prakṛti* or nature. The concept of *guṇa* is notoriously complicated and, some may say, slippery. The essay mentions in a footnote that even Max Müller found it difficult to understand the concept, but found Indian philosophers so clear about it that no explanation was needed.[82] The essay suggests that these qualities are of two kinds: *guṇas* that control *ajñāna* or the absence of knowledge (in a person) and *aprakāśa* or the non-manifest (in nature) are classified as *tamaḥ*.

---

[77] Ibid., p. 212.
[78] Ibid., pp. 1, 3.
[79] Ibid., p. 179.
[80] Ibid., pp. 212–13.
[81] Ibid.
[82] Max Müller, quoted in Bose, 'Sattva, Rajaḥ, Tamaḥ', p. 3.

The second kind of *guṇa* controls *jñāna* or knowledge (in human personality) and the manifest (in nature). These *guṇas* can, in turn, be of two types: *bahirmukha*, literally outer-directed or extroversive and *antarmukha*, inner-directed or introversive. The essay identified the former as *rajaḥ*; and the latter as *sattva*.[83] Bose summarized his argument in the following manner:

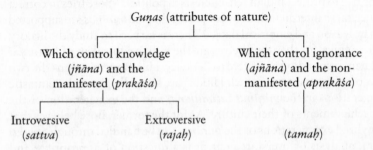

Guṇas (attributes of nature)

Which control knowledge (*jñāna*) and the manifested (*prakāśa*)

Which control ignorance (*ajñāna*) and the non-manifested (*aprakāśa*)

Introversive (*sattva*)   Extroversive (*rajaḥ*)   (*tamaḥ*)

It is not clear whether Bose borrows the second-order dichotomy— between extroversion and introversion—from Carl Jung, who had published his work on personality types in 1923.[84] The work should have reached Calcutta by the time Bose wrote his essay in 1930. On the other hand, the impact of Jung on the first generation of Indian psychoanalysts was limited, despite the overlap between his theories and aspects of traditional Indian thought. This is surprising when one remembers that Bose and some of his associates were well-versed in traditional philosophy and should have found Jung especially attractive. As inexplicable seems the fact that, though Jung visited India in 1938 and it was a triumphant visit, Bose probably did not meet him.[85]

Were these measures of the loyalty of the Indian group to psychoanalytic orthodoxy, as Hartnack assumes?[86] Were Indian psychoanalysts repelled by Jung's inadequate knowledge of Indian traditions, as some of them were to later claim? Or did Freud meet some deeper needs in Indians, who were searching at the time not so much for in-house criticisms as for a critical theory adequately discontinuous with a psychologically minded culture and able to serve as a radical critique of it? Probably the latter;

[83]Bose, '*Sattva, Rajaḥ, Tamaḥ*', p. 3.

[84]Carl G. Jung, *Psychological Types* (New York: Harcourt Brace, 1923).

[85]Hartnack, 'Psychoanalysis and Colonialism', p. 93; Bose's student Charuchandra Bhattacharya says that Bose probably met Jung but did not have any extended exchange with him.

[86]Ibid.

Jung probably was too close to India to serve as a base for social criticism or to avoid cultural incorporation of the kind Bose nearly brought off in the case of Freud. We shall come back to this point.

What emerges clearly is the hierarchy Bose imposes on the entire set of *guṇas*. Like Freud, he believes that the unconscious and the non-manifest (together constituting the *tamaḥ*) represent an inferior level of personality functioning. Unlike Freud and Jung but like a true Hindu, Bose extends this hierarchy to extroversion and introversion. In his model, the extroverted or *rājasika* becomes inferior to the introverted, seen as definitionally more *sāttvika*.[87] However, the hierarchy has no social-evolutionist thrust, of the kind that permeates the work of psychologists such as Abraham Maslow. Nowhere does Bose imply that only after the basic needs of a person have been met can he or she graduate to intro-version as part of a developmental profile.[88] As in Jung, the hierarchy remains in essence a classificatory scheme.

Bose goes on to say that the *ātmā* or self is *bhūmā* or all-pervasive; it pervades all nature.[89] Compared to *ātmā*, nature is narrower and more limited. And it is not so much the knowledge of self but the relationship between self and nature that is the stuff of genuine knowledge. The *śāstrakāras* or writers of sacred texts in India were primarily concerned, according to Bose, with this relationship. For the knowledge of this rela-tionship can be truly emancipatory.[90] I should emphasize that the few concepts verging on technical psychoanalytic terms in the paragraphs above are mine, not Bose's. The entire essay, though it provides an excel-lent indirect comparison between some aspects of the traditional Indian theory of the person and psychoanalysis, seems strangely oblivious of its own range. There is no direct mention of any psychoanalytic concept in the essay.

Bose offsets his typology of *guṇas* with the proposition that awareness of—or encounter with—the self is the same as the awareness of the ultimate reality of being and God. In his scheme, the *ātmāsakṣātkārī*, one who encounters one's own self, is automatically a *brahmasākṣātkārāī*, one who encounters/confronts the absolute, and *atmajñāna* (self-

---

[87]Bose, 'Sattva Rajaḥ, Tamaḥ', p. 3.
[88]See a discussion of this issue in Ashis Nandy, 'The Idea of Development: The Experience of Modern Psychology as a Cautionary Tale', in Carlos Mallmann and Oscar Nudler (eds.), *Human Development in Its Social Context: A Collective Exploration* (London: Hodder and Stoughton, 1986), pp. 248–59.
[89]Bose, 'Sattva, Rajaḥ, Tamaḥ', p. 3.
[90]Ibid.

knowledge) is *brahmajñāna* (knowledge of the absolute). One must, therefore, know *ātmā*; *ātmānam viddhi*, know thyself.[91]

Further, *antarmukha jñāna* or inner-directed knowledge is the knowledge of pure experience or awareness, whereas *bahirmukha jñāna* is material knowledge. 'From pure experience gradually grows pure knowledge . . . . In pure knowledge there is no plurality (*nānātva*). *Na iha nānāsti kiñcana*.'[92] This pure knowledge is self-knowledge and, therefore, knowledge of the absolute. It defines the nature of the soul. So the non-duality that sacrificed for the sake of the mind–body duality in Bose's concept of psychology is restored at another plane. (Elsewhere, Bose equates pure consciousness with the state of *samādhi* as described in Patañjali's *Yogasūtra*.)[93]

Obviously, Bose is here trying to locate contemporary psychology in the Indian experience and to legitimize the discipline as a natural outgrowth of traditional knowledge. As it happens, the space thus created for psychology also accommodates a heavily textual version of Advaita as the core of Indian consciousness. The psychologist is the ultimate scientist because he or she tries to look within. Psychology is *sāttvika*; so is the psychologist's work. The work of the psychiatrist and the psychotherapist, like that of the physicist and the chemist, is applied or instrumental and, hence, *rājasika*.[94] When counterpoised against Bose's formal emphasis on the therapeutics of psychoanalysis, this proposition makes strange reading. It is as if, after justifying psychoanalysis in terms of its *sāttvika* content, Bose is pleading for a less exalted *rājasika* role for it.

The second proposition of the essay is to define the individual as the ultimate unit of intellectual and, presumably, social analysis. Bose quotes from the *Kauṣītaki Upaniṣad*:

Do not try to understand speech; try to understand the speaker. Do not try to know smell; try to know the smeller. Do not try to know beauty; try to know the beautician; do not try to understand words; try to understand the listener . . . . do not try to know the deed (*karma*); try to know the doer (*kartā*). Do not try to understand the mind; try to understand the thinker.[95]

As opposed to the first proposition, which is clearly identifiable with aspects of Vedantic thought, the second goes directly against some of the

[91]Ibid.

[92]Ibid., pp. 3–4.

[93]Girindrasekhar Bose, quoted in Hartnack, 'Psychoanalysis and Colonialism', p. 98.

[94]Bose, '*Sattva, Rajaḥ, Tamaḥ*', p. 5.

[95]*Kauṣītaki Upaniṣad*, tr. Sitānāth Tattvabhuśana, quoted in Bose, '*Sattva, Rajaḥ, Tamaḥ*', p. 4.

most influential readings of the Vedanta. For Bose does not emphasize essence or platonic quality; he emphasizes the carrier of the essence. One suspects that he needed this sanction for using the individual as the basic unit of analysis both as a psychologist and as an urban Indian being constantly exposed to a wide variety of new institutions ideologically wedded to individualism.

A few other propositions emerge from '*Mānuṣer Mana*' as by-products of Bose's unselfconscious attempt to break out of the regime of the positive sciences. Science has become a fashionable word, Bose says, and it is invoked as an 'explanation' even for magical episodes in the Indian epics and rituals by Indians defensively seeking to give the episodes some respectability in contemporary times. This is natural, Bose feels, for wherever a science becomes popular, it produces its counterpoint, an *apavijñāna* (false or bad science).[96] To avoid the pitfalls of such cheap scientism, he justifies psychoanalysis, and psychology in general, in larger philosophical terms.

To Bose it is natural that psychology is a new science, the last science to crystallize as a separate discipline, for human beings are more interested in the outside world than in the inner.[97] According to the *Kaṭhopaniṣad*, God has created human beings as *bahirmukha*: our sense organs are oriented to externalities. A few serene persons (*dhīravyakti*) very occasionally cross the barrier of attachment to the outside world, to face and examine the self. From the wishes of this minority arises the need for *ātmadarśana*. According to the sacred texts *ātmajñana* or self-knowledge is impossible unless the mind becomes inner-directed.[98]

> *Parāñcikhāni vyatṛnat svayambhūḥ*
> *Tasmāt parāk paśyati nāntarātman*
> *Kaściddhīrāḥ pratyagātmānamaikṣa-*
> *dāvṛtta cakṣuramṛtattvamicchan*

Hence the small number of psychologists in the world. Bose implies that most people, being extroverted, are driven by emotions like anger and fear; when angry and fearful, we do not examine the internal changes in us.[99]

In other words, from the point of view of the Hindu *śāstras*, psychology is the highest of the sciences.[100] The growth of psychology is not merely

[96]Bose, '*Mānuṣer Mana*', pp. 339, 349.
[97]Ibid., p. 339.
[98]Ibid.
[99]Ibid.
[100]Ibid., p. 340.

an expression of the intrinsic power of the Indian civilization but also a marker of the intellectual and cultural maturity of Indians. This growth has a disciplinary meaning, too. Bose believes that as a science develops, its boundaries are better defined. By defining the boundaries of psychology more clearly, he is helping the science to grow.[101]

'*Mānuṣer mana*', a slighter essay, makes three other points. First, it relates psychological awareness to the study of sensibility and draws the readers' attention to the scientific works of Jagadis Chandra Bose which show that there can be sensibility even in inert objects. After Jagadis Chandra, to assert the presence of such sensibility is no longer a form of mysticism, the essay claims.[102] Second, there is an untearable (*acchedya*) chain of causality which ties together the entire material world.[103] This makes causality—presumably a scientific category—a special case of and intrinsic to the monistic vision of life. Third, at a more practical level, the essay affirms that the idea of the unconscious unburdens the individual of the need to believe in superstitions such as ghosts. Acceptance of the unconscious does not secularize one's world, for the unconscious is not particularly incompatible with spirituality, but it cures one of pseudo-spirituality:

Human beings usually try to attain happiness by extending their control over the external world. All the material sciences help men in this endeavour. The Hindu *śāstras* advise that there is no permanent happiness in external objects; genuine happiness comes from restraint over mind (*manaḥsanyama*). The serene person (*dhīraprajña*) is happy under all circumstances. To keep the mind under control, many advices/suggestions are given for rituals, institutions and asceticisms. Reduction of ignorance [unconscious?] is a way of attaining happiness and peace. The scientist of the unconscious (*nirjñānvit*) assures us that when the dammed instincts subside, the conflicts of mind dissolve and all sorrows are eliminated. Till now, the source of peace for the disturbed mind, tortured by mourning, anxiety, tiredness, lay in the moral lessons given by the religions. In this respect, the material scientist had to admit defeat at the hands of the religious preachers. Today, psychology, by offering human beings words of assurance and peace, has moved ahead to establish the dignity of science.[104]

Thus, the fate of the science of the unconscious, human happiness, and the dignity of science converge in the step-wise unravelling and

---

[101]Ibid.
[102]Ibid., pp. 346–7.
[103]Ibid., p. 347.
[104]Ibid., p. 353.

transcendence of the *guṇas*. According to the *śāstras*, Bose acknowledges, all three *guṇas* are hindrances to self-realization but, of the three, inner-directedness poses the least problem.[105] Ultimately though, he says, one must rise above one's attachment to the way—even when it is inner-directedness and even when it goes with the analytic attitude—to reach one's destination.[106] But, in the meanwhile, unravelling the *tāmasika guṇas* by focusing on inner experiences must become an important part of the agenda of any worthwhile theory of consciousness. Psychology, when it establishes the dignity of science, is presumably no longer a positivist science, but science as a philosophy of consciousness. It emancipates science from its own straitjacket, as Jagadis Chandra Bose's plant physiology has done.

Apparently the latent critical–moral stance of early psychoanalysis in India came from this tacit equation between the *tāmasika guṇas* and the instinctual impulses. Analytic interpretation became not merely a cognitive venture or an instrument of therapy, but also a moral statement and a form of social criticism. Freud did not like to view his infant science as a philosophy of life and he would have shuddered to think of it as a moral statement—Philip Rieff or no.[107] Some of Freud's first patients were even made to feel that 'he was not at all interested in politics, ethics or philosophy of life'.[108] And the admiring Fritz Wittels, despite his belief that the master was 'too profound a person not to grasp the need for a *Weltanschauung*',[109] could not avoid confronting Freud's own statement made in 1926: 'I must confess I am not at all partial to the fabrication of *Weltanschauungen*. Such activities may be left to philosophers.[110]

Bose had no such inhibitions when writing in the vernacular. His attempts to limit the critical–moral role of psychoanalysis and his stress on the therapeutic role of the discipline were not evidently the whole story. Nor, for that matter, was Freud's avoidance of philosophy and

---

[105]Ibid., p. 5.

[106]Ibid.

[107]Philip Rieff, *Freud: The Mind of the Moralist* (New York: Doubleday, 1959).

[108]Roazen, *Freud and His Followers*, p. 512.

[109]Fritz Wittels, *Freud and His Time: The Influence of the Master Psychologist on the Emotional Problems of Our Lives* (London: Peter Owen, 1956), p. 52.

[110]Sigmund Freud, 'Inhibitions, Symptoms and Anxiety' (1925), in James Stretchy (ed.), *The Standard Edition of the Complete Psychological Works of Sigmund Freud* (London: Hogarth, 1959), 20, pp. 75–175; see p. 96. Freud had already declared a year earlier, 'even where I refrained from observation, I carefully avoided approach to actual philosophy. Constitutional incapacity rendered such self-restraint easy for me.' Sigmund Freud (1925), quoted in Wittels, *Freud and His Time*, p. 50.

world-views. I like to believe that the work of Berkeley-Hill and Daly had shown Bose that the declared value-neutrality of psychoanalysis was no guarantee against latent moral judgements tilted in favour of the powerful. But one can never be sure that the Indian read his British colleagues that way. What we know for certain is that at least one part of Bose, a part that was a not-too-secret self either, would have ceased to be what it was if it gave up its philosophical and ethical moorings. Like early analysts such as Wilhelm Reich and Karen Horney who sought an element of social criticism in their therapeutics even at the cost of therapeutic 'finesse' and methodological 'sanity', Bose would have found psychoanalytic ego psychology in particular and the highly professionalized psychoanalysis of the Anglo-Saxon world in general, anti-analytic. This despite the subsequent career of the discipline in his own country, a career that he himself helped to shape.

IV *The Fate of Psychology*

Girindrasekhar Bose was not the only person to create a space for western psychology in Indian public life and the culture of healing. Nor were his works, especially his English works, free of inelegance, crudity and simplification. But he was certainly the most colourful and robust figure to emerge in the world of Indian psychology in the first half of this century. No one since his time has moved back and forth so daringly and freely between the implicit psychology of traditional Indian thought, academic psychology, and psychoanalysis.

He obtained this freedom by operating at two levels: by emphasizing the organizational needs and the therapeutic role of psychoanalysis for his western and westernizing pan-Indian audience and by disembedding the discipline from its cultural moorings in the West to relocate it in Indian high culture and in the bicultural lifestyle of the urban middle classes in colonial India.

The first was by design, and it made him into yet another high priest of the-transfer-of-technology model that reigned supreme in the academic circles of India at the time. The latter was by default and that unintended dissent gave him his intellectual robustness. But the dissent, by the logic of his life experiences and personality, had to remain partial. Bose did believe the Sanskritic tradition to be the core of Indianness and, his exposure to and assessment of the little traditions of India being what they were, he could not help looking at the world of knowledge through the eyes of the babu. On the other hand, even this partial dissent paid him rich dividends. Though he often was 'too logical' and 'mechanical'—

the judgement was Freud's—when writing in English, he wrote in Bengali as if he had anticipated the adage of Christopher Lasch that, in an age that had forgotten theory, 'theory had to begin in remembrance'.[111]

As this narrative has shown, the memories Bose chose to excavate were not random ones. They were selected and shaped by his personality, which in turn mirrored the experiences of a civilization and the anguish of an age and a class. Naturally, the memories had their own half-life. While they let modern psychology go native and acquire a moral standing in local terms, they also narrowed the discipline's social base. This base sustained the young discipline as a sectarian profession and therapeutic technique, not as a cultural critique. Like many other imported systems of knowledge and some of the new theologies, reform movements, and refurbished cults in South Asia that began spectacularly and then withered away, psychology, too, gradually lost its sense of adventure and wider social appeal to become a 'proper' vocation.

During his lifetime, however, Bose did manage to keep it a significant presence in Indian intellectual life. That would have been a harder task had he not been living in Calcutta in near-total isolation from the day-to-day culture of psychoanalysis in Europe and North America. For the isolation allowed Bose to take advantage of a contradiction in the European culture of science which got telescoped into Freud's self-definition and which the late nineteenth-century Viennese medicine man was never able to reconcile in his life or work. It was this contradiction that made Freud's vision a Shakespearian one for some like Lionel Trilling.

The contradiction was defined by a number of polarities, not all of them orthogonal: the metaphysical versus the applied or the narrowly empirical; the clinical versus the experimental; the intuitive and aesthetic versus the tough-minded and the objective; and, above all, between Freud the holistic healer and social critic inspired by the romantic tradition of science versus Freud the heroic, masculine scientist-engineer and pioneer of a new theoretical school, self-consciously speaking the language of hard-eyed positivism.[112] Some of these polarities were to survive in a

---

[111]Christopher Lasch, 'Introduction', in Russell Jacoby, *Social Amnesia: A Critique of Conformist Psychology from Adler to Laing* (Hassock, U.K.: Harvester 1975), pp. vii–xv; see p. vii.

[112]A roughly comparable dichotomy is between critical and professionalized psychoanalysis used by Kirsner in 'Is There a Future?' Kirsner's dichotomy hinges on his understanding of where Freud's real interest lay. He quotes Freud's statement that the analytic relationship is based on 'a love of truth' and the prime interest of psychoanalysis is to find out what resistances this love of truth meets and the 'mental, theoretical and institutional formations based on our need to *avoid* the truth' (ibid.,

few of his followers and in the disciplinary culture they built, though they had to drive underground the culturally less acceptable ends of the polarities, for fear of the social and professional costs of their dissenting philosophy and politics.[113]

But first a word on Freud's self-definition as a scientist. Freud was the product of a culture of science within which German romanticism was not quite dead. For though he lived well into the twentieth century, he really belonged to the previous one. By his own admission, he decided to study medicine after reading Goethe's evocative essay on nature, and he was exposed through his friend Wilhelm Fliess to romantic medicine, many of the assumptions of which came from the *naturphilosophie* of Schelling.[114] The exposure was deep enough for Robert Holt to trace to it one entire genre of Freud's work. Holt calls the genre 'phylogenetic theory' and includes in it books such as *Totem and Taboo*, *Beyond the Pleasure Principle*, *Group Psychology and the Analysis of the Ego*, *The Future of an Illusion*, *Civilization and its Discontents*, and *Moses and Monotheism*.

Holt's paper was published in 1963 and there is in the author, as in Freud, a clear touch of ambivalence towards such speculative stuff. Within ten years, Iago Gladston is already less apologetic on behalf of Freud and considers the romantic tradition so central to Freud as to call him 'an ethologist and ecological and holistic scientist'.[115]

The culture of science that sustained Freud as a holistic scientist was, however, one into which the experimental method and the idiom of positivism had made heavy inroads. George Rosen succinctly evokes the changing culture of science when Freud was a student and a young researcher, especially the way four young experimentalists—Ernst Brucke, Emil du Bois-Reymond, Hermann Helmholtz, and Carl Ludwig—came to set the tone of late nineteenth-century German science.[116] Within

---

p. 181). Professionalized psychoanalysis, on the other hand, is heavily dependent on what Freud calls 'therapeutic ambition', which he sees as 'only half way useful for science'. For such ambition is 'too tendentious' (ibid., p. 182).

[113]See. e.g., Russell Jacoby, *The Repression of Psychoanalysis: Otto Fenichel and the Political Freudians* (New York: Basic Books, 1983).

[114]Robert R. Holt, 'Two Influences on Freud's Scientific Thought: A Fragment on Intellectual Biography', in Robert W. White (ed.), *The Study of Lives: Essays in Honour of Henry A. Murray* (New York: Atherton, 1963), pp. 364–87.

[115]Iago Gladston, 'Freud and Romantic Medicine', in Cioffi, *Freud*, pp. 103–23; see pp. 109–10.

[116]George Rosen, 'Freud and Medicine', in Jonathan Miller (ed.), *Freud: The Man, His World, His Influence* (London: Weidenfeld and Nicolson, 1972), pp. 21–39; see esp. pp. 27–9.

twenty-five years these four men had realized their youthful dream: they had not merely become the leaders of scientific physiology in the German language area, they and their students were a major influence in the entire western community of medical researchers. As it happened, it was in Brucke's laboratory that young Freud honed his self-concept as a scientist. Holt, in fact, considers it ironic that the 'attraction to a poetic, metaphysical, grandiosely encompassing approach to nature led Freud into medicine and thus into the University of Vienna Medical School, a hotbed of physicalistic physiology'.[117]

The heart of the project of the four researchers was their tough-minded experimentalism. They had prised out the disciplines of physiology and pathology from the clinic and relocated them in the laboratory. These were now independent basic sciences which employed the precise methods of the natural sciences. Clinical observations were now at a discount. Rosen writes:

Brucke and his friends were in the forefront of a generational movement. They were members of a generation of young physicians who insisted that medical problems receive scientific treatment based more on laboratory experimentation and less on clinical observation . . . .

Underpinning this mode of thought was a philosophical position . . . . Life was equated with matter and energy, so that their genesis and development had to be studied and explained in material terms, that is, in terms of the chemical and physical forces that determine these processes, and thus ultimately on the basis of the impersonal, objective laws of nature. Intention and purpose had no place in such an approach to biological phenomena. This doctrine, comprising positivism, mechanism and materialism, was the philosophy to which Freud was exposed during his formative years as a medical student and young physician. Transmitted to him by those with whom he had chosen to identify, it was a major factor in the formation of his mode of thought and his self-image as a scientist.[118]

Beyond these exposures lay Freud's own need for social recognition and self-acceptance. Recent work suggests that his family background was one of East European Jews exposed to Hassidic influence. Later his family moved from eastern Europe to Germanic countries, first Czechoslovakia and then Austria. But the earlier exposures did not entirely wear off; he had a much more traditional upbringing than he ever publicly admitted. As a result he struggled not merely with his Jewish self as denigrated by the gentile world but also with his non-Germanic self which

[117]Holt, 'Two Influences on Freud's Scientific Thought', p. 370.
[118]Rosen, 'Freud and Medicine', pp. 28–9.

was looked down on by German Jews as open to non-rational mystical influences.[119]

The basic contradiction in Freud, therefore, was between the inner logic of clinical work which demanded a set of categories that came from myths, fantasies, and self-analysis, and a philosophy of science which demanded a different language of self-expression. The conflict between his emotions and reason sharpened the contradiction. Billa Zanuso goes so far as to suggest that 'there is not a single trait of his character, not a decision he made nor an incident in his life, that cannot be interpreted in two different ways' due to this conflict.[120]

For an outsider to the western world these fissures within Freud opened up immense possibilities, some of them invisible to those close to Freud culturally. The most important was the scope to construct a Freud who could be used as a radical critic of the savage world and, at the same time, a subverter of the imperial structures of thought that had turned the South into a dumping ground for dead and moribund categories of the Victorian era. Whether the possibility was fully explored by the likes of Bose or not is, of course, another issue.

Before we deal with that issue, let me spell out the nature of the conflict within Freud himself in some more detail.

As a school of thought, psychoanalysis acquired its political thrust from being part of the western critical tradition. It was a tradition to which a galaxy of thinkers from Giovanni Vico to Frederich Nieztsche to Karl Marx had contributed. As part of the tradition, Freud expanded the Enlightenment vision of a desirable society and sharpened its major methodological weapon, demystification.

However, this participation in the Enlightenment project was overlaid by certain insecurities and ambivalences in Freud towards the relationship between science and philosophy. Even a person as blinkered as Jones, who spent all his life reading and defending Freud as a hard-boiled positivist, admitted that as a young man, Freud had an early but 'thoroughly checked tendency to philosophize'.[121] Only after a decade-long détour by way of the medical–biological sciences had Freud been

---

[119]Yosef Hayim Yerushalmi, *Freud's Moses: Judaism Terminable and Interminable* (New Haven: Yale University Press, 1991). I am grateful to Alan Roland for drawing my attention to this part of the story.

[120]Billa Zanuso, *The Young Freud: The Origins of Psychoanalysis in Late Nineteenth-Century Viennese Culture* (Oxford: Basil Blackwell, 1986), pp. 64–86, esp. pp. 73–5.

[121]Ernest Jones, quoted in Roazen, *Freud and His Followers*, p. 24.

able, at an advanced age, to return to the problems of philosophy and religious psychology.[122] Holt is truer to the grain of psychoanalysis when he turns to the problem. He points to the

many indications that Freud's earlier inclination towards speculative psychology was something against which he felt a very strong need to defend himself . . . . [The] involvement of conflict and defence is perhaps more convincing when one reflects that Freud took no less than five courses in philosophy . . . during his eight years in the university, when he was supposedly studying medicine.[123]

Others have contextualized this defensiveness by identifying cultural influences on Freud that had an older, 'less respectable' pedigree, against which, too, he had to defend himself. David Bakan, for instance, has made an impressive case that Jewish mystical traditions found identifiable, if convoluted, expression in the master's work.[124] Still others have discovered in Freud the negation of at least some aspects of the Enlightenment culture of science. Some of them have used the discovery to denigrate psychoanalysis as anti-positivist and counter-modernist.[125] However, as the nineteenth-century concept of science itself has suffered a decline, scholars in recent decades have been more tolerant of these 'disreputable' aspects of psychoanalysis. Thus, unlike his forebears, Gladston is neither derisive nor defensive when he says:

Freud has been compared to Darwin, to Newton, and to Copernicus. I concur in these comparisons. Yet, to my mind there is one man he truly resembles— not in any other respect—but in the signature of his personality—that man is Paracelsus.[126]

Nor is Friederich Heer hesitant to admit that Freud's tragic vision implied a rejection of 'the simplest Anglo-American belief in the virtues of progress.'[127]

Freud himself, however, having driven underground his other self, worked hard to retain and use the idiom of tough-minded psychology.

---

[122]Sigmund Freud to Fredrich Eckstein, quoted in McGrath, *Freud's Discovery*, p. 94.

[123]Holt, 'Two Influences on Freud's Scientific Thought', p. 371.

[124]David Bakan, *Sigmund Freud and the Jewish Mystical Tradition* (Princeton, N.J.: Van Nostrand, 1958).

[125]For example, Hans J. Eysenck, *Fact and Fiction in Psychology* (Baltimore: Penguin, 1965); and *The Decline and Fall of the Freudian Empire* (London: Viking, 1985).

[126]Gladston, 'Freud and Romantic Medicine', p. 121.

[127]Friedrich Heer, 'Freud the Viennese Jew', tr. W.A. Littlewood, in Miller, *Freud*, pp. 22–39; see p. 24.

He was always fearful that psychoanalysis might otherwise be accepted
not as a positive science but as a cultural artefact or philosophical specu-
lation. One suspects that he avoided developing a world-view because he
feared the outlines of the world-view he sensed within himself, 'Is
Freud ... a metaphysician?', Egon Friedell asks and goes on to answer, 'Yes,
but he does not know it'.[128] Perhaps Freud knew but feared the knowledge.

The world-view Freud disowned was 'rooted in the culture of the late
German Enlightenment with its interest in the exploration of dreams,
emotions, and other mysterious phenomena in man's inner world.'[129]
To the first psychoanalyst, seeking academic credibility, that world-view
must have looked overly open to the culture of science associated with
the German romantic tradition. He could warmly endorse Bose's work,
blatantly philosophical though it was, because that was what the Hindus
were known for and could get away with. He himself had to be more
circumspect.

This other—and according to Bruno Bettelheim, more mature and
humanistic—Freud, who emerged from the shadows only when he was
in his late fifties, was unknown in the popular cultures of the West and
the East during the days psychoanalysis was spreading to distant corners
of the globe.[130] To most western-educated Indians, as to much of the
Anglo-American world, what mattered were the comparisons being made
between Freud, on the one hand, and Copernicus, Newton, and Darwin,
on the other. These comparisons invoked connections that made
psychoanalysis a positive science, an exportable technology, and an index
of progress. They tied mainstream psychoanalysis not merely to the
European Enlightenment, but also to the triumphalism of nineteenth-
century European science. The other psychoanalysis survived, as did the
other Freud, in the cracks of the modern consciousness, as reminders of
an underside of the discipline that, regrettably, existed but should not be
owned up.

As it happened, the Enlightenment vision, of which the dominant
culture of psychoanalysis and the positivist sciences were now valued parts,
came to India neither through apolitical cognitive choices nor through
'natural' cultural diffusion. They came to India through colonialism,
riding piggy-back on Baconian science, the utilitarian theory of progress,

[128]Egon Friedell, quoted in Rosen, 'Freud and Medicine', pp. 23–4.

[129]McGrath, *Freud's Discovery*, p. 93.

[130]According to Bettelheim, this was mainly due to the destruction of the
European traditions of psychoanalysis by the rise of the Nazis and shift in the locus
of psychoanalytic activities to the Anglo-Saxon cultures and the faulty English
translations through which Freud's works came to be known in large parts of the
world. Bruno Bettelheim, *Freud and Man's Soul* (London: Fontana, 1985).

evangelical Christianity, and their practical extension, the British colonial theory of a civilizing mission. Together they sought to systematically subvert a way of life and devalue all surviving native systems of knowledge. When the vision won over sections of the Indian middle classes, it also won over people who, however creative in other ways, were to constitute an emerging class of intellectual compradors. As if the new psychological man in India had to be, by definition, a colonial subject. As if psychology had to be, by definition again, the latest in a series of techniques of retooling Indians into a prescribed version of the nineteenth-century European.

Bose's vernacular self tried to find a way out of the predicament by rediscovering an older version of psychological man in a traditionally psychologically minded society. He probably hoped that this discovery would anchor the new discipline outside the colonial progressivist discourse. It did not. In his own professional life, there were signs that the culture of Indian psychology was being integrated within the dominant global culture of psychology, its 'fangs' safely removed. By the time Bose died in 1953, he was already being seen both in India and abroad as a pioneer whose days were past. It is not insignificant that when he died many of the major international journals of psychoanalysis did not publish obituaries. Such slights did not burden Indian psychoanalysts overmuch. Even in Calcutta, where it all began, any 'critical engagement with received theory' was soon almost to disappear.[131]

For the moment, let us not ask whether or not such a colonial connection was inevitable for Enlightenment values, given their links with three processes that were to ensure the creation and substantiation of the concept of the Third World as a territorial and cultural category in the post-colonial dispensation—the search for the absolute secularization and objectification of the world and for total control of nature, including human nature, through science; the primacy given to history as a form of consciousness and as a way of constructing the past; and the hierarchy of cultures and social evolutionism written into the bond the Enlightenment forged between power and knowledge. The fact remains that the Enlightenment vision—especially its progeny, the Baconian philosophy of science—did systematically underwrite in Asia and Africa colonial theories of progress and the stratarchy of cultures and races.[132] Granting the emancipatory role this vision might have played in Europe, it was

[131]Kakar, 'Stories From Psychoanalysis', p. 433.

[132]Jatinder K. Bajaj, 'Francis Bacon, the First Philosopher of Modern Science: A Non-Western View', in Ashis Nandy (ed.), *Science, Hegemony and Violence: A Requiem for Modernity* (New Delhi: Oxford University Press, 1988), pp. 24–67.

impossible to ignore its racist content and oppressive associations for the Southern world.

Any serious critique of cultures in British India had to take into account this anomaly. Even when accepting psychoanalysis as emancipatory in principle, such a critique had to turn it into a means of concurrently criticizing the native culture and the packaged progressivist discourse available as a legitimating ideology for colonial domination. That is, the analytic attitude, which Philip Rieff believes lies at the heart of the Freudian project,[133] had to bear a dual responsibility in India. It had to be self-critical at two planes: it had to demystify aspects of Indian culture and it had to demystify the proxy-West, constituted by the interlocking cultures of the colonial state and westernized middle-class Indians.

Many psychoanalysts—and social critics—chose the easy way out. Their 'self criticism' was directed against non-modern India, as if they were an organic part of it, and they exempted every category dear to westernized, middle-class India from criticism. As against them, Girindrasekhar Bose unwittingly—probably against himself—owned up this dual responsibility of the Indian psychoanalyst. This may be the other reason for his urgent attempt to reread psychoanalysis as a revised version or logical conclusion of some of the older theories of consciousness in India.

Bose's rereading was backed by two methodological deviations from mainstream psychoanalysis, both prompted by the need to situate the new science in an old cultural milieu.

Freud was fond of saying that he had not discovered the unconscious; it had been discovered by some of the great minds of antiquity. All he had done was invent a method of studying it. He had in mind the technique of free association, which evolved in response to two felt needs. One was the need to venture beyond the limits of the method of hypnosis with which he had started his career; the second was the need to go beyond the method of introspection developed by experimental psychologists such as Wilhelm Wundt and E.B. Titchener towards the end of the nineteenth century. This method, European academic circles now felt, had run its course. Freud himself said,

It is . . . an illusion to expect anything from intuition and introspection; they can give us nothing but particulars about our own mental life, which are hard

---

[133]Philip Rieff, *The Triumph of the Therapeutic: Uses of Faith after Freud* (New York: Harper, 1968).

to interpret, never any information about the questions which religious doctrine finds it so easy to answer.[134]

Bose did not feel burdened by either of the two needs. He never felt called upon to transcend the techniques of either hypnosis or introspection. He was not fully exposed to the culture of academic psychology in the West, and such tides and ebbs in methodological fashion might have looked to him, undersocialized to the modern academe, as sectarian ones. He had been a hypnotist himself and, to him, free association did not supersede hypnosis, but built on it. Most psychoanalysts believed, following Freud, that hypnosis disguised, psychoanalysis revealed.[135] Wittels acts as their spokesman when the says:

Hypnosis is one of the states in which the secondary function is put out of action. The secondary function is delivered over to the hypnotist. He assumes the testing of reality, decides between fantasy and actuality, logical and ethical problems, and precisely in the degree in which the medium renounces his own use of the secondary function.[136]

It is difficult to believe that Bose, a practising psychoanalyst and one of the editors of the *International Journal of Psychoanalysis*, was not aware of Wittels' argument. More likely, Bose sensed the presence of, and was impressed by, Freud's other, less socialized self, more open to methodological adventures. As early as 1905, emphasizing the ancient origins of psychotherapy, Freud had said, 'There are many ways and means of practising psychotherapy. All that lead to recovery is good.'[137]

[134]Sigmund Freud, 'The Future of an Illusion' (1929), *Standard Edition*, 21, pp. 5–58. This statement of Freud flatly contradicts Bettelheim's claim that psychoanalysis is an introspective psychology wrongly converted into a behavioural one in the United States (*Freud and Man's Soul*, p. 54). But the contradiction is only apparent, for the introspection that Bettelheim talks about is not the kind Freud had in mind when he rejected introspection but of the kind that Freud endorsed in the case of Bose.

[135]Sigmund Freud, 'Lecture XXVIII: Analytic Therapy', *Standard Edition*, 1963, 16, pp. 448–53.

[136]Wittels, *Freud and His Time*, p. 302.

[137]Sigmund Freud, 'On Psychotherapy' (1905), *Standard Edition*, 7, p. 259. In any case, there were probably limits to Freud's enthusiasm for psychoanalytic *therapy*. At least on one occasion he is said to have remarked, 'Neurotics are a rabble (*Gesindel*), good only to support us financially and to allow us to learn from their cases: psychoanalysis as a therapy may be worthless'. J. Dupont (ed.), *The Clinical Diary of Sandor Ferenczi*, trs. M. Balint and N.Z. Jackson (Cambridge, Mass.: Harvard University Press, 1988), quoted in Rudnytsky, 'A Psychoanalytic Weltanschauung', p. 291.

Fourteen years afterwards, he was to restate that faith in a context that must have sounded strikingly familiar to Bose:

It is possible to foresee that at some time or other the conscience of society will awake and remind it that the poor man should have just as much right to assistance for his mind . . . .

We shall then be forced by the task of adapting our technique to the new conditions . . . . It is very probable, too, that the large-scale application of our therapy will compel us to alloy the pure gold of analysis freely with the copper of direct suggestions; and hypnotic influence, too, might find a place in it again . . . .[138]

As for introspection, Bose never disowned it. To him, to view introspection as only a method of psychology was a trivialization. Introspection had behind it the authority of at least two thousand years of India's past, besides the association with some European philosophers found relevant by Indians (such as David Hume, George Berkeley and John Stuart Mill). It was a method that had shown its possibilities over and over again. Fifty years of academic psychology in one cultural region of the world could not wipe out those possibilities.

Hartnack notes Bose's commitment to introspection, but fails to gauge its full meaning. When Bose said in 1938, surveying the work done in psychology in India during the previous twenty-five years, 'psychological truth can *only* be discovered through introspection',[139] he was in effect conveying four messages: that he was unaware that the free-associative method had grown partly in reaction to introspection in western psychology and he saw free association mainly as an extension of introspection; that to him, the discipline of psychology was inextricably associated with introspection, which in turn represented insight in its grandest philosophical sense; that, as a trained academic psychologist, he was aware of but uninterested in the transient western academic debates on method; that though he casually used the language of progressivism he had acquired from his western education, he judged all techniques in terms of the philosophical quest that had continued unbroken in his

[138]Sigmund Freud, 'Lines of Advance in Psychoanalytic Therapy' (1919), *Standard Edition*, 17, pp. 157–68; see pp. 167–8. Jahoda in *Freud and the Dilemmas*, p. 26, adds that, after Freud's death, 'some psychoanalysts reverted to hypnosis and could overcome its disadvantages, even its boredom'.

[139]Girindrasekhar Bose, 'Progress in Psychology in India during the past Twenty-five Years', in B. Prasad (ed.), *The Progress of Science in India during the Past Twenty-Five Years* (Calcutta: Indian Science Congress Association, 1938), pp. 336–52; see p. 345. Quoted in Hartnack, 'Psychoanalysis and Colonialism', pp. 97–8. Italics mine.

society over the centuries, unimpeded by the rise and fall of dynasties and regimes. To Bose, 'India's ancient learned men had a genius for introspective meditation and the Indian psychologist has that heritage. In this respect, he enjoys an advantage over his colleagues in the West.'[140]

It is facile to call this merely an expression of nationalism. It should rather be read partly as a statement of intent, a construction of the past oriented to a preferred future and serving as a critique of an imperfect present.

Was the tradition of introspection so dominant in Indian civilization? Was traditional India that psychologically minded and was colonized India its true heir? When Bose opted for psychoanalysis, was it psychoanalysis he opted for? When he anticipated the other Freud whom historians of ideas identified only some three decades later, what empirical and conceptual clues did he use? Or was he reading Freud, too, as a classical text open to diverse interpretations, because he had more freedom as a *bhāsyakāra*, a traditional commentator on texts partly cut off from the modern West, than a formal psychoanalyst?

These questions remain unanswered in this essay. The issues they raise, I am aware, are debatable ones. Without prejudging the issues or fore-closing the debates, however, it is still possible to propose that, at one level of the intellectual culture Bose created, such questions were less than important. Bose, at this level, true to his vocation, was not con-cerned with unearthing the objective past, but with working through the remembered past. He seemed to know that, as with the individual, in some societies at some points of time the past flows out of the present as easily as in other societies, at other points of time, the present flows out of the past.

[140]Ibid.

*Earlier published in Ashis Nandy, *The Savage Freud and Other Essays on Possible and Retrievable Selves* (New Delhi: Oxford University Press, 1995).

15

~~~~

The Scope and Limits of Dissent
India's First Environmentalist and His Critique of the DVC

THE DAMODAR VALLEY Corporation or DVC in eastern India is one of the largest and most ambitious river-valley projects in South Asia. It was built at a time when, in the newly-independent countries of the South, the building of large dams was a matter of national pride and an affirmation of a country's technological autonomy and political equality with the West.[1] In this self-affirmation, the main role was played by the state. Technocrats and planners chose to believe that they were the main actors in the play and urban, middle-class India saw them as such. However, the political establishment usually viewed such technocrats and planners as substitutable functionaries or easily available legitimizers, dutifully providing a comfortable role model for Indian youth.

The DVC is still a massive presence in the eastern Indian landscape, though only four of its eight projected dams have been completed till now and everyone knows that the other four will never be built. Though covering an area of not less that 9357 square miles and a population of

[1] From the beginning of the Five Year Plans in 1952 till 1979, the Government of India spent about Rs 200,000 million, a sizeable 15 per cent of India's entire developmental expenditure, on dams and related canals. Of the dams built, 1554 could be classified as large dams and a hefty 58.37 per cent of them were in Maharashtra and Gujarat alone: *Registrar of Large Dams in India* (New Delhi: CBIP, 1979), quoted in Jayanta Bandopadhyay, *Ecology of Drought and Water Scarcity: Need for an Ecological Water Resource Policy* (Dehradun, U.P.: Research Foundation for Science and Environment. n.d.), p. 11.

half-a-million, the project no longer appears so august, even to the less technologically minded. Indeed, the appeal of the DVC nowadays resides not so much in its actual achievements as in its being a surviving symbol of the romance of planning and the early, superbly optimistic, techno-scientific vision of Indian nationalism. Built in the 1950s, during the early years of independent India, the DVC is now mainly the pride of an earlier generation of western-educated nationalists. To adapt Jawaharlal Nehru's grandiloquent, now-clichéd description of mega-dams, the DVC remains another of those 'temples of modern India' which has, to spite its committed priests, lost most of its devotees. It is of interest today mainly to archaeologists and temple architects.

Apart from the four multipurpose storage dams (Maithon, Tilaiya, Panchet, and Konar), the DVC includes, among other things, two barrages (one of them the controversial structure at Farakka), a huge power station at Bokaro and a smaller one at Chandrapura, a well-known fertilizer factory at Sindri, and a few by-now important townships. Together the complex has always invoked—and was designed to invoke—the memory of its better-known counterpart, the Tennessee Valley Authority in Missourie. The American experience actually served as a model for the Indian planners.[2] A book published by the DVC's Chief Information Officer in 1958, the well-known Bengali writer, Amal Home, states:

Sponsoring the DVC bill in Parliament, Shri N.V. Gadgil, the then Minister for Works, Mines and Power, described how the conception of the Damodar Valley Project was inspired by the romance of the TVA, which had ushered in an era of prosperity in the Tennessee Valley by taming the wayward Tennessee river in the U.S.A.[3]

Note the use of the term 'wayward'. It is perfectly compatible with the image of some of the larger, more turbulent rivers in folk-tales and memories in eastern India, where rivers are revered as powerful demonic mothers with a touch of wayward, insane violence. They protect and nurture when in a good mood but can turn malevolent and homicidal when not propitiated properly or out of sheer whimsy. That image has not only persisted, but it has powered many contemporary efforts to

[2]Records of the debates in the Constituent Assembly on the Damodar Valley Corporation Bill reveal the imposing psychological presence of the Tennessee Valley scheme in all plans pertaining to the Damodar Valley. An American expert, W.L. Voorduin, was by far the most important member of the Central Technical Power Board and wrote the main position paper for the Board.

[3]Amal Home (ed.), *D.V.C. in Prospect and Retrospect* (Calcutta: DVC, 1958), p. 7.

contain or tame rivers in that part of the world. Asit Sen's Bengali film *Panchatapa* (based on a popular novel by Ashutosh Mukhopadhyay) and even Kamakshiprasad Chattopadhyaya's brief poem, '*Nadi chokh ragrai*', on the dreams that dams can be, both set against the construction of the DVC, are near-perfect examples of the core fantasy that underlay middle-class India's perception of dams in the 1950s and 1960s.

I

Times change. And instead of looking like fearsome, moody matriarchs presiding over the lives of millions, Indian rivers are now more like tired, vulnerable, abandoned mothers facing lonely deaths. It is easy to criticize the DVC today when the TVA itself has come under harsh if not bitter scrutiny.[4] In fact, given that the DVC is in many ways a self-conscious copy of the TVA, its flaws and its failures seem even more glaring today. For they seem to be products of an embarrassing form of mimicry in which the ex-colonial culture of India specialized. Such imitation, however elegant and successful, discomfits many. And there are often reasons to be embarrassed. It is said that the Bhilai steel plant in hot and dusty central India, where the winter temperature rarely falls below 55°F, has a roof modelled on a Russian prototype, designed to withstand heavy snowfall. The DVC may not have acquired anything so impressive, but all around the area covered by it lie evidences of hopes unfulfilled and botched romantic visions of a modern, eastern-Indian utopia. I am told that till the 1970s one could glimpse a few steam launches, lying unused, that had been purchased in the 1950s for the pleasure cruises of tourists, expected to throng the area after the project had been completed. (The idea, one suspects, was borrowed from Krishnarajasagara dam near Mysore. Krishnarajasagara might well be the only mega-dam in the world the entertainment value of which is higher than its value as a source of water and hydroelectricity; the dam is now famous as a backdrop for song-and-dance sequences in commercial Indian movies.)

Two important points, however, should be made here for the sake of those exposed to the growing disenchantment with large projects such as the DVC. First, to adapt the argument of J.K. Bajaj about another controversial dam, Tehri, at the foothills of the Himalayas, the DVC was conceived over sixty years ago in the 1940s, and time has already

---

[4]For instance, William U. Chandler, *The Myth of TVA: Conservation and Development in the Tennessee Valley, 1933–1983* (Cambridge, Mass.: Ballinger Publishing, 1984).

extinguished much of the passion for such gigantism. If one was planning the DVC today, one would probably consider it a 'worthless exercise . . . for nobody takes such risks for such small gains.'[5] In the meanwhile, however, an entire generation of planners, development economists, engineers, scientists, administrators and even journalists, social scientists, and writers have derived a part of their life's meaning from dreaming, building or legitimizing projects such as the DVC. Now that they face the possibility that their earlier optimism was misplaced and their vision faulty, they frantically defend the optimism and the vision and the meaning of life in which these are embedded. Criticism of dams has become equivalent to criticism of one's painfully constructed self for many.

Second, it is known that for long stretches of its life the cost of maintaining the DVC has been higher than the value of its products economically, environmentally and in terms of energy use. It is also known that direct and indirect state subsidies have made the project a white elephant, and that the energy the DVC produces is almost entirely thermal and not hydroelectric (as the project promised to produce).[6] Yet, certain kinds of criticism of the project have still not been ventured, not because they do not apply or have not been thought of, but because the empirical basis for such criticism has been wiped out by time.

Thus, nobody makes a fuss about the hundreds of communities, many of them tribal, ousted from the areas where the DVC dams were built, even though such criticism is now routine in the case of all large dams.[7] The ease with which land was acquired for the DVC, mainly from

[5]J.K. Bajaj, quoted in T.M. Mukundan, 'The Dams on Narmada and Bhagirathi: Need for a Review' (Madras: Centre for Policy Studies, 1992), mimeo.

[6]Though the DVC has three thermal and three hydel power stations, the former together have a capacity of 1545 MW and the latter of 104 MW. *A Profile of Damodar Valley Corporation: Forty Years of Service, 1948–88* (Calcutta: DVC, n.d.), p. 4.

[7]Though the issue of displacement came up in the Constituent Assembly during the debate on the Damodar Valley Corporation Bill, compare for instance the low-key debate on the subject and the systematic use of this issue by those opposed to the Narmada Sagar project. Edward Goldsmith, Nicholas Hildyard and Denys Trussell (eds.), *The Social and Environmental Effects of Large Dams* (Camelford, Cornwall, UK: The Wadebridge Ecological Centre, 1984–92), Vols. 1–3; Claude Alvares and Ramesh Billorey, *Damming the Narmada: India's Greatest Planned Environmental Disaster* (Penang: Third World Network/Appen, 1988); Darryl D'Monte, *Temples or Tombs? Industry versus Environment, Three Controversies* (New Delhi: Centre for Science and Environment, 1985); Enakshi Ganguly Thukral (ed.), *Big Dams, Displaced People: Rivers of Sorrow, Rivers of Change* (New Delhi: Sage, 1992); and Mridula Singh, *Displacement by Sardar Sarovar and Tehri* (New Delhi: Multiple Action Research Group, 1992); Raajen Singh (ed.), *Dams and Other Major Projects: Impact on and Response of Indigenous People* (Goa: CCA-URM, 1988).

cultivators, can be gauged from Table 15.1. Few government initiatives in India have shown such a high rate of success.[8]

The people uprooted by the DVC, according to unofficial estimates about 150,000 strong, are now scattered.[9] Decultured and apparently well-settled, they now seem reconciled to their new life and have already sired a new generation which, like other such uprooted peoples, have learnt to use the dominant idiom of Indian public life. Even when some of them speak of their displacement and deculturation, there is a touch of instrumentality about it. Exposed to and knowledgeable about land prices, market demands, and the world of development in general, they are less unhappy about the fact that they were displaced from their traditional abode and ecological niche than about the paltry compensation they were paid, according to the conventions then prevalent. At least some of them would have agreed with the dedicated socialist planner

TABLE 15.1: *Land Acquisition—Targets and Achievement (hectares)*

Project	Target	Achieved	Per cent
Tilaiya	10,743	10,743	100.00
Konar	3,734	3,734	100.00
Maithon	10,785	10,785	100.00
Bokaro	673	491	72.96
Chandrapura	764	509	66.62
Transmission & Distribution	101	101	100.00
Hotwar	127	127	100.00
Panchet Tail Pool Dam	–	51	--
Over-all	35,831	34,361	95.90

Source: *Statistical Handbook 1980–81* (Calcutta: Statistical Branch, DVC, Ministry of Energy, 1981), Vol. 19, Table 8.3, ch. 8. Over-all figures are not column totals in the original tables. Perhaps because land acquired for unfinished projects have not been separately listed.

[8]This achievement is contextualized by a strange anomaly. When the DVC was built, it was hailed as a major developmental breakthrough because the project was being supposedly located in one of the poorest parts of India. Yet, Bengal at the time was India's richest state and Bihar was only a few steps behind. (Both states are now among the poorest in India.) The value of highly fertile land in the two states was among the highest in the country. Indeed, the politicians probably knew better. Leaders in many other states were said to be jealous about this windfall to the two eastern states in the form of the DVC and its 'natural' by-products for the local politicians and bureaucrats in terms of power, patronage and money.

[9]According to official data, at least 93,874 persons belonging to 21,310 families and 306 villages were displaced. *Statistical Handbook 1980–81* (Calcutta: Statistical Branch DVC, Ministry of Energy, 1981), Vol. 19, Table 8.4, ch. 8.

and influential policy-maker of the period, Pitambar Pant, who once reportedly said in a plan document that India's 'tribal brethren' were expected to make the necessary sacrifices for the future prosperity and happiness of the country.[10] Only they would now like to be paid a hefty compensation as a token of the country's gratitude. Nobody of course asked their tribal brethren at the time they were displaced if they were keen to make the sacrifice nor informed them beforehand of the true dimensions of the sacrifice involved.

In the larger, pan-Indian political culture within which the DVC was built, there was not much audible dissent. There could not be. The building of dams was no mere technological feat. As Shiv Viswanathan argues in the case of the well-known pioneer in the area, M. Visvesvaraya (1861–1962), dam building was also character building in the technological vision implicit in many versions of Indian nationalism. It involved containing and directing untamed, 'natural' energy. Decades ago, when in school, I had gone on an organized tour of the DVC lasting some three weeks along with twenty-five other students of science, engineering, humanities and medicine. A generous Rotary Club of Calcutta had sponsored the trip, and I still remember the enthusiasm and spirit of public service with which the sponsors and the high officials of the DVC explained to the young visitors the grandeur and niceties of the project. There was no doubt or scepticism in the air; no one had one serious critical comment to offer to even vaguely threaten the smooth execution of the master plan of a master project. The attitude of not only the committed business tycoons and plant managers or engineers, but that of the entire development community was that of the clergy explaining the complexities of an apparently ornate ritual to the ignorant but eager laity. Most disagreements to them seemed to arise from innocence and a few from more loathsome motives.[11] Neither that clergy nor its docile laity can now be expected to disown the past without disowning their own selfhood and self-created world.

In that heady, optimistic atmosphere Kapilprasad Bhattacharjee (1904–89) ventured his criticisms of the Damodar Valley Corporation in the late

---

[10]Quoted by Jaidev Sethi in an informal presentation made on Indian development at the India International Centre, 1989.

[11]That certitude and self-righteousness persist. Even today, critics of the Tehri and the Narmada Sagar dams in India are seen as traitors in the pay of the enemies of the country, even when they are respected Gandhians and freedom fighters like Baba Amte and Sundarlal Bahuguna. Some journalists have even popularized the term 'environmental terrorists' for them.

1950s and early 1960s. He was not the first to do so. K.B. Roy, a Calcutta-based engineer and specialist on rivers, had already openly criticized the DVC, as had a few others. Indeed, for a short while, Bhattacharjee was enthusiastic about the DVC and even wrote a letter to the editor of *The Hindustan Standard* supporting the project. But he soon changed his mind and was one of the first in the world and certainly the first in South Asia to develop a systematic technical and social critique of large dams. Neither the term environmentalism nor the idea of the social audit of mega-technology was then a part of mainstream public discourse and, during much of his life, though he had a reasonably large readership, few saw him as a pioneering environmental activist. Indeed, for many he was a dangerous and evil presence who, like Professor Moriarty in the Sherlock Holmes stories, knew the science of multipurpose water-management projects like the DVC but used that knowledge to benefit the enemies of the country.[12] This reading was strengthened by the fact that Bhattacharjee had at one time supported the DVC publicly.

Kapil Bhattacharjee was born in a lower middle-class Brahmin family of Telenipara in the Hooghly district of West Bengal, a place not far from Calcutta or from the banks of the Hooghly, one of the majestic rivers that were to be affected by the DVC. The family originally belonged to Dakshineshwar, another town on the banks of the Hooghly, close to the city of Calcutta. It was a town made famous by the nineteenth-century mystic Ramakrishna Paramhamsa. Kapil was the eldest of four brothers and three sisters. His father was a railway clerk and his grandfather a priest who made his living by taking groups of pilgrims to Gangasagar. Two of Kapil's elder brothers had died soon after birth and he was born after a *manat* made to the ancient sage Kapil. Hence the name Kapilprasad (Kapil's gift/benediction). Thus, for all practical purposes, Kapil was brought up as the first-born. The death of his brothers also ensured him

---

[12] The following is from a news item published in India's largest-selling newspaper at the time (*Ananda Bazar Patrika*, 7 November 1961):

> The central government's attention has been drawn to the propaganda being spread by a group of people that the Farakka Barrage will be harmful for West Bengal. The state government has been instructed by the central government to find out details about the leader of this propaganda. It has been also revealed that Pakistan, taking advantage of this propaganda, is conducting an anti-India propaganda internationally . . . .

> . . . the person [Kapil Bhattacharjee] leading the propaganda [who] touts himself as an experienced engineer has published sometime ago a pamphlet called *The Harmful Effects of the Farakka Barrage* and a Pakistani spy collected few copies of the booklet and sent them to the Pakistani government.

an especially protected, pampered childhood. He never quite acquired, his wife Tilottama believes, the capacity to stand physical hardship. Like his father, he had a nasty temper but an otherwise easy-going manner—a combination that, Tilottama thinks in retrospect, conformed to the family style of the Bhattacharjees.

When Kapil was young, his father was transferred to Katihar, in the adjacent state of Bihar. The elder Bhattacharjee liked the town and wanted to stay on there after retirement. His hand was forced when he was sacked from his job—reportedly because he beat up his English boss on being insulted—and the family decided to make Katihar their home. It was from there that Kapil matriculated in 1921. He did his Intermediate Science course (a preparatory course that allowed one to join degree courses) from the TNG College in Bhagalpur, which was close to Katihar, and went to Calcutta to study civil engineering at the Bengal Engineering College, Shibpur, from where he graduated in 1928.

Coming from a family of modest means, Kapil's first priority after graduation was to achieve economic self-sufficiency, and he established a private firm in civil engineering at Bhagalpur. He also got married in 1930. His wife, Alokmayee, belonged to another Bengali Brahmin family settled in Bihar; she was the daughter of an advocate who practised in Patna. Kapil's married life was sad, if eventful. Their first children, twins, died soon after birth. Their third child, a son, was born in 1932. At around this time, Alokmayee began to show signs of mental illness, to be diagnosed later as schizophrenia. Probably in the beginning the illness did not seem serious, for they had a second child, a girl, in 1936. However, soon afterwards Kapil began distancing himself from his wife, for he had in the meanwhile fallen in love with Tilottama who came from a large, well-to-do family of famous writers, some of whom were also well-known public figures. Her father, Surendranath Gangopadhyay, was a writer, her uncle Upendranath a novelist and the editor of the trendy literary journal, *Vichitra*, and her father's cousin, Saratchandra Chattopadhyay, was India's most popular novelist of all times. The young, struggling engineer might have been keen to shed his first wife.

Divorce at the time was not a popular option; in 1937 Kapil simply sent Alokmayee back to her natal family. Unable to take care of her at home, they in turn sent her to the well-known mental hospital at Ranchi, where she spent the rest of her life. Her son and daughter and their families were the only ones to visit her there once in a while. Kapil never visited or met her again and, it seems, tried hard to forget his first brush with marriage. He even kept it a secret from Tilottama that he had a daughter from his first marriage, born after his first wife had fallen ill. Alokmayee died at Ranchi in 1984.

As for his professional life, for about five years after his graduation, Kapil worked on inconsequential projects of various kinds. He then had a break. He got a chance to go to Paris for further studies with financial support from a well-known local patron of education, Dipnarayan Singh of Bhagalpur. Paris must have been a strange experience for the young engineer brought up in a small railway colony, but Kapil was not over-awed by it. Within a year he had picked up excellent French and opened an engineering firm in collaboration with a German friend. He also came under the influence of a French expert on hydrology and water management. Those were, however, difficult and unpredictable days in Europe and a strange set of events ended Bhattacharjee's sojourn at Paris. In 1935 he was reportedly contacted by Adolf Hitler through an intermediary. The French police came to know this and informed the British police, who in turn warned his father. The worried father sent him a cable saying he was seriously ill. Kapil rushed home, never to return to Paris. He resumed work as a civil engineer at Bhagalpur.

Kapil and Tilottama got married in 1936. Kapil, despite his odd brush with politics in Paris, had never really been political, but his second wife had been exposed to the freedom movement and the Indian National Congress through her family, mainly her father. It was probably because of her that Kapil later on began to take some interest in active politics. Also, Kapil had been reared in a bicultural Bengali–Bihari atmosphere at the margin of poverty; Tilottama's family, though it belonged to Bhagalpur, was proudly Bengali and conspicuously bourgeois. But perhaps for that same reason it lacked, Tilottama herself says, something of the warmth and kindness of the Bhattacharjees.

Kapil had been a good student throughout and had won a number of scholarships and awards. Everyone who knew him expected him to be a successful engineer. Once he returned from an internationally-known university, he was expected to settle down with a good job or set up a private practice, especially since he had family responsibilities. At first he seemed all set to fulfil these expectations. But already other concerns and interests had begun to occupy his mind. He had always been a serious reader; now he began to write, too. Some of the translations he did from French and some stories he published were later put together in two Bengali books: *Tin Peg Whiskey* and *Ghasetimaler Tabedari*.

Bhattacharjee had a rather complicated career as a professional engineer. He was in and out of a large number of jobs. Some of his more important appointments were his tenure at the Calcutta Municipal Corporation in the late 1930s; his work for Beton Arm as a civil engineer who pioneered the use of reinforced concrete in India and subsequently as an army contractor building roads at Ranchi during the Second World

War; his association with a tea company at Jorhat and Dibrugarh in Assam; and his work as a shipbuilder during the 1950s. Many of these were routine jobs, but some of the experience did not go waste. They helped him tangentially afterwards, it is said, when he became interested in the overlapping fields of dams, irrigation, hydrology and water management.

As early as 1939, Bhattacharjee had published an essay in the Bengali newspaper *Jugantar* in which he explored the idea of a network of waterways to relieve traffic congestion in the city of Calcutta. He also wrote, at about the same time, a letter to the editor of the *Statesman*, protesting against the construction of the Hirakud dam in Orissa, probably the first instance of public protest against dams in the modern sector in India. Over the years, such interests pushed him towards science journalism, and his prime interest became the faulty planning and execution of the DVC. This work depended little on any planned empirical research: it was mainly based on his immense reading, his exposure to the French hydrologist in Paris, his early acquaintance with some of the rivers that were later to be dammed, his varied experiences as a civil engineer, and random observations. His intellectual style always remained a Brahminic mix of the amateur and the professional.

It was around this time that Bhattacharjee drifted towards a vague form of radicalism, tinged with nationalism of the kind Subhas Chandra Bose's Forward Block represented. Gradually, given the intellectual atmosphere in Calcutta at the time, he moved closer to Marxism. According to most accounts, it was an uncritical, orthodox, unrepentant form of Leninism, that being the dominant creed in the circles in which he had begun to move. (Though his daughter, herself a part of the Left movement during her student days, now doubts if he ever truly turned a Marxist.) However, Marxism in Bengal, being part of the European cosmopolitanism imported by the Indian literati, carried a Brahminic imprint and Bhattacharjee, given his temperament and upbringing, might not have found it entirely uncongenial. Having been an apolitical person for much of his life, he probably picked up the outlines of his ideology from the group around *Svadhinata*, a Bengali newspaper which served as the official mouthpiece of the Communist Party of India and a newspaper that for a while published his columns. Kapil's son, Pradyumna, was seriously active in the communist movement and played an important role in establishing a relationship between his father and the party newspaper. Kapil himself probably did not have the necessary political background or exposure to critically evaluate the psychological and philosophical structure of the ideology he was opting for. Leninism was in the air in the intellectual circles of Calcutta and that might have been good enough for him. And his remained basically the radicalism of the 1930s—hard, ultra-positivist, subservient to the ideas of universal science, human engineering and linear history, and unrelieved, according to some, by any self-doubt or even any sense of humour. Like many others of his generation, he seemed to have lived happily with his idealistic, romantic commitment to historical materialism. His own fiction and the stories he chose to translate from French seem to hint at another informal ideological substratum, but that is beyond the scope of this study.

After more than twenty years of environmental activism and defying his thirty-year-long affair with Leninism, Bhattacharjee spent the last years of his life working mainly for the human rights movement. Though an old-style radical, he had become increasingly aware of the need for such a movement in eastern India where the concern with human rights had been relatively weak. The ruthlessness of law-enforcing agencies in the early 1970s, trying to root out Maoist militancy in urban Bengal, made him aware of the need for such a body, especially as some other prominent citizens, including a few leading lights of the Left, had refused to take a public position on the issue. At the age of sixty-eight, Bhattacharjee agreed to chair the Association for Protection of Democratic Rights (APDR). By the time of his death, he had managed in his usual tenacious fashion to give the movement some teeth.

However, by this time, the widespread public rejection of his position on large dams had made Bhattacharjee a disappointed, withdrawn, silent, perhaps somewhat sullen person. He had probably also come to regard his environmental activism as a futile, misconceived project. For the human rights activism of his later years never covered the victims of mega-dams, not even those displaced by the DVC. When he died in 1989, though movements against large dams had already broken out all over South Asia and environmentalism had become globally fashionable, his own environmental activism had become a vague, distant memory even for the younger generation of Greens.

II

'Environmentalists should agitate, but within the defined parameters.'

Kamal Nath, Minister of Environment, Government of India.
Quoted in *India Today*, 15 September 1993

Bhattacharjee's critique of the DVC was a three-tiered exercise, though it is doubtful if he himself ever saw it as that. There is in it a multi-layered, shadowy fourth tier that he sometimes used to preface his other, 'more serious', scientific criticisms of the project.

At the most manifest plane, the critique offered a bizarre conspiracy theory. He of course did not see it as bizarre; he was confident enough about it to start his famous 1953 lecture, '*Damodar Parikalpanar Samaskar Chai*', with a reading of this conspiracy.[13]

Bhattacharjee's argument on this theme is not easy to follow. He starts with the statement that the research of people like the physicist Meghnad Saha and his associates in India spurred the Viceroy, Lord Wavell, to first plan in the mid-1940s a multi-purpose project for the river Damodar that would mainly produce hydroelectricity. Bhattacharjee reminds his readers that Germany had just been defeated in the Second World War; the secrets of nuclear weaponry and the scientists who knew these secrets in Germany had been captured by the Allies. However, the British empire had no way of 'applying' this knowledge for military purposes. Also, whereas in the United States the TVA had started functioning, Britain herself lay devastated by German wartime bombing.[14] The 'shrewd' British prime minister, Winston Churchill, therefore, had no option but to allow the Americans to build nuclear weapons. Once the atom bombs were dropped on Japan, Churchill's 'faithful disciple' Lord Wavell 'suddenly decided to implement the multi-purpose project planned for the river Damodar'.[15] Within two years of the decision to build the DVC, the pact to transfer British power to the Indian National Congress was signed, and 'Britain's ongoing business continued to flourish' in India.[16] In 1948 work began on the DVC, planned within the framework of imperial self-interest; in the next six years between 440 and 450 million rupees was spent on the project 'of which 210 million was spent reportedly on buying materials from Britain and the United States.'[17] For Bhattacharjee, the clinching piece of evidence was that an obviously happy and satisfied Viscout Swinton, then British Secretary of Commonwealth Relations, had not merely congratulated but 'thanked' the Government of India for the DVC.

Even to the reader overly alert to imperial designs, this might appear to be a tenuous, if not paranoiac theory of conspiracy.[18] But those were

---

[13]Kapil Bhattacharjee, '*Damodar Parikalpanar Samaskar Chai*', in *Svadhin Bharate Nadnadi Parikalpana* (Calcutta: Kalam, 1986), pp. 14–30; see pp. 17–21, and pp. 23–6.
[14]Ibid., p. 20.
[15]Ibid.
[16]Ibid., pp. 20–1.
[17]Ibid., p. 21.
[18]The DVC did, however, have military significance. The American member of the Central Technical Power Board, Voorduin, did not try to hide this and indeed,

the early years of the cold war and the intellectual climate in modern India, as elsewhere, was filled with suspicion, stereotypes and scapegoating. More complex theories of the complicity of the First World in the sack of the Third World, through the global project of development, were to come into vogue later.[19] Bhattacharjee himself was to produce more refined theoretical formulations. However, it must also be admitted that he was ideologically closest to a form of radicalism that thrived on conspiracy theories of all hues; somehow or other, he felt he had to establish evidence of the direct, blatant exploitation of the Third World by the First, even if convincing only the few already proselytized.

At the second plane, Bhattacharjee is a modern, internal critic of the technological dream that sired the DVC, a dream that itself came to be symbolized by the DVC and the Bhakra–Nangal projects for nearly four decades.

At this plane, Bhattacharjee argues that before British rule India was never known as primarily an agricultural society ('*krishipradhan desh*'), though it was famous for its agricultural wealth. Pre-British India was also known as an industrial and trading nation.[20] Bhattacharjee refers to the 'consensus' of historians that to sustain imperial rule and exploitation, Britain reduced India to an agricultural society by making the huge majority of the country's people dependent on agriculture.[21]

Bhattacharjee saw the DVC as the direct continuation of that style of governance. It exploited the fear of the destructive floods of the Damodar to sell the idea of a technological 'marvel' that would bring about dramatic large improvements in the standard of living in east India, even though in reality it was to devastate India's economic future. First, the project reduced valuable fertile land in the name of digging canals to supply water, especially in the three districts of West Bengal—Hooghly, Howrah and Burdwan—where population density at that time was between 200

---

as if to spite Bhattacharjee, ended his memorandum to the CTPB by referring to the 'great' role of the DVC as a national defence agency. See W.L. Voorduin, 'The United Development of the Damodar River: Preliminary Memorandum', *Preliminary Memorandum on the Unified Development of the Damodar River* (1947) (Reprint Calcutta: DVC, 1985), pp. 7–35.

[19]For a more sophisticated statement of imperial domination through a project like the DVC, see the work of two young environmental activists, Hemant and Ranajiv (eds.), *Jab Nadi Bandhi* (Madhupur, Bihar: Jayaprakash Adhyayan ebam Anusandhan Kendra, 1991), pp. 8–11.

[20]Bhattacharjee, '*Damodar Parikalpanar Samaskar Chai*', p. 15.

[21]Ibid.

TABLE 15.2: *Nature of Land Acquired for Submergence*

Project	Land Acquired (Ha.)	Cultivated land (%)	Wasteland (%)	Total (%)
Tilaiya	6,508	49.14	50.86	100.00
Konar	2,722	31.45	68.55	100.00
Maithon	9,609	66.56	33.44	100.00
Panchet	7,275	54.16	45.84	100.00
Total	26,114	55.10	44.90	100.00

Source: *Statistical Handbook 1980–81*, Table 8.1, ch. 8.

TABLE 15.3: *Nature of Land Acquired for the Power Projects and Hotwar Estate*

Project	Land Acquired (Ha.)	Cultivated Land (%)	Wasteland (%)	Total (%)
Bokaro	424	91.13	18.87	100.00
Chandrapura	490	100.00	0.00	100.00
Transmission & Distribution	101	100.00	0.00	100.00
Hotwar	127	100.00	0.00	100.00
Total	1142	92.99	7.01	100.00

Source: *Statistical Handbook 1980–81*, Table 8.2, ch. 8.

and 300 per square mile and where three to four crops per year were common.[22] Instead of recovering fallow land or land eroded by river, the new DVC canals led to the loss of large tracts of fertile land. And the people knew it. (See the official figures on land lost due to submergence and construction of power stations alone in Tables 15.2 and 15.3. To get a fuller picture, one should add the arable land lost to the new townships and the industrial units. The tables also confirm that more cultivated land was lost to the DVC than wasteland.)

Also, as part of the DVC, a factory was being built at Sindri for 'artificial' chemical fertilizers and things were so arranged that people would be forced to buy these fertilizers at outrageous prices.[23] Bhattacharjee hoped that ordinary citizens would see through such trickery. He expected that the very fact that agriculturists and other affected sectors or targeted

[22]Ibid., p. 16.
[23]Ibid., p. 25.

beneficiaries were not involved in the planning of the DVC would soon alert people to the destructiveness of such plans, which were actually meant to enrich only a few compradors. These kinds of developmental plans, he felt, were the brainwaves of people who had learnt to parrot imperial ideas and had been nurtured by them.[24] As it happened, like many later environmentalists, Bhattacharjee was to be disappointed: articulate citizens, led by massive propaganda to believe that the DVC would build an earthly paradise through magical technology in eastern India, were to see Bhattacharjee as a maverick critic, sometimes as a traitor.

By this time the reader might have gathered that, unlike many of the recent environmental activists in India, Bhattacharjee was an open votary of the urban–industrial vision. He granted that the DVC would lead to some amount of industrialization and he considered that a positive contribution of the project.[25] He also had no quarrel with the multi-purpose nature of the DVC.[26] To this extent, one might say, he was an internal critic not only of modern technology but also of Indian development, a pioneer of the movement for what would now be called sustainable development. All he wanted were 'alternative' modes of water management for actualizing roughly the same goals that were the stated goals of India's official development policy.

Not surprisingly, Bhattacharjee's sharpest barbs were reserved for experts such as C.A. Bentley, William Wilcocks and C. Addams-William, who had suggested as early as the 1920s and 1930s that something like the DVC was necessary for the good of Indian peasants. Bhattacharjee saw the plea as a prescription for keeping India a backward, agricultural country. He felt that Wilcocks, famous the world over for building a dam on the Nile, had been responsible for reducing Egypt to a backward, underindustrialized country supplying agricultural products to Britain. 'Likewise in 1928–30, the goal of Sir William Wilcocks was to increase the volume of India's agricultural products and the size of her peasant population to serve the military and imperial purposes of the British.'[27]

That is why a major—perhaps the first—concern of Bhattacharjee was the survival of Calcutta port. One of his main criticisms of the DVC was that it would lead to the silting of the Hooghly and ensure the death of Calcutta. 'Before everything else, it is necessary to protect the port

[24]Ibid.
[25]Bhattacharjee, 'Introduction', in *Svadhin Bharate Nadnadi Parikalpana*, pp. 9–13; see p. 13.
[26]Ibid., p. 25.
[27]Ibid., p. 24.

TABLE 15.4: *Performance of the DVC at the End of the First Phase of the Project (1956)*

Sector	Estimate	Actual
Irrigation (acre)	10,000,000	3,000,000
Hydroelectricity (kW)	146,000	8,000
Thermal electricity (kW)	150,000	28,000
Expense (million Rs)	550	1,000

Source: Bhattacharjee, *Bangladesher Nadnadi*, pp. 78–9.

of Calcutta,' he repeatedly said. If Calcutta port could not entertain seafaring ships, the city of Calcutta and the industrial area around it were doomed. If Calcutta died, not merely the districts of Burdwan, Hooghly, Howrah and Midnapur but the entire states of West Bengal, Bihar, Assam and Orissa would become the victims of utter misery.[28] He wanted the work on DVC's Maithon and Panchet dams to be stopped for at least five years, till an appropriate scientific plan for saving the port of Calcutta had been devised.[29]

Bhattacharjee developed this argument in another well-known essay.[30] He said there that between 1954 and 1959, thanks to the DVC, the maximum discharging capacity of the Bhagirathi-Hooghly had come down from 50,000 cusecs to 20,000 cusecs, a decline of 60 per cent. This he read as the death-knell of Calcutta.[31] He believed that the planning authorities, out of 'a false sense of status', hoodwinked the public by 'shrewdly' building the Farakka barrage and diverting between 20,000 and 30,000 cusecs of Ganges water into the Hooghly and the Bhagirathi. This they claimed, dishonestly, would maintain the navigability of the river and its discharging capacity.[32] The building of a new port at Haldia was acknowledgement enough that the port of Calcutta was dead. But Bhattacharjee did not expect the Haldia port to survive either, for it also would die from the silting of river-beds.[33]

[28]Ibid., p. 29.
[29]Ibid. The future of the city of Calcutta was a lifelong preoccupation for Bhattacharjee. At different times he toyed with ideas about improving Calcutta's water supply and providing cheap housing for the city's middle class.
[30]Bhattacharjee, *'Damodar Upatakya Parikalpana: Paschim Banger Viparjaya'*, in *Svadhin Bharate Nadnadi Parikalpana*, pp. 31–7.
[31]Ibid., p. 31.
[32]Ibid., p. 33. This argument did not anticipate that the roots of India's tension with Bangladesh over the sharing of river waters would lie in this project.
[33]Ibid., pp. 33–4. The consistent tendency of the DVC experts to underestimate

Despite being a part-time writer of fiction and a translator of Maupassant, Bhattacharjee was not particularly psychologically minded. He had no inkling of the emerging culture of the Indian middle class, getting increasingly globalized and unable to give up, as unworkable, the progressivist dream that had come to define its vision of India's future. For the self-interest of this expanding middle class intermeshed with the dream. The Leninist crudities in his conspiracy theory of the origins of the DVC could have been more a product of his refusal to acknowledge the primacy of human subjectivity in some areas of public life than of any paranoiac element in his personality. For it was clear by the end of the 1950s, if not by the mid-1950s, that the DVC was not doing well. The data on the performance of the project, released after the completion of the first phase of the project, which Bhattacharjee himself deployed so skilfully, were widely available. The project officials, the dam enthusiasts, and the development community might have had a vested interest in ignoring or underplaying these data (see Table 15.4), but the newspaper-reading public did not. But they paid scant attention to them. As if the DVC was a crucial part of their self-definition which, if disowned, would bring down an entire world-view and an entire vision of a good society and desirable future. The enchantment of the dominant model of modernization still held in India and many were willing to face self-destruction rather than face any threat to their painfully-constructed self-definition.

At the third plane, Bhattacharjee seemed to defy his own public self and long-term commitment to the urban–industrial vision, his blatant scientism and even his own favourite theory of progress. At this plane he occasionally broke out of his self-created straitjacket of modernism to defend the traditional systems of knowledge in his part of the globe. This respect for the increasingly marginalized systems of knowledge in his community was probably, to Bhattacharjee, the least accessible area of his own personality, where his diagnosis of the DVC, stripped of its ideological moorings, converged with the shared knowledge of his community, transmitted over generations, outside the range of vision of technocrats and development experts. And he certainly was not alert

---

siltation, despite past experience and data, remains one of the more curious aspects of the whole story. Thus, for two of the older dams, Maithon and Panchet, the annual rates of siltation were expected to be 684 and 1982 acre feet respectively. The observed rates turned out to be 5980 and 9533. Bharat Dogra, 'The Indian Experience with Large Dams', in Goldsmith, Hildyard and Trussell, *The Social and Environmental Effects of Large Dams*, vol. 2, pp. 201–8; see p. 201.

to the sacralized concepts of water and river that framed these alternative knowledge systems.[34]

According to Bhattacharjee, in precolonial days, that is, till the first half on the eighteenth century, those who stayed near the banks of the last hundred miles of the Damodar, from *puranic* or epic times onwards, used the floods to supply fertilizers to their land, mainly in the form *pali* (alluvial soil).[35] The practice had been in use for at least 400 years. Also, the region did not suffer from any shortage of rainfall and, according to experts such as William Wilcocks and C. Addams-Williams, the monsoon floods brought in billions of fish eggs and tadpoles to the rice fields, which survived on mosquito eggs. This not merely helped control malaria, but the inhabitants had a plentiful, cheap supply of protein in the form of fish.[36] The experts admitted that the partial damming of the Damodar and subsequent check on floods had already reduced the fertility of land and easy availability of fish.[37]

Bhattacharjee granted that the practice of building embankments/ bunds for the Damodar was nearly 4000 years old. These structures were never high and, in any case, the peasants cut them occasionally for reasons of agriculture at times of floods. (Bhattacharjee usually used the Bengali term *bandh* which, depending on the context, could mean dam, barrage, embankment or dyke and even subsumes under it the Anglo-Indian *bund*, derived from the same source as *bandh*, and the southern Bengali *bhedi*; one has sometimes to guess the specific meaning from the context and by comparing his English and Bengali writings.) That controlled use of floods—and dams—was managed by the peasants collectively; the state did not play much part in it. So the peasants did not even have to pay any tax or levy for their privilege; their gains were seen as part of nature's bounty.[38] Wilcocks guessed, Bhattacharjee says, that the ancient

---

[34]I have in mind especially the kinds of sensitivity that is sought to be captured in the West, successfully or otherwise, in works such as Theodor Schwenk, *Sensitive Chaos* (London: Rudolph Steiner, 1976); and Theodor Schwenk and Wolfram Schwenk, *Water—The Element of Life*, tr. Marjorie Spock (New York: Anthroposophic Press, 1989).

[35]Bhattacharjee, '*Damodar Parikalpanar Samaskar Chai*', p. 21.

[36]Ibid.

[37]Strangely, not only in this instance but in many others, Bhattacharjee depended heavily on these much maligned writers for his understanding of the hydrological regime of eastern India, especially on C.A. Bentley, *Malaria and Agriculture in Bengal* (1925); William Wilcocks, *Ancient System of Irrigation in Bengal* (1938); *Report of the Damodar Flood Enquiry Committee*, Vols. 1 and 2 (1944).

[38]Bhattacharjee, '*Damodar Parikalpanar Samaskar Chai*', p. 22. Bhattacharjee did not take into account and probably did not want to take into account, traditional

kings of the region had taken the help of Babylonian experts to build some of the embankments and canals of the region.

The maintenance of these structures stopped in the eighteenth century, when Maratha raids became frequent in Bengal. Afterwards, when the Raj was established, the British did not understand the importance of maintaining these *bunds* and their proper use. They presumed they were only checks against floods, and that the canals were only a means of water supply.[39] The situation worsened when Lord Cornwallis introduced the Permanent Settlement system in eastern India in 1793.[40] The *bunds* that had been under the control of the peasants came under the control of the new landlords created by the system (who had no idea of the traditional water management system). Bhattacharjee does not add that they were often the upper-caste urban rich investing in land the new wealth they had acquired through their connection with the colonial political economy. These new landlords had no deep or time-tested relationships with their own land, the peasants in their domain or, for that matter, with agriculture as a way of life; they were mainly moved by ideas of safe investments and social status.

Though peasants discontented with the new system tried to affirm their traditional rights by often cutting open the *bunds* secretly at night, the image of the Damodar as a destructive river that annually flooded large areas gradually consolidated itself, thanks to the misuse or non-use of traditional flood-management techiques.[41] Malaria too established itself as an annual epidemic in eastern India at around the same time.[42]

The DVC was shaped by this distorted perception of an established agro-ecological system. Instead of an elaborate, costly affair like the DVC, Bhattacharjee therefore suggested the proper maintenance of old canals, tanks, lakes and other storage systems and waterways. They were more than adequate, he felt, for irrigational purposes. Even some small, troublesome sections of the Damodar could be turned into lakes by changing the nature of the embankments already built.[43] Nothing more needed to be done by way of flood-control. Here Bhattacharjee comes dangerously close to contemporary ideas of limits to modern science and

---

cultural means of coping with floods as a natural calamity. There are clues to them in M.Q. Zaman, 'Ethnography of Disasters: Flood and Erosion in Bangladesh', *Eastern Anthropologist*, 1994, 47(2), pp. 129–55.

[39]Bhattacharjee, *Damodarn Parikalpanar Samaskar Chai*', p. 22.

[40]Ibid., pp. 22–3.

[41]Ibid., p. 23.

[42]Ibid.

[43]Ibid., p. 28.

technology, and in his 'saner' moments he may not have been very happy about it.

I must hasten to re-emphasize that this aspect of Bhattacharjee—respect for the traditional systems of knowledge and for the life-support systems that backed that knowledge—was less accessible to him and somewhat incongruent with his public self. That self was essentially one of a counter-expert who offered an alternative technological solution rather than an alternative world-view. For a clue to this public and dominant self, one has to see only the one-page summary of his well-considered suggestions in '*Damodar Upatakya Parikalpana*'.[44] They are all basically technocratic, harsh though the term may sound when applied to a person as far-sighted and ecologically sensitive as him. In practice, Bhattacharjee was like a modern medical doctor, alert enough to hit upon the incidence and causes of iatrogenic ailments but who, driven by his own inner needs, has constantly to look for new drugs and surgical procedures to cure the new ailments. There are not many hints in his works, voluminous though they are, that he believed in the limits of human intervention in nature. As I have said, in retrospect, it is easier to read him as a pioneer of the movement for sustainable development than as a radical critic of the idea of development itself.

Nothing reveals this more clearly that the missing or, rather disowned, fourth and fifth levels in his critique of the DVC (see Figure 15.1). I have mentioned that Kapil Bhattacharjee was not a typical product of urban

FIGURE 15.1: *Layers of Critical Awareness in Kapil Bhattacharjee*

Critique of western imperialism and the West's neocolonial designs
Critique of the scientific basis of the DVC, its faulty planning and threats to the survival of Calcutta port
Critique of mindless destruction of established traditional technology of the region

Critique of attacks on the little cultures of communities, their technological traditions, micro-ecologies and micro-economics	Critique of modern science and technology, the totalism of urban-industrialism and developmentalism

Critique of desacralization of nature; accepting rivers as 'civilizational boons'

---

[44]Bhattacharjee, '*Damodar Upatakya Parikalpana*', pp. 36–7.

TABLE 15.5: *Internal Refugees Created by Indian Development*

Project	Displaced	Rehabilitated	Remaindered
Coal/Other mining	17,40,000	4,40,000	13,00,000
Dams	1,00,00,000	30,00,000	70,00,000
Industry	20,00,000	6,50,000	13,50,000
Sanctuaries/National Parks	6,00,000	2,00,000	4,00,000
Other	20,00,000	6,50,000	13,50,000
Total	1,63,40,000	49,40,000	1,14,00,000

Source: *Social Action*, July–September, 1988. Quoted in Hemant and Ranajiv, *Jab Nadi Bandhi*, p. 97. Note the entry of environmentalism into the picture—a case of environmentalism itself creating new iatrogenic environmental problems. Most of the 600,000 displaced by the creation of sanctuaries and national parks are recent cases of internal refugees. So they constitute a small but more significant proportion of the total today than the figures suggest.

India. He had spent some of his formative years in semi-rural small towns of Bihar. Also, part of his practical training as a student of engineering was a stay in Ranchi where Kapil developed warm relationships with a number of families belonging to the Munda tribe. So there is at least a good chance that he had seen first-hand or heard of tribal communities ousted from their traditional abodes for the sake of various development projects—the forests cleared, the villages relocated, and little cultures destroyed. At least 150,000 refugees had been created by the DVC who, being unorganized and lacking political clout, had received less than adequate compensation for the land they had lost.[45] Most of them were

[45]ECAFE figures on a typical case suggest that the purchase price of land then was a little less than Rs 900 per acre (U.S. $42.60) and compensation was calculated on that basis. United Nations Economic Commission for Asia and the Far East, *A Case Study of the Damodar Valley Corporation and its Projects* (Bangkok: ECAFE, 1960), Flood Control Series No. 16, p. 62. According to social anthropologist B.K. Roy Burman, the compensations were higher at the beginning; they declined later in response to advice from the World Bank.

At first, the DVC authorities built houses for the displaced, but the houses had little to do with the concept of housing of the displaced, who in many cases tore them down 'to better accommodate their way of life' (ibid., p. 64). Later on, the DVC ascertained in advance what the displaced wanted, cash settlement or compensation in the form of a house or land; 92 per cent chose cash and 'the remaining families took cash compensation to build houses for themselves and some even elected to do their own reclaiming' (ibid.). It is said that a large proportion of the displaced families, with little familiarity with the market economy, quickly burnt up their money without being able to build any tangible vocation or asset.

One indicator of the poor bargaining power of the displaced and the social ambience of the time was DVC's ability to acquire 96 per cent of the targeted land without much problem. See Table 15.1.

tribals. They were a part of the more than 15 million internal refugees created by Indian development, of whom only about 5 million were to be rehabilitated; the rest being considered fit for remaindering (see Table 15.5).[46] Bhattacharjee, though a pioneer in human-rights activism in his later years had almost nothing to say about that part of the story.

Likewise, Bhattacharjee must have seen something of the cultures of the tribes disappearing before the advancing juggernaut of the DVC. He must have seen the traditional artisan skills, healing systems, and the art of forest management implicit in the lifestyle of many forest-dwelling communities, and even the environmental awareness that characterized peoples such as the Santhal, Munda, Oraon, and Kol.[47] Yet, there is no hint in his works that he recognized the range of the pain and suffering of the tribals. One might say that he was never as alert to the cultural and communal fate of the communities uprooted and decultured by the DVC as he was to the fate of Calcutta and the urban–industrial future of West Bengal.

The reasons for this partiality are not hard to guess. Like many bhadraloks of his generation, Bhattacharjee thought himself to be a stepson of the modern West and the European Enlightenment. He shared the anxieties of a class that had been sired by the West and had always felt that it had been infantilized and exiled from its natural and rightful inheritance by an exploiting, scheming, jealous father, imperial in goals and style. The class therefore spent its creative life trying to separate the 'true' modern West with its 'true' heritage of the Enlightenment from the false West, violent and expropriatory. The former they wanted to own up; the latter they rejected. Within such a framework there could

[46]This figure could be a gross underestimation and may represent the number of people on whom rehabilitation data are available. According to another estimate, 21.6 million people—roughly the population of all the Scandinavian countries put together—have been displaced only by the construction of dams in India. Gayatri Singh, 'Displacement and Limits to Legislation', in Singh, *Dams and Other Major Projects*, pp. 91–7; see p. 91.

According to another study, of the 70 million tribals in India belonging to some 212 tribes, 15 per cent have been displaced by development projects, so that they could themselves be developed and turned into 'skilled human resources'. Smithu Kothari, 'Theorizing Culture, Nature and Democracy in India' (Delhi: Lokayan, 1993), mimeo. A little less than half of all the invisible refugees created by Indian development are tribals.

[47]Most of the displaced were Santhals, a tribe that has probably paid the most heavily for the development and modernization of India. The tragedy of the Santhals, as it has unfolded over the last two centuries thorugh western colonialism and the growth of a modern political economy in India, is fit subject for an epic. The DVC has reportedly displaced at least 50,000 Santhals. Other tribes that have suffered include the Kols, one of the oldest in India.

be no harm in mimicking Europe and North America, for that represented a step towards equality, adulthood and the universal principles the West had discovered earlier than other civilizations.

For Bhattacharjee, the moral rejection of the West's record outside the West, therefore, had to go hand-in-hand with efforts to internalize the 'technology' of dominance the West had developed, so that one would not be hoodwinked once again or caught in the imperial game as a hapless victim. This technology of dominance was seen to include a sharp scepticism towards the pre-industrial and non-industrial worlds, viewed as expendable luxuries or artificially-promoted pastoral utopias, and a clear rejection of social visions that did not accept the western-style modern, urban–industrial society as the ultimate goal of all Southern societies. All other visions were bound to look dangerous to Bhattacharjee, for they could be shown to be incapable of withstanding the masculine, technicized, this-worldly rationalism that powered the imperial West.

There was another aspect to the disowned self of Bhattacharjee. The revised version of his Bengali collection of essays, *Bangladesher Nadnadi o Parikalpana* (1955), begins with two elegant comments on the millennia-old place of the river Rupnarayan in the life of eastern India, and his unpublished ms, 'Hydrological Regime in Eastern India', begins with a handsome acknowledgement of the role of rivers in the cultural self-definitions of Bihar, Orissa, West Bengal, Bangladesh, Nepal, and Assam. Yet Bhattacharjee probably saw such comments and acknowledgement as indulgences he was entitled to.[48] Usually he defined the civilizational role of rivers on stark, secular lines that had little to do with the traditional categories and meanings of river in the region. Though he always chose to speak on behalf of the people, 'the idea of preserving the sanctity of environment, and especially of the great rivers that since almost the beginning of mankind have been defining features of certain civilizations' was beyond his world-view.[49] He saw himself as a secular rationalist and a progressive and could never take the position that rivers like the Ganga were a 'civilizational boon' that could be left out of cost–benefit analyses and large-scale techno-social interventions, and considered inviolable. Nor could he, even when he talked of the loss of

[48]Kapil Bhattacharjee, *'Paschim Banger Jivane Rupnarayan Nader Bhumika'* and *'Bangladesher Nadnadi Sambandhe Sadharan Katha'* in *Bangladesher Nadnadi o Parikalpana* (1955) (expanded 2nd ed., Calcutta: Vidyodaya Library, 1959), pp. iii–ix, 1–9; and 'Hydrological Regime in Eastern India', mimeo.

[49]Mukundan, 'The Dams on Narmada and Bhagirathi'.

cultivable land and top soil, mobilize from within himself a sensitivity to the life of the soil akin to that of someone like Daniel Hillel.[50]

Central to this secular rationalist view of the world was Third-World Marxism. A devoted child of the Enlightenment and committed to a full-blown theory of progress, Marx when invited into the savage world did not remain merely a bearded prophet of equality and justice. He was turned into a symbol of transcending that part of one's own cultural self that had become associated with humiliation, victimization and self-contempt. The savage Marx was not only a protest against inequality, exploitation and the bourgeois sham in which they were packaged, but a philosopher–activist who allowed one to exteriorize one's anger and project onto others the unacceptable parts of one's own self—expropriatory, greedy, hyper-competitive, ruthlessly materialistic and open to the enticements of bourgeois hedonism.[51] (That rejected self could then find expression in a distorted or pathological form under propitious circumstances. Perhaps the discovery of pathetic collections of French wines, Russian caviar, designer clothes, and American currency in the secret basements and vaults of the puritanic, orthodox–Marxist leaders of East Europe's collapsing communist regimes is part of the same story of self-hatred coated in self-righteousness.)

Marx in the Southern world also legitimized a Europe that had already been internalized by a significant section of the Southern élite, on grounds other than those Lord Macaulay had so thoughtfully spelt out in colonial India in the early nineteenth century. Macaulay dreamt of natives who would inherit the earth in the tropics by virtue of being European in thought and emotions beneath their darker skins. Marx suggested that another internalized Europe, brought about by colonial conquest, would supply the principles and frames of dissent to help contain or counter the depredations of imperial Europe. The only concession that second Europe demanded in return was that all other forms of resistance, rooted in the world-view of the violated, be jettisoned as ineffective, effeminate, superstitious or romantic. Marx in the tropics might have fought for the dispossessed and exiled, but he also decultured and alienated. To this positivist Marx, the cultural inheritance and the ecological niche of the tribal communities submerged by the rising

---

[50]Daniel J. Hillel, *Out of the Earth: Civilization and the Life of the Soil* (New York: The Free Press, 1991).

[51]This awareness is reflected in a rudimentary form in Daniel Bell, 'After the Age of Sinfulness: Lukacs and the Mystical Roots of Revolution', *The Times Literary Supplement*, 26 July 1991, pp. 5–7.

waters of the newly-built dams of the DVC were nothing more than embarrassingly humble artifacts and practices. They could be easily preserved as curios in the interstices of the modern world for the sake of the scholarly and the curious. In the meanwhile, the tribes themselves were expected to dutifully merge themselves in the mainstream culture of resistance defined by the industrial trade unions.

During the first half of this century, two persons pioneered environmentalism in South Asia. They may not have been the only environmentalists in a country where ecological concerns were often a cultural inheritance or, as in the case of some forms of Gandhism, an implicit component of a political ideology that did not even use the term environment. But the two I have in mind were the eponymic figures who mounted a lonely struggle to rediscover nature and the biosphere for modern Indians, awed by the dazzling achievements and power of an industrialized, arrogantly imperial West. The first of the two, Radhakamal Mukherji (1889–1968), was primarily an academic; he 'found' environmentalism as part of a lonely intellectual journey. That part of the story has been well-told by Mamkootam Kuriakose in his unpublished essay on Mukherji.[52] The other, Kapil Bhattacharjee, as I hope I have shown here, came to environmentalism through his practical concern for the survival of modern Bengal as represented by the cultural and socio-economic fate of the port city of Calcutta and its industrial suburbs.

India is not only its villages; it has a tradition of some 4000 years of urban living and Bhattacharjee's broad concerns did enjoy substantial cultural legitimacy. But he was not able to see, despite his obvious moral passion, that this heritage of urban living intermeshed intricately with a kaleidoscopic maze of lifestyles ranging from the better-known peasant cultures of India to the lesser known micro-cosmos of a myriad of interdependent communities, castes, and tribes. Not only did Bhattacharjee belong to a class that considered itself the wronged stepchild of Enlightenment Europe, but a class that had, through deliberate choice, disavowed its cultural parents and kinsfolk within India. To him, Indian modernity, as represented by Calcutta and its industrial suburbs, was not merely a part of a larger civilizational mosaic that also had a place for the small, the humble and the less vocal. To him, that modernity deserved a place at the centre of the Indic civilization and was being unjustly denied its right by a conspiratorial West and its accomplices in India.

---

[52]M. Kuriakose, 'Radhakamal Mukherji: Pioneer in Ecological Studies' (Delhi: Department of Sociology, Delhi School of Economics, 1980) mimeo.

This disavowal of important aspects of one's cultural self brings me to one particular form of the politics of dams that a 'progressivist' ideology has to be blind to. This is the massive use of the idea of modern science to legitimize large dams by politicians, technocrats, contractors, and development experts. The use of the idea of Baconian science as the ultimate court of appeal helps identify all scepticism of technology as obscurantist and romantic, even in situations where available data seem inconsistent with large-scale intervention in nature.

This scientism of the protagonists of mega-technology is not a disease that can be cured by empirical data, however voluminous and rich. The real interests of politicians and developmentalists, Kapil Bhattacharjee came very close to acknowledging, are not vested in the right kind of dam but in the idea of the dam itself. A mega-technological project is a major political–economic and psychotherapeutic intervention in a community's life and self-definition. It is often a major source of distributing patronage through contracts, political financing, building new networks of political obligations, generating politically powerful blue- and white-collar specialist jobs.[53] It is also often a technology of electoral mobilization and a means through which an impression of grand political performance can be created. Such a project gradually becomes an end in itself and cultivates a certain forgetfulness about its effects on the life-support systems of the community. Hence the addictive appeal of the bonding of science, development and state intervention in progressivist ideologies. These ideologies try to see through, demystify or deconstruct all ideologies except the ones that will, if successfully demystified, destroy the ideational basis and the certitudes of progressivism itself.

---

[53]This is indirectly acknowledged in 'The Politics of Damming', in Goldsmith, Hildyard and Trussell, *The Social and Environemntal Effects of Large Dams*, Vol. 1, ch. 19.

*This essay was first presented at a conference on the Greening of Economics at Bellagio, 2–6 August 1993.

Politics of the Future

16

Reconstructing Childhood
A Critique of the Ideology of Adulthood

I

THERE IS NOTHING natural or inevitable about childhood. Childhood is culturally defined and created; it, too, is a mater of human choice. There are as many childhoods as there are families and culture, and the consciousness of childhood is as much a cultural datum as patterns of child-rearing and the social role of the child. However, there are political and psychological forces which allow the concept of childhood and the perception of the child to be shared and transmitted. And it is with the political psychology of this shared concept and this transmission that I am concerned in the following analysis.

In the modern world, the politics of childhood begins with the fact that maturity, adulthood, growth, and development are important values in the dominant culture of the world. They do not change colour when describing the transition from childhood to adulthood. Once we have used these concepts and linked the processes of physical and mental change to a valued state of being or becoming, we have already negatively estimated the child as an inferior version of the adult—as a lovable, spontaneous, delicate being who is also simultaneously dependent, unreliable and wilful and, thus, as a being who needs to be guided, protected and educated as a ward. Indirectly, we have also already split the child into two: his childlikeness as an aspect of childhood which is approved by the society and his childishness as an aspect of childhood which is disapproved by the society. The former is circumscribed by those aspects of childhood which 'click' with adult concepts of the child; the latter by those which are independent of the adult constructions of the child. Childlikeness is valued, sometimes even in adults. Childishness is frowned upon sometimes even in children.

In much of the modern world, the child is not seen as a homunculus, as a physically smaller version of the adult with a somewhat different set of qualities and skills. To the extent adulthood itself is valued as a symbol of completeness and as an end-product of growth or development, childhood is seen as an imperfect transitional stage on the way to adulthood, normality, full socialization and humanness. This is the theory of progress as applied to the individual life-cycle. The result is the frequent use of childhood as a design of cultural and political immaturity or, it comes to the same thing, inferiority.[1] Much of the pull of the ideology of colonialism and much of the power of the idea of modernity can be traced to the evolutionary implications of the concept of the child in the western world-view. Much of the modern awe of history and of the historical can also be traced to the same concept. Let me give two examples from the two centuries of British colonialism in India.

No better representative can be found than James Mill (1773–1836) for the sincerity of purpose which some social reformers brought into the culture of British rule in India. The nineteenth-century liberal and Utilitarian thinker's view of his private responsibility as a father meshed with his view of Britain's responsibility to the societies under its patriarchal suzerainty.[2] Mill chose to provide, almost single-handed, an intellectual framework for civilizing India under British rule. Yet he was no xenophobe. In fact, he saw the Indian empire as a training ground and an opportunity for both colonizers and colonized. Only there was a clear difference between his perceptions of the two sets of trainees. He saw Britain as the elder society guiding the young, the immature and, hence, primitive Indian society towards adulthood or maturity, and he felt that Indian culture required more fundamental restructuring than that required by relatively advanced western cultures. It is thus that he provided his powerful, if indirect, ideological defence of British imperialism.

Mill's gentle civilizational mission was not the only metaphor of childhood that legitimized colonialism. Cecil Rhodes put it more clearly and,

---

[1] Ashis Nandy, *The Intimate Enemy: Loss and Recovery of Self under Colonialism* (New Delhi: Oxford University Press, 1983), chapter 1.

[2] For a fascinating indirect description of the interlinkages among father–son relationship, the liberal idea of progress, and inter-cultural relationship, see Bruce Mazlish, *James and John Mill: Father and Son in the Nineteenth Century* (New York: Basic Books, 1975).

one might add, darkly: 'The native is to be treated as a child and denied franchise. We must adopt the system of despotism . . . in our relations with the barbarous of South Africa.'[3] I am unable to believe that the equation Rhodes made between childhood and barbarism was only a matter of racism. It also conveyed, I suspect, a certain terror of childhood. Rhodes was one of those persons who sensed—and had to sense— that children could be dangerous. Not merely do children define childhood, they also symbolize, once we have seen through our constructions of childhood, a persistent, living, irrepressible criticism of our 'rational', 'normal', 'adult' visions of desirable societies. Whoever does not know that 'childhood is the promise of a new world—and that new world can only be destroyed before it is born'?[4] Colonial ideology required savages to be children, but it also feared that savages could be like children.

Rudyard Kipling (1865–1936) sought to establish a relationship between the metaphor of childhood and British imperialism on an altogether different plane. He was another one of those pathetic adults who wanted to reclaim, through his utopian vision of British rule, a lost childhood that had once been his own. Kipling, who was brought up primarily as an Indian child and whose experience in England as a child had been devastatingly cruel, spoke of the Indian as 'half savage and half child'—the former requiring civilization, the latter socialization. As I have argued elsewhere, to the extent the Indian was half child, he represented Kipling's own Indian childhood and his Indian experiences which he wanted to recover as an adult in his heroes; to the extent the Indian was half savage, he represented Kipling's fear of his authentic Indianized self, a self he wanted to disown for the sake of his inauthentic English— and imperialist—self, with the help of his overemphasis on laws and rules, unconditional obedience to authority, and his idea of legitimate violence inflicted or suffered for a cause.[5]

Mill and Kipling only used the growing ideological links between evolutionism and biological stratification in their culture.[6] The doctrine of progress, in the guise of models of biological and psychological development, had already promoted in post-medieval Europe, particularly in the nineteenth century, the use of the metaphor of childhood as a major justification of all exploitation. As Calvinism and the spirit of

[3]Cited in Chinweizu, *The West and the Rest of Us* (London: NOK, 1978), p. 403.
[4]Evgeny Bogat, 'Boys and Girls', in *Eternal Man: Reflections, Dialogues, Portraits* (Moscow: Progress Publishers, 1976), pp. 279–87; see p. 282.
[5]See Nandy, *The Intimate Enemy*.
[6]Ibid.

Protestantism consolidated their hold over important aspects of the European consciousness, the growth of the idea of the adult male as the ultimate in God's creation and as the this-worldly end-state for everyone was endorsed by the new salience of the productivity principle and Promethean activism, both in turn sanctified by far-reaching changes in Christianity. By about the sixteenth century the imagery of the child Christ, like that of the androgynous Christ, started becoming recessive in European Christianity. Instead, it was a patriarchal God, with a patriarchal relationship with his suffering and atoning son, that became the dominant mode in the culture. In such a culture, the child's physical weakness was already being seen as coeval with his moral and emotional weakness which needed to be corrected with the help of maturer persons. Without this correction, the child was seen to stand midway between the lower animals and humanity. In a culture in which nature, including non-human living beings, was seen as a lower stratum of God's creation, meant for man, the chosen species of God, the child as a being closer to nature was naturally considered usable—economically, socially and psychologically.

In his well-known work, Lloyd deMause faults Philippe Aries for suggesting that childhood, as we know it, is a modern creation.[7] De Mause argues that children have been ill-treated throughout history, and the modern world, if anything, is somewhat kinder to the child. He is here stating an old argument which offsets modern violence against various traditional forms of institutionalized violence.

De Mause is partly correct. Viewed from this side of history, the tradition of childhood is indeed the tradition of neglect, torture and infanticide. So-called parental care and education have often been a cover for the widespread social and psychological exploitation of children. Many past societies saw children as the property of their parents, sometimes without any legal protection against parental oppression. This in turn legitimized every variety of institutional violence. Mutilation of children in some societies—in the form of castration, circumcision or beautification through folk surgery—was the norm, rather than the exception. Terrorization of children for fun or for ensuring conformity was widespread. So were sodomy and other sexual abuse of children. Often these took place with the full consent not only of the victim's parents but also of society. And, above all, infanticide was not only common; it was often

---

[7]Lloyd deMause, 'The Evolution of Childhood', in Lloyd deMause (ed.), *The History of Childhood* (New York: Harper, 1975), pp. 1–76; see pp. 5–6; Philippe Aries, *Centuries of Childhood: A Social History of Family Life* (New York: Knopf, 1962).

a way of life. It took place in the 'civilized' West and in 'pacifist' India till the middle of the nineteenth century. (Indirect female infanticide exists in many pockets of India and other traditional Third-World societies even now.)

All this does suggest that mankind has progressed towards better treatment of children and that modern societies have been kinder to children than traditional societies. Such an argument, however, ignores the qualitative changes in human oppression brought about by new, impersonal, centralizing and uniformizing forces released by the modern state system, technology and, more recently, by a social consciousness dominated by mass communications. It ignores that anomic, mechanical, dispassionate, 'banal' oppression, to adapt Hannah Arendt's overworked term, is mainly a contribution of our times to the global culture. Unlike the traditional or savage oppressor, the modern oppressor is empty within. He lives with a schizoid sense of unreality of his self and that of others. He himself is an instrument; he uses others as instruments; his reason is instrumental and he legitimizes his actions in terms of instrumentality. In sum, he lives in a world of instruments, instrumentalities and instrumentation. Such a world induces a sharp discontinuity between the oppressor and the oppressed, who no longer share the same framework of values as in the medieval witch-hunt or in pre-modern feudal land relations. They speak to each other from two sides of a soundproof glass wall. The estimated 1000 children who die every year at the hands of their parents in Britain—or the estimated casualty rate in the United States, ranging between 200,000 and 500,000 for physical abuse and between another 465,000 and 1,175,000 for severe neglect and sexual abuse—are not victims of mystification, black magic or false religious values (as in ritual child sacrifice or indirect female infanticide in India) or of poverty leading to neglect or murder.[8] They are victims of meaninglessness, the collapse of inter-generational mutuality, unlimited individualism and a system which views children as intrusions into what is increasingly considered the only legitimate dyad in the family—namely the conjugal unit. They are victims of a world-view which sees the child as an inferior, weak but usable version of the fully productive, fully performing, human being who owns the modern world.

[8]Richard J. Light, 'Abused and Neglected Children in America: A Study of Alternative Policies', *Harvad Educational Review*, 1973, 43, pp. 566–7, quoted in Gilbert Y. Steiner, with the assistance of Pauline H. Milius, *The Children's Cause* (Washington, D.C.: Brookings Institute, 1976), pp. 85–9; see p. 85–6. Steiner quotes Senator Harrison Williams as follows: 'It has become clear that brutality against children by their parents has been dramatically and tragically increasing' (p. 87).

Aries is, after all, not so specious when he speaks of childhood as a product of the post-medieval consciousness. Modern childhood did come into its own with the growth of industrialism, the spread of Protestant values, the emergence of modern technology and consolidation of colonialism. Children formed one of the first social groups on which the model of the brave new world promised by these forces was tried out. For the first time in important parts of the world, normal modern adulthood could no longer be conceptualized without conceptualizing its opposite, modern childhood.

The resulting construction of childhood was not a matter of genuine false-consciousness. It did not arise from real limits to human awareness at a particular time or space. On the contrary, it involved a refusal to admit easily available data and experiences incongruent with the new ideology. If it was a false consciousness, it had built-in resistance to the recognition of its falsity.

For instance, when the industrial revolution gave rise to widespread use of child-labour in England, it also produced apologists of child-labour who wrote ornate, flowing prose on the good that industrial employment did to the child. Children slaving in the mills for more than twelve hours a day supposedly learned the virtues of productive work, thrift, honesty and discipline.[9] But many of these apologists also sensed that it was not incidental that the 'moral growth' of the allegedly reprobate, unsaved and savage children also helped a labour-scarce economy and produced wealth for their employers. Parents who habitually sent their children to other families to work as domestic servants and in exchange took in others' children for the same purpose, as in eighteenth-century England, mostly knew what they were doing. It was not genuine unconsciousness; it was primarily rational cost-calculations with a very thin, easily penetrable, veneer of rationalization.

I do not wish to underplay the suffering of the child in non-modern societies. Nor do I want to split hairs on the actual quanta of oppression involved in different societies and times. But I do doubt the glib assumptions of a theory of progress, which is surreptitiously applied to

[9]Exactly as the employers of child labourers in south Indian match and fireworks factories have recently produced elegant justifications for their employment practices in response to an indictment published by a civil rights worker. See the controversy following the publication of Smithu Kothari, 'There's Blood on Those Matchsticks: Child Labour in Shivakasi', *Economic and Political Weekly*, 2 July 1983, *18*, pp. 1191–1202; and 'Facts about Shivakasi Child Labour', *Indian Express*, 14 February 1983.

life-cycles of both persons and societies. I am conscious that if the early industrial societies introduced economies of scale in the exploitation of children, most other societies, too, have tried their hand at social and emotional exploitation of their children. There is a continuity between the pre-modern and modern societies, maintained through the social inculcation in the child of culturally preferred adaptive devices such as what psychoanalysis calls the mechanisms of ego defence.[10] Though euphemistically called training in cultural values and cognitive styles, and seen as products of family socialization and organized education, there can be little doubt that many elements of such training would have been described as institutionalized brainwashing if the trainees were adults.

In spite of this continuity between the traditional and the modern ill-treatment of the child, the modern world-view is distinctive in stressing four special uses of children. Each of these uses can also be found in traditional cultures, but modern technology and communications and the spread of the values of modern life—particularly the growing instrumental view of interpersonal relationships—have given them a new reach and legitimacy.

First, there is greater sanction now for the use of the child as a projective device. The child today is a screen as well as a mirror. The older generations are allowed to project into the child their inner needs and to use him or her to work out their fantasies of self-correction and national or cultural improvement. For instance, parents may try to realize through the child their own status ambitions or to negate through him or her their own sense of economic and psychological insecurity, or they may 'bring up' the child as a double who has marital, professional and other life choices no longer open to them. Such a system can be both effective and lasting, because parents constitute the immediate environs of the child. The society, too, perceives them as providing a benevolent capsulating context for childhood. So when a parent acts out his or her inner conflicts on the child or tries to face the oppressions of society by using the child as a shield, he or she has the support of the entire society. Bruno Bettelheim once said that neither Hamlet's father nor King Lear had any business to impose on their progenies, on Hamlet and Cordelia respectively, the responsibility of avenging the wrongs done to the earlier generation. The parents in both cases tried to put reins on the next generation and 'saddle it with a burden of gratitude'. Hamlet's father, like Lear, 'put a

---

[10]One could read this as the main thrust of the large number of culture and personality studies done in the late 1940s and 1950s.

private burden on his child's too weak shoulders'. And it is poetic justice, Bettelheim says, that Cordelia, willing to serve age by forgoing her right to a life of her own, suffers destruction along with her father.[11]

Unlike young adults such as Hamlet and Cordelia, younger children do not often have the option of breaking out of the social or educational 'traps' set for them. Their physical, emotional and socio-economic vulnerability does not give them much chance of escape and they have to play out the institutional games devised for them. In many societies, by the time they gain social and economic autonomy, it is already too late for psychological autonomy;[12] they continue to carry within them the passions, hates and loves of their earliest authorities. Even when oppression becomes obvious and, thus, some subjective basis for a search for autonomy is created, as in Shakespeare's *Romeo and Juliet*, the society may turn on the young with some savagery to ensure that the search is not actualized in practice. At one time, this probably was the ultimate meaning of all blood feuds and all attempts to settle historical scores. Today, it is the source of all attempts to use children to satisfy the grandest of personal and national aspirations.

Second, as already noted, childhood has become a major dystopia for the modern world. The fear of being childish dogs the steps of every psychologically insecure adult and of every culture which uses the metaphor of childhood to define mental illness, primitivism, abnormality, underdevelopment, non-creativity and traditionalism. Perfect adulthood, like hyper-masculinity and ultra-normality, has become the goal of most over-socialized human beings, and modern societies have begun to produce a large number of individuals whose ego-ideal includes the concept of adult maturity as defined by the dominant norms of the society. (Evgeny Bogat makes the important point that while every child is unique and while one expects that 'differences among persons and differences in character should become more apparent as people grow older . . . this is not the case. The differences sadly fade away, leaving only the memory of the wonderfully unique world of childhood.'[13]) Thus, the idea of childhood as a dystopia subtly permeates most popular myths about the lost utopia of childhood and most compensatory ideas about the beauties of child-like innocence and spontaneity. As Lloyd deMause points out in a

---

[11]B. Bettelheim, 'The Problem of Generations' in E.H. Erikson (ed.), *Youth: Change and Challenge* (New York: Basic, 1963), pp. 64–92; see pp. 69–70.

[12]This might look like an argument applicable only to modern societies, but even in traditional societies the search for psychological autonomy persists, even though more frequently in the sphere of the sacred than that of the secular.

[13]Bogat, 'Boys and Girls', p. 285.

different context, the idea of childhood as a lost utopia—found not in autobiographies but mainly in literature, myths and fantasies—is often built out of small episodes in remembered childhoods to serve as a wish-fulfilling fantasy and as a defence against traumatic childhood memories.[14] More dominant is the idea of a fearsome childhood to which one might any time regress.

Third, with greater and more intense cross-cultural contacts, childhood now more frequently becomes a battleground of cultures. This is specially true of many Third World societies where middle-class urban children are often handed over to the modern world to work out a compromise with cultures successfully encroaching upon the traditional lifestyle. For instance, even traditional rural parents may begin to send their children to modern urban schools for western education—partly to fulfil their status ambitions and partly to create a manageable bicultural space or an interface with the modern world within the family. Nobody who has read the lives of the reformers, political leaders and writers of nineteenth-century India can fail to notice that the Indian middle-class child became, under the growing cultural impact of British rule, the arena in which the battle for the minds of men was fought between the East and the West, the old and the new, and the intrinsic and the imposed. The autobiographies of Rabindranath Tagore and M.K. Gandhi provide excellent accounts of childhood as an area of adult experimentation in social change in mid-nineteenth-century India.[15] Both exemplify how the authors as children bore the brunt of conflicts precipitated by colonial politics, westernized education and exogenous social institutions.

Nineteenth-century Indian childhood was not an exception. Throughout the Southern world children are being made a means of reconciling the past and the present of their societies. With the accelerating pace of social change, even in many modern societies children are expected to help their elders cope with the contradictory social norms introduced into the society by large-sale technocultural changes, and to vicariously satisfy their elders' needs for achievement, power and self-esteem. (These are the needs a modern society implants in all its members but can allow only a handful to satisfy. The mythology of modernity rests on the belief that these needs can be satisfied if only an individual works hard, is adaptable and psychologically healthy. That is, there is no insurmountable institutional constraint on anyone having a sense of achievement, potency

[14]deMause, 'The Evolution of Childhood'.
[15]See Rabindranath Tagore, *Chhelebela* (Calcutta: Visvabharati University, 1944); M.K. Gandhi, *An Autobiography or The Story of My Experiments with Truth* (Ahmedabad: Navjeevan, 1927).

and personal worth; all failures in this respect, the modern belief goes, are actually failures of culpable individuals, not of structures.) As the modern society typically promises to meet these needs in exchange for productive, impersonal, monetized, industrial work in a competitive setting, the culture of productive work gradually takes over all other areas of life. It is in the modern society that we see the remarkable spectacle of even the child's early attainments in the area of sphincter control, speech, literacy and school-work becoming instruments of parental drive for performance, competition, productivity and status. This is the tacit politics in the psychopathology of everyday life in many societies today.

Fourth, societies dominated by the principle of instrumental reason and consumerism mystify the idea of childhood more than the idea of the child. This differential mystification ensures that the idea of the child is more positively cathected than the real-life child. The image of the child is in fact split and those aspects of childhood which are incongruent with the culture of adult life are defined as part of a natural savage childhood and excluded from the mythological idea of the child as a fully innocent, beautifully obedient, self-denying and non-autonomous being. In its most extreme form, the child is appreciated when he or she is least genuinely childlike or authentic—in fact, only when he or she meets the adult's concept of a good child.

The concept of a good child, derived from the objective and subjective demands of adults, finds expression in various ways. For instance, in many traditional societies such as the Indian and the Chinese, the child may be seen as reincarnation of some familial spirit, most frequently of one's parents' parents.[16] But even when the child is seen as a good omen or as the incarnation of a good spirit, there may be a touch of instrumentality to it. Thus, a male child in a patriarchal system may be seen as a means of ensuring the continuity of lineage. He may be expected to prepare himself to look after the welfare of his ancestors, and ensure their safe passage to the life after death or look after their after-life comforts from this world through proper rituals and other religious ceremonies.

Modern parents also see children as sources of economic security, old-age insurance and as allies in the cruel world of competition, work and day-to-day politics. Many cultures and individuals have elaborate defences against recognizing this aspect of their relationship with children. Of course, all interdependence is not tainted. Economic and social mutuality is no less legitimate than psychological mutuality. But when

---

[16]deMause even has a name for this; he calls it the reversal reaction. See his 'The Evolution of Childhood'.

cultures help individuals to repress the contractual aspects of the adult-child relationship and help institutionalize a totally benevolent, self-sacrificing concept of parenthood, social consciousness gets used to perceiving only a one-way flow of material benefits from parents to the child. The child, too, is socialized to such perceptions of benevolence and sacrifice and is constantly expected by the outside world as well as by his inner self to make reparative gestures towards his parents.

Thus, we seem to have come full circle to the first use of childhood we have described. If Hamlet seems too mythical a figure telling too apocryphal a story, every age has produced its version of the myth of the obligated progeny sacrificing his life to right real or imaginary wrongs done to his parents or to his parents' generation.[17]

II

Until recently, in most societies, high birth and high mortality rates ensured a plurality or near-plurality of children in the population. When the ideology of adulthood is superimposed on such social profiles, it beautifully sanctifies a subtle abridgement of democratic rights. Even in societies not dominated by this ideology—in societies where the child has often enjoyed a certain dignity, autonomy and, as in India, a clear touch of divinity[18]—the encroachment of the modern world on the traditions of nurture and child-rearing is helping to turn the childhood of the Third World into an ethnic variant of the First World's.

Thus, children are getting homogenized as a target as well as a metaphor of oppression and violence. Their story is becoming, to borrow Elise Boulding's expression for the history of women, another underside of history. Though some awareness of the role of the child in human civilization is reflected in religions and myths, it is mostly the lesser minds of the modern times that have emphathized with the child: an occasional Engels, not Marx, examining the political economy of the family and, indirectly, of childhood; an occasional Dickens, not Dostoevsky or Thomas Mann, anticipating twentieth-century authoritarianism in the treatment meted out to the nineteenth-century child.

[17]Only recently did Zulfikar Ali Bhutto, accused of political murder and condemned to death by a military junta in Pakistan, write from his death cell: 'My sons will not be my sons if they do not drink the blood of those who dare to shed my blood'. Z.A. Bhutto, *If I am Assassinated*, (ed.) Pran Chopra (New Delhi: Vikas, 1979).

[18]For example, on the Indian tradition of child rearing, see Sudhir Kakar, *Indian Childhood: Cultural Ideals and Social Reality* (New Delhi: Oxford University Press, 1979).

It is an indicator of the power of modern consciousness that even Gandhi's Gandhism failed when it came to his own children. Though his model of social change was a majestic indictment of the metaphor of childhood legitimizing colonialism and modernity, his attempt to introduce the concept of social intervention or service in the Indian world-view did presume a non-traditional, almost Calvinist concept of the sinful, selfish child who had to be moulded into a socially useful being. Corollary-wise, in his personal life, too, Gandhi forced his sons to live in a way that would concretize his own concept of the ideal child and atone for their birth in the sin of sexuality.[19] In consequence, Gandhi's eldest son Haridas was fully destroyed. He tried his hardest not to play out Gandhi's scenario for an eldest son's life, preferring to pursue to its nadir a lifestyle defined by blind negation of his enveloping father.[20] Alcohol, prostitutes, rejection of Hinduism, and a self-centred hedonism were not only the passions of Haridas but also his flawed instruments of a self-destructive search for autonomy. In the process, he provided a classic instance of Oedipal conflict in a culture which had traditionally shown a low salience of such conflicts.

If Gandhi, too, partly gave in to the modern concept of childhood, one can imagine the universalizing and homogenizing power of the concept. Here was a man who had not only rejected the ideology of modernity but had also defied the implied homology between the adult–child relationship and the West–East encounter under colonialism. Yet he was unable to extend his dissent against the ideology of adulthood from aggregates to persons, as he did so successfully in the case of the man–woman relationship and the ideology of hypermasculinity.[21]

For intimations of that other dissent against the ideology of adulthood one is forced to turn, paradoxically, to the best-known ideologue of normality and adulthood of our century, Sigmund Freud. Unlike Gandhi, Freud was totally oblivious of the larger political use being made of the ideology of adulthood. But then he was perfectly aware of the micropolitics of the family and that of the process of socialization.

It was Freud who first spelt out for the moderns the way exploitation of children ensures the persistence of a tortured childhood within each adult as a flawed consciousness. He called such consciousness abnormal

---

[19]See on this subject Erik H. Erikson, *Gandhi's Truth* (New York: Norton, 1969); Robert Payne, *The Life and Death of Mahatma Gandhi* (New York: Dutton, 1968).

[20]Payne, *Mahatma Gandhi*.

[21]See my 'The Final Encounter: The Politics of the Assassination of Gandhi', in *At the Edge of Psychology* (New Delhi: Oxford University Press, 1980), pp. 70–98.

personality, one which could not own up the remnants of an oppressed childhood within it, because it also included norms internalized from the ideology of adulthood. Psychopathology, in such a model, is a *double entendre*. It is an apparently apolitical, rational attempt to cope with inescapable memories of oppression, the so-called reality principle being not, as social consensus and psychiatric expertise would have it, a value-neutral objectivity, but a compromised apperception of reality erected by the inescapable structures of oppression. Secondly, psychopathology is a non-critical adaptation to the pathology of a fractured interpersonal world where the unreality of conventional reality and the abnormality of conventional normality organize a child's early environment.[22]

The double meaning of psychopathology is one of Freud's major legacies. Patriarchal and conservative in personal life and overtly committed to normality and adulthood, Freud left behind in this dialectics of meaning an instrument of dissent from the ideology of normality and adulthood. It was this legacy which made the social critic Freud, in spite of all attempts to institutionalize him as a positivist applied psychologist, a reluctant political rebel and visionary of a just world. In that rebellious, 'savage' Freud, a part of the culture of modern science suspended its social-evolutionism—to affirm that childhood and adulthood were not two fixed phases of the human life-cycle (where the latter had to inescapably supplant the former) but a continuum which, while diachronically laid out on the plane of life history, was always synchronically present in each personality. And that the repression of children in the name of socialization and education was the basic model of all 'legitimate' modern repression, exactly as the ideology of adulthood (including the glorification of work, performance and productivity as normal and mature) was the prototypical theory of progress, designed to co-opt on behalf of the oppressors the visions of the future of their victims. Admittedly, the metaphor of oppression was not used by Freud, impressed as he was by the rather simple, mechanistic versions of historicism and scientism (which blunted the critical edge of his concepts such as infantile sexuality, civilization as repression, and the reality principle). But, then, all social criticism does not have the obligation to be either self-aware or self-consistent.

In sum, Freud implied (*a*) that the use of children for acting out the emotional conflicts of adulthood, in turn built on the ruins of an

---

[22]In the neo-Freudian literature, the most detailed development of these themes are of course in Herbert Marcuse, *Eros and Civilization* (New York: Beacon, 1955); and R.D. Laing, *The Divided Self* (London: Tavistock, 1960). Both perspectives are compatible with a number of major traditional theories of madness.

oppressed childhood, distorted the world of the child; (*b*) that 'mental illness' was only a means of protecting oneself from the inescapable arbitrary victimhood experienced in childhood; and (*c*) that the oppression of socialization was the root of the civilizational discontents of our times and the ultimate psychopathology of everyday life. The repression within, to use a by now worn-out expression, invariably found its social counterpart in repression without.

I suspect that the early hostility to Freud was only partly due to his concept of infantile sexuality, which in any case was implied in the western concept of the savage, sinful child. Freud's stress on such sexuality only provided a humane interpretation of the fearful awareness that was already there in the recesses of the western mind. The hostility to Freud was also due to his theories which hinted at the oppressiveness of the idea of adulthood and the hollowness of the theory of progress when applied to a person's life-cycle. Human childhood, Freud's metapsychology seemed to suggest, was the basic design of a society where physical and material dominance set the pace for emotional and cultural life, by forcing human subjectivity to adapt to the physical and material dependency of the child. It is the modern childhood-which-survives-childhood from which Freud sought to liberate his civilization.[23]

On this plane, Freud tried to do for the person what Gandhi tried to do for the aggregate: to free humanity from the institutionalized violence which used the metaphor of childhood and the doctrine of progress as spelt out in the dominant post-medieval concept of history. Both tacitly agreed that childhood was a culture, a quality of living and a distinctive collection of cognitive skills, emotional and motivational patterns which modernity sought to disown or repress. Liberating the child or the savage was, thus, a means of liberating the adult and the civilized from the straitjacket of 'normal' adulthood and civility.[24]

I doubt if any other ideological formulation could have been more subversive of the language of modernity at that point of time. The formulation sought not only to protect the child and the savage but also to alter the language of social change and to unmask the universalism of modernity as only another legitimacy for ethnocides. If we see children as carriers of a culture which is politically and socially vulnerable but is

[23]Cf. Bogat, 'Boys and Girls', p. 284: 'The earlier a person leaves childhood the more infantilism there will be within him later on.' And also 'Mankind will retain its genius if it can somehow succeed in preserving the child within itself.' 'The Great Lesson of Childhood', in Bogat, *Eternal Man*, pp. 288–93, see p. 290.

[24]Nandy, *The Intimate Enemy*, ch. 1.

nonetheless intrinsically valuable, we also change the nature of our search for secular salvation. Analogously, cultures have a right to live not because they can be saved or promoted to a higher state of civilization but because of the alternatives they give us in their distinctive philosophies of life. Because ultimately they *are* willing to live out these alternatives on our behalf.

Freud was not a cultural relativist. In this model, childhood can be assessed in terms of the unique orientation to the natural and interpersonal worlds it represents. Cultural criticism of childhood, too, is legitimate; only it has to be ventured in the context of the biological, environmental and interpersonal demands of childhood—that is, in the context of both the psycho-ecology of childhood and the politics of cultures in our times. The model fears the arrogance of parents or societies which presume to 'bring up' their children; it sees family as a psycho-social space within which the culture of the adult world intersects and, sometimes, confronts the world of the child. Ideally, this sharing of space should take place on the basis of mutual respect. That it does not is a measure of our fear of losing our own selfhood through our close contacts with cultures which dare to represent our other selves, as well as a measure of our fear of the liminality between the adult and the child which many of us carry within ourselves. This is the liminality Freud worked through in his interpretation of psychopathology. This is also the liminality Gandhi had to face openly while battling the ideology of colonialism.

Liberation from the fear of childhood is also liberation from the more subtly institutionalized ethnocentrism towards past times. Elsewhere, I have discussed the absolute and total subjection of the subjects of history, who can neither rebel against the present times nor contest the present interpretations of the past. I have argued that the corollary of the modern attitude to the child is the tendency of the modern child within each modern adult to apply to past times the same doctrine of progress which is applied to the child by the adult.[25] The other name of modern childhood is personal history. Not knowing this is to be caught in the causality of history; knowing this is to reduce history to non-causal remembered past.[26] The struggle to disown one's 'childish' past in personal life is also an attempt to disown one's collective past as a pre-history or as a set of primitivism and traditions. The struggle to own up the child within oneself

[25]'Towards a Third World Utopia', in this volume. Also Nandy, *The Intimate Enemy*, chapter 1.
[26]Cf. Earnest Keen, 'The Past in the Future: Consciousness and Tradition', *Journal of Humanistic Psychology*, 1978, *18*, pp. 5–18.

is an attempt to restore wholeness in ruptured human relationships and experiences.

Is all attempt to improve or educate children, then, also an attempt to self-improve? Is every violation of children an attempt to self-destruct? Perhaps. One accepts in children what one accepts in oneself; one hates in children what one hates in oneself. Turn this into a conscious process and what looks like educating and rearing children turns out to be a pathetic attempt to compensate for unfulfilled and unrealized self-images and private ideals. Children, too, bring up their elders.

I must not end this argument leaving the impression that there is something intrinsically glamorous about childhood, or even about the innocence and victimhood of the child. That glamorization, too, is a defence against feared memories of childhood. The use of the child as a symbol of counter-cultures or utopias has often been a correlate of the use of the child as a symbol of dystopias. Children represent the contradictions and pathologies of cultures as part of an inescapable struggle for self-preservation. Adults, too, may sometimes need to be protected from them. Though the need for such protection has not arisen in the past, it may do so in the future. The vulnerability of the child in the past was primarily physical. As the importance of physical power diminishes in modern social relations, the power relations between age groups may change in the same way that it is changing between the sexes. So, while the inequality between the adult and the child may not automatically decline, it may come to depend less on brute force and more on institutions, technologies and the politics of age in the future. (Witness for instance the case of the youth. The youth 'revolutions' of the late 1960s in the West were also an effort to institutionalize the growing power of the youth in the western political economy as consumers and as voters who were becoming more numerous and mobilizable both in absolute terms and in comparison with other sections of the population.)

Until now the main force behind the ill-treatment of children has been the social structures and processes which have forced large sections of men and women to lose their self-esteem, and then forced them to seek that lost self-esteem through their children. From the violence-prone Spartan society (which saw its children only as future warriors for Sparta and, to test their 'toughness', exposed a large proportion of them to death at birth), to the English miners at the time of the industrial revolution (working fifteen to eighteen hours a day and coming back to beat up or rape their own children), violated, brutalized adulthood has been the other side of violated, brutalized children.

We thus come full circle. If violated men and women produce violated children, violated children in turn produce violated adults. Fortunately, this apparently vicious circle can be read the other way too. The ideology of adulthood has hidden the fact that children see through our hypocrisy perfectly and respond to our tolerance and respect fully.[27] Our most liberating bonds can be with our undersocialized children. And the final test of our skill to live a bicultural or multicultural existence may still be our ability to live with our children in mutuality. A plea for the protection of children is, thus, a plea for an alternative vision of the good society on the one hand, a vision in which the plurality of cultures and paradoxically that of visions themselves are granted, and a plea for recognizing the wholeness of human personality on the other.

[27]See an interesting indirect development of these themes in Eleonora Masini, 'Children's Images of the Future', paper presented at the meeting of World Order Models Project, Poona, India, July 1978.

*Earlier published in Ashis Nandy, *Traditions, Tyranny, and Utopias: Essays in the Politics of Awareness* (New Delhi: Oxford University Press, 1987).

17

Towards a Third World Utopia

Alas, having defeated the enemy, we have ourselves been defeated . . . .
The . . . defeated have become victorious . . . . Misery appears alike prosperity,
and prosperity looks like misery. This our victory is twined into defeat.

The Mahabharata[1]

I

THEORIES OF SALVATION do not save. At best, they reshape our social consciousness. Utopias, too, being ideas about the end-product of salvation,
cannot hope to do more. They, too, can only promise a sharper awareness and critique of existing cultures and institutionalized suffering—
the surplus suffering which is born, not of the human condition, but of
faulty social institutions and goals.

In this sense, all utopias and visions of the future are a language.
Whether majestic, tame, or down-to-earth, they are an attempt to communicate with the present in terms of the myths and allegories of the
future. When such visions are vindictive, they are a warning to us; when
they are benign or forgiving towards the present, they can be an encouragement. Like history, which exists ultimately in the minds of the historian
and his believing readers and is thus a means of communication, utopian

[1]*The Mahabharata*, Sauptik Parva: 10; Slokas 9, 12, 13, trans. Manmatha Nath
Dutt (Calcutta: Elysium, 1962), p. 20.

or futurist thinking is another aspect of—and a comment upon—the existent, another means of making peace with or challenging man-made suffering in the present, another ethic apportioning responsibility for this suffering and guiding the struggle against it on the plane of contemporary consciousness.[2]

Thus, no utopia can be without an implicit or explicit theory of suffering. This is especially so in the peripheries of the world, euphemistically called the Third World. The concept of the Third World is not a cultural category; it is a political and economic category born of poverty, exploitation, indignity and self-contempt. The concept is inextricably linked with the efforts of a large number of people trying to survive, over generations, quasi-extreme situations.[3] A Third-World utopia—the South's concept of a decent society, as Barrington Moore might call it—must recognize this basic reality.[4] To have a meaningful life in the minds of men, such a utopia must start with the issue of man-made suffering which has given the Third World both its name and its uniqueness. This essay is an inter-civilizational perspective on oppression, with a less articulate psychology of survival and salvation as its appendage. It is guided by the belief that the only way the Third World can transcend the sloganeering of its well-wishers is, first, by becoming a collective representation of the victims of man-made suffering everywhere in the world and in all past times; second, by internalizing or owning up the outside forces of oppression and, then, coping with them as inner vectors; and third, by recognizing the oppressed or marginalized selves of the First and the Second Worlds as civilizational allies in the battle against institutionalized suffering.[5]

The perspective is based on three assumptions. First, that as far as the core values are concerned, goodness and right ethics are not the monopoly

[2]Such utopianism is of course very different from the ones Karl Popper or Robert Nozick have in mind. See Karl Popper, 'Utopia and Violence', in *Conjectures and Refutations: The Growth of Scientific Knowledge* (London: Routledge and Kegan Paul, 1978), pp. 355–63; and Robert Nozick, *Anarchy, State and Utopia* (Oxford: Basil Blackwell, 1974), Part III.

[3]I have in mind the extremes Bruno Bettelheim describes in his 'Individual and Mass Behaviour in Extreme Situations' (1943), in *Surviving and Other Essays* (New York: Alfred Knopf, 1979), pp. 4–83.

[4]Barrington Moore, Jr., 'The Society Nobody Wants: A Look Beyond Marxism and Liberalism', in Kurt H. Wolff and Barrington Moore, Jr. (eds.), *The Critical Spirit: Essays in Honour of Herbert Marcuse* (Boston: Beacon, 1968), pp. 401–18.

[5]Though this is not relevant to the issues I discuss in this essay, the three processes seem to hint at the cultural–anthropological, the depth–psychological and the Christian-theological concerns with oppression respectively.

of any civilization. All civilizations share some basic values and such cultural traditions as derive from man's biological self and social experience. The distinctiveness of a complex civilization lies not in the uniqueness of its values but in the gestalt which it imposes on these values and in the weights it assigns to its different values and sub-traditions. So, certain traditions or cultural strains may, at a certain point of time, be recessive or dominant in a civilization, but they are never uniquely absent or exclusively present. What looks like a human potentiality which ought to be actualized in some distant future, is often only a cornered cultural strain waiting to be renewed or rediscovered.

Second, that human civilization is constantly trying to alter or expand its awareness of exploitation and oppression. Oppressions which were once outside the span of awareness are no longer so, and it is quite likely that the present awareness of suffering, too, will be found wanting and might change in the future. Who, before the socialists, had thought of class as a unit of repression? How many, before Freud, had sensed that children needed to be protected against their own parents? How many believed, before Gandhi's rebirth after the environmental crisis in the West, that modern technology, the supposed liberator of humankind, had become its most powerful oppressor? Our limited ethical sensitivity is not a proof of human hypocrisy; it is mostly a product of our limited cognition of the human situation. Oppression is ultimately a matter of definition, and its perception is the product of a world-view. Change the world-view, and what once seemed natural and legitimate becomes an instance of cruelty and sadism.

Third, that imperfect societies produce imperfect remedies of their imperfections. Theories of salvation are always soiled by the spatial and temporal roots of the theorists. Since the solutions are products of the same social experiences that produce the problems, they cannot but be informed by the same consciousness and, if you allow a psychologism, unconsciousness. Marx wrote about the process of declassing oneself and about breaking through the barriers of ideology and false consciousness; Freud, about the possibility of working through one's personal history, or, rather, the defences against such history. I like to believe that these intellectual folk heroes of our times were only reflecting an analytic attitude that allows a human aggregate to work through its own past, and to critically accept, reject or use that past as a part of the aggregate's living tradition. Contrary to what they themselves believed, our heroes were reflecting a continuity with the tradition of exegesis-as-criticism that was associated with some mythopoeic traditions as well as with some forms of classical scholasticism. It is perhaps in human nature to try to design—even if with only limited success—a future unfettered by the past and, yet, inevitably informed with the past.[6]

II

What resistance does a culture face in working through its remembered past and through the limits that past sets on its world-view? What are the psychological techniques through which the future is controlled or pre-empted by an unjust system or by the experience of injustice? What are the inner checks that a society or civilization erects against eliminating man-made suffering? What can liberation from oppression in the most utopian sense mean? What is minimum freedom and what is maximum?

We cannot even begin to answer these questions without recognizing three processes which give structured oppression its resilience.

The first is the anti-psychologism which oppression breeds and from which it seeks legitimacy. The fear of soft answers to hard questions is a fear of cultures which refuse to give an absolute value to hardness itself. Many years ago Theodor Adorno and his associates had found a link between authoritarian predisposition and anti-psychologism (which they, following Henry Murray, called anti-intraceptiveness).[7] Implicit in that early empirical study of authoritarianism was the recognition that one of the ways an oppressive social system can be given some permanence is by promoting a tough-mindedness which considers all attempts to look within to the sources of one's consciousness, and all attempts to grant any autonomy to culture or mind, as something compromising, soft-headed and emasculating. Twenty-five years afterwards Adorno recast that argument in broader cultural terms:

Among the motifs of cultural criticism one of the most long-established and central is that of the lie: that culture creates the illusion of a society worthy of man which does not exist; that it conceals the material conditions upon which all human works rise, and that, comforting and lulling, it serves to keep alive the bad economic determination of existence. This is the notion of culture as

[6]I have argued elsewhere that whereas the modern West has specialized in speaking the language of discontinuity or creative breaks, at least some traditional societies have chosen to speak the language of continuity or renewal. See Ashis Nandy, *The Intimate Enemy: Loss and Recovery of Self under Colonialism* (New Delhi: Oxford University Press, 1983).

[7]T.W. Adorno, Else Frenkel-Brunswik, Daniel J. Levinson and R. Nevitt Sanford, *The Authoritarian Personality* (New York: Harper, 1950).

ideology . . . . But precisely this notion, like all expostulation about lies, has a suspicious tendency to become itself ideology . . . . Inexorably, the thought of money and all its attendant conflicts extend into the most tender erotic, the most sublime spiritual relationships. With the logic of coherence and the pathos of truth, cultural criticism could therefore demand that relationships be entirely reduced to their material origin . . . . But to act radically in accordance with this principle would be to extirpate, with the false, all that was true also, all that however importantly strives to escape the confines of universal practice, every chimerical anticipation of a nobler condition, and so to bring about directly the barbarism that culture is reproached for furthering indirectly . . . . Apart from this, emphasis on the material element, as against the spirit as a lie, has given rise to a kind of dubious affinity with that political economy which is subjected to an immanent criticism, comparable with the complicity between police and underworld. Since utopia was set aside and the unity of theory and practice demanded, we have become all too practical . . . . Today there is growing resemblance between the business mentality and sober critical judgement.[8]

In a peculiar reversal of roles, the vulgar materialism Adorno describes is now an ally of the global structure of oppression. It colludes with ethnocide because culture to it is only an epiphenomenon. In the name of shifting the debate to the real world, it reduces all choice to those available within a single culture, the culture affiliated to the dominant global system. In such a world, ruled by a structure that has co-opted its manifest critics, the search for freedom may have to begin in the minds of men, with a defiance of those cultural themes which endorse oppression by themselves endorsing the conventional defiance of oppression. As we know, oppression to be known as oppression must be felt to be so, if not by the oppressors and the oppressed, at least by some social analyst somewhere.

There is a second issue involved here. Theories of liberation built on ultra-materialism invariably inherit a certain extraversion. The various perspectives upon the future emerging from the women's liberation movement, from debates on the heritability of IQ and from the North–South conflicts all provide instances of how certain forms of anti-psychologism are used to avoid the analysis of deeper and long-term results of cruelty, exploitation and authoritarianism. The idea that the problem is exclusively the political position of women and not the politics of femininity as a cultural trait, the idea that racial discrimination begins and ends with the racial difference in IQ and does not involve the definition of intelligence as only productive intelligence and as a substitute for

[8]T.W. Adorno, *Minima Moralia*, trans. E.F.N. Jephcott (London: NLB, 1977), pp. 43–4.

intellect, the belief that North–South differences involve only unequal exchange of material goods and not unequal exchange in theories of salvation themselves—these are all significant tributes to a global culture which is constantly seeking new and more legitimate means of short-changing the peripheries of the world. Yet, most debates around these issues assume that the impact of political and economic inequality is skin-deep and short-term. Remove the inequality and oppression, they say in effect, and you will have healthy individuals and healthy societies all around.

This anti-psychologism, partly a reaction to the over-psychologization of the age of the psychological man, is another means of belittling the long-term cultural and psychological effects of violence, poverty and injustice—effects which persist even when what is usually called political and economic oppression is removed. Continuous suffering inflicted by fellow human beings, centuries of inequity and deprivation of human dignity, generations of poverty, long experience of authoritarian political rule or imperialism, these distort the cultures and minds, especially the values and the self-concepts, of the sufferers and those involved in the manufacturing of suffering. Long-term suffering also generally means the establishment of powerful justifications for the suffering in the minds of both the oppressors and the oppressed. All the useful modes of social adaptation, creative dissent, techniques of survival, and conceptions of the future transmitted from generation to generation are deeply influenced by the way in which large groups of human beings have lived and died, and have been forced to live and forced to die. It is thus that institutionalized suffering acquires its self-perpetuating quality.

In sum, no vision of the future can ignore that institutional suffering touches the deepest core of human beings, and that societies must work through the culture and psychology of such suffering, in addition to its politics and economics. This awareness comes painfully, and each society in each period of history builds powerful inner defences against it. Per-haps it is in human nature to try to vest responsibility for unexplained suffering in outside forces—in fate, in history or, for that matter, in an objective science of nature or society. When successful, such an effort concretizes and exteriorizes evil and makes it psychologically more man-ageable. When unsuccessful, it at least keeps questions open. Predictably, every other decade we have a new controversy on nature versus nurture, a new incarnation of what is presently called sociobiology, and a new biological interpretation of schizophrenia. Biology and genetics exte-riorize; psychology owns up.

The second process is a certain continuity between the victors and the victims. Though some awareness of this continuity has been a part of our consciousness for many centuries, it is in this century—thanks primarily to the political technology developed by Gandhi and the cultural criticisms ventured by at least some Marxist thinkers and some interpreters of Freud—that this awareness has become something more than a pious slogan. Though all religions stress the cultural and moral degradation of the oppressor and the dangers of privilege and dominance, it is on the basis of these three eponymous strands of consciousness that a major part of our awareness of the subtler and more invidious forms of oppression (which make the victims willing participants and supporters of an oppressive system) has been built. The most detailed treatment of the theme can be found in Freudian metapsychology. It presumes a faulty society which perpetuates its repression through a repressive system of socialization at an early age. Its prototypical victim is one who, while trying to live an ordinary 'normal' life, gives meaning and value to his victimhood in terms of the norms of an unjust culture. Almost unwillingly Freud develops a philosophy of the person which sees the victims as willingly carrying within him his oppressors.

In other words, Freud takes repression seriously. He does not consider human nature a fully open system which can easily wipe out the scars of man-made suffering and can thus effortlessly transcend its past. Like all history, the history of oppression has to be worked through. This piercing of collective defences is necessary, Freud could be made to say, because human groups can develop exploitative systems within which the psychologically deformed oppressors and their psychologically deformed victims (both seeking secondary psychological gains) find a meaningful lifestyle and mutually potentiating cross-motivations. Such cross-motivations explain the frequent human inability to be free even when unfettered, a tendency which Erich Fromm, as early as in the 1940s, called the fear of freedom.

That is the warning contained in Bruno Bettelheim's and Victor Frankl's psychoanalytic accounts of the Nazi extermination camps based on their personal experiences.[9] Both describe how some of the victims internalized the norms of the camps and became the exaggerated, pathetic, but dangerous, versions of their oppressors. Losing touch with reality out of the fear of inescapable death and trying to hold together a collapsing world, they internalized the norms and world-view of their oppressors

---

[9]Bettelheim, 'Individual and Mass Behaviour'; and Victor E. Frankl, *Man's Search for Meaning* (New York: Pocket Book, 1959). See also the excellent summary of related studies by Barrington Moore, Jr., *Injustice: The Social Bases of Obedience and Revolt* (New York: Macmillan, 1978), pp. 64–77. Moore also covers the untouchables of India from this point of view, pp. 55–64.

and willingly collaborated with them, thus giving some semblance of meaning to their meaningless victimhood, suffering and death, and to the degradation and satanism of their tormentors. Elsewhere Bettelheim affirms that this was, everything said, an instance of the death drive wiping out the victim's will to live.[10] It is possible to view it also as part of a dialectic which offsets the ego defence called 'identification with the aggressor' against the moral majesty of the human spirit which, when faced with the very worst in organized repression, would rather give up the last vestiges of self-esteem and see itself as an object of deserved suffering than believe that another social group could deliberately inflict suffering without any perceivable concern for justice.[11] The killers in this case of course skilfully built upon this resilience of the victim's social self, particularly the persistence of his moral universe, and used it as a vital element in their industry of suffering.[12] The Nazis, one is constrained to admit, knew a thing or two about organized violence.

The third process which limits human visions of the future is the refusal to take full measure of the violence which an oppressive system does to the humanity and to the way of life of the oppressors. Aimé Césaire says about colonialism that it 'works to *decivilize* the colonizer, to *brutalize* him in the true sense of the word'.[13] And, that decivilization and that brutalization one day come home to roost: 'no one colonizes innocently, . . . no one colonizes with impunity either'.[14] If this sounds like the voice of a black Cassandra speaking of cruelties which take place only outside the civilized world, there is the final lesson Bettelheim derives from his study of the European holocaust: 'So it happened as it must: those beholden to the death drive destroy also themselves.'[15] Admittedly we are here close to the palliatives promoted by organized religions, but even in their vulgarized forms religions do maintain some touch with the eternal verities of human nature. At least some of the major

[10]Bettelheim, 'The Holocaust—One Generation Later', in *Surviving*, pp. 84–104.

[11]That this is not merely wishful thinking is partly evidenced by Helen Fein, *Accounting for Genocide: National Responses and Jewish Victimization during the Holocaust* (New York: Free Press, 1979), chapter 12. Gerda Klein says so movingly, 'Why? Why did we walk like meek sheep to the slaughter house? Why did we not fight back? . . . I know why. Because we had faith in humanity. Because we did not really think that human beings were capable of committing such crimes.' *All But My Life* (New York: Hill and Wang, 1957), p. 89, quoted in Terence Des Pres, *The Survivor* (New York: Oxford University Press, 1976), p. 83.

[12]Adorno, *Minima Moralia*, p. 108.

[13]Aimé Césaire, *Discourse on Colonialism*, trans. Joan Pinkham (New York and London: Monthly Review Press, 1972), p. 11. Italics in the original.

[14]Ibid., p. 170.

[15]Bettelheim, 'The Holocaust', p. 101.

faiths have never faltered in their belief that oppressors are the ultimate victims of their own systems of violence; that they are the ones whose dehumanization goes farthest even by the conventional standards of everyday religion and everyday morality. We have come here full circle in post-modern, post-evolutionary, social consciousness. It is now fairly obvious that no theory of liberation can be morally acceptable unless it admits the continuities between its heroes and its villains and perhaps even its chroniclers.

This general continuity between the slaves and the masters apart, there are, however, the more easily identifiable secondary victims: the human instruments of violence and oppression. Their brutalization is planned and institutionalized;[16] so is the displaced hostility they attract as a 'legitimately' violent sector protecting those more central to the system. The ranks of the army and the police in all countries come from the relatively poor, powerless or low-status sectors of society. Almost invariably, imperfect societies arrive at a system under which the lower rungs of the army and the police are some of the few channels of mobility open to the plebians. That is, the prize of a better life is dangled before the deprived socio-economic groups to encourage them to willingly socialize themselves into a violent, empty lifestyle. In the process, a machine of oppression is built; it has not only its open targets but also its dehumanized cogs. These cogs only seemingly opt for what Herbert Marcuse calls 'voluntary servitude': mostly they have no escape.

Though India is one country which was colonized and ruled with the help of Indians—under colonialism the number of white men in India rarely exceeded 50,000 in a population of about 300 million—I shall pick my example of this other oppression from another society in more recent times. The American experience with the Vietnam war shows that even anti-militarism, in the form of draft-dodging or other forms of collective protest, can become a matter of social discrimination. Pacifism can be classy. The better-placed dodge more skilfully the dirty world of military violence. In the case of Vietnam, this doubly ensured that most of those who went to fight were the socially under-privileged—men who were already hurt, bitter and cynical. As is well known, a disproportionately large number of them were blacks, who neither had any respite from the system nor from their progressive, privileged fellow citizens protesting the war and feeling self-righteous. They were people who had seen and

---

[16]See, for example, Chaim F. Shatan, 'Bogus Manhood, Bogus Honor: Surrender and Transfiguration in the United States Marine Corps', *Psychoanalytic Review*, 1977, 66, pp. 585–610.

known violence and discrimination—manifest as well as latent, direct as well as institutional, pseudo-legitimate as well as openly illegitimate. Small wonder, then, that in Vietnam many of them tried to give meaning to possible death and injury by developing a pathological over concern with avenging the suffering of their compatriots or 'buddies', by stereotyping the Vietnamese or the 'commies', or by being aggressive nationalists. The Vietnam war on this plane was a story of one set of victims setting upon another, on behalf of a reified, impersonal system of violence.[17]

III

An insight into these processes helps us visualize utopias different from the ones yielded by a straight interpretation of some of the Third-World cultures. This does not mean that cultural patterns or cosmologies are unimportant. It means that the experience of man-made suffering is a great teacher. Those who maintain, or try to maintain, their humanity in the face of such experience perhaps develop the skill to give special meaning to the fundamental contradictions and schisms in the human condition—such as the sanctity of life in the presence of omnipresent death; the legitimate biological differences (between the male and the female, and between the adult, the child and the elderly) which become stratificatory principles through the pseudo-legitimate emphases on productivity, performance and potency; and the search for spirituality and religious sentiment, for human values in general, in a world where the search almost always ends up as a new sanction for the infliction of new forms of suffering. Like Marx's 'hideous heathen god who refuses to drink nectar except from the skulls of murdered men', human consciousness has used the experience of oppression to sharpen its sensitivities and see meanings which are otherwise lost in the limbo of over-socialized thinking.

One element in their vision which many major civilizations in the Third World have protected with care is the refusal to think in terms of clearly opposed, exclusive, Cartesian dichotomies. For long, this refusal has been seen as an intellectual stigmata, the final proof of the cognitive inferiority of the non-white races. (Except at those moments when the idea of holism comes home to roost in someone like General Smuts or

---

[17]This issue has been approached from a slightly different perspective in Maurice Zeitlin, Kenneth Lutterman and James Russell, 'Death in Vietnam: Class, Poverty and Risks of War', in Ira Katznelson, Gordon Adams, Philip Brenner and Alan Wolfe (eds.), *The Politics and Society Reader* (New York: David McKay, 1974), pp. 53–68.

Heinrich Himmler seeking in the idea a marker of European supremacy.) The defensive Third-World response to the issue has ranged all the way from those who hold the West guilty of not living up to its own values (Césaire, for one, mentions the 'barbaric repudiation' by Europe of Descartes' charter of universalism: 'Reason . . . is found whole and entire in each man'[18]) to those who repudiate the values themselves—who would like Césaire to admit that Descartes is not the last word on the intellectual potentials of humankind or to endorse Leopold Senghor when he declares on behalf of the non-whites: 'I feel, therefore I am'. Rarely has the range of responses included the non-Cartesian reply that what was once a cultural embarrassment may have already become a reason for hope.

Many have shed tears over the genetic or social gap between intellect and passions in the Homo sapiens—the way our moral capacities have not kept up with our cognitive skills or our left brain with the right. Arthur Koestler and Julian Jaynes are only the last in a long line of thinkers to feel that in this matter nature and evolution have let us down.[19] Perhaps what looks like a failure of nature is after all one civilization's death wish. Perhaps reason and morality are bound to part company dramatically in a culture in which reason has to be defined so narrowly. Let us not forget that Freud had, unwittingly and by implication, worked out a psycho-pathology and a name for the 'Cartesian sickness'; he called it isolation, an ego defence which isolates reason from feelings.[20] It is a defence which turns into an inner technology Hölderlin's maxim, 'If you have understanding and a heart, show only one. Both they will damn, if both you show together.'[21]

It is remarkable in this context that, despite all the indignity and oppression they have faced, many defeated cultures refuse to draw a clear line between the victor and the defeated, the oppressor and the oppressed, the rulers and the ruled.[22] They recognize that the gap between cognition

---

[18]Césaire, *Discourse*, pp. 35, 51–2.

[19]Arthur Koestler, *The Ghost in the Machine* (London: Pan, 1976), ch. 18; and Julian Jaynes, *The Origin of Consciousness in the Breakdown of the Bicameral Mind* (Boston: Houghton Miflin, 1976).

[20]See a fuller discussion of this subject in 'Science, Authoritarianism and Culture', in this volume.

[21]J.C.F. Hölderlin, quoted in Adorno, *Minima Moralia*, p. 197.

[22]The post-Renaissance western preoccupation with clean divisions or oppositions of this kind is of course a part of the central dichotomy between the subject and the object, what Ludwig Binswanger reportedly calls 'the cancer of all psychology up to now'. Charles Hampden-Turner, *Radical Man* (New York: Double-day Anchor, 1977), p. 33. For 'psychology' in the Binswanger quotation, one must of course read 'modern western psychology'.

and affect tends to get bridged outside the Cartesian world, whether the gap be conceived as an evolutionary trap or as a battle between two halves of the human brain. Drawing upon the non-dualist traditions of their religions, myths and folkways, these cultures try to set some vague, half-effective limits on the objectification of living beings and on the violence which flows from it. They try to protect the faith—increasingly lost to the modern world—that the borderlines of evil can never be clearly defined, that there is always a continuity between the aggressor and his victim, and that liberation from oppressive structures outside has at the same time to mean freedom from an oppressive part of one's own self.[23] This can be read as a near-compromise with the powerful and the victorious; it can be read as cultural resistance to the 'normal', the 'rational' and the 'sane'.

The cleansing role Frantz Fanon grants to violence in his vision of a postcolonial society sounds so alien to many Africans and Asians mainly because it is insensitive to this cultural resistance.[24] Fanon admits the internalization of the oppressor. But he calls for an exorcism in which the ghost outside has to be finally confronted in violence, for it carries the burden of the ghost within. The outer violence, Fanon suggests, is the only means of making a painful break with a part of one's own self.

If Fanon had more confidence in his culture he would have sensed that his vision ties the victim more deeply to the culture of oppression than any collaboration can. Cultural acceptance of the major technique of oppression in our times, organized violence, cannot but further socialize the victims to the basic values of his oppressors. Once given intrinsic legitimacy, violence converts the battle between two visions of the human society into a contest for power and resources between two groups sharing the same frame of values. Perhaps if Fanon had lived longer, he would have come to admit that in his method of exorcism lies a partial answer to two vital questions about the search for liberation in our times, namely, why dictatorships of the proletariat never end and why revolutions always

[23]See, for example, an interesting cultural criticism of Hinduism by a person as humane and sensitive as Albert Schweitzer (*Hindu Thought and its Development*, New York: Beacon, 1959) for not having a hard, concrete concept of evil. For discussions of the debate around this issue, see W.F. Goodwin, 'Mysticism and Ethics: An Examination of Radhakrishnan's Reply to Schweitzer's Critique of Indian Thought', *Ethics*, 1957, 67, pp. 25–41; and T.M.P. Mahadevan, 'Indian Ethics and Social Practice', in C.A. Moore (ed.), *Philosophy and Culture: East and West* (Honolulu: University of Hawaii, 1962), pp. 579–93.

[24]Frantz Fanon, *The Wretched of the Earth* (Harmondsworth: Penguin, 1967); and *Black Skin, White Masks* (New York: Grove Press, 1967).

devour their children. Hatred, as Alan Watts reminds us at the cost of being trite, is a form of bondage, too.

In our times, no one understood better than Gandhi this stranglehold of the history of oppression on the human future. That is why for him the meek are blessed only if they are, in Rollo May's terms,[25] authentically innocent, and not pseudo-innocents living out the values of an oppressive system for secondary psychological gains. Gandhi acted as if he knew that non-synergic systems, driven by zero-sum competition and search for power, control and masculinity, forced the victims to internalize the norms of the system, so that when they displaced their exploiters, they built a system which was either an exact replica of the old one or a tragi-comic version of it. Hence, his concept of non-violence and non-cooperation. It stresses that the aim of the oppressed should be, not to become a first-class citizen in the world of oppression instead of a second- or third-class one, but to build an alternative world where he can hope to win back his humanity. He thus becomes a non-player for the existing system—one who plays another game, refusing to be either a player or a counter-player. Perhaps this is what Erik Erikson means when he suggests that Gandhi's theory of conflict resolution imputes an irreducible minimum humanity to the oppressors and militantly promotes the belief that his humanity could be actualized.[26]

The basic assumption here is that the dehumanized tyrant is as much a victim of his system as those tyrannized; he has to be liberated, too. The Gandhian stress on austerity and pacifism comes as much from the traditional Indian principles of renunciation and monism as from a deep-seated, early Christian belief in the superiority of the culture of the victims and from an effort to identify with that culture both as a defiance and as a testament. All his life, Gandhi sought to free the British as much as the Indians from the clutches of imperialism; the caste Hindu as much as the untouchable from untouchability. In this respect, too, he was close to some forms of Marxism and Christianity. Father F. Gutierrez, trying to reconcile Marxism and Christianity, almost inadvertently captures the spirit of Gandhi when he says:

One loves the oppressors by liberating them from their inhuman condition as oppressors, by liberating them from themselves. But this cannot be achieved

---

[25]Rollo May, *Power and Innocence: A Search for the Sources of Violence* (New York: Delta, 1972).

[26]Erik H. Erikson, *Gandhi's Truth: On the Origins of Militant Nonviolence* (New York: Norton, 1969).

except by resolutely opting for the oppressed, i.e. by combating the oppressive classes. It must be real and effective combat, not hate.[27]

This two-tier identification with the aggressor, which Gandhi so effortlessly made, is the obverse of the identification with the victim which allows a freer expression of aggressive drive. The Gandhian vision defies the temptation to equal the oppressor in violence and to regain one's self-esteem as a competitor within the same system. The vision builds on an identification with the oppressed which excludes the phantasy of the superiority of the oppressor's lifestyle, so deeply embedded in the consciousness of those who claim to speak on behalf of the victims of history. The vision includes the sensitivity that even those fighting an exploitative system may internalize the norms of the system and even when openly resisting the exploiters, even when speaking of the loneliness, mental illness or decadence of the victorious, may continue to believe that the privileged are powerful not merely economically but culturally and, thus, deserve to invite jealousy or hatred, not compassion.[28]

I have tried to understand how Gandhi's future began in the present, why he viewed the global struggle against oppression as a dialectic between inter-group and within-person conflicts, and why his utopia was, in Abraham Maslow's sense, a eupsychia.[29] For better or for worse, this is the age of false consciousness; it is the awareness of the predicament of self-awareness which has shaped this century's social thinking and helped the emergence of the psychological man. In this age, Gandhi's concept of self-realization could be seen as the most serious effort to locate within the individual and in action the subject–object dichotomy (humanity as the maker of history versus humanity as the product of history; humanity as a self-aware aspect of nature versus humanity as a product of biological evolution; the ego or reality principle versus the id or pleasure principle; praxis versus dialectic or process).[30] Such a concept

[27]G. Gutierrez, *A Theology of Liberation* (New York: Orbis Books, Maryknoll, 1973), p. 276.

[28]The obverse of this is of course the oppressors' search for the 'proper' worthy opponent among the oppressed. For an analysis of such a set of categories in an oppressive culture, see Nandy, *The Intimate Enemy*, chapter I.

[29]In fact, Gandhi was clearly influenced by important strands of Indian traditions which did stress such interiorization and working through. Being an internal critic of his tradition, he therefore had to do the reverse too, namely, exteriorize the inner attempts to cope with evil as only an internal state. His work as a political activist came from that exteriorization.

[30]This formulation is derived from the somewhat casual comments made by

of self-realization is a challenge to the post-Enlightenment split in the vision of the liberated man. For two and a half centuries—starting probably with Giovanni Vico—the modern human sciences have worked with a basic contradiction. Reacting to various forms of pre-modern fatalism, they have sought to make humanity the maker of its own fate— or history—by making humanity an object of the modern incarnations of fate—of natural sciences, social history, evolutionary stages and cumulative reason. Gandhi seemed to sense that this over-correction could only be remedied by world-views which re-emphasized a person's stature as a subject, seeking a more humble participation in nature and society. These are world-views in which a person is a subject by virtue of being a 'master' of nature and society *within*. They acknowledge the continuities between the suffering outside and the suffering within, and for them the self includes the experiences of the sufferings of both the self and the non-self.[31]

Using this sensitivity, Gandhi, more than anyone else in this century, tried to actualize in politics what the more sensitive social thinkers and literateurs had already rediscovered for the contemporary awareness— that any culture of oppression is only overtly a triad of the oppressor, the victim and the interpreter. Covertly the three roles merge. A complex set of identifications and cross-identifications makes each actor in the triad represent and incorporate the other two. This view—probably expressed in its grandest form in the ancient epic on greed, violence and self-realization, Mahabharata—is the flip side of Marx, who believed that even the cultural products thrown up by the struggle against capitalism and by the enemies of capitalism were flawed by their historical root in an imperfect society.[32] On this plane, Gandhian praxis is the logical extension of radical social criticism, for it insists that the continuity between

---

Neil Warren in his 'Freudians and Laingians', *Encounter*, March 1978, pp. 56–63; see also Philip Rieff, *The Triumph of the Therapeutic* (New York: Harper, 1966).

[31]Though some western scholars like Alan Watts would like to see such location of others in the self as a typically eastern enterprise—e.g. Alan Watts, *Psychotherapy East and West* (New York: Ballantine, 1969), this has been occasionally a part of western philosophical concerns, too. See, for instance, Jose Ortega y Gasset, *Meditations on Quixote* (New York: Norton, 1967). Within the Marxist tradition Georg Lukacs has argued that in the area of cognition and in the case of the proletariat at least, the subject–object dichotomy is eliminated to the extent self-knowledge includes molar knowledge of the entire society. Georg Lukacs, *History and Class-Conciousness* (London: Marlin, 1971).

[32]Many of Marx's disciples sought to place Marx outside history and culture, while he himself knew better. See 'Evaluating Utopias' in this volume, where I have briefly discussed how far any theory of salvation, secular or otherwise, can shirk the responsibility for whatever is done in its name.

the victim, the oppressor and the observer must be realized in action, and that one must refuse to act as if some constituents in an oppressive system were morally uncontaminated.

To sum up, a violent and oppressive society produces its own special brands of victimhood and privilege and ensures a certain continuity between the victor and the defeated, the instrument and the target, the interpreter and the interpreted. As a result, none of these categories remain pure. So even when such a culture collapses, the psychology of victimhood and privilege continues and produces a second culture which becomes, over time, only a revised edition of the first. Not to recognize this is to collaborate with violence and oppression in their subtler forms. This is what most social activism and analysis begin to do once the intellectual climate becomes hostile to manifest cruelty and expropriation.

IV

A second example of the non-dual consciousness of man-made suffering can well be the refusal of many cultures to translate the principles of biopsychological continuities, such as sex and age, into principles of social stratification. Many of the major eastern civilizations, in spite of all their patriarchal elements, see a continuity between the masculine and the feminine, and between infancy, adulthood and old age. Perhaps this is not all a matter of 'traditional wisdom'. At least in some cases it is a reaction to the colonial culture which assumed clear breaks between the male and the female, the adult and the child, and the adult and the elderly, and then used these biological differences as the homologues of secular political stratifications. In the colonial ideology, the colonizer became the tough, courageous, openly aggressive, hyper-masculine ruler and the colonized became the sly, cowardly, passive–aggressive, womanly subject. Likewise, the culture of the colonizer became the prototype of a mature, complete, adult civilization while the colonized became the mirror of a more simple, primitive, childlike cultural state. In some cases, confronted with their own ability to subjugate complex ancient civilizations, the historically-minded colonial cultures were forced to define the colonized as the homologue of the senile and the decrepit, deservedly falling under the suzerainty—and becoming the responsibility—of more vigorous cultures.

Once again I shall invoke Gandhi, who built an articulate frame of political action to counter the models of manhood and womanhood implicit in the colonial situation in India.

British colonialism in India, drawing strength from aspects of the 'mother culture', made an explicit order out of what it felt was the major strength of the western civilization vis-à-vis the Indian. It declared masculinity to be superior to femininity which, in turn, it saw as superior to effeminacy. It then gave a structural basis to this cultural stratarchy by emphasizing the differences between the so-called martial and non-martial races of India. The obverse of this stratarchy was a similar stratarchy in some Indian sub-traditions which acquired a new cultural ascendancy in British India. One example can be the various religious reform movements which stressed kshatriya-hood as the future core of postcolonial Hinduism.

There were many forms of reaction to this cultural order: some Indians desperately sought instances of hyper-masculinity in the Indian past; others accepted the order and sought to excel their rulers in martial valour. Gandhi's response was to posit two alternative sets of relationships against the imperial ideology and its native versions. In one, masculinity was seen to be at par with femininity and the two had to be transcended or synthesized for attaining a higher level of public functioning. Such 'bisexuality' or 'trans-sexuality' was seen as not merely spiritually superior both to masculinity and to femininity, as in many Indian ascetic traditions, but also politically more creative. Gandhi's second model saw masculinity as inferior to femininity which, in turn, was seen as inferior to femininity in man. Here the assumption was that femininity in men, especially in the form of maternity, provided a self-critical masculinity, which could subvert the values of the modern civilization more successfully than the mere affirmation of the rights of women.

I have discussed the psychological and cultural contexts of these concepts in some detail elsewhere.[33] All I want to add here is that the formal equality which is often sought by various movements fighting for the cause of women is qualitatively different from the synergy Gandhi sought. For the former, power, achievement, productivity, work, control over social and natural resources are seen as fixed quantities on which men have held a near monopoly and which they must now share equally with women. For Gandhi, these values are indicators of a system dominated by the masculinity principle, and the system and its values must both be seen as standing in the way of a non-oppressive world. To fight for mechanical equality, Gandhi seems to suggest, is to accept or internalize the norms of the existing system and to pay homage to masculine values under the guise of pseudo-equality.

[33]Ashis Nandy, 'Woman versus Womanliness: An Essay in Social and Political Psychology', *At the Edge of Psychology: Essays in Politics and Culture* (New Delhi: Oxford University Press, 1980), pp. 32–46; and *The Intimate Enemy*.

Similarly with age. While societies which have built upon the traditions of hyper-masculinity have conceived of adulthood as the ultimate in the human life-cycle because of its productive possibilities, many of the older cultures of the world, left out of the experience of the industrial and technological revolutions, refuse to see childhood as merely a preparation for, or an inferior version of, adulthood. Nor do they see old age as a decline from full manhood or womanhood. On the contrary, each stage of life in these cultures is seen as valuable and meaningful in itself. No stage is required to derive its legitimacy from some other stage of life, nor need it be evaluated in terms of categories entirely alien to it. It has been said in recent times that alternative visions of the human future must derive their ideas of spontaneity and play from the child.[34] Implied in this very proposal is the tragedy of western adulthood which has banished spontaneity and play to a small reservation called childhood, to protect the adult world from contamination. Spontaneity, play, directness of experience, and tolerance of disorder are for children or their homologues, the primitives in their sanctuaries.[35] Power, productive work and even revolutions are for mature adults and their homologues, the advanced historical societies with their experience with modern urban-industrialism and ripened revolutionary consciousness.

The dominance of the productivity principle in the modern West and the unending search for the new or the novel is a direct negation of visions which see age as giving a touch of wisdom to social consciousness and transmitting to the next generation valued elements of culture, elements which cannot be precisely formulated or transmitted as packaged products, but must be handed down to the young in the form of shared experiences. Old age is seen by the moderns primarily as a problem of management of less productive or non-productive lives. With the decline

---

[34]See a strong plea for this in Johan Galtung, 'Visions of Desirable Societies', written for a seminar on Alternative Visions of Desirable Societies, Mexico City, 1978. This of course is complementary to the idea of 'graceful playfulness' in Ivan Illich; see his *Tools for Conviviality* (Glasgow: Fontana/Collins, 1973). For the same awareness within 'proper' Marxism, see Evgeny Bogat, 'The Great Lesson of Childhood', *Eternal Man: Reflections, Dialogues, Portraits* (Moscow: Progress Publishers, 1976), pp. 288–93. The somewhat prim psychoanalytic idea of 'regression at the service of the ego' can also be viewed as an indirect plea for the acceptance of the same principle. It is possible to hazard the guess that these are all influenced in different ways by the association Christ made between childhood and the kingdom of God. That association survives within Christianity in spite of what Lloyd deMause considers to be the faith's overall thrust. See Lloyd deMause, 'The Evolution of Childhood', in *History of Childhood* (New York: Harper Torchbook, 1975), pp. 1–74.

[35]See 'Reconstructing Childhood' in this volume.

in physical prowess in men and sexual attractiveness in women, the self-image of the modern man or woman becomes something less than that of a complete human being. The pathetic worship of youth and the even more pathetic attempts to defend oneself against the inner fears of losing youthfulness and social utility—sometimes with the help of pseudo-respectful expressions such as 'senior citizens'—are produced not merely by rampant consumerism and limitless industrialism but also by a world-view associated with complex systems of oppression trying to deny the reflective or contemplative strains in the human civilization. Gerontocracy may be a false alternative to such a world-view, but it none-theless provides another baseline for envisioning an alternative cosmology in which age and sex would not serve as principles of social ordering, and in which respect for the qualities of old age would give completeness to youth and young adulthood, too.

V

This brings me to my third example of a non-dual vision of 'positive freedom': the cultural refusal in many parts of the savage world to see work and play as clearly demarcated modalities of human life. Many oppressed cultures, in trying to keep alive an alternative vision of a normal civilization and resisting some of the modern forms of man-made suffering, have sought to defy the modern concept of productive work and the totally instrumental concept of knowledge which goes with it. Once again I shall invoke the experience with modern colonialism, not so much because it is a shared legacy of the Third World but because it did better than most other exploitative systems of the modern era in terms of having an articulate ideology, a culturally rooted legitimacy and in avoiding counterproductive violence. That colonialism was, for this very reason, one of the most dangerous forms of institutionalized violence is part of the same argument. It is not accidental that while the British empire in India lasted two centuries, the Third Reich existed for a paltry decade. Successful institutionalization of a large-scale oppressive system is not an easy achievement. It needs something more than martial skills and nihilistic passions; it needs some awareness of human limits.

One belief the colonial cultures invariably promoted was that the sub-ject communities had a contempt for honest work, that they consisted of indolent shirkers who could not match the hard work or single-minded pursuit of productive labour of the colonizers. This was a belief sincerely held by the rulers. But sincerity in such matters, one knows, is only a defence against recognizing one's deeper need to justify a political economy which expects the subject community to work without dignity, without an awareness of being exploited, and without meaningful work goals.

The oppressed, I have argued, is never a pure victim. One part of him collaborates, compromises and adjusts; another part defies, 'non-cooperates', subverts or destroys, often in the name of collaboration and under the garb of obsequiousness. (The second part of the story creates problems for the social sciences. The modern tradition of social criticism is unidirectional. It can demystify some forms of dissent and show them to be non-dissent. It has no means of demystifying some forms of collaboration to discover secret defiance underneath. For modern social criticism equates interpretation with debunking, and this debunking must always reveal the base of 'evil' beneath the superstructure of the 'good'.) The colonized soon learnt, through that subtle communication which goes on between the rulers and the ruled, to react to and cope with the obsessive concept of productive work brought into the colonial cultures by some European and Christian sub-traditions.[36] At a certain level of awareness, the subjects knew they could retaliate, tease and defy their oppressors—'fools attached to action', as the Bhagavad Gita might have called them—by refusing to share the imposed concepts of the sanctity of work and such work-values as productivity, control, predictability, discipline and utility. The differences between work and play, stressed by a repressive conscience which had to idealize colonialism as a civilizational mission, could only be resisted through an unconscious non-cooperation which included 'malingering', 'shirking' and 'indiscipline'. If this vaguely reminds the reader of the folk response of American Blacks to slavery,[37] it only shows that there is something in the experience of man-made suffering which cuts across cultures and across the folk and the classical. In India at least the much-venerated Gita was waiting to be 'misused' by those caught on the wrong side of history:

> Who dares to see action in inaction,
> and inaction in action
> he is wise, he is yogi,
> he is the man who knows what is work.[38]

---

[36]On activity and work as the first postulates of a Faustian civilization, see a brief statement in Roger Garaudy, 'Faith and Liberation', in Eleonora Masini (ed.), *Visions of Desirable Societies* (London: Pergamon, 1983), pp. 47–60.

[37]Cf. E.D. Genovese, *Roll, Jordan Roll: The World the Slaves Made* (New York: Pantheon, 1974). See also Moore, *Injustice*, pp. 465–6.

[38]*The Bhagavad Gita*, IV: 18, transcreated by P. Lal (New Delhi: Orient Paperback, 1965), p. 33.

This may not be the Brahminic scholar's idea of the true meaning of the *sloka*, but what are religious texts for, if they cannot provide popular guides to survival?

If colonialism sought to do away with the human dignity of its subjects, the subjects unconsciously tried to protect their self-esteem by subverting the dignity of their rulers, by forcing the rulers to use naked force to make their subjects work, produce and be 'useful'. That is the way helpless victims are often forced to control and monitor their oppressors and to maintain an 'internal locus of control'. In their near-total impotency, they strip the authorities of the pretences to civilized authority, humane governance and, ultimately, self-respect. That is the inner logic of all domination. It ensures that if the victims are sometimes pseudo-innocent part-victims, the victors too are all too often pseudo-autonomous part-victors.

Rejection of the principle of productivity and work also means rejection of the concept of workability. Many defeated cultures have pre-served with some care the banished awareness of the First and Second Worlds: that knowledge is valuable not because it is applicable, useful or testable, but also because it represents aesthetics, relatedness to man and nature, and self-transcendence. Certain intuitive and speculative modes of perception have come naturally to these cultures, giving rise, on the one hand, to an institutionalized dependence on music, literature, fine arts and other creative media for the expression of social thought and scientific analysis; on the other, to dependence upon highly speculative, deductive, mathematical and, even, quantitative empirical modes of think-ing as vehicles of normative passions and as expressions of religious or mystical sentiments. I have in mind here not the feeling man which Leopold Senghor offsets against the Cartesian man of the West, but cultures which refuse to partition and affect, both as a matter of conviction and as a technique of survival.[39]

This blurring of the boundaries between science, religion and the arts is also of course a defiance of the modern concept of classification of knowledge.[40] It represents an obstreperous refusal to be converted to the modern world-view and accepting the imperialism of categories the world-view has established. It defies the total autonomy of technology and the idea of workability which has come to dominate all modern

[39]For a fuller treatment of the psychology of partitioning cognition and affect, see 'Science, Authoritarianism and Culture' in this volume.

[40]See on this subject J.P.S. Uberoi, *Science and Culture* (New Delhi: Oxford University Press, 1979).

systems of knowledge. Defeated cultures know that technology now legitimates modern science and it is the spirit of instrumentality which gives a sense of personal potency, self-esteem, social status and political power in the modern sector. Technology, these cultures know, has cannibalized science.

As opposed to this culture of instrumentality, which 'works' with a concept of a universal, perfectly objective, cumulative science and admits at best only the existence of peripheral folk-sciences from which modern science may occasionally pick up scraps of information, the marginalized parts of the world—the second-class citizens of the Third World, marginalized even in their own societies—protect their dignity by viewing the world of science as an area of a number of coexisting, universal ethnosciences, one of which has become dominant and usurped the status of the only universal and the only contemporary science.[41] Various traditional systems of medicine, artisan skills which retain the individuality of the producer and refuse to draw a line between art and craft, agricultural practices which have resisted the destructive pull of modern agronomy—these are not only aspects of a resilient cultural self-affirmation; these are indicators of a spirit which defies the power of a way of life which seeks to cannibalize all other ways of life. The Third World has a vested interest in refusing to grant sanctity to a science which sees human beings and nature as the raw material for vivisectional experimentation. What seems an irrational, impractical or unworkable resistance to the products of modern science and technology in the peripheries of the world is often a deeply rooted suspicion of the instrumental vision of sectors which live off these peripheries and a desperate attempt to preserve alternative concepts of knowledge, technique and work in the interstices of the savage world.

VI

Fourth, the experience of suffering of some Third World societies has added a new dimension to utopianism by sensing and resisting the oppression which comes as 'history'. By history as oppression I mean not only the limits which our past always seems to impose on our visions of the future, but also the use of a linear, progressive, cumulative, deterministic concept of history—often carved out of humanistic ideologies—to

[41]See Ashis Nandy, 'Science in Utopia: Equity, Plurality and Openness', *India International Centre Quarterly*, 1983, 10(1), pp. 47–59.

suppress alternative world-views, alternative utopias and even alternative self-concepts. The peripheries of the world often feel that they are victimized not merely by partial, biased or ethnocentric history, but by the idea of history itself.

One can give a psychopathological interpretation of such scepticism towards history, often inextricably linked with painful, fearsome memories of man-made suffering. Defiance of history may look like a primitive denial of history and, to the extent the present is fully shaped by history in the modern perception, denial of contemporary realities. But, even from a strictly clinical point of view, there can be reasons for and creative uses of ahistoricity. What Alexander and Margarete Mitscherlich say about those with a history of inflicting suffering also applies to those who have a history of being victims:

A very considerable expenditure of psychic energy is necessary to maintain this separation of acceptable and unacceptable memories; and what is used in the defence of a self anxious to protect itself against bitter qualms of conscience and doubts about its worth is unavailable for mastering the present.[42]

The burden of history is the burden of such memories and anti-memories. Some cultures prefer to live with it and painfully excavate the anti-memories and integrate them as part of the present consciousness. Some cultures prefer to handle the same problem at the mythopoetic level. Instead of excavating for the so-called real past, they excavate for other meanings of the present, as revealed in traditions and myths about an ever-present but open past. The anti-memories at that level become less passionate and they allow greater play and lesser defensive rigidity.

What seems an ahistorical and even anti-historical attitude in many non-modern cultures is often actually an attempt on the part of these cultures to incorporate their historical experiences into their shared traditions as categories of thinking, rather than as objective chronicles of the past.[43] In these cultures, the mystical and consciousness-expanding modes are alternative pathways to experiences which in other societies are sought through a linear concept of a 'real' history. In the modern context these modes can sometimes become what Robert J. Lifton calls 'romantic totalism'—a post-Cartesian absolutism which seeks to replace

---

[42]Alexander Mitscherlich and Margarete Mitscherlich, 'The Inability to Mourn', in Robert J. Lifton and Eric Olson (eds.), *Explorations in Psychohistory: The Wellfleet Papers* (New York: Simon and Schuster, 1974), pp. 257–70, quotation on p. 262.

[43]See a fuller discussion of these themes with reference to Gandhi's world-view in Nandy, *The Intimate Enemy*.

history with experience.[44] But that is not a fate which is written into the origins of these modes. If the predicament is the totalism and not the romance, the *history* of civilizations after Christopher Columbus and Vasco da Gama also shows that that totalism can also come from a history which seeks to replace experience. Especially so when, after the advent of the idea of scientific history, history has begun to share in the near-monopoly science has already established in the area of human certitude. Albert Camus once drew a line between the makers of history and the victims of history. The job of the writer, he said, was to write about the victims. For the silent majority of the world, the makers of history also live in history and the defiance of history begins not so much with an alternative history as with the denial of history as an acreage of human certitude.

In their scepticism of history, the ahistorical cultures have an ally in certain recessive orientations to the past in the western culture, which have re-emerged in recent decades in some forms of structuralism and psychoanalysis, in attempts to view history either as semiotics or as a 'screen memory' with its own rules of dream-work. As we well know, the dynamics of history, according to these disciplines, is not in an unalterable past moving towards an inexorable future; it is in the ways of thinking and in the choices of present times.[45]

The rejection of history to protect self-esteem and ensure survival is often a response to the structure of cognition history presumes. The more scientific a history, the more oppressive it tends to be in the experimental laboratory called the Third World. It is scientific history which has allowed the idea of social intervention to be cannibalized by the ideal of social engineering at the peripheries of the world. For the moderns, history has always been the unfolding of a theory of progress, a serialized expression of a telos which, by definition, cannot be shared by communities on the lower rungs of the ladder of history. Even the histories of oppression and the historical theories of liberation postulate stages of growth which, instead of widening the victims' options, reduce them. No wonder that

---

[44]Robert J. Lifton, *Boundaries: Psychological Man in Revolution* (New York: Simon and Schuster, 1969), pp. 105–6. On a different plane, Alvin Gouldner has drawn attention to the close links between utopianism and ahistoricity. See his *The Dialectic of Ideology and Technology: The Origins, Grammar and Future of Ideology* (London: Macmillan, 1976), pp. 88–9.

[45]I need hardly add that within the modern idea of history, too, this view has survived as a latent—and, one is tempted to add, unconscious—strain. From Karl Marx to Benedetto Croce and from R.G. Collingwood to Michael Oakeshott, philosophers of history have often moved close to an approach to history which is compatible with traditional orientations to past times.

till now the main function of these theories has been to ensure the centrality of the cultural and intellectual experiences of a few societies, so that all dissent can be monitored and framed in the idiom of domination.

The ethnocentrism of the anthropologist can be corrected; he is segregated from his subject only socially and, some day, his subjects can talk back. The ethnocentrism towards the past mostly goes unchallenged. The dead do not rebel, nor can they speak out. So the subjecthood of the subjects of history is absolute, and the demand for a real or scientific history is the demand for a continuity between subjecthood in history and subjection in the present. The corollary to the refusal to accept the primacy of history is the refusal to chain the future to the past. This refusal is a special attitude to human potentialities, an alternative form of utopianism that has survived till now as a language alien to, and subversive of, every theory which in the name of liberation circumscribes and makes predictable the spirit of human rebelliousness.

VII

As my final example, I shall briefly discuss the so-called dependency syndrome in some Third World cultures. When offset against the Occidental man's unending search for autonomy or independence, it is this syndrome in the non-western personality which allegedly explains the origin, meaning and resilience of colonial subjugation.

Such explanations have been savagely attacked by both Césaire and Fanon as racist psychoanalysis. Césaire quotes the following words of Octave Manoni as virtually final proof of the western psychologist's prejudice against all oppressed cultures:

It is the destiny of the Occidental to face the obligation laid down by the commandment *Thou shalt leave thy father and thy mother*. This obligation is incomprehensible to the Madagascan. At a given time in his development, every European discovers in himself the desire . . . to break the bonds of dependency, to become the equal of his father. The Madagascan, never! He does not experience rivalry with the paternal authority, 'manly protest', or Adlerian inferiority— ordeals through which the European must pass and which are civilized forms . . . of the initiation rites by which one achieves manhood.[46]

I have not been able to locate this passage in Manoni's *Prospero and Caliban* and do not know in which context it occurs.[47] Nor do I know

---

[46]Octave Manoni, quoted in Césaire, *Discourse*, p. 40. Italics in the original.
[47]O. Manoni, *Prospero and Caliban: The Psychology of Colonization*, trans. Pamela Powesland, 2nd ed. (New York: Praeger, 1964).

Manoni's politics which presumably can provide the other context of these sentences. Thus, I have to accept at face value Césaire's and Fanon's plaint that Manoni vends 'down-at-heel clichés' to justify 'absurd preju-dices' and 'dresses up' the old stereotype of the Negro as an overgrown child.

Yet, I have a nagging suspicion that a third view on the subject is sustainable. That view would recognize that the modern West has not only institutionalized a concept of childhood shaped by the ideology of masculine, non-dependent adulthood and societies which represent such adulthood, it has also popularized a devastatingly sterile concept of au-tonomy and individualism which has increasingly atomized the western individual. Many non-western observers of the culture of the modern West—its lifestyle, literature, arts and its human sciences—have been struck by the way contractual, competitive individualism—and the utter loneliness which flows from it—dominates the western mass society. From Friedrich Nietzsche to Karl Marx to Franz Kafka, much of western social analysis, too, has stood witness to this cultural pathology. What once looked like independence from one's immediate authorities in the family, and defiance of the larger aggregates they represented, now looks more and more like a Hobbesian world-view gone rabid. The individual in the mass society is not only in an adversary relationship with everyone else, his individuality increasingly depends upon his becoming an inde-pendent consumption unit to which 'machines' would sell consumables and from which other machines would get work in order to produce more consumables. To the extent Manoni imputes to the Madagascan some degree of anti-individualism, to the extent the Madagascan is not a well-demarcated person, he unwittingly underscores the point that modern individualism—and the insane search for absolute autonomy it has unleashed—cannot be truly separated from the thirst for colonies, *Lebensraum* and domination for the sake of domination. In an inter-dependent world, total autonomy for one means the reduction of the autonomy of others.

Hence, while the much-maligned dependency complex may not be the best possible cultural arrangement in the face of modern oppression, it could be seen as a more promising baseline for mounting a search for more genuine social relatedness and for maturer forms of individuality than the one which now dominates the world. The baseline may not meet the exacting standards of the westernized critics of the West in the Third World, it may not yield the virile anti-imperialism by which they swear, but those who have lived for centuries with only the extremes of related-ness and dependency will never guess that in a world taken over by the autonomy principle and by the extremes of individualism, dependency and fears of abandonment could represent a hope and a potentiality. The pathology of relatedness has already become less dangerous than the pathology of unrelatedness. What looks like an 'ego wanting in strength' in the Malagasy or a case of a 'weak ego' in the Indian can be viewed as another kind of ego strength. What looks like poor independence training in the non-achieving societies and 'willing subservience' and 'self-castration' in the Hindu may be read also as an affirmation of basic relatedness and a recognition of the need for some degree of reverence in human relations.[48] At one place in his *Discourse on Colonialism*, Césaire traces Nazism to Europe's bloodstained record in the colonies. Nazism, he says, was only a way of life coming home to roost.[49] Césaire seems unaware that some have already traced Nazi satanism to the unrestrained spread in Europe, over the previous century, of the doctrines of amoral realpolitik and *sacro egoismo* and of the 'morals of a struggle that no longer allows for respect'.[50] All that remains to be done is to relate the colonial impulse, too, to the search for non-reverential autonomy and total individualism, even though the same search is now part of many anti-colonial ideologies.

VIII

I have chosen these examples to describe what I have called the indissoluble bond between the future of the peripheries of the world and that of the apparently autonomous, powerful, prosperous, imperial centres. This is necessarily an essay on the continuity between winners and losers, seen from the losers' point of view. The reader must have noticed that each of the examples I have given also happens to be a live problem in exactly those parts of the world which are commonly considered privileged. The various forms of neo-Marxism, the various versions of

[48]For instance, Manoni, *Prospero and Caliban*, p. 41; G. Morris Carstairs, *The Twice Born: A Study of a Community of High-Caste Hindus* (Bombay: Allied Publishers, 1971), p. 160. I have of course in mind a galaxy of other well-motivated academics and writers, such as, to give random examples, David C. McClelland and David G. Winter, *Motivating Economic Achievement* (New York: Basic Books, 1969); Alex Inkeles and Donald H. Smith, *Becoming Modern* (London: Heinemann, 1974); Nirad C. Chaudhuri, *The Continent of Circe* (London: Chatto and Windus, 1965); V.S. Naipaul, *India: A Wounded Civilization* (London: André Deutsch, 1977); and *Among the Believers: An Islamic Journey* (London: André Deutsch, 1981).

[49]Césaire, *Discourse, passim*.

[50]Friedrich Meinecke and Gerhard Ritter, quoted in Renzo De Felice, *Interpretations of Fascism*, trans. Brenda H. Everett (Cambridge, Mass.: Harvard University, 1977), pp. 17–18.

the women's liberation movement, the numerous attempts to build alternative philosophies of science and technology by giving up the insane search for total control and predictability are but a recognition that the gaps between the so-called privileged and underprivileged of the world are mostly notional. As the peripheries of the world have been subjected to economic degradation and political impotency and robbed of their human dignity with the help of Dionysian theories of progress, the First and the Second Worlds too have sunk deeper into intellectual provincialism, cultural decadence and moral degradation. In my version of an old cliché, no victor can be a victor without being a victim. In the case of nation-states as much as in the case of two-person situations, there is an indivisibility of ethical and cognitive choices. If the Third World's vision of the future is handicapped by its experience of man-made suffering, the First World's future, too, is shaped by the same record.

The reader might also have noticed that I have tried to give moral and cultural content to some of the common ways in which the savage world has tried to cope with modern oppression and then projected these common ways as possibilities or opportunities. How far is this justified? After all, as one popular argument goes, history is made through the dirty process of political economy; it has no place for human subjectivity or for any defensive moralizing about human frailties and attempts to make a virtue out of necessity. Perhaps, in line with some non-modern traditions of interpretation, I could be allowed to argue that the so-called ultimate realities of political economy too could be further demystified to obtain clues to new moral visions of the human future. The frailties of human nature produced by a given social arrangement in the context of a given political economy, too, can begin to look like the baseline of a new society, once another social arrangement is envisioned. The frailty of human frailties, too, is an open question and an open text. I take heart from a brain researcher who has recently said, summing up comparative zoological work on evolution, that there also is a 'survival of the weak', and the weak do inherit the world.[51]

Such an approach is not negated by the blood-drenched history of man-made suffering in the Third World—I am speaking of possibilities and opportunities, not offering a prognosis based on a trend analysis. Exactly as one cannot stop the magical mystery tours of the Third World undertaken by many First-World environmentalists (in defiance of the

[51]Paul D. MacLean, 'The Imitative–Creative Interplay of Our Three Mentalities', in Harold Harris (ed.), *Astride the Two Cultures: Arthur Koestler at 70* (New York: Random House, 1976), pp. 187–213.

totalist anthropocentrism and the arrogant ecocidal world-conception they see around them) by drawing attention to the poor conservationist record of the Third World. For what is being proposed is a new cultural self-expression of an ancient man–nature symbiosis, not a statistical projection of the past or the present into the future.

I hope all this will not be seen as an elaborate attempt to project the sensitivities of the Third World as the future consciousness of the globe or a plea to the First World to wallow in a comforting sense of guilt. Nor does it, I hope, sound like the standard doomsday 'propheteering' which often prefaces fiery calls to a millennial revolution. All I am trying to do is to affirm that ultimately it is not a matter of synthesizing or aggregating different civilizational visions of the future. Rather, it is a matter of admitting that while each civilization must find its own authentic vision of the future and its own authenticity in future, neither is conceivable without admitting the experience of co-suffering which has now brought some of the major civilizations of the world close to each other. It is this co-suffering which makes the idea of cultural closeness something more than the chilling concept of One World which nineteenth-century European optimism popularized and promoted to the status of a dogma.[52]

The intercultural communion I am speaking about is defined by two intellectual coordinates. The first of them is the recognition that the 'true' values of different civilizations are not in need of synthesis. They are, in terms of basic biopsychological needs, already in reasonable harmony and capable of transcending the barriers of particularist consciousness. The principle of cultural relativism—that I write on the possibilities of a distinct eupsychia for the Third World is a partial admission of such relativism—is acceptable only to the extent it accepts the universalism of some core values of humankind. Anthropologism is no cure for ethnocentrism; it merely pluralizes the latter. Absolute relativism can also become an absolute justification of oppression in the name of ethnic tolerance, as it often becomes in the 'apolitical' anthropologist's field report.

---

[52]As Fouad Ajami recognizes, 'The faith of those in the core in global solutions came up against the suspicions of those located elsewhere that in schemes of this kind the mighty would prevail, that they would blow away the cobwebs behind which weak societies lived . . . . In a world where cultural boundaries are dismantled, we suspect we know who would come out on top.' See Fouad Ajami, 'The Dialectics of Local and Global Culture: Islam and Other Cases', paper presented at the meeting of the group on Culture, Power and Transformation, World Order Models Project, Lisbon, 1980, mimeographed. Ajami advises us to walk an intellectual and political tightrope, avoiding both the 'pit of cultural hegemony' and 'undiluted cultural relativism'.

The second coordinate is the acknowledgement that the search for authenticity of a civilization is always a search for the other face of the civilization, either as a hope or as a warning. The search for a civilization's utopia, too, is part of this larger quest. It needs not merely the ability to interpret and reinterpret one's own traditions but also the ability to involve the often-recessive aspects of other civilizations as allies in one's struggle for cultural self-discovery, the willingness to become allies to other civilizations trying to discover their other faces, and the skills to give more centrality to these new readings of civilizations and civilizational concerns. This is the only form of a dialogue of cultures which can transcend the flourishing intercultural barters of our times.

*Earlier published in Ashis Nandy, *Tradition, Tyranny, and Utopias: Essays in the Politics of Awareness* (New Delhi: Oxford University Press, 1987).

18

~mm~

Shamans, Savages and the Wilderness
On the Audibility of Dissent and the Future of Civilizations

WE ARE LIVING in a global civilization, even if it does not look to us sufficiently global. This civilization has certain features and 'ground rules' and those who want to consolidate, transcend or dismantle it, must first identify them.

Foremost among the rules are a few laws of obedience that come in many guises, only two of which I shall touch upon here. The first is the peculiarly narrow and specific form dissent has to take, to be audible or politically 'non-co-optable' in our times. The second is the strange inaudibility that plagues those who, by design or by default, have become citizens of the dominant global culture. In the first section of this paper, we shall discuss the former; in the second, the latter. I shall then suggest that the two can be conceptually collapsed and the Third World can be made to represent that collapsed category, but the reader need not accept that part of the story.

The Dissent of the Shaman

If the first criterion of a global civilization is that all other surviving civilizations define themselves with reference to it, the signs today are all too clear. The old classification between the historical and ahistorical societies may not have broken down, but all large ahistorical societies now have sizeable sections of population that have become, through a process of over-correction, entirely captive to the historical mode. They

not only would like to rewrite their own histories but to live up to someone else's history. It is a remarkable feature of our times that so many
individuals and collectivities are willing and are even eager to forego their
right to design their own futures. Some societies do not any longer have a
workable concept of the future. They have a past, a present and someone
else's present as their future. 'The entire East', Rabindranath Tagore said
more than fifty years ago, is 'attempting to take into itself a history which
is not the outcome of its own living.'[1]

Some other societies have done even better; they have got rid of parts
of their past and present, or rewritten the rest from the point of view of
their borrowed futures. Their journey from the past to the present now
reads remarkably like similar journeys undertaken by other—usually
west European—societies during the last three hundred years. They are
the success stories in the global civilization today; they can be called the
new historical societies.

More than forty years ago, Ruth Benedict wrote her *Chrysanthemum
and the Sword*.[2] In that book, written during the Second World War
and published soon after, she identified a configuration of cultural and
personality characteristics which could be identified as the source of
Japanese authoritarianism and militarism. Less than twenty years later
Robert Bellah, then in his earlier incarnation, wrote of the Protestant-
ethics-like elements in Japanese culture—as a clue to Japan's growing
economic muscle.[3] As it happened, some of the elements on which Bellah
focused were not terribly different from the ones that to Professor Benedict
had looked so dangerous. Within another decade, Herman Kahn, the
technocratic oracle, wrote another book on Japan, this time a highly
adulatory one.[4] Trying to explain the success of what he predicted would
soon be world's third superpower, Kahn stumbled on many of the same
traits Benedict and Bellah had touched upon, only with a sense of awe
and a touch of admiration and zeal.

It is easy to explain all this away by saying that nothing succeeds like
success. It is more difficult to admit that all criteria, except the ones handed
down to us by the dominant global consciousness, are being either pre-
empted or rendered obsolete. On the one hand, Japan's developmental

---

[1]Rabindranath Tagore, *Nationalism* (Madras: Macmillan, 1985), p. 64.

[2]Ruth Benedict, *Chrysanthemum and the Sword* (New York: Penguin Books,
1967).

[3]Robert N. Bellah, 'Reflections on the Protestant Ethic Analogy in Asia', *The
Journal of Social Issues*, 1963, 19(1), pp. 52–60.

[4]Herman Kahn, *Emerging Japanese Superstate: Challenge and Response* (New
York: Prentice-Hall, 1971).

success has silenced its internal cultural critics and reconstructed Japan's past from the point of view of her preferred future; on the other, it has given Japan a new set of criteria of self-evaluation from the present global civilization, including parts of a brand-new identity.

The same case can be made about the well-known 'failures' within the present global civilization. Thanks to her defeat in the game of development, Bangladesh today, to use a cliché, is an 'international basket case'. Her all other self-definitions are facing extinction. And you have to only read the Indian press and listen to the lament of the Indian literati today to know how unhappy the modern Indians are that many aberrant self-definitions still persist in Indian society and how much they, the modern Indians, derive psychological security from the fact that at least the political ultra-élite in India at the moment seems fully immersed in the global mass culture of politics.

The recovery of the other selves of cultures and communities, selves not defined by the dominant global consciousness, may turn out to be the first task of social criticism and political activism and the first responsibility of intellectual stocktaking in the first decades of the coming century. But that recovery may not be easy. As I have said, radical dissent today constantly faces the danger of getting organized into a standardized form. It begins to borrow from the dominant world-view to sustain itself, to reach out to the mainstream, to model itself on the previously successful and popular. Whether revolution consumes its children or not, it certainly follows an Orwellian logic to produce a new priesthood— may be a revolutionary priesthood but a priesthood nonetheless—to somehow attain respectability within the present global culture. We shall come back to this issue later in this essay, albeit through a different route.

The only way out, at this moment, seems to be that of the shaman. The shaman not as the heroic symbol of all non-co-optable dissent but the shaman as a more modest symbol of resistance to the dominant politics of knowledge, the shaman as one whose style of negation and whose categories do not make any sense centre-stage but always seem to touch the disempowered in the wings. A shaman is not an expert and he or she cannot be produced through or co-opted by institutional processes. Coming out of a transformative experience and, then, claiming to be a testimony to another way of looking at reality and intervening in it, the shaman is a combination of a mystic healer and an exorcist who identifies demons—popular or unpopular, traditional or modern. The shaman has one foot in the familiar, one foot outside; one foot in the present, one in the future or, as some would put it, in the timeless.

The shaman waits—this shaman I am speaking of, not the anthropologist's favourite subject—till the right moment and the right candidates come, to reproduce him or herself. Because the moment the shaman uses the available institutional instrumentalities, he or she becomes a part of the everyday world, a priest—someone who has power and perhaps, even charisma, but is not subversive. A priest is never subversive. The priest helps consolidate a culture, whether as a priest to a revolutionary movement or as a high priest in art. He or she might have a subversive past but it is only a past, and nothing is as dead as the past in a historical society.

The shaman *can* survive in a historical society but with difficulty. Usually as a relic of the past, surviving in the present under sufferance and waiting to be superseded by interpreters who will, rationally and systematically, explain shamanism or, if it does not stand up to critical scrutiny, consign it to history, identifying it as belonging to an earlier stage of the evolution of consciousness. The shaman may even manage to survive in a historical society as a lunatic, a schizophrenic who should be psychiatrically committed or, if that becomes politically embarrassing, met with deafening silence.

However, it is possible to argue that once you explain a shaman properly, you turn him or her into a *guru* or, worse, a priest, an odd eccentric priest may be, but a priest nevertheless. The difference between the shaman and the priest is in some ways akin to the one George Steiner, I am told, has drawn somewhere between books and texts. The shaman here is the text, the priest the book. A text can be read in many more ways than a book can ever be. In our times, Marx, Freud and Gandhi are examples of persons who have produced or have become texts. Most of their disciples, though, have consistently tried to turn them into books, closed ones at that.

Alternatively, the shaman can assume a prophetic voice, partly outside the society and entirely outside the metropolis. Unlike the priest, the shaman can afford to be irresponsible, immature and irrational. The shaman's responsibility is ultimately to an inner vision, or, as many would put it, to an inner vision of truth. Yet, it can be argued that the shaman is actually the repressed self of the society; articulating some possibilities latent in a culture, possibilities which the 'sane', the 'mature' and the 'rational' cannot self-consciously express or seriously pursue.

Probably, I am being unfair. The sane, the rational and the mature, too, will like to explore the shamanic possibilities, but only if the hazards can be foreseen or, at least, cast in the language of probability theory. Unfortunately, the shaman can give certainty only within the shamanic world, not within ours. The choice he or she offers is nothing less than a choice between two worlds.

It can be argued that the shaman also forces a choice between civilizations and cultures. As one who esteems civilizational categories, I say this with a touch of sadness. The concept of civilization carries with it a connotation of civility and the city. It conveys, however indirectly, high culture. The idea of culture is a more modest affair; it can cover the political structure of the African Bushmen, the art of the Navahos, or the dying healing system of the Santhals of eastern India. The shaman's whole existence is a defiance of civility and the city. But then, one may say, taking off from William Thompson, that if history represents an oscillation between the city and the wilderness, and by implication between civilizations and cultures, the shaman is a living warning that in that oscillation the wilderness—the insurrection of the little cultures, as some call it—may have to be taken seriously. Owning up the shaman can be made to mean the responsibility to own up that oscillation, too.

Perhaps, in the present global culture, the shaman, taken metaphysically as the opposition to the king and the priest, remains the ultimate symbol of authentic dissent, representing the utopian and transcendental aspects of the child, the lunatic, the androgynous, and the artist. In this sense, he remains the least socialized articulation of the values of freedom, creativity, multiple realities and an open future. At a time when mass culture and media dominate the world capitals, the shaman tries to transcend the manifest reality and the straitjacket of commonsense. True, this expression of defiance uses a language of transcendence or utopianism. But that is partly because the shaman has to force us to move beyond the accessible world of knowledge to the mysterious world of those who remain the undersocialized critics of the present global civilization.

I do not want to push this metaphor too far, for using the shaman as the ultimate symbol of non-co-optable dissent has its hazards. The shaman's concept of collectivity includes a fear of organization and structured dissent. The shaman often is too anarchic, too individualistic, and too suspicious of all formal political processes. But I do want to underscore that, before envisioning the global civilization of the future, one must first own up the responsibility of creating a space at the margins of the present global civilization for a new, plural, political ecology of knowledge. In that ecology, there will certainly have to be a place for our favourite priests and anti-priests but also for a variety of moonstruck shamans, ever ready to lead us into adventures of ideas which, in 'normal' everyday life, must look like lunatics' visions or children's fantasies. Not that the visions or fantasies are ever likely to be realized—a shaman's vision is never realizable in everyday life; it only resonates in the lives of other shamans or prospective shamans and in the dreams of those to whom he or she is not merely a harmless lunatic—but because the shaman experiments with experiences on behalf of us all. The shaman's dissent is against the conventionality of everyday life and thought.

This does not mean that the shaman does not carry a cultural baggage. Shamans are also human. They are not outside time or space, though they may believe otherwise. Moreover, they rarely love shamans belonging to other tribes. But they do usually consider the world large enough for different kinds and they do usually know how to live with one another. Their empiricism in these matters is derived from life, not books. Their admirers are the ones who find it more arduous to tolerate other shamans and their followers. Karl Marx, who never really ceased to be a shaman, could congratulate Abraham Lincoln on the abolition of slavery in the United States because he was less constrained than the later Marxists by the nature of the system over which Lincoln presided. Human suffering was real to Marx; he tried to look at it directly, not through the pages of books, not even when they were his own.

Liberation for Those Who do not Speak the Language of Liberation

Oddly enough, the problem of inaudibility, to which we shall now turn, is not entirely orthogonal to the problem of audibility. They intertwine in strange ways.

Fiodor Dostoevsky has reportedly claimed somewhere that there are two classes of people in the world: the anthropologists and the subjects of anthropological study. Over the last two hundred years, one subset in the anthropologists' world have learnt to speak the language of liberation—a secularized version of the language of liberation once pre-eminent in much of the Christendom. Today, the power of the language has become so enormous that nearly all dissent within the modern world and the modernized Third World has to be cast in the language, to be heard or taken seriously.

In the world of the subjects of anthropology, the rhetoric of liberation is a new import. It is not usually taken seriously and it is often seen as esoteric radical chic. There are concepts akin to 'liberation' in some of the major civilizations of the world—the Sanskritic concepts of *moksa* and *mukti* are obvious examples—but they neither enjoy the same political clout nor the intellectual stature to move the social and political activists. In fact, many indigenous concepts akin to liberation often carry strong connotations of a theory of transcendence and/or other-worldliness.

Predictably, a plethora of social activists since the last century have been trying to teach the objects of anthropological enquiry, scattered all over the world, the beauties of liberation. From St Marx in the nineteenth century to comrade Mao Ze Dong in the twentieth, from Christian missionaries in the savage world to Reverend Paulo Freire among the volatile, noisy Latin Americans, none has let slip an opportunity to teach the language of liberation to those who do not speak it.

This language of liberation, as it has grown over the last 150 years, is inextricably linked to the idea of revolution. Revolution is what brings about fundamental or radical changes in a society and, thus, the liberation of oppressed peoples. Its votaries, therefore, see revolution as opposed to both status quo and reform. However, the revolutionaries are usually harshest not on the defenders of status quo but on the defenders of reform. To the partisans of revolution, reform is a false mode of transformative politics, dangerous because it can become an easy substitute for revolution. The best that the idea of reform does, this line of argument goes, is to provide a safe internal critique of a faulty social system and, thus, strengthen the system.

To those who do not use the language of liberation and/or revolution, these debates read like fruitless hair-splitting. For neither do these outsiders view change as intrinsically valuable nor do they see any sustainable philosophical ground to presume a one-to-one relationship between any language of change and the processes of change.

These outsiders are also vaguely aware that the break in linear time a revolution is supposed to represent has a self-contradictory quality about it. Revolution in contemporary times is seen as located in history and the break in time it represents is supposed to be a break in history. Yet, once you have said that, you are faced with the fact that, ever since the concept of revolution has entered the lexicon of social intervention, after every revolution, the effort of both the partisans and the critics of the revolution has been to establish, *ex post facto*, that there really was no break, that the revolution was inevitable and the historical process was leading up to it. History, thus, gobbles up the idea of the 'break in history' intellectually.

Some understanding of this process informs the modern awareness, too, though the popular saying 'a revolution consumes its children' does not convey the full implication of the proposal being ventured here, namely that it is not revolution but the language of continuity which consumes the language of change. Once this implication is accepted, the proposal

brings us back to the language and world-view of those who refuse—
or are unable—to speak the language of change, history, revolution and
liberation but who nevertheless, in their own way and with the help of
their own categories, resist domination and theorize about it.

The other main argument of this part of the paper is that the attempts to introduce the language of liberation to those who do not speak
it, as a precondition for the latter qualifying for what the moderns call
liberation, is a travesty of even the normatives of the modern concept of
liberation. (Though it is perfectly compatible with the social evolutionism underpinning the concept.) I am not at the moment entering the more
serious objection to the modernist demand—the demand that the victim
must learn the oppressor's language and world-view before qualifying
as a proper dissenter—that the post-seventeenth century concept of dissent itself is a prototypical pathology of the Enlightenment vision of the
human future, a vision which sees itself as the last word in human self-
realization and a logical culmination of the Baconian project of building
modern science as the ultimate legitimation of domination, by giving
modern scientific rationality absolute priority over democratic rights and
over the subjective and objective experiences of man-made suffering.

The modern world, including the modernized Third World, is built
on the suffering and brutalization of millions. These victims, rebellious
only when in their eyes the stakes and the options are right, seek justice
and empowerment. If the moderns want to call this search a search for
liberation, it is their lookout and their tryst with their morality. To the
lesser mortals, being constantly sought to be liberated by a minority within
the modern world, the resistance to the categories imposed on them by
the dominant culture of global politics, including the categories imposed
by the dominant language of dissent, is part of the struggle for survival.

This resistance takes many shapes in the savage world. It may take
the form of a full-blooded rejection of the modern world's deepest faith,
scientific rationality. It may take the form of a subtle subversion of the
modern world's fondest—I almost said cleverest—charity, development.
One can never be sure and the strength of the resistance lies in the fact
that one can never be sure.

Note that I am not here concerned with the viability or otherwise
of either modern science or development, nor with the substantive
justifiability of these rejections. I may have something to say about them
but this is not the place. I am here concerned with the politics of these
rejections, the way the growing hostility to these cognitive and pro-
grammatic ventures, among those whom science and development are
supposed to benefit, tells one something about the power relations of

knowledge and the politics of knowledge-based social transformation in our times. I am proposing here that, for a large part of the world, the negation of certain universals of knowledge is a natural *political* consequence of the nature of dominance exercised in our times. For domination today is rarely justified through oracles, ritual superiority, or claims to birthrights; domination is now more frequently justified in terms of better acquaintance with universal knowledge and better access to universal modes of acquiring knowledge. In the world of awareness in which we live, without such things as scientific rationality, laboratory experiments and analytic reasoning, without the acquisition of a progressivist, social–evolutionist idiom and without a proper historical consciousness, reportedly no human being is any more fully human. All oppressed, to acquire the right to our attention and sympathy, have to first show that they are the truly deserving oppressed and are not a part of the flora and fauna of the Southern world—timeless, unindividuated and living in a mythopoetic world.

The more sensitive modern counter-response to such 'irrational', 'infantile' and 'atavistic' political response to the favourite slogans of the dominant global culture (provided the counter-response is not as dismissive as it usually is) has been to split the concepts being challenged or resisted. Thus, for instance, there is now a modern science reportedly dominated by the establishment and a modern science reportedly emancipatory or liberative. The former constitutes the mainstream; it is wedded to militarism, capitalism and giganticism. The latter is a form of dissent; it is non-conventional, futuristic and egalitarian. Similarly, development has been split into two: conventional development and 'another' development. The latter has many aliases; it is often called alternative development, sustainable development, ecodevelopment or indigenous development.

I am in great sympathy with many of these efforts to generate alternatives. I have personal links with a few of them. But I cannot for that reason deny that most of the efforts are also products of the same worldview which has produced the mainstream concepts of science, liberation and development. Nor can I deny that the political logic of the battle of minds demands that the victims of the oppressive forces in our times first attack the domination of the ideas of modern scientific rationality, history and progress as the organizing principles of all social intervention and then, only then, seriously consider if some elements from them can be safely accommodated in a post-modern science or in a post-development world.

This does not mean that internal criticisms have no value at this point of time. This means that internal criticisms are internal criticisms. They do not exhaust all criticisms. They certainly do not exhaust the criticisms of human violence and oppression which are implicit in the ways of life, myths, legends and, above all, in the spontaneous defiance and rebellions of the oppressed. These self-expressions are not usually cast in the language of liberation; even less frequently can they be accommodated in a proper theory of liberation. We, standing outside, can try to translate these self-expressions into our language and construct for ourselves a theory of liberation out of the 'primitive', 'populist' theories of oppression and spontaneous acts of subversion, but these are our needs, not theirs.

It is with that awareness that we may have to try to give voice or, at least, to create the space for those who will give voice, to the victims of man-made sufferings in the coming decades. The awareness does not deny that man-made suffering is a joint product of the lifestyles, systems of knowledge and theories of liberation populating the world in which we the moderns live. It insists that those trying to give voice to the voiceless must recognize that, after nearly four centuries of presence on the world stage and after about two centuries of hegemony, the culture of modern Europe and North America no longer arouses the enthusiasm which, as a critique of traditions, it once aroused in the Third World. The first generation of social reformers in the colonized societies hoped to use modernity as a vector within the Asian and African traditions, something which would, by providing an outsider's critique, help them recover certain recessive aspects of these traditions and give more strength and vivacity to the traditions. It is now fairly obvious that such controlled use of modernity has not been possible in the savage world. Modernity is not only triumphant in the Southern hemisphere; it has taken over as an imperial principle in human consciousness in society after society. What was dissent has now become the establishment.

As an in-house criticism of that mainstream, the theories of liberation may have to learn a lot. They will certainly have to be, as a part of the ruling world-view, more modest. As an aspect of the modern world's concept of sane, mature, scientific dissent, with only the romantic traditions of nineteenth-century Europe to give them a touch of unmanageability or untameability, these theories have the idea of historical inevitability to back them up and they can hope to ride piggy-back on the urban–industrial vision of life and mass culture. For that same reason, however, these theories must recognize the existence of dissent that is not only 'insane' and 'infantile' but which flouts the first canon of all post-Enlightenment theories of knowledge, namely that a dissent to qualify as dissent must be fully translatable into the idiom of modernity.

I doubt if the rebellious spirit of humanity can be ever fully captured in what is essentially one civilization's concept of rebellion in a particular point of time. What is dissent if it has no place for the unknown, the childlike and the non-rational? And what is the intellectual's job-definition if it does not include the ability to be in a minority and at the borderlines of the knowable?

One last word on the inaudibility of dissent. Everyone is for the liberation of some group or other in the 'civilized' world. The idea of liberation now cuts across most modern ideologies and has become the common currency over a large cultural terrain. But the enthusiasm for liberating others has only infrequently been matched by any respect for the categories, particularly the native 'half-baked' theories of oppression used by the others. For, to accept such home-brewed theories is to, in effect, cut out the role of the experts on revolution and de-expertize dissent. That is why there is such limited acceptance, among the theorists of liberation, of the categories of those who supposedly are waiting to be led to their liberation by some specialist group or other.

On second thought, this is less surprising than it seems. Ideologues are always ambivalent towards the peoples whose cause they take up. Ideologues are always embarrassed by their targeted beneficiaries, allegedly stuck in an earlier stage of history and disinclined to show much interest in the good turn going to be done to them by the ideologues. Horror of horrors, even when the benefits are delivered to them, the beneficiaries conceptualize the benefits in their own way. As a result, their gratefulness to their liberators, too, is often shockingly close to zero. Understandably so. Human nature being what it is, while everyone likes to be a social engineer, few like to be the objects of social engineering.

Such cynicism of the savage world, towards our favourite rhetoric of dissent, may not be such a great loss. For all we know, it may widen our choices and keep the options for future generations more open. In matters of human futures there probably can be no final word. And while the quest for freedom is perennial, the present language of liberation need not be so. In fact, as the temporal and spatial limitations of the language become more obvious, that which looks like a hopeless case of dislexia may turn out to be a 'natural' cognitive advantage. In the sense that those who are thoroughly socialized in the presently dominant language of global communications may find it harder to re-educate themselves than those who start from scratch. In the meanwhile, it is possible to venture the proposal that to survive beyond the tenure of the modern knowledge systems, the language of liberation will have to take into account, respectfully, the quests for freedom which are articulated in other languages and in other forms, sometimes even through the language of silence.

Who knows, those who force the language of liberation to take into account these other languages and forms may have in future a special place in the calculations of those to whom the language of liberation is only a useful but flawed instrument to actualize the human quest for freedom? But then, so long has the language of liberation been grounded in the nineteenth-century thirst for certitude and objectivist interpretations of the human enterprise that it has probably lost the capacity to make place within itself for the unknown, the unclear and the less than rational. Yet, not recognizing that human freedom has always thrived on a mixture of the two—the certain and the uncertain, the clear and the unclear, the objective and the subjective, the rational and the non-rational—is not merely a form of politics of knowledge designed to marginalize large parts of the cultures of the oppressed the world over, it is a form of politics of knowledge which seeks to abridge the concept of human freedom itself.

Re-Imagining the Third World

The implication of the argument thus far is this: openness to voices, familiar or strange, may well have to be the first criterion of the shared self which transcends nation-states, communities, perhaps even cultures themselves. A direct, sharp awareness of man-made suffering, a genuine empirical feel for it, may be the second. (Philosophers who say that we cannot feel the toothache of others may be right, but we *can* cognize the ache and use that cognition as the *reductio* of our conceptual frames.) I have tried to convey here that the two issues and the attendant responsibilities—listening to voices and renewing the awareness of the surplus suffering produced by faulty social institutions—are interrelated. For all theories of suffering—in this secular age, we prefer to call them theories of oppression—can become mandates for the infliction of new forms of suffering which, because they are cast in the language of the latest theory of oppression, can then be neither seen nor heard.

Perhaps, human ingenuity in matters of social domination being what it is, we may have to learn to feel safe with transience of such theories, even when they seem grounded in forms of rationality and scientific truth which look perennial. Perhaps, in the future, social and political theories will be expected to include some minimum checks against themselves, perhaps even an element of self-destructiveness. In the meanwhile, we cannot afford to forget that the one and half million Cambodians who died in the 1970s in the last great genocide of our times, died for the sake of an allegedly perfect theory of oppression and human liberation. They had only one consolation, before dying like so many flies, that the theory was custom-made for them in a university no less than Sorbonne. Only forty years ago, when records for genocide were being thoughtfully set up for the *Guinness Books of Records* in Auschwitz, Dresden and Hiroshima, a galaxy of biologists, doctors, nuclear physicists, and social theorists had provided not only the scientific but also the moral wherewithal of doing, what Heinrich Himmler used to call, one's dirty but necessary duty to the dominant idea of a global civilization.

I shall now briefly turn to two concepts which have begun to recur in virtually every contemporary analyses of man-made suffering, either as indicators of the tragic possibilities inherent in the present global civilization or as touchstones for judging all visions of the future. The first is the concept of the Third World, the second that of backwardness. I shall suggest that the concepts can be reworked to respond to the problems of audibility and the loss of the feel for direct experience of suffering.

The audible dissent of the shaman, who defies the given formats of defiance, and the inaudible dissent of those, who cannot and sometimes would not cussedly vocalize their protest, converge in the symbolism of the Third World. For the shaman's natural habitat is a 'backward', 'uncivil', 'retrogressive' culture; his natural clientele are those inhabiting the mosquito-ridden, steamy backwaters of Asia, Africa, and South America. The shaman is the protest of the non-protesting.

Let us admit straightaway that the concept of the Third World is a disaster. The concept defines neither a shared political economy nor a common political ideology. Apart from the fact that most of the Third World is desperately poor and ruled by despots who live off it as systematically as does the First World, most other identifiers of the Third World are either claptraps or propaganda.

But perhaps one can give meanings or associations to the idea of the Third World which would transcend its internal contradictions and existential realities, perhaps even the dishonesty of its rulers. One can build on the fact that the Third World *has* become the Other of the First, in a way the Second World ceased to be long ago. The Second World could compete with the First in space programmes or in summer Olympics but most people are now convinced, rightly or wrongly, that the Second World gave up rather early the ambition of being anything but a poor man's version of the First World, more egalitarian perhaps, but nothing more adventurous than that.

The otherness of the Third World opens up—alas, only theoretically—many possibilities. The Third World can claim to be the upholder of traditions, of cultures outside the present global culture, waiting for its prodigal brothers to come back and admit their profligacy. Of course, it is true that the Third World is not prodigal partly because it has been never given its due share of the patrimony in the first place. Most of the Third World has never had the chance to be anything but austere. It also has ambitions to live it up; only it cannot afford to do so. But then, is it not possible to claim that austerity, even when hypocritically espoused, has a role to play in a world hell-bent on squandering away its natural and cultural inheritance? After all, such hypocrisy at least keeps alive the values of conservation and diversity for future generations to build on.

The Third World can be redefined as a concept of trusteeship, a concept analogous to the one Gandhi used in the sphere of economics. The Third World is what holds in trust the rejected selves of the First and the Second Worlds the way gene banks hold in trust germ-plasms which in the future may provide a base-line for exploring new as well as old possibilities, in case the presently-dominant strains exhaust themselves. The Third World is not only the trustee of memories, it is the dirty frontier of the dominant style of 'doing' intellectual work today; it is where experiments are possible and lost causes pursued. The Third World is where the shaman survives and, in some cases, thrives.

Is there a Third World? The question cannot be answered the way the gifted writer from Trinidad, Shiv Naipaul, tried to answer it in his last book.[5] For an honest answer, the question must be reworded. For our purposes, it ought to be: can we discover a Third World to widen choices in the matter of human futures?

Now, a different set of formulations become available to us which could serve both as a set of propositions about the nature of the present global civilization and as a set of possibilities in another.

For instance, the Third World can now become a reminder—to those whom George Aseniero calls the new Leibnitzians—that everything is not well with this, the allegedly best of all possible worlds. Like beggars in my native Calcutta, who in their utter degradation haunt the citizen who believes that he or she lives in the best of all possible worlds, the Third World could be a source of moral discomfort to the wealthy and the powerful, not only in the First and Second Worlds but also in the Third. The public-spirited, professional social workers may not like to encourage vagrancy by giving alms to beggars, but the professionals may never guess

[5]Shiv Naipaul, *An Unfinished Journey* (New York: Penguin Books, 1987).

how beggary could keep alive political and moral issues by making the smug and the narcissistic cringe and recoil from the social reality around them.

You are of course protected from the same reality in another way if you take an eagle's-eyeview of the Third World, for then you miss no detail and waste no compassion. Many experts do so. The citizens of the Third World, though, live in the Third World; they have to survive. They have to blur out many of the details around them to live their versions of a normal life. Is the first kind of numbing different from the second? Ruth Prawer Jhabwala, the high-priestess of Orientalist fiction on India today, does not think so. India, the new Kipling has declared in the Introduction to her new collection of short stories, is not merely terribly poor but also terribly backward.[6]

Terribly poor, yes. But why terribly backward? Mrs Jhabwala has no clear answer, but seems to suggest that many Indians develop elaborate defences, so as not to be emotionally flooded by the suffering around them. In a small scale, they do what victims and collaborators under duress always do to ensure survival and protect their sanity in an extreme situation, be it in a concentration camp or in a society under oppressive rule. They numb themselves to suffering, to use Robert Lifton's term, in a way which resembles, in howsoever a muted form, the more dangerous numbing that takes place in their oppressors. In any case, why do they, the backward Indians, have to be more of their brother's keepers than the First World intellectuals—or for that matter, Third World intellectuals in the First World—in an age of high-speed global communications? Why should moral responsibility stop at the frontiers of a nation-state? Does a Mizo tribal from Northeast India have more access to information about destitution in the slums of Bombay than an upper middle-class housewife at Manhattan? Once again, Mrs Jhabwala has no answer. We have to take it from her on faith that India is very backward and the moral responsibility for it is solely that of the Indian passport-holders.

This note seeks to expand accountability, not limit it. The loss of the capacity for guilt and the loss of the sense of responsibility that grows out of guilt, this note believes with Lifton, may turn out to be in the contemporary world a greater threat to human survival than the vicissitudes of unconscious guilt against which Freud warned humanity in *Civilization and its Discontents*.[7] Indians and others of their ilk *are*

[6]Ruth Prawer Jhabwala, *Out of India* (New York: Simon and Schuster, 1987).

[7]Robert J. Lifton, 'The Concept of the Survivor', *The Future of Immortality and Other Essays for a Nuclear Age* (New York: Basic Books, 1987), pp. 231–43, see pp. 237–8.

responsible, probably more than others are. But everyone is accountable, some for immunizing themselves to human suffering, others for generating, running and living off the systems which generate the suffering. The Third World is often a target of supervision and patronage, but it can be made a symbol of planetary intellectual responsibility, even despite the Third World. The experience of the Third World can be turned into something more than the record of its individual nation-states. It can be read as a text on survival which hides a code of transcendence.

Probably, even in the matter of nation-states, the Third World may have something to say to our age. Not through their spectacular success in the science of nation-building but through their less-than-spectacular failure in it. The main problem with the nation-states is not their resistance to reforms which encroach on their sovereignty but their refusal to abdicate their status as the ultimate unit of political analysis. The problem is cognitive, not political, though it can be called a problem in the politics of knowledge. It is the inability of those exposed to the mass culture of global politics to think in terms of categories even partly independent of the idea of nation-state which triggers Mrs Jhabwala's lament about Indian insensitivity to suffering. Indian poverty is Indian responsibility, and Indian responsibility means the responsibility of the subjects of the Indian nation-state. The lament is simultaneously a by-product and a justification of an entire generation's attempt to absolutize state-boundaries. Within the boundaries, the state is supposed to act as a focus of all major moral and political awareness and be the source of all ameliorative action.

Compromises with sovereignty many states at some points of time are willing to make. They do it when they are defeated in wars; they do it when they are weak and at the mercy of other states; they do it even for larger political-economic gains (as in the case of the European Union). The United Nations, ramshackle or senile though it may look today— what with its mimic-state status, its international civil servants, its development experts and cultural impresarios—was built out of such compromises. But like the Government of India which, after driving out the IBM and Coca-Cola from India in the late 1970s, dutifully encouraged Indian private enterprise to make a grand success of two brand-new, 'indigenous' corporations called the IDM and Campa Cola, the United Nations represents only an edited version of the present global nation-state system. For the United Nations itself has acquired many of the trappings of a modern state. Its building blocks are nation-states and its unit of analysis is the nation-state.

Many call this way of thinking 'statism'. This is not an appropriate term, but it does convey that a state in the Third World can come to represent something more than the state conceptualized by at least some of the anti-imperialist movements over the last one hundred years. (Nationalism, as it is commonly understood in the modern world, is however perfectly compatible with statism.[8]) I shall, however, following Ernest Gellner and others, distinguish between patriotism and anti-imperialism on the one hand and nationalism, on the other, seeing the latter as a sub-species of the domain covered by the first two concepts. (Seventy-five years ago, a number of South Asian thinkers—Rabindranath Tagore being the most prominent among them—had used the same distinction creatively in public discourse. However, in the regnant global culture of knowledge, that is neither here nor there, given that the likes of Gellner, have already in practice collapsed all three categories under nationalism and declared all thought associated with it to be shoddy.) Nationalism as a sub-species of patriotism need not occupy the entire space belonging to patriotism. And it can be argued that at least some of the anti-colonial movements in the Third World were moved primarily by the spirit of patriotism but, after winning independence, lost out to nationalism. It can be even argued that it is the spirit of nationalism which helped spread the idea of an imperial state, internalized from the colonial experience, in many of these societies. Colonialism may have vanished from the world scene but its smile lingers in the air.

This distinction has become important because the spirit of anti-imperialism that was sweeping the world only fifty years ago has been finally overpowered by the clenched-teeth nationalism in which Europe used to once specialize, through a process which Sigmund Freud would have loved to identify as a perfect clinical case of identification with the aggressor.

It is possible that statism and the perverted, self-destructive form of nationalism which goes with it, too, will reach their dead-ends in the Third World. Not because of enlightened internationalism, but because of the contradiction which has arisen between such statism and the democratic principle and because the defiance of the nation-state has become the *sine qua non* of survival for many in the Third World and in the Third Worlds within the First and the Second—the indigenous

---

[8]On such nationalism, two distinct but not incompatible recent works are Ernest Gellner's *Nations and Nationalism* (Ithaca: Cornell University Press, 1983); and Benedict Anderson's *Imagined Communities: Reflections on the Origin and Spread of Nationalism* (London : Verso, 1983).

peoples, the minorities, the political dissenters, who do not or cannot use the language of global mainstream and are partly or wholly outside the market, economically and/or psychologically. While we debate the priniciples of sovereignty, what the nation-state should or should not give up for the sake of a more humane and equitable world order in the future, the nation-states are increasingly at war with the citizens of the Third World and are being subverted by their own logic. Remember the 22-carat, solid-gold bath tub of the expatriate cabinet minister of one of the African states which the Lloyds of London could not afford to insure some years ago.

Sustainable politics is usually unheroic. The shamans, therefore, may not ultimately win; sanity and maturity *may* ultimately come to rule the best of all possible worlds; but, in the meanwhile, the onus will be on our generation to decide or at least debate whether this century's dominant faiths do represent the next century's ideas of sanity and maturity. That is what some of us are trying to do.

*Earlier published in *Alternatives* 14(3) 1989.

Index